CORE LITERACY LIBRARY

Teaching Reading Sourcebook

UPDATED SECOND EDITION

Bill Honig, Linda Diamond,
Linda Gutlohn

CONTRIBUTING AUTHORS: *Carrie L. Cole, Pamela Beard El-Dinary, Roxanne F. Hudson, Holly B. Lane, Jacalyn Mahler, Paige C. Pullen*

Arena Press NOVATO, CALIFORNIA

BERKELEY, CALIFORNIA

Arena Press
20 Leveroni Court
Novato, California 94949
800-422-7249
www.AcademicTherapy.com

Consortium on Reaching Excellence in Education, Inc. (CORE)
2550 Ninth Street, Suite 102
Berkeley, California 94710
888-249-6155
www.corelearn.com

ISBN: 978-1-57128-690-1
Print Number: 15 14 13 12 11 10 09 08 07 06
Library of Congress Control Number: 2012941438

CREDITS
Editorial Director: Linda Gutlohn
Book Design and Production: Lucy Nielsen
Marketing: Christine Fleming McIsaac
Contributors: Frances Bessellieu, Susan Blackaby, Catherine Boote, Carrie L. Cole, Pamela Beard El-Dinary, Jan E. Hasbrouck, Roxanne F. Hudson, Holly B. Lane, Jacalyn Mahler, Christine Fleming McIsaac, Paige C. Pullen, Small Planet Communications, Glenda Taylor
Editorial: Shelle Epton, Lawrence DiStasi, Tom Hassett, David Sweet, Lynn Trepicchio

For their valuable contributions to scientifically based reading instruction, special acknowledgment is given to Marilyn J. Adams, Anita L. Archer, James F. Baumann, Isabel L. Beck, Andrew Biemiller, Cathy Collins Block, Douglas W. Carnine, Linnea C. Ehri, Douglas Fuchs, Linda B. Gambrell, Michael F. Graves, John T. Guthrie, Jan E. Hasbrouck, Edward J. Kame'enui, Louisa C. Moats, Michael Pressley, Taffy E. Raphael, Tim Rasinski, S. Jay Samuels, John Shefelbine, Deborah C. Simmons, Steven Stahl, Joseph K. Torgesen, Rebecca Treiman, and Joanna P. Williams.

ACKNOWLEDGMENTS
For each of the following selections, grateful acknowledgment is made for permission to adapt and/or reprint original or copyrighted material.

Fran Avni: "There's a Starfish Hidden Under My Bed," by Fran Avni. Copyright © 1997 by Fran Avni. Reprinted by permission of Fran Avni. For information about the audiocassette "I'm All Ears," school concerts, and workshops, contact Fran Avni at 510-595-9132 or FAVNI@aol.com.

Cambridge University Press: "Selected Statistics for Major Sources of Spoken and Written Language," from "Vocabulary Simplification for Children: A Special Case of 'Motherese'?" by Donald P. Hayes and Margaret G. Ahrens in *Journal of Child Language,* Vol. 15, No. 2 (June 1988), pp. 395–410. Reprinted with the permission of Cambridge University Press.

International Reading Association: "Variation in Amount of Independent Reading" figure from Anderson, R. C. (1996). "Research Foundations to Support Wide Reading." In V. Greany (ed.) *Promoting Reading in Developing Countries.* Newark, DE: International Reading Association. Adapted from R. C. Anderson, P. T. Wilson, and L. G. Fielding (1988), "Growth in Reading and How Children Spend Their Time Outside School," *Reading Research Quarterly* 23 (3), pp. 285–303. Reprinted by permission of Richard C. Anderson and the International Reading Association.

Lawrence Erlbaum Associates, Inc.: "Correlation Between Decoding and Comprehension in the Connecticut Longitudinal Study," from "The Case for Early Reading Intervention" by Barbara R. Foorman, David J. Francis, Sally E. Shaywitz, Bennett A. Shaywitz, and Jack M. Fletcher, in *Foundations of Reading Acquisition and Dyslexia: Implications for Early Intervention,* edited by Benita A. Blachman. Copyright © 1997 by Lawrence Erlbaum Associates, Inc. Reprinted by permission of Barbara R. Foorman and Lawrence Erlbaum Associates, Inc.

LinguiSystems, Inc.: "The Hungry Thing" activity, adapted from "The Hungry Thing" activity in *The Sounds Abound™ Program* developed at the Stern Center for Language and Learning by Orna Lenchner and Blanche Podhajski. Copyright © 1998 by LinguiSystems, Inc. Adapted by permission of LinguiSystems, Inc., East Moline, IL. 800-776-4332.

John Ross: "Albert Einstein Asks a Question," by John Ross. Copyright © 1999 by John Ross. Used by permission of the author.

San Francisco Mime Troupe: "TV Dinner," by the San Francisco Mime Troupe. Script by Joaquin Aranda, Daniel Chumley, and Joan Holden. Based on a story by Sophia and Kate Chumley. Songs by Bruce Barthol. Copyright © 1979 by the San Francisco Mime Troupe. Adapted by permission of The San Francisco Mime Troupe. 415-285-1717.

Ann Seidler: "The Hungry Thing," by Jan Slepian and Ann Seidler. Copyright © 1967 by Ann G. Seidler and Janice B. Slepian. Currently out of print. Reprinted by permission of Ann G. Seidler.

Illustration Credits: Art Parts™

Photo Credits: JupiterImages (pp. 760, 761)

CONTENTS

SECTION I:
Word Structure

SECTION II:
Early Literacy

SECTION III:
Decoding and
Word Recognition

SECTION IV:
Reading Fluency

SECTION V:
Vocabulary

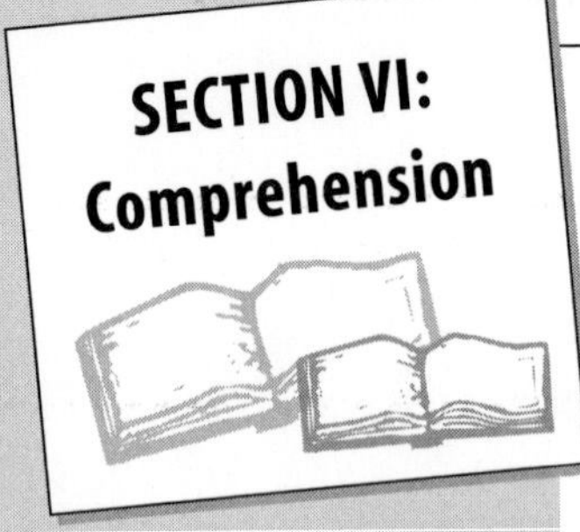
SECTION VI:
Comprehension

For printable PDFs of the Resources section, go to www.corelearn.com/SB2Resources.html

For educators at every level, the *Teaching Reading Sourcebook* is a comprehensive reference about reading instruction. Organized according to the elements of explicit instruction (what? why? when? and how?), the Sourcebook includes both a research-informed knowledge base and practical sample lesson models.

what?

a thorough but concise graphic explanation of research-based content and best practices

why?

a readable summary of scientifically based research, selected quotes from researchers, and a bibliography of suggested reading

when?

information about instructional sequence, assessment, and intervention strategies.

how?

sample lesson models with suggestions for corrective feedback; providing a bridge between research and practice, and making explicit instruction easy

The *Teaching Reading Sourcebook, Updated Second Edition* combines the best features of an academic text and a practical hands-on teacher's guide. It is an indispensable resource for teaching reading and language arts to both beginning and older struggling readers.

WHAT? • WHY? • WHEN? • HOW?

- User-friendly text
- Plentiful charts and tables

Connect to Theory

- Interactive activities for the reader
- Opportunities to review and interpret content

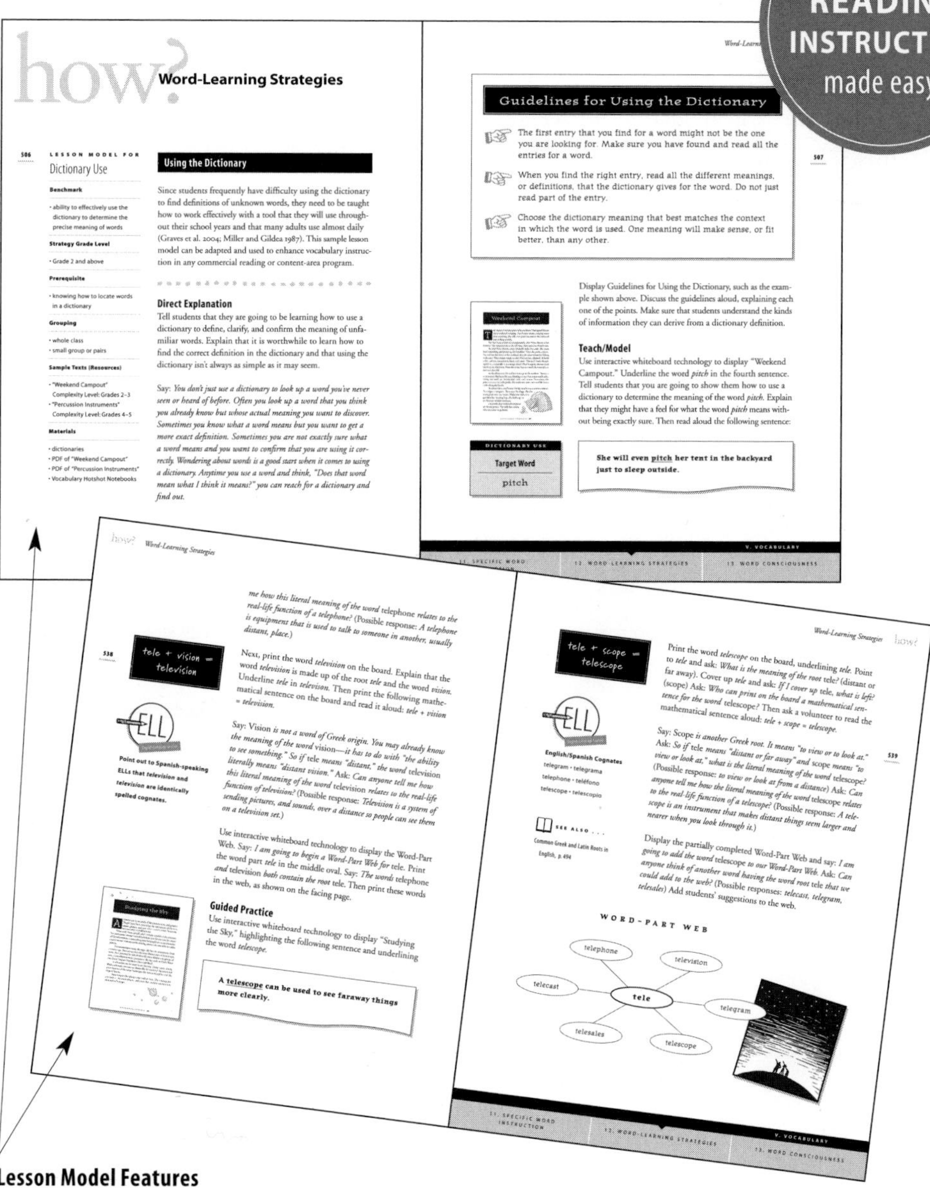

Lesson Model Features

- Focus and materials sidebar
- Explicit instruction
- Clear explanation
- Teacher modeling
- Useful background information
- Identification of research base
- Support for English-language learners
- Suggestions for corrective feedback

RESOURCES

The Resources section provides reproducible sample texts, activity masters, and teaching charts designed to be used in conjunction with sample lesson models. Sample texts include literary and informational texts that provide a context for explicit instruction.

The *Teaching Reading Sourcebook* can be used by . . .

- **elementary teachers** to enhance reading instruction in core reading programs
- **middle and high school teachers** to enhance language arts and content-area instruction
- **college professors and students** as a textbook for pre-service teacher education
- **providers of professional development** as an educational resource tool
- **school or district administrators** to support and facilitate effective literacy instruction
- **literacy coaches** as a resource for implementation
- **teachers of English-language learners (ELLs)** to support reading acquisition
- **teachers of older struggling readers** for research-based strategies tailored to individual needs
- **new teachers** as a comprehensive foundation for reading instruction

Discover . . .

THE SOURCEBOOK COMPANION

website

www.sourcebookcompanion.com

a valuable online resource for teacher educators

CCSS ABOUT THE COMMON CORE STATE STANDARDS AND THE TEACHING READING SOURCEBOOK

The Common Core State Standards do not tell teachers how to teach, but they do help teachers figure out the knowledge and skills their students should have . . . .

—*Common Core State Standards Initiative, 2012*

CCSS

How the Sourcebook can be useful for implementing the Common Core . . .

- It provides a bridge between the Standards and evidence-based instruction.
- It encompasses the Reading strand, especially Foundational Skills.
- It extensively covers Vocabulary Acquisition and Use in the Language strand.
- It enhances understanding of Common Core's Appendix A: Research Supporting Key Elements of the Standards.
- It emphasizes reading of informational text: 8 out of 12 Sample Texts are informational.

The *Teaching Reading Sourcebook* has always supported educators in bridging the gap between evidence-based reading research and actionable instructional strategies. Now the Sourcebook also supports educators' efforts in understanding, transitioning to, unpacking, and implementing the Common Core State Standards for English Language Arts. In the Updated Second Edition, new features seamlessly connect and clarify the Sourcebook's alignment to the Common Core.

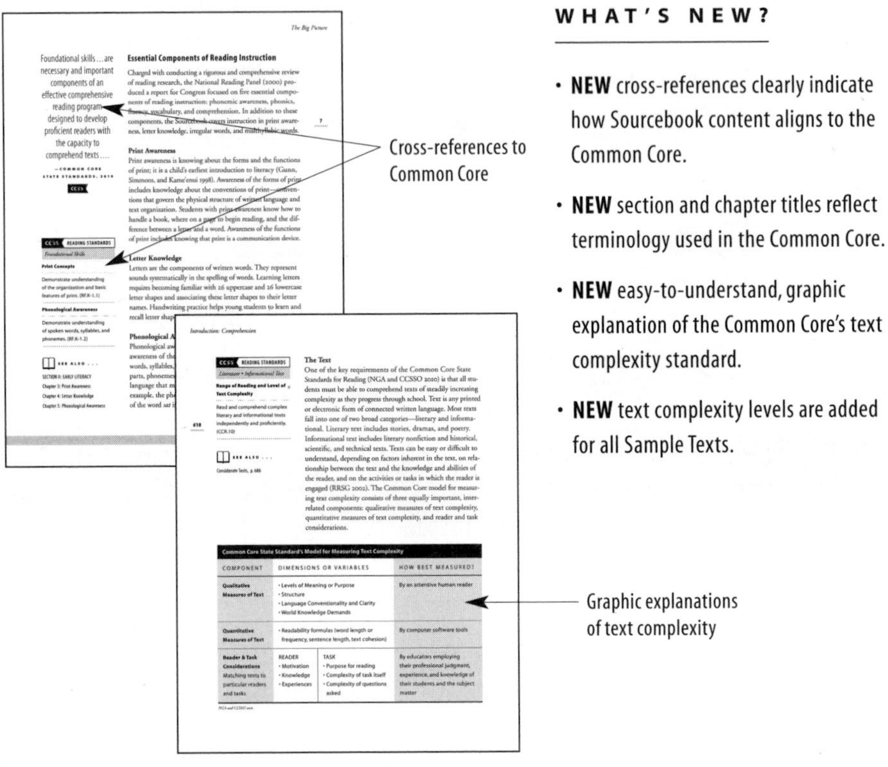

WHAT'S NEW?

- **NEW** cross-references clearly indicate how Sourcebook content aligns to the Common Core.
- **NEW** section and chapter titles reflect terminology used in the Common Core.
- **NEW** easy-to-understand, graphic explanation of the Common Core's text complexity standard.
- **NEW** text complexity levels are added for all Sample Texts.

NEW Charts and Tables Further Elicit Understanding of the Common Core

- Organization of the Common Core State Standards for English Language Arts, p. xvii
- Quick Reference: Where to Find the Common Core in the Sourcebook, p. xvii
- Correlation: Sourcebook Sample Lesson Models to Common Core State Standards, pp. xviii–xix
- Common Core State Standard's Model for Measuring Text Complexity, p. 610
- Qualitative Measures of Text Complexity: Literary and Informational Text, p. 611

Available Online

Detailed Correlations to the Common Core
www.sourcebookcompanion.com/correlations.html

Download complete grade-specific correlations demonstrating how the *Teaching Reading Sourcebook, Updated Second Edition* aligns to the Common Core State Standards for English Language Arts.

CCSS Organization of the Common Core State Standards for English Language Arts

Strands	College and Career Readiness (CCR) Anchor Standards	Grade-Specific Standards
READING: Literature (RL) READING: Informational Text (RI)	• Key Ideas and Details (1, 2, 3) • Craft and Structure (4, 5, 6) • Integration of Knowledge and Ideas (7, 8, 9) • Range of Reading and Level of Text Complexity (10)	Grades K–5 Grades 6–12
READING: Foundational Skills (RF)	• Print Concepts (1) • Phonological Awareness (2) • Phonics and Word Recognition (3) • Fluency (4)	Grades K–5
WRITING (W)	• Text Types and Purposes (1, 2, 3) • Production and Distribution of Writing (4, 5, 6) • Research to Build and Present Knowledge (7, 8, 9) • Range of Writing (10)	Grades K–5 Grades 6–12
SPEAKING AND LISTENING (SL)	• Comprehension and Collaboration (1, 2, 3) • Presentation of Knowledge and Ideas (4, 5, 6)	Grades K–5 Grades 6–12
LANGUAGE (L)	• Conventions of Standard English (1, 2) • Knowledge of Language (3) • Vocabulary Acquisition and Use (4, 5, 6)	Grades K–5 Grades 6–12

National Governors Association Center for Best Practices and Council of Chief State School Officers, 2010.

See next page for correlations of Sourcebook Sample Lesson Models to CCSS

CCSS Quick Reference: Where to Find the Common Core in the Sourcebook

COMMON CORE STATE STANDARDS FOR ENGLISH LANGUAGE ARTS		TEACHING READING SOURCEBOOK, UPDATED SECOND EDITION	
STRAND	**CCR ANCHOR STANDARD**	**SECTION**	**CHAPTER**
READING: Foundational Skills	• Print Concepts	II: Early Literacy	3. Print Awareness 4. Letter Knowledge
	• Phonological Awareness	II: Early Literacy	5. Phonological Awareness
	• Phonics and Word Recognition	III: Decoding and Word Recognition	6. Phonics 7. Irregular Word Reading 8. Multisyllabic Word Reading
	• Fluency	IV: Reading Fluency	9. Fluency Assessment 10. Fluency Instruction
READING: Literature **READING: Informational Text**	• Key Ideas and Details • Craft and Structure • Integration of Knowledge and Ideas • Range of Reading and Level of Text Complexity	VI: Comprehension	14. Literary Text
		VI: Comprehension	15. Informational Text
LANGUAGE	• Conventions of Standard English	II: Early Literacy	4. Letter Knowledge
		III: Decoding and Word Recognition	6. Phonics 7. Irregular Word Reading 8. Multisyllabic Word Reading
	• Vocabulary Acquisition and Use	V: Vocabulary	11. Specific Word Instruction 12. Word-Learning Strategies 13. Word Consciousness
		VI: Comprehension	14. Literary Text 15. Informational Text

CCSS Correlation: Sourcebook Sample Lesson Models to Common Core State Standards

TEACHING READING SOURCEBOOK			COMMON CORE STATE STANDARDS							
			READING						LANGUAGE	
CHAPTER	SAMPLE LESSON MODEL	PAGE	RF.1	RF.2	RF.3	RF.4	RL	RI	L.1,2	L.4,5,6
3. Print Awareness	Print Referencing in Shared Storybook Reading	78	x				x	x		
4. Letter Knowledge	Letter Names and Shapes: Uppercase Letters	96	x							
	Handwriting: Uppercase Letter Forms	99							x	
	Letter Names and Shapes: Lowercase Letters	103	x							
	Handwriting: Lowercase Letter Forms	107							x	
	Letter-Sound Strategy	110	x	x	x					
5. Phonological Awareness	The Hungry Thing	128		x						
	Phonological Medley	132		x						
	Salad Toss	137		x						
	Critter Sitter	140		x						
	Bridge Game	143		x						
	Sound Match	146		x						
	Odd One Out	149		x						
	Simon Says	151		x						
	Say-It-and-Move-It	154		x						
	Elkonin Sound Boxes	156		x						
6. Phonics	Integrated Picture Mnemonics	196	x	x	x				x	
	Introducing Consonant Digraphs	200			x					
	Introducing Short Vowels	204			x					
	Reading and Writing CVC Words	208			x				x	
	Reading and Writing CCVC Words	214			x				x	
	Reading and Writing CVCe Words	221			x				x	
	Reading and Writing Words with Vowel Combinations	226			x				x	
	Reading and Writing Words with Phonograms	232			x				x	
	Method for Reading Decodable Text	235			x	x	x	x		
7. Irregular Word Reading	Sound-Out Strategy	252			x				x	
	Spell-Out Strategy	255			x				x	
8. Multisyllabic Word Reading	Introducing Open and Closed Syllables	272			x					
	Syllable Division Strategy: VC/CV	276			x				x	
	Syllable Division Strategy: VCV	283			x					
	Syllable Segmentation Strategy	292			x				x	
	Syllasearch Procedure	298			x				x	
	Introducing Affixes	304			x					
	Flexible Strategy for Reading Big Words	308			x				x	
	Root Word Transformation Strategy	314			x				x	
9. Fluency Assessment	Assessment of ORF Rate and Accuracy	340				x				
	Digital Graphing of ORF Scores	349				x				
	Assessment of Prosodic Reading	355				x				
10. Fluency Instruction	Timed Repeated Oral Reading	374				x				
	Partner Reading	384				x				
	Phrase-Cued Reading	391				x				
	Readers Theatre	398				x	x			

CCSS Correlation: Sourcebook Sample Lesson Models to Common Core State Standards

TEACHING READING SOURCEBOOK			COMMON CORE STATE STANDARDS							
			READING						LANGUAGE	
CHAPTER	SAMPLE LESSON MODEL	PAGE	RF.1	RF.2	RF.3	RF.4	RL	RI	L.1,2	L.4,5,6
11. Specific Word Instruction	Text Talk: Read-Aloud Method	436					X	X		X
	Meaning Vocabulary: Direct Explanation Method	443					X	X		X
	Method for Independently Read Text	453					X	X		X
	Introducing Function Words	462							X	X
	Concept Picture Sort	467								X
	Semantic Map	470								X
	Semantic Feature Analysis	474								X
	Possible Sentences	478								X
	Word Map	481								X
	Keyword Method	484								X
12. Word-Learning Strategies	Using the Dictionary	506								X
	PAVE Procedure	511				X				X
	Concept of Definition Map	516								X
	Compound Words	521			X					X
	Word Families	524								X
	Word-Part Clues: Prefixes	527			X					X
	Word-Part Clues: Suffixes	533			X					X
	Word-Part Clues: Roots	537			X					X
	Context Clues	541				X	X	X		X
	Introducing Types of Context Clues	545				X	X	X		X
	Applying Types of Context Clues	551				X	X	X		X
	Introducing The Vocabulary Strategy	555				X	X	X		X
	Practicing The Vocabulary Strategy	562				X	X	X		X
13. Word Consciousness	Animal Idioms	580					X			X
	Latin and Greek Number Words	584			X					X
	Antonym Scales	588								X
	Web Word Web	592								X
	Five-Senses Simile Web	595					X			X
	Poetry as Word Play	598					X			X
	Vocabulary Hotshot Notebook	601								X
14. Literary Text	Dialogic Reading: Picture Book Read-Aloud Method	648					X	X		
	Story Structure	651					X			
	TSI (Transactional Strategies Instruction)	659					X	X		X
	Book Club: Writing in Response to Literature	677					X			
15. Informational Text	QAR (Question-Answer Relationships)	702					X	X		
	Strategies for Summarizing	711					X	X		
	CSR (Collaborative Strategic Reading)	720				X		X		X
	QtA (Questioning the Author)	733					X	X		
	CORI (Concept-Oriented Reading Instruction)	739						X		X

KEY Common Core State Standards

RF.1	Print Concepts	**RL**	Literature
RF.2	Phonological Awareness	**RI**	Informational Text
RF.3	Phonics & Word Recognition	**L.1,2**	Conventions of Standard English
RF.4	Fluency	**L.4,5,6**	Vocabulary Acquisition and Use

Note: RF stands for Reading: Foundational Skills.

The Big Picture

motivation
scientific approach
reading deficit
differentiated
instruction

The Big Picture

> Democracy... can survive and flourish only with a literate citizenry.
>
> —THOMAS JEFFERSON

The Reading Deficit

Literacy is an essential skill needed to participate in today's world. Whether we are reading a ballot, a map, a train schedule, a driver's test, a job application, a text message, a label on a medicine container, or a textbook, reading is required to fully function in our society. Unfortunately, an enormous proportion of young citizens cannot read well enough to adequately function or to expand their knowledge about the world. This situation is especially distressing because we now know that the majority of students can learn to read regardless of their backgrounds (Lyon 2002).

The State of Reading Today

The focus on learning to read has never been greater. The latest National Assessment of Educational Progress (NAEP) indicates that fourth- and eighth-grade reading scores are abysmally low. According to the achievement-level results in reading, 68 percent of fourth graders and 68 percent of eighth graders scored at or below the basic level of reading achievement.

NAEP Achievement Levels

basic
partial mastery of knowledge and skills fundamental for proficient academic performance

proficient
solid academic performance

advanced
superior academic performance

NAEP Achievement-Level Results in Reading

GRADE	Below Basic	Basic	Proficient	Advanced
Grade 4	34%	34%	25%	7%
Grade 8	25%	43%	29%	3%

National Center for Education Statistics 2011.

Source

Common Core State Standards Initiative

http://www.corestandards.org

Educational standards help teachers ensure their students have the skills and knowledge they need to be successful by providing clear goals for student learning.

—COMMON CORE STATE STANDARDS INITIATIVE, 2012

CCSS

Sources of Reading Failure

Neurological factors (brain metabolism)

Familial factors (environment)

Socioeconomic factors (poverty)

Instructional factors (teaching)

Common Core State Standards

The Common Core State Standards (CCSS) for English Language Arts (National Governors Association Center for Best Practices and Council of Chief State School Officers 2010) are the culmination of an extended, broad-based effort to create the next generation of K–12 standards to help ensure that all students are college and career ready in literacy no later than the end of high school. The Standards aim to be research and evidence based, aligned with college and work expectations, rigorous, and internationally benchmarked. Until now, most states have had their own set of English language arts standards, meaning public education students at the same grade level in different states have been expected to achieve at different levels. It is believed that common standards will provide more clarity about and consistency in what is expected of student learning across the country. They will allow states to share information effectively and will help provide all students with an equal opportunity for an education that will prepare them to go to college or enter the workforce, regardless of where they live.

What's Not Working?

With all this focus on reading and education, one might wonder why scores have not dramatically changed for the better. Research suggests that using ineffective teaching methods along with instructional strategies that are without "enough research evidence" limit student mastery of essential skills and new concepts (Rosenshine 2012; Moats 2007; Sweet 2004). For example, even though extensive research clearly shows that students, regardless of their learning difficulties, reach higher and faster achievement with systematic and explicit instruction, this type of instruction is still not always used (Gill and Kozloff 2004).

LEFT HEMISPHERE OF THE BRAIN

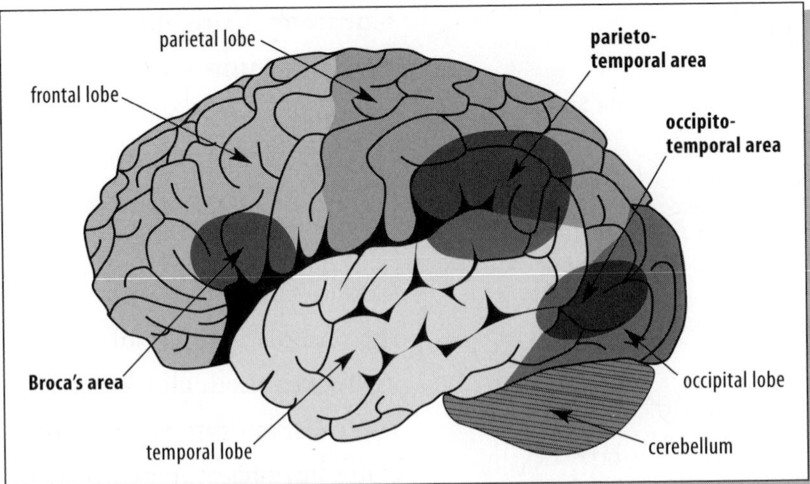

DYSLEXIA
a language-based learning disability that is neurological in origin

The Brain and Reading

Brain research is an area of scientific investigation looking for the best ways to teach students how to read. Functional magnetic resonance imaging (fMRI) technology has allowed scientists to track brain activity. Researchers have discovered that the brain activation patterns of students with dyslexia and other poor readers are different from those of good readers.

Areas for Skilled Reading

Broca's area

Parieto-temporal area

Occipito-temporal area

Brain Geography

The brain is made up of two mirror-image sides, or hemispheres. Each hemisphere of the brain is divided into four lobes, or sections: frontal, parietal, temporal, and occipital. The left hemisphere of the brain is associated with speech, language processing, and reading. Within the left hemisphere, the frontal lobe controls speech, reasoning, planning, regulating emotions, and consciousness; the parietal lobe controls sensory perceptions as well as links spoken and written language to memory; the temporal lobe is involved in verbal memory; and the occipital lobe is important in the identification of letters (Hudson, High, and Al Otaiba 2007; Shaywitz 2003).

Within and between these lobes, there are areas that are especially important for skilled reading: Broca's area, the parieto-temporal area, and the occipito-temporal area (Shaywitz 2003). Broca's area is important for the organization, production, and manipulation of language and speech (Joseph, Nobel, and Eden 2001). The parieto-temporal area analyzes words by pulling them apart and linking the letters to their sounds—conscious, effortful decoding (Shaywitz 2003). The occipito-temporal area identifies words rapidly and automatically on sight, instead of analyzing them sound by sound.

At all ages, good readers show a consistent pattern: strong activation in the back of the brain with lesser activation in front.

—SHAYWITZ, 2003

How the Brain Reads

In her research, Shaywitz (2003) found that the parieto-temporal and occipito-temporal areas in the back of the brain are especially important to skilled reading but have different roles. The parieto-temporal system's slow, analytic, step-by-step decoding function seems to be relied upon more by beginning readers. In contrast, the occipito-temporal area is the "express pathway to reading."

According to Shaywitz (2003), during brain imaging skilled readers show the highest level of activation of the occipito-temporal area. It is the hub where, for example, all the relevant incoming information about a word—how it looks, how it sounds, and what it means—is tightly bound together and stored. After a reader has analyzed and correctly read a word several times, then he or she forms a neural model of that specific word that is then stored permanently in the occipito-temporal area. After that, just seeing the word in print immediately activates the neural model and all the relevant information about that word. This all happens automatically, without the reader's conscious thought or effort.

Source

Proust and the Squid

Proust and the Squid: The Story and Science of the Reading Brain (2007) by Maryanne Wolf. New York: Harper Perennial.

As they read, good readers activate the back of the brain and also, to some extent, the Broca's area in the front of the brain, an area that helps in slowly analyzing a word. On the other hand, poor readers underutilize the areas in the back of the brain. Evidence-based reading instruction in phonemic awareness and phonics can change brain activity in struggling readers and assist in the activation and use of the areas in the back of the brain (Shaywitz et al. 2004; Aylward et al. 2003).

> Research—when it is based on sound scientific observation—provides reliable information about what works and why and how it works.
>
> —REYNA, 2004

Scientific Approach to Reading Instruction

The term *scientifically based reading instruction* was first defined in the Reading Excellence Act of 1998 as "the application of rigorous, systematic, and objective procedures to obtain valid knowledge relevant to reading development, reading instruction, and reading difficulties." According to Stanovich and Stanovich (2003), reflective teachers use scientific thinking every day—they "inquire into their own practice and . . . examine their own classrooms to find out what works best for them and their students."

How to Recognize Effective Research

Educators can use three simple questions to distinguish between research that confirms the effectiveness of an instructional practice and research that does not: (1) Has the research been published in a peer-reviewed journal? (2) Have the research results been replicated by other scientists? (3) Is there a consensus that the research findings are supported by other studies?

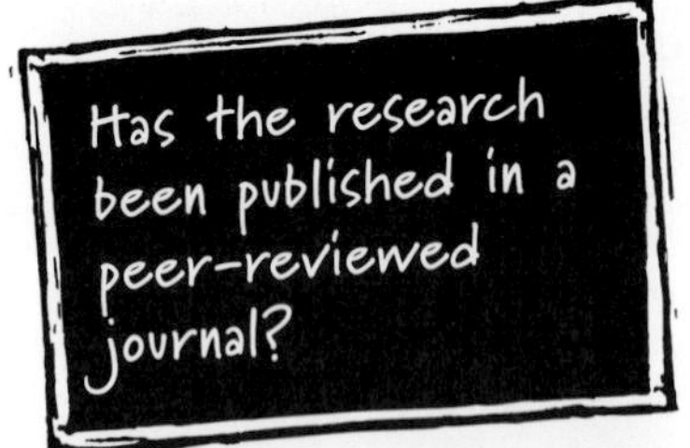

INDEPENDENT PEER REVIEW Articles published in peer-reviewed journals have gone through a process of review. This process of quality control exposes ideas and experimentation to examination and criticism by other scientists in the same field.

Have the research results been replicated by other scientists?

REPLICATION OF RESULTS BY OTHER SCIENTISTS To be considered scientifically based, a research finding must be presented in a way that enables other researchers to reach the same results when they repeat the experiment. True scientific knowledge is public and open to challenge.

CONSENSUS WITHIN THE RESEARCH COMMUNITY Scientists do not simply evaluate data from a single study; they evaluate data from many studies. Research findings are most often accepted after the scientific community agrees that sufficient evidence has converged to support one finding over another.

Foundational skills... are necessary and important components of an effective comprehensive reading program designed to develop proficient readers with the capacity to comprehend texts....

—COMMON CORE STATE STANDARDS, 2010

CCSS

Essential Components of Reading Instruction

Charged with conducting a rigorous and comprehensive review of reading research, the National Reading Panel (2000) produced a report for Congress focused on five essential components of reading instruction: phonemic awareness, phonics, fluency, vocabulary, and comprehension. In addition to these components, the Sourcebook covers instruction in print awareness, letter knowledge, irregular words, and multisyllabic words.

Print Awareness

Print awareness is knowing about the forms and the functions of print; it is a child's earliest introduction to literacy (Gunn, Simmons, and Kame'enui 1998). Awareness of the forms of print includes knowledge about the conventions of print—conventions that govern the physical structure of written language and text organization. Students with print awareness know how to handle a book, where on a page to begin reading, and the difference between a letter and a word. Awareness of the functions of print includes knowing that print is a communication device.

Letter Knowledge

Letters are the components of written words. They represent sounds systematically in the spelling of words. Learning letters requires becoming familiar with 26 uppercase and 26 lowercase letter shapes and associating these letter shapes to their letter names. Handwriting practice helps young students to learn and recall letter shapes (Ehri and Roberts 2006; Berninger 1999).

Phonological Awareness

Phonological awareness is an umbrella term that includes the awareness of the larger parts of spoken language, such as words, syllables, and onsets and rimes—as well as the smaller parts, phonemes. A phoneme is the smallest unit of spoken language that makes a difference in a word's meaning. For example, the phonemes /s/ and /f/ are different; the meaning of the word *sat* is different from the meaning of the word *fat*.

CCSS READING STANDARDS

Foundational Skills

Print Concepts

Demonstrate understanding of the organization and basic features of print. (RF.K-1.1)

Phonological Awareness

Demonstrate understanding of spoken words, syllables, and phonemes. (RF.K-1.2)

SEE ALSO . . .

SECTION II: EARLY LITERACY

Chapter 3: Print Awareness

Chapter 4: Letter Knowledge

Chapter 5: Phonological Awareness

According to the National Reading Panel (2000), phonemic awareness instruction is most effective when students are taught to use letters as they manipulate phonemes.

CCSS READING STANDARDS

Foundational Skills

Phonics and Word Recognition

Know and apply grade-level phonics and word analysis skills in decoding words. (RF.K-5.3)

SEE ALSO . . .

SECTION III: DECODING AND WORD RECOGNITION

Chapter 6: Phonics

Chapter 7: Irregular Word Reading

Chapter 8: Multisyllabic Word Reading

Phonics

Phonics is a method of instruction that teaches students the systematic relationship between the letters and letter combinations (graphemes) in written language and the individual sounds (phonemes) in spoken language and how to use these relationships to read and spell words. Phonics instruction—which is intended for beginning readers in the primary grades and for older students who are struggling to read—can help students learn how to convert the printed word into its spoken form (National Reading Panel 2000). This process, called decoding, involves looking at a word and connecting the letters and sounds and then blending those sounds together. Phonics instruction also helps students to understand the alphabetic principle—written letters represent spoken sounds. In other words, letters and sounds work together in systematic ways to allow spoken language to be written down and written language to be read.

Irregular Word Reading

Not all words are regular or can be read by sounding them out. An irregular word contains one or more sound/spelling correspondences that a student does not know and therefore cannot use to decode the word. Within a reading program, there are basically two types of irregular words: words that are permanently irregular and words that are temporarily irregular (Carnine et al. 2006). Some of the most common words in English are irregular. These high-frequency words appear often in printed text and therefore are crucial for comprehension.

CCSS READING STANDARDS

Foundational Skills

Fluency

Read with sufficient accuracy and fluency to support comprehension. (RF.1-5.4)

SEE ALSO . . .

SECTION IV: READING FLUENCY

Chapter 9: Fluency Assessment

Chapter 10: Fluency Instruction

CCSS LANGUAGE STANDARDS

Vocabulary Acquisition and Use

Determine or clarify the meaning of unknown and multiple-meaning words and phrases. (CCR.4)

Demonstrate understanding of figurative language, word relationships, and nuances in word meanings. (CCR.5)

Acquire and use accurately a range of general academic and domain-specific words and phrases. (CCR.6)

SEE ALSO . . .

SECTION V: VOCABULARY

Chapter 11: Specific Word Instruction

Chapter 12: Word-Learning Strategies

Chapter 13: Word Consciousness

Multisyllabic Word Reading

While phonics instruction gives students the basic tools to decode most single-syllable words, explicit instruction in recognizing syllables and morphemes gives students additional strategies for reading longer multisyllabic words. To read words in text fluently and accurately, the brain's orthographic processor must learn to "see" common letter patterns and recurring word parts (Moats 2005). In multisyllabic words, these multi-letter patterns, or "chunks," may be syllables, affixes, or phonograms (Ehri 2002).

Fluency

According to Hudson, Lane, and Pullen (2005), reading fluency is made up of at least three key elements: "*accurate* reading of connected text at a conversational *rate* with appropriate *prosody* or expression." Each of these elements—accuracy, rate, and prosody—has a clear connection to reading comprehension. Differences in reading fluency distinguish good readers from poor; a lack of reading fluency is a good predictor of reading comprehension problems (Stanovich 1991). Teachers can think of reading fluency as a bridge between the two major components of reading—decoding and comprehension.

Vocabulary

Vocabulary is the knowledge of words and word meanings. It occupies an important position both in learning to read and in comprehending text (National Reading Panel 2000). According to Michael Graves (2000), there are four components of an effective vocabulary program: (1) wide or extensive independent reading to expand word knowledge, (2) instruction in specific words to enhance comprehension of texts containing those words, (3) instruction in independent word-learning strategies, and (4) word consciousness and word-play activities to motivate and enhance learning. Not surprisingly, vocabulary development is especially important for English-language learners (ELLs).

CCSS READING STANDARDS

Literature • Informational Text

Key Ideas and Details

Craft and Structure

Integration of Knowledge and Ideas

Range of Reading and Level of Text Complexity

TEXT COMPLEXITY
the inherit difficulty of reading and comprehending a text combined with reader and task variables

SEE ALSO . . .

SECTION VI: COMPREHENSION

Chapter 14: Literary Text

Chapter 15: Informational Text

SEE ALSO . . .

Comprehensive Reading Model, p. 743

Comprehension

Reading comprehension is the process of extracting and constructing meaning from written texts. It has three key elements—the text, the reader, and the activity and related tasks (RAND Reading Study Group 2002; Snow 2003). Good comprehension instruction requires teachers to consider all of these factors. More important, it involves showing students how these factors affect their understanding when reading. Recent innovations in comprehension instruction have been built on a foundation of what good readers do. Research has shown that the effective reading processes, or strategies, of good readers can be explicitly taught and that doing so improves comprehension (National Reading Panel 2000).

Reading Assessment

Scientifically based research studies have repeatedly demonstrated the value of regularly assessing students' reading progress (e.g., Fuchs and Fuchs 1999; Shinn 1998). Reliable and valid assessments help monitor the effectiveness of instruction. An assessment is reliable if it provides a dependable, consistent measurement of a particular trait or ability; it is valid if it actually measures that trait or ability (Torgesen 2006).

Types of Assessment

There are basically four types of assessments—screening, progress monitoring, diagnostic, and outcome. Screening assessments identify those students who are at risk for reading difficulty. If screening results indicate a potential difficulty, the student is usually provided with additional support and increased progress monitoring. In cases where screening results indicate a severe reading problem, immediate diagnostic evaluation may be warranted. Diagnostic assessment is usually reserved for students who, according to progress monitoring, fail to respond to additional support (Hosp, Hosp, and Howell 2007).

Reading Assessments

TYPE	PURPOSE	ADMINISTRATION
▸ **Screening**	• To identify students who are at risk for reading difficulty and may benefit from additional support • To determine the most appropriate starting point for instruction	• To elementary students, at the beginning of the school year or semester • To middle- and high-school students at the end of the previous school year
▸ **Progress Monitoring**	• To determine whether students are making adequate progress • To determine whether instruction needs to be adjusted	• To students reading at the expected level, three times a year • To students reading below the expected level, biweekly • To students reading significantly below the expected level, weekly or biweekly
Curriculum Embedded	• To measure the extent to which students have learned the material taught in a specific reading program	
General or External	• To measure critical reading skills (phonemic awareness, phonics, fluency, vocabulary, or comprehension) in general • To predict success in meeting grade-level standards by the end of the year	
▸ **Diagnostic**	• To pinpoint a student's specific area of weakness • To provide in-depth information about students' skills and instructional needs	• Only after other forms of assessment reveal that an individual student is reading below the expected level or not making sufficient progress
▸ **Outcome**	• To provide a bottom-line evaluation of the overall effectiveness of a reading program	• To all students, at the end of the school year or semester

SEE ALSO . . .

Comprehensive Reading Model, p. 743

Comprehensive Assessment Plan

Assessment not only directs students' reading development, but also supports educators by helping them to make instructional decisions and monitor program implementation (Diamond 2005). According to Torgesen (2006), a comprehensive assessment plan is "a critical element of an effective school-level plan for preventing reading difficulties." The plan has four main objectives which correspond roughly to the types of assessment: (1) to *identify* students at the beginning of the school year who are at risk for reading difficulties and who may need extra support or intervention, (2) to *monitor* students' progress during the school year to determine whether the at-risk students are making adequate progress and to identify any other students who may be falling behind, (3) to *collect* student assessment data that inform instruction, and (4) to *assess* whether instruction is sufficient enough to ensure that all students achieve grade-level expectations.

SEE ALSO . . .

Chapter 9: Fluency Assessment

Curriculum-Based Measurement (CBM)

Curriculum-based Measurement (CBM) is an assessment tool that usually includes a set of standard directions, a timing device, a set of passages, scoring rules, standards for judging performance, and record forms or charts (Hosp et al. 2007). With CBM students are tested on the curriculum they are being taught. Because CBM emphasizes repeated measurement over time, it is often used for progress monitoring. Reading CBM consists of oral reading fluency (ORF) and maze passage reading. In ORF CBM, students read aloud from a passage for one minute. In Maze CBM, students read a passage silently for one minute. In the passage, every seventh word has been replaced with a word choice. As they read, students choose the one out of three words that makes sense within the sentence context.

Stumbling Blocks to Becoming a Proficient Reader

Difficulty learning to read words accurately and fluently

Insufficient vocabulary, general knowledge, and reasoning skills to support comprehension of written language

Absence or loss of initial motivation to read, or failure to develop a mature appreciation of the rewards of reading

Snow, Burns, and Griffin 1998.

MATTHEW EFFECTS

A term used to describe a negative spiral in which good readers get increasingly "richer" in reading ability, while nonproficient readers get increasingly "poorer."

Downward Spiral of Reading Failure

Early assessment is one of the best ways to prevent the downward spiral of reading failure; it serves to identify students who need extra help in reading before they experience serious failure—or "catch them before they fall" (Torgesen 1998). The sooner an intervention occurs, the more likely students will regain ground (Torgesen 1998, 2004). Studies show that students who are poor readers at the end of first grade almost never acquire average-level reading skills by the end of elementary school (Francis et al. 1996; Shaywitz et al. 1999; Torgesen and Burgess 1998). This delayed development of reading skills affects students' exposure to text. Having less exposure to text prevents readers from fully developing language, vocabulary, and background knowledge, therefore adding to the downward spiral in which students have a difficult time ever catching up (Stanovich 1986, 1993). Stanovich calls this phenomenon the "Matthew effects," in which students who learn to read early continue improving and thus get "richer." But students who do not learn to read early continue to struggle, faced with harder and harder text, and so become "poorer" and increasingly distanced from the students "rich" in reading ability. The term refers to a Bible verse in the Book of Matthew.

The Fourth-Grade Slump

According to Jeanne Chall's stages of reading development (1983, 1996), reading is a process that changes as the reader becomes more able and proficient. Generally, Stages 1 and 2 (Grades 1–3) are characterized as a period when students are "learning to read," and Stages 3–5 (Grades 4 and above) are characterized as a period of "reading to learn." In the learning-to-read stage, students typically read simple texts containing familiar words within their oral vocabularies and knowledge base. In the reading-to-learn stage, students read increasingly more demanding academic texts containing challenging words and complex concepts beyond their oral vocabularies and knowledge base. In the critical transition period, from Stage 2 to Stage 3, from "learning to read" to "reading to learn," teachers have often noticed an apparently sudden drop-off in reading scores, particularly for socioeconomically disadvantaged students (Chall and Jacobs 2003). This phenomenon has been referred to as the "fourth-grade slump." To combat the fourth-grade slump, Chall and Jacobs (2003) recommend focusing on vocabulary development to expand students' word knowledge along with reading fluency and automaticity.

One of the most compelling findings from recent reading research is that children who get off to a poor start in reading rarely catch up.

—TORGESEN, 1998

Motivation and Interest in Reading

There is often a decline in motivation and interest in reading in students who at first had difficulty in learning to read (Eccles et al. 1993; McKenna, Kear, and Ellsworth 1995). According to Torgesen et al. (2007), this lack of motivation has "two unfortunate consequences, both of which have a direct impact on the growth of reading proficiency in adolescents." The first consequence is that students with low motivation and interest in reading do not read as much. The second is that students who are less motivated to read are usually less interested in fully understanding what they are reading (Guthrie et al. 2004).

SEE ALSO . . .

Fundamentals of Comprehension, p. 609

Motivation and Engagement with Reading, p. 695

Anderson (1996) suggests that "reading books may be a cause, not merely a *reflection,* of students' level of reading proficiency." In a study of fifth graders, Anderson, Wilson, and Fielding (1988) found a positive relationship between the amount of students' out-of-school, independent reading and measures of reading comprehension, vocabulary, and reading speed. The table on the facing page shows staggering differences in fifth graders' reading habits; students in the 90th percentile spent more than 200 times as many minutes reading than students in the 10th percentile.

SEE ALSO . . .

Section V: Vocabulary

Academic Language

Dutro and Moran (2003) define academic language as "the language of texts, of academic discussion, and of formal writing." It is the advanced form of language needed to communicate successfully in formal, often academic, situations. Many skills

Variation in Amount of Independent Reading

Percentile Rank [a]	Minutes of Reading per Day		Words Read per Year	
	BOOKS	TEXT [b]	BOOKS	TEXT [b]
98	65.0	67.3	4,358,000	4,733,000
90	21.2	33.4	1,823,000	2,357,000
80	14.2	24.6	1,146,000	1,697,000
70	9.6	16.9	622,000	1,168,000
60	6.5	13.1	432,000	722,000
50	4.6	9.2	282,000	601,000
40	3.2	6.2	200,000	421,000
30	1.8	4.3	106,000	251,000
20	.7	2.4	21,000	134,000
10	.1	1.0	8,000	51,000
2	0	0	0	8,000

[a] *Percentile rank on each measure separately.* [b] *Books, magazines, and newspapers.*
Anderson, Wilson, and Fielding 1988.

To be successful academically, students need to develop the specialized language of academic discourse that is distinct from conversational language.

—FRANCIS ET AL., 2006

are wrapped up in the concept of academic language. Components of academic language include vocabulary knowledge, syntax (sentence architecture), and rules of grammar. Academic vocabulary consists of both specialized, content-specific words such as *phoneme* or *morpheme* and highly utilized terms such as *cognitive* or *diagnostic*.

In terms of exposing students to new academic vocabulary, speech is far more limited than written language. According to an analysis by Hayes and Ahrens (1988), students are more likely to encounter a word outside their academic vocabularies from a printed text than from a television show or a conversation with a college-educated adult. In fact, the text of a children's book contains more rare words than does any kind of oral language. The table on the following page shows selected statistics from Hayes and Ahrens' analysis.

Selected Statistics for Major Sources of Spoken and Written Language (Sample Means)	RANK OF MEDIAN WORD	RARE WORDS PER 1,000
1. Printed texts		
Abstracts of scientific articles	4,389	128.0
Newspapers	1,690	68.3
Popular magazines	1,399	65.7
Adult books	1,058	52.7
Comic books	867	53.5
Children's books	627	30.9
Preschool books	578	16.3
2. Television texts		
Popular prime-time adult shows	490	22.7
Popular prime-time children's shows	543	20.2
Cartoon shows	598	30.8
Mr. Rogers and *Sesame Street*	413	2.0
3. Adult speech		
Expert witness testimony	1,008	28.4
College graduates to friends, spouses	496	17.3

Hayes and Ahrens 1988.

Differentiated Instruction

SEE ALSO . . .

Comprehensive Reading Model, p. 743

Students come to school with a wide variety of skills, abilities, and interests as well as varying proficiency in English and other languages. Some students struggle, while others are right on level or even above it. Diverse learners demand instruction that supports their special needs. This differentiated instruction meets the needs of students with reading difficulties, students with disabilities, advanced learners, and English-language learners.

Levels of Learners

Using assessment data, teachers can plan appropriate instruction that supports students' diverse needs. The needs of these learners can be categorized into four different levels: advanced, benchmark, strategic, and intensive. Based on these levels, teachers can target additional skill instruction and intervention.

Levels of Learners	
Advanced Learners	Students who consistently exceed grade-level expectations
Benchmark Learners	Students who meet grade-level expectations and occasionally may need differentiated instruction
Strategic Learners	Students who are below grade-level expectations but will make progress with targeted assistance
Intensive Learners	Students who are significantly below grade-level expectations and require substantial intensive intervention

Struggling Readers

- **Aliterate**
- **Functional illiterate**
- **Illiterate**

Adolescent Struggling Readers

Struggling readers belong to the strategic and intensive groups of learners. Adolescent struggling readers fall into three categories: aliterate, functional illiterate, and illiterate. *Aliterate* refers to students who can read fairly well but choose not to—reading bores them and they see no purpose in engaging in it. *Functional illiterate* refers to students who have some reading skills, though these skills are insufficient for competent performance in everyday tasks, such as reading a bus schedule or telephone directory. *Illiterate* refers to students who are totally unable to read a simple sentence in any language. According to Curtis and Longo (1999), the only hope for improvement of functional illiteracy and illiteracy is "direct instruction in the processes, knowledge, and skills students have not yet had the opportunity to acquire."

English-Language Learners (ELLs)

The U.S. Department of Education defines ELLs as "national-origin-minority students who are limited-English proficient." In the last twenty years, the population of ELLs has grown 169 percent. Projected to be 30 percent of the school-aged population by 2015, ELLs are one of the fastest-growing groups in the nation's schools (Francis et al. 2006). They speak more than 400 languages, Spanish being the most prevalent at 79 percent.

Acquiring reading skills in a second language is similar to the process of acquiring reading skills in a first language.

—FRANCIS ET AL., 2006

Based on limited available research on acquiring literacy in a second language, the National Literacy Panel on Language-Minority Children and Youth (August and Shanahan 2006) published the following findings:

- As is for native English speakers, the essential components of effective reading instruction—phonological awareness, phonics, fluency, vocabulary, and text comprehension—have a positive influence on the literacy development of ELLs.
- Instruction in the essential components of reading is necessary—but not sufficient—for teaching ELLs to read and write proficiently in English. ELL students need more work in oral language development, vocabulary, and text comprehension than native English speakers.
- ELLs enter classrooms with varying degrees of oral proficiency and literacy in their first language. Tapping into first-language literacy can confer advantages to ELLs and can be used to facilitate literacy development in English.

English-Language Learners

Language	Estimated Students
Spanish	3,598,451 (79%)
Vietnamese	88,906 (2%)
Hmong	70,768 (1.6%)
Chinese, Cantonese	46,466 (1%)
Korean	43,969 (1%)

Kindler 2002.

Educating English-language learners has become both a challenge and a necessity across the country. In *Practical Guidelines for the Education of English Language Learners: Research Based Recommendations for Instruction and Academic Interventions* (Francis et al. 2006), the authors make the following recommendations for planning effective reading instruction and interventions for ELLs: (1) build decoding skills through early, explicit, and intensive instruction in phonological awareness and phonics, (2) offer additional opportunities for the development of in-depth vocabulary knowledge, (3) provide the strategies and knowledge necessary to comprehend challenging literary and informational texts, (4) focus instruction in reading fluency on vocabulary and increased exposure to print, (5) supply significant opportunities for students to engage in structured, academic talk, and (6) ensure that independent reading is structured and purposeful, with good reader–text match.

I

SECTION I

Word Structure

CHAPTER 1

Structure of English

CHAPTER 2

Structure of Spanish

CHAPTER

1

Structure of English

what? why? when? how?

what?

Phonemes

PHONEME
the smallest unit of spoken language that makes a difference in a word's meaning

SEE ALSO . . .

Chapter 5: Phonological Awareness
Chapter 6: Phonics

Phoneme Categories

The English-language alphabet has 26 letters that are used singly and in combination to represent about 42 to 44 different sounds, or phonemes. In Greek, *phon* means "sound"; *eme* means "an element or little piece of something." A phoneme is the smallest unit of spoken language that makes a difference in a word's meaning. For example, the phonemes /p/ and /s/ are different; the word *pit* has a different meaning from *sit.* Linguists disagree on the actual number of phonemes, or sounds, in the English language. The number varies according to dialect, individual speech patterns, changes in stress, and other variables.

Consonant Phonemes

There are about 25 consonant phonemes, or sounds. Eighteen consonant phonemes, such as /d/ and /t/, are represented by a single letter. Seven phonemes, such as /ch/ and /sh/, are represented by two letters. The letters *c, q,* and *x* do not have a unique phoneme assigned to them. The sounds that they represent are more commonly represented by other letters and spellings: the sound /k/ or /s/ for *c,* the sounds /kw/ for *qu,* and the sounds /ks/ for *x.*

Vowel Phonemes

The vowel letters *a, e, i, o,* and *u* are used singly and in combination to represent the different sounds. Including *r*-controlled vowels, there are about 18 vowel phonemes, or sounds.

Consonant Phonemes (Standard American English)

Phoneme	Key Word	Phoneme	Key Word	Phoneme	Key Word
/b/	bus	/n/	no	/ch/	chair
/d/	dot	/p/	pen	/sh/	shoe
/f/	fan	/r/	red	/zh/	television
/g/	gold	/s/	city, six	/th/	think
/h/	hat	/t/	tent	/TH/	this
/j/	giraffe, jog	/v/	van	/hw/	what
/k/	cat, key	/w/	web	/ng/	wing
/l/	log	/y/	you		
/m/	milk	/z/	zebra		

Vowel Phonemes (Standard American English)

Phoneme	Key Word	Phoneme	Key Word	Phoneme	Key Word
/ā/	take	/i/	rib	/o͝o/	good
/ē/	teeth	/o/	pot	/oi/, /oy/	oil
/ī/	tie	/u/	nut	/ou/, /ow/	house
/ō/	rope	/ə/	ago	/ûr/	girl
/a/	bat	/aw/	saw	/är/	art
/e/	egg	/o͞o/, /yo͞o/	tube, cube	/ôr/	or

what?

Consonant Phoneme Classifications

10 Most Frequent Consonant Phonemes

/r/, /t/, /n/, /s/, /l/, /k/, /d/, /m/, /p/, /b/

Hanna et al. 1966.

Consonant sounds may be classified according to place of articulation, manner of articulation, and whether they are voiced or unvoiced. To produce a consonant sound, vocal airflow is either partially or completely obstructed as it moves through the mouth. All consonants are not equally accessible in spoken language (Moats 2005).

Consonant Phoneme Classifications	
Place of Articulation Where in the mouth is the sound produced?	▸ Lips closed (bilabial) ▸ Upper front teeth on lower lip (labiodental) ▸ Tongue between teeth (dental) ▸ Tongue on ridge behind upper teeth (alveolar) ▸ Tongue against roof of mouth (palatal) ▸ Tongue against soft palate in back of throat (velar) ▸ Throat open (glottal)
Manner of Articulation How is the sound produced?	▸ **Stops (plosives)** Airflow is stopped completely for a short time. ▸ **Nasals** Air is forced through the nasal cavity; mouth is closed. ▸ **Fricatives** Air is forced through a narrow space, creating friction. ▸ **Affricates** A sequence of a stop and a fricative; airflow is stopped completely and then released. ▸ **Glides** glide immediately into the vowel that always follows; airflow is not obstructed. ▸ **Liquids** seem to float in the mouth; difficult to produce in isolation or to separate from the preceding vowel sound.
Voiced or Unvoiced Sounds	▸ **Voiced** The vocal cords vibrate. ▸ **Unvoiced** The vocal cords do not vibrate.

Consonant Phoneme Articulation *(boldface phoneme indicates voiced sound)*

Place \ Manner	Stops	Nasals	Fricatives	Affricates	Glides	Liquids
Lips (bilabial)	**/b/** /p/	**/m/**				
Teeth on lip (labiodental)			**/v/** /f/			
Tongue between teeth (interdental)			**/TH/** /th/			
Ridge behind teeth (alveolar)	**/d/** /t/	**/n/**	**/z/** /s/			**/l/** **/r/**
Roof of mouth (palatal)			**/zh/** /sh/	**/j/** /ch/	**/y/**	
Back of throat (velar)	**/g/** /k/	**/ng/**			**/hw/** /wh/	
Throat (glottal)					/h/	

Based on Moats 2005.

Consonant Phonemes

Continuous Sounds sounds that can be produced for several seconds without distortion	/f/, /l/, /m/, /n/, /r/, /s/, /v/, /w/, /y/, /z/
Stop Sounds sounds that can be produced for only an instant	/b/, /d/, /g/, /h/, /j/, /k/, /p/, /t/

what?

Vowel Phoneme Classifications

Vowels are a class of open, unobstructed speech sounds that are not consonants.

—MOATS, 2000

American English has 15 vowel phonemes plus at least three *r*-controlled vowel combinations that are often classified as vowels (Moats 2005). Vowels can be classified according to place of articulation: tongue position (front to back, high to low) and lip position (wide and smiling, rounded and wide open, rounded and partially open). Pronunciation of a vowel may vary according to regional and dialect differences.

In the chart on the facing page, vowels are arranged according to their proximity to one another in articulation (Moats 2000, 2005). Beginning with /ē/, the position of the tongue moves from front to back and drops from high to low. Tongue position affects lip position. Lip position changes one step at a time from wide and smiling to rounded and wide open: /ē/, /i/, /ā/, /e/, /a/, /ī/, /o/. After /u/, the lips close slowly until they are rounded and partially open. To see how lip position changes, look in a mirror while saying the vowel sequence in order.

Some vowel sounds do not fit into the general sequence. A diphthong sound shifts in the middle as the lips change position from the rounded to smile. A schwa (ə) is an indistinct vowel sound—an empty vowel with no identity. In English, the vowel in an unstressed syllable often "reduces" to a schwa. In *r*-controlled vowels, the letter *r* affects the sound of the vowel(s) that precedes it. The vowel(s) may become totally combined with *r* (*bird, her, fur*), may be slightly separated from *r* (*far, for*), or may keep its original sound (*hair, hear, hire*).

Vowel Articulation

Tongue position

Lip position

10 Most Frequent Vowel Phonemes

/ĭ/, /ə/, /a/, /e/, /ō/, /ē/, /ā/, /o/, /ī/, /u/

Hanna et al. 1966.

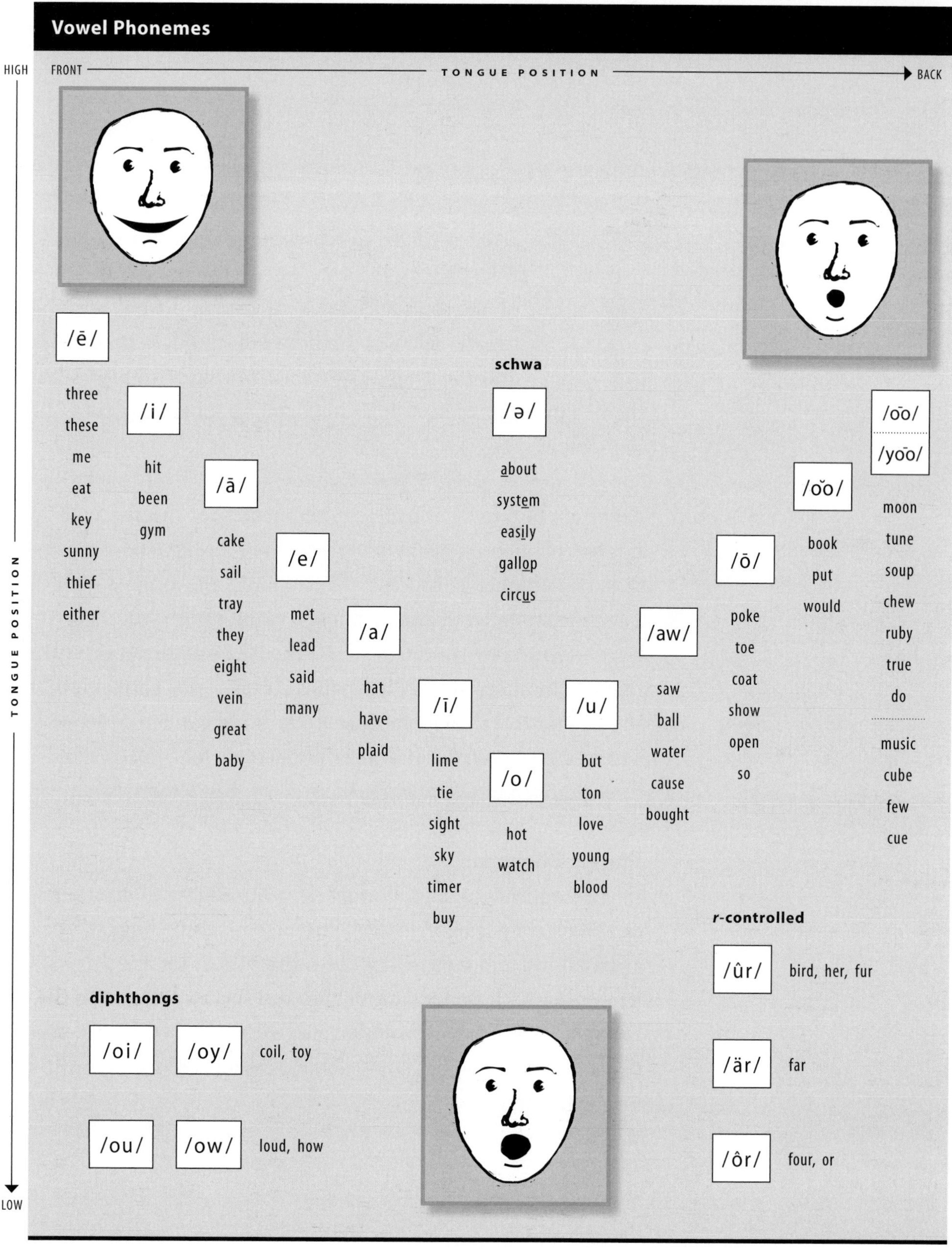
Vowel Phonemes
HIGH
FRONT
TONGUE POSITION
BACK
/ē/
three
these
me
eat
key
sunny
thief
either
/i/
hit
been
gym
/ā/
cake
sail
tray
they
eight
vein
great
baby
/e/
met
lead
said
many
/a/
hat
have
plaid
/ī/
lime
tie
sight
sky
timer
buy
schwa
/ə/
about
system
easily
gallop
circus
/o/
hot
watch
/u/
but
ton
love
young
blood
/aw/
saw
ball
water
cause
bought
/ō/
poke
toe
coat
show
open
so
/ŏo/
book
put
would
/ōo/
/yōo/
moon
tune
soup
chew
ruby
true
do
music
cube
few
cue
r-controlled
/ûr/
bird, her, fur
/är/
far
/ôr/
four, or
diphthongs
/oi/
/oy/
coil, toy
/ou/
/ow/
loud, how
TONGUE POSITION
LOW

Based on Moats 2005.

what?

Sound/Spellings

28

SOUND/SPELLING
a phoneme/grapheme pairing

SEE ALSO . . .

Chapter 6: Phonics

Letters are used to represent or stand for sounds. A letter is a *grapheme,* or written representation, of one sound. Phonics instruction involves teaching the relationship between sounds (phonemes) and the spellings (graphemes) used to represent them. These are referred to as phoneme/grapheme pairings, or sound/spellings.

There are hundreds of different graphemes for the 42 to 44 English phonemes. Many phonemes are represented by more than one grapheme, or letter. For example, the long-*e* sound can be represented by the spellings *e, ea, ee*; the /b/ sound can be represented by the letter *b*; and the /sh/ sound can be represented by the letters *sh.* The word *sat* has three phonemes (/s/ /a/ /t/) and three graphemes (*s, a, t*) represented by three letters. The word *chop* has three phonemes (/ch/ /o/ /p/) and three graphemes (*ch, o, p*) represented by four letters.

Phonic Elements

In the English language, phonic elements and generalizations can be used to categorize the common sound/spellings, which are used to form words. For the most part, after the single-letter phonic elements (consonants and short vowels), it is the multiple spelling representations for the same sounds that students find challenging. The phonic elements are summarized on the facing page.

Phonic Elements (Sound/Spelling Categories)	
Single Consonants	(b, c, d, f, g, h, j, k, l, m, n, p, q, r, s, t, v, w, x, y, z)
Consonant Blends	Two consonants that appear together in a word, with each retaining its sound when blended. (Examples: fl, gr, sp, mp)
Consonant Digraphs	Two consonant letters that together stand for a single sound. (Examples: sh, th, wh)
Silent Consonants	Two consonant letters may represent the sound of only one of them. The other consonant is "silent." (Examples: gn, kn, wr)
Short Vowels	(a, e, i, o, u)
Long Vowels	(ā, ē, ī, ō, ū) Long vowels occur at the end of an open syllable.
Long Vowels with Silent *e*	(a_e, e_e, i_e, o_e, u_e)
***r*-Controlled Vowels**	The letter *r* affects the sound of the vowel(s) that precedes it. (Examples: er, ir, ur, ar, or)
Vowel Digraphs*	Also known as vowel pairs. These pairs make one sound. (Examples: ai in *bait,* ee in *feet,* ie in *pie,* oa in *coat*)
Variant Vowel Digraphs*	Sounds that are not commonly classified as long or short vowels. (Examples: aw, au, o͝o, o͞o)
Diphthongs*	A blend of vowel sounds in one syllable. (Examples: oi in *boil,* oy in *toy,* ow in *now,* ou in *cloud*)
Schwa (ə)	The vowel sound sometimes heard in an unstressed syllable.

*These vowel pairings are sometimes referred to as *vowel teams.*

Common Consonant Sound/Spellings				
Phoneme	**Initial Position***	**Key Word**	**Final Position***	**Key Word**
/b/	b	bat	b	hub
			bb	ebb
/ch/	ch	chop	ch	beach
	t	future		
			tch	match
/d/	d	day	d	bad
			dd	add
			ed	loved
/f/	f	fat	f	beef
			ff	off
			gh	laugh
			lf	calf
	ph	phone	ph	graph
/g/	g	get	g	big
			gg	egg
	gh	ghost	gh	burgh
			gue	plague
/h/	h	how		
	wh	who		
/hw/	wh	what		
/j/			dge	dodge
	g	gem		
			ge	cage
	j	jump		

*Initial or final position in a syllable

Based on Hanna et al. 1966.

Common Consonant Sound/Spellings

Phoneme	Initial Position*	Key Word	Final Position*	Key Word
/k/	c	cat		
	ch	choir		
			ck	clock
	k	kite		
			lk	walk
/l/	l	let	l	pail
			ll	wall
/m/			lm	calm
	m	mat	m	ham
			mb	lamb
			mn	hymn
/n/	gn	gnat	gn	sign
	kn	knock		
	mn	mnemonic		
	n	net	n	man
			nn	inn
/ng/	n (medial)	bank		
			ng	sing
/p/	p	pet	p	top
/r/	r	rat		
	rh	rhyme		
	wr	write		

*Initial or final position in a syllable
Based on Hanna et al. 1966.

CONTINUED ▷

Common Consonant Sound/Spellings

Phoneme	Initial Position*	Key Word	Final Position*	Key Word
/s/	c	cent		
			ce	face
	ps	psychology		
	s	sat	s	bus
	sc	scene		
			ss	kiss
/sh/	ci	social		
	sh	shoe	sh	rash
			ssi	mission
	ti	action		
/t/			ed	skipped
	t	tip	t	fit
			tt	putt
/th/	th	thank	th	path
/TH/	th	this	th	bathe
/v/	v	vine		
			ve	love
/w/	w	wave		
/y/	i	senior		
	y	yellow		
/z/			es	goes
			s	has
	z	zoo		
			zz	buzz
/zh/	g	regime		
	s	usual		
	si	fusion		

*Initial or final position in a syllable

Based on Hanna et al. 1966.

Initial Consonant Blend Sound/Spellings

	Sounds	Spelling	Key Word
L - BLENDS	/bl/	bl	block
	/cl/	cl	clip
	/fl/	fl	flow
	/gl/	gl	glad
	/pl/	pl	plan
	/sl/	sl	slap
R - BLENDS	/br/	br	brat
	/cr/	cr	crow
	/dr/	dr	drain
	/fr/	fr	free
	/gr/	gr	green
	/pr/	pr	pray
	/tr/	tr	train

	Sounds	Spelling	Key Word
S - BLENDS	/sk/	sc	scan
	/sk/	sk	skate
	/sm/	sm	small
	/sn/	sn	snow
	/sp/	sp	spell
	/st/	st	star
	/sw/	sw	sway
3 - LETTER	/skr/	scr	scream
	/spl/	spl	splash
	/spr/	spr	spring
	/skw/	squ	squash
	/str/	str	strap

Final Consonant Blend Sound/Spellings

Sounds	Spelling	Key Word
/kt/	ct	fact
/ft/	ft	raft
/ld/	ld	wild
/lf/	lf	self
/lk/	lk	milk
/lp/	lp	help
/lt/	lt	quilt
/mp/	mp	damp

Sounds	Spelling	Key Word
/nd/	nd	bend
/nk/	nk	sink
/nt/	nt	rent
/pt/	pt	kept
/sk/	sk	desk
/sp/	sp	crisp
/st/	st	best

Common Vowel Sound/Spellings									
/ā/	a (favor)	a_e (late)	ai (bait)	ay (say)	ea (steak)	ei (veil)	ey (they)	eigh (sleigh)	
/ē/	e (me)	ee (feet)	ea (bead)	y (many)	ie (field)	e_e (these)	ey (key)	i_e (machine)	ei (receive)
/ī/	i_e (time)	i (minor)	y (try)	i (mild)	ie (pie)	igh (high)	y_e (type)		
/ō/	o (so)	o_e (hope)	oa (coat)	ow (low)	oe (toe)	ou (soul)	ew (sew)		
/a/	a (sat)	a_e (have)	ai (plaid)						
/e/	e (pet)	ea (head)	ai (said)	a (many)					
/i/	i (six)	y (gym)	e (pretty)	i_e (give)	ee (been)	ui (build)	a_e (senate)		
/o/	o (log)	a (watch)							
/u/	u (but)	o (ton)	o_e (love)	ou (young)					
/ə/	a (alone)	e (system)	i (easily)	o (gallop)	u (circus)				
/ûr/	ur (turn)	ir (girl)	er (her)	or (work)					
/är/	ar (car)	are (are)	ear (heart)						
/ôr/	or (or)	our (four)	ar (war)						
/aw/	aw (saw)	au (cause)	a[l] (walk)	a[ll] (ball)	ough (cough)	augh (caught)			
/oi/ **/oy/**	oi (boil)	oy (toy)							
/ou/ **/ow/**	ou (cloud)	ow (now)							
/o͞o/ **(yo͞o)***	oo (hoot)	u (ruby) (music)*	ue (blue) (cue)*	ew (new) (few)*	u_e (tube) (cube)*	o (do)	ou (soup)		
/o͝o/	oo (book)	u (put)	o (wolf)	ou (would)					

Most Frequent English Sound/Spellings

It is useful to know which sound/spellings are important enough to teach and which, because of their lower frequency in words, can be learned on an as-needed basis. The following chart shows the most frequent spellings of the 43 phoneme sounds covered in this book. The percentages provided in parentheses are based on the number of occurrences in which each sound/spelling appeared in the 17,000 most frequently used single and multisyllabic words (Hanna et al. 1966).

Sound/Spelling Frequency

Sound	Spellings
CONSONANTS	
/b/	b (97%), bb
/d/	d (98%), dd, ed
/f/	f (78%), ph (12%), ff, lf, gh
/g/	g (88%), gg, gue, gh
/h/	h (98%), wh (2%)
/j/	g (66%), j (22%), dg
/k/	c (73%), k (13%), ck, ch
/l/	l (91%), ll
/m/	m (94%), mm, mb, lm, mn
/n/	n (97%), nn, kn, gn, mn
/p/	p (96%), pp
/r/	r (97%), rr, wr, rh
/s/	s (73%), c (17%), ss, sc
/t/	t (97%), tt (3%), ed
/v/	v (99.5%)
/w/	w (92%)
/y/	i (55%), y (44%)
/z/	s (64%), z (23%), es, zz
/ch/	ch (55%), t (31%), tch (11%)
/sh/	ti (53%), sh (26%), ci, ssi
/zh/	si (49%), s (33%), g (15%)
/th/	th (100%)
/TH/	th (100%)
/hw/	wh (100%)
/ng/	ng (59%), n (41%)
VOWELS	
/ā/	a (45%), a_e (35%), ai, ay
/ē/	e (70%), ea (10%), ee (10%), e_e, i_e, i, ie
/ī/	i_e (37%), i (37%), y (14%), igh, ie, y_e
/ō/	o (73%), o_e (14%), oa, ow
/a/	a (97%), a_e, ai
/e/	e (91%), ea, a
/i/	i (68%), y (23%), i_e, a_e
/o/	o (94%), a
/u/	u (86%), o, ou
/ə/	o (27%), a (24%), i (22%), e (13%), ou, u
/ûr/	er (40%), ur (26%), ir (13%)
/är/	ar (89%), are, ear
/ôr/	or (41%)
/aw/	a (22%), au (19%), aw (10%), ough, augh
/oi/	oi (62%), oy (32%)
/ou/	ou (56%), ow (29%)
/o͞o/	oo (38%), u (21%), o, u_e, ou, ew, ue
/yo͞o/	u (69%), u_e (22%), ew, ue
/o͝o/	u (54%), oo (31%), ou, o

Based on Hanna et al. 1966.

Syllables

SYLLABLE
a word or part of a word pronounced as a unit

SEE ALSO . . .
Chapter 8: Multisyllabic Word Reading

A syllable is a word or part of a word pronounced as a unit. Each syllable contains only one vowel sound. There are six common types of syllables found within English words and four useful principles of syllable division.

Most Useful Syllable Division Principles

Division	Examples	Description
VC/CV	rab•bit nap•kin	**Two Consonants Between Two Vowels** If two consonants come between two vowels, divide between the consonants. The first vowel sound will be short.
V/CV (75%) VC/V (25%)	mu•sic clos•et	**One Consonant Between Two Vowels** If a word has one consonant between two vowels, divide the word after the first vowel and give the vowel its long sound. If this division does not produce a recognizable word, then divide the word after the consonant and give the vowel its short sound.
VC/CCV VCC/CV	hun•dred ink•well ath•lete	**Three Consonants Between Two Vowels** Keep the letters in a consonant blend or digraph together in the same syllable.
Consonant–*le*	wig•gle ri•fle	**Consonant–*le* Forms a Separate Syllable** If the first syllable ends with a consonant, try the short sound for the first vowel. If the first syllable ends with a vowel, try the long sound.

Based on Moats 2005.

Common Types of Syllables		Examples	
Syllable Type	**Description**	**Single Syllable**	**Multisyllable**
Closed	A syllable ending in one or more consonants and having a short-vowel sound spelled with one vowel letter. VC, CVC, CCVC, CVCC	dump fish men	picnic rabbit
Open	A syllable ending with a long-vowel sound spelled with one vowel letter. CV, CCV	me she	robot veto
Vowel Combination	A syllable with a short-vowel, long-vowel, or diphthong sound spelled with a vowel combination, such as *ai, ea, ee, oi,* or *oo.* CVVC, CCVVC, CVVCC	boil bread rain spoon teeth	baboon canteen complain heavy poison
***r*-Controlled**	A syllable containing a letter combination made up of a vowel followed by the letter *r,* such as *ar, er, ir, or,* and *ur.* The vowel–*r* combination is one welded sound that cannot be segmented.	far fern first for fur	perfect purchase snorkel target thirsty
Vowel–Consonant *e*	A syllable with a long-vowel sound spelled with one vowel letter followed by one consonant and a silent *e.* VCe, CVCe, CCVCe	fuse hide mole Pete race	amuse erase provide stampede tadpole
Consonant–*le*	A final, separate syllable containing a consonant followed by the letters *le.*	NA	apple table

Most Common Syllables in the Most Frequent English Words							
ing	er	i	y	de	en	u	per
ly	ed	tion	ter	com	an	ti	to
es	re	e	ex	o	ty	ri	
in	a	con	al	di	ry	be	

Based on Sakiey et al. 1980.

what?

Onset-Rime

ONSET-RIME
the two parts of a syllable

Levels of Phonological Awareness, p. 117

A syllable has two parts: the onset and the rime. The onset is the part of the syllable that comes before the vowel. It may be a consonant, consonant blend, or digraph. The rime is the vowel and everything after it. For example, in the one-syllable words *sing, bring,* and *thing,* the rime is *–ing* and the onsets are *s, br,* and *th.* Since the rime contains the vowel, all syllables have a rime. However, all syllables do not have an onset; for example, *I, it,* and *out.*

Onset and Rime

Word	Onset	Rime
I	_	I
it	_	it
out	_	out
sing	s	ing
bring	br	ing
thing	th	ing

PHONOGRAM
nonlinguistic term for rime

Phonograms

Phonogram is a nonlinguistic term sometimes substituted for rime. In the word *back, –ack* is the phonogram; it is also the rime.

SEE ALSO . . .

Phonograms, p. 186

A relatively small number of phonograms can be used to generate a large number of words. Wylie and Durrell (1970) point out that nearly 500 primary-grade words can be derived from only 37 "rhyming" phonograms.

Phonograms

ack	ail	ain	ake	ale
ame	an	ank	ap	ash
at	ate	aw	ay	eat
ell	est	ice	ick	ide
ight	ill	in	ine	ing
ink	ip	ir	ock	oke
op	ore	or	uck	ug
ump	unk			

Based on Wylie and Durrell 1970.

Phonograms

ack: back, black, crack, flack, hack, jack, knack, lack, pack, quack, rack, sack, slack, stack, tack, track

ail: bail, fail, frail, grail, hail, jail, mail, nail, pail, quail, rail, sail, snail, tail, trail, wail

ain: brain, chain, drain, gain, grain, lain, main, pain, plain, rain, slain, sprain, stain, strain, swain, train, twain, vain

ake: bake, brake, cake, drake, fake, flake, lake, make, quake, rake, sake, shake, snake, stake, take, wake

Phonograms

ale: bale, gale, hale, kale, male, pale, sale, scale, shale, stale, tale, vale, wale, whale

ame: blame, came, fame, flame, frame, game, lame, name, same, shame, tame

an: ban, bran, can, clan, fan, man, pan, plan, ran, scan, span, tan, than, van

CONTINUED ▷

Phonograms
ank: bank, blank, clank, crank, dank, drank, flank, frank, lank, plank, prank, rank, sank, shank, spank, stank, swank, tank, thank, yank
ap: cap, chap, clap, flap, gap, lap, map, nap, pap, rap, sap, scrap, slap, snap, strap, tap, trap, wrap, yap, zap
ash: bash, brash, cash, clash, crash, dash, flash, gash, gnash, hash, lash, mash, rash, sash, slash, smash, splash, stash, thrash, trash
at: bat, brat, cat, chat, drat, fat, flat, gnat, hat, mat, pat, rat, sat, scat, slat, spat, sprat, that, vat
ate: crate, date, fate, gate, grate, hate, late, mate, pate, plate, rate, skate, slate, spate, state
aw: caw, claw, craw, draw, flaw, gnaw, haw, jaw, law, maw, paw, raw, saw, slaw, squaw, straw, taw, thaw, yaw
ay: bay, bray, cray, day, flay, fray, gay, gray, hay, jay, lay, may, nay, pay, play, pray, quay, ray, say, slay, spay, splay, spray, stay, stray, sway, tray, way

Phonograms
eat: beat, bleat, cheat, cleat, eat, feat, heat, meat, neat, peat, pleat, seat, teat, treat, wheat
ell: bell, cell, dell, fell, hell, jell, knell, quell, sell, shell, smell, spell, swell, tell, well, yell
est: best, blest, chest, crest, fest, guest, jest, nest, pest, quest, rest, test, vest, west, zest
ice: dice, lice, mice, nice, price, rice, slice, spice, splice, thrice, trice, twice, vice
ick: brick, chick, click, crick, flick, hick, kick, lick, nick, pick, prick, quick, sick, slick, stick, thick, tick, trick, wick
ide: bide, bride, chide, glide, hide, pride, ride, side, slide, snide, stride, tide, wide
ight: blight, bright, fight, flight, fright, knight, light, might, night, plight, right, sight, slight, tight
ill: bill, chill, dill, drill, fill, gill, grill, hill, kill, mill, pill, quill, shrill, sill, skill, spill, still, thrill, till, will
in: bin, chin, din, fin, gin, grin, kin, pin, shin, sin, skin, spin, tin, thin, win
ine: brine, dine, fine, line, mine, nine, pine, shine, spine, swine, tine, thine, vine, wine

Phonograms
ing: bring, cling, ding, fling, king, ping, ring, sing, sling, spring, sting, string, swing, thing, wing, zing
ink: blink, brink, clink, drink, fink, ink, kink, link, mink, pink, rink, sink, slink, stink, think, wink
ip: blip, chip, clip, dip, drip, flip, grip, hip, kip, lip, nip, pip, quip, rip, ship, sip, skip, slip, strip, tip, trip, whip, zip
ir: fir, sir, stir, whir
ock: block, chock, clock, cock, crock, dock, flock, frock, hock, jock, knock, lock, mock, pock, rock, shock, smock, sock, stock
oke: bloke, broke, choke, coke, joke, poke, smoke, spoke, stoke, stroke, woke, yoke
op: cop, chop, crop, drop, flop, fop, glop, hop, lop, mop, plop, pop, prop, shop, slop, sop, stop, top

Phonograms
ore: bore, chore, core, fore, gore, lore, more, pore, score, shore, snore, sore, spore, store, swore, tore, wore, yore
or: for, nor
uck: buck, chuck, cluck, duck, luck, muck, pluck, puck, shuck, snuck, struck, stuck, suck, truck, tuck
ug: bug, chug, drug, dug, hug, jug, lug, mug, plug, pug, rug, slug, smug, snug, thug, tug
ump: bump, chump, clump, dump, frump, grump, hump, jump, lump, plump, pump, rump, slump, stump, sump, thump, trump
unk: bunk, chunk, clunk, dunk, drunk, flunk, funk, hunk, junk, lunk, punk, skunk, slunk, spunk, stunk, sunk, trunk

what?

Morphemes

MORPHEMES
word-part clues; the meaningful parts of words
- root words
- prefixes
- suffixes
- Greek and Latin roots

SEE ALSO . . .

Morphemic Analysis, p. 490

Morphemes are the meaningful parts of words. They are often referred to as word-part clues. In Greek, *morphos* means "form or structure"; *eme* means "an element or little piece of something." The majority of morphemes in English came from one of three ancient languages: Greek, Latin, or Anglo-Saxon. A morpheme may be one syllable (*pig*) or more than one syllable (*elephant*). It may be a whole word or a part of a word. There are two basic types of morphemes: *free* and *bound. Free morphemes* can stand alone as words; they do not have to be combined with other morphemes to make words. *Bound morphemes* must be attached to, or "bound" to, other morphemes to make words.

Anglo-Saxon Root Words

Anglo-Saxon root words are free morphemes. A root word, or base word, is a single word that cannot be broken into smaller words or word parts. Anglo-Saxon root words are words from which many other words are formed.

COMPOUND WORDS Compound words are composed of two Anglo-Saxon root words. The meaning of some compound words can be derived from the meanings of the two smaller words that comprise them: for example, *doghouse* and *bluebird.* Other compound words have a meaning that differs from the meaning of the two smaller words: for example, *butterfly* and *airline.*

Types of Morphemes	
Free Morphemes Can stand alone as words	Anglo-Saxon root words: *help, play, run*
Bound Morphemes Cannot stand alone as words	• Prefixes: *dis–, in–, re–, un–* • Derivational suffixes: *–ful, –less, –ly* • Inflectional suffixes: *–ed, –es, –ing, –s* • Greek roots: *bio, graph, scope* • Latin roots: *dict, ject, struct*

Affixes

Affixes are bound morphemes. This group of word parts includes prefixes and two kinds of suffixes: derivational and inflectional.

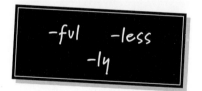

PREFIXES Prefixes are word parts that are "fixed" to the beginning of root words. They usually alter the meaning of the root word to which they are attached.

DERIVATIONAL SUFFIXES Derivational suffixes are word parts that are "fixed" to the end of root words. Like prefixes, they usually alter the meaning of the root word to which they are attached. It may also change the root word's part of speech, pronunciation, or spelling.

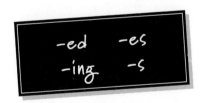

INFLECTIONAL SUFFIXES Inflectional suffixes, or endings, are word parts that are "fixed" to the end of root words. They usually change the form of a root word but not its part of speech. If the root word is a noun, the suffix may show possession (*hers*), or plurality (*boxes*). If the root word is a verb, the suffix may show tense (*walked*), active or passive voice (*it was driven*), or state (*she had been singing*). If the root word is an adjective, the suffix may show comparison (*louder, loudest*).

Greek and Latin Roots

Greek and Latin roots are also bound morphemes. Most Greek roots appear in combination with each other. Most Latin roots appear in combination with one or more affixes.

Most Frequent Prefixes

Prefix	Meaning	Example	Percent
un–	not	unfriendly	26%
re–	again, back	redo, return	14%
in–, im–, il–, ir–	not	injustice, impossible	11%
dis–	not, opposite of	disagree	7%
en–, em–	cause to	encode, embrace	4%
non–	not	nonsense	4%
in–, im–	in, on	inhabit, imprint	4%
over–	too much	overdo	3%
mis–	wrong	misfire	3%
sub–	under	submarine	3%
pre–	before	prefix	3%
inter–	between	interact	3%
fore–	before	forecast	3%
de–	not, opposite	deactivate	2%
trans–	across	transport	2%
super–	above	superstar	1%
semi–	half	semicircle	1%
anti–	against	antiwar	1%
mid–	middle	midway	1%
under–	below	undersea	1%
All others			3%

Based on White, Sowell, and Yanagihara 1989.

Most Frequent Suffixes			
Suffix	**Meaning**	**Example**	**Percent**
–s, –es	more than one	books, boxes	31%
–ed	past-tense verbs	hopped	20%
–ing	verb form/present participle	running	14%
–ly	characteristic of	quickly	7%
–er, –or	one who	worker, actor	4%
–ion, –tion, –ation, –ition	act, process	occasion, attraction	4%
–able, –ible	can be done	comfortable	2%
–al, –ial	having characteristics of	personal	1%
–y	characterized by	happy	1%
–ness	state of, condition of	kindness	1%
–ity, –ty	state of	infinity	1%
–ment	action or process	enjoyment	1%
–ic	having characteristics of	linguistic	1%
–ous, –eous, –ious	possessing the qualities of	joyous	1%
–en	made of	wooden	1%
–er	comparative	higher	1%
–ive, –ative, –itive	adjective form of a noun	plaintive	1%
–ful	full of	careful	1%
–less	without	fearless	1%
–est	comparative	biggest	1%
All others			7%

Based on White, Sowell, and Yanagihara 1989.

Common Latin Roots

Root	Meaning	Example	Root	Meaning	Example
aud	hear	audible	man	hand	manual
bene	well, good	benefit	mem	mind	memory
centi	hundred	centipede	migr	move	migrate
contra	against	contrary	mit, miss	send	submit/mission
cred	believe, trust	credible	ped	foot	pedal
dict	tell	dictate	pop	people	popular
duct	lead	conduct	port	carry	transport
equi	equal	equitable	rupt	break	erupt
extra	outside	extravagant	sign	mark	signal
fac	make	factory	spect	see	inspect
fig	form	figure	sta/stat	stand	statue
flec	flex, bend	flexible	struct	build, form	construct
form	shape	formulate	trac/tract	pull	tractor
fract	break	fracture	urb	city	suburb
init	beginning	initial	vid/vis	see	video/visible
ject	throw	reject	voc	voice	vocal
junct	join	junction	volv	roll	revolve

Common Greek Roots

Root	Meaning	Example	Root	Meaning	Example
amphi	both	amphibian	micro	small	microscope
astro	star	astronaut	mono	single	monorail
auto	self	automatic	ology	study of	morphology
biblio	book	bibliography	opt	eye	optical
bio	life	biology	para	beside	parallel
chron	time	chronic	phil	love	philosophy
geo	earth	geology	phon	sound	phonograph
graph	write, record	autograph	photo/phos	light	photograph
hemi	half	hemisphere	pod	foot	podiatrist
hydr	water	hydraulic	psych	mind, soul	psychic
hyper	over	hyperactive	scope	see	microscope
ist	one who	dentist	sphere	ball	hemisphere
logo	word, reason	logic	syn	together	synonym
macro	large	macrobiotic	tele	from afar	telephone
mech	machine	mechanic	therm	heat	thermometer
meter	measure	barometer			

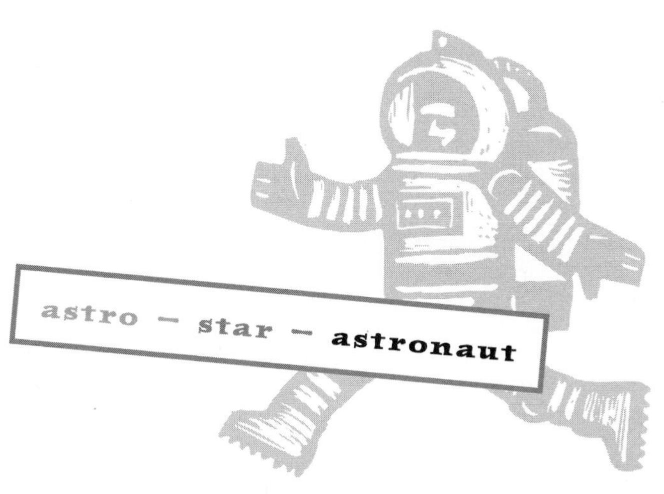

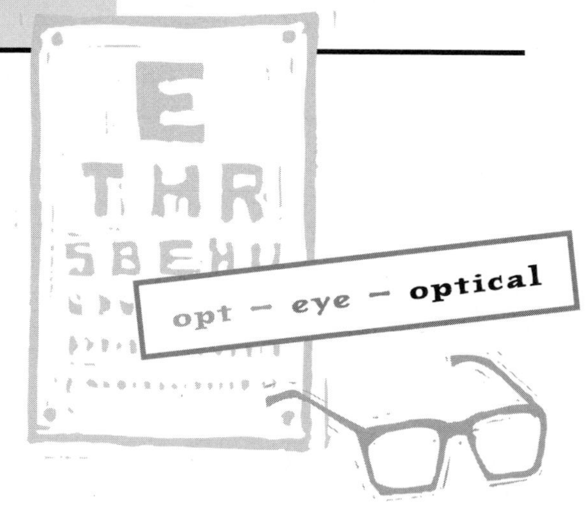

CHAPTER

2

Structure of Spanish

what?

Spanish Letter/Sound System

Most Spanish speakers in North, Central, and South America pronounce both *ll* and *y* as /y/.

Spanish Phonic Elements with Positive Transfer to English, p. 62

From a phonetic standpoint, Spanish is a much simpler language than English. There is a nearly one-to-one correspondence between the 22 phonemes in the Spanish that is spoken in the Americas and the 29 letters that represent these sounds. One significant difference between Spanish and English is the ease with which students are able to learn the letter/sound correspondences of the five Spanish vowels. Each vowel letter has a distinct and relatively consistent sound that forms the nucleus of every syllable. The five vowels are categorized as open (/a/), semi-open (/e/, /o/), and closed (/i/, /u/), depending on how wide the mouth is opened and the position of the tongue and lips. Because of the grapheme/phoneme consistency and structural importance of vowels, beginning Spanish readers are taught vowel letters and their corresponding sounds before they are introduced to consonant letters and their sounds.

The phonetic variations of Spanish consonants are a challenge for many beginning readers. As the chart of Spanish consonants later in this chapter shows, the *c* and *g* (like their English counterparts) have both a "hard" and a "soft" sound (e.g., *cocina* and *gigante*). In addition, the Spanish consonant phonemes /s/, /b/, and /y/ have more than one spelling. Students typically take several years to master these contrasts, drawing on visual memory specific to words or word families (Moran and Calfee 1993). Although the spelling of the consonant phonemes /k/, /g/, and /x/ varies, it follows predictable rules that are governed by the vowel sound that follows the consonant phoneme. Therefore, students can be taught how to use syllabic context to decode and spell words with these sounds.

Spanish Vowels

Vowel Type	Letter	Phoneme*	Key Words	Notes
Open	a	/a/	ama, casa	This is the short-*o* sound in *father* and *spa.*
Semi-Open	e	/e/	edad, mesa	This is the short-*e* sound in *messy.***
	o	/o/	oso, mono	This is the long-*o* sound in *no* and *old.*
Closed	i	/i/	iba, niña	This is the long-*e* sound in *machine.*
	u	/u/	uno, duda	This is the long-*oo* sound in *ruby* and *July.*
	y	/i/	y	This is the long-*e* sound in *city.*

*Phonemes are represented by phonetic symbols used in Spanish. **Commonly taught in U.S. schools as the long-*a* sound in *weigh*.

Spanish Vowel Combinations

Hiatos	*Hiatos* are two consecutive vowels that appear in different syllables. There is a pause between two distinct sounds.
	▸ One open and one semi-open, or two semi-open
	ae ao ea eo ee oa oe
	Key words: trae, real, leo, cree, toalla
	▸ One open or semi-open, and one accented closed
	ía íe ío úa úe úo aí eí oí aú eú
	Key words: día, río, actúo, país, leí, Raúl
Diptongos	*Diptongos* are two consecutive vowels that appear in the same syllable. The sounds are blended together.
	▸ One open or semi-open, and one closed
	ai/ay ei/ey oi/oy au eu ou
	ia ie io ua ue uo
	Key words: baile, voy, aunque, lluvia, cielo, cuando, puede
	▸ Two closed
	iu ui/uy
	Key words: ciudad, ruido, muy
Triptongos	*Triptongos* are three consecutive vowels that are blended within one syllable.
	▸ Open or semi-open, and two closed
	iai iei iau ioi uai/uay uei/uey uau
	Key words: apreciáis, miau, averiguáis, buey, guau

Spanish Consonants			
Letter	**Phoneme***	**Key Words**	**Notes**
b	/b/	boca, baño	
c	/k/	cama, cosa, cuna	Phoneme /k/ is spelled *c* before *a, o,* and *u* and *qu* before *e* and *i.*
	/s/	cena, cita	
ch	/ch/	chato, ocho	
d	/d/	deja, dos	Similar to /th/ between vowels (*nada*) and at the end of words (*pared*)
f	/f/	fiesta, fecha	
g	/g/	gato, guerra, guía	Hard *g* before *a, o, ue, ui*
	/x/	giro, gente	Spanish phoneme /x/ is a guttural sound, similar to English /h/.
h	silent	hijo, hermano	
j	/x/	jabón, rojo, jugo dije, jinete	Spanish phoneme /x/ is spelled *j* before *a, o,* and *u.* It can be spelled *j* or *g* before *e* and *i.* (See note for phoneme /x/ spelled *x.*)
l	/l/	loma, malo	
ll	/y/	llama, pollo	Although *ll* and *y* represent two distinct phonemes, most Spanish speakers say both /y/.
m	/m/	más, ama	
n	/n/	nido, una	
ñ	/ñ/	año, niño	Phoneme /ñ/ has a sound similar to that of the letters *ni* in the English word *onion.*

*A simplified system of phonetic symbols has been used to represent the sounds of *ch, ll, ñ, rr,* and *y.*

CONTINUED ▷

Spanish Consonants			
Letter	**Phoneme***	**Key Words**	**Notes**
p	/p/	papá, pera	
q	/k/	queso, quita	For /kw/ sound in Spanish, *cu* + vowel
r	/r/	oro, cara	More forcibly rolled than English /r/
	/rr/	rosa, alrededor, barro	Initial *r* has /rr/ sound, as does *r* after *l, n,* or *s.* When phoneme /rr/ occurs between two vowels, it is spelled *rr*
s	/s/	sapo, silla, mesa	Similar to the *s* of *cause* when followed by *b, d, g, l, m, n*
t	/t/	tú, todo, pata	Softer than English /t/
v	/b/	vaca, oveja	There is no Spanish phoneme /v/.
x	/s/	xilófono	The letter *x* can be pronounced four different ways.
	/x/	México	
	/gs/	excavar	
	/ks/	taxi	
y	/y/	yema, yo	
z	/s/	zapato, paz	
k	/k/	kilogramo, kiosco	Only appears in words of foreign origin
w	/o͞o/ or /b/	wat, wáter	Only appears in words of foreign origin

*A simplified system of phonetic symbols has been used to represent the sounds of *ch, ll, ñ, rr,* and *y.*

Spanish Consonant Blends

	Sounds	Spelling	Key Words
R - BLENDS	/br/	br	brazo, abrigo
	/cr/	cr	crema, crudo
	/dr/	dr	drama, dragón
	/fr/	fr	frío, ofrece
	/gr/	gr	gris, agregar
	/pr/	pr	primo, aprende
	/tr/	tr	traigo, atrás

	Sounds	Spelling	Key Words
L - BLENDS	/bl/	bl	blusa, habla
	/cl/	cl	clase, aclara
	/fl/	fl	flaco, flores
	/gl/	gl	globo, glaciar
	/pl/	pl	plancha, pluma
	/tl/	tl	nahautl, tlacuache

llama

Spanish Consonant Digraphs

Phoneme	Spelling	Key Words	Notes
/ch/	ch	choque, ancho	Usually taught as part of the Spanish alphabet
/y/	ll	llama, calle	Usually taught as part of the Spanish alphabet
/rr/	rr	perro, barril	

Spanish Sound/Spelling Sequence

SEE ALSO . . .

General Sequence for Teaching Phonic Elements, p. 178, for information about the English sound/spelling sequence

Explicit Spanish phonics instruction has been shown to improve Spanish-speaking students' reading achievement in both Spanish and English (Carrillo 1994; Durgunoglu, Nagy, and Hancin-Bhatt 1993). Although there is no "set in stone" sequence for teaching Spanish sound/spelling relationships, the following are some general guidelines:

- Unlike phonics instruction in English, Spanish phonics instruction should begin with the five vowels.
- Instruction should progress from simple to more complex sounds. Consonant sounds should be taught before digraphs (*ch, ll, rr*), blends (*cr, tr, bl, pl,* etc.), and vowel combinations (*hiatos* and *diptongos*).
- Consonants should be taught in combination with vowels so that students can apply what they learn to decodable text. Instruction should begin with the consonants that are most useful in generating and decoding Spanish words.
- The sequence of instruction should stagger consonant sounds to vary the type of articulation:
  - Bilabial (/p/, /b/, /m/)
  - Labiodental (/f/)
  - Dental (/t/, /d/)
  - Alveolar (/s/, /n/, /l/, /r/, /rr/)
  - Palatal (/ch/, /ñ/, /y/)
  - Velar (/k/, /x/, /g/)

In addition, students should receive systematic instruction that includes constant review and repetition of sound/spelling relationships. With these guidelines in mind, the following chart presents a possible sequence of Spanish phonics instruction.

Suggested Spanish Sound/Spelling Sequence		
Vowels	Initial vowel	o, a, i, u, e
Consonants and Consonant Digraphs	Open syllables with	m, s, p, t, c (/k/), n, b, l, f, r (initial) & rr, g (/g/), d, v, ch, ñ, j, ll, r (medial), c (/s/), g (/x/), y, q, gu + *e* or *i* (/g/), z, h, güe & güi, k, x, w
	Closed syllables ending in	l, m, n, r, s, d, z, x
Consonant Blends	Open syllables with	cr, pr, tr, br, gr, fr, bl, cl, fl, pl
	Closed syllables with	cr, pr, tr, br, gr, fr, bl, cl, fl, pl
Vowel Combinations	Hiatos	ae, ea, ee, eo
	Diphthongs in open syllables	ia, ie, ua, ue, ui & uy, io, ai & ay, oy
	Diphthongs in closed syllables	ie, ua, ue

what?

Spanish Syllable Types and Patterns

SEE ALSO . . .

Syllables, p. 36, for information about English syllable types and patterns

Spanish is in many respects a syllabic language: the spoken language is built upon a relatively small collection of distinctive syllables, and the printed language is easily decoded syllable by syllable (Moran and Calfee 1993). The vast majority of Spanish syllables fall into two categories: open CV (55.94 percent) and closed CVC (20.16 percent) (Guirao and Manrique 1972).

In Spanish, the guiding principle in syllable division is to make syllables end in a vowel as far as possible, so a single consonant between vowels is joined to the vowel or vowels that follow: *ca•la•ba•za.* The digraphs *ch, ll, rr* are considered single consonants and never separated: *ca•rre•te•ra.* Prepositional prefixes form separate syllables, except when the prefix is followed by *s* + a consonant: *con•sul•tar* vs. *cons•tan•te.* Vowels forming a diphthong or triphthong must not be separated: *llu•via.* Hiatos as well as diphthongs and triphthongs that are dissolved by an accent mark form separate syllables: *le•er* and *dí•a.* The liquids *l* and *r* when preceded by any consonant other than *s* are not separated from that consonant unless the consonant is part of a prefix: *a•bra•zo* vs. *sub•ra•yar.* Two separate consonants standing between vowels are divided: *pron•to.*

Spanish Syllable Types		
Syllable Type	**Definition**	**Key Words**
Open	An open syllable ends in a vowel. In Spanish, most syllables are open and begin with a consonant.	la, de, ojo, hilo, sopa, corre, abeja, bonito, muchacho, graciosa
Closed	A closed syllable ends in a consonant.	el, ir, vez, pon, árbol, tambor, saltan, barcos, puentes, comparten

Spanish Syllable Patterns (from Most to Least Frequent)		
Pattern	**Division**	**Key Words**
CV	CV/C	so • pa, mu • cha • cho
CVC	CVC/C	ven • der, tor • men • tas
V	V/CV, CV/V	u • va, e • cha, tí • o, le • a
CCV	CCV/C CCV/CC	cla • se, glo • bos pro • ble • ma
VC	VC/C	us • ted, ár • bol, im • por • tan • tes
CCVC	CCVC/C	gran • de, cris • tal
VCC	VCC/CC VCC/C	abs • trac • to ins • pi • rar
CVCC	CVCC/C	cons • tan • te, pers • pec • ti • va
CCVCC	CCVCC/C	trans • for • mar

globos

what?

English/Spanish Language Differences

SEE ALSO . . .

Pronunciation of English and Spanish Letter Names, p. 85

The following chart identifies important differences between English and Spanish phonology and orthography. Teachers of Spanish-speaking students can use this information to better understand students' performance in both reading and spelling. When teachers recognize that a particular error is a result of a student correctly applying the rules of Spanish, they can work with the student to identify differences between the two language systems and thereby build on the student's existing repertoire of literacy skills.

English/Spanish Language Differences	
b & v	In Spanish *b* and *v* are pronounced with the same sound, like the letter *b* in *balloon*. Therefore, students may have problems spelling words with the letter *v*.
c, s, z	In Spanish the following letters have the same sound, like the sound of the letter *s* in *sent:* •*c* preceding *e* or *i* •*s* •*z* Students may be confused when spelling words with any of these three letters.
ch & sh	The *sh* digraph does not exist in Spanish. Therefore, students may pronounce *sh* as /s/ and have difficulty spelling words with *sh*, possibly substituting *ch*. The *ch* consonant digraph is usually taught as part of the Spanish alphabet. It has the /ch/ sound in *cheese*.
Double Consonants	The only double consonants in Spanish where both letters are pronounced are *cc*—pronounced like /ks/ in *accent*—and *nn*. In Spanish *ll* and *rr* are not considered double consonants because they represent a single sound. English words containing double consonants may be difficult to read and spell.
-ed	The variations in the sound of *-ed* in past-tense verbs may be confusing, especially when *-ed* has the soft-*t* sound as in *wrapped*.

English/Spanish Language Differences	
Final Consonant Blends	Because Spanish words do not usually end with final consonant blends, English words that do may cause confusion in spelling. Students will generally pronounce the first consonant and not the second. The most common combinations that can create difficulties are *ng, nd, st, nk, mp, nt, ft,* and *rl.*
g* & *j	In Spanish, *g* before *e* or *i,* and *j* represent a strong guttural sound with no equivalent in English. The English *h* has a sound that most closely approximates the Spanish consonant sound /x/. Students may pronounce words such as *general* as *heneral, giraffe* as *hiraffe,* and *juvenile* as *huvenile.* These pronunciation differences can lead to spelling confusion.
h (initial position)	The only silent letter in Spanish is *h.* Students may not write the letter *h* in the initial position of words and may not pronounce it when reading.
k	In Spanish, the letter *k* is found only in words of foreign origin and may, therefore, be unfamiliar to students. They may use the letter *c* or *qu* followed by *e* or *i* to write the sound for the letter *k.*
Plurals	English plural words are likely to cause problems in both pronunciation and spelling for Spanish-speaking students. First, the pronunciation of the final *–s* in English varies. It can have the /s/ sound of *books* or the /z/ sound of *stores.* Second, students may have problems writing the plurals of English words ending in consonants, as most take *–s* and not *–es* as is the case in Spanish.
q	The /kw/ sound in the English word *question* is always written *cu* plus a vowel in Spanish. The letter *q* always appears with *ue* or *ui* in Spanish and has the /k/ sound as in *kite.*
***s*-Blends**	There are no Spanish words that begin with *s*-blends. A vowel always precedes consonant clusters with *s,* so Spanish-speaking students may add the sound of the letter *e* (/ā/) when they pronounce words that begin with *sc, sk, sl, sm, sn, sp, sq, st,* or *sw.*
th	The *th* digraph does not exist in Spanish spoken in the Americas. Students may pronounce *th* as *d* since its sound is similar to the soft *d* in Spanish. For example, *that* might become *dat.*
Vowels	In Spanish, vowels have a single and relatively invariable sound: •*a* as in *spa* •*e* as in *weigh* •*i* as in *marine* •*o* as in *open* •*u* as in *tune* Spanish-speaking students may have trouble with the various English vowel sounds and vowel combinations, substituting them with Spanish vowel sounds and combinations.
w* & *wh	The letter *w* and the digraph *wh* do not exist in Spanish, except in words of foreign origin. The pronunciation of the letter *w* depends on the language the word comes from and is either the /o͞o/ or /b/ sound. This may cause confusion in spelling. In addition, students may pronounce and write *wh* as *w.*

what?

Spanish/English Cross-Language Transfer

For those Spanish-speaking ELLs who are literate in their first language, much of their native language reading skills can be applied to their reading in the second language.

Students who can read in Spanish have mastered a number of important skills. Even beginning Spanish readers have learned that letters represent the different sounds of spoken language and that individual sounds can be blended into meaningful units. Rather than being a deficit, literacy in Spanish provides a strong foundation for learning English phonics.

As teachers introduce Spanish readers to English phonics, they can draw on a large number of phonic elements that are common to both languages. The following chart lists these common sound/spelling patterns.

Spanish Phonic Elements with Positive Transfer to English*		
/b/ spelled *b*	/m/ spelled *m*	/ch/ spelled *ch*
/d/ spelled *d*	/n/ spelled *n*	*l*-blends (bl, cl, fl, gl, pl)
/f/ spelled *f*	/p/ spelled *p*	*r*-blends (br, cr, dr, fr, gr, pr, tr)
/g/ spelled *g* in *ga, go, gu*	/s/ spelled *s* and *c* in *ce, ci*	/ō/ spelled *o*
/g/ spelled *gu* in *gue, gui*	/t/ spelled *t*	/o͞o/ spelled *u*
/k/ spelled *c* in *ca, co, cu*	/y/ spelled *y*	diphthong /oi/ spelled *oi, oy*
/l/ spelled *l*		

*Sound/spelling patterns are the same in both languages.

Certain features of the Spanish letter/sound system are likely to cause difficulties for students who are transitioning from reading in Spanish to reading in English. Teachers can use the following chart to identify these elements with "negative transfer" and help students understand the differences between Spanish and English. In addition, there are many features of the English sound/spelling system that don't exist in Spanish. The second chart lists the phonic elements that have no counterparts in Spanish and thus have "zero transfer."

Spanish Phonic Elements with Negative Transfer to English*
▸ *g* before *e* and *i*, and *j* represent the guttural sound /x/, similar to English /h/.
▸ *h* is a silent letter.
▸ *ll* is a consonant digraph, usually taught as part of the Spanish alphabet. Most Spanish speakers pronounce *ll* as /y/.
▸ *que* and *qui* are pronounced /k/, never /kw/.
▸ *rr* is a consonant digraph that represents the forcibly rolled phoneme /rr/.
▸ *v* is pronounced /b/.
▸ *z* is pronounced /s/ by Spanish speakers in the Americas.
▸ The five Spanish vowels are relatively invariable in sound:
a represents the short-*o* sound in *watch* and *father.*
e represents the long-*a* sound in *eight.*
i represents the long-*e* sound in *machine.*
o represents the long-*o* sound in *no, old, rose.*
u represents the long-*u* sound in *July, tube.*

English Phonic Elements with Zero Transfer from Spanish**
▸ all short vowels and schwa
▸ long vowels with silent *e*
▸ long-vowel digraphs and double vowels (except the diphthongs *oy* and *oi*)
▸ /j/ spelled *j* and *g* in words like *jump, giant,* and *cage*
▸ /k/ spelled *k* (In Spanish, the letter *k* only appears in a small number of borrowed words.)
▸ /w/ (Letter *w* only appears in Spanish in a limited number of borrowed words and is pronounced /b/ or /o͞o/.)
▸ /v/ spelled *v*
▸ digraphs *sh, th, wh, ph, gh, -ng*
▸ *s*-blends
▸ consonants in final position (A limited number of consonants can appear at the end of Spanish words: *n, s, l, m, r, x, t, d, z, j.*)
▸ final consonant blends
▸ three-letter consonant blends

*Letter/sound correspondences are different. **Sound/spelling patterns do not exist in Spanish.

what?

English/Spanish Cognates

COGNATES
words in two languages that share a similar spelling, pronunciation, and meaning

FALSE COGNATES
pairs of words that are spelled the same or nearly the same in two languages but do not share the same meaning

Cognates are words in two languages that share a similar spelling, pronunciation, and meaning. Students often can draw on their knowledge of words in their native language to figure out the meanings of cognates in English. Because of their common Latin and Greek roots, as well as the close connections between English and the Romance languages, English and Spanish share a large number of cognate pairs. English/Spanish cognates fall into several different categories: cognates that are spelled identically, cognates that are spelled nearly the same, cognates that are pronounced nearly the same, and false cognates. False cognates are pairs of words that are spelled identically or nearly the same in two languages but do not share the same meaning.

English/Spanish Cognates Spelled Identically

English	Spanish	English	Spanish	English	Spanish
accidental	accidental	confusion	confusión	hotel	hotel
animal	animal	coyote	coyote	idea	idea
area	área	director	director	metal	metal
banana	banana	doctor	doctor	natural	natural
banjo	banjo	extra	extra	piano	piano
cable	cable	flexible	flexible	radio	radio
cafeteria	cafetería	gas	gas	television	televisión
cereal	cereal	honor	honor	terrible	terrible
chocolate	chocolate	hospital	hospital	triple	triple
color	color				

English/Spanish Cognates Spelled Nearly the Same

English	Spanish	English	Spanish	English	Spanish
accident	accidente	distance	distancia	part	parte
active	activo/activa	discrimination	discriminación	perfect	perfecto/perfecta
adult	adulto/adulta	family	familia	planet	planeta
adventure	adventura	favorite	favorito/favorita	plant	planta
artist	artista	future	futuro	plate	plato
brilliant	brillante	history	historia	police	policía
cause	causa	important	importante	program	programa
class	clase	insect	insecto	possible	posible
cognate	cognado	map	mapa	restaurant	restaurante
culture	cultura	minute	minuto	temperature	temperatura
different	diferente	music	música	tomato	tomate
dinosaur	dinosaurio				

bicicleta

English/Spanish Cognates Pronounced Nearly the Same

English	Spanish	English	Spanish	English	Spanish
baby	bebé	equal	igual	north	norte
bicycle	bicicleta	famous	famoso/famosa	object	objeto
blouse	blusa	fruit	fruta	park	parque
breeze	brisa	group	grupo	peace	paz
coast	costa	hour	hora	route	ruta
common	común	interesting	interesante	surprise	sorpresa
desert	desierto	leader	líder	telephone	teléfono
difficult	difícil	lemon	limón		

English/Spanish False Cognates

English	Spanish	English	Spanish
actual	actual (current)	camp	campo (countryside)
arena	arena (sand)	embarrassed	embarazada (pregnant)
mayor	mayor (older)	exit	éxito (success)
once	once (eleven)	fabric	fábrica (factory)
pan	pan (bread)	football	fútbol (soccer)
papa	papa (potato)	lecture	lectura (reading)
pie	pie (foot)	rare	raro (odd)
pretender	pretender (to try)	rope	ropa (clothing)
red	red (net)	soap	sopa (soup)
sensible	sensible (sensitive)	vase	vaso (drinking glass)
Spelled Identically		Spelled Nearly the Same	

Sources

***NTC's Dictionary of Spanish Cognates Thematically Organized* (1999) by Rose Nash. New York: McGraw-Hill.**

***NTC's Dictionary of Spanish False Cognates* (1996) by Marcial Prado. New York: McGraw-Hill.**

SECTION II

Early Literacy

CHAPTER 3

Print Awareness

CHAPTER 4

Letter Knowledge

CHAPTER 5

Phonological Awareness

Introduction

EARLY LITERACY

> Early childhood literacy is . . . the single best investment for enabling children to develop skills that will likely benefit them for a lifetime.
>
> —DICKINSON & NEUMAN, 2006

CCSS READING STANDARDS

Foundational Skills

Print Concepts

Phonological Awareness

SEE ALSO . . .

Chapter 3: Print Awareness

Chapter 4: Letter Knowledge

Chapter 5: Phonological Awareness

LITERACY KNOWLEDGE developed in the early years can be an excellent predictor of students' later reading success. Print awareness, letter knowledge, and phonological awareness form a foundation on which literacy learning rests. Although these skills are often thought of as discrete and very different from one another, they are interrelated and work together to form what is considered early literacy development.

Print awareness is one of the earliest introductions to literacy. Young children begin to learn about print as parents or other adults read to them. Print awareness includes the understanding, for example, of how to hold a book, that print conveys meaning, and which direction printed text should be read. Eventually, children become aware that the written symbols on the page represent spoken words. This understanding provides the impetus to learn more about print, including knowledge about the letters of the alphabet.

Letter knowledge includes knowing the names and the shapes of the letters as well as knowing the sounds each letter represents. Alphabet knowledge, it is thought, is largely a matter of rote memorization. In English, as in other alphabetic languages, the relationship between the names and the shapes of the letters is largely arbitrary. However, letter sounds and their names do have a logical connection in that most letter names contain the sound of the letter. It is the knowledge of letter sounds that is most important in the reading process. Letter knowledge works in concert with another early literacy skill, phonological awareness, to form an important concept called the alphabetic principle—that letters and sounds work together to form words. Just knowing letter sounds without an understanding of the alphabetic principle is futile.

Phonological awareness is the understanding that speech flow can be broken into smaller units of sound such as words, syllables, onsets and rimes, and phonemes. Phonological awareness is a particularly robust predictor of later reading achievement. Ultimately, understanding that a spoken word can be broken into individual sounds, or *phonemic awareness,* is necessary to be able to read words in print. When combined with letter knowledge, phonemic awareness forms the foundation of word reading ability, or the alphabetic principle.

Although each chapter in this section is devoted to only one early literacy domain, these three domains are interrelated and are developed simultaneously, rather than in a linear fashion. For example, the research reviewed suggests that phonological awareness and letter knowledge influence each other as they develop. Learning the names of English letters may foster students' phonological awareness by alerting them to the similarities in sound among the letters' names. Learning the letters' sounds may improve students' phonemic awareness by helping them detect a phoneme within a letter name. In the following chapters, the research described provides additional support for the interrelatedness of these three early literacy domains. Each is critical on its own merit but must work in concert with one another to ultimately ensure later reading success.

CHAPTER

3

Print Awareness

what?

Print Awareness

> The classroom should be print rich, and the print should be varied, functional, and significant to students.
>
> —ADAMS, 1990

PRINT AWARENESS understanding and appreciation of the *forms* and the *functions* of printed language

CCSS READING STANDARDS

Foundational Skills

Print Concepts

Demonstrate understanding of the organization and basic features of print. (RF.K-1.1)

Print is everywhere—in books, on signs, on labels, in logos. Print awareness is knowing about the forms and the functions of print (Gunn, Simmons, and Kame'enui 1998). Awareness of the forms of print includes knowledge about the conventions of print—conventions that govern the physical structure of written language and text organization. Students with print awareness know how to handle a book, where on a page to begin reading, and the difference between a letter and a word. Awareness of the functions of print includes knowing that print is a communication device. Knowing that printed words are symbols for words in spoken language helps students to bridge the gap between oral and written language. Through engagement with print in their everyday environments, students come to understand that the function of print differs according to its purpose or use in different text forms. Print awareness plays an integral part in the process of learning to read; it is a child's earliest introduction to literacy.

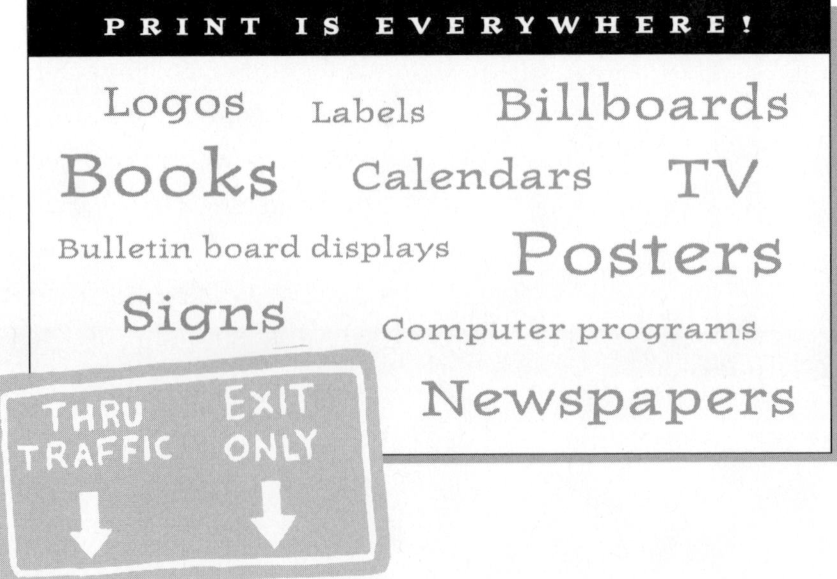

PRINT IS EVERYWHERE!
Logos
Labels
Billboards
Books
Calendars
TV
Bulletin board displays
Posters
Signs
Computer programs
Newspapers
THRU TRAFFIC
EXIT ONLY

Elements of Print and Book Awareness	
Functions of Print	• Print carries meaning. • Print can be used for different purposes. • Print corresponds to speech, word for word.
Conventions of Print	• Print is print, no matter in what form it appears. • Printed words are made up of letters (concept of word). • Printed words are separated by spaces (word boundaries). • Sentences in print are made up of separate words. • Sentences start with capital letters and end with punctuation marks. • Text is read from left to right with a return sweep to the next line. • Lines of text are read from top to bottom of the page. • When one page of text is read, the story continues on the following page.
Book Conventions	• A book has a front cover and a back cover. • A book has a spine. • A book is held right side up. • A book has a title and a title page. • A book has an author; some books have pictures created by an illustrator. • A book has pages. The left page of a book is read before the right page. • Pages are turned one at a time in a sequence from front to back.

SEE ALSO . . .

LESSON MODEL: Print Referencing in Shared Storybook Reading, p. 78

Print-Referencing Cues

Ask questions about print.

Make comments about print.

Pose requests about print.

Point to print when talking about the story.

Track print when reading.

Ezell and Justice 2000.

Print Referencing

Print referencing is a read-aloud strategy that can be used to direct students' attention to the forms, features, and functions of written language (Justice and Pullen 2003). Explicit or implicit print-referencing cues are embedded within shared storybook reading. The cues can be nonverbal (such as pointing to print or tracking print when reading) or verbal (such as asking questions about print, making comments about print, or posing requests about print) (Justice and Ezell 2004). According to Justice and Pullen (2003), verbal and nonverbal references to print in book reading routines encourage a "child's explicit and implicit interactions with and attention to oral and written language."

why?

Print Awareness

> Adults sometimes forget that children have to learn the most basic conventions that govern written language, such as spaces that separate words.
>
> —BURNS, GRIFFIN & SNOW, 1999

Although printed words may be all around them, some children arrive at school with relatively little exposure to the uses, methods, or pleasures of print. A child's awareness of the forms, functions, and uses of print provides the foundation upon which reading and writing abilities are built (Adams 1990; Mason 1980). According to numerous research studies, assessments measuring a child's understanding of print concepts have successfully predicted future reading success (Pullen and Justice 2003).

For most children, the ability to understand how print works does not emerge automatically and unaided. This understanding comes about through active intervention by adults who point out the conventions and features of print and printed materials (Pullen and Justice 2003). A language- and print-rich environment provides many opportunities for students to develop their early literacy experiences (Teale and Sulzby 1996). In general, a student in a low-socioeconomic-status (SES) classroom encounters less print on the walls and other surfaces of the classroom, has fewer books and magazines in the classroom library, and receives fewer references to classroom environmental print (Duke 2000a). In a study by Duke (2000a), the types of school print environments and literacy experiences may contribute to relatively lower levels of literacy achievement among low-SES students.

Research Findings . . .

Global awareness of the forms, functions, and uses of print provides not just the motivation but the basic conceptual backdrop against which reading and writing may best be learned.

—ADAMS, 1990

Adult-child shared storybook reading experiences that involve discussion about print increase children's knowledge of important print concepts.

—JUSTICE & EZELL, 2000

The performance of children on tests designed to measure concepts about print has been found to predict future reading achievement and to be strongly related to other, more traditional measures of reading readiness and achievement.

—TUNMER ET AL., 1988

Suggested Reading . . .

A Child Becomes a Reader (2006) by Bonnie B. Armbruster, Fran Lehr & Jean Osborn. Jessup, MD: National Institute for Literacy.

Concepts About Print (2000) by Marie M. Clay. Portsmouth, NH: Heinemann.

Engaging Children with Print: Building Early Literacy Skills Through Quality Read-Alouds (2010) by Laura M. Justice & Amy E. Sofka. New York: Guilford.

Preventing Reading Difficulties in Young Children (1998) edited by Catherine E. Snow, M. Susan Burns & Peg Griffin. Washington, DC: National Academies Press.

Starting Out Right: A Guide to Promoting Children's Reading Success (1999) edited by M. Susan Burns, Peg Griffin & Catherine E. Snow. Washington, DC: National Academies Press.

Teaching Our Youngest (2002) by the Early Childhood–Head Start Task Force. Washington, DC: U.S. Department of Education and U.S. Department of Health and Human Services.

when?

Print Awareness

> It is important to keep in mind that many children enter school quite well versed in the nature and purpose of print, so print concepts instruction should be provided only for those children who need it.
>
> —VELLUTINO, 2003

Promote Print Awareness

Create a print-rich classroom environment.

Provide plenty of read-aloud experiences.

Embed print-referencing cues in shared storybook reading.

When to Teach

Print knowledge is acquired by most children during the preschool years. At a very young age, children begin building concepts about print through literacy-based interactions with the adults in their lives. In preschool and Kindergarten, the enhancement of students' print awareness should be a central goal (Adams 1990). By the end of Kindergarten, students should have developed basic concepts of print (Snow, Burns, and Griffin 1998).

By the end of Kindergarten, a student

- knows the parts of a book and how books are held and read;
- identifies a book's title and understands what authors and illustrators do;
- follows print from left to right and from top to bottom of a page when stories are read aloud;
- understands the relationship between print and pictures;
- understands that the message of most books is in the print and not the pictures;
- knows the difference between letters and words;
- knows that sentences in print are made up of separate words;
- knows that there are spaces between words in print;
- knows that print represents spoken language and contains meaning (Armbruster, Lehr, and Osborn 2002).

When to Assess and Intervene

In Kindergarten, assess print awareness three times: in the fall, winter, and spring. During instruction, identify students who

Who Is at Risk?

Students who have little at-home experience with books and reading

need additional support and determine whether the pace of instruction should be increased, be decreased, or remain the same. Clay (2000) suggests that the lowest-achieving students should receive help and careful monitoring in the first six months of school.

Informal assessments provide opportunities for students to demonstrate their understanding of print concepts and book-handling skills. Because students may find it far easier to show rather than talk about print concepts, teachers should use assessment techniques that ask students to "point to" or "show" parts of a book. Generally, such assessments should take place one-on-one in a quiet, comfortable environment.

Examples of Informal Assessment Questions	
Place a closed storybook on a table and ask:	• Can you show me how to hold this book? • Can you show me the front cover of the book? • Can you show me the title of the book?
Open the storybook and ask:	• Can you show me a word? • Can you show me a space? • Can you tell me how many words are in this sentence? • Can you show me where I should start reading? • Can you show me which way I should go when I read? • When I come to the end of this line, where do I go next? • Can you point to each word as I read it?

Purpose	✓ Print-Awareness Assessment	Publisher
Screening	Phonological Awareness Literacy Screening (PALS) ▸ PALS–PreK: Print and Word Awareness ▸ PALS–K: Concept of Word	University of Virginia http://pals.virginia.edu
Screening Diagnostic	TPRI Early Reading Assessment ▸ Book & Print Awareness	Texas Education Agency http://www.tpri.org
Diagnostic	Test of Early Reading Ability, 3rd Edition (TERA-3) ▸ Subtest: Conventions	Pro-Ed

how? Print Awareness

LESSON MODEL FOR
Print Awareness

Benchmarks

- ability to recognize that print carries meaning
- ability to understand and use book-component vocabulary
- ability to turn the pages in a book
- ability to track text from left to right and top to bottom
- ability to recognize a word
- ability to recognize the spaces between words

Strategy Grade Level

- Pre-K – Kindergarten

Grouping

- whole class
- small group
- individual

Print Referencing in Shared Storybook Reading

According to Justice and Ezell (2004), "print referencing is an adult's use of nonverbal and verbal cues to direct a child's attention to the forms, features, and functions of written language." Print referencing uses the adult-child shared storybook reading context to maximize students' learning opportunities (Justice and Pullen 2003). The strategy is most effective if it is used with big books or regular-sized illustrated storybooks in which print is a salient, or highly noticeable, feature (Justice and Lankford 2002). Salient print features include large bold print, 20 words or fewer per page, patterned or predictable text, and print embedded within the illustrations (Justice and Kaderavek 2002; Justice and Ezell 2002). This sample lesson model can be adapted and used to enhance print awareness instruction during any shared storybook reading experience.

THE NOISY DOG
woof!
arf!
by Simon Dibley
Illustrated by Art Fisher
night he howls at the moon.
But he is as quiet as a mouse when he's in his doghouse.

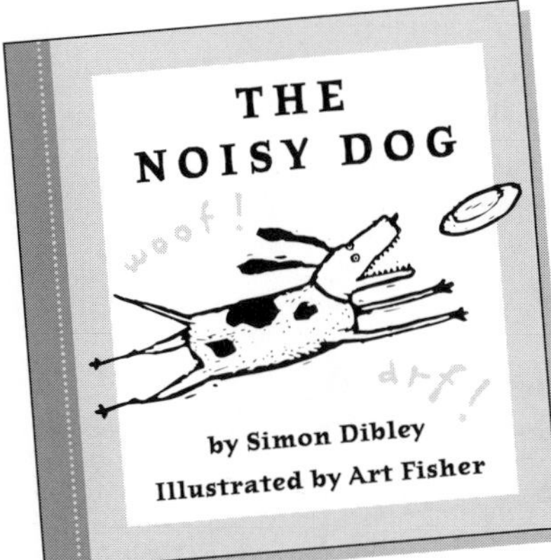

Teach/Model

Talking About Books: Cover, Title, Author, and Illustrator

Show the front cover of a book. Say: *Let's look at the front of the book. This is called the cover.* Ask: *What do you call the front of a book?* (the cover) Explain that on the cover you usually can find the name of the book, who wrote it, and who drew the pictures.

Say: *The name of a book is called the title.* Point to the title. Say: *The title, or name, of the book is right here.* Point to each word as you read the title aloud. Then have students repeat the title as you point to each word. Ask: *What do you call the name of a book?* (the title)

Say: *A person who writes a book is called the author.* Point to the author's name. Say: *The author's name is right here.* Point to each word as you read the author's name aloud. Then have students repeat the name as you point to each word. Ask: *What do authors do?* (write books)

Say: *The person who makes the pictures that go with a story is called an illustrator.* Point to the illustrator's name. Say: *The illustrator's name is right here.* Point to each word as you read the illustrator's name aloud. Then have students repeat the name as you point to each word. Ask: *What do illustrators do?* (make the pictures that go with a story)

Text Directionality

Show students the front cover of the book again and say: *We start reading a book from the front.* Ask: *Who can show me where I should start reading?* (Student should point to cover.) Say: *Starting at the front of the book, we turn one page at a time.* Demonstrate turning the pages one at a time. Ask: *Can someone help me hold the book and turn the pages?*

Marie Clay (1993) suggests that teachers avoid using directional terms, such as left-to-right, if possible. Model directionality as often as student needs help.

Open the book to the first spread and point to the top left of the page. Say: *I am going to start reading the page here. Then I'll go this way.* Sweep to the right with your finger. Read aloud the sentence while tracking, or moving your finger under each word as you read. Say: *Look, I just read the words on this page. These words help tell the story. It says, "Our dog is a very noisy dog."* Again read the sentence aloud while tracking.

Point to the left-hand page again. Say: *I finished reading this page.* Point to the right-hand page. Say: *Now I'm going to read this page.* Ask: *Which page should I read next?* (Student points to the right-hand page.) Say: *I am going to start reading here.* Point to the first word in the sentence on the right-hand page. Then read the sentence aloud while tracking. Ask: *Who can show me where to start reading?* (Student points to the word *He.*) Ask: *Now which way do I go?* (Student points from left to right.) Ask: *Where do I go after that?* (Student points to the word *when* at the beginning of the next line.)

Concept of Word

Read aloud the sentence while tracking: *"At night he howls at the moon."* Then point to the word *he*. Say: *This is a word.* Point to the word *howls*. Say: *This is another word. Words are separated by empty spaces.* Point to the empty space between *he* and *howls*. Ask: *Who can point to a word?* Ask: *Who can point to a space between words?*

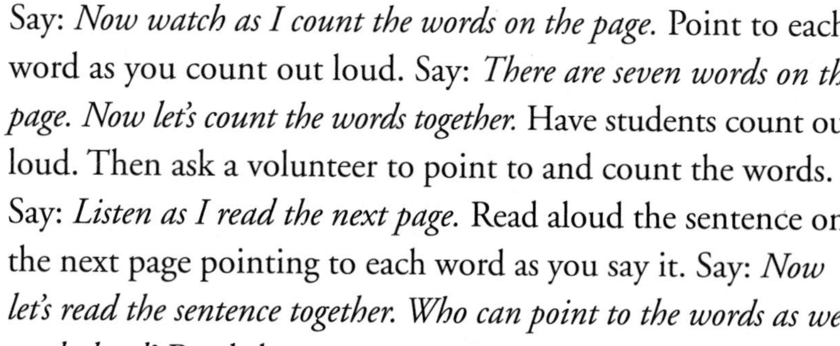

Say: *Now watch as I count the words on the page.* Point to each word as you count out loud. Say: *There are seven words on this page. Now let's count the words together.* Have students count out loud. Then ask a volunteer to point to and count the words. Say: *Listen as I read the next page.* Read aloud the sentence on the next page pointing to each word as you say it. Say: *Now let's read the sentence together. Who can point to the words as we read aloud?* Read the sentence again.

Since too much print referencing during reading can detract from students' enjoyment, Justice and Ezell (2004) suggest three to five print references during the reading of a storybook.

Point to the right-hand page. Say: *What do you see on this page?* (a doghouse) Say: *Watch as I point to the word that names what you see in the picture.* Point to the word *doghouse* and say *doghouse*. Ask: *Who can point to the word that names the doghouse in the picture?*

At night he howls at the moon.

But he is as quiet as a mouse when he's in his doghouse.

OBSERVE & ASSESS

Questions for Observation	Benchmarks
(Place a closed storybook on a table.) Can you show me the front cover of this book?	Student can recognize the cover of a book.
(Open the storybook.) Can you show me a word? A space?	Student can recognize individual words and word boundaries.
(Open the storybook.) Can you show me where I should start reading on this page?	Student can locate the starting point for reading text.
(Open the storybook.) Can you show me which way I should go when I read?	Student can track lines of text from left to right.
(Open the storybook.) When I come to the end of this line, where do I go next?	Student can sweep from the end of one line to the beginning of the next.

woof! woof! woof!

CHAPTER 4

Letter Knowledge

what? why? when? how?

what?

Letter Knowledge

> Letter names supply convenient verbal labels that uniquely identify each letter and that are important if a child is to understand the language of literacy.
>
> —SHARE, 2004

CCSS READING STANDARDS

Foundational Skills

Print Concepts

Recognize and name all upper- and lowercase letters of the alphabet. (RF.K.1d)

Letter Knowledge

Letter names

Letter shapes

Letter sounds

Letter formation (handwriting)

Letters are the components of written words. They represent sounds systematically in the spelling of words. Learning letters requires becoming familiar with 26 uppercase and 26 lowercase letter shapes and associating these letter shapes to their letter names. In English, the relationship between the shapes and the names of the letters is largely arbitrary. As a result, young students have no choice but to memorize the links between letter shapes and names (Treiman and Kessler 2003). One way to help young students learn and recall letter shapes is through handwriting practice (Ehri and Roberts 2006; Berninger 1999).

The learning of letter sounds is quite different from the learning of letter shapes and names (Treiman and Kessler 2003). The relationship between the names and sounds of letters is *not* arbitrary in English or any other alphabetic system. Most letter names contain their sounds; for example, the letter name *b* begins with its most frequent sound, /b/, and the letter name *f* ends with its most frequent sound, /f/. Rather than memorize letter-sound correspondences in a rote fashion, young students can detect a letter-sound within a letter name.

Letter-Name Iconicity

All known letter-name systems are iconic—the names of the letters contain the sound that the letter represents (Treiman and Kessler 2003). For example, in both English and Spanish the name of the letter *b* contains /b/. In English, there are only two totally noniconic letter names: the name of the letter *h* and the name of the letter *w*. (The letter *y* is considered iconic because it can stand for /ī/.)

All languages show iconicity in their letter names.

—TREIMAN & KESSLER, 2003

SEE ALSO . . .

Spanish Letter-Sound System, p. 50

Pronunciation of English and Spanish Letter Names

Letter	English	Spanish
a	/ā/	/o/
b	/b/ /ē/	/b/ /ā/
c	/s/ /ē/	/s/ /ā/
d	/d/ /ē/	/d/ /ā/
e	/ē/	/ā/
f	/e/ /f/	/e/ /f/ • /ā/
g	/j/ /ē/	/h/ /ā/
h	/ā/ /ch/	/o/ • /ch/ /ā/
i	/ī/	/ē/
j	/j/ /ā/	/h/ /ō/ • /t/ /o/
k	/k/ /ā/	/k/ /o/
l	/e/ /l/	/ā/ • /l/ /ā/
m	/e/ /m/	/e/ /m/ • /ā/
n	/e/ /n/	/e/ /n/ • /ā/
o	/ō/	/ō/
p	/p/ /ē/	/p/ /ā/
q	/k/ /yū/	/k/ /o͞o/
r	/är/	/e/ /r/ • /ā/
s	/e/ /s/	/e/ /s/ • /ā/
t	/t/ /ē/	/t/ /ā/
u	/yo͞o/	/o͞o/
v	/v/ /ē/	/o͞o/ • /b/ /ā/
w	/d/ /ə/ • /b/ /ə/ /l/ • /yo͞o/	/o͞o/ • /b/ /ā/
		/d/ /ō/ • /b/ /l/ /ā/
x	/e/ /ks/	/ā/ • /k/ /ē/ /s/
y	/w/ /ī/	/ē/ • /g/ /r/ /ē/ • /ā/ • /g/ /o/
z	/z/ /ē/	/s/ /ā/ • /t/ /o/

How much do you know about the iconicity of letter names? In the chart above, English and Spanish letter names are segmented into individual phonemes. Use this information to answer the following questions. (See Answer Key, p. 800.)

Which English consonant letter names begin with the sound that the letter frequently stands for? Which English consonant letter names end with the sound that the letter frequently stands for?

Letter Characteristics

Characteristics of letters can affect students' learning of letter names. These characteristics include the similarity in appearance of a letter to other letters and the number of phonemes a letter name shares with other letters.

SEE ALSO . . .

LESSON MODELS

Letter Names and Shapes: Uppercase Letters, p. 96

Letter Names and Shapes: Lowercase Letters, p. 103

Letter Shapes That Are Visually Similar

A factor that affects the learning of letter names is the extent to which the visual form, or shape, of the target letter looks like those of other letters (Treiman and Kessler 2003). The more alike the appearance of two letters is, the more likely students will confuse them. In a recent study, researchers found that similarity of letter shapes was the strongest single determinant of confusion errors (Treiman, Kessler, and Pollo 2006). When introducing a potentially confusing letter, make sure that it is mastered prior to the introduction of the other letter in the visually similar pair.

In learning lowercase letter names, a factor is whether the shape of the lowercase letter is almost identical in uppercase. Since uppercase letters tend to be learned before lowercase letters, a lowercase letter that is a smaller version of a previously known uppercase letter may be easier to recognize than one that appears quite different (Treiman and Kessler 2003).

Visually Similar Letters

Letter Shape	Letters whose form shares 50 percent or more of strokes in target letter's form	B-D, B-P, B-R, E-F, F-P, G-O, K-X, M-N, M-W, O-Q, O-U, P-R, U-V, V-Y
	Letters whose overall form is identical or similar to target letter's form when rotated, flipped, or reversed	b-d, b-p, b-q, d-g, d-q, e-a, g-q, g-y, i-j, i-l, k-x, m-n, n-c, n-h, p-q, u-v, u-w, u-y, w-m, y-v
Letter Case	A letter pair whose forms are almost identical in upper- and lowercase	Cc, Kk, Oo, Pp, Ss, Uu, Vv, Ww, Xx, Zz

Based on Treiman and Kessler 2003; Boles and Clifford 1989.

Children often begin by learning the name of the first letter of their own first name.

—TREIMAN ET AL., 2006

Letter Names That Are Phonologically Similar

The phonological characteristics of letter names also affect students' learning (Treiman and Kessler 2003). Phonological similarity is defined as "the number of phonemes that pairs of letter names share in the same position" (Treiman et al. 2006). For example, the letter name *p* shares a phoneme with the letter name *b* but does not share any phonemes with the letter name *f*.

Phonologically SImilar Letter Names		
Letter Name	**Shared Phoneme**	**Position in Name**
b, c, d, g, p, t, v, z	/ē/	final
j, k	/ā/	final
f, l, m, n, s, x	/e/	initial

Letters That Are Both Phonologically and Visually Similar

Students are especially likely to confuse letters that have similar names as well as similar shapes (Treiman et al. 2006). For example, the uppercase letters *B* and *D* are similar in both name and shape and therefore students often interchange them. The lowercase letters *h* and *n* are less often confused; they are similar in shape but dissimilar in name.

Phonologically and Visually Similar Letters	
Letter Case	**Letter Pair**
Uppercase	B-D, B-P, M-N
Lowercase	b-d, b-p, d-g, m-n

bd BD mn MN

Children appear to use letter names to help learn and remember letter sounds.

—TREIMAN ET AL., 2006

SEE ALSO . . .

LESSON MODEL: Letter-Sound Strategy, p. 110

Use of Letter Names to Learn Letter Sounds

Certain properties of a letter's name affect students' ability to learn its sound (Treiman 2005; Treiman et al. 1998). The letter-sound correspondence for a letter whose name contains its relevant phoneme is learned more easily than the letter-sound correspondence for a letter whose name does *not* contain its relevant phoneme (Share 2004). Treiman et al. (1998) found that students were better at identifying a letter's sound when it was at the beginning of a letter name than when it was at the end or not in the name at all. Students acquire these phonological clues by implicitly noticing that the relationship between a letter's name and the sound that it makes is not arbitrary (Treiman et al. 1998). They have the most difficulty with those letters for which the sound is not in the name at all, as with *h* and *w*. In a study by Treiman, Weatherston, and Berch (1994), some Kindergarteners used the letter *y* to spell words beginning with /w/, such as *win*. When questioned, students said that the letter y made the sound /w/.

Letter-Name Properties and Their Utility in Learning Letter Sounds

Useful	• Letter sound at beginning of letter name	b, d, j, k, p, t, v, z
	• Letter sound at end of letter name	f, l, m, n, r, s, x
	• Long-vowel letter sound *is* letter name	a, e, i, o, u
Less Useful	• Soft letter sound at beginning of letter name	c /s/, g /j/
	• Similar letter sound at beginning of letter name	q /k/
	• Less frequent letter sound at end of letter name	y /ī/
Not Useful	• Letter sound *not* in Letter name	h, w
	• Short-vowel letter sound *not* in letter name	a, e, i, o, u
	• Most frequent letter sound *not* in letter name	c /k/, g /g/, y /y/

Based on Treiman and Kessler 2003.

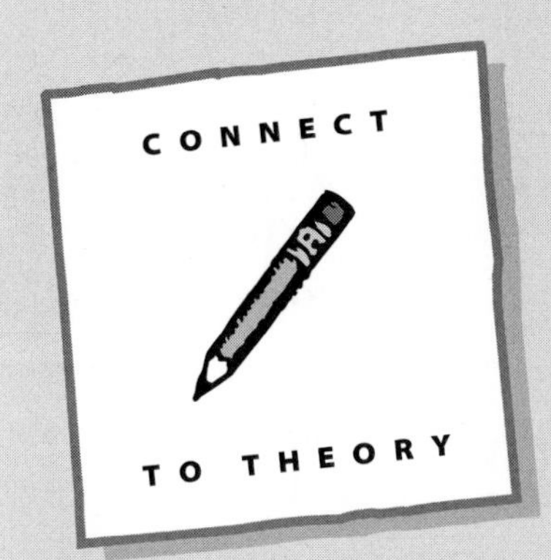

According to researchers Treiman (2005) and Share (2004), it is easier for students to learn a particular letter-sound correspondence if the letter's sound happens to be in the letter's name. Based on this research, what are the implications for instruction? Is it necessary to devote the same amount of instructional time to teaching each new letter-sound correspondence?

Explain why or why not.

(See Answer Key, p. 800.)

CCSS LANGUAGE STANDARDS

Conventions of Standard English

Print all upper- and lowercase letters. (L.K-1.1a)

Handwriting

As students are taught how to recognize letters, they should also learn how to write those letters. Handwriting introduces primary-grade students to the letter forms found in printed text. In the earliest grades, handwriting is linked to basic reading and spelling achievement. To become proficient in the task of handwriting, young students need explicit instruction in letter formation with plenty of guided practice (Wolf 2005).

LESSON MODELS

Handwriting: Uppercase Letter Forms, p. 99

Handwriting: Lowercase Letter Forms, p. 107

Manuscript Letter Forms

There are many forms of print handwriting, but the one most often recommended is one that uses a continuous stroke (Spear-Swerling 2006; Wolf 2005; Slingerland 1971). A continuous stroke reduces the opportunity for reversals, which may occur when a student lifts the pencil (Wolf 2005). In a continuous-stroke letter, the strokes are retraced whenever possible and the pencil is lifted from the paper only when necessary. All lowercase manuscript letters can be formed with a continuous stroke, except for letters *f, i, j, k, t, x,* and *y.*

Lowercase Manuscript Letter Forms

a b c d e f g

h i j k l m n

o p q r s t u

v w x y z

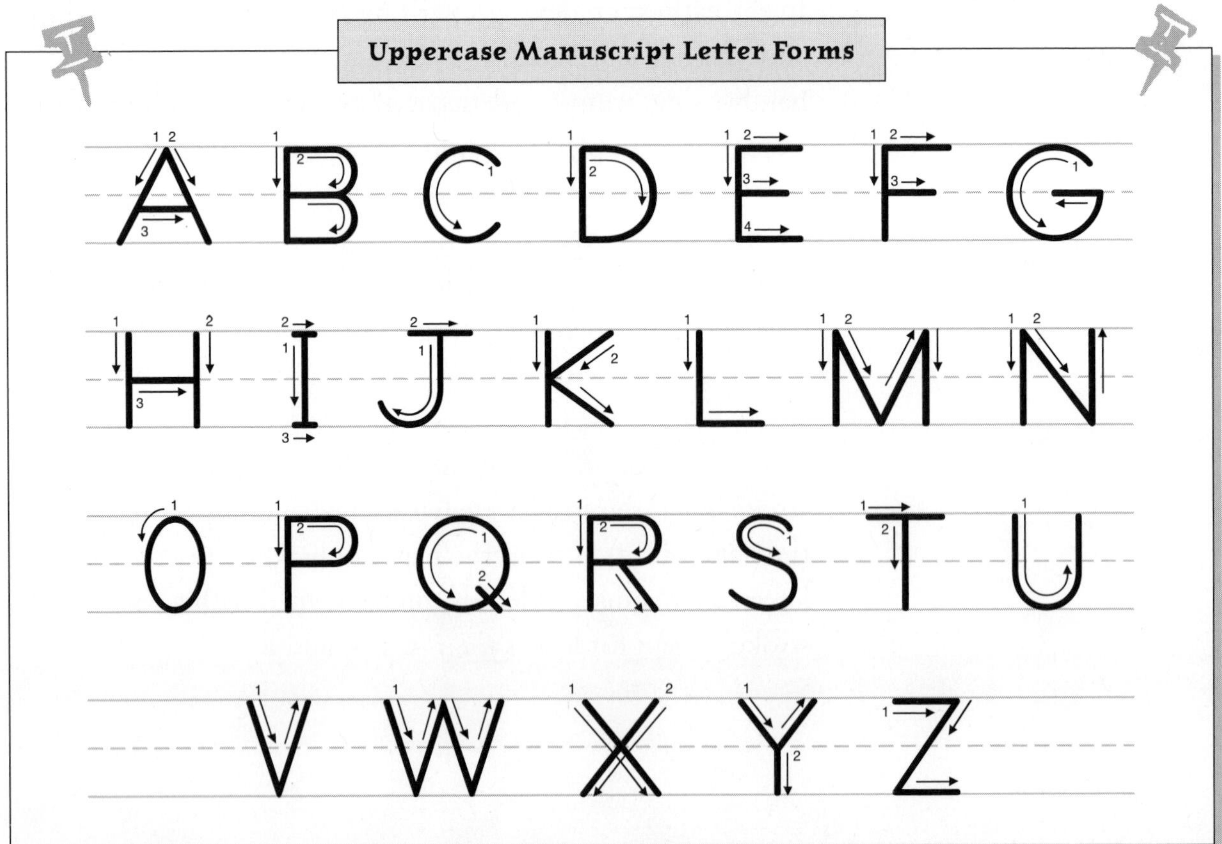

Adapted from *Practical Guide to Handwriting: Manuscript* (2007) by Michael Milone. Novato, CA: Academic Therapy Publications.

Technological advances do not eliminate the need for explicit teaching of handwriting.

—SPEAR-SWERLING, 2006

Handwriting Habits

Students should be aware of proper . . .

- **posture**
- **paper position**
- **pencil grip**

Suggestions for Teaching Handwriting

Louise Spear-Swerling (2006) and Beverly Wolf (2005) offer the following suggestions for teaching handwriting:

- Teach the consistent formation of letters using a continuous stroke whenever possible.
- Teach proper handwriting posture, paper position, and pencil grip.
- Teach similarly formed letters together in a sequence that takes into account both ease of formation and frequency in words.
- Focus initially on teaching the motor pattern for forming a letter rather than how to write it on paper with perfect legibility or size.
- Utilize arrow cues to help students remember how to form letters.
- Verbalize consistent, precise directions for writing each letter shape or stroke.

why?

Letter Knowledge

> Knowing letter names provides a springboard for learning and remembering letter-sound relationships.
>
> —ALLEN, NEUHAUS & BECKWITH, 2005

Letter knowledge has a foundational role in literacy development. Knowing letter names allows students to label letter shapes. Learning the names of English letters may foster phonological awareness by alerting students to the similarities in sound among the letter names (Treiman 2005). Because the phoneme that a letter represents is usually heard in its name, knowing the names of letters may make it easier for students to master the sound/spelling correspondences necessary for efficient decoding (Share 2004; Treiman and Kessler 2003). According to Treiman et al. (2006), letter knowledge also helps students to "make some sense of printed words, such as *jail,* where the entire name of one or more of the letters is heard in the spoken word." If students can instantly and effortlessly recognize letters, they can give all their attention to other emergent literacy tasks (Hall and Moats 1999). Fluent letter naming leads to word-reading accuracy and fluency, and to reading comprehension (Neuhaus 2003). According to Adams (1990), "a student who can recognize most letters with confidence will have an easier time learning about letter sounds and word spellings than a student who still has to work at remembering what is what." Likewise, handwriting practice aids letter recognition development and fluent handwriting leads to better composition skills (Graham and Harris 2005).

Research Findings . . .

A child's ability to identify the letters of the alphabet by name is one of the best predictors of how readily he or she will learn to read.

—TREIMAN, KESSLER & POLLO, 2006

Reading depends first and foremost on visual letter recognition.

—ADAMS, 1990

*The general system of English letter names (*w *and* y *excepted) may be surprisingly well adapted to the task of providing both unique identifiers for English graphemes and aids to letter-sound learning.*

—SHARE, 2004

Kindergarten letter identification is almost as successful at predicting later reading skill as an entire reading readiness test.

—SNOW, BURNS & GRIFFIN, 1998

Suggested Reading . . .

Beginning to Read: Thinking and Learning About Print (1990) by Marilyn Jager Adams. Cambridge, MA: MIT Press.

Handbook of Early Literacy Research, Volume 2 (2006) edited by David K. Dickinson & Susan B. Newman. New York: Guilford.

Handwriting Research and Resources (2008). Columbus, OH: Zaner-Bloser.

Multisensory Teaching of Basic Language Skills, 3rd Edition (2011) edited by Judith R. Birsh. Baltimore, MD: Paul H. Brookes.

Phonics from A to Z: A Practical Guide, 2nd Edition (2006) by Wiley Blevins. New York: Scholastic.

Reading Readiness Skills Manual (2002) by Neuhaus Education Center. Bellaire, TX: Neuhaus Education Center.

Words Their Way: Word Study for Phonics, Vocabulary, and Spelling Instruction, 5th Edition (2012) by Donald R. Bear, Marcia Invernizzi, Shane Templeton & Francine Johnston. Boston: Allyn & Bacon.

when?

Letter Knowledge

An important step in learning about letters is mastering the associations between the letters' upper- and lower-case forms and their names.

—TREIMAN & KESSLER, 2003

ABC

Letter Knowledge

Recite or sing the alphabet.

Recognize and name all upper- and lowercase letters.

Independently write all upper- and lowercase letters.

Identify the sound a letter makes.

When to Teach

The alphabet has a conventional order, which many children learn from an early age. Through informal experiences, most children learn to sing or recite at least part of the alphabet in order by age three and the entire alphabet song by age five (Worden and Boettcher 1990). When children start school, however, they need formal instruction that will help them name, recognize, and write the letters (Ehri and Roberts 2006). This formal instruction should be systematic and planned.

There is no consensus on the best sequence for teaching letters. According to Hall and Moats (1999), students appear to acquire letter knowledge in a sequence that begins with letter names, then letter shapes and formation, and finally letter sounds. Special attention should be given to the pacing of letter introduction. The research showing that students use their knowledge of letter names to make inferences about letter sounds has some important implications for instruction. According to Treiman and Kessler (2003), students "need more time to learn the sounds of some letters than others." For example, their research suggests that students have more trouble learning the sound of a letter like *w*, which is not phonologically similar to its letter name, than the sound of a letter like *b*, which is. Therefore, the common practice of spending the same amount of instructional time on each letter—the "letter-of-the-week" approach—may not be effective. Treiman and Kessler (2003) ask, "Why not spend more time on the harder letters and less time on the easier letters?"

Informal Experiences Learning Letters

Singing alphabet songs

Reciting alphabet rhymes

Reading alphabet books

Playing alphabet games

Manipulating alphabet letters

Ehri and Roberts 2006.

SEE ALSO . . .

CORE Literacy Library

Assessing Reading: Multiple Measures, 2nd Edition

When to Assess and Intervene

Letter Naming Fluency

Research indicates that emergent readers must not only be able to accurately identify the letters of the alphabet, but they must also be able to do so in and out of sequence and with automaticity (Adams 1990). Letter naming fluency assessments evaluate how fluently a student can name visually presented uppercase and lowercase letters in one minute. The speed and accuracy with which students identify letters not only measures whether students can identify the letters, but how *thoroughly* students have learned them. This type of assessment is usually administered in Kindergarten in the fall, winter, and spring, and in first grade in the fall.

Handwriting Skills

Assessment of handwriting should incorporate observations of execution, legibility, and speed of writing (Spear-Swerling 2006). Execution includes correct and consistent pencil hold, posture, and letter formation. Legibility involves the readability of letters, as well as spacing within and between words. Beyond the primary grades, writing speed contributes to students' ability to complete tasks efficiently (Graham and Harris 2005).

Purpose	✓ Letter-Knowledge Assessment	Publisher
Screening	Phonological Awareness Literacy Screening (PALS) ▸ PALS–K: Alphabet Knowledge	University of Virginia, http://pals.virginia.edu
Screening Progress Monitoring	AIMSweb® Test of Early Literacy (TEL) ▸ Letter-Naming Fluency ▸ Letter Sound Fluency	Pearson http://aimsweb.com
Screening Progress Monitoring	DIBELS® Next ▸ Letter Naming Fluency (LNF)	Sopris West http://dibels.org
Screening Progress Monitoring Diagnostic	easy CBM™ ▸ Letter Names	Riverside Publishing http://easycbm.com

Letter Knowledge

LESSON MODEL FOR

Letter Recognition

Benchmark

- ability to recognize uppercase letter names and shapes

Strategy Grade Level

- Pre-K – Grade 1

Prerequisite

- ability to recite the traditional alphabet song

Grouping

- whole class
- small group

Materials

- alphabet letter cards
- chart paper
- materials for selected activities

For first graders, teach lowercase letters first because they are more predominant in reading text.

Letter Names and Shapes: Uppercase Letters

In Kindergarten, it is generally recommended that uppercase letters be taught before lowercase letters (Hall and Moats 1999). This is because uppercase letters are more distinguishable than lowercase letters. An exception to this guideline may be made for identically shaped pairs of upper- and lowercase letters (e.g., *Cc, Pp, Ss*). These pairs of upper- and lowercase letters may be introduced at the same time (Carnine et al. 2006). Students often confuse uppercase letter shapes that are visually similar (e.g., *B-D, B-P, M-N*); these letters should not be introduced in proximity (Treiman et al. 2006). This sample lesson model targets uppercase letter *P.* The same model can be adapted and used to enhance uppercase letter recognition instruction in any commercial reading program.

Sing the Alphabet Song

When singing the traditional version of the alphabet song, students often slur the letters *L, M, N, O, P*. Lead students in singing the alphabet to different melodies, such as "Mary Had a Little Lamb" or "Old McDonald Had a Farm."

Teach/Model

Display an alphabet card for the uppercase letter *P.* Point to the card and say: *This is the letter* P. *It has a straight line down and then goes up and around.* With your finger, trace the letter from top to bottom and then back up and around. Say: *This is the letter* P. Ask: *What is the name of this letter?* (P) Point to the letter as students respond. Next, direct students' attention to at least two other examples of uppercase letter *P.* The letter could be displayed somewhere in the classroom environment or in a big book. Follow the same procedure for each new example, pointing to the letter and tracing the lines.

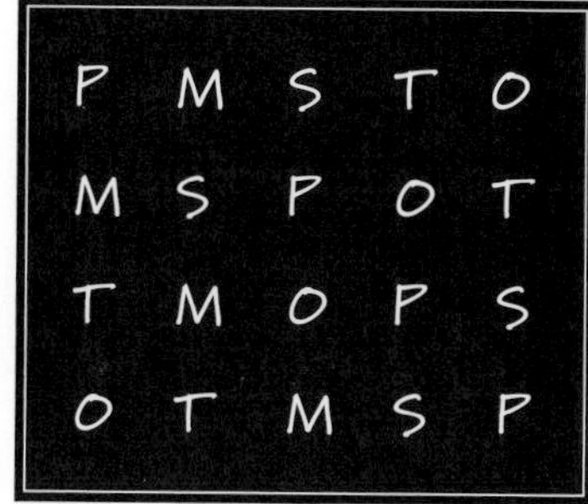

Letter Naming Automaticity

Choose four or five previously introduced uppercase letters. Print them on the board or on chart paper as shown at left. There should be four lines of letters repeated in random order.

Say: *Let's all practice saying the names of the letters together. When I point to the left of a letter, I want everyone to think about the letter name—think about it in your head. When I tap under the letter, I want everyone to say the letter name aloud. I'll show you how.* Point to the left of the letter *P,* pause two seconds for "thinking time," and then tap under the letter to signal that students should respond by saying "P." Follow the same procedure, pointing to each letter from left to right. Make sure that each student in the group is responding. When the group is consistently answering all items correctly, call on individual students to identify specific letters.

CORRECTIVE FEEDBACK If a student or students respond incorrectly, model the correct response for the entire group. Say the name of the letter. Then ask: *What is the name of this letter?* Tap under the letter as students respond. To ensure mastery and automaticity, back up two letters before the error and continue according to the procedure described above.

Activities for Cumulative Review

ALPHABET CENTER Set up an alphabet center. Provide students with access to letters in many forms, such as alphabet blocks, books, and letter cards, and a variety of materials to make letters, such as alphabet stencils and stamps. Allow students time to explore and use the materials.

LETTER PATH Create a construction paper "letter stone path" around the classroom. Print an uppercase letter on each stone. Have students "walk" the alphabet each day, saying aloud each letter name. You can also call out the letter names, asking students to stand on the appropriate stone (Blevins 2006).

GUESS WHAT GAME Give each pair of students a set of uppercase plastic letters in a container. Tell the first player in the pair to draw a plastic letter from the container and then, with eyes closed, identify the letter by feeling its shape. If the letter is named correctly, the first player keeps the letter. If the letter is not named correctly, it goes back into the container. The second player now takes a turn. Continue the game until all letters have been named. The student with the most letters at the end of the game is the winner (Neuhaus Education Center 2002).

OBSERVE & ASSESS

Questions for Observation	Benchmarks
(Pointing to an uppercase letter) What is the name of this letter?	Student can recognize uppercase letter names and shapes.
(Sliding finger under a line of uppercase letters) Can you tell me the names of these letters?	Student can recognize uppercase letters in random order. Later, student can name letters in a set time limit.

LESSON MODEL FOR

Handwriting

Benchmark

- ability to independently write uppercase letter forms

Strategy Grade Level

- Pre-K – Grade 1

Prerequisite

- ability to correctly form vertical, horizontal, slanted, and curved lines

Grouping

- whole class
- small group

Materials

- alphabet wall cards, for reference
- number 2, or softer, pencils
- copies of handwriting worksheet

Sources

Handwriting Strokes

- Handwriting Without Tears® http://www.hwtears.com
- Neuhaus Education Center http://www.neuhaus.org

Handwriting: Uppercase Letter Forms

According to Louise Spear-Swerling (2006), "students should learn a highly consistent way to form a given letter every time they write it." Teach letter formation using a continuous stroke (without lifting the pencil from the paper) when possible. When teaching handwriting, group together letters that begin in the same place and use the same type of strokes. For example, uppercase letters *F, E, D, P, B, R, N,* and *M* all begin in the top left corner with a vertical line down (Olsen 2003). This sample lesson model, which targets uppercase letter *P,* is based on handwriting lessons developed by the Neuhaus Education Center. The same model can be adapted and used to enhance handwriting instruction for other uppercase letters in any commercial reading program.

Teach/Model

Handwriting Habits

For handwriting instruction to be effective, students must first know the proper handwriting posture, paper position, and pencil grip (Wolf 2005; Hofmeister 1992). Lack of attention to these habits will lead to poor handwriting. Model for students and then ask them to demonstrate the following handwriting habits:

POSTURE Sit at a desk with your feet flat on the floor and your back straight. Lean slightly forward with your lower arms resting on the desk. Hold your head straight, not tilted.

PAPER POSITION If you are right-handed, place the paper directly in front of you and slant it downward to the left. Place your free, or left, hand on the top of the paper to hold

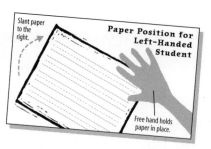

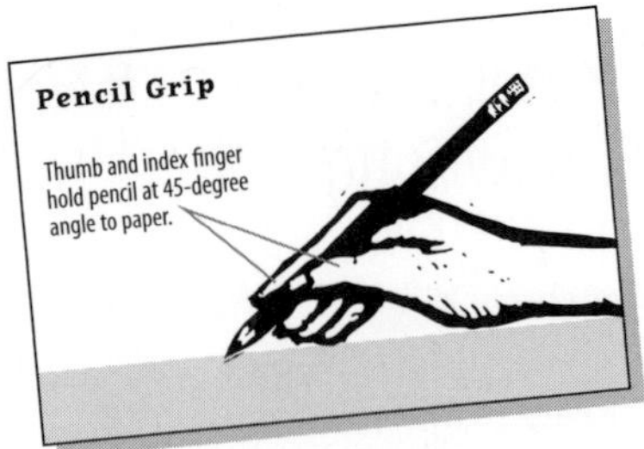

Handwriting Habits

Posture

Paper Position

Pencil Grip

it in place. If you are left-handed, slant the paper downward to the right and place your free, or right, hand on the top of the paper to hold it in place.

PENCIL GRIP About 1 inch from the point, rest the pencil on the first joint of your middle finger. Use your thumb and index finger to hold the pencil in place at a 45-degree angle to the paper.

Review the four types of lines used to make letters: vertical, horizontal, slanted, and curved. Then pass out magnetic letters to students and ask them to identify the types of lines in each letter.

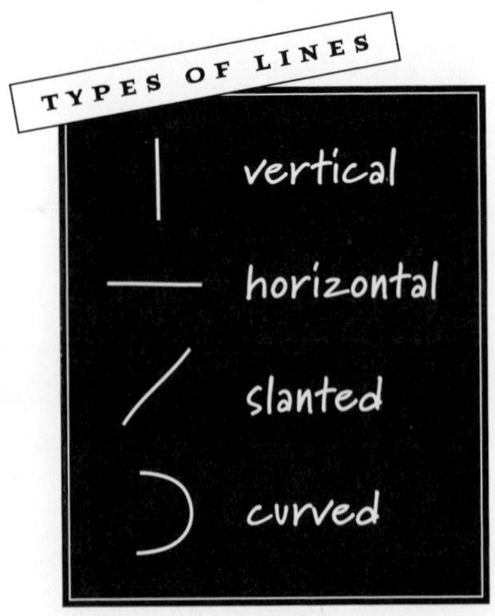

Letter Formation

Stand in front of the board. Say: *Today we're going to practice writing uppercase letter* P. Print the letter *P* on the board, one to two feet high, describing the letter strokes while forming the letter. For example, say: *This is uppercase letter* P. *Watch me write it. Down, up, around.*

Say: *Now I'm going to skywrite the letter* P. *I'm going to pretend my first two fingers are a magic pencil. I'll use my magic pencil to write uppercase* P *in the air.* Facing the board, extend your writing arm and first two fingers. Rest your nonwriting hand on the shoulder of your writing arm. While forming the letter in the air, say: P. *Down, up, around.*

Say: *Now it's your turn to skywrite. Stand up and get out your magic pencil. Get ready to write uppercase* P *in the air. Remember to start at the top. Ready, name the letter.* P. *Down, up, around.* Have students practice skywriting by following your hand motions as you skywrite the letter in the air. Repeat procedure two more times. Then say: *Now let's trace the letter* P *on our desks with our pointing finger. Remember to start at the top. Ready, name the letter.* P. *Down, up, around.* Repeat the same procedure two more times.

P down up around

P

Guided Practice

Give each student a handwriting worksheet. A sample worksheet for uppercase *P* is shown above.

TRACE LETTER FORM WITH FINGER Direct students' attention to the letter *P* on the top line of the worksheet. Say: *The arrows will help you remember how to make the letter* P. *Start at the top, and then go down, up, and around.* Then on the next line have students put their pointing finger at the top of the letter *P*. Say: *I want you to name the letter as you trace it with your pointing finger.* Pause as students name the letter *P* and trace it with their finger. Repeat the same procedure two more times.

TRACE LETTER FORM WITH PENCIL Say: *Get ready to trace the same letter* P *three times with your pencil. Remember to start at the top.* Have students put their pencil point at the top of the letter *P*. Say: *Get ready. Name the letter.* Pause as students name the letter *P* and trace with their pencil. Repeat the same procedure two more times.

COPY LETTER FORM WITH FINGER Say: *Using your pointing finger, practice copying the letter* P. Have students place the tip of their pointing finger on the dot to the right. Say: *Get ready. Name the letter.* Pause as students name the letter *P* and then write it with their finger.

COPY LETTER FORM WITH PENCIL Say: *Now, make a copy of the letter* P *with your pencil.* Have students place the tip of their pencil on the next dot to the right. Say: *Get ready. Name the letter.* Pause as students name the letter *P* and then write it with their pencil. Then direct students to complete the handwriting worksheet by copying the letter *P* five more times. Remind students to name the letter as they write it.

OBSERVE & ASSESS

Questions for Observation	Benchmarks
Can you show me how you sit when you write? Can you show me how you place your paper? Can you show me how you hold your pencil?	Student exhibits correct and consistent handwriting habits.
Can you show me how you write uppercase letter *P*?	Student can independently write a legible uppercase letter using correct letter formation.

LESSON MODEL FOR

Letter Recognition

Benchmarks

- ability to recognize lowercase letter names and shapes
- ability to match uppercase and lowercase letters

Strategy Grade Level

- Pre-K – Grade 1

Prerequisite

- ability to recognize uppercase letter names and shapes, both in and out of sequence

Grouping

- whole class
- small group

Materials

- alphabet big book
- alphabet letter cards for uppercase *T* and lowercase *t*
- chart paper
- materials for selected activities

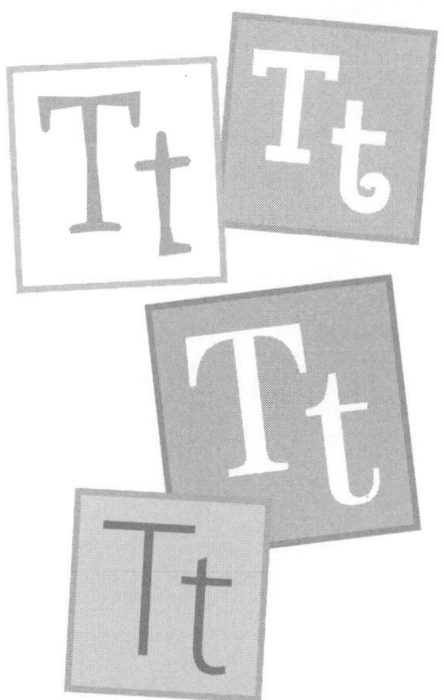

Letter Names and Shapes: Lowercase Letters

As with uppercase letter shapes, students often confuse lowercase letter shapes that are visually similar (e.g., *b-d, b-p, d-g, m-n*); these letters should not be introduced in proximity (Treiman et al. 2006). Alphabet books provide an excellent opportunity for students to hear, say, and see the alphabet. Bus and van IJzendoorn (1988) found that reading alphabet books to students was positively correlated with their ability to name the letters. To develop letter recognition, students should be able to match uppercase and lowercase letters (Bear et al. 2000). This sample lesson model targets lowercase letter *t*. The same model can be adapted and used to enhance lowercase letter recognition instruction in any commercial reading program.

Read an Alphabet Big Book

Ask students to listen carefully as you read aloud an alphabet big book. Read the book in its entirety, without pauses, so students can enjoy the language and illustrations. Then go back and point to target uppercase letters and ask: *What is the name of this letter? What do you notice about its shape?*

Teach/Model

Open an alphabet big book to the page for uppercase and lowercase *Tt*. Say: *Today we are going to learn a lowercase letter. First, let's review the uppercase letter.* Point to the uppercase letter *T* and ask: *What is this letter?* (T) Say: *Yes, this is uppercase* T. *It has a straight line down and then crosses at the top.* With your finger, trace the letter from top to bottom and then cross at the top. Now point to lowercase *t*. Say: *This is lowercase* t. *It is smaller than uppercase* T. *It also has a straight line down, but crosses in the middle.* Ask: *What is the name of this letter?* (t) Next, direct students' attention to at least two other examples of lowercase letter *t*. The letter could be displayed somewhere

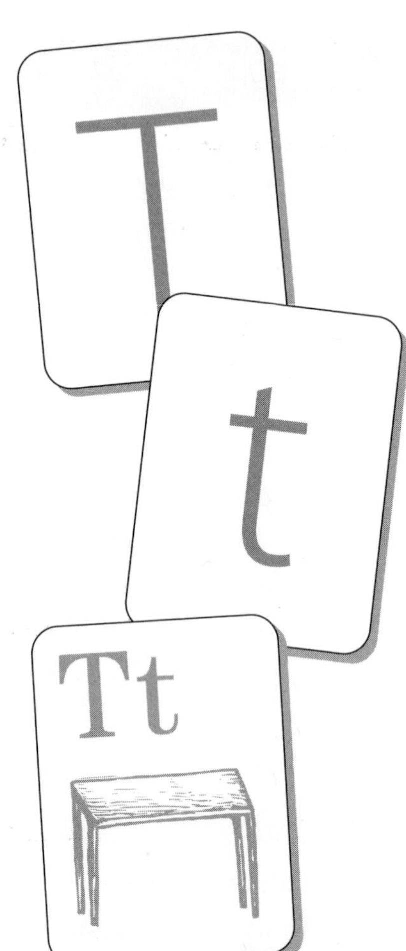

in the classroom environment or in a big book. Follow the same procedure for each new example, pointing to the letter and tracing the lines.

Show the alphabet letter card for uppercase *T*. Ask: *What is the name of this letter?* (T) Say: *Yes, this is uppercase* T. Then show the alphabet letter card for lowercase *t*. Ask: *What is the name of this letter?* (t) Say: *Yes, this is lowercase* t. Display the cards together, side by side. Say: *These uppercase and lowercase letters match. They both show* Tt. Hold up the alphabet letter card for lowercase *t*. Ask: *Can someone find in our big book the uppercase match to this letter?* Repeat the same procedure for uppercase *T*, finding a lowercase match.

Letter Naming Automaticity

Choose four or five previously introduced uppercase and lowercase letters. Print them on the board or on chart paper as shown below. There should be four lines of letters repeated in random order.

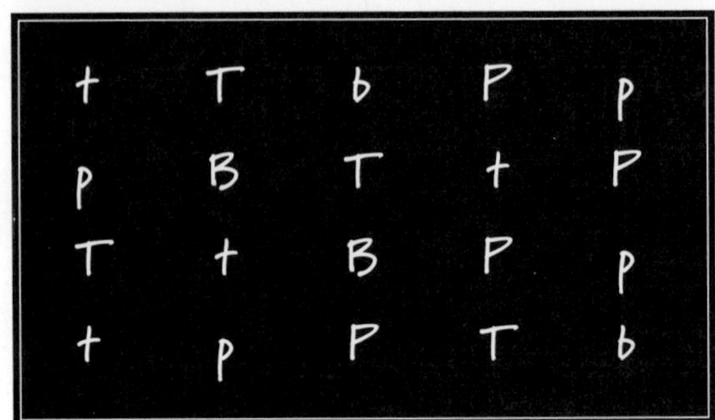

Say: *Let's all practice saying the names of the letters together. When I point to the left of a letter, I want everyone to think about the letter name—think about it in your head. When I tap under the letter, I want everyone to say the letter name aloud. I'll show you how.* Point to the left of the letter *t*, pause two seconds for "thinking time," and then tap under the letter to signal that students should respond by saying "t." Follow the same procedure, pointing to each letter from left to right. Make sure that each student in the group is responding. When the group is consistently answering all items correctly, call on individual students to identify specific letters.

CORRECTIVE FEEDBACK

CORRECTIVE FEEDBACK If a student or students respond incorrectly, model the correct response for the entire group. Say the name of the letter. Then ask: *What is the name of this letter?* Tap under the letter as students respond. To ensure mastery and automaticity, back up two letters before the error and continue according to the procedure described above.

Letter Matching Activities for Cumulative Review

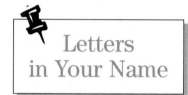

Letters in Your Name

LETTERS IN YOUR NAME Spell out a student's name with uppercase letter cards. Then give the student a mixed set of matching lowercase letter cards. Ask the student to match the lowercase letters to the uppercase letter in his or her name. Point to each uppercase and lowercase letter and ask the student to name them (Bear et al. 2000).

ALPHABET CONCENTRATION Make a set of eight to ten pairs of matching uppercase and lowercase letter cards. Place the letter cards facedown in a square array. Have players turn over two cards at a time. If the uppercase and lowercase letters match, the player gets to keep the cards and take another turn. The game is over when all the cards have been matched. The winner is the player with the most cards.

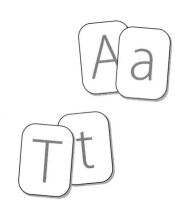

Alphabet Concentration

Questions for Observation	Benchmarks
(Pointing to a lowercase letter) What is the name of this letter?	Student can recognize lowercase letter names and shapes.
(Sliding finger under a line of lowercase letters) Tell me the names of as many letters as you can.	Student can recognize upper-case letters in random order. Later, student can name letters in a set time limit.
(Pointing to an uppercase letter) What is the name of this letter? Can you find the matching lowercase letter?	Student can match the upper-case and lowercase letters.

LESSON MODEL FOR

Handwriting

Benchmark

- ability to independently write lowercase letter forms

Strategy Grade Level

- Pre-K – Grade 1

Prerequisite

- ability to correctly form uppercase letters

Grouping

- whole class
- small group

Materials

- alphabet wall cards, for reference
- number 2, or softer, pencil
- copies of handwriting worksheet

Sources

Handwriting Strokes

- Handwriting Without Tears® http://www.hwtears.com
- Neuhaus Education Center http://www.neuhaus.org

Handwriting: Lowercase Letter Forms

The teaching sequence for handwriting instruction is based on how easy a letter is to form, how the letter is formed, and frequency of letter use. Letters that use the same stroke are generally grouped together for instruction (Olsen 2003); for example, lowercase letters *a, d, g* and *p, r, n, m, h, b*. After introducing the lowercase letters that are identical in shape to their uppercase form, introduce lowercase *t*. Lowercase *t* is almost like uppercase *T*, but it is crossed lower (Olsen 2003). This sample lesson model, which targets lowercase letter *t*, is based on handwriting lessons developed by the Neuhaus Education Center. The same model can be adapted and used to enhance handwriting instruction for other lowercase letters in any commercial reading program.

Review Handwriting Habits

Model and review proper handwriting habits. (Refer to Handwriting Habits, p. 99.) Then ask volunteers to demonstrate a range of correct and incorrect habits, asking the class to identify the correct posture, paper position, or pencil grip.

Teach/Model

Stand in front of the board. Say: *Today we're going to practice writing lowercase letter* t. Print the letter *t* on the board, one to two feet high, describing the letter strokes while forming the letter. For example, say: *This is lowercase letter* t. *Watch me write it. Down, cross.*

Say: *Now I'm going to skywrite the letter* t. *I'm going to pretend my first two fingers are a magic pencil. I'll use my magic pencil to write lowercase* t *in the air.* Facing the board, extend your writing arm and first two fingers. Rest your nonwriting hand on the shoulder of your writing arm. While forming the letter in the air, say: t. *Down, cross.*

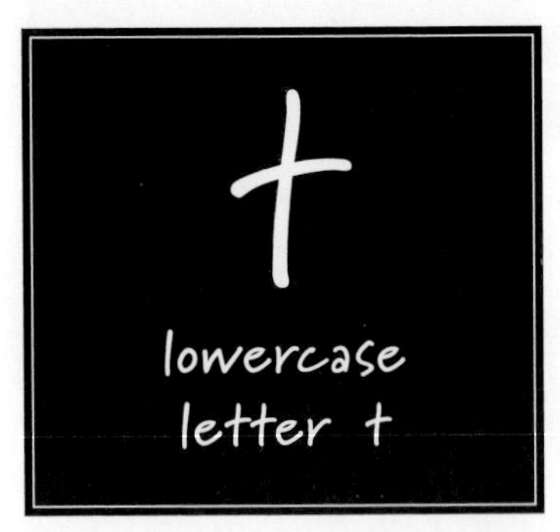

Say: *Now it's your turn to skywrite. Stand up and get out your magic pencil. Get ready to write lowercase* t *in the air. Remember to start at the top. Ready, name the letter.* t. *Down, cross.* Have students practice skywriting by following your hand motions as you skywrite the letter in the air. Repeat the procedure two more times. Then say: *Now let's trace the letter* t *on our desks with our pointing finger. Remember to start at the top. Ready, name the letter.* t. *Down, cross.* Repeat the same procedure two more times.

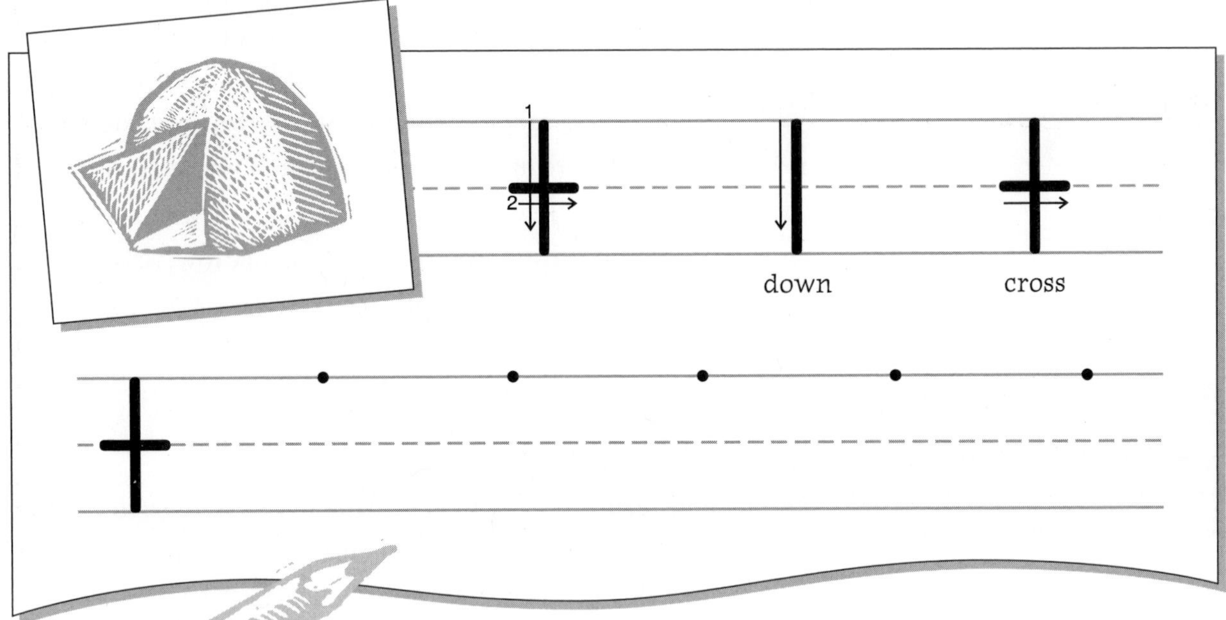

Guided Practice

Give each student a handwriting worksheet. A sample worksheet for lowercase *t* is shown above.

TRACE LETTER FORM WITH FINGER Direct students' attention to the letter *t* on the top line of the worksheet. Say: *The arrows will help you remember how to make the letter* t. *Start at the top, and then go down and cross.* Then on the next line have students put their pointing finger at the top of the letter *t*. Say: *I want you to name the letter as you trace it with your pointing finger.* Pause as students name the letter *t* and trace it with their finger. Repeat the same procedure two more times.

TRACE LETTER FORM WITH PENCIL Say: *Get ready to trace the letter three times with your pencil. Remember to start at the top.* Have students put their pencil point at the top of the letter *t*. Say: *Get ready. Name the letter.* Pause as students name the letter *t* and trace with their pencil. Repeat the same procedure two more times.

COPY LETTER FORM WITH FINGER Say: *Using your pointing finger, practice copying the letter* t. Have students place the tip of their pointing finger on the dot to the right. Say: *Get ready. Name the letter.* Pause as students name the letter *t* and then write it with their finger.

COPY LETTER FORM WITH PENCIL Say: *Now, make a copy of the letter* t *with your pencil.* Have students place the tip of their pencil on the next dot to the right. Say: *Get ready. Name the letter.* Pause as students name the letter *t* and then write it with their pencil. Then direct students to complete the handwriting worksheet by copying the letter *t* five more times. Remind students to name the letter as they write it.

Questions for Observation	Benchmarks
Can you show me how you sit when you write? Can you show me how you place your paper? Can you show me how you hold your pencil?	Student exhibits correct and consistent handwriting habits.
Can you show me how you write lowercase letter *t*?	Student can independently write a legible lowercase letter using correct letter formation.

LESSON MODEL FOR

Letter-Sound Correspondence

Benchmarks

- ability to use letter names to detect letter sounds
- ability to produce a sound associated with a letter

Strategy Grade Level

- Pre-K – Grade 1

Prerequisites

- knowledge of letter names
- ability to isolate phonemes in spoken words

Grouping

- small group
- individual

Materials

- chart paper

Use of Letter Names to Learn Letter Sounds, p. 88

Letter-Sound Strategy

Students can use their knowledge of letter names to help them learn and remember the corresponding letter sounds (Treiman 2005; Share 2004). According to Ehri and Roberts (2006), this means that letter names and sounds can be taught together—there is no need to decide which element to teach first. This sample lesson model focuses on a strategy to make students aware that a letter's name can often help them in detecting the sound the letter makes. The same model can be adapted and used to enhance letter-knowledge and letter-sound instruction in any commercial reading program.

Review: Letter Naming Automaticity

On the board or on chart paper, print previously introduced uppercase and lowercase letters. There should be four lines of letters repeated in random order as shown below.

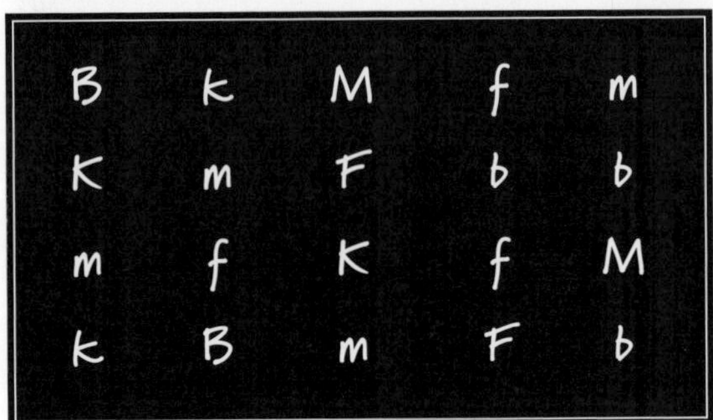

Say: *Let's all practice saying the names of the letters together. When I point to the left of a letter, I want everyone to think about the letter name—think about it in your head. When I tap under the letter, I want everyone to say the letter name aloud.* Point to the left of the letter *B,* pause two seconds for "thinking time," and then tap under the letter to signal that students should respond by saying "B." Follow the same procedure, pointing to each letter from left to right. Make sure all students are responding.

When the group is consistently answering all items correctly, call on individual students to identify specific letters.

CORRECTIVE FEEDBACK

CORRECTIVE FEEDBACK If a student or students respond incorrectly, model the correct response for the entire group. Say: *The name of this letter is* B. Tap under the letter *B* and ask: *What is the name of this letter?* (B)

INITIAL SOUND IN LETTER NAMES

Students are usually better at identifying letter sounds when the letter's name begins with that sound than when it ends with the sound or is not in the name at all (Treiman and Kessler 2003).

Teach/Model

Say: *Letters stand for sounds. I'm going to show you how knowing a letter's name can help you to learn and remember a sound the letter stands for.* Print the letter *b* on the board. Ask: *What is the name of this letter?* (b) Say: *Yes,* b. *Listen as I say* b *a sound at a time, /b/ /ē/. Now you say it one sound at a time with me, /b/ /ē/. The sound the letter* b *stands for is the first sound in its name, /b/.* Ask: *What sound does the letter* b *stand for?* (/b/) Ask: *How can you remember the sound?* (It's the first sound in the letter name.) Say: *Yes, /b/ is the first sound in the letter name* b. Repeat the same procedure with the letter name *k* (/k/ /ā/).

Guided Practice

On the board or on chart paper, print letters that have their sound at the beginning of their names, for example:

Letter Sound at the Beginning of Letter Name

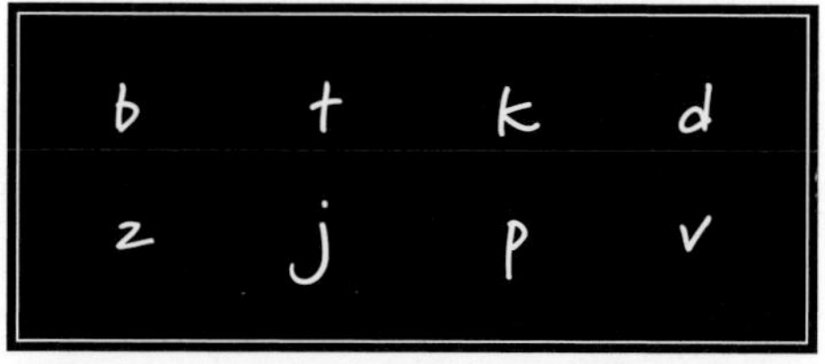

Point to the letter *b*. Ask: *What is the name of this letter?* (b) Say: *Listen as I say* b *a sound at a time, /b/ /ē/.* Ask: *What is the first sound in the letter name* b? (/b/) Ask: *What sound does the letter* b *stand for?* (/b/) Point under the letter *b* as students respond. Follow the same procedure, pointing to the rest of the letters from left to right. Make sure each student in the group is responding. When the group is consistently answering all items correctly, call on individual students to identify the letter sounds.

CORRECTIVE FEEDBACK

CORRECTIVE FEEDBACK Students are especially likely to confuse letters that have similar names as well as similar shapes, such as *b* and *d* or *b* and *p*. If a student or students respond incorrectly, model the correct response for the entire group. For example, point to the letter *b* and say: *Listen as I say* b *a sound at a time, /b/ /ē/. The sound the letter* b *stands for is the first sound in its name, /b/. What's the first sound in* b? (/b/)

FINAL SOUND IN LETTER NAMES

Teach/Model

Say: *Some letters stand for the sound at the end of their names.* Print the letter *m* on the board. Ask: *What is the name of this letter?* (m) Say: *Yes,* m. *Listen as I say* m *a sound at a time, /e/ /m/. Say the letter name* m *a sound at a time with me, /e/ /m/. The sound the letter* m *stands for is the last sound in its name, /m/.* Ask: *What sound does the letter* m *stand for?* (/m/) Ask: *How can you remember the sound?* (It's the last sound in the letter name.) Say: *Yes, /m/ is the last sound in the letter name* m. Repeat the same procedure with the letter name *f* (/e/ /f/).

Guided Practice

On the board or on chart paper, print letters that have their sound at the end of their names, for example:

Letter Sound at the End of Letter Name

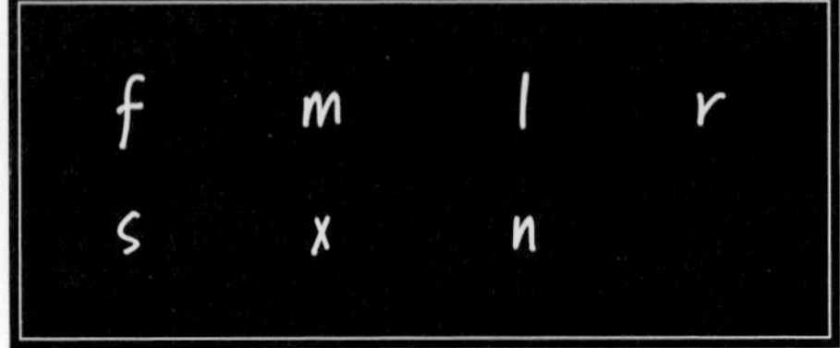

Point to the letter *f.* Ask: *What is the name of this letter?* (f) Say: *Listen as I say* f *a sound at a time, (/e/ /f/).* Ask: *What is the last sound in the letter name* f*?* (/f/) Ask: *What sound does the letter* f *stand for?* (/f/) Point under the letter *f* as students respond. Follow the sâme procedure, pointing to the rest of the letters from left to right. Make sure each student in the group is responding. When the group is consistently answering all items correctly, call on individual students to identify the sounds.

CORRECTIVE FEEDBACK Students are especially likely to confuse letters that have similar names as well as similar shapes, such as *m* and *n.* If a student or students respond incorrectly, model the correct response for the entire group. For example, point to the letter *m* and say: *Listen as I say* m *a sound at a time, /e/ /m/. The sound the letter* m *stands for is the last sound in its name, /m/. What's the last sound in* m*?* (/m/)

OBSERVE & ASSESS

Questions for Observation	Benchmarks
(Point to the letter b.*)* What sound does the letter *b* stand for? (/b/) How did you remember the sound? (It's the first sound in the letter name.)	Student can associate a letter sound with a letter name.
(Point to the letter m.*)* What sound does the letter *m* stand for? (/m/) How did you remember the sound? (It's the last sound in the letter name.)	Student can associate a letter sound with a letter name.

CHAPTER

5

Phonological Awareness

what?
why?
when?
how?

what? Phonological Awareness

> Phonological awareness instruction should never be considered an end in itself. It should always be conducted with its connections to decoding in mind.
>
> —LANE & PULLEN, 2004

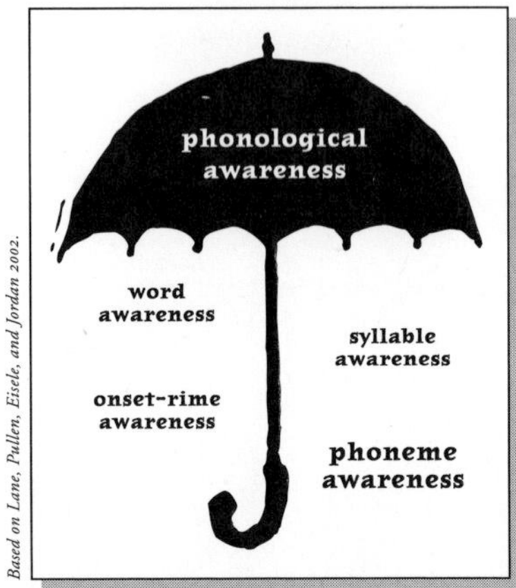

Based on Lane, Pullen, Eisele, and Jordan 2002.

Phonological awareness is an umbrella term that includes the awareness of the larger parts of spoken language, such as words, syllables, and onsets and rimes—as well as the smaller parts, phonemes. A phoneme is the smallest unit of spoken language that makes a difference in a word's meaning. For example, the phonemes /s/ and /f/ are different; the meaning of the word *sat* is different from the meaning of the word *fat.*

Phonemic awareness, the ability to detect, identify, and manipulate phonemes in spoken words, is the most sophisticated and essential level of phonological awareness. It is both a reliable predictor of later reading achievement and a result of learning to read (Bishop 2003; Bus and van IJzendoorn 1999; Ehri et al. 2001; O'Connor and Jenkins 1999). Phonemic awareness instruction improves phonics skills and phonics instruction improves phonemic awareness; the relationship is reciprocal (Lane and Pullen 2004).

Phonemic awareness is *not* the same as phonics. Phonemic awareness is the understanding that *spoken* language can be broken into phonemes. Phonics is the understanding of the relationship between phonemes and graphemes, the letters that represent the sounds in *written* language. Instruction in phonemic awareness and phonics tends to overlap. According to the National Reading Panel (2000), phonemic awareness instruction is most effective when students are taught to use letters as they manipulate phonemes. The panel (2000) also noted "that when phonemic awareness is taught with letters, it qualifies as phonics instruction."

Phonemes, or speech sounds, combine to form syllables and words. Some words, such as *I* or *a,* have only one phoneme, but most words contain more than one. The word *may* has two phonemes (/m/ /ā/), *read* has three phonemes (/r/ /ē/ /d/), and *speech* has four phonemes (/s/ /p/ /ē/ /ch/).

Count and then identify the phonemes in each of these words:

ice own top let face easy meets

Now reverse the sequence of phonemes by saying each word backward. For example, if you say *may* backward, it becomes *aim.* Remember to think of the sounds, not the letters.

(See Answer Key, p. 800.)

Levels of Development

Word Level

Syllable Level

Onset-Rime Level

Phoneme Level

SEE ALSO . . .

Phonemes, p. 22
Consonant Phoneme Classifications, p. 24
Vowel Phoneme Classifications, p. 26
Syllables, p. 36
Onset-Rime, p. 38

Levels of Phonological Awareness

Phonological awareness can be broken into four developmental levels: word, syllable, onset-rime (intrasyllable), and phoneme. As students progress through the levels, they learn to blend, segment, and manipulate words, syllables, and onsets and rimes. This instruction lays a strong foundation for the development of phonemic awareness, helping students learn to pay attention to the way language sounds, in addition to what it means (Blachman 2000).

At the phoneme level, students attend to the smallest units of sound. Ultimately, phoneme blending and segmenting are the most critical phonological skills. According to the National Reading Panel (2000), segmenting words into phonemes and blending phonemes into words contributes more to learning to read and spell well than any of the other phonological awareness skills.

Phonological Awareness Skills by Level

LEVEL	SKILL NAME	DESCRIPTION	EXAMPLE
WORD	**Sentence Segmentation**	Given a sentence or phrase, student taps one time for every word in the sentence.	Tap one time for every word you hear in the sentence: *I like pizza.*
WORD	**Blending**	Given two smaller words, student blends them together to form a compound word.	Listen as I say two small words: *dog . . . house.* Can you put the two words together to make a bigger word? (doghouse)
WORD	**Segmentation**	Given a compound word, student breaks the word into the two smaller words.	Can you clap the word parts in *doghouse*? (dog•house) How many times did you clap? (two)
WORD	**Deletion**	Given a compound word, student deletes one of the smaller words.	Say *doghouse*. Now say *doghouse* without the *house*. (dog)
SYLLABLE	**Blending**	Given a word broken into syllables, student blends the word parts together to create the whole word.	Can you put these word parts together to make a whole word: *pock•et*? (pocket)
SYLLABLE	**Segmentation**	Given a whole word, student breaks the word into syllables.	Can you clap the word parts in *pocket*? (pock•et) How many times did you clap? (two)
SYLLABLE	**Deletion**	Given a whole word, student deletes one of the syllables.	Say *pepper*. Now say *pepper* without the *er*. (pep)
ONSET-RIME	**Recognize Rhyme**	Given a pair of words, student determines whether they rhyme.	Do these two words rhyme: *ham, jam*? (yes)
ONSET-RIME	**Generate Rhyme**	Given a word, student says a word that rhymes.	Tell me a word that rhymes with *nut*. (cut)
ONSET-RIME	**Categorization**	Given a set of three or four words, student finds the word that does not rhyme.	Which word does not belong: *mat, sun, cat, fat*? (sun)
ONSET-RIME	**Blending**	Given a word broken into onset and rime, student blends the sounds together to create the whole word.	What whole word am I trying to say: /b/. . . /ig/? (big)
ONSET-RIME	**Segmentation**	Given a word, student breaks the word into onset and rime.	Can you say *big* in two parts? (/b/. . . /ig/)

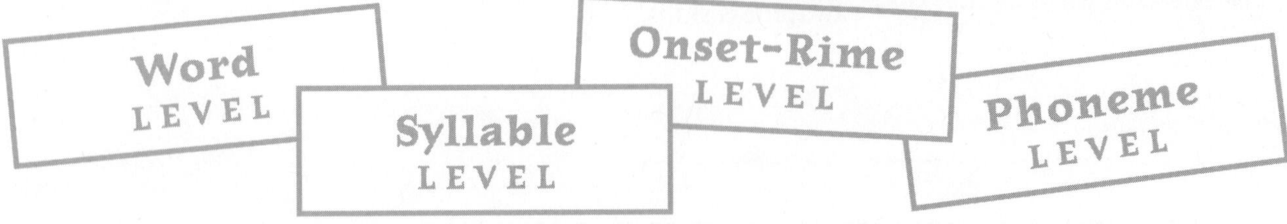

Phonological Awareness Skills by Level *(continued)*

LEVEL	SKILL NAME	DESCRIPTION	EXAMPLE
PHONEME	**Isolation**	Given a word, student recognizes individual sounds in the word.	What is the first sound in *van*? (/v/) What is the last sound in *van*? (/n/) What is the middle sound in *van*? (/a/)
	Identity	Given a word, student selects the word that has a common sound from a set of three or four different words.	Which word has the same first sound as *car*: *fan, corn,* or *map*? (corn)
	Categorization	Given a set of three or four words, student recognizes the word that has the "odd" sound.	Which word does not belong: *bus, ball, mouse*? (mouse)
	Blending	Given a word separated into phonemes, student combines the sounds to form a whole word.	What word is /b/ /i/ /g/? (big)
	Segmentation	Given a whole word, student separates the word into individual phonemes and says each sound.	How many sounds in *big*? (three) Can you say them sound by sound? (/b/ /i/ /g/)
	Deletion	Given a word, student recognizes the word that remains when a phoneme is removed from that word.	What is *spark* without the /s/? (park)
	Addition	Given a word, student makes a new word by adding a phoneme.	What word do you have if you add /s/ to the beginning of *park*? (spark)
	Substitution	Given a word, student makes a new word by replacing one phoneme for another.	The word is *rug*. Change /g/ to /n/. What's the new word? (run)

Adapted from Lane and Pullen 2004.

Blending and Segmentation Skills Across the Levels

LEVELS ⟶	WORD	SYLLABLE	ONSET-RIME	PHONEME
Blending Given a word separated into phonemes, student combines the sounds to form a whole word.	Listen as I say two small words: *dog • house.* Can you put the two words together to make a bigger word? (doghouse)	Can you put these word parts together to make a whole word: *pock • et?* (pocket)	What whole word am I trying to say: /b/ . . . /ig/? (big)	What word is /b/ /i/ /g/? (big)
Segmentation Given a whole word, student separates the word into individual phonemes and says each sound.	Can you clap the word parts in *doghouse*? (dog • house) How many times did you clap? (two)	Can you clap the word parts in *pocket*? (pock • et) How many times did you clap? (two)	What is the first part of *big*? (/b/) What is the last part of *big*? (/ig/) Can you say *big* in two parts? (/b/. . . /ig/)	How many sounds are in *big*? (three) Can you say them sound by sound? (/b/ /i/ /g/)

CCSS READING STANDARDS

Foundational Skills

Phonological Awareness

Demonstrate understanding of spoken words, syllables, and phonemes. (RF.K-1.2)

Lesson Models

PHONEME
the smallest unit of spoken language that makes a difference in a word's meaning

PHONEMIC AWARENESS
the ability to detect, identify, and manipulate phonemes in spoken words

Effective Phonological Awareness Instruction

Phonological awareness should be taught by teachers who have adequate knowledge about the structure of language (Moats 2000). Not all types of phonological awareness instruction are equally effective. To maximize the effectiveness of instruction, here are some general guidelines:

- Phonological awareness instruction should be explicit. Instruction should include clear explanations, teacher modeling of tasks, and sufficient opportunity for student practice (Cunningham 1990; Foorman and Torgesen 2001).

- Phonological awareness instruction should be systematic. It should progress from easier to more difficult tasks. For example:

  Segmenting words or syllables is easier than segmenting phonemes.

  Isolating initial phonemes in words is easier than isolating final or medial phonemes in words.

  Blending or segmenting words with two phonemes is easier than blending or segmenting words with three or four phonemes.

  Blending words with continuous sounds is easier than blending words with stop sounds. For example, *sun* is easier to blend than *dip*.

- Phonological awareness instruction should be conducted in small groups (Foorman and Torgesen 2001; National Reading Panel 2000). Small-group instruction allows for sufficient teacher attention to individual needs.

- For most students, the entire phonological awareness program need not last more than 20 hours over the school year. Each session, or lesson, should probably not exceed 30 minutes in length (National Reading Panel 2000). Additional instruction may be required for struggling readers.

The development of phonological awareness is not strictly language specific. The skills involved in building an awareness of the sound structure of words in a native alphabetic language can be transferred and applied to learning a second alphabetic language (Gillon 2004).

- A phonemic awareness lesson should target no more than one or two skills at a time. All lessons should support instruction in phoneme blending and segmentation (National Reading Panel 2000).
- To make sounds less abstract and more concrete, phonemic awareness instruction that provides markers for phonemes is helpful in teaching students how to manipulate phonemes in speech (Ehri and Roberts 2006). Concrete markers include cubes, chips, buttons, and blocks.
- Phonological awareness instructional techniques should be engaging, interesting, and motivating, making use of games and other interactive activities.
- In phonemic awareness activities, phonemes should be pronounced correctly in a manner that will make them "blendable." This is especially relevant when pronouncing stop sounds—sounds that cannot be pronounced, or held out, for several seconds without distortion (Lane and Pullen 2004).

Blendable Sounds

Stop Sounds

/b/ • /d/ • /g/ • /h/
/j/ • /k/ • /p/ • /t/

Continuous Sounds

/f/ • /l/ • /m/ • /n/
/r/ • /s/ • /v/ • /w/
/y/ • /z/ • /a/
/e/ • /i/ • /o/ • /u/

SEE ALSO . . .

Consonant Phoneme Classifications, p. 24

Blendable Sounds

STOP SOUNDS A stop sound is a sound that can be pronounced for only an instant. Avoid adding an /uh/ when producing stop consonant sounds. In other words, don't say /kuh/ /a/ /tuh/ and expect students to blend those sounds to make *cat*. Say the sounds as quickly as possible in the way they are pronounced at the end of words (Pullen 2005). Because it is nearly impossible to pronounce the voiced stop consonants /b/, /d/, and /g/ in isolation without a vowel sound attached, model saying these sounds followed by an extremely brief short *i* sound (Lane and Pullen 2004). For example, pronounce /b/ as /bi/ and /d/ as /di/.

CONTINUOUS SOUNDS A continuous sound is a sound that can be pronounced for several seconds without any distortion. Continuous sounds can be held out and therefore are easy to blend together.

why?

Phonological Awareness

> Acquiring phonemic awareness is a means rather than an end. Phonemic awareness is not acquired for its own sake but rather for its value in helping children understand and use the alphabetic system to read and write.
>
> —NATIONAL READING PANEL, 2000

To benefit from phonics instruction, students must first possess a fundamental level of phonological awareness. Therefore, according to Lane and Pullen (2004), "improvements in phonological awareness can and usually do result in improvements in reading ability." Students with strong phonological awareness are likely to become good readers, but students with weak phonological skills will likely become poor readers (Blachman 2000). It is estimated that the vast majority—more than 90 percent—of students with significant reading problems have a core deficit in their ability to process phonological information (Blachman 1995).

The understanding that speech sounds can be segmented and blended is necessary to make connections between speech and print. Without the capacity to attend to the individual sounds in words, it is extremely difficult to match sounds to letters and decode words. According to Adams (1990), a child's level of phonemic awareness at school entry is widely considered the strongest single determinant of his or her later reading achievement. Phonemic awareness can be developed through instruction and doing so significantly accelerates students' subsequent reading and writing achievement (Ball and Blachman 1991).

Research Findings . . .

Phoneme awareness performance is a strong predictor of long-term reading and spelling success and can predict literacy performance more accurately than variables such as intelligence, vocabulary knowledge, and socioeconomic status.

—GILLON, 2004

Over the years, educational research has identified many reliable predictors of later reading performance, but phonological awareness is one of the few factors that teachers are able to influence significantly.

—LANE & PULLEN, 2004

The most common cause of children's early difficulties in acquiring accurate and fluent word recognition skills involves individual differences in their phonological knowledge and skills.

—TORGESEN, 2002

The reason for teaching children to analyze phonemes in words is so they can connect letters to phonemes when they read or write words.

—EHRI & ROBERTS, 2006

Suggested Reading . . .

Phonemic Awareness in Young Children (1998) by Marilyn Jager Adams, Barbara Foorman, Ingvar Lundberg & Terri Beeler. Baltimore, MD: Paul H. Brookes.

Phonological Awareness Assessment and Instruction: A Sound Beginning (2004) by Holly B. Lane & Paige C. Pullen. Boston: Allyn & Bacon.

Phonological Awareness: From Research to Practice (2007) by Gail T. Gillon. New York: Guilford.

Proust the Squid: The Story and Science of the Reading Brain (2007) by Maryanne Wolf. New York: HarperCollins.

Put Reading First: The Research Building Blocks for Teaching Children to Read, 3rd Edition (2006) by Bonnie Armbruster, Fran Lehr & Jean Osborn. Jessup, MD: National Institute for Literacy.

Speech to Print: Language Essentials for Teachers, 2nd Edition (2010) by Louisa Cook Moats. Baltimore, MD: Paul H. Brookes.

when?

Phonological Awareness

The impact of phonemic awareness instruction may be greatest in preschool and Kindergarten, and may become smaller beyond first grade.

—EHRI ET AL., 2001

For English-language learners, phonemic awareness is just as crucial for learning to read as it is for English-only learners (Chiappe, Siegel, and Gottardo 2002).

When to Teach

For most students, learning to attend to individual phonemes comes more easily following experiences at the less advanced word, syllable, and onset-rime levels of phonological awareness. In general, begin with larger sound units and move progressively to smaller units. It is not essential for students to fully master all of the phonological skills at a particular level before moving on to the next level. As students move into phoneme-level skills a variety of tasks are necessary to provide ample practice. According to the National Reading Panel (2000), instruction is more effective when it focuses on one or two phoneme manipulations, rather than when it combines multiple types of manipulations in one lesson. It is important to logically sequence skills from easier to more difficult. Generally, instruction in blending pho-nemes should begin before phoneme segmentation; instruction in phoneme isolation and identity should begin before phoneme-by-phoneme segmentation; and instruction in phoneme deletion, addition, and substitution should begin after phoneme segmentation (Lane and Pullen 2004; Pullen 2005).

The National Reading Panel (2000) concluded that decisions about the amount of phonemic awareness instruction should be influenced by situational factors, such as the goals of instruction, how many skills are being taught, whether letters are included, and students' prior phonological skills. They also concluded that more instruction is not necessarily better. Here are some general recommendations:

Amount of Instruction

All Students

KINDERGARTEN About 10 to 15 minutes per day

GRADE 1 About 10 minutes per day for the first three months of the school year

Intervention

KINDERGARTEN An additional 15 minutes per day, three or four times per week, for about 10 weeks

GRADE 1 An additional 15 minutes per day, three or four times per week, for as long as needed

GRADES 2 AND ABOVE About 15 minutes per day, three or four times per week, for as long as needed

Throughout Kindergarten, students should receive at least 10 to 15 minutes per day of phonological awareness instruction (Foorman et al. 1997a). Instruction can take place as one lesson, or tasks may be broken into informal activities throughout the day. For example, call on students to line up for lunch according to the first sound in their name. For students who need further assistance, provide instruction in a small-group setting for an additional 15 minutes per day, three or four times per week, for about 10 weeks. The National Reading Panel (2000) determined that small-group phonological awareness instruction produced greater gains than individual or large-group instruction.

In the first grade, students should receive instruction 10 minutes per day for about the first three months of school, in conjunction with phonics instruction. For students who need further assistance, provide instruction in a small-group setting for an additional 15 minutes per day, three or four times per week, as long as needed.

In second grade and above, phonemic awareness instruction is usually only necessary for students who do not automatically recognize words and who are not reading at grade level. For students who need further assistance, provide instruction in a small-group setting for an additional 15 minutes per day, three or four times per week, for as long as needed.

Phonemic Awareness with Letters

Although plentiful evidence exists to support the inclusion of letters in phonemic awareness instruction, the appropriate time to begin incorporating letters is less clear (Ehri and Roberts 2006). Some students become confused when they try to learn letter sounds and the processes for blending and segmenting them at the same time (Stahl 1992).

To make the transition to letters smooth, ensure that students can successfully blend and segment consonant-vowel-consonant words without letters first. Also, check to see that students know most of the letter names and many of the sounds that go with the letters before including letters in phonemic awareness instruction. That is, alphabet instruction and phonemic awareness instruction should remain separate until a clear trajectory toward mastery of both is established. At that point, including letters can accelerate progress (Snow, Burns, and Griffin 1998).

When to Assess and Intervene

> The most reliable and informative method of assessing phonological awareness is in-depth, individual testing.
>
> —LANE & PULLEN, 2004

Begin phonological awareness assessment in mid-Kindergarten and continue to assess it throughout the early elementary grades, as needed. Generally, once a student demonstrates decoding ability, assessment of phonological awareness is no longer necessary. For students who have low decoding skills in first and second grades, the best approach is to assess their phonological awareness before teaching it. Assessment will indicate which students need the instruction and which do not, or which students need to be taught rudimentary levels of phonemic awareness, such as phoneme isolation, or which are ready for more advanced levels, such as phoneme blending and segmentation (Ehri et al. 2001).

For students who have fallen behind in phonemic awareness, intensive intervention may be appropriate. Intensive intervention is characterized by more explicit modeling, smaller groups, additional time, or extra practice on new skills. Intervention may also include attention to the manner in which sounds are articulated. For some students, a focus on how sounds are produced provides a physical connection that makes the abstract notion of isolating sounds in words more understandable (Heilman, Voeller, and Alexander 1996).

SEE ALSO . . .

CORE Literacy Library

Assessing Reading: Multiple Measures, 2nd Edition

Older Struggling Readers

Phonological awareness may contribute less to older, normally developing readers but may make a big difference for older students who have failed to make normal progress in learning to read (Ehri et al. 2001). If a student continues to struggle with decoding in the upper grades, assessment in phonological awareness may still be appropriate. Lack of foundational skills can interfere with development of skilled decoding. Intervention for older students should focus on the specific areas of weakness (Mercer and Mercer 2004).

Purpose	✓ Phonological-Awareness Assessment	Publisher
Screening	Phonological Awareness Literacy Screening (PALS) ▸ PALS–K: Rhyme Awareness, Beginning Sound Awareness ▸ PALS 1–3: Level C, Phonemic Awareness	University of Virginia http://pals.virginia.edu
Screening Progress Monitoring	AIMSweb® Test of Early Literacy (TEL) ▸ Phoneme Segmentation Fluency	Pearson http://aimsweb.com
Screening Progress Monitoring	DIBELS® Next ▸ First Sound Fluency (FSF) ▸ Phoneme Segmentation Fluency (PSF)	Sopris West http://dibels.org
Screening Progress Monitoring Diagnostic	easy CBM™ ▸ Phonemic Awareness	Riverside Publishing http://easycbm.com
Screening Progress Monitoring Diagnostic	TPRI Early Reading Assessment ▸ Phonemic Awareness	Texas Education Agency http://www.tpri.org
Diagnostic	Comprehensive Test of Phonological Processing (CTOPP)	Pro-Ed
Diagnostic	Early Reading Diagnostic Assessment®, 2nd Edition (ERDA)	Pearson
Diagnostic	First Performances™ Fox in a Box®, 2nd Edition ▸ Phonemic Awareness	CTB/McGraw-Hill
Diagnostic	Lindamood Auditory Conceptualization Test, 3rd Edition (LAC-3)	Pro-Ed
Diagnostic	Test of Phonological Awareness, 2nd Edition: PLUS (TOPA-2+)	Pro-Ed

LESSON MODEL FOR

Rhyming

Benchmarks

- ability to recognize words that rhyme
- ability to generate rhyming words

Strategy Grade Level

- Pre-K – Grade 1

Grouping

- small group

Materials

- picture cards of foods: bean, beet, corn, fish, fig, ham, jam, meat, milk, nut, peach, pear, peas, rice, roll, soup
- large envelope that says "Feed Me" on one side and "Thank You" on the other with string attached so that it can hang around a student's neck

Sources

- *The Hungry Thing* (2001) by Jan Slepian and Ann Seidler. New York: Scholastic.
- Activity adapted from *The Sounds Abound™ Program* (1998) by Orna Lenchner and Blanche Podhajski. East Moline, IL: LinguiSystems, www.linguisystems.com.

The Hungry Thing

According to Bryant (1990), the recognition of rhyme may be the entry point to phonological awareness. By working with rhyme, students begin to attend to the way language sounds, separate from its meaning. This sample lesson model is based on the *The Hungry Thing,* a children's book by Jan Slepian and Ann Seidler. It focuses on single-syllable words that begin with single consonants. Once students become adept with this type of word, use the same model with single-syllable words beginning with digraphs or blends. This lesson model can be adapted and used to enhance phonological awareness instruction in any commercial reading program.

Develop Oral Language

Because it is very difficult to work with sounds in an unfamiliar word, it is important that students know the food names used in this lesson model. To ensure that students develop in-depth knowledge of the food names, refer to the sample lesson models in Section V: Vocabulary.

Teach/Model

RHYME RECOGNITION Explain to students that they are going to learn about rhyming words. Say: *Rhyming words are two or more words that sound the same in the middle and at the end. Listen carefully as I say these two rhyming words:* ham-jam. Jam *has /am/.* Ham *has /am/. They both have /am/, so they rhyme*. Ask: *Do* ham *and* jam *rhyme?* (yes) *What makes them rhyming words?* (They sound the same in the middle and at the end.) Follow the same procedure with another rhyming word pair, such as *meat-beet.*

To clarify what is and what is not a rhyme, say: *Now listen carefully as I say two more words:* rice-roll. *Let's see.* Rice *has /ice/, but* roll *has /oll/. So* rice *and* roll *do not rhyme.* Ask: *Do* rice *and* roll *rhyme?* (no) Follow the same procedure with word pairs *toast-roast* and *fish-fig.*

RHYME GENERATION Say: *If I wanted to come up with words that rhyme with* fig, *what part of the word would stay the same? The /ig/ would stay the same, as in the words* big *and* dig. Display three food picture cards: *nut, peach, bean.* Have students identify the foods pictured on the cards. Say: *I'm going to name the food on the card. Then I'm going to say a word that rhymes with the food name. Point to the picture of a* nut. Say: *This is a* nut. *A word that rhymes with* nut *is* cut. Nut *has* /ut/. Cut *has* /ut/. *They both have /ut/, so they rhyme*. Follow the same procedure with *peach (beach)* and *bean (green).*

Small-Group Guided Practice

Explain to students that you are going to tell them a story about a Hungry Thing who comes to town. The people in the town want to feed the Hungry Thing. They ask it what it wants to eat. For some reason, the Hungry Thing can't say the name of the food it wants to eat. Instead, it can only say a word that rhymes with the name of that food.

Before telling the story, select one student to be the Hungry Thing. Hang the "Feed Me" sign around the student's neck. Then pass out the food picture cards. Have students sit in a circle with their food picture cards facing up in front of them. Have each student say the name of the food on his or her card.

The Hungry Thing

	NARRATION	ACTION/PROMPT
1	Once upon a time there was a Hungry Thing that came into the town of (school location) and pointed to a sign around its neck that said "Feed Me."	Prompt the Hungry Thing to point to its sign.
2	And the townspeople asked, "What would you like to eat?"	
3	The Hungry Thing answered, "Pilk."	Supply a nonsense word that rhymes with a food named on one of the picture cards.
4	"What is pilk?" the townspeople asked.	Pause and then prompt students to look at the picture cards for a food name that rhymes with *pilk*.
5	And a student in [classroom name] said, "Pilk rhymes with . . .	Direct the student who has the food name that rhymes with *pilk* (milk) to say the name of the food and to then put the card into the Hungry Thing's "Feed Me" envelope.
6	milk!"	
7	Then the Hungry Thing wiped its mouth and pointed again to the "Feed Me" sign.	Prompt the Hungry Thing to point to the sign.
8	And the townspeople asked, "Now what would you like to eat?"	Repeat lines 3 through 6 until all students have fed the Hungry Thing.
9	Then the Hungry Thing wiped its mouth, turned the sign around, pointed to it, and said, "Thank you."	Prompt the Hungry Thing to wipe its mouth, turn the sign around, point to it, and say, "Thank you."

Feed Me

Thank You

Say: *I'm going to tell you the story of the Hungry Thing. Listen carefully because each time the Hungry Thing asks for food, you must check to see if the name of the food on your picture card rhymes with what the Hungry Thing says it wants to eat. For example, the words* pilk *and* milk *rhyme. So if the Hungry Thing says it wants* "pilk," *whoever has the milk picture card would "feed" it to the Hungry Thing. To feed the Hungry Thing, you must put your picture card into the Hungry Thing's "Feed Me" envelope.* Then lead students through the following interactive story.

CORRECTIVE FEEDBACK

CORRECTIVE FEEDBACK If a student responds incorrectly, model the correct response. For example, say: *Listen carefully:* pilk *has /ilk/, but* peas *has /eas/. So* pilk *and* peas *do not rhyme. We need to find a food name that has /ilk/ in the middle and at the end. What food name rhymes with* pilk*?* (milk)

OBSERVE & ASSESS

Questions for Observation	Benchmarks
Do these two words rhyme: *ham, jam?*	Student can recognize words that rhyme.
A word that rhymes with *nut* is *cut*. Tell me another word that rhymes with *nut*.	Student can generate rhyming words.

LESSON MODEL FOR

Word-Part Blending, Segmentation, and Deletion

Benchmarks

- ability to blend word parts in a two-syllable compound word
- ability to segment and count word parts in a two-syllable compound word
- ability to delete a word part from a two-syllable compound word and to recognize the word that remains

Strategy Grade Level

- Pre-K – Grade 1

Grouping

- small group

Materials

- pairs of picture cards that form compound words: dog, house; tooth, brush; rain, coat; foot, ball; door, bell; pan, cake; pea, nut
- picture cards of compound words: doghouse, toothbrush, raincoat, football, doorbell, pancake, cupcake, peanut, hotdog, grapefruit, popcorn, sailboat, starfish

SEE ALSO . . .

LESSON MODEL: Compound Words, p. 521

Phonological Medley

According to Lane and Pullen (2004), "the most fundamental level of phonological awareness is the word level. At the word level, two-syllable compound words provide a good starting point for skill instruction in blending, segmentation, and deletion. This sample lesson model, which is divided into three parts, can be adapted and used to enhance phonological awareness instruction in any commercial reading program.

Develop Oral Language

Because it is very difficult to work with sounds in an unfamiliar word, it is important that students are familiar with the meaning of the compound words used in this lesson model. To ensure that students develop in-depth knowledge of the compound words, refer to the sample lesson models in Section V: Vocabulary.

BLEND WORD PARTS: DOGHOUSE

Teach/Model

On a dry-erase board or chalkboard tray, display the picture cards of the dog and the house as shown below.

Point to the picture card of the dog and say: *This is a dog.* Point to the picture card of the house and say*: This is a house.* Slide the two picture cards together and say: *When I put the two word parts together and say them fast, I make a new word,* doghouse. Ask: *What is the word when I say the two parts fast?* (doghouse) Now, display the picture card of the doghouse next to the picture cards of the dog and the house. Point to the doghouse and say: *A house that a dog lives in is a* doghouse. Ask: *What is a house that a dog lives in?* (a doghouse). Follow the same procedure with the word *toothbrush.*

Small-Group Guided Practice

Display the following picture cards and identify their names: rain, coat; foot, ball; door, bell; and pan, cake. Say: *We're going to play a game with these picture cards. I'll show you how.* Give a volunteer the picture card of the coat. Say*: Listen as I say two word parts:* rain . . . coat. Hold up the picture card of rain and say: *I have the* rain *picture card.* Ask: *Who has the* coat *picture card?* Direct the volunteer to come to the front of the classroom. Place the picture card of rain on the dry-erase board or chalkboard tray. Direct the volunteer to place the picture card of the coat to the right of the picture card of rain and to create a small space between the cards. Say: *Listen as we say the word parts.* Point to the picture card of rain and say *rain.* Prompt the volunteer to point to his or her picture card and say *coat.*

Slide the two picture cards together and say: *Now everyone say the two word parts fast. What's the word?* (raincoat). Place the picture card of the raincoat next to the picture cards of rain and the coat. Point to the picture card of the raincoat and ask: *What is a coat that you wear in the rain?* (a raincoat) Now pass out all the picture cards to students and follow the same procedure to make the following compound words: *football, doorbell, cupcake, peanut, hotdog, grapefruit, pancake, popcorn.*

SEGMENT WORDS: YUMMY, YUMMY

Teach/Model

Display picture cards of a cupcake and a peanut. Point to the cupcake and say: *This is a cupcake. There are two word parts in* cupcake, cup *and* cake. *Listen carefully as I say and clap each of the words parts in* cupcake. Demonstrate by clapping the word parts as you say them. Pause briefly between the two parts. Say: *I just clapped two times. How many times did I clap?* (two) *There are two word parts in* cupcake, cup *and* cake. Repeat the procedure with the word *peanut.*

Small-Group Guided Practice

Display the following picture cards: cupcake, peanut, popcorn, hotdog, grapefruit, and pancake. Say: *Now we will practice clapping word parts as we say the chant "Yummy, Yummy." When it is your turn to name a food that you like to eat, you can choose one of the foods on the picture cards. I'll show you how.* Using the picture card of the popcorn, chant "Yummy, Yummy," as shown below. Then repeat the chant, asking students to take turns choosing a picture card and reciting the line "I like [food pictured on card]" while clapping the word parts. Continue until every student has had a turn to choose and recite.

Class chants: Yummy, yummy, rub your tummy.
What's a treat you like to eat?
(Students rub their tummies.)

Student chants: I like pop•corn.
(Student supplies a food name,
clapping the word parts as they are said.)

Class chants: [Student's name] likes pop•corn.
(Class repeats food name, clapping the word parts.)

DELETE WORD PARTS: STARFISH

Teach/Model

Draw a picture of a football on the board. Then say: *This is a football. Let's say the word together:* football. Clap the two word parts as you say *foot • ball.* Ask: *How many times did I clap?* (two) *How many word parts do you hear in the word* football? (two) Draw two lines below the picture of the football. Put a self-stick note on the line to the left. Point to the self-stick note and say: *The first word part in* football *is* foot. *What is this word part?* (foot) Put a self-stick note on the line to the right. Point to the self-stick note on the line to the right and say: *The last word part in* football *is* ball. *What is this word part?* (ball)

Say: *Now watch carefully as I take away one of the word parts.* Take away the self-stick note on the line to the left and say: *When I take away the* foot *in* football, *the word part that is left is* ball. *What word part is left?* (ball) Put the self-stick note back on the line to the left and say: *Now I am going to take the last word part away.* Take away the self-stick note on the line to the right and say: *When I take away the* ball *in* football, *the word part that is left is* foot. *What word part is left?* (foot) Follow the same procedure with the word *rainbow.*

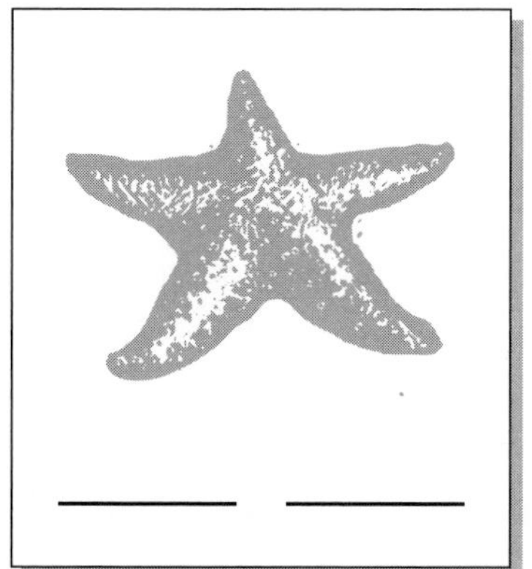

Small-Group Guided Practice

Teach students the chant "There's a Starfish Hidden Under My Bed." Display the picture of the starfish. Using the clapping and self-stick-note procedure described above, chant the rhyme slowly. As you chant, remember to remove the note that represents the deleted syllable *star.*

CONTINUED ▷

There's a Starfish Hidden Under My Bed

There's a starfish hidden under my bed
STARFISH *(clap, clap)*, STARFISH *(clap, clap)*
Someone took the star — What's left instead?
Someone took the star — What's left instead?
(remove self-stick note)
It's just a . . . fish! A fish!

"There's a Starfish Hidden Under My Bed" (1997) by Fran Avni.

Then chant the rhyme again, this time removing the note that represents the deleted syllable *fish.*

Someone took the fish—What's left instead?
It's just a … star! A star!

Repeat the same procedure with other pictures and words, such as *sailboat, doorbell,* and *pancake,* each time varying the deleted word part.

OBSERVE & ASSESS

Questions for Observation	Benchmarks
Listen as I say two small words: *dog•house.* Can you put the two words together to make a bigger word? (doghouse)	Student can blend the syllables in a two-syllable compound word.
Can you clap the word parts in *cupcake?* (cup•cake) How many times did you clap? (two)	Student can segment and count the syllables in a two-syllable compound word.
Say *starfish.* Now say *starfish* without the *fish.* (star)	Student can delete a syllable from a two-syllable compound word and recognize the word that remains.

LESSON MODEL FOR

Syllable Segmentation and Blending

Benchmarks

- ability to clap and count syllables in two- and three-syllable words
- ability to say each syllable in two- and three-syllable words
- ability to orally blend syllables into a whole word

Strategy Grade Level

- Pre-K – Grade 1

Grouping

- small group

Materials

- pictures or models of vegetables whose names have two or three syllables: carrot, lettuce, pepper, radish; cucumber, celery, potato, tomato
- brown construction paper for salad bowls
- colored markers

Salad Toss

The ability to segment syllables usually precedes the ability to segment phonemes, and most students acquire this skill with minimum instruction (Liberman, Shankweiler, and Liberman 1989). Some research has shown, however, that it is not necessary or valuable for students to learn the term *syllable*. What is critical, however, is for them to be able to understand the concept of syllables and how to manipulate them (Lane and Pullen 2004). This sample lesson model can be adapted and used to enhance syllable awareness instruction in any commercial reading program.

Develop Oral Language

Because it is very difficult to work with sounds in an unfamiliar word, it is important that students know the meaning of salad and the food names used in this lesson model. To ensure that students develop in-depth knowledge of salad and the food names, refer to the sample lesson models in Section V: Vocabulary.

Teach/Model

Attach two brown paper salad bowls to a bulletin board. In one bowl, draw two dots and a carrot. In the other bowl, draw three dots and a tomato.

Say: *Here are two salad bowls.* Point to the salad bowl with the carrot in it. Ask: *What vegetable is in this bowl?* (a carrot) Say:

That's right. I am going to clap as I break the word carrot *into parts.* Demonstrate by clapping the word parts as you say *car • rot.* Then say: *I just clapped two times. The word* carrot *has two word parts. Now clap and say the word parts with me:* car • rot. *Great.* Ask: *How many times did we clap?* (two) *How many word parts are in* carrot*?* (two) *Now I am going to say the parts again, one at a time. Listen carefully because I am going to ask you to put the parts together to make a whole word:* car • rot. Ask: *What is the whole word?* (carrot) Repeat the procedure with *tomato* (to • ma • to). Be sure students recognize that *tomato* has three word parts.

Small-Group Guided Practice

VEGGIE SALADS Say: *Now we are going to fill up the salad bowls.* Show the picture or model of a pepper. Ask: *What is the name of this vegetable?* (pepper) Say: *Clap the word parts in* pepper *with me.* (pep • per) Ask: *How many word parts did you clap*? (two) Point to the two-dot bowl. Ask: *How many word parts are in* carrot*?* (two) Point to the three-dot bowl. Ask: *How many word parts are in* tomato*?* (three) Say: *We're going to put the pepper in the bowl with the carrot because* pepper *and* carrot *both have two word parts. Say and clap the two words with me.* (pep • per, car • rot) Ask: *How many times did we clap for each word?* (two times) Say: *That's right.* Ask: *Can anyone help me draw a picture of a pepper in the salad bowl?*

Show the picture or model of a cucumber. Ask: *What is the name of this vegetable?* (cucumber) Say: *Clap the word parts in* cucumber *with me.* (cu • cum • ber) Ask: *How many word parts did you clap?* (three) Ask: *In which bowl should I put the cucumber—the bowl with the pepper or the bowl with the tomato?* (the bowl with the tomato) Say: *That's right. We're going to put the cucumber in the bowl with the tomato because* tomato *and* cucumber *both have three word parts.* Ask: *Can anyone help me draw a picture of a cucumber in the salad bowl?* Now repeat the same procedure using pictures or models of a head of lettuce, a radish, a potato, and a bunch of celery.

CORRECTIVE FEEDBACK

CORRECTIVE FEEDBACK If a student responds incorrectly, model the correct response. For example, say: *Listen carefully as I count the word parts in* cucumber*: (cu • cum • ber). I clapped three word parts. Now you clap with me: (cu • cum • ber). How many word parts did you clap?* (three) *Yes, the word* cucumber *has three word parts.*

For Spanish-speaking students, use the following two- and three-syllable names of fruit: *higo, pera, piña, uva, melon; manzana, sandía, banana,* and *naranja.*

CRAZY SALADS Give students practice segmenting word parts of two- and three-syllable words other than names of vegetables. Attach two more paper salad bowls to a bulletin board. On one bowl, draw or attach two dots, and on the other, three dots. Invite students to make "crazy salads" by drawing or cutting out pictures of objects whose names have two or three syllables to put in the bowls. For example, students might place "ingredients" such as a spider, a skateboard, and a pencil into the two-dot bowl. They might place items such as a computer, an elephant, and a bicycle into the three-dot bowl. Be sure students cut out or draw only objects that they can easily name. Have students identify the items they add to the salad, clapping out the word parts as they put the pictures into the appropriate salad bowl.

OBSERVE & ASSESS

Questions for Observation	Benchmarks
Can you put these word parts together to make a whole word: *cu•cum•ber*? (cucumber)	Student can blend syllables to form a whole word.
Can you clap the word parts in *cucumber*? (cu•cum•ber) How many times did you clap? (three)	Student can segment and count the syllables in a three-syllable word.

LESSON MODEL FOR

Onset-Rime Blending

Benchmark

- ability to blend onset-rime to produce one-syllable words

Strategy Grade Level

- Pre-K – Grade 1

Grouping

- small group

Materials

- pictures or plastic models of animals whose names have one syllable, for example: bat, bear, bee, bird, cat, cow, deer, duck, fish, fox, frog, goat, goose, hen, horse, mouse, pig, shark, sheep, skunk, snake, swan, toad, wolf
- kitchen items whose names have one syllable: cup, fork, glass, knife, lid, pan, plate, pot, spoon
- a hand puppet (one that is not an animal)

SEE ALSO . . .

Onset-Rime, p. 38

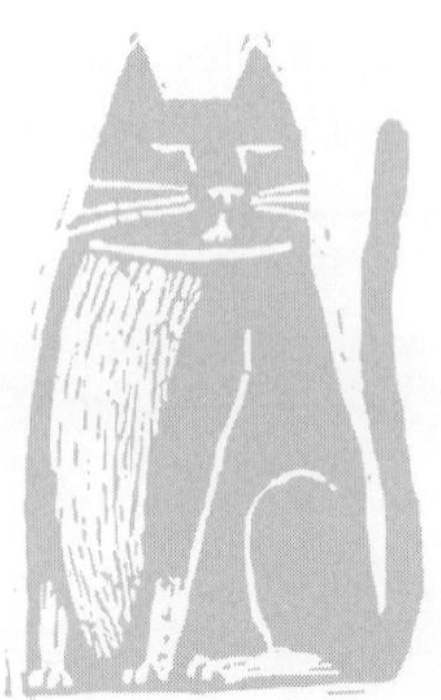

Critter Sitter

Syllables can be divided into smaller units called onset and rime. For example, in the one-syllable word *rime*, /r/ is the onset and /ime/ is the rime. Onset-rime is an essential and instructionally useful level of analysis between syllables and phonemes (Adams 1990). Instruction in onset-rime is an important intermediary step for many students (Treiman 1992). This sample lesson model can be adapted and used to enhance onset-rime instruction in any commercial reading program.

Develop Oral Language

Because it is very difficult to work with sounds in an unfamiliar word, it is important that students can identify the names of the animals and kitchen items used in this lesson model. To ensure that students develop in-depth knowledge of these names, refer to the sample lesson models in Section V: Vocabulary.

Teach/Model

Introduce students to the puppet, Critter Sitter. Then say: *Critter Sitter works at the zoo taking care of animals.* Critter *is another word for animal. Critter Sitter talks in a funny way. It does not say a whole word at one time. Listen carefully. When Critter Sitter says /k/ . . . /at/, it means* cat. Repeat the onset and rime for *cat* and then ask: *What word is Critter Sitter trying to say?* (cat) Say: *Listen as Critter Sitter says another word: /f/ . . . /ox/. The word is* fox. Repeat the onset and rime for *fox* and then ask: *What word is Critter Sitter trying to say?* (fox)

Small-Group Guided Practice

CATCH THE CRITTERS Draw a picture of a large cage on the board. Display pictures or models of the animals. Then say: *Critter Sitter has a big problem at the zoo. Some of the animals, or critters, have escaped. To get them back into their cages, Critter Sitter needs to call the critters by name. Since Critter Sitter talks in a funny way, it needs your help to catch the critters.*

Hold up the Critter Sitter puppet. Explain that Critter Sitter is going to say the name of the critter that it needs to catch. Hold up the picture or model of the bat. Critter Sitter says: *I need to catch the /b/. . . /at/.* Ask: *What animal does Critter Sitter want to catch?* (bat) Say: *That's right, the bat.* Now, set the picture or model of the bat below the cage and hold up another animal picture or model. Critter Sitter says: *Now I need to catch the /sn/. . . /ake/.* Ask: *What animal does Critter Sitter want to catch?* (snake) Say: *That's right, the snake.* Put the picture or model of the snake below the cage. Continue until all of the critters have been "captured."

CORRECTIVE FEEDBACK If a student responds incorrectly, model the correct response. Say: *My turn. Critter Sitter wants to catch the /b/. . . /at/. The word is* bat. *Your turn.* Ask: *What animal does Critter Sitter want to catch?* (the bat)

KITCHEN HELPERS Display the kitchen items on a desk or table. Explain that Critter Sitter likes to cook, but also it likes having lots of kitchen helpers. Say: *I'll be the first helper.* Critter Sitter says: *Please hand me a /k/. . . /up/.* Say: *Cup. Here's a cup.* Give Critter Sitter the cup. Say: *Now I want you to be Critter Sitter's helpers.* Critter Sitter says: *Please hand me a /f/. . . /ork/.* Ask: *What does Critter Sitter want?* (He wants a fork.) Ask: *Who wants to give Critter Sitter the fork?* Repeat the same procedure with remaining items: spoon, plate, pot, and bowl.

OBSERVE & ASSESS

Question for Observation	Benchmark
What whole word am I trying to say: /p/. . . /ot/? (pot)	Student can blend onset and rime to produce a one-syllable word.

LESSON MODEL FOR

Phoneme Isolation

Benchmarks

- ability to isolate the initial sound in a one-syllable word
- ability to isolate the final sound in a one-syllable word

Strategy Grade Level

- Pre-K – Grade 1

Grouping

- small group

Materials

- toy animals or pictures of animals: ant, ape, bat, bee, bird, cat, deer, dog, fish, fox, goat, goose, horse, mole, moose, mouse, mule, pig, rat, seal, toad, wolf, worm

Bridge Game

Phoneme isolation requires students to recognize individual sounds in words. Because it is easier to isolate an initial sound, instruction on an initial sound should precede that of a final sound. To eliminate confusion between the final sound of a syllable and the final sound of a word, begin instruction with one-syllable words. This sample lesson model, which is based on the work of Zhurova (1963), targets initial and final /m/. The same model can be adapted and used to enhance phoneme isolation instruction for other initial and final phonemes in any commercial reading program.

Develop Oral Language

Because it is very difficult to work with sounds in an unfamiliar word, it is important that students can identify the animals used in this lesson model. To ensure that students develop in-depth knowledge of these animal names, refer to the sample lesson models in Section V: Vocabulary.

Teach/Model

INITIAL SOUND Hold up the toy mouse or a picture of a mouse. Say: *This is a mouse.* Ask: *What is the name of this animal?* (mouse) Say: *Listen carefully while I say the word again,* mouse. Repeat the word, this time accentuating the initial sound, *mmmouse.* Say: *The first sound in* mouse *is /mmm/. Say the first sound with me, /mmm/.* Ask: *What's the first sound in mouse?* (/mmm/) *Good.* Repeat the same sequence of instruction with other one-syllable animal names.

FINAL SOUND Hold up the toy worm or a picture of a worm. Say: *This is a worm.* Ask: *What is the name of this animal?* (worm) Say: *Listen carefully while I say the word again,* worm. Repeat the word, this time accentuating the final sound, *wormmm.* Say: *The last sound in* worm *is /mmm/. Say the last sound with me, /mmm/.* Ask: *What's the last sound in* worm? (/mmm/) *Good.* Repeat the same sequence of instruction with other one-syllable animal names.

INTERVENTION STRATEGY Some students may need help isolating the sound of the letter. Say: *Let's see how we make the sound /mmm/ with our mouths. Let's say the sound again.* (/mmm/) Say: *Tell me how your lips move when you say /mmm/.* (They come together.) Say: *Yes, they come together. Does any air come out?* (no) Say: *Try holding your nose. Can you still say /mmm/?* (no) Say: *That is because the air comes through your nose when you make the sound /mmm/.*

Small-Group Cumulative Guided Practice

To play the Bridge Game, students should be familiar with the initial and final sounds in each of the animal names. Prepare to play the game by creating a bridge out of chairs or other props.

Give each student a toy animal or a picture of an animal. Have each student say the name of his or her animal. Have students stand in a line on one side of the bridge while you stand on the other side. Tell students that you are the lion who guards the bridge. Say: *To cross the bridge, you need to answer two questions: What animal are you? What is the first sound in your name? Let's begin.* Say: *I am the lion who guards the bridge!* Ask the first student in line: *What animal are you?* (moose) *What is the first sound in your name?* (/mmm/) *Excellent. You may cross my bridge.* Repeat the same procedure until all of the animals have crossed the bridge.

CORRECTIVE FEEDBACK If a student responds incorrectly, model the correct response. Say: *The first sound in moose is /mmm/. Say the sound with me, /mmm/.* Ask: *What is the first sound in moose?* (/mmm/) Say: *Good. You may cross the bridge.*

When all the students (or animals) have crossed the bridge, go to the opposite side and tell students that it is now time for the animals to return to their homes.

Explain to students that the lion will ask again for the name of the animal, but this time instead of asking for the first sound in the animal name, the lion will ask for the last sound. Say: *Let's try it.* Call on the first student and say: *I am the lion who guards the bridge!* Ask: *What animal are you?* (goat) *Excellent. What is the last sound in your name*? (/t/) *Very good. You may cross back over my bridge.* Repeat the same procedure until all of the animals have returned home.

CORRECTIVE FEEDBACK If a student responds incorrectly, model the correct response. Say: *The last sound in* goat *is /t/. Say the sound with me, /t/.* Ask: *What is the last sound in* goat*?* (/t/) Say: *Good. You may cross the bridge.*

INTERVENTION STRATEGY Some students may need help isolating the sound of the letter. Say: *Let's see how we make the sound /t/ with our mouths. Let's say the sound again.* (/t/) Ask: *Did you feel a lot of air come out?* (yes) Say: *Try to close your lips and say /t/. Can you do it?* (no) Say: *Another part of your mouth makes /t/. Can you feel what part?* (the tongue) Ask: *Where is your tongue when you say the /t/ sound at the end of* bat*?* (At the top of your mouth behind your teeth.)

Questions for Observation	Benchmarks
What is the first sound in *moose*? (/mmm/)	Student can isolate the initial sound in a one-syllable word.
What is the last sound in *moose*? (/sss/)	Student can isolate the final sound in a one-syllable word.

LESSON MODEL FOR

Phoneme Identity

Benchmarks

- ability to isolate initial and final sounds in words
- ability to recognize and match the same sound in different words
- ability to generate words with the same initial and final sounds

Strategy Grade Level

- Pre-K – Grade 1 and/or Intervention

Grouping

- small group

Materials

- classroom objects: ball, book, can, doorknob, hat, lightbulb, marker, pen

As you say *book,* be sure to emphasize and enunciate clearly the initial sound without "bouncing" it by saying *b-b-b.*

Sound Match

Phoneme identification requires students to recognize the common sound in different words. Students should be able to identify a target sound in the initial position, before the same sound is introduced in the final position. After introducing a sound in both initial and final positions, move on to the next target sound. This sample lesson model targets initial and final /b/. The same model can be adapted and used to enhance phoneme identification instruction for other initial and final phonemes in any commercial reading program.

Develop Oral Language

Because it is very difficult to work with sounds in an unfamiliar word, it is important that students can identify the names of the objects used in this lesson. To ensure that students develop in-depth knowledge of the object names, refer to the sample lesson models in Section V: Vocabulary.

Teach/Model

INITIAL SOUND Hold up a book. Say: *I want you to listen carefully for the first sound in* book. Say the word *book* again, emphasizing the initial sound. Say: *The first sound in* book *is /b/.* Ask: *What is the first sound in* book? (/b/) Say: *That's right. The first sound in* book *is /b/.*

To adapt this lesson model for Spanish-speaking students, display a pencil (*lápiz*), a book (*libro*), and a pair of scissors (*tijeras*).

When selecting distracters, be sure that their initial sounds are easily distinguishable from the target sound—or not easily confused such as /b/ and /p/.

INTERVENTION STRATEGY

If three-choice problems are too difficult, use two-choice problems. When students are ready, move on to three-choice problems.

Say: *Now we are going to listen for words that have the same first sound as* book. Display a hat, a marker, and a ball. Say: *Listen carefully as I identify the object whose name has the same first sound as* book. Hold up the hat. Say: *This is a hat. The first sound in* hat *is /h/.* Ask: *What is the first sound in* hat*?* (/h/) Say: *Listen carefully:* hat */h/,* book */b/.* Hat *and* book *do not have the same first sound.* Ask: *Do* hat *and* book *have the same first sound?* (no) Repeat the same procedure with the marker. Then, hold up the ball. Say: *This is a ball. The first sound in* ball *is /b/.* Ask: *What is the first sound in* ball*?* (/b/) Say: *Listen carefully:* ball */b/,* book */b/.* Ball *and* book *have the same first sound.* Ask: *Do* ball *and* book *have the same first sound?* (yes) Point to all three objects. Ask: *Which one of these object names has the same first sound as* book*:* hat, marker, *or* ball*?* (ball) Hold up the ball and say: *That's right.* Book *and* ball *have the same first sound, /b/.*

FINAL SOUND Point to a doorknob. Say: *I want you to listen carefully for the last sound in* knob. Say the word *knob* again, emphasizing the final sound. Say: *The last sound in* knob *is /b/.* Ask: *What is the last sound in* knob*?* (/b/) Say: *That's right. The last sound in* knob *is /b/.*

Say: *Now we are going to listen for words that have the same last sound as* knob. Display a pen, a lightbulb, and a can. Say: *Listen carefully as I identify the object whose name has the same last sound as* knob. Hold up the pen. Say: *This is a* pen. *The last sound in pen is /n/.* Ask: *What is the last sound in* pen*?* (/n/) Say: *Listen carefully:* pen */n/,* knob */b/.* Pen *and* knob *do not have the same last sound.* Ask: *Do* pen *and* knob *have the same last sound?* (no) Repeat the procedure with the lightbulb and the can. Point to all three objects. Ask: *Which one of these object names has the same last sound as* knob: pen, bulb, *or* can*?* (bulb) Hold up the bulb and say: *That's right.* Knob *and* bulb *have the same last sound /b/.*

Small-Group Guided Practice

Say: *We are going to play a game called I Spy. I'll show you how.* Hold up a book and say: *I spy something in the room whose name has the same first sound as* book. Ask: *Do you see anything in the room whose name has the same first sound as* book*?* Have students find and name the object, for example, a balloon. Then say: *Yes, balloon!* Ask: *What is the first sound in* book *and* balloon? (/b/) Say: *Very good. The first sound in* book *and* balloon *is /b/.* After playing this game with initial sounds, play it with final sounds.

CORRECTIVE FEEDBACK If a student responds incorrectly, model the correct response. For example, say: *Listen carefully:* book */b/,* light */l/.* Light *does not have the same first sound as* book. *Let's see if we can find an object whose name has the same first sound as* book. *I spy a* balloon. *Listen carefully:* book */b/,* balloon */b/.* Book *and* balloon *have the same first sound.*

OBSERVE & ASSESS

Questions for Observation	Benchmarks
What is the first sound in *book*? (/b/) What is the last sound in *book*? (/k/)	Student is able to identify initial and final sounds in words.
Which word has the same first sound as *book*: *hat, ball,* or *marker*? (ball) Which word has the same last sound as *knob*: *pen, bulb,* or *can*? (bulb)	Student is able to match the same sound in different words.
Name an object whose name has the same first sound as *book*. (balloon) Name an object whose name has the same last sound as *knob*. (bulb)	Student is able to generate words with the same initial or final sound.

LESSON MODEL FOR

Phoneme Categorization

Benchmark

- ability to isolate the initial sound in words
- ability to recognize the picture or word that has the odd initial sound in a set of three one-syllable words

Strategy Grade Level

- Pre-K – Grade 1 and/or Intervention

Grouping

- small group

Materials

- sets of picture cards: bus, ball, mouse; cow, car, hat; fish, foot, tent; milk, mop, cup; lamp, lips, ring; pot, pig, bean; soup, sun, dog; duck, door, egg
- pocket chart

Odd One Out

Phoneme categorization is an oddity task requiring students to recognize a word with the odd phoneme, or sound, in a set of three or four words. Instruction should begin with initial sounds, followed by final sounds. Work with medial sounds should begin after students are skilled with initial and final sounds (Lane and Pullen 2004). This sample lesson model targets initial sounds. The same model can be adapted and used to enhance phoneme categorization instruction in any commercial reading program.

Develop Oral Language

Because it is very difficult to work with sounds in an unfamiliar word, it is important that students can name the pictures on the picture cards used in this lesson model. To ensure that students develop in-depth knowledge of the picture names, refer to the sample lesson models in Section V: Vocabulary.

Teach/Model

Display the following picture card set: bus, ball, mouse. Say: *The name of one of these pictures does not belong with the others. It begins with a different sound. Listen carefully as I say each picture name and its first sound.* Point to the picture card of the bus. Say: *This is a bus. The first sound in* bus *is /b/.* Point to the

picture card of the ball. Say: *This is a ball. The first sound in* ball *is /b/.* Point to the picture card of the mouse. Say: *This is a mouse. The first sound in* mouse *is /m/.* Then say: *bus, ball, mouse.* Bus *and* ball *begin with /b/.* Mouse *begins with /m/.* Mouse *does not belong. It does not have the same first sound as* bus *and* ball, */b/. Now you say the words with me.* Point to each picture card as students identify it. Ask: *Which word does not belong?* (mouse) Say: *Good.* Mouse *doesn't belong because it doesn't have the first sound /b/.* Repeat the same procedure with picture card sets cow, car, hat; fish, foot, tent.

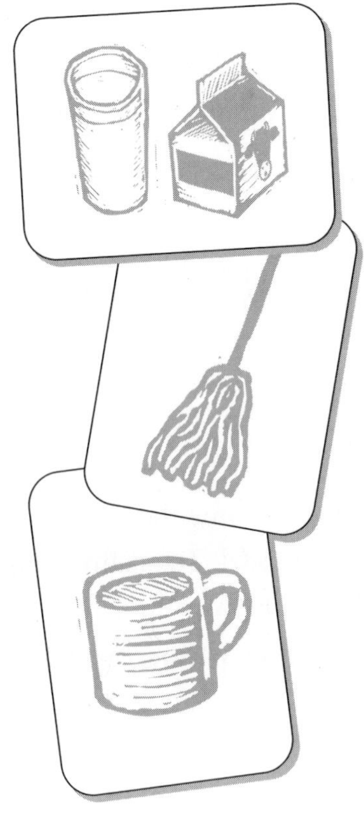

Small-Group Guided Practice

Display the following picture card sets in a pocket chart, three to a row: milk, mop, cup; lamp, lips, ring; pot, pig, bean; soup, sun, dog; duck, egg, door. Say: *Now it's your turn to figure out which picture name does not belong. Let's try it.* Ask a volunteer to come to the front. Direct the volunteer to point to each picture card on the first row and say its name: *milk, mop, cup.* Remind students to listen carefully to the first sound in each picture name. Ask the volunteer: *Can you point to the card and say the picture name that does not belong*? (cup) Say: *Yes,* cup *begins with a different sound than* milk *or* mop. Milk *and* mop *begin with /m/.* Repeat the same procedure with the remaining picture card sets until all students have had a turn.

CORRECTIVE FEEDBACK If a student responds incorrectly, model the correct response. For example, say: *Listen carefully:* milk */m/,* mop */m/,* cup */k/.* Cup *doesn't belong. It begins with /k/, a different sound than* milk *or* mop, */m/.* Milk *and* mop *begin with /m/.* Ask: *What word doesn't belong?* (cup).

Question for Observation	Benchmark
What word does not belong: *bus, ball, mouse*? (mouse)	Student can recognize a word that has the odd initial sound in a set of three one-syllable words.

LESSON MODEL FOR

Phoneme Blending

Benchmark

- ability to blend spoken phonemes to form one-syllable words

Strategy Grade Level

- Pre-K – Grade 1

Grouping

- small group

Materials

- hand puppet

Simon Says

Blending and segmenting phonemes are the two phonemic awareness skills most useful for the acquisition of decoding skills (National Reading Panel 2000). Phoneme blending requires students to listen to a sequence of separately spoken sounds and then to combine them to form a word. An effective method for teaching students the concept of phoneme blending is to use a puppet that speaks in "secret language" (Lane and Pullen 2004). The idea is that the puppet can only say words one sound at a time. This sample lesson model can be adapted and used to enhance instruction in phoneme blending in any commercial reading program.

Simon Says

Develop Oral Language

Because it is very difficult to work with sounds in an unfamiliar word, it is important that students know the body-part names used in this lesson. To ensure that students develop in-depth knowledge of body part names, play a practice game of Simon Says.

Leader: Simon says, "Close your eyes."
(Students close their eyes.)

Leader: Simon says, "Wiggle your finger."
(Students wiggle a finger.)

Leader: "Nod your head."
(Students do nothing.)

Leader: Simon says, "Lift your foot."
(Students lift a foot.)

Be sure to pause briefly before pronouncing the next sound, and avoid adding an /uh/ when pronouncing a consonant sound.

Blendable Sounds, p. 121

Teach/Model

Introduce students to the puppet. Say: *This is Simon. Simon likes to talk in a funny way. He likes to say words one sound at a time. Listen as Simon says the sounds in the word.* Hold up the puppet and in a Simon voice say: */n/ /ō/ /z/.* Then say in your own voice: *The word is* nose. Ask: *What word does Simon mean when he says the sounds /n/ /ō/ /z/?* (nose) *Good. Let's try another one.* Hold up the puppet and say: *Simon says /n/ /ē/. The word is* knee. Ask: *What word does Simon mean when he says the sounds /n/ /ē/?* (knee) Say: *That's correct,* knee.

Small-Group Guided Practice

Say: *Now it's your turn to figure out what Simon is saying. Listen as Simon says the sounds in a word.* Hold up the puppet and say: *Simon says /ar/ /m/.* Ask: *What word is Simon trying to say?* (arm). Repeat with /l/ /e/ /g/, *leg.*

Review the rules of Simon Says. Then say*: Now we are going to play Simon Says, but this time I will talk like Simon. After I say the sounds, you will say the word and then perform the action. Remember, you move only when Simon says so. Let's try it.* Play the role of leader, using the example below.

Leader: Simon says, "Touch the tip of your /n/ /ō/ /z/."
What's the word? (nose)
(Students touch the tip of the nose.)

Leader: Simon says, "Blink your /ī/ /z/."
What's the word? (eyes)
(Students blink their eyes.)

Leader: Simon says, "Shake your /l/ /e/ /g/."
What's the word? (leg)
(Students shake a leg.)

Shake your /l/ /e/ /g/

Leader: Touch your /n/ /e/ /k/.
What's the word? (neck)
(Students make no movement.)

Leader: Simon says, "Touch your /t/ /ō/ /z/."
What's the word? (toes)
(Students touch their toes.)

Continue the game, using other one-syllable body-part names in the following sequence: arm, knee, lips, wrist, foot, heel, head, hand, and waist.

CORRECTIVE FEEDBACK If a student responds incorrectly, model the correct response. For example, say: *My turn. Simon says touch your /n/ /ō/ /z/. The word is* nose. Touch your nose. Say: *Your turn. Simon says touch your /n/ /ō/ /z/.* Ask: *What's the word?* (nose) Say: *Yes,* nose.

Question for Observation	Benchmark
What word is */n/ /ō/ /z/*? (nose)	Student can blend spoken phonemes to form a whole word.

LESSON MODEL FOR

Phoneme Segmentation and Blending

Benchmarks

- ability to segment spoken phonemes in one-syllable words
- ability to blend spoken phonemes to form one-syllable words

Strategy Grade Level

- Pre-K – Grade 1 and/or Intervention

Prerequisite

- ability to blend spoken phonemes

Grouping

- small group

Activity Master (Resources)

- Say-It-and-Move-It Board

Materials

- copies of Say-It-and-Move-It Board
- manipulatives: small cubes or buttons

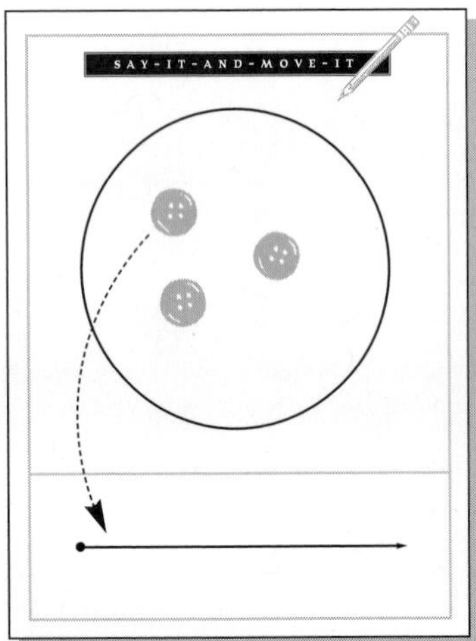

Say-It-and-Move-It

Phoneme segmentation requires students to break a word into its separate sounds. Teaching how to segment words into sounds helps students learn to spell (Armbruster, Lehr, and Osborn 2001). This sample lesson model is based on the say-it-and-move-it activities described in *Road to the Code* (Blachman et al. 2000). This sample lesson model targets two-phoneme words. The same model can be adapted for three- or four-phoneme words and used to enhance instruction in phoneme segmentation and blending in any commercial reading program.

Develop Oral Language

Because it is very difficult to work with sounds in an unfamiliar word, it is important that students know the meaning of the words used in this lesson model. To ensure that students develop in-depth knowledge of the words, refer to the sample lesson models in Section V: Vocabulary.

Teach/Model

Display the Say-It-and-Move-It Board. Place two buttons in the circle at the top of the board. Tell students that you are going to show them how to play a game called Say-It-and-Move-It. To play the game, you will first say a sound in a word and then move a button that represents the sound. Say: *Here is the first word:* egg. Ask: *What word did I say?* (egg) Say: *Listen and watch me as I play.* Then say the first sound in *egg,* /eee/. As you are saying /eee/, simultaneously slide a button out of the circle and down to the black dot on the arrow. Point to the button and say: */eee/.* Now say: */g/.* As you are saying /g/, simultaneously slide the remaining button out of the circle and down to the arrow, placing it to the immediate right of the first button. Point to the second

button and say: */g/*. Ask: *How many buttons did I move?* (two) Say: *Now I'll say the whole word fast,* egg. Slide your finger under the buttons from left to right as you say the word *egg* normally. Repeat the same procedure with the following words: *eat* (/ē/ /t/) and *ice* (/ī/ /s/).

Small-Group Guided Practice

Give each student a Say-It-and-Move-It Board and two counters. Tell them that they are going to play Say-It-and-Move-It with you. Tell students to place their counters in the circle at the top of the board. Say: *The first word is* me. Ask: *What's the word?* (me) Say: *Now let's say it and move it.* Remind students to slide a counter down to the arrow as they say each sound in the word. (/mmm/ /ēēē/) Then ask: *How many counters did you move?* (two) Then ask students to slide their finger under the two counters and to say the word fast. (me) Finally, direct students to move their two counters back inside the circle and get ready for the next word. Repeat the same procedure with the following words: *ape* (/ā/ /p/), *low* (/l/ /ō/), *zoo* (/z/ /o͞o/), *say* (/s/ /ā/), *knee* (/n/ /ē/), *tie* (/t/ /ī/), *day* (/d/ /ā/), *new* (/n/ /o͞o/).

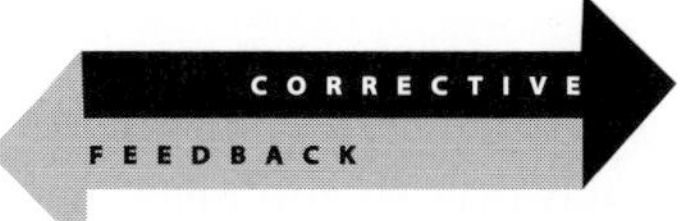

CORRECTIVE FEEDBACK If a student responds incorrectly, model the correct response. For example, say: *Let's try this again. Watch me say it and move it.* Then ask the student to say it and move it with you. Next, ask the student to say it and move it independently.

Questions for Observation	Benchmarks
How many sounds in *up*? (two) Can you say them? (/u/ /p/)	Student can segment spoken words into sounds.
Can you say */u/ /p/* fast? (up)	Student can blend spoken sounds to form whole words.

LESSON MODEL FOR

Phoneme Segmentation and Blending

Benchmarks

- ability to segment spoken phonemes in one-syllable words
- ability to blend spoken phonemes to form one-syllable words

Stratgey Grade Level

- Pre-K – Grade 1 and/or Intervention

Prerequisite

- ability to blend spoken phonemes

Grouping

- small group

Activity Master (Resources)

- Elkonin Card

Materials

- copies of Elkonin Card
- crayons or markers
- self-stick notes

To adapt this lesson for Spanish-speaking students, use three-phoneme Spanish words, such as the following: *sol* (sun), *pan* (bread), and *pez* (fish).

Elkonin Sound Boxes

Elkonin (1963), a Russian psychologist, was one of the earliest researchers to link phonemic awareness to reading. He developed a method that involves the use of Elkonin boxes—a card with a picture and boxes that represent the number of phonemes in the picture name. This sample lesson model targets the segmentation of three-phoneme words. The same model can be adapted for two- or four-phoneme words and used to enhance instruction in phoneme segmentation and blending in any reading program.

Oral Language

Because it is very difficult to work with sounds in an unfamiliar word, it is important that students can name the pictures on the cards used in this lesson model. To ensure that students develop in-depth knowledge of the picture names, refer to the sample lesson models in Section V: Vocabulary.

Teach/Model

Display the Elkonin Card. Draw a sun in the picture frame at the top. Place a self-stick note below each box in the grid.

Point to the picture of the sun and say: *What is this?* (the sun) *Yes, this is the sun.* Say: *The three boxes under the picture each stand for a sound in* sun. *I'm going say the sounds in* sun *slowly and move a paper square as I say each sound. Listen.* Say /sss/ and move a self-stick note into the first box on the left. Say /uuu/ and move a self-stick note into the middle box. Say /nnn/ and quickly move the third self-stick note into the last box. Say: *Listen as I say the word slowly.* Then segment the word slowly as you point to each square while saying the sound, /sss/ /uuu/ /nnn/. Say: *Now I'll say the word fast.* Slide your finger under the grid from left to right as you say the word normally, *sun.* Then say: *Watch as I count the squares.* Count aloud as you point to each square. Say: *I counted three squares. There are three sounds in* sun. Ask: *How many sounds in* sun*?* (three) Repeat the same procedure with the word *moon.*

Small-Group Guided Practice

Give each student a copy of the Elkonin Card and three self-stick notes. Say: *We're going to do this one together.* On your copy, print the number ten in the picture frame and put a self-stick note below each box in the grid. Have students do the same.

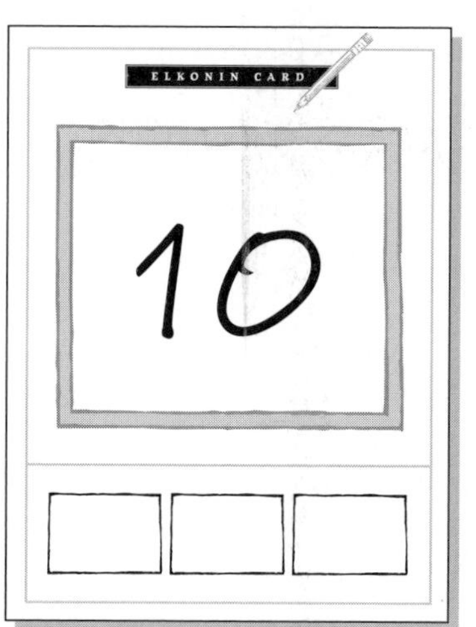

Point to the number ten. Ask: *What is this number?* (ten) Say: *Now it's your turn to move the squares into the boxes as we say the sounds in* ten. Point to the first box and say: *Remember to start here.* Say: */t/.* Direct students to move a square into the first box as they say /t/ along with you. Say: */eee/.* Direct students to move a square into the middle box as they say /eee/ along with you. Say: */nnn/.* Direct students to quickly move a square into the last box as they say /nnn/ along with you. Say: *Let's say the word slowly.* Have students segment the word slowly as you point to each square from left to right, /t/ /eee/ /nnn/. Ask: *Can you say the whole word fast?* Slide your finger under the grid from left to right as students say the word normally, *ten.*

Ask: *How many squares are there?* (three) Ask: *How many sounds in ten?* (three) Say: *Yes, there are three sounds in* ten, */t/, /e/, /n/.* Repeat the same procedure with other three-phoneme words, such as *hat, cup, kite, bed, mop,* and *foot.*

INTERVENTION STRATEGY For students having difficulty hearing the individual sounds, prompt them to watch your lips as you pronounce each sound, or let them observe themselves in a mirror to help detect each sound visually.

Questions for Observation	Benchmarks
How many sounds in *cat*? (three) Can you say them? (/k/ /a/ /t/)	Student can segment spoken words into sounds.
Can you say /k/ /a/ /t/ fast? (cat)	Student can blend spoken sounds to form whole words.

III

SECTION III

Decoding and Word Recognition

CHAPTER 6

Phonics

CHAPTER 7

Irregular Word Reading

CHAPTER 8

Multisyllabic Word Reading

Introduction

DECODING AND WORD RECOGNITION

CCSS READING STANDARDS

Foundational Skills

Phonics and Word Recognition

DECODING
the ability to convert a word from print to speech

SEE ALSO . . .

Chapter 6: Phonics

Chapter 7: Irregular Word Reading

Chapter 8: Multisyllabic Word Reading

Learning to read words is fundamental to understanding text. Although proficient readers use multiple strategies for figuring out unfamiliar words, the most reliable strategy is decoding, the ability to convert a word from print to speech (Adams 1990). To ensure the development of proficiency in reading, students must be taught to decode regular words, to identify irregular words, and to use word parts to read multisyllabic words. This requires a strong foundation of print awareness and phonological awareness. The Road to Reading Words illustrates how awareness of spoken language (phonological awareness) merges with written language to contribute to automatic word recognition.

The three chapters in this section are all related to learning to read words. To clarify how these word reading skills contribute to proficient reading, Marilyn Jager Adams (1990) and Linnea Ehri (2002) provide explanations of how the reading process works.

The Road to Reading Words

SPOKEN LANGUAGE

Awareness of Words
(phonological awareness)

Awareness of Syllables and Onset-Rimes
(phonological awareness)

Awareness of Phonemes
(blending and segmentation)

Concepts About Print
(print awareness)

Letter Names and Shapes
(letter knowledge)

Sound/Spelling Correspondences
(blending)

Chunks Within Words
(phonograms, syllables, affixes)

Automatic Word Recognition
(all word types)

WRITTEN LANGUAGE

Based on Lane 2006.

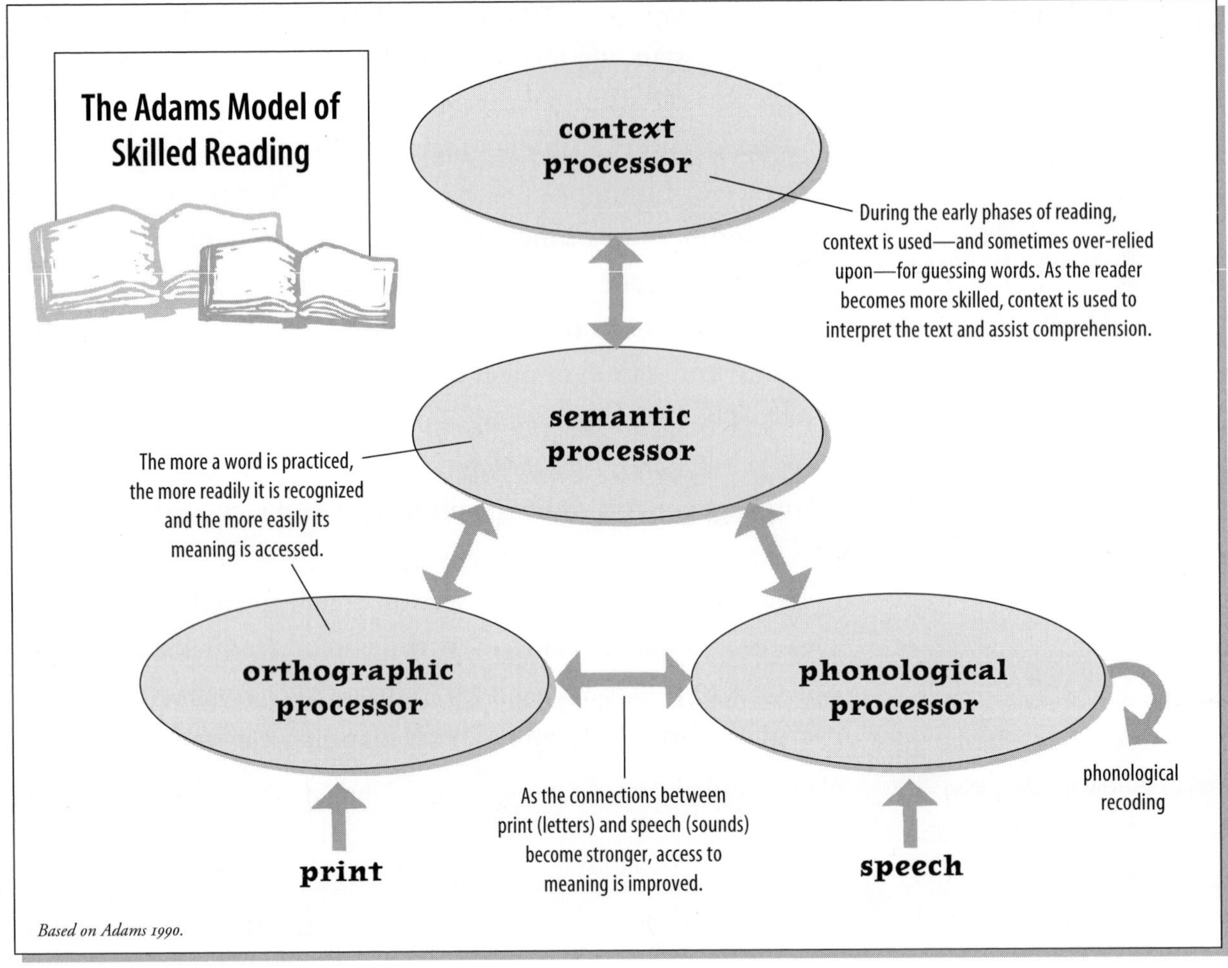
The Adams Model of Skilled Reading
context processor
During the early phases of reading, context is used—and sometimes over-relied upon—for guessing words. As the reader becomes more skilled, context is used to interpret the text and assist comprehension.
semantic processor
The more a word is practiced, the more readily it is recognized and the more easily its meaning is accessed.
orthographic processor
phonological processor
phonological recoding
print
As the connections between print (letters) and speech (sounds) become stronger, access to meaning is improved.
speech

Based on Adams 1990.

The Adams Model of Skilled Reading

Marilyn Jager Adams (1990, 2001) explains the skilled reading process as a network of connections among four processors: the orthographic processor, which accesses the visual information from the print; the phonological processor, which contributes information from speech sounds; the semantic processor, which considers possible meanings and selects the correct one; and the context processor, which constructs an ongoing and coherent interpretation of the text.

In the diagram above the semantic processor is in the center of the model. Each of the other processors contributes to the development of meaning in the semantic processor. For proficient

In order for students to read and comprehend text, they must be able to read most of the words accurately.

—EHRI & SNOWLING, 2004

reading to occur, all of the processors must be working and the connections among them must be well developed. This "connectionist" approach to thinking about the reading process is helpful in understanding the complexity of the skills readers must master.

Beginning readers must connect the printed form of a word with the spoken form, either by reading the word aloud or by subvocalizing the word in their head. This connection of the letters (orthographic information) with the sounds (phonological information) to form words is known as decoding. Connecting both the printed and spoken forms of a word allows the reader to access the word's meaning (semantic information). Recognizing the orthographic and phonological forms, along with the rest of the context provided in the text, allows for comprehension. Therefore, decoding is essential for comprehension.

Phases of Word Recognition Development

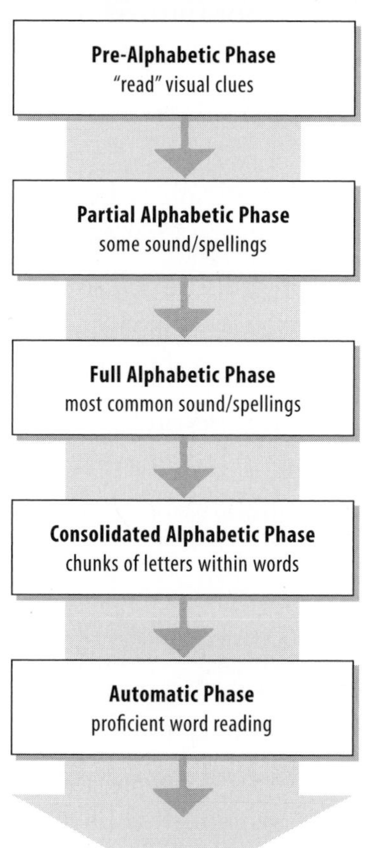

Ehri's Phases of Word Recognition Development

The model of reading that Adams (2001) describes is the skilled reading process, one in which the processors work simultaneously and in concert with one another through strong connections. For most students, skilled reading doesn't just happen overnight. Learning to read words is a complex process. Linnea Ehri's research has done much to reveal what occurs during the process of learning to recognize words (Ehri and McCormick 1998; Ehri 2002; Ehri and Snowling 2004). According to Ehri, word recognition develops in five phases: pre-alphabetic, partial alphabetic, full alphabetic, consolidated alphabetic, and automatic. The goal of moving students through these phases is to develop their sight word vocabularies. Ehri (2002) defines sight word as any word practiced enough to be read from memory. This definition of sight word is somewhat different from other commonly used definitions, which consider sight words to be simply high-frequency or irregularly spelled words.

SEE ALSO . . .

SECTION II: EARLY LITERACY

Chapter 3: Print Awareness

Chapter 4: Letter Knowledge

Chapter 5: Phonological Awareness

Pre-Alphabetic Phase

All readers begin in the pre-alphabetic phase. Before learning to recognize the letters of the alphabet or the sounds that are associated with those letters, a child depends on other visual cues to "read" words. Most often, this is demonstrated when the child "reads" a well-known logo. In books, this phase is evident when a child who has heard a story read aloud can retell the story, using the pictures as cues. Students in preschool and Kindergarten are typically in the pre-alphabetic phase. During this phase, meaning is accessed through rudimentary connections between visual cues and the spoken words represented by those cues. To progress beyond this phase, a child must acquire some letter knowledge and phonemic awareness.

WITHIN THE ADAMS MODEL During this phase, the initial connection is made among the orthographic processor (processing of visual cues such as logos), the phonological processor (processing of spoken words), the semantic processor (processing of meaning), and the context processor (processing of story content).

...to learn to read, all students must know the letters of the alphabet, understand their linguistic significance ... and learn the logic and conventions governing their use.

—ADAMS, 2001

Partial Alphabetic Phase

The second phase is called the partial alphabetic phase because students know at least some letters and sounds. During the partial alphabetic phase, students use their still-limited sound/spelling knowledge to figure out words. A student in this phase may guess a word on the first letter or the first and last letters; few words can be identified reliably. To move beyond the partial alphabetic phase, a student must know all the letters of the alphabet and at least the most common sounds associated with each letter.

WITHIN THE ADAMS MODEL Beginning readers tend to rely heavily on context (usually the pictures in a book) to guess what a word is. Letters exert little influence on the word that is guessed, because students lack knowledge of sound/spelling correspondences. Using context to help figure out words can

Having English as a second language does not necessarily result in difficulty acquiring word-reading skills.

—FRANCIS ET AL., 2006

be helpful and build confidence, but overreliance on context during this phase can slow the development of word reading. In the partial alphabetic phase, the connections between the orthographic and phonological processors shift from the recognition of visual cues to the initial linking of letters and sounds. These connections, along with the context provided by the pictures, allow for meaning to develop in the semantic processor. Unfortunately, because all the letters and sounds in words are not used, the meaning developed may be inadequate or inaccurate.

Full Alphabetic Phase

The next phase is called the full alphabetic phase because students in this phase have extensive knowledge of the alphabetic system. A student in this phase recognizes letters and sounds, uses this knowledge to read words, and, while reading a word, attends to each letter in the word. As students begin this phase, their decoding, while accurate, is typically slow and laborious. With practice, their decoding becomes more proficient and automatic. They become familiar with the most common sound/spellings and multiletter patterns, such as vowel digraphs, consonant blends, and phonograms. In addition, they begin to recognize more words from memory. Independent reading becomes possible during this phase.

WITHIN THE ADAMS MODEL During the full alphabetic phase, connections between the orthographic and phonological processors are strengthened, and access to meaning is increased. By the time a reader reaches this phase, reliance on context to figure out individual words wanes. The reader realizes that the visual (orthographic) and auditory (phonological) information—that is, the sound/spellings—is sufficient to read words and access meaning (semantic information). During this phase, context is used more broadly to help the reader interpret the text coherently. The reader begins using phonological recoding. Practice with phonological recoding strengthens the connections among the processors and promotes word recognition.

PHONOLOGICAL RECODING
the process of transforming sounds to pronunciations during decoding

Consolidated Alphabetic Phase

Students in the consolidated alphabetic phase begin to rely less on individual sound/spellings and more on the multiletter patterns, or chunks within words. They retain multisyllabic words in memory as a string of consolidated units such as syllables, affixes, or phonograms. Students begin to use analogy from known patterns to recognize words, and their sight word knowledge steadily increases.

WITHIN THE ADAMS MODEL During the consolidated alphabetic phase, connections between the orthographic and phonological processors continue to be strengthened, and word meaning becomes more easily accessible and context becomes more coherent. As the reader moves into this phase, the orthographic and phonological processors are working so efficiently that it becomes easier to process words as a series of chunks or recognizable multiletter patterns. This signifies that the connections between the processors are strengthening. Information sent to the semantic processor is more reliable and allows for improved access to meaning. As the connections become very strong, the processes become automatic, and the reader reaches reading proficiency, or the automatic phase.

> More resources are available for comprehension, if word identification processes occur relatively effortlessly.
>
> —HUDSON, LANE & PULLEN, 2005

Automatic Phase

Once a reader has learned to decode words, the word recognition process becomes more automatic through practice. Ehri and McCormick (1998) explain that the majority of words readers encounter during this phase will be part of their sight vocabularies, or practiced sufficiently to have been committed to memory. When an unfamiliar word appears in text, the reader has multiple strategies available to identify the word. A reader at this phase reads words fluently, and that fluent word recognition allows the reader's attention to focus on the meaning of the text.

WITHIN THE ADAMS MODEL During the automatic phase, the orthographic, phonological, semantic, and context processors are working effortlessly, and the connections among them are strong.

Decoding Is Connected with All Aspects of Reading

SEE ALSO . . .

Section II: Early Literacy

Section V: Reading Fluency

Section VI: Vocabulary

Section VII: Comprehension

The ability to read words is connected with all aspects of reading. Learning to decode words early and well is essential to the development of reading proficiency. Reading proficiency relies on reading words accurately and automatically. Reading words requires knowledge of letters, understanding of sound/spelling correspondences, and phonemic blending skills. When these word-reading skills are well developed and automatic, fluent reading becomes possible, and the reader's attention can be fully devoted to text comprehension. Reading also expands vocabulary, and in turn vocabulary impacts decoding. That is, the more one reads, the more words one learns, and the more words one knows, the easier it is to decode new words.

The Connecticut Longitudinal Study demonstrates that first-grade decoding ability continues to be a major factor in comprehension as students progress through the grades (Shaywitz et al. 1992). It is not surprising that reading comprehension is highly correlated with how well students can read words. However, the fact that a substantial portion of the variance in ninth graders' reading comprehension can be explained by first-grade decoding skill is remarkable. These data demonstrate that early decoding ability continues to have an impact in the upper grades. Ultimately, learning to read words is essential for comprehending text.

CONTINUED ▷

Correlation Between Decoding & Comprehension (in the Connecticut Longitudinal Study)

COMPREHENSION / DECODING	GRADE 1	GRADE 2	GRADE 3	GRADE 4	GRADE 5	GRADE 6	GRADE 7	GRADE 8	GRADE 9
GRADE 1	.89								
GRADE 2	.75	.83							
GRADE 3	.70	.74	.77						
GRADE 4	.64	.71	.74	.73					
GRADE 5	.58	.63	.68	.67	.70				
GRADE 6	.59	.65	.67	.68	.66	.69			
GRADE 7	.53	.61	.65	.65	.67	.68	.69		
GRADE 8	.49	.58	.62	.62	.64	.65	.65	.63	
GRADE 9	.52	.58	.60	.62	.60	.63	.63	.61	.63

Foorman et al. 1997b.

CHAPTER 6

Phonics

what?
why?
when?
how?

what?

Phonics

> The aim of phonics instruction is to help children acquire alphabetic knowledge and use it to read and spell words.
>
> —EHRI, 2004

PHONICS
instruction in the relationship between letters and the sounds they represent

DECODING
the ability to convert a word from print to speech

ALPHABETIC PRINCIPLE
the understanding that written letters represent spoken sounds and that these sounds go together to make words

Phonics is a method of instruction that teaches students the systematic relationship between the letters and letter combinations (graphemes) in written language and the individual sounds (phonemes) in spoken language and how to use these relationships to read and spell words. Phonics instruction—which is intended for beginning readers in the primary grades and for older students who are struggling to read—can help students learn how to convert the printed word into its spoken form (National Reading Panel 2000). This process, called decoding, involves looking at a word and connecting the letters and sounds and then blending those sounds together. Phonics instruction also helps students to understand the alphabetic principle—written letters represent spoken sounds. In other words, letters and sounds work together in systematic ways to allow spoken language to be written down and written language to be read.

Systematic and Explicit Phonics Instruction

From 1997 to 1999, the National Reading Panel conducted a meta-analysis to review and evaluate research on the effectiveness of various approaches for teaching children to read (Ehri et al. 2001; National Reading Panel 2000). According to the panel's findings, students who received systematic and explicit phonics instruction were better readers at the end of instruction than students who received nonsystematic or no phonics instruction (Ehri 2006; Armbruster, Lehr, and Osborn 2001).

Findings of the National Reading Panel	
Systematic and Explicit Phonics Instruction:	• significantly improves students' reading and spelling in Kindergarten and Grade 1.
	• significantly improves students' ability to comprehend what they read.
	• is beneficial for all students, regardless of their socioeconomic status.
	• is effective in helping to prevent reading difficulties among students who are at risk.
	• is beneficial in helping students who are having difficulty learning to read.

National Reading Panel 2000; Armbruster et al. 2001.

CCSS READING STANDARDS

Foundational Skills

Phonics and Word Recognition

Know and apply grade-level phonics and word analysis skills in decoding words. (RF.K-5.3)

Just because a program has a scope and sequence doesn't mean it's systematic. The instruction must be cumulative.

—BLEVINS, 2006

Understanding the terms *systematic* and *explicit* is important to planning and implementing effective phonics instruction. The hallmark of *systematic* phonics instruction is teaching a set of useful sound/spelling relationships in a clearly defined, carefully selected, logical instructional sequence (Armbruster et al. 2001). Systematic phonics lessons are organized in such a way that the logic of the alphabetic principle becomes evident, newly introduced skills are built on existing skills, and tasks are arranged from simplest to most complex. According to Marilyn Adams (2001), "the goal of systematic instruction is one of maximizing the likelihood that whenever children are asked to learn something new, they already possess the appropriate prior knowledge and understandings to see its value and to learn it efficiently." *Explicit* instruction refers to lessons in which concepts are clearly explained and skills are clearly modeled, without vagueness or ambiguity. According to Carnine et al. (2006), "instruction is explicit when the teacher clearly, overtly, and thoroughly communicates to students how to do something." Learning phonics through explicit teaching requires less inference and discovery on the part of students and is therefore more within their grasp (Chall and Popp 1996).

Approaches to Phonics Instruction

There is more than one approach to teaching phonics. Several approaches are described below.

Synthetic phonics is especially effective as a method that classroom teachers can use to teach beginners to read.

—NATIONAL READING PANEL, 2000

SEE ALSO . . .

Onset-Rime, p. 38

Synthetic Phonics

In this systematic and explicit approach, students learn how to transform letters and letter combinations into sounds and then blend (synthesize) the sounds together to form recognizable words. Furthermore, students are provided with practice materials in the form of short decodable books or stories. These texts contain words that offer students an opportunity to use the sound/spelling relationships they have learned or are learning.

Analogy Phonics

In this approach, students learn how to use a phonogram, or rime, in a familiar word to identify an unfamiliar word having that same rime. They first recognize that the rime of the unfamiliar word is identical to that of the familiar word. Then they decode the unfamiliar word by first pronouncing the shared rime and then blending it with the new onset. For example, to teach the unfamiliar word *brick* the teacher might first introduce the rime *–ick* in the familiar word *kick.* The teacher would then point out that both *kick* and *brick* contain *–ick,* and ask students to pronounce *–ick* and blend it with the onset *br* to make *brick.*

Analytic Phonics

In this approach, instruction begins with the identification of a familiar word. The teacher then introduces a particular sound/spelling relationship within that familiar word. For example, the teacher might print the word *mat* on the board and point out to students that the sound in the middle of *mat* is /a/. The teacher would identify other words that have the same medial sound as in *mat* (e.g., *fat, tan, bag*) and then ask volunteers to read the whole words aloud, without blending the individual sounds.

Embedded Phonics

In this approach, phonics instruction is embedded in the context of "authentic" reading and writing experiences. Phonic elements are introduced informally when the teacher senses that students need to know them. Instruction focuses on teaching students to predict the identities of words using a variety of "word-solving skills." These skills include using context, pictures, familiar word parts, and the first or last letters of words (Fountas and Pinnell 1996). For example, if a student has trouble identifying a word while reading, the teacher might ask: *Do you know another word that starts with those letters?*

Differentiate between the following pairs of descriptions in which one sentence is an example of synthetic phonics and the other is a nonexample. For each pair of sentences, first identify the example of synthetic phonics and then identify the approach described in the other sentence. (See Answer Key, p. 800.)

1a. Students first identify a word and then the teacher introduces a sound/spelling within that word.
1b. First the teacher introduces new sound/spellings and then students blend the previously taught sound/spellings together to form a recognizable word.

2a. The teacher explicitly introduces sound/spellings for students to use for decoding unfamiliar words.
2b. The teacher explicitly introduces phonograms for students to use for decoding unfamiliar words.

3a. Student reading texts are derived from a program's phonics instruction. Phonic elements are introduced in a clearly defined sequence and practiced in connected text.
3b. A program's phonics instruction is derived from the student reading texts. Phonic elements are introduced informally based on opportunities presented in the text.

Good Phonics Instruction

Develops understanding of the alphabetic principle

Incorporates phonemic awareness

Provides sufficient practice in reading words

Leads to automatic word recognition

Is one part of a comprehensive reading program

Stahl, Duffy-Hester, and Stahl 1998.

Phonics instruction need not be boring, especially if the instruction is kept brisk, to the point, and does not take an excessive amount of time each day.

—STAHL, DUFFY-HESTER & STAHL, 1998

SEE ALSO . . .

Chapter 5: Phonological Awareness

AUTOMATICITY
the ability to recognize a word effortlessly and rapidly

Good Phonics Instruction

Steven Stahl and colleagues (1998) reviewed basic principles underlying word learning and phonics instruction and made several recommendations. Here is a description of some of their basic principles of good phonics instruction.

Good phonics instruction develops understanding of the alphabetic principle. To be able to decode words, it is necessary to have an understanding of the alphabetic principle. Successful beginning readers understand the systematic relationship between letters and sounds in words (Adams 1990).

Good phonics instruction incorporates phonemic awareness. Phonemic awareness and phonics have a mutually beneficial reciprocal relationship. Phonemic awareness instruction improves phonics skills, and phonics instruction improves phonemic awareness (Lane and Pullen 2004). Good phonics instruction should incorporate a variety of phonemic awareness tasks, especially when introducing individual sound/spellings. Instruction in these tasks should be taught with letters.

Good phonics instruction provides sufficient practice in reading words. The ultimate purpose of phonics instruction is for students to learn to read words. Successful phonics instruction provides a great deal of practice in reading words containing the sound/spelling correspondences that are taught. There are three main types of practice: reading words in isolation, reading words in decodable texts, and writing words from dictation.

Good phonics instruction leads to automatic word recognition. In order to read successfully and comprehend text, students need to be able to decode words quickly and automatically. Instruction should provide students repeated opportunities to develop automaticity through practice in reading words in isolation and in decodable text.

Phonics instruction by itself does not help students acquire all the processes they need to become successful readers.

—NATIONAL READING PANEL, 2000

Good phonics instruction is one part of a comprehensive reading program. Phonics instruction is only one part of a total reading program. According to the National Reading Panel (2000), "phonics should not become the dominant component in a reading program, neither in the amount of time devoted to it nor in the significance attached." Reading instruction should include phonics, so that students can learn how to decode, but must also develop the other aspects of reading, such as vocabulary and comprehension.

Explicit Phonics Lesson Sequence	
1. Develop Phonemic Awareness	A variety of phonemic awareness activities help students make sense of the alphabetic principle and develop their phonics skills. Letters are incorporated into this explicit instruction.
2. Introduce Sound/Spelling	Phonic elements are explicitly taught in isolation.
3. Blend Words	Blending includes explicit instruction and practice in sounding out and reading words. Routines include sound-by-sound, continuous, spelling-focused, and whole word blending.
4. Build Automatic Word Recognition	Activities to develop automaticity focus on the rapid and effortless decoding and reading of words in isolation.
5. Apply to Decodable Text	Opportunities to practice reading and rereading decodable texts also develop automaticity. Decodable texts contain a high proportion of the words that are made up of previously taught sound/spelling correspondences.
6. Word Work for Decoding and Encoding	A range of activities leads students to practice sound/spelling patterns by building, manipulating, and sorting words. Word-work activities include word sorting, Elkonin boxes with letters, word building, and dictation.

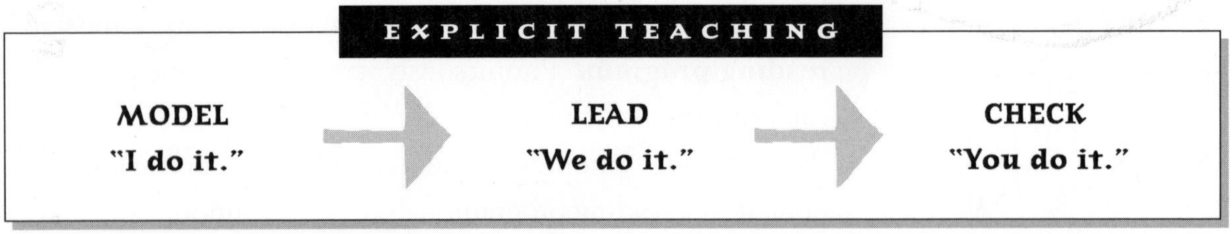

EXPLICIT TEACHING

MODEL		LEAD		CHECK
"I do it."	→	"We do it."	→	"You do it."

> The manner in which a teacher presents lessons is as important as the instructional design underlying the content being presented.
>
> —CARNINE ET AL., 2006

Effective Instructional Techniques

According to Carnine et al. (2006), certain lesson presentation techniques have been shown to improve student engagement and contribute to instructional efficiency. Here is an overview of some of these techniques. For examples, refer to the lesson models in this chapter and section of the Sourcebook.

CORRECTIVE FEEDBACK Student errors should be corrected immediately. When a student answers incorrectly, stop and immediately model the correct response for the entire group—do not single out the student who made the mistake.

MONITORING Monitor students to make sure that they are paying attention and responding correctly. In a group situation, monitor performance by watching students' mouths and eyes.

PACING Lively pacing keeps students attentive. The key is not to have "downtime" after students give a response.

SIGNALING The effective use of signals makes it clear when students are to respond in unison. Hand signals include pointing, scooping, looping, and sweeping. Never signal while you're talking; talk first and then signal.

Phonics teaching is a means to an end.

—NATIONAL READING PANEL, 2000

Phonics Scope & Sequence

Educators are not in agreement about the order, or sequence, in which to introduce sound/spelling correspondences. Here are some guidelines to use when evaluating a reading program.

SOUND/SPELLING
a phoneme/grapheme pairing

- In terms of scope, a program should introduce a set of sound/spellings that occur most commonly in words. Although there are hundreds of different sound/spellings for English phonemes, only the most useful ones are important enough to warrant instruction.
- A program should introduce high-utility sound/spellings early in the sequence. This enables students to begin reading words as soon as possible. For example, the program should introduce /m/*m* and /a/*a* before /j/*j*, /y/*y*, /ks/*x*, or /z/*z*.
- A program's sequence should progress from simple to more complex sound/spellings. For example, single consonants and short vowels should be introduced before vowel digraphs and diphthongs.
- Along with single consonants, a program should introduce a few short vowels early in the sound/spelling sequence, so that words can be formed and read as early as possible. Here is an example of the beginning of a sound/spelling sequence of introduction: /a/*a*, /s/*s*, /m/*m*, /t/*t*, /i/*i*, /f/*f*.
- In a program's sequence, letters with easy-to-pronounce sounds should be introduced first. For example, continuous sounds at the beginning or middle of words are easier to pronounce and blend than stop sounds.
- In a program's sequence, letters having similar sounds and shapes should be separated. For example, lowercase letters *b* and *d* are similar in sound and in shape, and therefore are easily confused by students.

Common Consonant Sound/Spellings, p. 30
Common Vowel Sound/Spellings, p. 34
Most Frequent English Sound/Spellings, p. 35

Letter Characteristics, p. 86

SEE ALSO . . .

LESSON MODELS

Integrated Picture Mnemonics, p. 196

Introducing Consonant Digraphs, p. 200

Introducing Short Vowels, p. 204

Reading and Writing CVC Words, p. 208

Reading and Writing CCVC Words, p. 214

Reading and Writing CVCe Words, p. 221

Reading and Writing Words with Vowel Combinations, p. 226

SEE ALSO . . .

Phonic Elements (Sound/Spelling Categories), p. 29

Phonologically and Visually Similar Letters, p. 87

General Sequence for Teaching Phonic Elements

Based on their combined research of 50 years, Jeanne Chall and Helen Popp (1996) suggest the following general sequence for teaching phonic elements. The order is based on utility as well as ease of learning. The elements introduced first are also the most consistent and occur most frequently in the English language.

- single consonants and short vowels
- consonant digraphs
- long vowels with silent *e* (CVCe pattern)
- long vowels at the end of words or syllables
- *y* as a vowel
- *r*-controlled vowels
- silent consonants
- vowel digraphs (vowel teams)
- variant vowel digraphs and diphthongs

Choose a core reading program, an intervention program, or a supplemental phonics program and evaluate its first-grade phonics scope & sequence according to the guidelines and general sequence described above. Consider the following:

- Are more frequent sound/spellings introduced before less frequent sound/spellings?
- Is a combination of consonant and short-vowel sounds introduced early in a sequence?
- How many lessons separate the introduction of letters that both sound and look alike; for example, /b/*b* and /d/*d*?
- How does the overall scope & sequence of phonics elements compare with the General Sequence for Teaching Phonic Elements listed above?

After completing your evaluation, how does the program compare? What modifications might you suggest?

Approximately 50 percent of English words are completely regular.

—HANNA ET AL., 1966

Decoding Regular Words

Teaching students sound/spelling correspondences prepares them for decoding, the ability to convert a printed word to speech. To decode a word, students use the printed letters in the word to retrieve the sounds associated with those letters; for example, they see the letters *m-a-t* in the word *mat* and say /mat/. A crucial component of decoding is to be able to blend the individual sounds in a word together and come up with a recognizable word, or an approximate pronunciation of a word (Beck 2006). Blending has been described as the "heart and soul" of phonics instruction.

REGULAR WORDS
words in which each letter represents its most common sound

Many struggling readers and at-risk students need highly explicit and systematic instruction that begins with sounding out words orally and gradually transitions to a stage where students can recognize words automatically without sounding them out orally (Carnine et al. 2006).

SEE ALSO . . .

LESSON MODELS

Reading and Writing CVC Words, p. 208

Reading and Writing CCVC Words, p. 214

Reading and Writing CVCe Words, p. 221

Reading and Writing Words with Vowel Combinations, p. 226

In regular word reading, the first step is to orally blend the individual sound/spellings in a word. The next step is to put the individual sounds together to say the whole word. The final step involves students in blending the sound/spelling correspondences "in their heads," or silently producing the whole word.

SEE ALSO . . .

Blendable Sounds, p. 121

One-syllable regular words can be classified by type according to their relative difficulty to decode (Carnine et al. 2006). Words beginning with a continuous sound, such as *at* and *mop,* are generally easier for students to blend than words beginning with a stop sound, such as *dog* and *bag.*

Regular Word Types—Easy to Difficult

Word Type	Key Words
VC and CVC words beginning with a continuous sound	am, at, man, mop
VCC and CVCC words beginning with a continuous sound	ant, end, fill, sack
CVC words beginning with a stop sound	dog, bag
CVCC words beginning with a stop sound and ending with a consonant blend	jump, test
CCVC words beginning with a consonant blend	blob, frog
CCVCC, CCCVC, and CCCVCC words	slick, split, stress

Based on Carnine et al. 2006.

Choose a core reading program or an intervention program and evaluate the ease and difficulty of word types used for blending in its first-grade program. Locate and copy the first 20 words used in blending instruction. Then analyze the words according to their word type and whether they begin with a continuous or stop sound. How does the program's progression of word difficulty compare with the word-type progression shown above?

WORD	WORD TYPE	FIRST SOUND?
am	VC	continuous
at	VC	continuous
sap	CVC	continuous
tap	CVC	stop
ran	CVC	continuous
rat	CVC	continuous
cast	CVCC	stop
mist	CVCC	continuous
lip	CVC	continuous
list	CVCC	continuous
past	CVCC	stop

Blending Routines

Sound by Sound

Continuous

Whole Word

Spelling Focused

SEE ALSO . . .

LESSON MODELS

Model—Sound-by-Sound Blending, p. 209

Model—Continuous Blending, p. 215

Blending Routines

There is more than one routine, or strategy, to use when teaching or practicing blending. Instruction usually begins with sound-by-sound or continuous blending and then progresses to whole word and spelling-focused blending.

Sound-by-Sound Blending

1. m — /mmm/
2. ma — /aaa/
3. ma — /mmmaaa/
4. mat — /t/
5. mat — /mmmaaat/
6. mat — mat

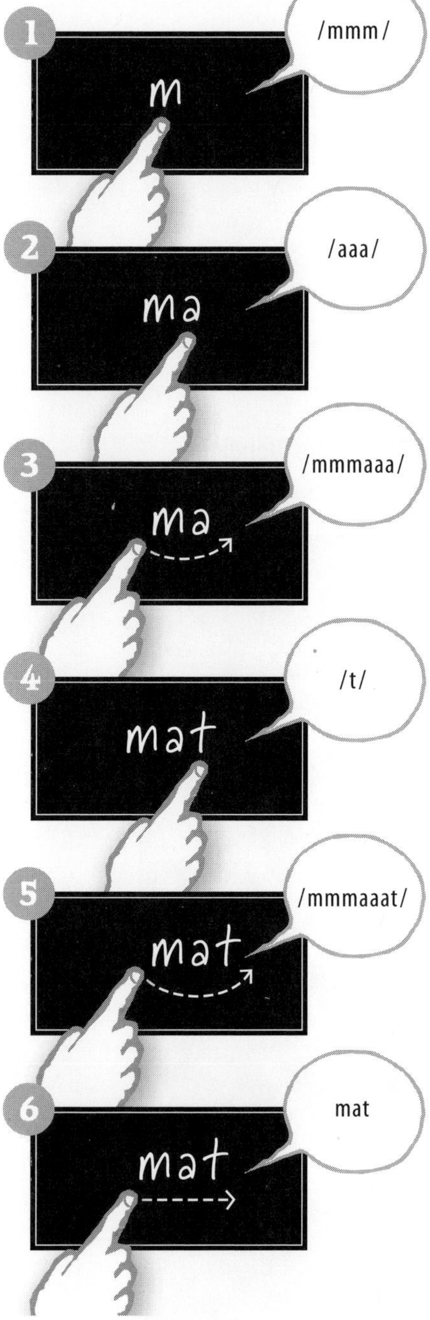

Continuous Blending

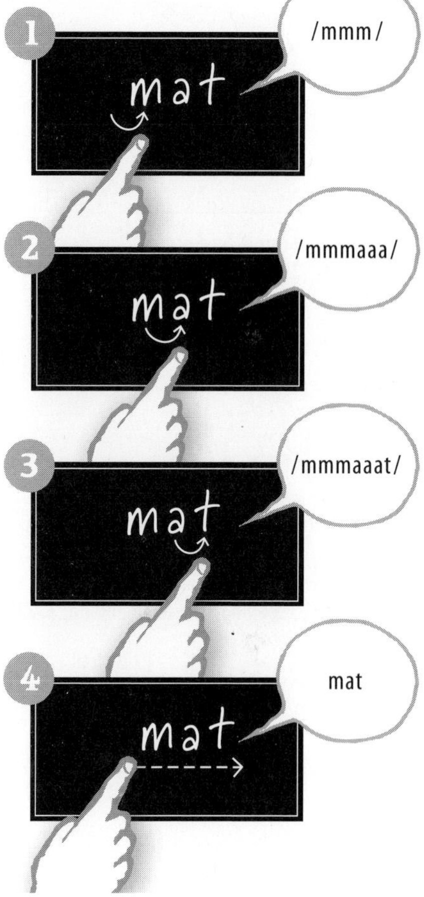

1. mat — /mmm/
2. mat — /mmmaaa/
3. mat — /mmmaaat/
4. mat — mat

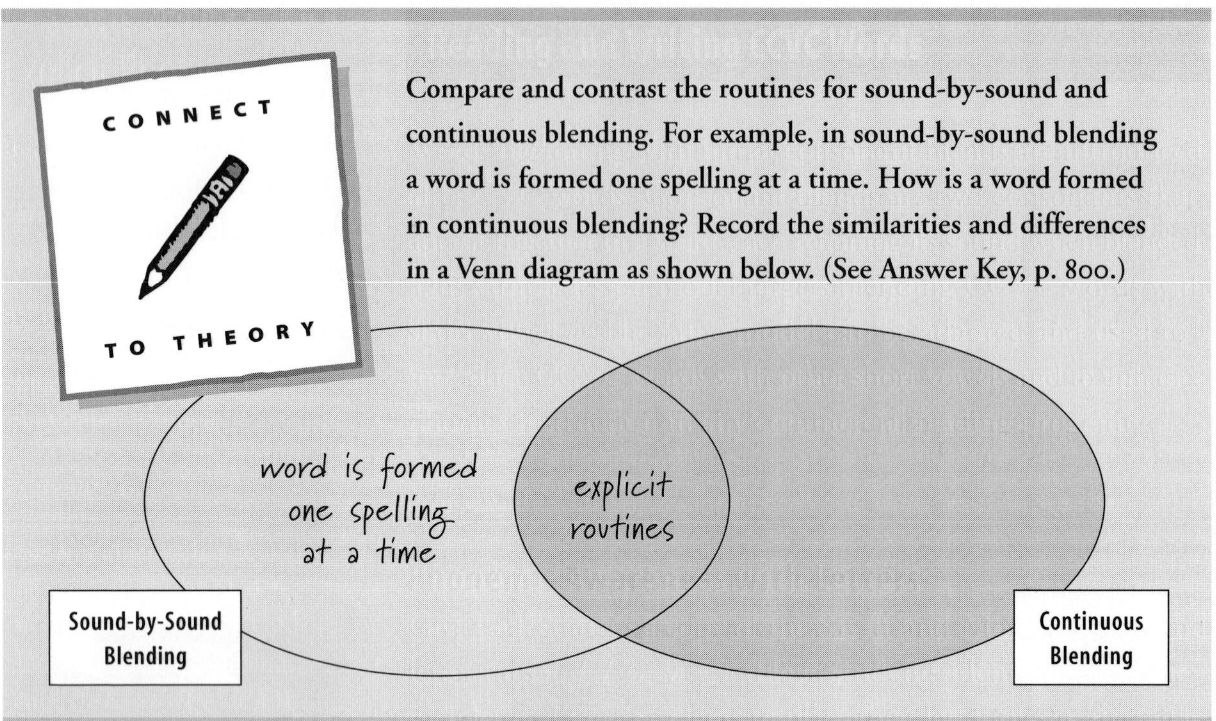

Compare and contrast the routines for sound-by-sound and continuous blending. For example, in sound-by-sound blending a word is formed one spelling at a time. How is a word formed in continuous blending? Record the similarities and differences in a Venn diagram as shown below. (See Answer Key, p. 800.)

SEE ALSO . . .

LESSON MODELS

Model—Whole Word Blending, p. 222

Model—Spelling-Focused Blending, p. 227

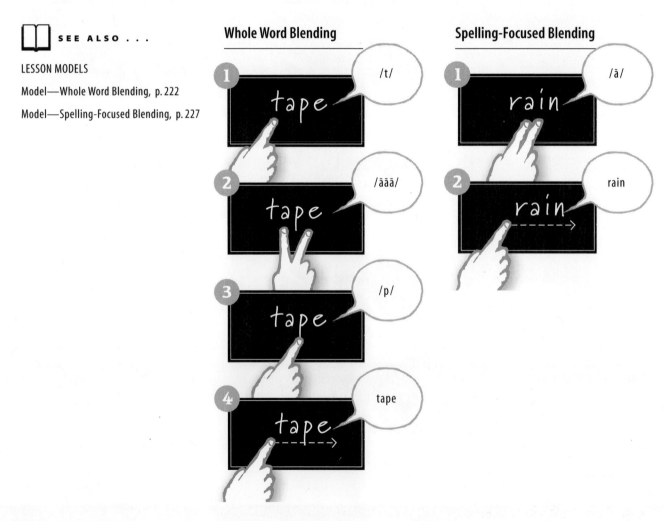

Whole Word Blending

1 tape /t/

2 tape /āāā/

3 tape /p/

4 tape tape

Spelling-Focused Blending

1 rain /ā/

2 rain rain

SEE ALSO . . .

LESSON MODEL: Word Reading Practice for Automaticity, pp. 218, 224, 229

SEE ALSO . . .

Chapter 4: Letter Knowledge

Chapter 5: Phonological Awareness

Section IV: Reading Fluency

Automatic Word Recognition

Good phonics instruction leads to automatic word recognition, being able to decode words quickly and effortlessly. Instruction should provide students repeated opportunities to develop automatic word recognition through practice in reading words in isolation and in decodable text (Stahl et al. 1998). Several subskills are required to develop automatic word recognition: students must be able to identify letter sounds quickly and effortlessly and be fluent in phonemic decoding (Wolf and Bowers 1999; Hudson et al. 2006). Without automatic word recognition skills, a student will not be able to develop reading fluency, an essential skill for comprehension (LaBerge and Samuels 1974).

The type of text for beginning readers does matter.

—BLEVINS, 2006

Decodable Text

Decodable text is reading practice material in which the majority of words are linked to phonics instruction using sound/spelling relationships and spelling patterns students have been taught. This type of controlled text also contains a proportion of previously taught irregular sight words, including high-frequency words and story words. It is important that decodable text be more than just phonetically connected; it should also be coherent and comprehensible—the words should be known well by beginning readers or belong to their grade-level oral vocabularies (Anderson et al. 1985; Kamil and Hiebert 2005).

Decodable text is an integral part of systematic and explicit phonics instruction. In a study by Blevins (2006), students who used decodable text in their early reading instruction get off to a stronger start in reading development. These short books or passages provide beginning readers with opportunities to apply what they are learning and to build automaticity, confidence, and fluency. Reading this type of text is an intervening step between students' acquisition of phonics knowledge and their ability to read authentic literature.

Text Types

Decodable Text

- controlled text
- emergent reader text

Predictable/Patterned Text

- repetitive or cumulative text patterns
- matching of text to illustrations

Authentic Text

- literature trade books in different genres

LESSON MODEL: Method for Reading Decodable Text, p. 235

SEE ALSO . . .

Chapter 7: Irregular Word Reading

How decodable must text be to support learning? Researchers have not pinned down the extent to which this type of text should be decodable, nor have they agreed upon a standardized list of criteria to define a wholly decodable word. Although some states require that the decodable text in K–2 core reading programs be 75 percent to 80 percent wholly decodable, these percentages have no empirical base (Foorman et al. 2004).

Decodable Text Analysis

One way to determine the decodability of a particular text is by examining the relationship between the instructional sequence of sound/spellings and the words in the text. An example of the text-analysis process follows, using an excerpt from a decodable text:

From *Bass Lake,* Sound Out Chapter Books (1999) by Matt Sims. Novato, CA: High Noon Books.

> **Gail and Sue like to hike.**
> **Every year they go to Bass Lake for a week.**
> **They fill their packs with all they will need.**
> **Then they hike in to the lake.**

For this example, assume that the following sound/spellings and irregular words have been previously taught.

- **Introduced Sound/Spellings:** All single consonants and short vowels; /k/*ck;* /th/*th;* /ā/*a_e, ai;* /ē/*ea, ee;* /ī/*i_e;* /ō/*o*
- **Introduced Irregular Words:** *a, all, for, the, their, they, to*

Based on the decodable text word types and the previously taught sound/spellings and irregular words, the analysis of the 32 words in this text excerpt reveals that 56 percent of the words are wholly decodable, 38 percent are introduced irregular words, and 6 percent are nondecodable words.

Decodable Text Word Types

Wholly Decodable Words

Words that can be identified on the basis of sound/spelling relationships and spelling patterns that have been previously taught

Irregular Words

Irregular words (e.g., high-frequency and story words) that are explicitly taught prior to reading text

Nondecodable Words

Words that are neither wholly decodable nor previously taught sight words

Decodable Text Analysis of *Bass Lake*		
Word Types	**Identified Words in Text**	**Percentage of Words in Text**
Wholly Decodable Words	and, Bass, fill, Gail, go, hike, hike, in, Lake, lake, like, need, packs, Then, week, will, with, year	18 words or 56%
Introduced Irregular Words	a, all, for, the, their, they, They, they, they, to, to, to	12 words or 38%
Nondecodable Words	Sue, every	2 words or 6%

Analyze the decodability of the same *Bass Lake* decodable text excerpt. This time, assume that the following sound/spellings and irregular words have been previously taught. These sound/spellings and irregular words are different from the previous example. What does this new analysis reveal? What are the percentages of the wholly decodable words and the irregular words? Explain your criteria for each of the nondecodable words.

- Introduced Sound/Spellings: All single consonants and short vowels; /k/*ck;* /or/*or;* /ā/*a_e;* /ē/*ee;* /ī/*i_e*
- Introduced Irregular Words: *a, all, every, the, their, they, to*

(See Answer Key, p. 800.)

Of the 286 phonograms that appeared in primary-level texts, 272 (95 percent) were pronounced the same in every word in which they were found.

—DURRELL, 1963

LESSON MODEL: Reading and Writing Words with Phonograms, p. 232

Onset-Rime, p. 38

Phonograms

As students learn how to use beginning sounds in the decoding process, they should also learn to use common phonograms or rime patterns (Cunningham 2005). A phonogram is a letter (or series of letters) that stands for a sound, syllable, syllable part, or series of sounds. A linguistic term sometimes used for phonogram is *rime.* Rime is generally used in combination with the term *onset.* Onset and rime refer to the two parts of a syllable.

Phonograms should never be the sole focus of early reading instruction. Phonogram instruction should build on the knowledge gained from systematic, explicit phonics instruction in sound/spelling correspondences. Students must know the sounds of the individual letters that make up the phonogram before being introduced to it as a unit. Beginning readers who rely primarily on phonograms to decode by analogy are less skilled at word identification than beginning readers who analyze words fully, sound by sound (Bruck and Treiman 1990).

Although they should not be the sole focus, phonograms should be included as a part of phonics instruction. In fact, knowing phonograms is a critical step for students in that they need to move beyond blending individual phonemes to more advanced decoding of chunks of words (Ehri 2002). Knowing about chunks of words, such as phonograms, reduces the number of connections a reader needs to decode a word (Ehri 2002). For example, to read the unfamiliar word *chain,* a reader only needs to make connections between the onset /ch/ and the phonogram or rime /ain/. In a study of decoding fluency, the naming of phonograms predicted how fluently a student was able to decode (Hudson et al. 2006). This may be because English is more regular at the level of rimes than it is at the phoneme level (Moats 2000; Treiman and Kessler 2003).

Word Work

Word Work for Encoding and Decoding

Word work is a broad term that describes a range of activities that leads students to practice sound/spelling patterns by building, manipulating, and sorting words. Word-work activities should provide opportunities for students to both encode and decode words and can be conducted with manipulative materials or through writing.

One advantage of word-work activities, particularly when using manipulative materials, is that they help to make the abstract concept of blending and segmenting more concrete for students (Pullen et al. 2005). In studies that have incorporated the use of written word work or word work with manipulative letters, students who received word-work instruction performed better on measures of phonological awareness and decoding than students who did not receive word-work instruction (Lane, Pullen, and Hudson 2006; Pullen et al. 2005; Pullen 2000).

Various types of word work can be incorporated into classroom instruction as whole class, small group, or individual activities. Examples of word work include word sorting, Elkonin boxes with letters, word building, and dictation.

SEE ALSO . . .

LESSON MODEL: Word Work: Picture Sort, pp. 202, 206

Word Sorting

Word sorting is a method for calling attention to word elements. It is an active process in which students categorize, or group, words and pictures within and across categories to reveal essential differences and similarities among the words. There are different kinds of sorts: closed, open, blind, writing, and speed. Each type serves a different instructional purpose (Bear et al. 2000).

Word or Picture Sorts	
Closed	Teacher defines key word or picture categories and models sorting procedure.
Open	Students define key word or picture categories.
Blind	Teacher defines key word or picture categories; teacher calls out a word that students do not see, then students point to the key word or picture with the same sound.
Writing	Teacher defines key word categories; teacher calls out a word, and students write the word below the key word with the same sound/spelling pattern.
Speed	Closed, open, blind, and writing sorts are completed within a particular time frame.

SEE ALSO . . .

LESSON MODELS

Elkonin Sound Boxes, p. 156

Word Work: Elkonin Boxes with Letters, p. 212

CCSS LANGUAGE STANDARDS

Conventions of Standard English

Spell words phonetically. (L.K.2d; L.1.2e)

Elkonin Boxes with Letters

In Elkonin box activities to develop phonemic awareness, students segment words into sounds using chips to represent the sounds. However, Elkonin boxes can also be used to help bridge the connection between phonemes and graphemes. Once students are able to segment phonemes and have knowledge of sound/spelling correspondences, they can move the actual letter(s), or grapheme, for each sound into the individual Elkonin boxes.

SEE ALSO . . .

LESSON MODEL: Word Work: Word Building, pp. 225, 234

Word Building

According to Isabel Beck (2006), word building is an activity that "supports decoding and word recognition by giving students opportunities to experience and discriminate the effects on a word of changing one letter." Within each word-building sequence, words are transformed progressively by substituting, inserting, or deleting letters. Each word in a sequence is different from the previous word by one letter, as in the sequence *ad, had, sad, sat, sit, it,* and *pit.*

Conventions of Standard English

Spell words phonetically. (L.K.2d; L.1.2e)

SEE ALSO . . .

LESSON MODELS
Word Work: Sound-by-Sound Dictation, p. 219
Word Work: Whole Word Dictation, p. 230

Dictation

Regular dictation of words containing patterns taught in phonics lessons is a useful way to assess student progress. It also develops students' auditory skills. There are basically two dictation methods: sound-by-sound dictation and whole word dictation. The sound-by-sound dictation method is similar to blending instruction in that the teacher dictates words to students, one sound at a time. The whole word dictation method gives students the opportunity to practice writing words with previously taught sound/spellings with less help from the teacher. The procedure is the same as that for sound-by-sound dictation, but rather than being guided to spell words sound by sound, students are prompted to "think about" the sounds they hear in the words and write the entire word.

why?

Phonics

> English is an alphabetic language in which there are consistent, though not entirely predictable, relationships between letters and sounds.
>
> —ANDERSON ET AL., 1985

Based on numerous studies, it has been confirmed that phonics instruction is the best and most efficient way to teach students the alphabetic principle (National Reading Panel 2000). English is an alphabetic language; thus, knowing how written letters represent spoken sounds gives readers a systematic method of reading unfamiliar words when they are encountered in text. It is important to note that phonics instruction is just a means to an end—fluent reading and writing. Students' ability to read words accurately and automatically enables them to focus on text comprehension because less mental energy is required to decode words and more mental energy can be devoted to making meaning from text (Freedman and Calfee 1984; LaBerge and Samuels 1974).

Research Findings . . .

Systematic phonics instruction helps students learn to read more effectively than nonsystematic phonics or no phonics instruction.

—NATIONAL READING PANEL, 2000

Systematic phonics instruction is effective in preventing reading difficulties among at-risk students and in helping children overcome reading difficulties.

—ARMBRUSTER, LEHR & OSBORN, 2001

Phonics instruction helps Kindergartners and first graders acquire the alphabetic knowledge they need to begin learning to spell.

—NATIONAL READING PANEL, 2000

Phonics instruction increases the ability to comprehend text for beginning readers and older students with reading disabilities.

—NATIONAL READING PANEL, 2000

That direct instruction in alphabet coding facilitates early reading acquisition is one of the most well-established conclusions in all of behavioral science.

—STANOVICH, 1994

Suggested Reading . . .

Beginning to Read: Thinking and Learning About Print (1990) by Marilyn Jager Adams. Cambridge, MA: MIT Press.

Making Sense of Phonics: The Hows and Whys (2006) by Isabel L. Beck. New York: Guilford.

Put Reading First: The Research Building Blocks for Teaching Children to Read, 3rd Edition (2006) by Bonnie Armbruster, Fran Lehr & Jean Osborn. Jessup, MD: National Institute for Literacy.

Reading Instruction for Students Who Are at Risk or Have Disabilities, 2nd Edition (2011) by William D. Bursuck & Mary Damer. Boston: Allyn & Bacon.

Speech to Print: Language Essentials for Teachers, 2nd Edition (2010) by Louisa C. Moats. Baltimore, MD: Paul H. Brookes.

Teaching Struggling and At-Risk Readers: A Direct Instruction Approach (2006) by Douglas W. Carnine, Jerry Silbert, Edward J. Kame'enui, Sara G. Tarver & Kathleen Jungjohann. Upper Boston: Allyn & Bacon.

Teaching Word Recognition: Effective Strategies for Students with Learning Difficulties (2007) by Rollanda E. O'Connor. New York: Guilford.

The Roots of Phonics: A Historical Introduction, Revised Edition (2009) by Miriam Balmuth. Baltimore, MD: Paul H. Brookes.

when?

Phonics

The right maxims for phonics are: Do it early. Keep it simple.

—ANDERSON ET AL., 1985

When to Teach

Phonics instruction exerts its greatest impact on beginning readers in Kindergarten and Grade 1 and therefore should be implemented at those grade levels (National Reading Panel 2000). Phonics instruction can begin as soon as students know the sounds of a few letters and should continue until students develop the ability to decode multisyllabic words with confidence and automaticity. The nature of instruction changes as students' skills develop, shifting from sound-by-sound decoding to automatic recognition of letter patterns.

In a study of phonics instruction, Torgesen et al. (2001) found that students who did not master or become fluent in phonics skills by the end of first grade continued to struggle in the future in other areas of reading. According to the National Reading Panel (2000), phonics helped to prevent reading difficulties in beginners at risk for developing reading problems. In fact, effects were significantly greater in first graders at risk for future reading difficulties than in older students who had already become poor readers. Using phonics instruction to remediate reading problems may be harder than using phonics initially to prevent reading difficulties. According to Linnea Ehri (2004), "when phonics instruction is introduced after students have already acquired some reading skill, it may be more difficult to step in and influence how they read because doing so requires changing students' habits." For example, students may need to learn to suppress the habit of figuring out a word by using context, illustrations, and the first letter of the word.

CCSS READING STANDARDS

Foundational Skills

Phonics and Word Recognition

KINDERGARTEN

Demonstrate basic knowledge of one-to-one letter-sound correspondences by producing the primary, or most frequent sound, for each consonant. (RF.K.3a)

Associate the long and short sounds with common spellings for the five major vowels. (RF.K.3b)

CCSS READING STANDARDS

Foundational Skills

Phonics and Word Recognition

GRADE 1

Know the sound/spelling correspondences for common consonant digraphs. (RF.1.3a)

Decode regularly spelled one-syllable words. (RF.1.3b)

Know final *–e* and common vowel team conventions for representing long vowel sounds. (RF.1.3c)

GRADE 2

Distinguish long and short vowels when reading regularly spelled one-syllable words. (RF.2.3a)

Know sound/spelling correspondences for additional common vowel teams. (RF.2.3b)

Identify words with inconsistent but common sound/spelling correspondences. (RF.2.3e)

Pacing

Research suggests that approximately two years of phonics instruction is typically sufficient for most students (National Reading Panel 2000). Because students differ in how quickly they develop phonics skills, there is no exact formula for how many sound/spellings to introduce per day or week. The pacing of phonics instruction is contingent upon student mastery. Thus, it is critical to adjust pacing to ensure student mastery. According to Carnine et al. (2006), introducing one new letter each second or third day may be an optimal pace for students with little beginning alphabet knowledge. For students who have more background knowledge, letters may be introduced at a quicker pace.

When to Assess and Intervene

Assessment and intervention for beginning readers should focus on understanding the alphabetic principle. Intervention for struggling beginning readers in Kindergarten and first grade should occur as soon as a reading problem is identified through assessment. For beginning readers, initial assessment should also include knowledge of sound/spelling correspondences and move gradually to decoding, including a student's ability to read simple CVC words. Researchers suggest that the best way to assess a student's ability to apply knowledge of sound/spelling correspondences in decoding words is to use measures of nonsense-word reading (Carver 2003; Share and Stanovich 1995). This is a good measure of decoding because when a student attempts to read a nonsense word, he or she must rely on phonemic decoding rather than memorization to pronounce the word.

Once beginning readers are able to use the decoding process to read unfamiliar words in print, they should begin developing automatic word recognition skill. Thus, in addition to measuring students' ability to decode words and nonsense words, it is important to measure students' level of decoding automaticity, which is defined by Berninger et al. (2006) as "effortless, context-free retrieval assessed by the rate of single word reading." According to Berninger et al. (2003), those students who have not developed automaticity by the beginning of second grade are at risk for reading failure. Moreover, Hudson et al. (2006) suggest that when students are unable to use the decoding process fluently, their accuracy in reading connected text suffers. Failing to achieve automaticity in decoding skill can have long-term detrimental effects on all aspects of a student's reading.

SEE ALSO . . .

Section IV: Reading Fluency

Section VI: Comprehension

Older Struggling Readers

Although intervention should begin early for students who struggle to acquire reading skills, some students will not learn to read in the primary grades. For older readers who are not yet reading fluently, who struggle to recognize individual words, and who consequently have weak fluency and comprehension, intensive intervention is critical. Some of these students, non-readers and very weak readers, will need basic phonics instruction coupled with phonemic awareness development; others will need instruction in word attack skills. For these students, assessment data are crucial to guide teachers in filling in the skill gaps. Like beginning readers, assessment and instruction for older readers who are struggling should include phonemic awareness, sound/spelling correspondences, and decoding.

SEE ALSO . . .

Chapter 8: Multisyllabic Word Reading

In addition to remediating phonemic decoding skills for older readers, as students advance into upper elementary and beyond, texts become more complex and require knowledge for decoding multisyllabic words. Thus, for older readers, assessment and instruction should go beyond simple phonics to include more advanced morphological and orthographic knowledge (Henry 2003).

Purpose	✓ Phonics Assessment	Publisher
Screening	CORE Literacy Library *Assessing Reading: Multiple Measures, 2nd Edition* ▸ CORE Phonics Survey	Arena Press
Screening	Test of Word Reading Efficiency, 2nd Edition (TOWRE-2) Subtest: Phonetic Decoding Efficiency (PDE)	Pro-Ed
Screening Progress Monitoring	AIMSweb® Test of Early Literacy (TEL) ▸ Letter Sound Fluency ▸ Nonsense Word Fluency	Pearson http://aimsweb.com
Screening Progress Monitoring	DIBELS® Next ▸ Nonsense Word Fluency (NWF)	Sopris West http://dibels.org
Screening Progress Monitoring Diagnostic	easy CBM™ ▸ Letter Sounds ▸ Word Fluency	Riverside Publishing http://easycbm.com
Screening Progress Monitoring Diagnostic	TPRI Early Reading Assessment ▸ Graphophonemic Knowledge ▸ Word Reading	Texas Education Agency http://www.tpri.org
Screening Diagnostic	Word Identification and Spelling Test (WIST) ▸ Word Identification ▸ Spelling ▸ Sound-Symbol Knowledge	Pro-Ed
Diagnostic	Diagnostic Assessments of Reading (DAR), 2nd Edition ▸ Word Recognition	Riverside Publishing
Diagnostic	Early Reading Diagnostic Assessment®, 2nd Edition (ERDA)	Pearson
Diagnostic	First Performances™ Fox in a Box®, 2nd Edition ▸ Phonics	CTB/McGraw-Hill
Diagnostic	Woodcock Reading Mastery Tests, 3rd Edition (WRMT™-III) ▸ Word Attack	Pearson

how? **Phonics**

LESSON MODEL FOR

Letter/Sound Correspondence

Benchmarks

- ability to produce a sound associated with a letter
- ability to write a letter that stands for a sound

Strategy Grade Level

- Kindergarten – Grade 1 and/or Intervention

Prerequisites

- Letter-Sound Strategy, p. 110
- ability to recognize and name all uppercase and lowercase letters

Grouping

- small group
- individual

Activity Master (Resources)

- Letter Picture Worksheet

Materials

- PDF and copies of Letter Picture Worksheet
- unlined paper

Integrated Picture Mnemonics

Knowing letter names can often help students in reading and spelling words, but there are cases in which letter names are no help at all or are misleading (Treiman and Kessler 2003). According to Ehri and Roberts (2006), mnemonics is an effective way for teaching students the sounds that are not present in letter names, such as short-vowel sounds and the single consonants *h, w,* and *y.* This sample lesson model, which is based on a study by Linnea Ehri and her colleagues (Ehri, Deffner, and Wilce 1984), targets consonant letter *h*. The same model can be adapted and used to enhance alphabet knowledge and sound/spelling correspondence instruction in any commercial reading program.

Review: Letter-Sound Strategy

Remind students that knowing a letter's name can help them to learn and remember a sound the letter stands for. Print the letter *p* on the board. Ask: *What is the name of this letter?* (p) *What is the first sound in the letter name* p*?* (/p/) Say: *Yes, /p/ is the first sound in the letter name* p*. The sound the letter* p *stands for is the first sound in its name.* Repeat the same procedure with letter name *t.* Now print the letter *s* on the board. Ask: *What is the name of this letter?* (s) *What is the last sound in the letter name* s*?* (/sss/) Say: *Yes, /sss/ is the last sound in the letter name* s*. The sound the letter* s *stands for is the last sound in its name.* Repeat the same procedure with letter name *m.*

Teach/Model

Tell students that there are some letter names that don't provide much help in learning or remembering the sound the letter stands for; for example, letter names *h, w,* and *y.* Explain that for these letters a picture shape can help them to remember what the letter looks like and a picture name can help them to remember the sound the letter stands for. Give each student a copy of the Letter Picture Worksheet for the letter *h.* Then use interactive whiteboard technology to display the worksheet.

Letter Picture Worksheet

1. Connect the Integrated Picture to a Letter Sound
2. Make a Copy of the Integrated Picture
3. Trace the Letter and Make It into an Integrated Picture
4. Write the Letter and Connect It to the Picture Name

1. Connect the Integrated Picture to a Letter Sound

Point to the integrated picture of the house. Say: *This is a house. The house is drawn in the shape of the letter* h. Ask: *What is this?* (house) Say: *The first sound in* house *is /h/.* Ask: *What is the first sound in* house? (/h/) Say: *The sound the letter* h *stands for is the first sound in* house, */h/. Watch as I trace the picture of the house.* Model tracing the picture of the house on the whiteboard; then direct students to trace over the picture of the house in Box 1 of their worksheet.

In Spanish, the letter *h* is silent. Therefore, Spanish-speaking students may not write the letter *h* in the initial position of words and may not pronounce it when reading.

English/Spanish Language Differences, p. 60

2. Make a Copy of the Integrated Picture

Ask students to make a copy of the picture of the house in Box 2 of their worksheet. When they are finished, tell them to turn over their worksheet.

Now give students a blank piece of paper. Say: *On your paper, I want you to draw the same picture of the house again from memory—without looking at the picture on your worksheet.* When they are finished drawing, ask again: *What is the name of the picture?* (house) *What is the first sound in* house? (/h/)

3. Trace the Letter and Make It into an Integrated Picture

Now point out to students the shape of the letter *h* and its relationship to the mnemonic drawing of the house. Point to the letter *h* on the whiteboard. Tracing over the letter *h* on the whiteboard, say: *This is the letter* h. *It goes down, up, and over. The letter* h *stands for the first sound in* house, */h/.* Now tell students to trace the letter *h* in Box 3 of their worksheet.

Then say: *Watch as I draw a house on top of the letter* h. Model drawing the integrated picture of the house. Say: *In Box 3, I want you to draw a house on top of the letter* h. Ask: *What picture are you going to draw?* (a house) When they are finished drawing, ask: *What is the first sound in* house? (/h/) *What sound does the letter* h *stand for?* (/h/)

4. Write the Letter and Connect It to the Picture Name

Say: *The letter* h *stands for the /h/ sound. Watch as I print the letter* h. *It goes down, up, and over.* Print the letter *h* on the whiteboard. Say: *Now it's your turn to print the letter* h *on your worksheet.* After students print the letter *h,* say: *Thinking of a house and saying its first sound, /h/, will help you to learn and remember the sound of the letter* h.

Review

On the following day, before introducing a new letter and sound, review the letter *h*. Ask students to draw the integrated picture of the house again from memory. After they complete the picture, ask them to identify the first sound in *house*, (/h/). Then ask them to trace the letter in the picture of the house that makes the sound /h/. Finally, have them write the letter *h* two more times on their own.

Questions for Observation	Benchmarks
(Point to the letter h.*)* What sound does this letter stand for? (/h/)	Student can recall letter-sound correspondence.
(Point to the letter h.*)* What is the name of the picture that goes with this letter? (house)	Student can recall letter-sound mnemonic.
Can you write the letter that stands for the /h/ sound?	Student can recall letter shape.

LESSON MODEL FOR

Sound/Spelling Correspondence

Benchmarks

- ability to recognize consonant digraph sound/spelling correspondences
- ability to discriminate consonant digraphs in initial and final positions in words

Strategy Grade Level

- Kindergarten – Grade 1 and/or Intervention

Prerequisites

- ability to recognize and name all uppercase and lowercase letters
- ability to isolate the initial and final sounds in a word
- introduced sound/spellings: all single consonants

Grouping

- whole class
- small group
- individual

Materials

- picture cards: shark, shell, ship, shirt, shoe; bush, brush, dish, fish
- puppet
- small index cards (one per student)
- two large index cards
- pocket chart

Introducing Consonant Digraphs

This sample lesson model is primarily based on a method developed by Isabel Beck and described in her book *Making Sense of Phonics* (2006). It targets the sound/spelling correspondence for the consonant digraph /sh/*sh.* The same model can be adapted and used to introduce other consonant digraphs or single consonants and to enhance phonics instruction in any commercial reading program.

Phonemic Awareness

Display the following picture cards: ship, shell, shoe, dish, fish, and brush. Then introduce students to the puppet, Simon. Tell students that Simon likes to talk in a funny way; he says words one sound at a time. Hold up the puppet and in a Simon voice say: */sh/ /iii/ /p/.* Then point to the picture card of the ship and say in your own voice: *The word is* ship. Say: *Now you try it.* Hold up the puppet and in a Simon voice say: */sh/ /eee/ /lll/.* Ask: *What word is Simon trying to say? Can you point to the picture?* (shell) Say: *Yes,* shell. Repeat the same procedure with the following words: *shoe* (/sh/ /ōō/), *dish* (/d/ /iii/ /sh/), *fish* (/fff/ /iii/ /sh/), *brush* (/b/ /rrr/ /uuu/ /sh/).

For students having difficulty hearing the individual sounds, prompt them to watch your lips as you pronounce each sound, or let them observe themselves in a mirror to help detect each sound visually.

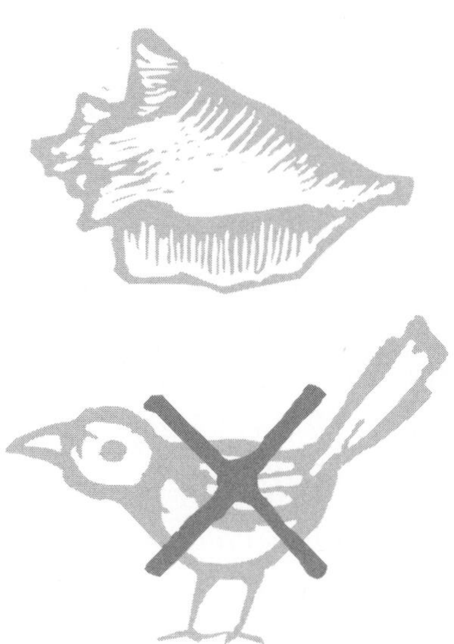

Teach/Model—Connect Spelling to Sound

Print the letters *sh* on the board. Point to the letters *s* and *h* with two fingers and say: *These are the letters* sh. *When the letters* s *and* h *are together, they stand for /sh/. The letters* sh *stand for the first sound in* ship *and the last sound in* fish. Ask: *What sound do the letters* sh *stand for?* (/sh/) *Each time I point to the letters* s *and* h, *I want you to say /sh/.* Point to the letters *s* and *h* two more times as students respond by saying "/sh/."

Guided Practice—Isolate Sound

INITIAL SOUND Give students a small index card and tell them to print the letters *sh* on it. Say: *The letters* sh *stand for the /sh/ sound. The first sound in* ship *and* shoe *is /sh/. I'm going to say some words. If the first sound in a word is /sh/, hold up your* sh *card and say /sh/. If the first sound in a word is not /sh/, put the card behind your back and don't say anything. The first word is* shell. Then follow the same procedure, having students discriminate the initial sound in the words *show, cat, lamp, shop, mouse, bird, ship,* and *shark.* Encourage students to think of other words for which the first sound is /sh/.

FINAL SOUND Have students use their *sh* card again. Say: *The letters* sh *can also stand for the last sound in a word. The last sound in* fish *and* brush *is /sh/. I'm going to say some words. If the last sound in a word is /sh/, hold up the* sh *card and say /sh/. If the last sound in a word is not /sh/, put the card behind your back and don't say anything. The first word is* rash. Then follow the same procedure, having students discriminate the final sound in the words *dish, let, box, wish, push, thumb, fish,* and *brush.* Encourage students to think of other words for which the last sound is /sh/.

The *sh* digraph does not exist in Spanish. Therefore, Spanish-speaking students may pronounce *sh* as /s/.

SEE ALSO . . .

English/Spanish Language Differences, p. 60

Word Work: Picture Sort

Print *sh*___ and ___*sh* on two large index cards, as shown below:

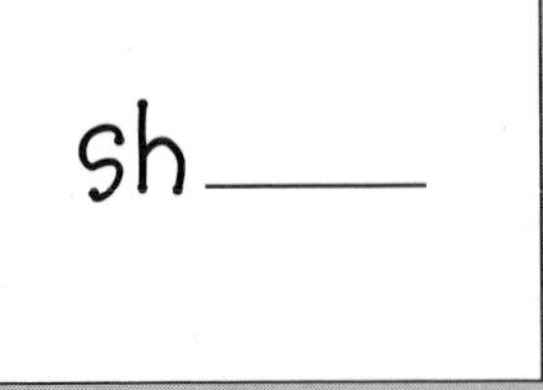

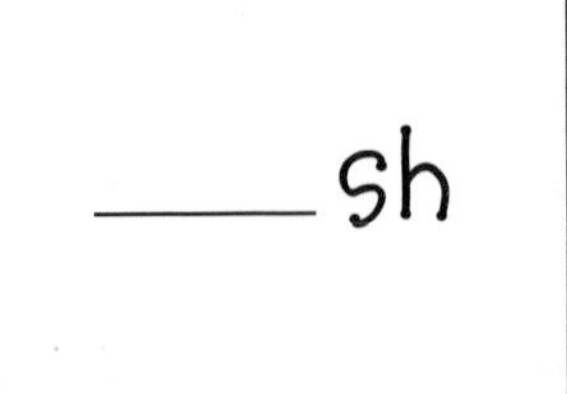

Explain to students that they are going to do a picture sort. Tell them that you will show them a picture and say its name. They will listen and then decide if /sh/ is the first or last sound in the picture's name. Place the card with *sh*___ in the top left corner of a pocket chart. Point to the card and say: *If /sh/ is the first sound in the picture's name, we will put the picture here, below this card.* Place the card with ___*sh* in the top right corner of the pocket chart. Point to the card and say: *If /sh/ is the last sound in a picture's name, we will put the picture here, below this card. Let's try one.* Show the picture card of the shirt. Say: *This is a shirt.* Ask: *What's the name of this picture?* (shirt) Ask: *Is /sh/ the first or last sound in* shirt? (first sound) Say: *Because /sh/ is the first sound in* shirt, *I'll put the picture card of the shirt here.* Place the picture card of the shirt below the card with *sh*___. Follow the same procedure with the remaining picture cards: shoe, fish, shell, shark, dish, bush.

Sound/Spelling Practice for Automaticity

Print four or five previously introduced single consonants and digraphs on the board or on chart paper as shown below. There should be at least four lines of letters repeated in random order.

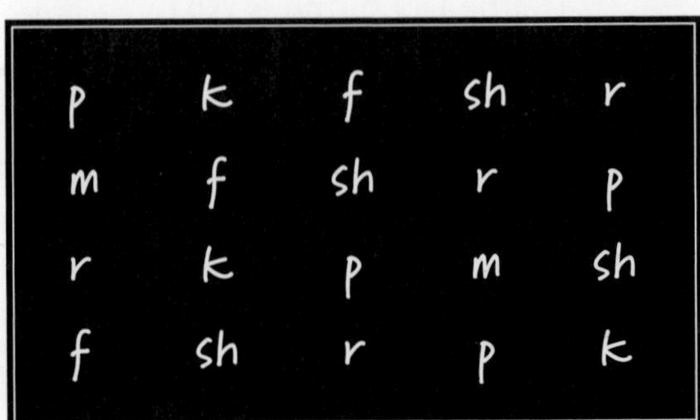

Say: *Let's practice saying the sounds for these letters. When I point to the left of a letter or letters, I want everyone to think about the sound. When I tap under the letter or letters, I want everyone to say the sound aloud.* Point to the left of the letter *p,* pause two seconds for "thinking time," and then tap under *p* to signal that students should respond by saying "/p/." Follow the same procedure, pointing to each letter or letters from left to right. Make sure that each student in the group is responding. When the group is consistently answering all items correctly, call on individual students to identify specific sounds.

CORRECTIVE FEEDBACK If a student or students respond incorrectly, model the correct response for the entire group. For example, point to the digraph *sh* with two fingers and say: *The sound is /sh/.* Point to the left of *sh* and ask: *What's the sound?* Tap under the letters with two fingers as students respond /sh/. To ensure mastery and automaticity, back up two sound/spellings before the error and continue according to the procedure described above.

OBSERVE & ASSESS

Questions for Observation	Benchmarks
(Point to the letters sh.*)* What is the sound for these letters? (/sh/)	Student can recognize consonant digraph sound/spellings.
In the word *shut,* is /sh/ the first sound or the last sound? (first sound)	Student can discriminate consonant digraphs in initial and final positions in words.

LESSON MODEL FOR

Sound/Spelling Correspondence

Benchmarks

- ability to recognize vowels and short-vowel sounds
- ability to discriminate short vowels in initial and medial positions in words

Strategy Grade Level

- Kindergarten – Grade 1 and/or Intervention

Prerequisites

- ability to recognize and name all uppercase and lowercase letters
- ability to isolate the initial and medial sounds in a word
- introduced sound/spellings: single consonants /m/*m*, /p/*p*, /s/*s*, /t/*t*

Grouping

- whole class
- small group
- individual

Materials

- small index cards (one per student)
- two large index cards
- pocket chart
- picture cards: ax, apple, bag, cat, bat, hat, cap, bath, map

Introducing Short Vowels

This sample lesson model is primarily based on a method developed by Isabel Beck and described in her book *Making Sense of Phonics* (2006). It targets the sound/spelling correspondence for /a/*a*. The same model can be adapted and used to introduce other short vowels and to enhance phonics instruction in any commercial reading program.

Phonemic Awareness

Say: *You're going to practice saying the sounds in words. Each time I hold up a finger, you will say a sound. Watch as I do one for you.* Hold up a closed fist, fingers facing toward you. Then say: *The word is* map. *Watch as I say the sounds in* map, */mmm/ /aaa/ /p/*. Hold up a finger as you say each sound. Ask: *How many sounds in* map*?* (three) Say: *Now it's your turn to say the sounds. Remember, each time I hold up a finger, you say a sound. The word is* cat. Ask: *What's the word?* (cat) *What are the sounds in* cat*?* (/k/ /aaa/ /t/) One at a time, hold up a finger to signal students to say a sound. Ask: *How many sounds in* cat*?* (three). Follow the same procedure with the words *at, add, map, sack, hat,* and *catch.*

Teach/Model—Connect Spelling to Sound

Print the letter *a* on the board. Point to the letter *a* and say: *This is the letter* a. *The letter* a *stands for the /a/ sound.* Ask: *What sound does the letter* a *stand for?* (/a/) Say: *The letter* a *stands for the first sound in* apple *and the middle sound in* cat. *Each time I point to the letter* a, *say /a/.* Point to the letter *a* two more times as students respond by saying "/a/."

Identifying a vowel sound in the medial position is much more difficult than identifying a vowel sound at the beginning of a word. In speech, phonemes usually overlap; for example, the /m/ in *map* still remains as you say the vowel sound /a/.

Guided Practice—Isolate Sound

INITIAL SOUND Give students a small index card and tell them to print the letter *a* on it. Say: *The letter* a *stands for the /a/ sound. The first sound in* apple *and* add *is /a/. I'm going to say some words. If the first sound in a word is /a/, hold up your* a *card and say /a/. If the first sound in a word is not /a/, put the card behind your back and don't say anything. The first word is* apple. Then follow the same procedure, having students discriminate the words *at, tree, apple, ask, actor,* and *bike.* Encourage students to think of other words for which the first sound is /a/.

If students are having trouble hearing the vowel sound in the middle of a word, hold out the medial sound so it's easier to hear; for example, /mmm/ /aaaa/ /p/.

MEDIAL SOUND Have students use their *a* card again. Say: The letter *a* can also stand for the middle sound in a word. *The middle sound in* cat *and* back *is /a/. I'm going to say some words. If the middle sound in a word is /a/, hold up the* a *card and say /a/. If the middle sound in a word is not /a/, put the card behind your back and don't say anything. The first word is* cat. Then follow the same procedure, having students discriminate the words *hat, bed, map, sack, fox,* and *pack.* Encourage students to think of other words for which the middle sound is /a/.

Word Work: Picture Sort

Print *a*___ and ___*a*___ on two large index cards, as shown below:

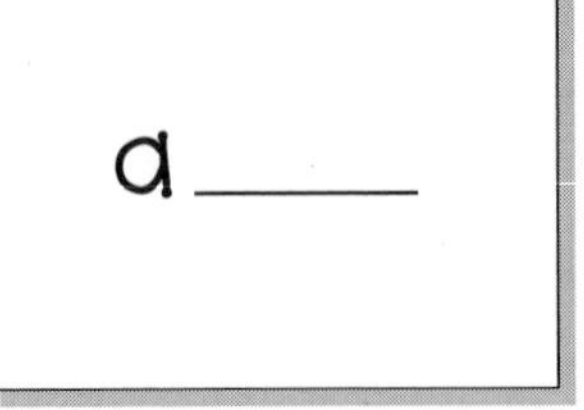

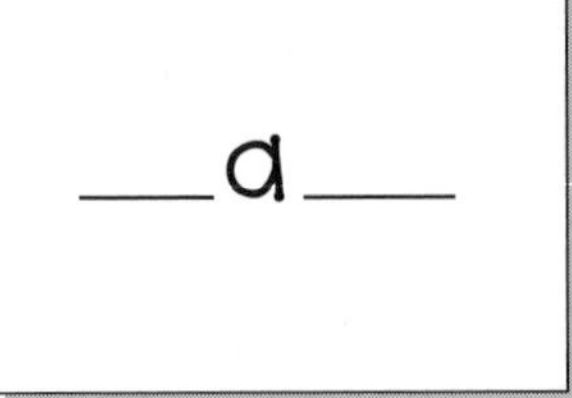

Explain to students that they are going to do a picture sort. Tell them that you will show them a picture and say its name. They will listen and then decide if /a/ is the first or middle sound in the picture's name. Place the card with *a*___ in the top left corner of a pocket chart. Point to the card and say: *If /a/ is the first sound in the picture's name, we will put the picture here, below this card.* Place the card with ___*a*___ in the top right corner of the pocket chart. Point to the card and say: *If /a/ is the middle sound in a picture's name, we will put the picture here, below this card. Let's try one.* Show the picture card of the hat. Say: *This is a hat.* Ask: *What's the name of this picture?* (hat) Ask: *Is /a/ the first or middle sound in* hat*?* (middle sound) Say: *Because /a/ is the middle sound in* hat, *I'll put the picture of the hat here.* Place the picture card of the hat below the card with ___*a*___. Follow the same procedure with the remaining picture cards: ax, cap, bath, map, bat, apple, cat, bag.

Spanish-speaking students may substitute a Spanish vowel sound for an English vowel sound.

Spanish Vowels, p. 51

Sound/Spelling Practice for Automaticity

Print four or five previously introduced sound/spellings on the board or on chart paper as shown below. There should be at least four lines of letters repeated in random order.

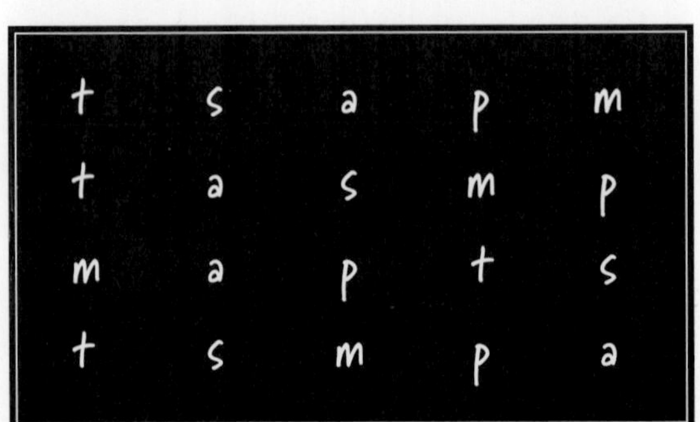

Say: *Let's practice saying the sounds for letters. When I point to the left of a letter, I want everyone to think about its sound. When I tap under the letter, I want everyone to say the sound aloud.* Point to the left of the letter *t,* pause for two seconds for "thinking time," and then tap under *t* to signal that students should respond by saying "/t/." Follow the same procedure, pointing to each letter from left to right. Make sure that each student in the group is responding. When the group is consistently answering all items correctly, call on individual students to identify specific sounds.

CORRECTIVE FEEDBACK If a student or students respond incorrectly, model the correct response for the entire group. Point to *a* and say: *The sound is /a/.* Point to the left of *a* and ask: *What's the sound?* Tap under the letter as students respond "/a/." To ensure mastery and automaticity, back up two sound/spellings before the error and continue according to the procedure described above.

OBSERVE & ASSESS

Questions for Observation	Benchmarks
(Point to the letter a.*)* What is the sound for this letter? (/a/)	Student can recognize short-vowel letter sounds.
In the word *map,* is /a/ the first sound or the middle sound? (middle sound)	Student can discriminate short vowels in initial and medial positions in words.

LESSON MODEL FOR

Explicit Phonics

Benchmarks

- ability to blend CVC words
- ability to spell CVC words

Strategy Grade Level

- Kindergarten – Grade 1 and/or Intervention

Prerequisites

- all previous Lesson Models in this chapter
- ability to isolate the initial or final sound in a one-syllable word
- introduced sound/spellings: /a/*a*, /m/*m*, /p/*p*, /s/*s*, /t/*t*

Grouping

- whole class
- small group
- individual

Materials

- letter cards *a, m, p, s, t* (one set per student)
- picture cards: ant, monkey, paper, seal, ten
- decodable text
- small dry-erase board
- dry-erase marker

Reading and Writing CVC Words

Explicit instruction in blending CVC words should begin after students know from four to six sound/spellings (Carnine et al. 2006). This sample lesson model targets reading and writing CVC words with the short vowel *a*. The same model can be adapted and used to introduce CVC words with other short vowels and to enhance phonics instruction in any commercial reading program.

Phonemic Awareness with Letters

Give each student letter cards *a, m, p, s,* and *t*. Say: *I'm going to name some pictures and I want you to tell me the first sound you hear in each picture name. Then I want you to hold up the letter that makes that sound. Let's try one.* Show the picture card of the seal. Say: *This is a seal.* Ask: *What's the name of this picture?* (seal) Say: *Yes, seal.* Ask: *What is the first sound in* seal*?* (/s/) Say: *Yes, /s/.* Ask: *Can you hold up the letter that makes the /s/ sound?* Monitor students as they hold up the letter *s*. Follow the same procedure with picture cards of the ant, monkey, paper, and number 10.

Model—Sound-by-Sound Blending

Say: *Today I am going to show you how to blend words sound by sound. Watch me blend the first word.*

1. Print the first letter in the word *mat* on the board. Say: *Sound?* Simultaneously point to the letter *m* and say: */mmm/.*

2. Print the letter *a* after the letter *m* on the board. Say: *Sound?* Simultaneously point to the letter *a* and say: */aaa/.*

3. Point just to the left of *ma* and say: *Blend.* Then scoop your finger under the *m* and *a* as you blend the sounds together without a break: */mmmaaaa/.*

4. Print the letter *t* after the letter *a* on the board. Say: *Sound?* Simultaneously point to the letter *t* and say: */t/.*

5. Point just to the left of *mat* and say: *Blend.* Then scoop your finger from left to right under the whole word as you slowly blend the sounds together without a break: */mmmaaat/.*

6. Finally, point just to the left of *mat* and say: *Now watch as I read the whole word.* Then quickly sweep your finger under the whole word and say *mat.* Say: *A mat is like a rug. It covers a floor and people can wipe their feet on it.* Mat.

Repeat the same routine with the word *pat.*

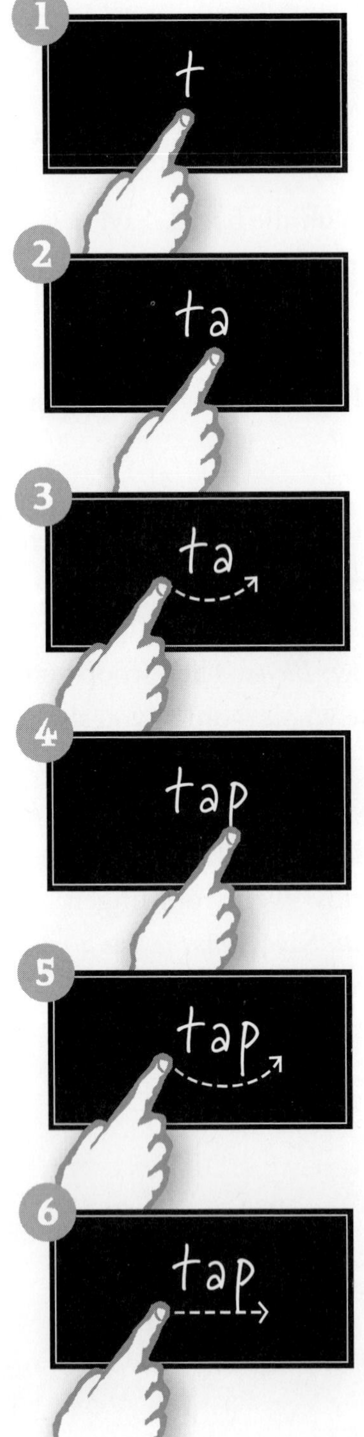

Lead—Sound-by-Sound Blending

Say: *Now I am going to lead you in sounding out words. You're going to sound out some words along with me.*

1. Print the first letter in the word *tap* on the board. Say: *Sound?* Point to the letter *t* and have students respond along with you: */t/.*

2. Print the letter *a* after the letter *t* on the board. Say: *Sound?* Point to the letter *a* and have students respond along with you: */aaa/.*

3. Point just to the left of *ta.* Say: *Blend.* Then scoop your finger under the *t* and *a* as you lead students in blending the sounds together without a break: */taaa/.*

4. Print the letter *p* after the letter *a* on the board. Say: *Sound?* Point to the letter *p* and have students respond along with you: */p/.*

5. Point to the left of *tap* and say: *Blend.* Then scoop your finger from left to right under the whole word as you lead students in slowly blending the sounds together without a break: *tap*.

6. Finally, point just to the left of *tap* and say: *Let's read the whole word.* Then quickly sweep your finger under the word as you lead students in saying the whole word: *tap*. Say: *I heard a light tap on the door,* tap.

Repeat the same routine with the words *Sam* and *Pat.*

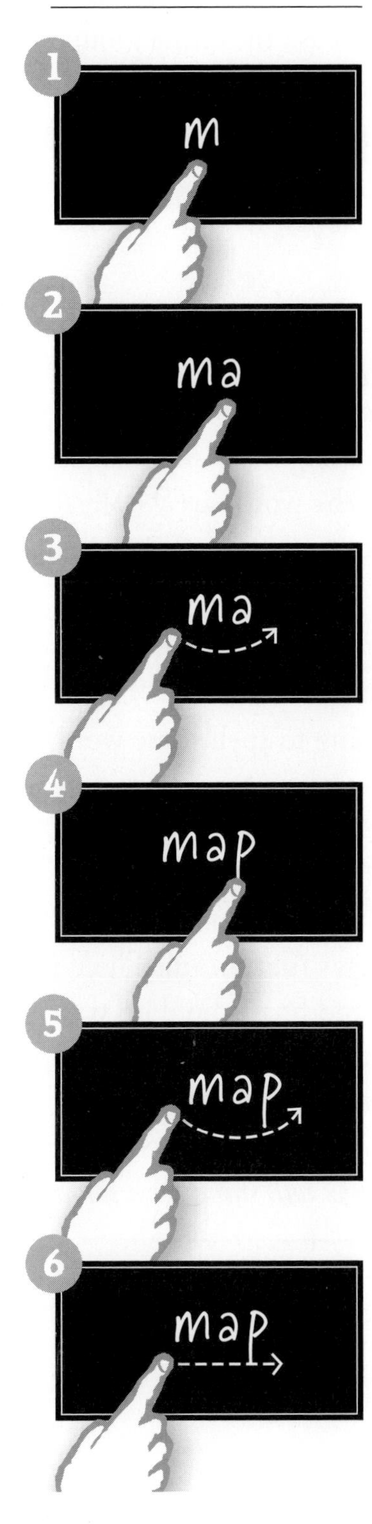

Check—Sound-by-Sound Blending

Say: *Now it's your turn to sound out words. Remember, when I point to a letter, say the sound for that letter. When I scoop my finger under the letters, blend the sounds together. When I sweep my finger under the word, say the whole word.*

1. Print the first letter in the word *map* on the board. Ask: *Sound?* Point to the letter *m* to signal students to respond. (/mmm/)

2. Print the letter *a* after the letter *m* on the board. Ask: *Sound?* Point to the letter *a* to signal students to respond. (/aaa/)

3. Point just to the left of *ma* and say: *Blend the sounds.* Then scoop your finger under the letters from left to right to signal students to respond. (/mmmaaaa/)

4. Print the letter *p* after the letter *a* on the board. Ask: *Sound?* Point to the letter *p* to signal students to respond. (/p/)

5. Point just to the left of *map* and say: *Blend the sounds.* Scoop your finger from left to right under the word as students blend the sounds together without a break. (map)

6. Finally, point just to the left of *map.* Quickly sweep your finger under the word to signal students to respond by saying the whole word. (map)

Repeat the same routine with the words *at, am, sat, mat, Sam, pat, Pam, sap,* and *tap*. When you are finished, develop students' vocabulary by going back and clarifying the meaning of any unfamiliar words. To build word reading automaticity, have students read the list of words again, this time at a faster pace and only with nonverbal signals.

CORRECTIVE FEEDBACK If a student or students respond incorrectly, stop immediately and model the correct response for the entire group and then ask the entire group to respond. For blending errors, first model blending the word and then lead students in blending it again. For sound/spelling errors, immediately say the correct sound, for example, /mmm/. Then point to the letter *m* and ask: *Sound?* (/mmm/) Say: *Yes, the sound is /mmm/.*

LESSON MODEL: Method for Reading Decodable Text, p. 235

Apply to Decodable Text

To ensure ample practice in sound/spelling correspondences, provide students with connected reading materials. Choose books or passages in which most of the words are wholly decodable and the majority of the remaining words are previously taught irregular words.

SEE ALSO . . .

LESSON MODEL: Elkonin Sound Boxes, p. 156

Word Work: Elkonin Boxes with Letters

Explain to students that they are going to spell some words. Say: *I am going to say a word and then together we will count how many sounds we hear in the word. The first word is* map, */mmmaaap/. I hear three sounds in* map. With your palm toward you, so students can see the progression from left to right, hold up your first finger as you say /mmm/, then hold up your second finger as you say /aaa/, and finally hold up your third finger as you say /p/. Then ask: *How many sounds in* map*?* (three) Say: *Now let's count the sounds again.* Have students hold up their fingers as they count along with you. Say: *Now I am going to draw three boxes. Each box will stand for a sound in* map.

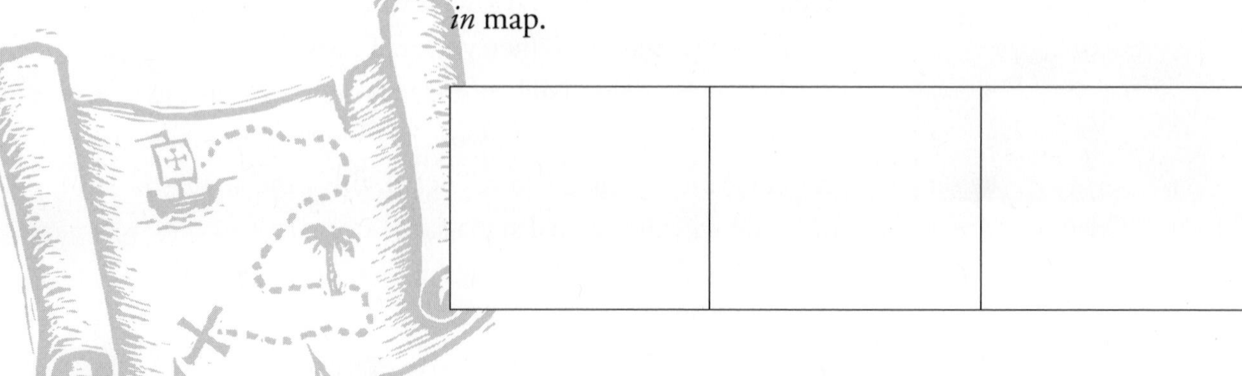

On a dry-erase board, draw a three-box grid as shown. Point to the first box in the grid and say /mmm/, point to the middle box and say /aaa/, and then point to the last box and say /p/. Say: *Now I will lead you in saying each sound in* map *as I print the spelling that stands for that sound.* Say: *The first sound in* map *is /mmm/.* Print the letter *m* into the first box as the students say /mmm/ along with you. Say: *The middle sound in* map *is /aaa/.* Print the letter *a* in the middle box as students say /aaa/ along with you. Say: *The last sound in* map *is /p/.* Print the letter *p* into the last box as students say /p/ along with you.

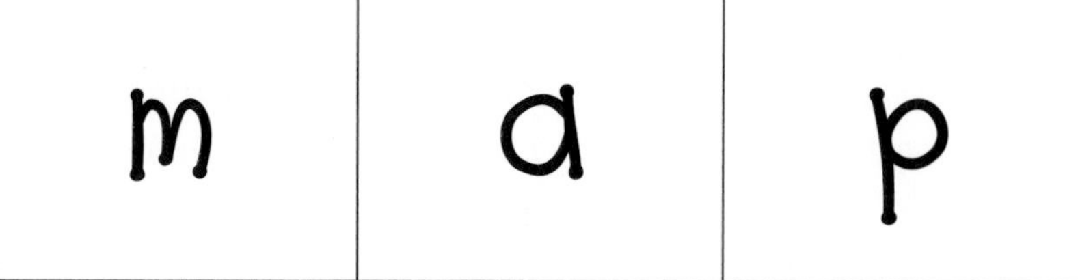

Say: *Now let's read the whole word.* Slide your finger under the grid from left to right as you lead students in saying the whole word: *map.* Say: *Now let's spell the word.* Point to each letter from left to right as you lead students in saying each letter name along with you. (m-a-p) Repeat the same procedure using the word *mat.* Then, following the same procedure with words such as *sap* and *sat*, ask volunteers to draw the grid and print the letters in the boxes.

Questions for Observation	Benchmarks
(Point to the word map.*)* Can you sound out this word?	Student can blend CVC words.
The word is *map.* Can you spell this word? (m-a-p)	Student can spell CVC words.

LESSON MODEL FOR

Explicit Phonics

Benchmarks

- ability to blend CCVC words
- ability to spell CCVC words

Strategy Grade Level

- Kindergarten – Grade 1 and/or Intervention

Prerequisites

- Say-It-and-Move-It, p. 154
- all previous Lesson Models in this chapter
- introduced sound/spellings: /a/*a*, /b/*b*, /k/*c*, /f/*f*, /g/*g*, /l/*l*, /m/*m*, /n/*n*, /p/*p*, /r/*r*, /s/*s*, /t/*t*

Grouping

- whole class
- small group
- individual

Activity Master (Resources)

- Say-It-and-Move-It Board

Materials

- copies of Say-It-and-Move-It Board
- letter tiles *a, f, l, m, p, s, t* (one set per student)
- decodable text
- small dry-erase boards (one per student)
- dry-erase markers (one per student)

Reading and Writing CCVC Words

Words beginning with initial consonant blends are introduced after CVC words. Consonant blends are two consonants that appear together in a word, each retaining its sound when blended. This sample lesson model targets blending CCVC words with short vowel *a*. The same model can be adapted and used to introduce CCVC words with other short vowels and to enhance phonics instruction in any commercial reading program.

Phonemic Awareness with Letters

Give each student a copy of the Say-It-and-Move-It Board and letter tiles *a, f, l, m, p, s, t*. Have students identify and name each letter. Direct students to place their letter tiles in the circle at the top of the board. Say: *We are going to play Say-It-and-Move-It with letters. Let's do the first one together.* Say: *The first word is* fat. Ask: *What's the word?* (fat) Say: *Now let's say it and move it. The first sound in* fat *is /fff/.* Ask: *What's the sound?* (/fff/) Say: *Yes, /fff/.* Ask: *What letter stands for /fff/?* (f) Direct students to slide the letter *f* down to the arrow as they say /fff/. Then use the same procedure for the middle sound /a/ and the last sound /t/.

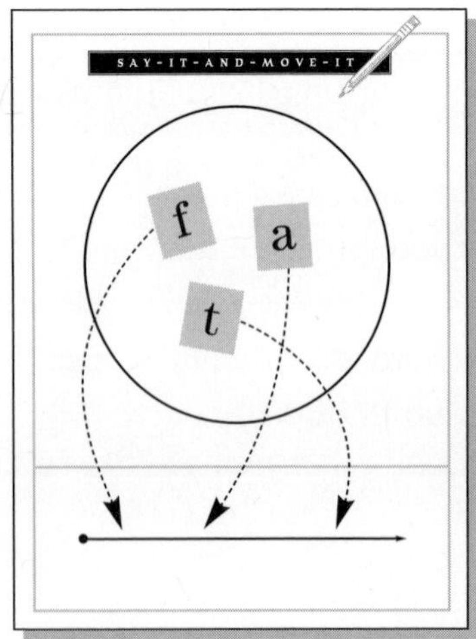

Say: *Now let's read the whole word.* Monitor students as they slide their finger under the tiles from left to right and say the word *fat*. Say: *Good. Let's try another.* Direct students to move their letter tiles back inside the circle and get ready for the next word. Repeat the same procedure with the following words: *mat, sat, sap, map, lap.*

MODEL
Continuous Blending

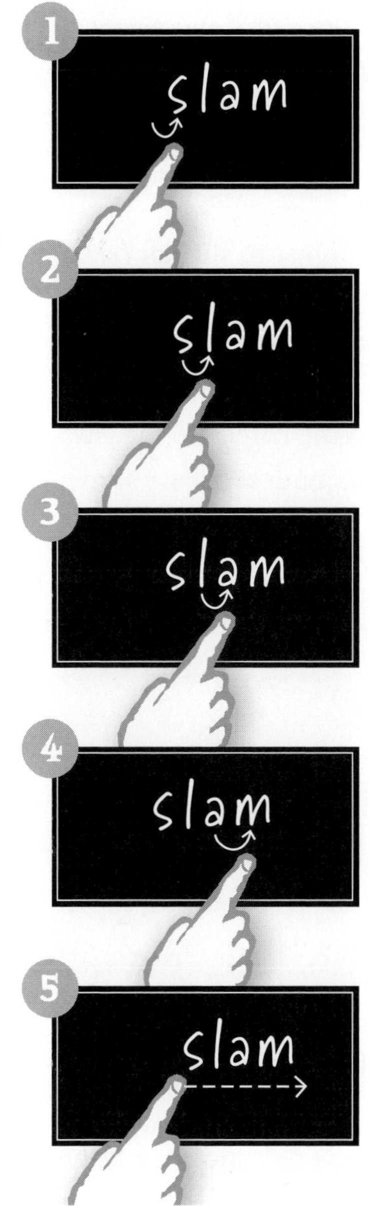

Model—Continuous Blending

Print the word *slam* on the board. Say: *Today I am going to show you how to sound out words. Watch me blend the sounds in the first word.* Point just to the left of *slam* and say: *I will blend this word.*

1. With your finger, make a loop from just to the left of *slam* to the letter *s.* Pointing to the letter *s,* say: */sss/. I'm going to keep saying this sound until I point to the next letter.*

2. Keep saying /sss/. With your finger, make a loop from the letter *s* to the letter *l.* Pointing to the letter *l,* say: */lll/.*

3. Keep saying /lll/. With your finger, make a loop from the letter *l* to the letter *a.* Pointing to the letter *a,* say: */aaa/.*

4. Keep saying /aaa/. With your finger, make a loop from the letter *a* to the letter *m.* Pointing to the letter *m,* say: */mmm/.*

5. Point just to the left of *slam* and say: *Now watch as I read the whole word.* Then quickly sweep with your finger under the whole word and say *slam.* Say: *To slam a door means "to shut it hard." When you slam a door, it usually makes a loud noise.* Slam.

Repeat the same routine with the word *trap.*

SLAM!

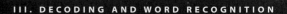

Point to continuous sounds (e.g., /a/*a*, /f/*f*, /l/*l*, /m/*m*, /s/*s*) for one or two seconds and to stop sounds (e.g., /p/*p*, /t/*t*) for only an instant.

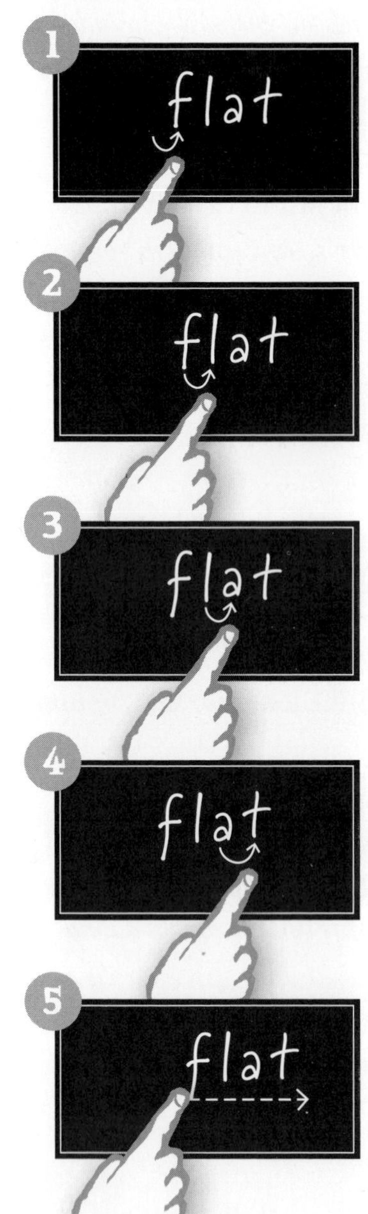

Lead—Continuous Blending

Print the word *flat* on the board. Say: *Now I am going to lead you in sounding out words. You're going to sound out some words along with me. Remember, we'll keep saying a sound until I point to the next letter.* Point just to the left of *flat* and say: *Let's blend this word.*

1. With your finger, make a loop from just to the left of *flat* to the letter *f*. Point to the letter *f* for one or two seconds and have students respond along with you: */fff/*.

2. With your finger, make a loop from the letter *f* to the letter *l*. Point to the letter *l* for one or two seconds and have students respond along with you: */lll/*.

3. With your finger, make a loop from the letter *l* to the letter *a*. Point to the letter *a* for one or two seconds and have students respond along with you: */aaa/*.

4. With your finger, make a loop from the letter *a* to the letter *t*. Point to the letter *t* for only an instant and have students respond along with you: */t/*.

5. Point just to the left of *flat* and say: *Read this word.* With your finger, sweep quickly under the word as you lead students in saying the whole word*: flat.*

Repeat the same routine with the words *flap* and *plan.* When you are finished, develop students' vocabulary by going back and clarifying the meaning of any unfamiliar words.

Check—Continuous Blending

Print the word *flag* on the board. Say: *Now it's your turn to sound out words. This time when I point to a letter, I want you to say its sound. Keep saying it until I point to the next letter. When I sweep my finger under the word, say the whole word.* Point just to the left of *flag* and say: *Blend this word.*

1. With your finger, make a loop from just to the left of *flag* to the letter *f.* Point to the letter *f* for one or two seconds to signal students to say the sound for the letter *f.* (/fff/)

2. With your finger, make a loop from the letter *f* to the letter *l.* Point to the letter *l* for one or two seconds to signal students to say the sound for the letter *l.* (/lll/)

3. With your finger, make a loop from the letter *l* to the letter *a.* Point to the letter *a* for one or two seconds to signal students to say the sound for the letter *a.* (/aaa/)

4. With your finger, make a loop from the letter *a* to the letter *g.* Point to the letter *g* for only an instant to signal students to say the sound for the letter *g.* (/g/)

5. Finally, point just to the left of *flag.* Quickly sweep your finger under the word to signal students to respond by saying the whole word. (flag)

Repeat the same routine with the words *grab* and *clap.* When you are finished, develop students' vocabulary by going back and clarifying the meaning of any unfamiliar words.

CORRECTIVE FEEDBACK If a student or students respond incorrectly, stop immediately and model the correct response for the entire group and then ask the entire group to respond. For blending errors, such as pausing between sounds, immediately say: *Don't stop between sounds. Listen to me blend*

the word without stopping. Model blending the word and then lead students in blending the word again. For letter-sound errors, immediately say the correct sound, for example, /aaa/. Then point to the letter *a* and ask: *What sound?* (/aaa/) Say: *Yes, the sound is /aaa/.*

Word Reading Practice for Automaticity

Automaticity is quick and effortless reading of words. It is achieved through corrected practice. Once students are adept at sounding out words vocally during blending instruction, they may be ready to sound out the words to themselves.

MODEL Print the following words on the board: *trap, plan.* Say: *I am going to show you how to read words without saying each sound out loud.* Point just to the left of *trap.* Then simultaneously point and loop from letter to letter while subvocalizing, or whispering, the sounds. Then say: *What's the word?* With your finger, sweep quickly from left to right under the word as you say it out loud: *trap*. Repeat the same procedure with *plan.*

LEAD Print the following words on the board: *snap, flat.* Say: *Now I am going to lead you in reading words without saying the sounds out loud. As I point and loop from letter to letter, we will sound out a word to ourselves.* Point just to the left of *snap.* Then simultaneously point and loop from letter to letter while leading students in whispering the sounds. Then say: *What's the word?* With your finger, sweep quickly under the word as you lead students in saying the whole word: *snap.* Repeat the same procedure with *flat.*

CHECK Print the following words on the board: *slam, flap, slap, brat, clap, grab.* Say: *Now it's your turn to sound out words. When I point to a word, sound it out to yourselves. When I sweep my finger under the word, read the whole word aloud.* Point just to the left of *slam.* Pause three seconds for students to sound out the word to themselves. Then say: *What's the word?* Quickly sweep your finger under the word. Follow the same routine with the rest of the words. When all the words have been read correctly, ask students to read them again in a different order with a two-second pause.

LESSON MODEL: Method for Reading Decodable Text, p. 235

Since there are no Spanish words that begin with *s*-blends, Spanish-speaking students may add the long-*a* sound when they pronounce words beginning with *sl*.

English/Spanish Language Differences, p. 60

Apply to Decodable Text

To ensure ample practice in sound/spelling correspondences, provide students with connected reading materials. Choose books or passages in which most of the words are wholly decodable and the majority of the remaining words are previously taught irregular words.

Word Work: Sound-by-Sound Dictation

Provide each student with a small dry-erase board and a dry-erase marker. Then follow the steps of the dictation procedure.

1. Introduce the Word

Say: *On our board, we are going to spell some of the words we just blended. Let's do the first word together. The first word is* slam. *If you slam the door too hard, the window will rattle.* Slam. Ask: *What's the word?* (slam)

2. Count the Sounds in the Word

Say: *Now let's say and count the sounds in* slam, */sss/ /lll/ /aaa/ /mmm/.* As you say each sound, hold up a finger and have students do the same. Ask: *How many fingers are we holding up?* (four) Ask: *How many sounds in* slam*?* (four) Say: *Yes, there are four sounds in* slam.

3. Spell the Word Sound by Sound

Say: *The first sound in* slam *is /sss/.* Ask: *What's the first sound in* slam*?* (/ss/) Say: *Yes, /sss/.* Say: *The letter* s *stands for the /sss/ sound.* Ask: *What letter stands for /sss/?* (s) Say: *Print the letter* s *on your board.* Ask: *What's the next sound in* slam*?* (/lll/) Say: *Yes, /lll/.* Ask: *What letter stands for /lll/?* (*letter* l) Say: *Print the letter* l *after the letter* s *on your board.* Ask: *What's the next sound in* slam*?* (/aaa/) Say: *Yes, /aaa/.* Ask: *What letter stands for /aaa/?* (*letter* a) Say: *Print the letter* a *after the letter* l *on your board.* Ask: *What's the last sound in* slam*?* (/mmm/) Say: *Yes, /mmm/.* Ask: *What letter stands for /mmm/?* (*letter* m) Say: *Print the letter* m *after the letter* a *on your board.*

4. Compare and Correct

To monitor students, print the word *slam* on your board. Show your board with the correct spelling of the word to students. Ask them to hold up their boards and compare their spelling with yours. After giving students an opportunity to make corrections, say: *Now, let's say and spell the word together,* slam . . . s-l-a-m.

Then coach students through the dictation procedure for the remaining words (*fat, flat, lap, flap, slap,* and *slat*) by reminding them to count the sounds in the word, spell the words sound by sound, and blend the word to check.

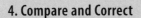

Questions for Observation	Benchmarks
(*Point to* slam.) Can you sound out this word?	Student can blend CCVC words.
The word is *slam*. Can you spell this word? (s-l-a-m)	Student can spell CCVC words.

LESSON MODEL FOR

Explicit Phonics

Benchmarks

- ability to blend CVCe words
- ability to spell CVCe words

Strategy Grade Level

- Grade 1 and/or Intervention

Prerequisites

- all previous Lesson Models in this chapter
- ability to discriminate letter names from letter sounds
- introduced sound/spellings: all single consonants and short vowels

Grouping

- whole class
- small group
- individual

Materials

- picture cards: cake, cap, cape, cat, gate, map, pan, van, wave
- decodable text
- small dry-erase board and dry-erase marker (one per student)

CVCe Patterns

a_e (tape)

e_e (Pete)

i_e (mine)

o_e (note)

u_e (rude)

Reading and Writing CVCe Words

In a CVCe pattern word, a single vowel is followed by a consonant, which, in turn, is followed by a final *e.* In approximately two-thirds of one-syllable CVCe words, the initial vowel stands for its long sound. In the other one-third, the initial vowel sometimes stands for its short sound, as in *give,* or for a sound that is neither short nor long, as in *done* (Carnine et al. 2006). This sample lesson model targets reading and writing CVCe words spelled *a_e.* The same model can be adapted to introduce other CVCe spelling patterns and to enhance phonics instruction in any commercial reading program.

Phonemic Awareness

Display the picture cards of the cap and the cape and name them. Point to the picture card of the cap and say: *The middle sound in* cap *is /a/.* Ask: *What is the middle sound in* cap? (/a/) Point to the picture card of the cape and say: *The middle sound in* cape *is /ā/.* Ask: *What is the middle sound in* cape? (/ā/)

Explain to students that they are going to do a picture sort. Tell them that you will show them a picture and say its name. They will listen and then decide if the picture name has the same middle sound as *cap* or *cape.* Show the picture card of the van. Say: *This is a van.* Ask: *What is the name of this picture?* (van) Ask: *Does* van *have the same middle sound as* cap *or* cape? (cap) Say: *Good. I'll put the picture of the van next to the picture of the cap.* Follow the same procedure with the remaining picture cards: pan, map, cat, cake, gate, wave.

Students should be aware that there are exceptions to this final-*e* rule. For example, in words such as *give* and *live* the vowel *i* represents the short-*i* sound—it does not say its name.

Introduce the CVCe Pattern

Print the word *tap* on the board and have students blend it. Point to the *a* in *tap* and ask students to say the sound of the letter. (/a/) Next, add an *e* to the end of *tap* to make *tape*. Point to the letter *a* in *tape* and say: *The name of this letter is* a *and the sound for this letter is /āāā/. The* e *at the end of* tape *tells us that the sound of the vowel is the same as the vowel's name, /ā/.* Point to the letter *a* again and ask: *How can we identify the sound of this vowel?* (The *e* at the end of the word tells us that the sound is the same as its name.)

Model—Whole Word Blending

Print the word *tape* on the board. Say: *Today I am going to show how to sound out words that end with the letter* e. *Watch me blend the sounds in the first word.*

Point just to the left of *tape* and say: *This word ends with the letter* e. *The letter* e *at the end of this word tells me that the sound of the vowel is the same as the vowel's name.* Point to the letter *a* and say: *The vowel's name is* a. *Its sound is /ā/. Now watch as I blend the word.*

1. Point to the letter *t* and say: /t/.

2. With two fingers, point to the letters *a* and *e* and say: /āāā/.

3. Point to the letter *p* and say: /p/.

4. Point just to the left of *tape* and say: *Now watch as I read the whole word.* Then quickly sweep your finger under the whole word and say *tape*. Say: *Tape is a sticky piece of plastic. I use tape to wrap a present.* Tape.

Repeat the same routine with the word *cane*.

Lead—Whole Word Blending

Print the word *rake* on the board. Say: *Now I am going to lead you in sounding out words. You're going to sound out some words along with me. Remember, the letter* e *at the end of this word tells us that the sound of the vowel is the same as the vowel's name.*

Point just to the left of *rake* and ask: *Is there an* e *at the end of this word?* (yes) Ask: *What does the* e *tell us?* (The sound of the vowel is the same as the vowel's name.) Point to the letter *a* and ask: *What sound does the vowel* a *stand for?* (/ā/)

1. Point to the letter *r* and have students respond along with you: */rrr/.*

2. With two fingers, point to the letters *a* and *e* and have students respond along with you: */āāā/.*

3. Point to the letter *k* and have students respond along with you: */k/.*

4. Point just to the left of *rake* and say: *Let's read this word.* Quickly sweep your finger under the word as you lead students in saying the whole word: *rake.*

Repeat the same routine with the words *tame* and *made.* When you are finished, develop students' vocabulary by going back and clarifying the meaning of any unfamiliar words.

Check—Whole Word Blending

Print the word *game* on the board. Say: *Now it's your turn to sound out words. Remember, an* e *at the end of a word tells us that the sound of the vowel is the same as the vowel's name. When I point to a letter, I want you to say its sound. When I sweep my finger under a word, say the whole word.*

CONTINUED ▷

Whole Word Blending

1. Point to the letter *s*. Ask: *Sound?* (/s/)

2. With two fingers, point to the letters *a* and *e*. Ask: *Sound?* (/ā/)

3. Point to the letter *m*. Ask: *Sound?* (/m/)

4. Point just to the left of *same*. Ask: *What's the word?* Quickly sweep your finger under the word to signal students to respond by saying the whole word. (same)

Repeat the same routine with the words *take* and *rate*. When you are finished, develop students' vocabulary by going back and clarifying the meaning of any unfamiliar words.

CORRECTIVE FEEDBACK If a student or students respond incorrectly, stop immediately and model the correct response for the entire group and then ask the group to respond. A common error is saying a CVC word instead of a CVCe word; for example, saying "sam" for *same*.

SEE ALSO . . .

Word Reading Practice for Automaticity, p. 218

Word Reading Practice for Automaticity

Print the following words on the board: *lake, tap, van, fade, cake, fake, lane, fad, vane, tap.* Say: *Now it's your turn to sound out words. When I point to a word, sound it out to yourselves. When I sweep my finger under the word, read the whole word aloud.* Point just to the left of *lake*. Pause three seconds for students to sound out the word to themselves. Then say: *What's the word?* Quickly sweep your finger under the word. Follow the same routine with the rest of the words. When all the words have been read correctly, ask students to read them again in a different order with a two-second pause.

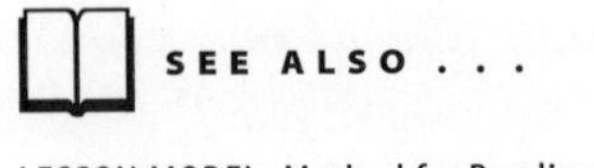

SEE ALSO . . .

LESSON MODEL: Method for Reading Decodable Text, p. 235

Apply to Decodable Text

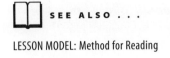

To ensure ample practice in sound/spelling correspondences, provide students with connected reading materials. Choose books or passages in which most of the words are wholly decodable and the majority of the remaining words are previously taught irregular words.

Word Work: Word Building

Say: *We are going to build some words.* Print the word *cane* on the board. Ask: *What's this word?* (cane) Say: *Watch as I change one letter in* cane *to make a new word.* Erase the *n* and replace it with *m.* Say: *I changed the* n *to* m. Ask: *What's the new word?* (came) Erase the *c* and replace it with *s.* Say: *I changed the* c *to* s. Ask: *What's the new word?* (same)

Give each student a small dry-erase board and dry-erase marker. Say: *Now it's your turn to build words. I'll tell you what letters to print on your board. The first letter is* g. *The next letter is* a. *The next letter is* t. *The last letter is* e. Ask: *What's the word?* (gate) Say: *Change the* g *to* l. Ask: *What's the new word?* (late) Continue by having students build more words, for example:
Say: *Change the* l *to* m. Ask: *What's the new word?* (mate)
Say: *Change the* t *to* k. Ask: *What's the new word?* (make)
Say: *Change the* k *to* l. Ask: *What's the new word?* (male)
Say: *Change the* m *to* s. Ask: *What's the new word?* (sale)

When word-building sequence is complete, ask a volunteer to read all the words aloud.

Questions for Observation	Benchmarks
(Point to the letter a *in the word* tape.*)* What is the sound for this letter? (/ā/)	Student can identify the vowel sound in a CVCe word.
(Point just to the left of tape.*)* Can you sound out this word?	Student can blend CVCe words.
The word is *tape.* Can you spell this word? (t-a-p-e)	Student can spell CVCe words.

LESSON MODEL FOR

Explicit Phonics

Benchmarks

- ability to blend words with vowel combinations
- ability to spell words with vowel combinations

Strategy Grade Level

- Grade 1 and/or Intervention

Prerequisites

- Letter-Sound Strategy, p. 110
- all previous Lesson Models in this chapter
- introduced sound/spellings: all single consonants and short vowels

Grouping

- whole class
- small group
- individual

Materials

- letter card *A* (one per student)

Reading and Writing Words with Vowel Combinations

A vowel combination is a group of consecutive letters that represents a particular vowel sound(s) in a number of words. Each vowel combination should first be introduced in isolation (Carnine et al. 2006). Vowel digraphs are vowel combinations. This sample lesson model targets reading and writing words with vowel digraphs *ai* and *ay*. The same model can be adapted and used to introduce other vowel combinations such as other vowel digraphs, diphthongs, variant vowels, and *r*-controlled vowels, and to enhance phonics instruction in any commercial reading program.

Phonemic Awareness with Letters

Give each student a letter card *A*. Have students identify the letter. Remind them that knowing the name of the letter *A* can help them to remember one sound that the letter *A* stands for, /ā/. Tell them that the name of the letter and the sound for the letter are the same. Have students repeat the letter sound. Say: *I'm going to say some words. If you hear the /ā/ sound in the word, hold up the letter* A *and say /ā/. If you do not hear the sound, put the card behind your back and don't say anything. The first word is* hay. Follow the same procedure with the words *paint, day, wake, dad, wag, stay, stack,* and *pat.*

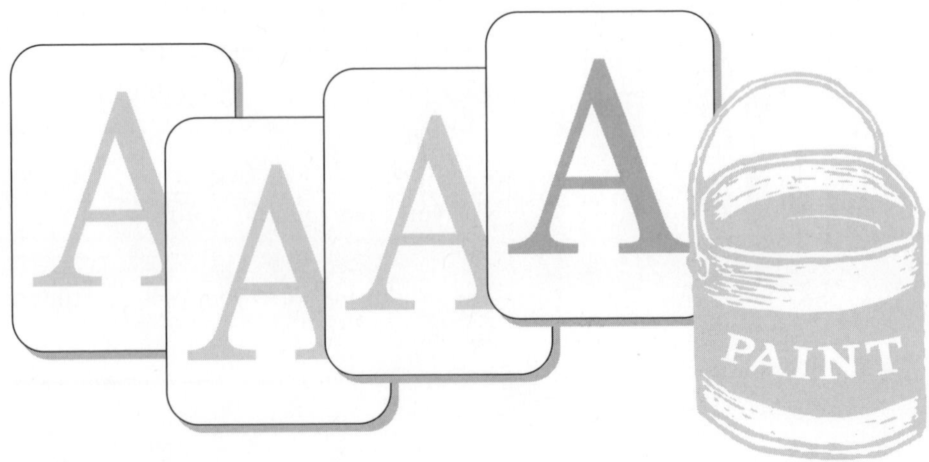

Vowel Combinations

r-controlled vowels

variant vowels

vowel digraphs

vowel diphthongs

vowel teams

SEE ALSO . . .

Phonic Elements (Sound/Spelling Categories), p. 29

Common Vowel Sound/Spellings, p. 34

MODEL
Spelling-Focused Blending

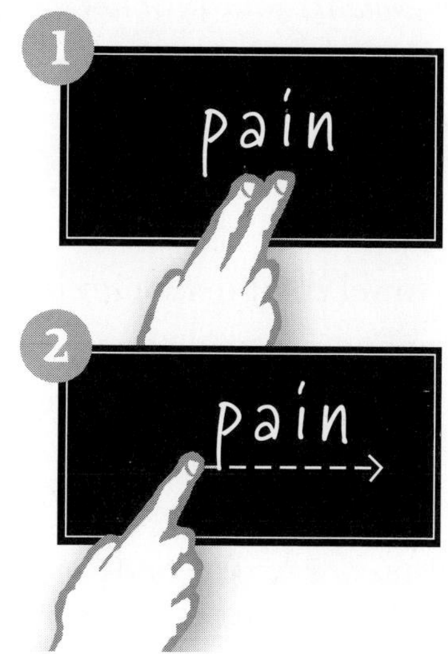

Introduce Vowel Combinations *ai* and *ay*

Print the word *rain* on the board. Say: *This word is* rain. Ask: *What's this word?* (rain) Point with two fingers together to vowel combination *ai*. Say: *When the letters* ai *are together in a word, they usually stand for /ā/.* Erase the *r* and *n* in *rain*. Say: *When I point to the letters* ai, *say /ā/.* Point with two fingers together to *ai*. Ask: *What sound does this vowel combination usually stand for?* (/ā/)

Print the word *pay* on the board. Say: *This word is* pay. Ask: *What's this word?* (pay) Point with two fingers together to vowel combination *ay*. Say: *When the letters* ay *are together in a word, they usually stand for /ā/.* Erase the *p* in *pay*. Say: *When I point to the letters* ay, *say /ā/.* Point with two fingers together to *ay*. Ask: *What sound does this vowel combination usually stand for?* (/ā/)

Model—Spelling-Focused Blending

Print the word *pain* on the board. Say: *Today I am going to show you how to read words with vowel combinations* ai *and* ay. *Watch me sound out the first word.*

1. Point with two fingers together to vowel combination *ai* in the word *pain*. Say: *Sound?* With two fingers together, simultaneously tap under the vowel combination *ai* and say: */ā/.*

2. Then point just to the left of *pain* and say: *Now watch as I read this word.* Pause for two seconds and then quickly sweep your finger under the whole word and say: The word is *pain*. Then ask: *What's the word?* (pain)

Now repeat the same routine with the word *say* and the vowel combination *ay*.

Lead—Spelling-Focused Blending

Print the word *may* on the board. Say: *Now I am going to lead you in sounding out words. You're going to sound out some words along with me. When I point to the vowel combination, we will say the sound. Then when I sweep my finger under the word, we will say the whole word.*

1. Point with two fingers together to *ay* in the word *may.* Say: *Sound?* To signal students to respond with you, simultaneously tap under the vowel combination and say: */ā/.*

2. Then point just to the left of *may* and say*: Let's read this word.* Pause for two seconds and then quickly sweep your finger under the whole word as you lead students in saying the word *may.*

Repeat the same routine with the word *sail* and the vowel combination *ai.*

Check—Spelling-Focused Blending

Print the word *ray* on the board. Say: *Now it's your turn to read words with vowel combinations. Remember, when I point to a vowel combination, say the sound. Then when I sweep my finger under the word, say the whole word.*

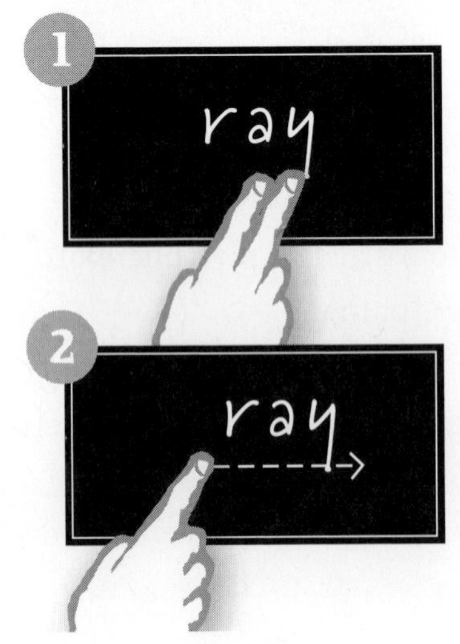

1. Point with two fingers together to vowel combination *ay* in the word *ray.* Ask: *Sound?* With two fingers together, tap under the vowel combination *ay* to signal student response. (/ā/)

2. Then point just to the left of *ray.* Pause for two seconds and ask: *What's the word?* Then quickly sweep your finger under the whole word to signal students to respond. (ray)

Repeat the same routine with the words *mail, hay,* and *maid.*

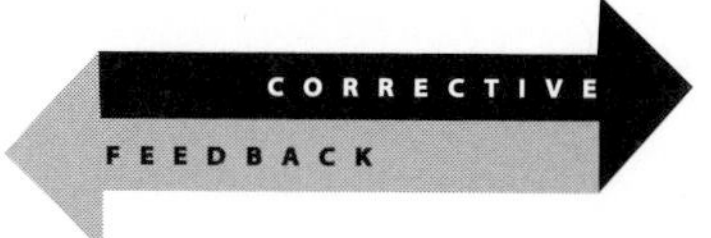

CORRECTIVE FEEDBACK If a student or students respond incorrectly, stop immediately and model the correct response for the entire group and then ask the entire group to respond. For blending errors, first model blending the word and then lead students in blending it again. For vowel combination errors, immediately say the correct sound, for example, /ā/. Then point with two fingers to the vowel combination *ai* and ask: *Sound?* (/ā/) Say: *Yes, the sound is /ā/.*

vane paid fad slip rat lake tray fake train made tap

Word Reading Practice for Automaticity

Word Reading Practice for Automaticity, p. 218

Print the following words on the board: *lake, paid, rat, slip, made, tray, train, fake, lane, fad, vane, tap.* Say: *Now it's your turn to sound out words. When I point to a word, sound it out to yourselves. When I sweep my finger under the word, read the whole word aloud.* Point just to the left of *lake.* Pause three seconds for students to sound out the word to themselves. Then say: *What's the word?* Quickly sweep your finger under the word. Follow the same routine with the rest of the words. When all the words have been read correctly, ask students to read them again in a different order with a two-second pause.

Apply to Decodable Text

LESSON MODEL: Method for Reading Decodable Text, p. 235

To ensure ample practice in sound/spelling correspondences, provide students with connected reading materials. Choose books or passages in which most of the words are wholly decodable and the majority of the remaining words are previously taught irregular words.

Word Work: Sound-by-Sound Dictation, p. 219

Word Work: Whole Word Dictation

This procedure is the same as that for sound-by-sound dictation, but rather than be guided to spell words sound by sound, students are prompted to "think about" the sounds they hear in the words.

1. Introduce the Word

Provide each student with a sheet of paper and a pencil. Say: *On your paper, we are going to spell some of the words we just blended. Let's do the first word together. The first word is* rain. Rain. *The dark clouds will probably bring some rain.* Rain. Ask: *What's the word?* (rain)

2. Count the Sounds in the Word

Say: *Now let's say and count the sounds in* rain, */rrr/ /ā/ /nnnn/.* As you say each sound, hold up a finger and have students do the same. Ask: *How many fingers are we holding up?* (three) Ask: *How many sounds in* rain*?* (three) Say: *Yes, there are three sounds in* rain.

3. Spell the Word Sound by Sound

Say: *Think about the three sounds in* rain. *Now, print the word* rain *sound by sound on your papers.*

4. Compare and Correct

To monitor students, print the word *rain* on the board. Ask students to hold up their papers and compare their spelling with yours. After giving students an opportunity to make corrections, say: *Now, let's say and spell the word together,* rain . . . r-a-i-n.

Then coach students through the dictation procedure for the remaining words: *wait, pain, plain, sail, may, way, pay,* and *play.*

OBSERVE & ASSESS

Questions for Observation	Benchmarks
(Point to the vowel combination ai *in the word* rain.*)* What is the sound for these letters? (/ā/)	Student can identify the sound for vowel combination *ai.*
(Point to rain.*)* Can you sound out this word?	Student can blend words with vowel combinations.
The word is *rain.* Can you spell this word? (r-a-i-n)	Student can spell words with vowel combinations.

LESSON MODEL FOR

Phonograms

Benchmarks

- ability to recognize common phonograms in words
- ability to blend onset and rime to produce a new word

Strategy Grade Level

- Grades 1 – 2 and/or Intervention

Prerequisites

- all previous Lesson Models in this chapter
- ability to blend onset and rime
- introduced sound/spellings: all single consonants and short vowels; /ī/ *igh*

Grouping

- whole class
- small group
- individual

Materials

- magnetic letters
- decodable text

Reading and Writing Words with Phonograms

Phonogram instruction should build on the knowledge gained from systematic, explicit phonics instruction in sound/spelling correspondences. Students must know the sounds of the individual letters that make up a phonogram, or rime, before being introduced to it as a unit. This sample lesson model targets the phonogram *–ight*. The same model can be adapted and used to introduce other common short- and long-vowel phonograms and to enhance phonics instruction in any commercial reading program.

Phonemic Awareness

Tell students that you want them to substitute one sound for another to make a new word.

Say: *The word is* sock. *Change /s/ to /l/.*
Ask: *What's the new word?* (lock)

Say: *The word is* lock. *Change /l/ to /r/.*
Ask: *What's the new word?* (rock)

Say: *The word is* rock. *Change /r/ to /d/.*
Ask: *What's the new word?* (dock)

Say: *The word is* mice. *Change /m/ to /d/.*
Ask: *What's the new word?* (dice)

Say: *The word is* dice. *Change /d/ to /r/.*
Ask: *What's the new word?* (rice)

Say: *The word is* rice. *Change /r/ to /n/.*
Ask: *What's the new word?* (nice)

SEE ALSO . . .

Onset-Rime, p. 38

Introduce the Phonogram *–ight*

Tell students that words can contain similar letter patterns and that recognizing these common patterns can help them to read words. Explain that one common letter pattern is *–ight.* Print the phonogram *–ight* on the board. Point with three fingers together to *igh* and say the sound, /ī/. Next, point to the letter *t* and have students say the sound, /t/. Quickly sweep your finger under the phonogram and say *–ight.* Have students say *–ight* with you and then on their own.

Print the word *light* on the board. Cover up the onset *l* and then identify the phonogram, or rime, *–ight.* Say: *These four letters form a common letter pattern, which is pronounced /ight/.* Ask: *What's the letter pattern?* (–ight) Follow the same procedure with the words *bright, night,* and *right.*

Onset-Rime Blending

Using magnetic letters, write the phonogram, or rime, *–ight.* Ask a volunteer to identify the letter pattern. Place the letter *f* before *–ight.* Point to the letter *f* and ask students to say the sound, /fff/. Now quickly sweep your finger under the onset *f* and rime *–ight* and pronounce the word *fight.* Then ask students to blend the onset and rime on their own. Repeat the same procedure with the onsets *fl (flight), m (might), s (sight), sl (slight),* and *t (tight).*

SEE ALSO . . .

LESSON MODEL: Method for Reading Decodable Text, p. 235

Apply to Decodable Text

To ensure ample practice of sound/spelling correspondences and phonograms, provide students with connected reading materials. Choose books or passages in which most of the words are wholly decodable and the majority of the remaining words are previously taught irregular words.

Word Work: Word Building

For this cumulative review activity, students must know the following sound/spellings: all single consonants, /s/*c*, /k/*ck*, /i/*i*, and /ī/*i_e*. Print the following phonograms on the board and have students identify them: *–ice, –ick, –ide, –ight, –ine,* and *–ip*. Challenge students to select a phonogram, or rime, and create as many one-syllable words as they can by adding an onset, such as a single consonant, consonant blend, or consonant digraph. For example, for the phonogram *–ice* they might list the words *dice, lice, mice, nice, price, rice, slice, splice, twice,* and *vice*. When students are finished, have them compare their lists of words.

Questions for Observation	Benchmarks
(Point to the word light.*)* Do you see a common letter pattern in this word? (yes, –ight)	Student can identify a phonogram in a word.
(Add an m *to* –ight.*)* What is this word? (might)	Student can blend onset and rime.

LESSON MODEL FOR

Decodable Text

Benchmark

- ability to accurately and fluently apply phonics knowledge to reading decodable text

Strategy Grade Level

- Kindergarten – Grade 1 and/or Intervention

Prerequisites

- all previous Lesson Models in this chapter
- introduced sound/spellings: all single consonants, short vowels, consonant digraphs, /k/*ck*, /ng/*ng*
- introduced irregular words *a, he, of, out, the, to, too, was*

Grouping

- whole class
- small group
- individual

Materials

- decodable text

Method for Reading Decodable Text

Decodable text is usually a small book or passage in which most of the words are wholly decodable and the majority of the remaining words are previously taught irregular words. These emergent reader texts provide an opportunity for students to practice and apply newly acquired phonics knowledge and to develop fluency and automaticity. In this sample lesson model, a sample story is used to represent decodable text found in a typical beginning reading program. The same model can be adapted and used to enhance the reading of decodable texts connected to any commercial reading program.

Review Irregular Words

Students should be able to automatically and accurately read all previously taught irregular words found in this story: *a, he, of, out, the, to, too,* and *was.* For instructional strategies to introduce and practice these words, refer to the sample lesson models in Chapter 7: Irregular Word Reading.

It was six.
The sun was
not up
Sam ha
get out
Sam fed his
cat. Then he
had ham
s.
Sam
by Simon Dibley
Illustrated by Art Fisher
SAMPLE STORY

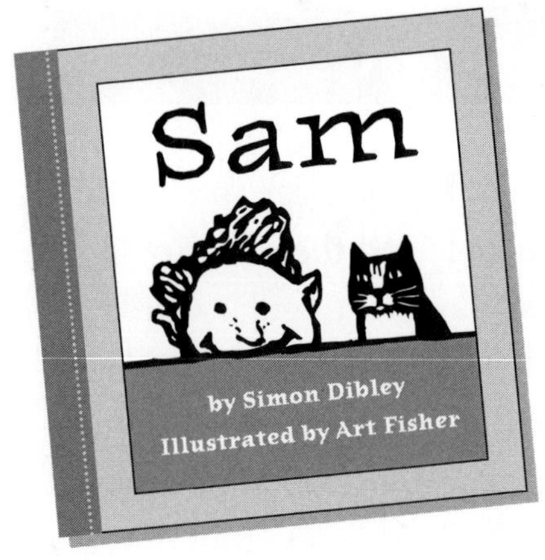

LESSON MODEL: Print Referencing in Shared Storybook Reading, p. 78

Introduce the Book

1. Identify the Title, Author, and Illustrator

Pass out the decodable book to each student. Say: *Today we're going to read a book together. First I will read with you, and then you will get a chance to read on your own.* Show the front cover of the book and say: *The name of a book is called the title.* Point to the title. Say: *The title of this book is* Sam. *Now you point to the title.* Monitor as students point to the title of the book. Ask: *What's the title of this book?* (*Sam*) Say: *Yes,* Sam.

Say: *A person who writes a book is called the author.* Point to the author's name and say: *Simon Dibley is the author of this book,* Sam. *Now you point to the author's name.* Monitor students as they point to the author's name. Ask: *Who is the author of this book?* (Simon Dibley) Ask: *What does an author do?* (writes books)

Say: *The person who makes the pictures that go with a story is called an illustrator.* Point to the illustrator's name and say: *Art Fisher is the illustrator of this book. Now you point to the illustrator's name.* Monitor students as they point to the illustrator's name. Ask: *Who is the illustrator of this book?* (Art Fisher) Ask: *What does an illustrator do?* (makes the pictures that go with a story)

Sound-by-Sound Blending, p. 181
Continuous Blending, p. 181

2. Browse the Book

Say: *Now it's time to browse the book. When we browse a book, we look at the illustrations and words to get an idea of what the story is about. We also look for any difficult words.* Allow students to quickly browse through the book. Have them share any difficult words they may have encountered while browsing. As they share these words, print them on the board. Then model blending the words using sound-by-sound or continuous blending.

SEE ALSO . . .

Research-Based Methods of Repeated Oral Reading, p. 365

Whole Group: Read the Book One Page at a Time

Lead students in reading each page twice before moving on to the next page—first with a whisper read, then with a choral read. Say: *Now we will read the book* Sam. *We'll read it one page at a time. First you will whisper read a page to yourself, and then we'll read aloud the same page together.*

 It was six. The sun was not up yet. Sam had to get out of bed.	Sam fed his cat. Then he had ham and eggs. 

1. WHISPER READ Say: *Watch as I whisper read the first page.* In a whisper voice, read: *"It was six. The sun was not up yet. Sam had to get out of bed."* While reading, be sure to track, or move your finger, under each word. Say: *Now it's your turn to whisper read. Everyone point under the first word of the page.* Pause for students to place their finger under the first word and then say: *Whisper read the page to yourself. Remember to point to each word as you read. Ready, begin.* Monitor students as they whisper read the page, providing help for specific students when needed.

2. CHORAL READ When more than half of the students have finished whisper reading the first page, say: *Now let's read aloud the same page together. Go back to the beginning of the page and point under the first word.* Pause for students to place their finger under the first word and then say: *Now everyone read aloud. Remember to point to each word as you read. Ready, begin.* Choral read the first page with students, ensuring that all students are responding and tracking under the words as they read.

Read the rest of the book with students in the same manner, first whisper reading and then choral reading each page.

Sam got his pack and cap. He got in a red van.

Sam met his pal Jan. Jan has a dog.

Sam swings and Jan jumps.

The dog can jump, too!

If a student or students consistently take more than two seconds to blend a word or words, provide additional blending instruction and practice. Using sound-by-sound or continuous blending, have students blend the words in isolation.

CORRECTIVE FEEDBACK If a student or students misidentify a word, model the correct response for the entire group. For example, point to the word *pal* and say: *Stop. The word is* pal. *Put your finger on the word.* Ask: *What's the word?* (pal) Say: *Yes,* pal. *Go back to the beginning of the sentence and reread it.*

Individual Turns: Read the Entire Book

Say: *Now we'll read the entire book, but this time I'll call on individual students to take a turn reading aloud. When someone is reading aloud, I want you to read along silently and point to each word as it is being read.* Have students take turns reading aloud a sentence or two at a time as the group listens and follows along. To encourage attentiveness, randomly call on students to read. Provide corrective feedback as needed.

Respond to Literal Questions

Encourage students to respond to the story. Ask literal questions about the story, such as:
When did Sam get out of bed? (He got out of bed at six.)
What did Sam eat for breakfast? (He had ham and eggs.)
What color is Sam's van? (The van is red.)
Who is Jan? (Jan is Sam's pal.)
What do Jan and her dog like to do? (They like to jump.)

As students tell the answer and show the sentence or page that supports their answer, encourage the rest of the class to point to the answer in the text. You might also have the volunteer read the sentence containing the answer to the question.

When answering questions, students should show what sentence or page supports their answers. Responses should be in complete sentences. Support vocabulary development by asking questions such as: *Sam got in a van. What are names of other types of transportation?* (cars, trucks, buses)

Partners: Reread the Entire Book

Assign students reading partners. Say: *You're going to practice reading the book two more times with your partner. You will take turns reading a page at a time. When you are the listener, remember to read along silently and point to each word as it is being read. If your partner makes a mistake, say the correct word. If you are the reader and your partner corrects you, stop. Be sure to repeat the word and then go back to the beginning of the sentence and reread it.* Allow students time to practice reading the book. Monitor students, listening to each pair read. If needed, provide more practice in small groups.

OBSERVE & ASSESS

Question for Observation	Benchmark
(Select a sentence.) Can you read this sentence out loud?	Student can read text accurately and fluently.

CHAPTER

7

Irregular Word Reading

what? why? when? how?

what?

Irregular Word Reading

An irregular word is basically a word that the student does not have the phonics skills to read.

—CARNINE ET AL., 2006

IRREGULAR WORDS
cannot be decoded by sounding out

REGULAR WORDS
can be decoded by sounding out

HIGH-FREQUENCY WORDS
regular and irregular words that appear often in printed text

Not all words are regular, or can be read by sounding them out. An irregular word contains one or more sound/spelling correspondences that a student does not know and therefore cannot use to decode the word. Because students can't sound out irregular words by applying their phonics knowledge, they have to learn to identify these words as wholes, or automatically by sight. Many of the most common (i.e., high-frequency) words in English are irregular.

Within a beginning reading program, there are basically two types of irregular words: words that are permanently irregular and words that are temporarily irregular (Carnine et al. 2006). Permanently irregular words contain one or more sound/spellings that are not pronounced conventionally and are unique to that word or a few words. For example, the word *said* (/sed/) is permanently irregular because short *e* spelled *ai* is a low-frequency sound/spelling that is generally not explicitly taught within a reading program's phonics scope and sequence. Other examples of this type of irregular word are *of, one, two, been, could,* and *once.*

Temporarily irregular words may be irregular at one point in a beginning reading program but may eventually become regular after all the sound/spellings in the word have been taught. In other words, as students learn more sound/spellings, some of the irregular words that they learned by sight become wholly decodable words. For example, in the early part of a reading program the word *for* may be considered an irregular word because the sound/spelling /or/*or* had not yet been taught. After /or/*or* is introduced in the reading program, the word *for* becomes wholly decodable.

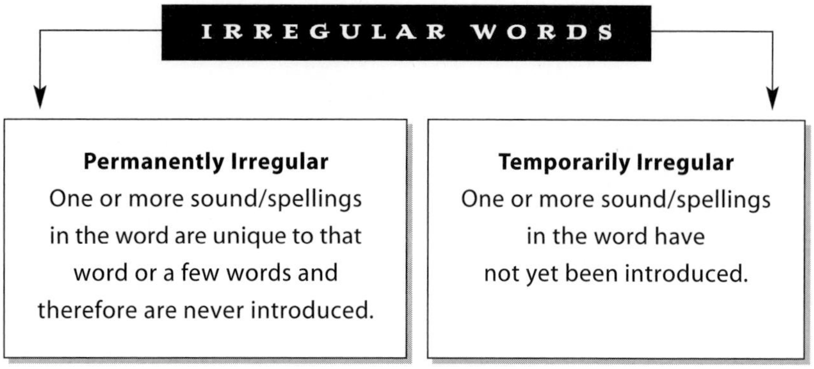

IRREGULAR WORDS

Permanently Irregular	**Temporarily Irregular**
One or more sound/spellings in the word are unique to that word or a few words and therefore are never introduced.	One or more sound/spellings in the word have not yet been introduced.

CCSS READING STANDARDS

Foundational Skills

Phonics and Word Recognition

Read common high-frequency words by sight. (RF.K.3c)

Recognize and read grade-appropriate irregularly spelled words. (RF.1.3g; RF.2.3f; RF.3.3d)

CCSS LANGUAGE STANDARDS

Conventions of Standard English

Use conventional spelling for frequently occurring irregular words. (L.1.2d)

Use conventional spelling for high-frequency and other studied words. (L.3.2e)

High-Frequency Irregular Words in Printed Text

Only 100 words account for approximately 50 percent of words in text used in schools and colleges (Zeno et al. 1995). Out of this list of 100 high-frequency words, almost 25 percent are permanently irregular. These high-frequency irregular words appear often in printed text and therefore are crucial for comprehension. They include function words (e.g., articles, prepositions, pronouns, and conjunctions) and are the grammatical glue that holds sentences together and cues a reader to sentence structure.

High-Frequency Word Lists
Dolch Basic Sight Vocabulary (Buckingham and Dolch 1936)
1000 Instant Words (Fry 2004)
The Educator's Word Frequency Guide (Zeno et al. 1995)
Basic Elementary Reading Vocabularies (Harris and Jacobson 1972)
The American Heritage Word Frequency Book (Carroll, Davies, and Richman 1971)

Most Frequent Words in School and College Text			
Words 1–25	**Words 26–50**	**Words 51–75**	**Words 76–100**
the	not	people	most
of	have	them	its
and	this	other	made
to	but	more	over
a	by	will	see
in	were	into	first
is	one	your	new
that	all	which	very
it	she	do	my
was	when	then	also
for	an	many	down
you	their	these	make
he	there	no	now
on	her	time	way
as	can	been	each
are	we	who	called
they	what	like	did
with	about	could	just
be	up	has	after
his	said	him	water
at	out	how	through
or	if	than	get
from	some	two	because
had	would	may	back
I	so	only	where

Most Frequent Words in School and College Text *(continued)*

Words 101–115	Words 116–130	Words 131–145	Words 146–160
know	work	should	life
little	any	small	three
such	go	old	went
even	use	think	those
much	things	take	own
our	well	still	help
must	look	place	every
before	another	find	here
good	around	off	house
too	man	different	might
long	great	part	between
me	same	found	never
years	came	us	home
day	come	world	thought
used	right	away	put

From *The Educator's Word Frequency Guide* (1995) by Susan M. Zeno, Stephen H. Ivens, Robert T. Millard, and Raj Duvvuri. Brewster, NY: TASA.

From the first column in the list of Most Frequent Words in School and College Text, identify the five words that could be considered permanently irregular—words that contain one or more sound/spellings unique to that word or a few words. Explain your selection. (See Answer Key, p. 800.)

Good readers in first grade require a minimum of four practice trials to retain irregular sight words in memory.

—REITSMA, 1983

SEE ALSO . . .

LESSON MODELS

Sound-Out Strategy, p. 252

Spell-Out Strategy, p. 255

Teaching Irregular Word Reading

The set of irregular words selected for instruction is generally drawn from the upcoming stories, passages, or other connected texts that students will be reading. Whether a word is permanently irregular, such as *two,* or temporarily irregular, such as *for,* new irregular words should be systematically and explicitly introduced. Instruction should focus students' attention on all the letters in a word.

Practice facilitates students' automatic recognition of irregular words. Since students require considerable exposure to an irregular word before they can be expected to recognize it on sight, previously taught words should be practiced and then cumulatively reviewed on a daily basis (Carnine et al. 2006; Chall and Popp 1996). Repeated exposure to these words in lists, grids, and connected text increases the probability of their automatic identification by sight and gives students opportunities to recognize them in isolation and in context.

The more difficult an irregular word, the more practice is necessary. There are two factors that determine the difficulty of an irregular word: (1) the number of irregularities in the pronunciation of its sound/spelling correspondences and (2) whether or not the word is in a student's oral vocabulary (Carnine et al. 2006). For example, the irregular word *would* will require more practice than *was,* and the irregular word *busy* will be easier for students to remember than *gauge.*

Word Banks and Word Walls

Word banks and word walls provide a method for teachers to organize irregular words that have been taught and learned so that students can practice them (O'Connor 2007). Students can each keep a personal word bank, or collection, of previously taught irregular words. Word walls are places to display previously taught words. The words can be grouped alphabetically or by similar letter patterns (e.g., *could, would, should*). They can be practiced as a whole class activity, in partners, or individually.

WORD WALL

A	B	C	D	E	F	G	H	I	J	K	L	M
and as are at all an about	be but by	can			for from		he his had have her	in is it if				
N	**O**	**P**	**Q**	**R**	**S**	**T**	**U**	**V**	**W**	**X**	**Y**	**Z**
not	of on or one out				she said some so	the to that they this their there	up		was with were when we what would		you	

SEE ALSO . . .

Selecting Words for English-Language Learners (ELLs), p. 425

Sequence of Introduction

Carnine et al. (2006) suggest the following factors to use when determining or evaluating the sequence of introduction of irregular words within a reading program.

WORD FREQUENCY Introduce high-frequency irregular words before low-frequency irregular words. If too many irregular words appear in an upcoming story, prioritize by teaching only the words that are more likely to appear in future reading.

WORD SIMILARITY Some pairs of irregular words are frequently confused by students, such as *of–off, there–their,* and *were–where.* These pairs of words should not be introduced too close to each other. Introducing the second potentially confusing word at a later time allows students to master the first irregular word.

SEE ALSO . . .

Phonograms, p. 38

WORD RELATIONSHIP Some pairs of irregular words belong to the same word family; they contain similar letter patterns, or phonograms. Irregular words that have a phonogram in common, such as *could, should,* and *would,* should be introduced in sets.

why? # Irregular Word Reading

> Instructional strategies for teaching irregular words are different from those used for teaching regular words.
>
> —HARRIS & VON HARRISON, 1988

Decoding is a highly reliable strategy for identifying regular words, but irregular words do not always conform to what is taught in phonics instruction. Beginning readers do not learn irregular words as quickly or accurately as regular words; they tend to read these words more slowly and inaccurately (Nation and Snowling 1998). Therefore, it is important to provide students with explicit instruction and systematic practice in identifying irregular words (Vellutino and Scanlon 2002). Since many of the frequently used function words in beginning reading texts are irregular, students must learn to identify these words as wholes. Although most function words contain little meaning, they affect the flow and coherence of text (Blevins 2006). Knowledge of these irregular words is necessary for fluent reading.

Research Findings . . .

The rewards for learning [high-frequency] words thoroughly and reliably are smoother, less effortful reading and perhaps a greater inclination to read independently (which in turn may also increase a student's store of instantly recognized words).

—O'CONNOR, 2007

. . . if developing readers cannot instantly identify [high-frequency] words, they are unlikely to become fluent because of the widespread presence of these words.

—PIKULSKI, 2006

. . . children don't learn "irregular" words as easily or quickly as they do "regular" words. . . . Therefore, children need to be taught "irregular" high-frequency words with explicit instruction.

—BLEVINS, 2006

Suggested Reading . . .

Multisensory Teaching of Basic Language Skills, 3rd Edition (2011) edited by Judith R. Birsh. Baltimore, MD: Paul H. Brookes.

Phonics from A to Z: A Practical Guide (2006) by Wiley Blevins. New York: Scholastic.

Research-Based Methods of Reading Instruction, Grades K–3 (2004) by Sharon Vaughn & Sylvia Linan-Thompson. Alexandria, VA: ASCD.

Teaching Struggling and At-Risk Readers: A Direct Instruction Approach (2006) by Douglas W. Carnine, Jerry Silbert, Edward J. Kame'enui, Sara G. Tarver & Kathleen Jungjohann. Boston: Allyn & Bacon.

Teaching Word Recognition: Effective Strategies for Students with Learning Difficulties (2007) by Rollanda E. O'Connor. New York: Guilford.

when?

Irregular Word Reading

It is important not to overwhelm children with too rapid an introduction of irregular words.

—CARNINE ET AL., 2006

CCSS READING STANDARDS

Foundational Skills

Phonics and Word Recognition

KINDERGARTEN
Read common high-frequency words by sight. (RF.K.3c)

GRADES 1-3
Recognize and read grade-appropriate irregularly spelled words. (RF.1.3g; RF.2.3f; RF.3.3d)

When to Teach

Irregular words need to be systematically introduced in a reasonable order, practiced, and then cumulatively reviewed. Introduce irregular words after students can read regular CVC words at a rate of about one word every three seconds. Waiting to introduce irregular words will strengthen students' reliance on identifying a word by sounding it out rather than by identifying it as a whole (Carnine et al. 2006). Irregular words, particularly high-frequency irregular words, are learned through repeated encounters in text (Carreker 2005). A new irregular word should be introduced at least one lesson before students read it in connected text (Simmons and Kame'enui 2000).

Although pace is a critical instructional consideration, there is little research on the exact number of words to introduce at a time. Carnine et al. (2006) observe that it is important not to overwhelm students by introducing too many words at once. Simmons and Kame'enui (2000) recommend starting out with one irregular word per lesson and then gradually progressing to no more than five to seven new words per lesson as students demonstrate their ability to retain and read the words in isolation and connected text. Student performance should determine the "right" number of irregular words to introduce at one time; the rate should be realistic. Some students may need extra practice to develop automaticity in reading irregular words.

Guidelines for Teaching Irregular Words

Introduce high-frequency words before low frequency.

Do not introduce too many words at once.

Introduce new words before they appear in connected text.

Cumulatively review previously taught words every day.

Provide opportunities for students to use the words.

When to Assess and Intervene

Teachers should assess students' mastery of high-frequency regular and irregular words to inform classroom instruction. The process for monitoring irregular words is similar to that of regular words. However, each type of word should be monitored separately (Vaughn and Linan-Thompson 2004). Frequently monitor student progress in the mastery of irregular words to determine whether students are in fact learning the words being taught. For students performing at or above grade level, monitor progress every four to six weeks. For students who are slightly below grade level, monitor progress every two weeks (Carnine et al. 2006). Monitor student progress weekly for those who are significantly below grade level. To monitor word reading automaticity, simply ask students to read aloud from a set of previously introduced irregular words. Teachers can also keep a record of any irregular words students have problems with while reading connected text.

Purpose	✓ Irregular Word Reading Assessment	Publisher
Screening	CORE Literacy Library *Assessing Reading: Multiple Measures, 2nd Edition* ▸ CORE Graded High-Frequency Word Survey	Arena Press
Screening	The Irregular Words Test (IWT)	Developed by John Shefelbine http://www.reg8.net/users/0031/docs/iiirregwords10_06.pdf

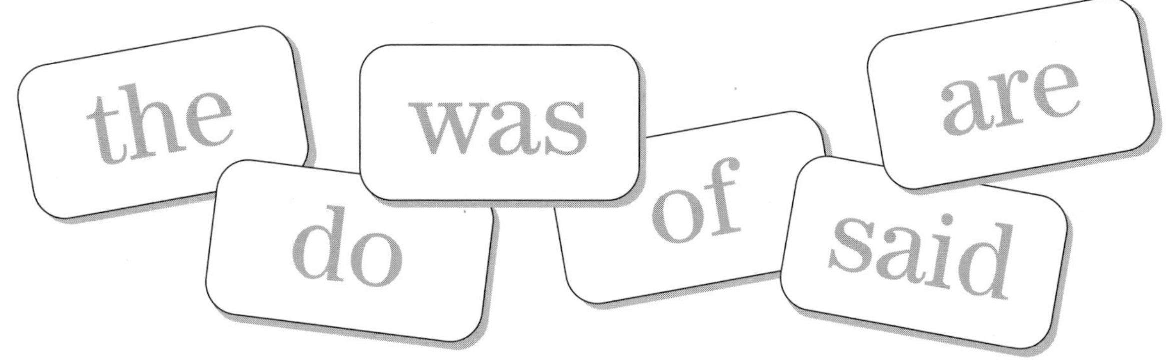

how?

Irregular Word Reading

LESSON MODEL FOR

Irregular Word Reading

Benchmarks

- ability to read and spell irregular words in which the sound/spellings are unique to that word or a few words
- ability to quickly and accurately identify irregular words

Strategy Grade Level

- Kindergarten – Grade 2 and/or Intervention

Prerequisite

- introduced sound/spellings: single consonants and short vowels

Grouping

- whole class
- small group
- individual

Materials

- word cards *do, of, said, to, was*
- magnetic letters (one set per student)
- small dry-erase boards and dry-erase markers (one per student)
- decodable text

Sound-Out Strategy

The sound-out strategy for introducing irregular words is based on a format described in *Teaching Struggling and At-Risk Readers: A Direct Instruction Approach* (Carnine et al. 2006). According to the authors of this book, the procedure for introducing the first 15 to 25 irregular words should require students to examine all the letters in a word and then point out the irregularity in one or more of the word's sound/spelling correspondences. This sample lesson model targets five irregular words. The same model can be adapted and used to introduce irregular words found in the connected texts of any commercial reading program.

Introduce Irregular Words

Tell students that they are going to learn how to read some irregular words. Explain that irregular words are tricky words that cannot be sounded out in the regular way. Display the word card for *was.* Point to *was* and say: *This is a tricky word. The word is* was. Ask: *What's the word?* Quickly sweep your finger under the whole word to signal students to respond. (was)

Say: *Now I'm going to sound out this word.* Using continuous blending, point to each letter and pronounce its most common sound, /wăăăsss/. Say: *That's how we sound out the word. But this is the way we say it, "wuz."* Point to your ear and ask: *How do we actually say it?* (/wuz/) Point again just to the left of *was* and say: *Now it's your turn to sound out this word the regular way—by saying the most common sound for each letter.* Point to each

letter as students pronounce its most common sound. Then point to one ear and say: *But how do we actually say the word? /wuz/.* Point to your ear again and say: *Again, how do we actually say it?* (/wuz/)

Follow the same procedure with the irregular words *do* (/dŏ/), *of* (/ŏv/), *said* (/sāid/), and *to* (/tŏ/).

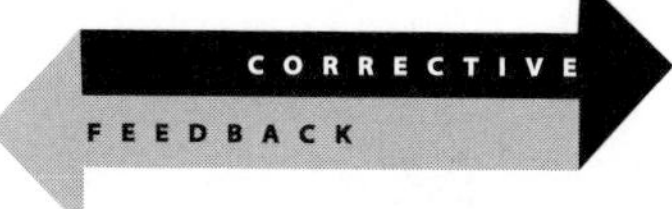

CORRECTIVE FEEDBACK If a student or students respond incorrectly, stop immediately and model the correct response for the entire group. For errors, such as saying "wăăăsss" for "wuz," point to your ear and say: *We actually say /wuz/.* Point to your ear again and ask: *How do we actually say it?* (/wuz/)

Practice Irregular Words

Provide each student with a set of magnetic letters and a magnetic surface. Display the word card for *was.* Ask students to identify the word. Then direct students to spell the word with magnetic letters. Next, have them touch each letter as they spell the word out loud. (w-a-s) Finally, tell them to say the word after they spell it. Repeat the same procedure with the irregular words *do, of, said,* and *to.*

Provide each student with a small dry-erase board and a dry-erase marker. Display the word card for *do.* Ask students to identify the word. Say: *I want you to write* do *as big as you can on your dry-erase board.* Then direct them to write *do* in a couple of different ways, such as writing it as small as they can or in all uppercase letters. Finally, have students write the word from memory. Repeat the same procedure with the irregular words *of, said, to,* and *was.*

do was
DO OF
Said
SAID
TO to

Word Reading Practice for Automaticity

Make a word recognition grid, like the one shown on the following page. Each of the five horizontal rows contains the same previously introduced irregular words in a different order.

WORD RECOGNITION GRID

was	do	said	of	to
do	was	of	to	said
said	to	was	do	of
of	do	said	was	to
to	of	do	said	was

Use interactive whiteboard technology to display the grid. Tell students that they are going to practice reading words that they have already learned. To warm up, point and sweep under each of the words in the top row and say, for example: *This word is* was. Then ask: *What's this word?* (was)

After the warm-up, say: *Now you are going to practice reading the words. When I point and sweep under a word, read it aloud. Ready?* Then point to each word in order, starting with the top row and working down and then across each row. Review troublesome words by pointing to them at random as students name them.

SEE ALSO . . .

LESSON MODEL: Method for Reading Decodable Text, p. 235

Apply to Decodable Text

To ensure ample practice of irregular words, provide students with connected reading materials. Choose books or passages in which most of the words are wholly decodable and the majority of the remaining words are previously taught irregular words.

Question for Observation	Benchmark
(Point to an irregular word.) What is this word?	Student can read an irregular word.

LESSON MODEL FOR

Irregular Word Reading

Benchmarks

- ability to read and spell words that are considered irregular because not all the sound/spellings in the words have been introduced yet
- ability to quickly and accurately identify irregular words

Strategy Grade Level

- Kindergarten – Grade 2 and/or Intervention

Grouping

- whole class
- small group
- individual

Materials

- word cards *and, for, in, is, the*
- magnetic letters (one set per student)
- small dry-erase boards and dry-erase markers (one per student)
- decodable text

Spell-Out Strategy

The spell-out strategy for introducing irregular words is based on a format described in *SIPPS* (Shefelbine and Newman 2004). This sample lesson model targets words that are irregular at one point in a reading program but may not be irregular permanently. The same model can be adapted and used to introduce irregular words in which the sound/spellings are unique to that word or a few words. Both types of irregular words are found in the connected texts of any commercial reading program.

Introduce Irregular Words

Tell students that they are going to learn to read some irregular words. Explain that irregular words cannot be sounded out in the regular way. Display the word card for *for.* Say: *Here's the first irregular word. This word is* for. *This book is for you.*

READ Point just to the left of *for.* Pause briefly and then ask: *What's this word?* Quickly sweep your finger under the whole word to signal students to respond. (for)

SPELL Point just to the left of *for.* Ask: *How do you spell* for*?* (f-o-r) Quickly point to each letter as students spell the word.

READ Point just to the left of *for.* Pause briefly and then ask: *What's this word?* Quickly sweep your finger under the whole word to signal students to respond. (for)

SPELL Point just to the left of *for.* Ask: *How do you spell* for*?* (f-o-r) Quickly point to each letter as students spell the word.

READ Point just to the left of *for.* Pause briefly and then ask: *What's this word?* Quickly sweep your finger under the whole word to signal students to respond. (for)

Repeat the same procedure for the irregular words *and, in, is,* and *the.*

CONTINUED ▷

CORRECTIVE FEEDBACK If a student or students respond incorrectly, simply tell them the word. Then repeat the entire routine again.

Practice Irregular Words

Provide each student with a set of magnetic letters and a magnetic surface. Display the word card for *for.* Ask students to identify the word. Then direct students to spell the word with magnetic letters. Next, have them touch each letter as they spell the word out loud. (f-o-r) Finally, tell them to say the word after they spell it. Repeat the same procedure with the words *and, in, is,* and *the.*

Provide each student with a small dry-erase board and a dry-erase marker. Display the word card for *in.* Ask students to identify the word. Say: *I want you to write* in *as big as you can on your dry-erase board.* Then direct them to write *in* in a couple of different ways, such as writing it as small as they can or in all uppercase letters. Finally, have students write the word from memory. Repeat the same procedure with the words *and, for, is,* and *the.*

Word Reading Practice for Automaticity

Make a word recognition grid, like the one shown on the facing page. Each of the five horizontal rows contains the same previously introduced irregular words in a different order.

Use interactive whiteboard technology to display the grid. Tell students that they are going to practice reading words that they have already learned. To warm up, point and sweep under each of the words in the top row and say, for example: *This word is* and. Then ask: *What's this word?* (and)

WORD RECOGNITION GRID

and	for	in	the	is
for	and	the	is	in
in	is	and	for	the
the	for	in	and	is
is	the	for	in	and

After the warm-up, say: *Now you are going to practice reading the words. When I point and sweep under a word, read it aloud. Ready?* Then point to each square in order, starting with the top row and working down and then across each row. Review troublesome words by pointing to them at random as students name them.

LESSON MODEL: Method for Reading Decodable Text, p. 235

Apply to Decodable Text

To ensure ample practice of irregular words, provide students with connected reading materials. Choose books or passages in which most of the words are wholly decodable and the majority of the remaining words are previously taught irregular words.

Question for Observation	Benchmark
(Point to an irregular word.) What is this word?	Student can read an irregular word.

CHAPTER

8

Multisyllabic Word Reading

what?

Multisyllabic Word Reading

Polysyllabic words are perceived as sequences of spelling patterns corresponding to syllabic units.

—ADAMS ET AL., 1990

CCSS READING STANDARDS

Foundational Skills

Phonics and Word Recognition

Use combined knowledge of all sound/spelling correspondences, syllabication patterns, and morphology (e.g., roots and affixes) to read accurately unfamiliar multisyllabic words in context and out of context. (RF.4-5.3a)

Students who can read single-syllable words often have difficulty with multisyllabic words (Just and Carpenter 1987). While phonics instruction gives students the basic tools to decode most single-syllable words, explicit instruction in recognizing syllables and morphemes gives students additional strategies for reading longer words. For students in fifth grade and beyond, knowing how to decode multisyllabic words is essential because most of the words they will encounter in print are words of seven or more letters and two or more syllables—"big" words (Nagy and Anderson 1984).

Pattern detection is an important word-recognition function of the brain; the same letter pattern (e.g., *–tion, –able*) can recur in different words (Cunningham 1998). To read words in text fluently and accurately, the brain's orthographic processor must learn to "see" common letter patterns and recurring word parts (Moats 2005). In multisyllabic words, these multiletter patterns, or "chunks," may be syllables, affixes, or phonograms (Ehri 2002). According to Adams (1990), "skilled readers' ability to recognize a long word depends on whether they can chunk it into syllables in the course of perceiving it." When skilled readers encounter a multisyllabic word, they automatically break it down into smaller units based on the brain's memory of common letter patterns found in other words (Adams 1990; Mewhort and Campbell 1981).

Syllabication

Syllabication is considered by some to be an important strategy that helps students read words.

—BHATTACHARYA & EHRI, 2004

Syllabication is the division of a multisyllabic word into separate syllables with each syllable containing one vowel sound. A syllable may contain more than one vowel letter, but the letters will represent only one vowel sound. The ability to segment and blend syllables facilitates the accurate and rapid identification of multisyllabic words (Ehri 1995). Syllabication strategies are much less likely to lead to the correct pronunciation of a multisyllabic word if the word's meaning is not known—that is, if the word is not in students' oral vocabulary (Shefelbine and Newman 2004). According to Moats (2005), "knowing what a word means will help students come up with its pronunciation after the sounds and syllables are decoded."

SYLLABLE
a word or part of a word pronounced as a unit

In past decades, students were taught a set of syllabication rules, but today research supports a shift from rigid rules to a more flexible approach to decoding longer words (Archer, Gleason, and Vachon 2003, 2006). According to Canney and Schreiner (1977), syllabication rules are too numerous and complex to remember and knowing them does not necessarily improve students' decoding skills. Chall and Popp (1996) also recommend not spending too much time on rules and generalizations. They believe that practice is the best way for students to gain insight and confidence about syllabication. Other researchers recommend that, instead of rules, students be taught more flexible strategies for reading longer words (Bhattacharya and Ehri 2004; Archer et al. 2003, 2006; Shefelbine 1990). In these approaches, students learn that they can be flexible in dividing a word into parts as long as they can ultimately make the word into a real, or recognizable, word (Archer et al. 2003, 2006).

There are basically three different research-based approaches to teaching students how to decode longer multisyllabic words (Archer et al. 2003). These approaches differ in how the words are broken down into decodable chunks, or syllable units: (1) using syllable types and division principles, (2) identifying affixes or word parts, and (3) using flexible syllabication strategies.

Common Types of Syllables		**Examples**	
Syllable Type	**Description**	**Single Syllable**	**Multisyllable**
Closed	A syllable ending in one or more consonants and having a short-vowel sound spelled with one vowel letter. VC, CVC, CCVC, CVCC	dump fish men	picnic rabbit
Open	A syllable ending with a long-vowel sound spelled with one vowel letter. CV, CCV	me she	robot veto
Vowel Combination	A syllable with a short-vowel, long-vowel, or diphthong sound spelled with a vowel combination, such as *ai, ea, ee, oi,* or *oo.* CVVC, CCVVC, CVVCC	boil bread rain spoon teeth	baboon canteen complain heavy poison
***r*-Controlled**	A syllable containing a letter combination made up of a vowel followed by the letter *r,* such as *ar, er, ir, or,* and *ur.* The vowel–*r* combination is one welded sound that cannot be segmented.	far fern first for fur	perfect purchase snorkel target thirsty
Vowel–Consonant *e*	A syllable with a long-vowel sound spelled with one vowel letter followed by one consonant and a silent *e.* VCe, CVCe, CCVCe	fuse hide mole Pete race	amuse erase provide stampede tadpole
Consonant–*le*	A final, separate syllable containing a consonant followed by the letters *le.*	NA	apple table

Sequence for Syllable-Type Instruction		
1. Closed	3. Open	5. Consonant–*le*
2. Vowel–Consonant *e*	4. Vowel Combination	6. *r*-Controlled

Based on Moats 2005.

SEE ALSO . . .

LESSON MODELS

Introducing Open and Closed Syllables, p. 272

Syllable Division Strategy: VC/CV, p. 276

Syllable Division Strategy: VCV, p. 283

Syllasearch Procedure, p. 298

SEE ALSO . . .

Spanish Syllable Types and Patterns, p. 58

Syllable Types and Division Principles

This approach emphasizes identifying and reading the six common types of syllables found within English words. Noah Webster regularized these types to justify the division of syllables in his 1806 dictionary. In this approach, students are introduced to the vowel sound within each common syllable type. According to Louisa Moats (2005), the knowledge of syllable types will help "students remember how to pronounce the vowels in new words." Henry (2003) suggests that students first practice the identification of syllable types in single-syllable words before identifying the syllables in multisyllabic words.

Open and closed syllables make up almost 75 percent of syllables in English words (Stanback 1992). For this reason, Shefelbine and Newman (2004) refer to these two types as "the basic building blocks of polysyllabic decoding." Shefelbine, Lipscomb, and Hern (1989) found a significant relationship between students' sight knowledge of open and closed syllables and students' ability to read multisyllabic words.

Referring to the Common Types of Syllables chart on the facing page and using the grid below, sort the following one-syllable words by syllable type.

top, heat, trade, clip, with, hi, go, broke, me, park, snow, side, twist, verb, toy, noun, thorn, hurt

(See Answer Key, p. 800.)

closed	vowel combination	consonant-*le*
open	**vowel-consonant *e***	***r*-controlled**

Most Useful Syllable Division Principles		
Division	**Examples**	**Description**
VC/CV	rab•bit nap•kin	**Two Consonants Between Two Vowels** If two consonants come between two vowels, divide between the consonants. The first vowel sound will be short.
V/CV (75%) **VC/V (25%)**	mu•sic clos•et	**One Consonant Between Two Vowels** If a word has one consonant between two vowels, divide the word after the first vowel and give the vowel its long sound. If this division does not produce a recognizable word, then divide the word after the consonant and give the vowel its short sound.
VC/CCV **VCC/CV**	hun•dred ink•well ath•lete	**Three Consonants Between Two Vowels** Keep the letters in a consonant blend or digraph together in the same syllable.
Consonant-*le*	wig•gle ri•fle	**Consonant-*le* Forms a Separate Syllable** If the first syllable ends with a consonant, try the short sound for the first vowel. If the first syllable ends with a vowel, try the long sound.

Based on Moats 2005.

> The best way we have found to teach and learn syllabication of long words is to be playful, correcting errors with cheer and laughing easily at humorous misreadings.
>
> —CHALL & POPP, 1996

Familiarity and flexibility with syllable-division principles help students to develop strategies for reading longer words (Carreker 2005). These principles help novice readers "see" the chunks, or patterns of letters, in multisyllabic words and guide correct pronunciation (Moats 2005). However, most syllable-division principles, rules, and generalizations are not reliable and thus are not worth teaching (Canney and Schreiner 1977). Certain more useful or reliable principles, nevertheless, are worthwhile pointing out because they do get readers closer to identifying a multisyllabic word by providing a way to approximate the pronunciation (Chall and Popp 1996; Blevins 2006).

> Spoken language syllable divisions often do not coincide with the conventions for dividing written syllables.
>
> —MOATS, 2005

Dictionary-Based Syllabication Rules

Use caution when looking up syllable breaks in a dictionary. Most dictionaries divide words according to how a printed word should be broken across lines of text, which sometimes has little to do with how the syllables in a spoken word are pronounced (Blevins 2001). When sounding out a word, it matters little, for example, whether a student pronounces *simple* as "simp • le" or "sim • ple." What is important is that each unit is pronounceable (Adams et al. 1990).

Other Syllable Division Principles

- Divide two-syllable compound words between the two smaller words (e.g., *in • side, pan • cake*).
- Inflectional endings such as *–ing, –er, –es, –ed,* and *–est* often form separate syllables.
- Never separate the letters in a consonant or vowel digraph, vowel diphthong, or *r*-controlled vowel across syllable divisions.
- One of the syllables in a multisyllabic word usually receives more stress, or emphasis. In two-syllable words, the stress usually falls on the first syllable (e.g., *mo'ment, fa'mous*). In the unstressed syllable, the vowel sound often is "reduced" to a schwa (e.g., *wa'gon, cac'tus*).

Referring to the syllable division chart on the facing page, sort the following two-syllable words according to common syllable division principles. (See Answer Key, p. 800.)

study, ancient, believe, system, distant, Minor, features, planets, science, center, accept, pictures, details, Saturn, people, models, solar, even, Major, craters, observed

VC/CV	V/CV	VC/V	VC/CCV	VCC/CV	Less Common

SEE ALSO . . .

Morphemes, p. 42

Morphemic Analysis, p. 490

Layers of the English Language, p. 577

SEE ALSO . . .

LESSON MODELS

Introducing Affixes, p. 304

Root Word Transformation Strategy, p. 314

Word Families, p. 524

Word-Part Clues: Prefixes, p. 527

Word-Part Clues: Suffixes, p. 533

Word-Part Clues: Roots, p. 537

Affixes as Syllables

Some researchers suggest teaching students to use root words and affixes to decode multisyllabic words (Venezky 1970; Chomsky 1970; McFeely 1974). Syllable divisions often occur between morphemic units of meaning—word parts. Word parts include root words, Greek and Latin roots, and affixes. According to Shefelbine and Newman (2004), affixes that function as syllables are worth teaching because they are "limited in number, occur frequently, and especially in the case of suffixes are reasonably consistent across words." Given that 80 percent of all words readers encounter have one or more affixes, Cunningham (1998) also suggests that "instant recognition and accurate pronunciation of affixes is the key to decoding long words."

In the part-by-part strategy, students are taught the pronunciation of an affix in isolation, asked to identify and say it in a word, and then instructed to read the whole word (Archer et al. 2003; Engelmann et al. 1999). The assumption is that students will develop a strategy for attacking multisyllabic words as a result of extensive practice in reading long words and being exposed to recurring letter patterns (Archer et al. 2003). According to Carnine et al. (2006), this type of instruction should begin with the introduction of the most common suffixes (*–s, –er, –est, –ing, –le, –ed, –y*).

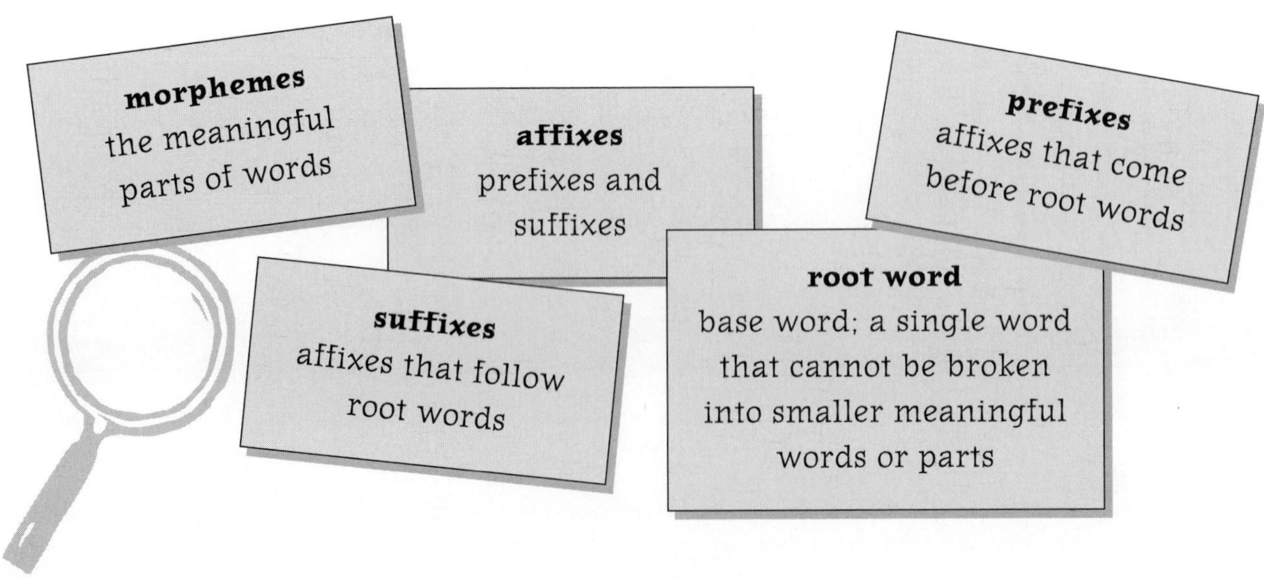

morphemes
the meaningful parts of words
affixes
prefixes and suffixes
prefixes
affixes that come before root words
suffixes
affixes that follow root words
root word
base word; a single word that cannot be broken into smaller meaningful words or parts

Students need to be taught flexible strategies for unlocking the pronunciation of long words.

—ARCHER ET AL., 2006

SEE ALSO . . .

LESSON MODELS

Syllable Segmentation Strategy, p. 292

Flexible Strategy for Reading Big Words, p. 308

Flexible Syllabication

Rather than using rigid, rule-directed syllabication to divide multisyllabic words into parts, students can be taught to recognize the parts in a flexible manner. They can segment multisyllabic words into graphosyllabic units (i.e., spelling units) or "chunks" that can be decoded (Bhattacharya and Ehri 2004; Archer et al. 2003, 2006). According to a research study by Bhattacharya and Ehri (2004), accurate decoding of multisyllabic words can take place when students form consolidated connections between the pronunciations and spellings of letter units, or syllables. This syllable segmentation strategy involves breaking words into spoken syllables, matching the spoken syllables to their spellings, and then blending the segments to form a recognizable word. In a program by Archer et al. (2006), the flexible strategy is based on the information that (1) a high percentage of multisyllabic words contain at least one prefix or suffix and (2) each syllable contains one vowel sound. To achieve a close approximation to the actual pronunciation of a word, the program teaches students to segment words into parts by identifying the affixes and then the vowel sounds in the rest of the word (Archer et al. 2006).

why?

Multisyllabic Word Reading

> Many big words occur infrequently, but when they do occur they carry much of the meaning and content of what is being read.
>
> —CUNNINGHAM, 1998

To progress in reading, students must have strategies for decoding big words. From fifth grade on, the average student encounters about 10,000 new words each year. Most of these words are multisyllabic (Nagy and Anderson 1984). Since the meaning of intermediate-grade content-area text is generally carried by multisyllabic words, the inability to decode these words in text has some definite consequences: the reader is unable to understand the vocabulary and therefore equally unable to extract meaning from what is being read (Perfetti 1986; Archer et al. 2003).

Syllabication is an important strategy for reading words (Shefelbine et al., 1989). Research suggests that word recognition difficulty stems from deficient analysis of syllable units in words (e.g., Bhattacharya 2006). While good readers accurately identify multisyllabic words by effortlessly breaking down the words into syllables, poor readers often identify multisyllabic words inaccurately by processing the letters within words, rather than the syllables (Bhattacharya 2006; Mewhort and Beal 1977; Scheerer-Neumann 1981). According to Shefelbine and Calhoun (1991), "low decoders correctly pronounced fewer affixes and vowel sounds, disregarded large portions of letter information, and were two to four times more likely to omit syllables." Several studies have shown that teaching students strategies for decoding longer words improves their decoding ability (Archer et al. 2006).

Research Findings . . .

An emphasis on multisyllabic word reading is critical because of the number of novel words introduced in intermediate and secondary textbooks and the potential for failing to learn from the material if the words can't be read.

—ARCHER ET AL., 2003

It turns out that skillful readers' ability to read long words depends on their ability to break the words into syllables. This is true for familiar and unfamiliar words.

—ADAMS ET AL., 1990

If students are going to be successful at inferring the meaning of derived words by analysis of morphemes, they first need to read the words accurately.

—CARLISLE & STONE, 2005

Suggested Reading . . .

Making Sense of Phonics: The Hows and Whys (2006) by Isabel L. Beck. New York: Guilford.

Reading Instruction for Students Who Are at Risk or Have Disabilities, 2nd Edition (2011) by William D. Bursuck & Mary Damer. Boston: Allyn & Bacon.

Teaching Phonics & Word Study in the Intermediate Grades (2001) by Wiley Blevins. New York: Scholastic.

Teaching Struggling and At-Risk Readers: A Direct Instruction Approach (2006) by Douglas W. Carnine, Jerry Silbert, Edward J. Kame'enui, Sara G. Tarver & Kathleen Jungjohann. Boston: Allyn & Bacon.

Teaching Word Recognition: Effective Strategies for Students with Learning Difficulties (2007) by Rollanda E. O'Connor. New York: Guilford.

Unlocking Literacy: Effective Decoding & Spelling Instruction, 2nd Edition (2010) by Marcia K. Henry. Baltimore, MD: Paul H. Brookes.

when?

Multisyllabic Word Reading

> Word reading accuracy depends on the decoding of syllable units in multisyllabic words.
>
> —BHATTACHARYA, 2006

CCSS READING STANDARDS

Foundational Skills

Phonics and Word Recognition

GRADE 1

Use knowledge that every syllable must have a vowel sound to determine the number of syllables in a printed word. (RF.1.3d)

Decode two-syllable words following basic patterns by breaking the words into syllables. (RF.1.3e)

Read words with inflectional endings. (RF.1.3f)

GRADE 2

Decode regularly spelled two-syllable words with long vowels. (RF.2.3c)

Decode words with common prefixes and suffixes. (RF.2.3d)

When to Teach

Researchers generally agree that instruction in multisyllabic word reading can begin after students have mastered the decoding of single-syllable words. Other prerequisites include the ability to pronounce common sound/spelling correspondences, especially vowel combinations, to identify open and closed syllables, and to pronounce affixes in isolation (Archer et al. 2003; Carnine et al. 2006; Moats 2005; Shefelbine and Newman 2004).

According to Carnine et al. (2006), the average number of syllables in the words students read increases steadily in the primary grades. By the end of Grade 1, students are reading mostly one- and two-syllable words. By the end of Grade 2, students are reading mostly two- and three-syllable words. By Grade 3, longer multisyllabic words appear in text.

When to Assess and Intervene

The inability to read multisyllabic words has long been recognized as a stumbling block for students with reading difficulties (Shefelbine 1990). Therefore, it is generally suggested that assessment in multisyllabic word reading should begin in mid-second grade in order to plan effective intervention. Students who have difficulty in reading multisyllabic words need to receive diagnostic assessment in order to determine whether the deficit in this area can be attributed to a deeper-seated issue; for example, difficulty in reading single-syllable words.

CCSS READING STANDARDS

Foundational Skills

Phonics and Word Recognition

GRADE 3

Identify and know the meaning of the most common prefixes and derivational suffixes. (RF.3.3a)

Decode words with common Latin [derivational] suffixes. (RF.3.3b)

Decode multisyllabic words. (RF.3.3c)

GRADES 4-5

Use combined knowledge of all sound/spelling correspondences, syllabication patterns, and morphology (e.g., roots and affixes) to read accurately unfamiliar multisyllabic words in context and out of context. (RF.4-5.3a)

Older Struggling Readers

Many middle- and high-school students have problems with reading accuracy. A large number of these students have mastered basic decoding skills but lack strategies for identifying multisyllabic words. They struggle to identify new words frequently encountered in content-area texts. Problems at this level arise both because students cannot confidently use a repertoire of multisyllabic word analysis strategies with these new words and because many of the new words are outside their vocabulary. It is not clear from current research the amount of explicit multisyllabic word instruction necessary for struggling readers after third grade (Torgesen et al. 2007).

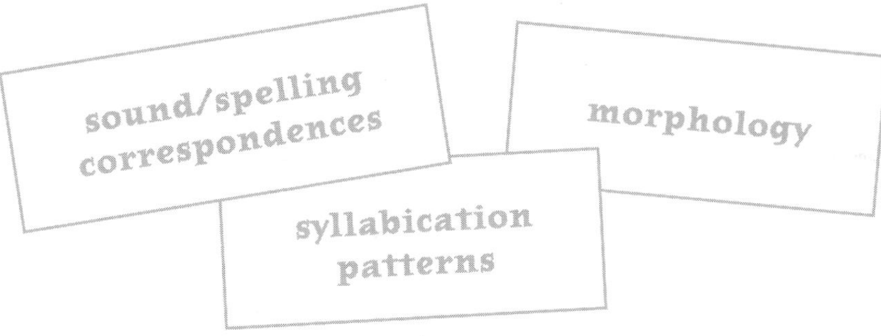

Purpose	Multisyllabic Word Reading Assessment	Publisher
Screening	CORE Literacy Library *Assessing Reading: Multiple Measures, 2nd Edition* ▸ CORE Phonics Survey	Arena Press
Screening	Test of Silent Word Reading Fluency (TOSWRF)	Pro-Ed
Screening Progress Monitoring	Test of Word Reading Efficiency (TOWRE) Subtests: ▸ Phonetic Decoding Efficiency (PDE) ▸ Sight Word Efficiency (SWE)	Pro-Ed
Screening Progress Monitoring Diagnostic	easy CBM™ ▸ Word Fluency	Riverside Publishing http://easycbm.com
Diagnostic	Woodcock Reading Mastery Tests, Third Edition (WRMT™-III) ▸ Word Attack ▸ Word Identification	Pearson

how?

Multisyllabic Word Reading

LESSON MODEL FOR

Reading Open and Closed Syllables

Benchmark

- ability to identify and read open and closed single syllables

Strategy Grade Level

- Grade 2 and above

Prerequisites

- ability to identify vowels and consonants
- ability to distinguish between short- and long-vowel sounds
- ability to decode one-syllable words
- knowledge of common sound/spelling correspondences

Grouping

- whole class
- small group or pairs
- individual

Materials

- none

Introducing Open and Closed Syllables

An open syllable ends in one vowel; the vowel sound is long. A closed syllable ends in at least one consonant; the vowel sound is short. Closed syllables are the most common type of syllable in English; they account for approximately 50 percent of the syllables in running text (Moats and Rosow 2003). This sample lesson model targets two syllable types: open and closed. The same model can be adapted and used to introduce other open and closed syllables and to enhance single-syllable or multi-syllabic word instruction in any commercial reading program.

Introduce the Syllable Types

Fold a piece of paper into fourths. Print the letter *m* in the first fourth and the letter *e* in the second fourth. Then, fold over the last fourth (it will cover the third fourth) and print the letter *n* in it.

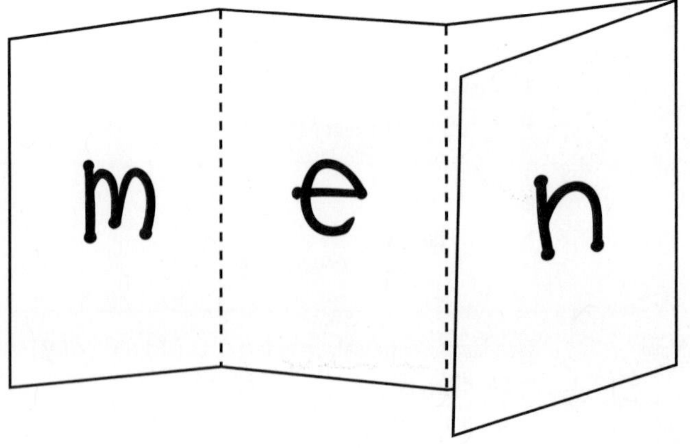

CLOSED SYLLABLES Say: *Every syllable has only one vowel sound. Look at this word.* Fold over the paper flap with the letter *n* to show the word *men.* Say: *The door is closed.* Ask: *What's this word?* (men) *Right. This one-syllable word is* men. *The consonant at the end of this word tells me that this is a closed syllable. In a closed syllable, a consonant "closes in" the vowel and the vowel sound is short, just as you read it.* Point to the letter *e* in *men.* Say: *This letter stands for /e/.* Point to *men* and say: *Let's say the word again.*

OPEN SYLLABLES Now, unfold the paper flap, or "open the door," to reveal the word *me.* Say: *I just opened the door.* Ask: *What's this word?* (me) Say: *Right. This one-syllable word is* me. *The single vowel at the end tells me that this is an open syllable. In an open syllable, the vowel sound is the same as the name of the letter, or long.* Point to the letter *e* in *me.* Say: *This letter stands for /ē/. The letter's name is the same as its sound.* Point to *me* and say: *Let's say the word again.*

Follow the same procedure with *hi/hit, so/sob, he/hen,* and *go/got.*

Teach/Model

Say: *Today you're going to learn to read open and closed syllables. To read the syllables, you will need to decide whether to say the long- or short-vowel sound. Watch as I show you how.*

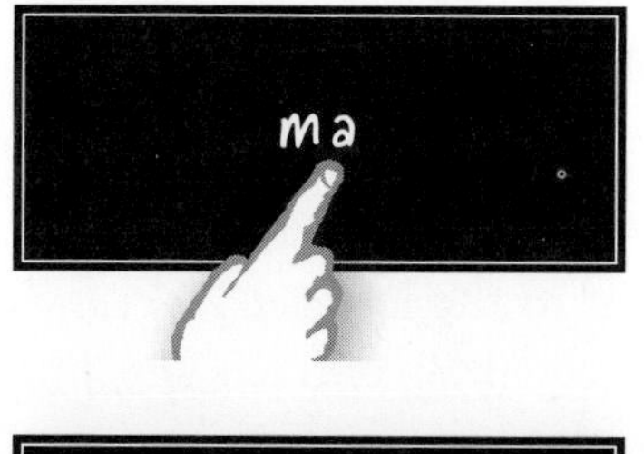

Print the syllable *ma* on the board. Point to *ma* and say: *There is a vowel at the end, so this is an open syllable.* Point to the letter *a* in *ma* and say: *This vowel sound is long. The long-vowel sound for this letter is /ā/.* Point just to the left of *ma* and say: *Listen as I read the syllable.* Sweep your finger under the syllable and say: *mā.*

CONTINUED ▷

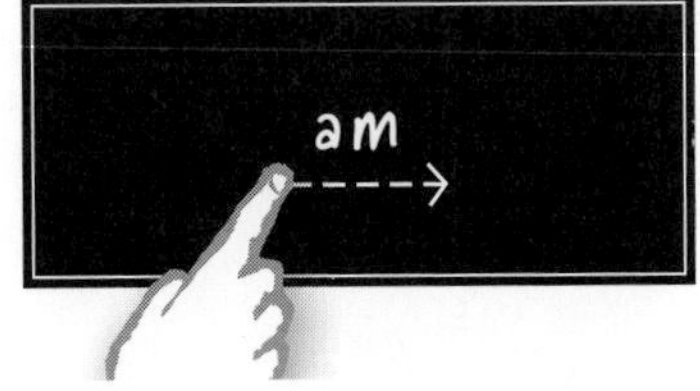

Now print the syllable *am* on the board. Point to *am* and say: *There is a consonant, not a vowel, at the end, so this is a closed syllable.* Point to the letter *a* in *am* and say: *This vowel sound is short. The short-vowel sound for this letter is /a/.* Point just to the left of *am* and say: *Listen as I read the syllable.* Sweep your finger under the syllable and say: *am.*

Guided Practice

Print the following lists of syllables on the board.

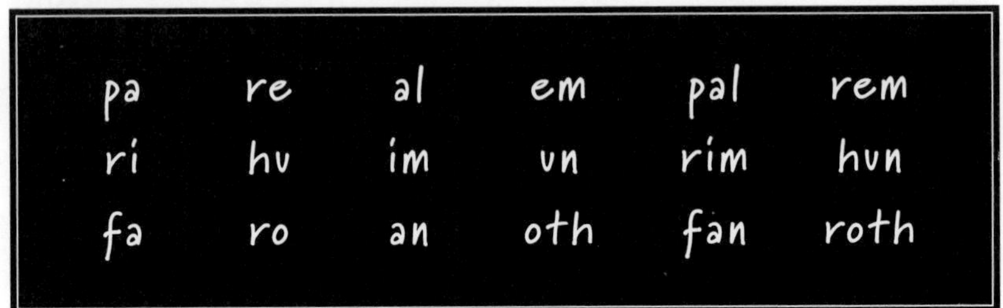

SEE ALSO . . .

Spanish Syllable Types, p. 59

Say: *Now it's your turn to decide how to pronounce the vowel sound in open or closed syllables. Remember, if there's a vowel at the end, the syllable is open and the vowel sound is long. If there's a consonant at the end, the syllable is closed and the vowel sound is short.*

Point to *pa* in the first column. Ask: *Is there a vowel or a consonant at the end?* (vowel) Point to the letter *a*. Ask: *Is this vowel sound long or short?* (long) Ask: *What's the vowel sound?* (/ā/) Point to *pa* again. Say: *Read.* Sweep your finger under the syllable as students respond. (pā) Follow the same procedure with the rest of the syllables in the column.

Point to *al* in the second column. Ask: *Is there a vowel or a consonant at the end?* (a consonant) Point to the letter *a*. Ask: *Is this vowel sound long or short?* (short) Ask: *What's the vowel sound?* (/a/) Point to *al* again. Say: *Read.* Sweep your finger under the syllable as students respond. (ăl) Follow the same procedure with the rest of the syllables in the column. Next read across each row, following the same procedure.

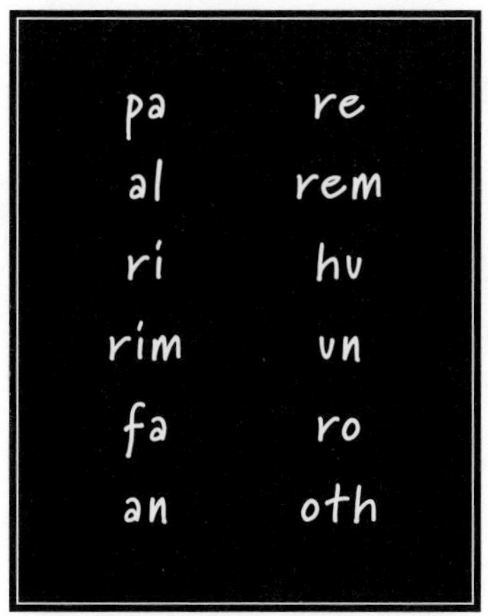

Word Work: Syllable Sort

For this closed sort, print the following syllables on the board: *pa, al, ri, rim, fa, an, re, rem, hu, un, ro,* and *oth.* Have students divide their papers in half lengthwise and label one column Open Syllables and the other Closed Syllables. Tell students that you want them to sort this list of syllables. Model the sort using the syllable *re.* Ask students to identify whether *re* is an open or closed syllable. (open) Call on a volunteer to tell you how they know. (There is a vowel at the end.) Direct students to write *re* in the column labeled Open Syllables. Have students sort the rest of the syllables on their own, writing each syllable in the appropriate column. Monitor students and provide assistance as needed. When students have finished, call on volunteers to read aloud the syllables in each list. Have them identify whether the vowel sound is long or short in each syllable.

Questions for Observation	Benchmarks
(Point to me.*)* Is this an open or closed syllable? (open) How do you know? (The vowel is at the end.) Is the vowel sound long or short? (long) Can you read this syllable? *(me)*	Student can identify and read open syllables.
(Point to men.*)* Is this an open or closed syllable? (closed) How do you know? (The vowel is not at the end.) Is the vowel sound long or short? (short) Can you read this syllable? *(men)*	Student can read open and closed syllables.

LESSON MODEL FOR

Reading Multisyllabic Words

Benchmarks

- ability to divide two-syllable words with the VCCV pattern
- ability to read two-syllable words with the VCCV pattern

Strategy Grade Level

- Grade 2 and above

Prerequisites

- Introducing Open and Closed Syllables, p. 272
- ability to recognize vowels and consonants
- ability to decode one-syllable words
- knowledge of common sound/spelling correspondences

Grouping

- whole class
- small group or pairs
- individual

Materials

- none

Syllable Division Strategy: VC/CV

In a word with the VCCV syllable pattern, two consonants come between two vowels and the word is divided between the two consonants. The first syllable of a VCCV word is closed and therefore contains a short-vowel sound. This sample lesson model for dividing multisyllabic words into syllables targets two-syllable words with the VCCV pattern. The same model can be adapted and used to introduce other VCCV words and to enhance multisyllabic word instruction in any commercial reading program.

Review: Open and Closed Syllables

Print two columns of open- and closed-syllable words on the board.

Tell students that they are going to review open and closed syllables. Then have them read aloud each column of words. Direct students' attention to the first column. Remind students that every syllable has only one vowel sound. Ask a volunteer to underline the vowel in each of the words. Ask: *Where's the vowel in each of these words?* (at the end) *Is the syllable open or closed?* (open) *Is the vowel sound long or short?* (long) Now direct students' attention to the second column. Ask a volunteer to underline the vowel in each of the words. Ask: *Where's the vowel in each of these words?* (not at the end) *What is at the end?* (a consonant) *Is the syllable open or closed?* (closed) *Is the vowel sound long or short?* (short)

STEPS FOR SYLLABLE DIVISION: VCCV

1. Identify and Label the Vowels
2. Identify and Label Any Consonants Between the Vowels
3. Look at the Pattern and Divide the Word
4. Identify the Syllable Types
5. Blend Each Syllable and Then Read the Whole Word

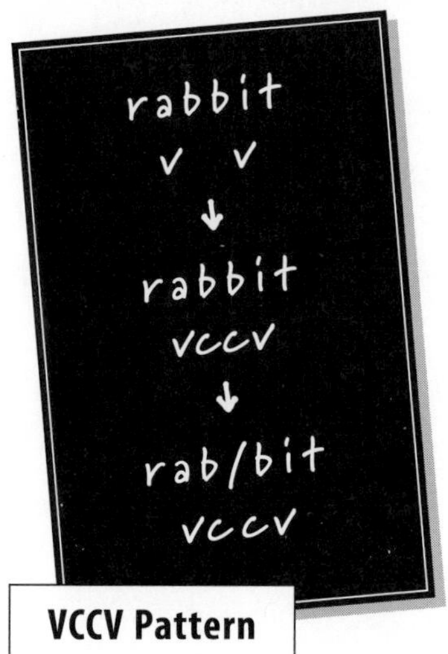

VCCV Pattern

Teach/Model

Display the Steps for Syllable Division, such as the example shown above. Explain to students that they are going to learn to read multisyllabic words using the steps in this strategy.

1. Identify and Label the Vowels

Print the word *rabbit* on the board. Point to the word and say: *Step 1 says to identify and label the vowels. I will label each vowel with a* v. Point to the *a* and say: *The first vowel in this word is* a. Print a *v* under the *a*. Then point to the *i* and say: *The next vowel in this word is* i. Print a *v* under the *i*.

2. Identify and Label Any Consonants Between the Vowels

Say: *Step 2 says to identify and label any consonants between the vowels. I will label each consonant with a* c. In the word *rabbit*, point to the two *b*'s between the vowels and say: *There are two consonants between the vowels* a *and* i. Print a *c* under each of the *b*'s.

278 **When dividing words into syllables, keep consonant blends and digraphs together.**

3. Look at the Pattern and Divide the Word

Say: *Step 3 says to look at the pattern and divide the word.* Point to the VCCV labels and say: *This word has the VCCV syllable pattern. There are two consonants between the vowels.* Ask: *How many consonants are between the vowels?* (two) Say: *If two consonants come between two vowels, divide between the two consonants.* Draw a front slash between the two *b*'s in *rabbit.*

4. Identify the Syllable Types

Say: *Step 4 says to identify the syllable types.* Point to the first syllable and say: *There is a consonant at the end of this syllable, so this is a closed syllable. The vowel sound will be short.* Point to the second syllable and say: *There is a consonant at the end of this syllable, so this is also a closed syllable. The vowel sound will be short.*

5. Blend Each Syllable and Then Read the Whole Word

Say: *Step 5 says to blend each syllable and then read the whole word.* Point just to the left of *rabbit* and say: *Now I'll blend each syllable.* Scoop your finger under the first syllable as you blend the sounds together and say: *rab.* Then scoop your finger under the second syllable as you blend the sounds together and say: *bit.* Point just to the left of *rabbit* and say: *Now I'll read the whole word.* Quickly sweep your finger under the whole word and say: *rabbit.* Point out to students that when you read the whole word, you only said the /b/ sound once.

Guided Practice

Explain to students that now it's their turn to follow the Steps for Syllable Division. Print the word *basket* on the board. Have students copy the word onto a sheet of paper.

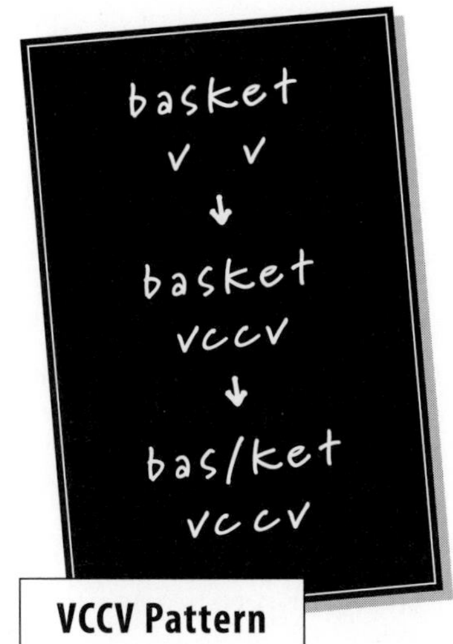

VCCV Pattern

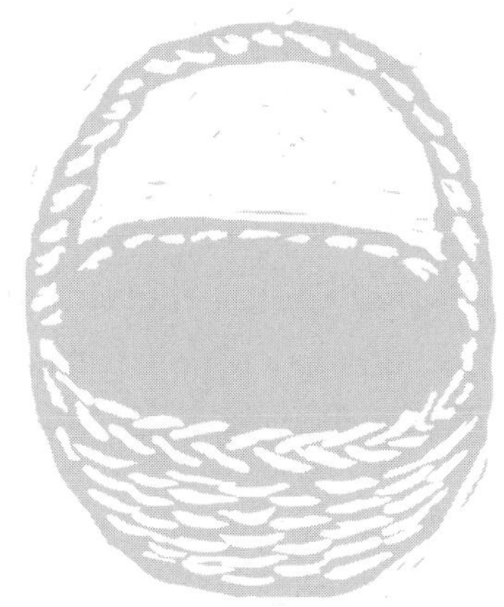

1. Identify and Label the Vowels

Say: *Step 1 says to identify and label the vowels. On your paper, label each vowel with a* v *and I will do the same.* Ask: *What is the first vowel?* (a) *What is the next vowel?* (e)

2. Identify and Label Any Consonants Between the Vowels

Say: *Step 2 says to identify and label any consonants between the vowels. On your papers, label each consonant with a* c *and I will do the same.* Ask: *How many consonants between the vowels?* (two) Ask: *What are the consonants?* (s and k)

3. Look at the Pattern and Divide the Word

Say: *Step 3 says to look at the pattern and divide the word. Look at how the word is labeled.* Ask: *What is the syllable pattern?* (VCCV) Ask: *Where do we divide a VCCV word?* (between the two consonants) Say: *Right. Draw a front slash between* s *and* k *and I will do the same.*

4. Identify the Syllable Types

Say: *Step 4 says to identify the syllable types.* Point to the first syllable *bas* and ask: *Is this syllable open or closed?* (closed) Ask: *How do you know?* (It ends in a consonant.) Ask: *Will the vowel sound be long or short?* (short) Point to the second syllable and ask: *Is this open or closed?* (closed) Ask: *How do you know?* (It ends in a consonant.) *Will the vowel sound be long or short?* (short)

CONTINUED ▷

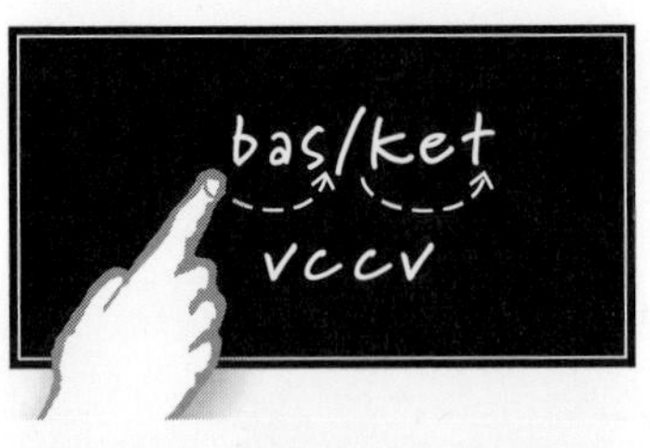

5. Blend Each Syllable and Then Read the Whole Word

Say: *Step 5 says to blend each syllable and then read the whole word.* Point just to the left of the first syllable and ask: *First syllable?* Scoop your finger under the first syllable as students blend the sounds together and respond. (bas) Point just to the left of the second syllable and ask: *Second syllable?* Scoop your finger under the second syllable as students blend the sounds together and respond. (ket) Point just to the left of *basket.* Quickly sweep your finger under the whole word to signal students to respond. (basket) Ask: *What's the whole word?* (basket) Repeat the same procedure with the words *classic, absent, plastic, gossip,* and *puppet.*

CORRECTIVE FEEDBACK If a student or students pronounce a word incorrectly, pronounce the word correctly for the entire group and then ask the entire group to respond. Explain your correct pronunciation of the word.

Apply to Connected Text

Provide opportunities for students to apply what they have learned about syllable division. Have students find examples of words with the VCCV syllable pattern in reading program or content area text. Ask them to pick one of the words and then show a classmate how to go about reading the word according to the Steps for Syllable Division.

Word Work: Dictation

This procedure is similar to the procedure for whole word dictation, but rather than spell each sound, students spell each syllable. Students will need a sheet of paper and a pencil.

1. Introduce the Word

Say: *Now we are going to practice spelling two-syllable words. We will spell each word one syllable at a time. The first word is* mitten. *I found a mitten in the snow.* Mitten. Ask: *What's the word?* (mitten)

2. Count the Syllables in the Word

Say: *Hold up one finger at a time while saying each syllable in* mitten *with me:* mit • ten. Ask: *How many syllables are in* mitten*?* (two) Ask: *What's the first syllable in* mitten*?* (mit) Ask: *What's the second syllable in* mitten*?* (ten)

mitten

3. Spell Each Syllable

Say: *The first syllable in* mitten *is* mit. *Think of the sounds in* mit *and then write the syllable on your papers.* Then say: *The second syllable in* mitten *is* ten. *Think about the sounds in* ten *and write the syllable on your papers.* Monitor students as they spell each syllable, providing guidance as needed.

mitten

4. Compare and Correct

Print the word *mitten* on the board. Ask students to compare their spelling with yours. After giving them an opportunity to make corrections, say: *Now, let's say and spell the word together.* Ask: *First syllable?* (mit . . . m-i-t) Ask: *Second syllable?* (ten . . . t-e-n). Repeat the same dictation procedure with the words *happen, plastic,* and *napkin.*

Word Reading Practice for Automaticity

Make a word recognition grid, like the one shown on the following page. In the grid, print in random order 20 words that contain the VCCV pattern. Repeat the words in a different order until the grid is full.

Use interactive whiteboard technology to display the grid. Tell students that they are going to practice reading words with the VCCV pattern. To warm up, point to *rabbit,* or the first word in the top row, and say: *Watch as I blend each syllable and then read the whole word.* Scoop your finger under the first syllable and say: */rab/.* Scoop your finger under the second syllable and say: */bit/.* Then quickly sweep your finger under

WORD RECOGNITION GRID

rabbit	puppet	crimson	common	absent
plastic	gossip	basket	candid	picnic
public	upset	ribbon	tennis	suffix
rotten	cactus	admit	dentist	exit
absent	picnic	suffix	exit	dentist
tennis	candid	common	crimson	basket
ribbon	admit	suffix	picnic	cactus
upset	gossip	puppet	rabbit	plastic
public	rotten	absent	tennis	admit
common	exit	ribbon	basket	public

the whole word and say: *rabbit.* Follow the same procedure with the rest of the words in the top row.

After the warm-up, say: *Now you are going to practice reading the words. First you will blend each syllable and then read the whole word. Ready?* Point to the first word, *rabbit.* Scoop your finger under the first syllable to signal students to respond. (/rab/) Scoop your finger under the second syllable to signal students to respond. (/bit/) Then sweep your finger under the whole word to signal students to respond. (rabbit) Follow the same procedure with the rest of the words, starting with the top row and working down and then across each row. Review troublesome words by pointing to them at random as students blend them.

Question for Observation	Benchmark
(Point to a two-syllable word with a VCCV pattern.) Can you show me how to use the Steps for Syllable Division to read this word?	Student can divide and read a two-syllable word.

LESSON MODEL FOR

Reading Multisyllabic Words

Benchmarks

- ability to divide two-syllable words with the VCV pattern
- ability to read two-syllable words with the VCV pattern

Strategy Grade Level

- Grade 2 and above

Prerequisites

- Introducing Open and Closed Syllables, p. 272
- ability to decode one-syllable words
- knowledge of common sound/spelling correspondences

Grouping

- whole class
- small group or pairs
- individual

Materials

- connected text

Syllable Division Strategy: VCV

In a word with the VCV syllable pattern, one consonant comes between two vowels. About 75 percent of the time, the word is divided before the consonant (i.e., V/CV), making the first syllable open and with a long-vowel sound (Moats 2005). About 25 percent of the time, the word is divided after the consonant (i.e., VC/V), making the first syllable closed and with a short-vowel sound. This sample lesson model for dividing multisyllabic words into syllables targets two-syllable words with the VCV pattern. The same model can be adapted and used to introduce other VCV words and to enhance multisyllabic word instruction in any commercial reading program.

Review: Open and Closed Syllables

Print two columns of open and closed syllables on the board.

be	beg
mo	mot
fi	fin
ri	riv
sa	sal

Tell students that they are going to review open and closed syllables. Then have them read aloud each column of syllables. Direct students' attention to the first column. Remind students that every syllable has only one vowel sound. Ask a volunteer to underline the vowel in each of the syllables. Ask: *Where's the vowel in each of these syllables?* (at the end) *Is the syllable open or closed?* (open) *Is the vowel sound long or short?* (long) Now direct students' attention to the second column. Ask a volunteer to underline the vowel in each of the syllables. Ask: *Where's the vowel in each of these syllables?* (not at the end) *What is at the end?* (a consonant) *Is the syllable open or closed?* (closed) *Is the vowel sound long or short?* (short)

STEPS FOR SYLLABLE DIVISION: VCV

1. Identify and Label the Vowels
2. Identify and Label Any Consonants Between the Vowels
3. Look at the Pattern and Divide the Word
4. Identify the First Syllable's Type
5. Blend Each Syllable and Then Read the Whole Word
6. If You Don't Recognize the Word, Divide It in a Different Way

Teach/Model—V/CV

Display the Steps for Syllable Division, such as the example shown above. Explain to students that they are going to learn to read two-syllable words using the steps in this strategy. Print the word *begin* on the board.

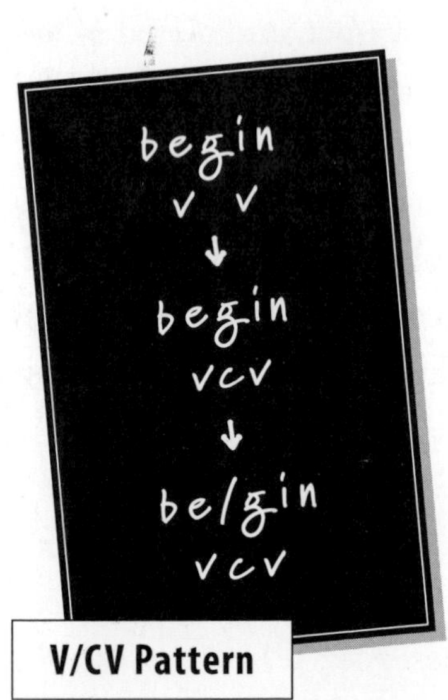

V/CV Pattern

1. Identify and Label the Vowels

Say: *Step 1 says to identify and label the vowels. I will label each vowel with a* v. Point to the *e* in *begin* and say: *The first vowel in this word is* e. Print a *v* under the *e*. Then point to the *i* and say: *The next vowel in this word is* i. Print a *v* under the *i*.

2. Identify and Label Any Consonants Between the Vowels

Say: *Step 2 says to identify and label any consonants between the vowels. I will label each consonant with a* c. Point to the *g* in *begin* and say: *There is one consonant between the vowels* e *and* i. Print a *c* under the consonant *g*.

3. Look at the Pattern and Divide the Word

Say: *Step 3 says to look at the pattern and divide the word.* Point to the VCV labels and say: *This word has the VCV syllable pattern. There is one consonant between the vowels.* Ask: *How many consonants are between the vowels?* (one) Say: *If one consonant comes between two vowels, first try to divide before the consonant.* Draw a front slash before the *g* in *begin.*

4. Identify the First Syllable's Type

Say: *Step 4 says to identify the first syllable's type.* Point to the first syllable in *begin* and say: *There is a vowel at the end of this syllable, so this is an open syllable. The vowel sound will be long.*

5. Blend Each Syllable and Then Read the Whole Word

Say: *Step 5 says to blend each syllable and then read the whole word.* Point just to the left of *begin* and say: *Now I'll blend each syllable.* Scoop your finger under the first syllable as you blend the sounds and say: */bē/.* Then scoop your finger under the second syllable as you blend the sounds and say: */gin/.* Point just to the left of *begin* and say: *Now I'll read the whole word.* Quickly sweep your finger under the whole word and say: *begin.* Ask: *Is this a real word that you recognize?* (yes) Say: *Yes. When you begin to do something, you start doing it.*

Teach/Model—VC/V

Display the Steps for Syllable Division, such as the example shown above. Explain to students that they are going to learn to read two-syllable words using the steps in this strategy. Print the word *closet* on the board.

1. Identify and Label the Vowels

Say: *Step 1 says to identify and label the vowels. I will label each vowel with a* v. Point to the *o* in *closet* and say: *The first vowel*

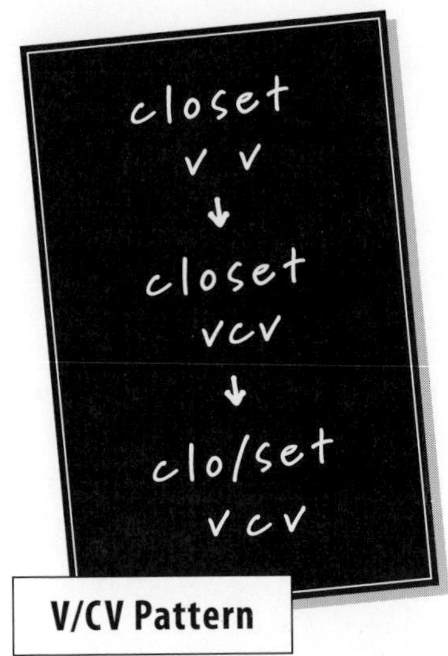

V/CV Pattern

in this word is o. Print a *v* under the *o*. Then point to the *e* and say: *The next vowel in this word is* e. Print a *v* under the *e*.

2. Identify and Label Any Consonants Between the Vowels

Say: *Step 2 says to identify and label any consonants between the vowels. I will label each consonant with a* c. Point to the *s* in *closet* and say: *There is one consonant between the vowels* o *and* e. Print a *c* under the consonant *s*.

3. Look at the Pattern and Divide the Word

Say: *Step 3 says to look at the pattern and divide the word.* Point to the VCV labels and say: *This word has the VCV syllable pattern. There is one consonant between the vowels.* Ask: *How many consonants are between the vowels?* (one) Say: *If one consonant comes between two vowels, first try to divide before the consonant.* Draw a front slash before the *s* in *closet.*

4. Identify the First Syllable's Type

Say: *Step 4 says to identify the first syllable's type.* Then point to the first syllable in *closet* and say: *There is a vowel at the end of this syllable, so this is also an open syllable. The vowel sound will be long.*

5. Blend Each Syllable and Then Read the Whole Word

Point to *closet.* Say: *Now I'll read each syllable.* Scoop your finger under the first syllable and say: */clō/.* Then scoop your finger under the second syllable and say: */zət/.* Point just to the left of *closet* and say: *Now I'll read the whole word.* Quickly sweep your finger under the whole word and say: *clōzet.* Say: *I don't recognize this word as I just pronounced it. I'm not sure it is a real word. I'm going to go to Step 6 and try dividing the word in a different way.*

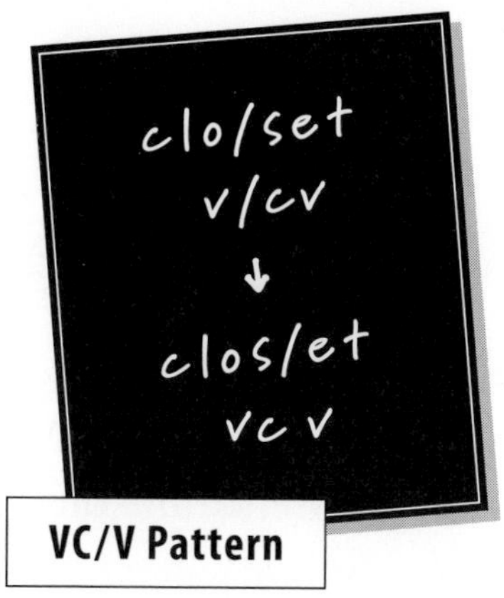

VC/V Pattern

6. If You Don't Recognize the Word, Divide It in a Different Way

Say: *Because I didn't recognize the word* clōzit, *I'm going to try dividing the word in a different way. This time, I will try dividing the word after the consonant.*

In *closet,* erase the front slash before the consonant *s* and draw a new front slash after the consonant *s.* Say: *Now I have to go back to Steps 4 and 5. Step 4 says to identify the first syllable's type.* Point to the first syllable in *closet* and say: *There is a consonant at the end of this syllable, so this is a closed syllable. The vowel sound will be short.* Say: *Step 5 says to blend each syllable and then read the whole word. Now I'll blend each syllable.* Point just to the left of *closet.* Scoop your finger under the first syllable as you blend the sounds and say: /*cloz*/. Then scoop your finger under the second syllable as you blend the sounds and say: /*et*/. Point just to the left of *closet* and say: *Now I'll read the whole word.* Quickly sweep your finger under the whole word and say: *closet.* Ask: *Is this a real word that you recognize?* (yes) Say: *Yes, a closet is a place to hang up your clothes.*

Guided Practice

Explain to students that now it is their turn to use the Steps for Syllable Division. Print the word *river* on the board. Have students copy the word on a sheet of paper.

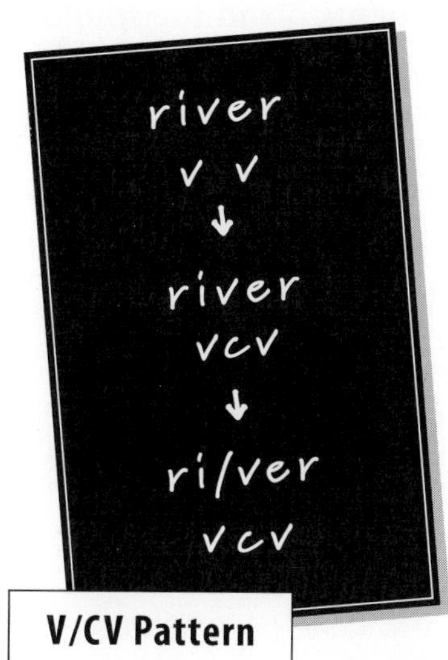

V/CV Pattern

1. Identify and Label the Vowels

Say: *Step 1 says to identify and label the vowels. On your paper, label each vowel with a* v *and I will do the same.* Ask: *What is the first vowel?* (i) *What is the next vowel?* (e)

2. Identify and Label Any Consonants Between the Vowels

Say: *Step 2 says to identify and label any consonants between the vowels. On your papers, label each consonant with a* c *and I will do the same.* Ask: *How many consonants between the vowels?* (one) Ask: *What is the consonant?* (v).

3. Look at the Pattern and Divide the Word

Say: *Step 3 says to look at the pattern and divide the word. Look at how the word is labeled.* Ask: *What is the syllable pattern?* (VCV) Ask: *Where do we first try dividing a VCV word?* (before the consonant) Say: *Right. Draw a front slash before the* v, *and I will do the same.*

4. Identify the First Syllable's Type

Say: *Step 4 says to identify the first syllable's type.* Point to the first syllable *ri* and ask: *Is this syllable open or closed?* (open) Ask: *How do you know?* (It ends in a vowel.) Ask: *Will the vowel sound be long or short?* (long)

5. Blend Each Syllable and Then Read the Whole Word

Say: *Step 5 says to blend each syllable and then read the whole word.* Point just to the left of the first syllable and ask: *First syllable?* Scoop your finger under the first syllable *ri* as students blend the sounds together and respond. (/rī/) Point just to the left of the second syllable and ask: *Second syllable?* Scoop your finger under the second syllable as students blend the sounds together and respond. (/ver/) Then point just to the left of *river* and ask: *What's the whole word?* Quickly sweep your finger under the whole word to signal students to respond. (rīver) Ask: *Is this a real word that you recognize?* (no) Ask: *What do you have to do?* (Try dividing the word after the consonant.) Say: *Okay, let's go to Step 6.*

VC/V Pattern

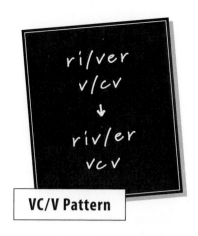

6. If You Don't Recognize the Word, Divide It in a Different Way

Have students erase the front slash before the consonant *v* in *river* and draw a new front slash after the consonant *v*. Say: *We have to go back to Steps 4 and 5. Step 4 says to identify the first syllable's type.* Point to the first syllable *riv* and ask: *Is this syllable open or closed?* (closed) Ask: *How do you know?* (It ends in a consonant.) Ask: *Will the vowel sound be long or short?* (short)

Say: *Step 5 says to blend each syllable and then read the whole word.* Point just to the left of the first syllable and ask: *First syllable?* Scoop your finger under the first syllable *riv* as students blend the sounds together and respond. (/riv/) Point just to the left of the second syllable and ask: *Second syllable?* Scoop your finger under the second syllable as students blend the sounds together and respond. (/er/) Then point just to the left of *river* and ask: *What's the whole word?* Quickly sweep your finger under the whole word to signal students to respond. (river) Ask: *Is this a real word that you recognize?* (yes) Say: *Yes, a river is a nice place to go swimming or fishing.* Repeat the same procedure with the words *final, melon,* and *motel.*

CORRECTIVE FEEDBACK If a student or students pronounce a word incorrectly, pronounce the word correctly for the entire group and then ask the entire group to respond. Explain your correct pronunciation of the word.

Apply to Connected Text

Provide opportunities for students to apply what they have learned about syllable division. Have students find examples of words with the VCV syllable pattern in reading program or content-area text. Ask them to pick one of the words and then show a classmate how to go about reading the word according to the Steps for Syllable Division.

Word Work: Syllable Pattern Sort

Tell students that they are going to sort words into two categories: Words with the V/CV Pattern and Words with the VC/V Pattern. Print the key words *music* and *seven* on the board. Have students repeat the words after you and then print them at the top of two separate columns on a sheet of paper. Next print the following words on the board: *label, open, magic, cabin, metal, even, total,* and *finish*. Tell students to use the Steps for Syllable Division: VCV to decide the appropriate column in which to write each of the words. When the sort is complete, ask students to read the words aloud.

Word Reading Practice for Automaticity

Make a word recognition grid, like the one shown below. In the grid, print in random order 20 words that contain the VCV pattern. Repeat the words in a different order until the grid is full.

WORD RECOGNITION GRID

closet	river	motel	final	pupil
melon	solo	total	satin	valid
frozen	salad	even	cozy	limit
rival	silent	panic	tiger	virus
limit	virus	valid	pupil	final
satin	cozy	tiger	panic	even
motel	river	solo	total	salad
silent	rival	limit	frozen	melon
closet	salad	even	pupil	satin
final	solo	river	virus	tiger

Use interactive whiteboard technology to display the grid. Tell students that they are going to practice reading words with the VCV pattern. To warm up, point to *closet,* or the first word in the top row, and say: *Watch as I blend each syllable and then read the whole word.* Scoop your finger under the first syllable and say: */kloz/.* Scoop your finger under the second syllable and say: */et/.* Then quickly sweep your finger under the whole word and say: *closet.* Follow the same procedure with the rest of the words in the top row.

After the warm-up, say: *Now you are going to practice reading the words. First you will blend each syllable and then read the whole word. Ready?* Point to the first word *closet.* Scoop your finger under the first syllable *clos* to signal students to respond. (/kloz/) Scoop your finger under the second syllable *et* to signal students to respond. (/et/) Then sweep your finger under the whole word to signal students to respond. (closet) Follow the same procedure with the rest of the words, starting with the top row and working down and then across each row. Review troublesome words by pointing to them at random as students blend them.

OBSERVE & ASSESS

Questions for Observation	Benchmarks
(Point to a two-syllable word with a V/CV pattern.) Can you show me how to use the Steps for Syllable Division to read this word?	Student can divide and read a two-syllable V/CV word.
(Point to a two-syllable word with a VC/V pattern.) Can you show me how to use the Steps for Syllable Division to read this word?	Student can divide and read a two-syllable VC/V word.

LESSON MODEL FOR

Reading Multisyllabic Words

Benchmarks

- ability to segment multisyllabic words into syllables
- ability to decode multisyllabic words
- ability to retain multisyllabic words in memory

Strategy Grade Level

- Grade 2 and above

Prerequisite

- knowledge of common sound/spelling correspondences

Grouping

- whole class
- small group or pairs
- individual

Materials

- none

Syllable Segmentation Strategy

This sample lesson model is based on a syllable segmentation strategy developed in a study by Alpana Bhattacharya and Linnea Ehri (2004). This form of syllable instruction focuses on application rather than rule learning. Only one syllabication rule is taught: each syllable contains only one vowel sound. In this strategy, different ways of dividing words into syllables are accepted as long as each syllable contains one and only one vowel sound (e.g., fin•ish or fi•nish). The same model can be adapted and used to segment other multisyllabic words and to enhance multisyllabic word instruction in any commercial reading program.

Review: What's a Syllable?

Explain to students that a syllable is a word part, or unit of pronunciation, and that every syllable has a vowel sound in it. Remind students that vowel sounds are usually spelled with the letters *a, e, i, o, u,* or *y,* or combinations of these letters such as *ea* or *ai.* Say: *You hear one, and only one, vowel sound in every syllable. For example, the word* radish *has two syllables,* rad *and* ish. *Each syllable has only one vowel sound, the /a/ in* rad *and the /i/ in* ish. Tell students that you are going to show them a strategy for reading words that have more than one syllable.

SYLLABLE SEGMENTATION STRATEGY

1. Pronounce the Written Word and Explain Its Meaning
2. Segment the Spoken Word into Syllables
3. Match the Spoken and Written Syllables
4. Blend the Syllables to Say the Whole Word

Teach/Model

Display the Syllable Segmentation Strategy, such as the example shown on the facing page. Explain to students that they are going to learn to read multisyllabic words using the steps in this strategy. Print the word *finish* on the board.

finish

1. Pronounce the Written Word and Explain Its Meaning

Say: *This word is* finish. Finish *means "to bring something to an end." When you finish doing something, you do the last part of it so that there is no more for you to do.*

2. Segment the Spoken Word into Syllables

Hold up one finger as you slowly say *fin.* Then hold up a second finger as you slowly say *ish.* Next, hold up the two fingers and say: *There are two syllables in the word* finish, fin *and* ish. *Listen as I say the word again,* finish.

finish

3. Match the Spoken and Written Syllables

Say: *The first syllable in* finish *is* fin. Underline the letters that stand for *fin.* Say: *The second syllable in* finish *is* ish. Underline the letters that stand for *ish.* Say: *Notice that in* finish *there is one vowel sound in each syllable, /i/ in* fin *and /i/ in* ish.

4. Blend the Syllables to Say the Whole Word

Say: *Now I will blend the syllables* fin *and* ish *to say the whole word.* Point just to the left of *finish* and then quickly sweep your finger under the whole word and say: *finish.*

Repeat the same procedure with the three-syllable word *microphone* (mi•cro•phone, mic•ro•phone).

Guided Practice

Explain to students that now it's their turn to follow the steps of the Syllable Segmentation Strategy. Print the word *violin* on the board.

1. Pronounce the Written Word and Explain Its Meaning

Ask: *What's this word?* (violin) Ask: *Do you know what a violin is?* (a musical instrument with strings)

CORRECTIVE FEEDBACK If a student or students fail to read the word correctly, say: *This word is* violin. *Now you read it.* If a student doesn't know a word's meaning, give the meaning of the word.

2. Segment the Spoken Word into Syllables

Say: *I want you to hold up one finger at a time while saying each syllable in* violin. After students have said the word and have held up three fingers, ask: *How many syllables in* violin*?* (three) Ask: *What's the whole word?* (violin)

CORRECTIVE FEEDBACK If a student or students segment a word incorrectly, stop immediately and model the correct response for the entire group and then ask the entire group to respond. For example, hold up three fingers and say: *There are three syllables in the word* violin. After modeling the correct response, say: *Now you copy me and do it just like that.*

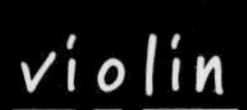

3. Match the Spoken and Written Syllables

Ask: *What is the first syllable in* violin*?* (vī) Ask a volunteer to underline the letters that stand for *vī*. Ask: *What is the second syllable in* violin*?* (ō) Ask the volunteer to underline the letter that stands for *ō*. Ask: *What is the third syllable in* violin*?* (lin) Ask the volunteer to underline the letters that stand for *lin*.

Say: *Each syllable has only one vowel sound.* Ask: *What is the vowel sound in the first syllable?* (/ī/) *The second syllable?* (/ō/) *The third syllable?* (/i/)

CORRECTIVE FEEDBACK If a student or students don't respond or respond incorrectly, stop immediately and model the correct response for the entire group and then ask the entire group to respond. For example, say: *Watch me say the syllables and find their spellings.* After modeling the correct response, say: *Now you copy me and do it just like that.*

4. Blend the Syllables to Say the Whole Word

Say: *Now I want you to blend the syllables to say the whole word.* Then point just to the left of *violin* and ask: *What's the whole word?* Sweep your finger under the whole word to signal students to respond. (violin)

CORRECTIVE FEEDBACK If a student or students respond incorrectly when reading the word, stop immediately and model the correct response for the entire group and then ask the entire group to respond. For example, say: *The word is* violin. *Now you read it.*

Repeat the same procedure with the three-syllable words *percentage* (per • cent • age, per • cen • tage) and *multiply* (mul • ti • ply, mult • i • ply, mul • tip • ly, mult • ip • ly).

Apply to Connected Text

Provide opportunities for students to apply what they have learned about reading multisyllabic words. Have students find examples of multisyllabic words in reading program or content area text. Ask them to pick one of the words and then show a classmate how to go about reading the word according to the steps in the Syllable Segmentation Strategy.

Word Work: Dictation

This procedure is similar to the procedure for whole word dictation, but rather than spell each sound, students will spell each syllable. Students will need a sheet of paper and a pencil.

1. Introduce the Word

Say: *Now we are going to practice spelling multisyllabic words. We will spell each word one syllable at a time. The first word is* gorilla. *A gorilla is a large ape, or type of monkey, that lives in Africa.* Gorilla. Ask: *What's the word?* (gorilla)

2. Count the Syllables in the Word

Say: *Hold up one finger at a time while saying each syllable in* gorilla *with me:* gor•il•la. Ask: *How many syllables are in* gorilla*?* (three) Ask: *What's the first syllable in* gorilla*?* (gor) *What's the second syllable in* gorilla*?* (il) *What is the third syllable in* gorilla*?* (la)

3. Spell Each Syllable

Say: *The first syllable in* gorilla *is* gor. *Think of the sounds in* gor *and then write the syllable on your papers.* Then say: *The second syllable in* gorilla *is* il. *Think about the sounds in* il *and then write the syllable on your papers.* Then say: *The third syllable is* la. *Think about the sounds in* la *and write the syllable on your papers.* Monitor students as they spell each syllable, providing guidance as needed.

4. Compare and Correct

Print the word *gorilla* on the board. Ask students to compare their spelling with yours. After giving students an opportunity to make corrections, say: *Now, let's say and spell the word together.*

First syllable? (gor, g-o-r) *Second syllable?* (il, i-l) *Third syllable?* (la, l-a). Repeat the same dictation procedure with the words *conclude* (con • clude), *target* (tar • get), and *violet* (vi • o • let).

OBSERVE & ASSESS

Questions for Observation	Benchmarks
Read the word. How many syllables do you hear?	Student can identify the number of syllables in spoken and written words.
(Point to a word with more than one syllable.) Read the word? Can you match the sounds of the syllables to the spellings in the word?	Student can match sounds of the syllables with spellings in the word.

LESSON MODEL FOR

Reading Multisyllabic Words

Benchmarks

- ability to analyze and synthesize multisyllabic words
- ability to decode multisyllabic words with consonant–*le* syllables

Strategy Grade Level

- Grade 2 and above

Prerequisite

- knowledge of common sound/spelling correspondences

Grouping

- whole class
- small group or pairs
- individual

Materials

- pocket chart
- word cards *battle, candle, fiddle, giggle, pebble, stable, staple, title, uncle*
- syllable cards *bat, can, fid, gig, peb, stab, stap, ti, un* (first syllables); *ble, cle, dle, gle, ple, tle* (second syllables)

Syllasearch Procedure

This sample lesson model is based on a research-based procedure designed by Isabel Beck and her colleagues to provide opportunities for students "to participate in the analysis and synthesis of multisyllabic words" (Beck, Roth, and McKeown 1985). A lesson sequence for Syllasearch is included in *Making Sense of Phonics: The Hows and Whys* (Beck 2006). This lesson model targets two-syllable words with consonant–*le* syllables. A consonant–*le* combination at the end of multisyllabic words is a whole syllable unit, even though the letter *e* after the *l* does not stand for a vowel sound. The same model can be adapted and used to analyze and synthesize words that contain other syllable types and to enhance multisyllabic word instruction in any commercial reading program.

Introduce Consonant–*le* Syllables

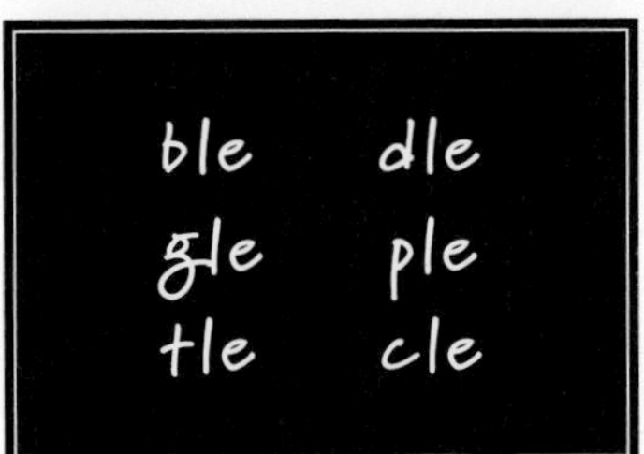

Print the most common consonant–*le* syllables on the board: *ble, dle, gle, ple, tle,* and *cle.* Tell students that many words end in this type of syllable: a consonant and the letters *le.* Underline the consonant in each syllable and say: *In these syllables, the* e *is silent and the* le *is pronounced* /əl/. Ask: *How is the* le *pronounced?* (/əl/) Say: *Let's read the syllables. When I point to the left of a syllable, blend the sounds in your head. When I sweep my finger under the syllable, read it aloud.* Point to the left of *ble.* Say: *Read.* Sweep your finger under the syllable to signal students to respond. (/bəl/) Repeat the same procedure until all syllables are read.

table

Print the word *table* on the board and underline *ble.* Point to the last syllable *ble* and say: *The last syllable in this word is the consonant–*le *syllable* b-l-e. *It stands for /bəl/.* Point to the first syllable *ta* and say: *The first syllable ends in a vowel so it is an open syllable and the vowel sound is long.* Ask: *How's the first syllable pronounced?* (/tā/) *How's the second syllable pronounced?* (/bəl/) *What's the whole word?* Sweep your finger under the whole word to signal students to respond. (table)

tumble

Print the word *tumble* on the board and underline *ble.* Point to the last syllable *ble* and ask: *What's the last syllable in this word?* (/bəl/) Point to the first syllable *tum* and say: *The first syllable ends in a consonant so it is a closed syllable and the vowel sound is short.* Ask: *How's the first syllable pronounced?* (/tum/) *How's the second syllable pronounced?* (/bəl/) *What's the whole word?* Sweep your finger under the whole word to signal students to respond. (tumble)

Words

fiddle
giggle
title
candle
battle
staple
stable
pebble
uncle

Teach the Procedure

Tell students that they are going to learn to play Syllasearch, which will help them to read big words quickly and easily. Explain that Syllasearch has three parts: Meet the Words, Find the Syllables, and Collect the Words.

1. Meet the Words

Display the following word cards in one column in a pocket chart: *fiddle, giggle, title, candle, battle, staple, stable, pebble,* and *uncle.* Say: *In order to play the game Syllasearch, you must first meet, or become acquainted with, this set of words, which all contain consonant–*le *syllables.* Read aloud the words and then ask students to say the words with you. Provide a very brief student-friendly definition or context sentence for any words you think may be unfamiliar to students.

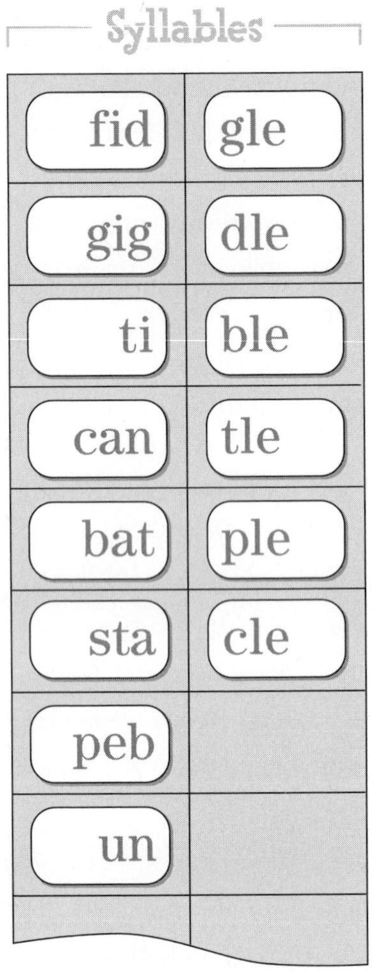

Syllables

fid	gle
gig	dle
ti	ble
can	tle
bat	ple
sta	cle
peb	
un	

2. Find the Syllables

Remove all the word cards from the pocket chart. Tell students that now it is time to find the syllables within the words. Show the first word card *fiddle.* Point to *fiddle* and say: *Remember, this word is* fiddle. Ask: *What's the word?* (fiddle) Say: *Listen as I read the first syllable in* fiddle. Scoop your finger under the first syllable and say: */fid/.* Ask: *What's the first syllable?* (/fid/) Ask: *Is* fid *an open or closed syllable?* (closed) Place the syllable card *fid* in the first column of the pocket chart. Say: *Listen as I read the second syllable in* fiddle. Scoop your finger under the second syllable and say: */dəl/.* Ask: *What's the second syllable?* (/dəl/) Place the syllable card *dle* in the second column, second row, of the pocket chart.

Using the arrangement shown at left, follow the same procedure with the rest of the word cards. If a syllable is repeated (e.g., the *tle* in *title* and *battle*), point out to students that the syllable is already displayed in the pocket chart. When the syllable cards have been identified and displayed, tell students that next they will collect the words.

3. Collect the Words

Display the syllable cards, as shown on the facing page. Tell students that now they are going to collect, or build, the words they previously met by combining a syllable card from the first column and a syllable card from the second column.

Say: *I will say one of the words that we just met. Then I will call on a volunteer to build that word using the syllable cards in the pocket chart. Let's try one. The first word I want a student to build is* title. Ask: *What word?* (title) Call on a volunteer to build the word *title.* The student should take one syllable card from each column to build the word and then form the word at the bottom of the pocket chart, as shown.

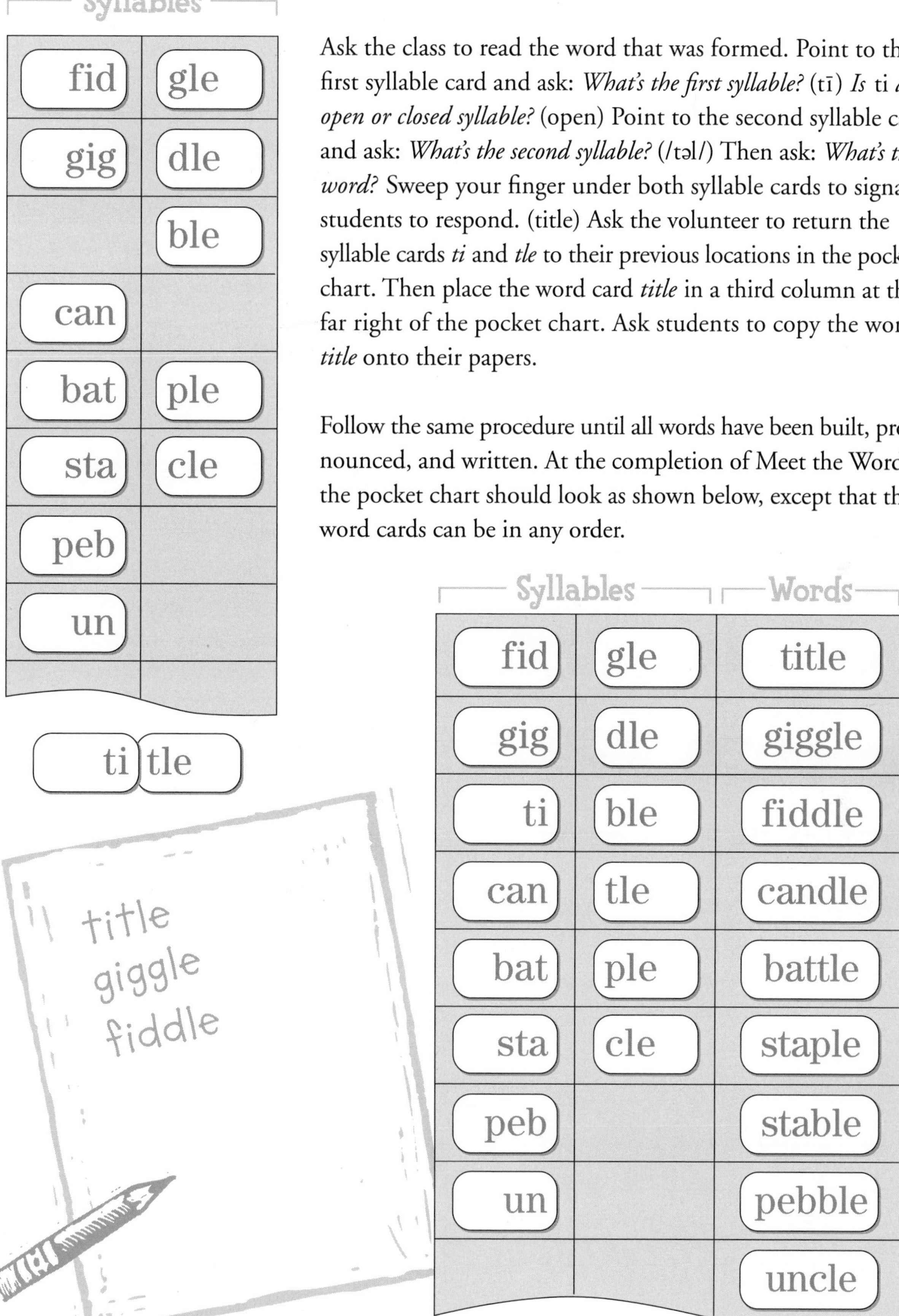

Ask the class to read the word that was formed. Point to the first syllable card and ask: *What's the first syllable?* (tī) *Is* ti *an open or closed syllable?* (open) Point to the second syllable card and ask: *What's the second syllable?* (/təl/) Then ask: *What's the word?* Sweep your finger under both syllable cards to signal students to respond. (title) Ask the volunteer to return the syllable cards *ti* and *tle* to their previous locations in the pocket chart. Then place the word card *title* in a third column at the far right of the pocket chart. Ask students to copy the word *title* onto their papers.

Follow the same procedure until all words have been built, pronounced, and written. At the completion of Meet the Words, the pocket chart should look as shown below, except that the word cards can be in any order.

can | ple

NONSENSE-WORD VERSION Tell students that now you want them to build nonsense words using the same syllable cards. Call on a volunteer to build a nonsense word by choosing a syllable card from each column. After the student builds the word, have the class identify the syllables and then pronounce the made-up word. For example, if a student builds the nonsense word *canple,* point to the first syllable card and ask: *What's the first syllable?* (can) *Is* can *an open or closed syllable?* (closed) Point to the second syllable card and ask: *What's the second syllable?* (/pəl/) Then ask: *What's the nonsense word?* Sweep your finger under the whole word as students respond. (/canpəl/) You may want to ask students to provide a creative definition for each of the nonsense words.

Word Reading Practice for Automaticity

Make a word recognition grid, like the one shown below. In the grid, print in random order 20 words that contain the consonant–*le* syllables. Repeat the words in a different order until the grid is full.

WORD RECOGNITION GRID

apple	tumble	battle	bridle	bugle
cradle	candle	ripple	noble	title
giggle	fable	giggle	staple	nibble
pebble	uncle	saddle	maple	cattle
bugle	title	nibble	cattle	maple
staple	noble	bridle	saddle	giggle
ripple	battle	apple	candle	fable
uncle	pebble	giggle	cradle	able
pebble	apple	saddle	bridle	cattle
bugle	maple	ripple	fable	cradle

Use interactive whiteboard technology to display the grid. Tell students that they are going to practice reading words with consonant–*le* syllables. To warm up, point to *apple,* or the first word in the top row, and say: *Watch as I blend each syllable and then read the whole word.* Scoop your finger under the first syllable and say: */ap/.* Scoop your finger under the second syllable and say: */pəl/.* Then quickly sweep your finger under the whole word and say: *apple.* Follow the same procedure with the rest of the words in the top row.

Point out to students that when they blend *apple* syllable by syllable they will pronounce each /p/ sound in the double consonant, but when they read the whole word they will pronounce the /p/ sound once.

After the warm-up, say: *Now you are going to practice reading the words. First you will blend each syllable and then read the whole word. Ready?* Point to the first word *apple.* Scoop your finger under the first syllable to signal students to respond. (/ap/) Scoop your finger under the second syllable to signal students to respond. (/pəl/) Then sweep your finger under the whole word to signal students to respond. (apple) Follow the same procedure with the rest of the words, starting with the top row and working down and then across each row. Review troublesome words by pointing to them at random as students blend them.

OBSERVE & ASSESS

Question for Observation	Benchmark
*(Point to a word with the consonant–*le *syllable type.)* Can you read this word?	Student can read words with the consonant–*le* syllable type.

LESSON MODEL FOR

Reading Multisyllabic Words

Benchmarks

- ability to identify common affixes in isolation
- ability to decode affixed words

Strategy Grade Level

- Grade 2 and above

Prerequisites

- ability to identify prefixes *pre–* and *re–*
- ability to identify suffixes *–er* and *–ful*
- knowledge of common sound/spelling correspondences

Grouping

- whole class
- small group or pairs
- individual

Materials

- connected text

SEE ALSO . . .

Most Frequent Prefixes, p. 44

Most Frequent Suffixes, p. 45

Introducing Affixes

According to Cunningham (1998), of the words readers are apt to meet, affixed words (i.e., words with a prefix and one or more suffixes) outnumber unanalyzable words by a factor of four to one. Therefore, the ability to recognize and pronounce affixes quickly and accurately in isolation is key to decoding longer words (Archer, Gleason, and Vachon 2003). Common prefixes and suffixes should be systematically introduced throughout the primary grades (Carnine et al. 2006). Each section of this sample lesson model is divided into two parts: prefixes and suffixes. Please note that in actual classroom lessons, it is not advisable to introduce new prefixes and suffixes at the same time. The same model can be adapted and used to introduce other affixes and to enhance multisyllabic word reading instruction in any commercial reading program.

Introduce the Affix in Isolation

PREFIXES Say: *Now we are going to learn about word parts we call prefixes. Prefixes always come at the beginning of words.* Print the prefix *un–* on the board. Point to *un–* and say: *This is the prefix* un–. Then ask: *What's the prefix?* (un–) Have students practice identifying the prefix in isolation over a period of several days.

SUFFIXES Say: *Now we are going to learn about word parts we call suffixes. Suffixes always come at the end of words.* Print the inflectional suffix *–ing* on the board. Point to *–ing* and say: *This is the suffix* –ing. Then ask: *What's the suffix?* (–ing) Have students practice identifying the suffix in isolation over a period of several days.

CORRECTIVE FEEDBACK If a student or students respond incorrectly, stop immediately and model the correct response for the entire group. For example, point under a prefix and say: *This prefix is* un–. Ask: *Everyone, what's the prefix?* (un–)

Teach/Model—Reading Words with Affixes

PREFIXES Say: *Today I am going to show you how to read words with the prefix* un–. *Watch me read the first word.* Print the word *unpack* on the board and underline the prefix *un–*. Ask: *Do prefixes come at the beginning or at the end of words?* (at the beginning) Point to the prefix *un–*. Say: *At the beginning of a word, these letters usually stand for the prefix* un–. Say: *Now watch as I read the word by parts.* Scoop your finger under *un–* and say: *The prefix, or word part, is* un–. Then scoop your finger under *pack* and say: *This word part is* pack. Point just to the left of *unpack* and say: *Now watch as I read the whole word.* Pause and then quickly sweep your finger under the whole word and say: *The word is* unpack. Then ask: *What's the word?* (unpack) Follow the same procedure with the words *unload* and *uncommon.*

SUFFIXES Say: *Today I am going to show you how to read words with the suffix* –ing. *Watch me read the first word.* Print the word *jumping* on the board and underline the suffix *–ing*. Ask: *Do suffixes come at the beginning or at the end of words?* (at the end) Point to the suffix *–ing*. Say: *At the end of a word, these letters usually stand for the suffix* –ing. Say: *Now watch as I read the word by parts.* Scoop your finger under *jump* and say: *This word part is* jump. Then scoop your finger under *–ing* and say: *This suffix, or word part, is* –ing. Point just to the left of *jumping* and say: *Now watch as I read the whole word.* Pause for two seconds and then quickly sweep your finger under the whole word and say: *The word is* jumping. Then ask: *What's the word?* (jumping) Follow the same procedure with the words *working* and *learning.*

Guided Practice—Reading Words with Affixes

unfair unsafe
uncover refill
uneasy preheat

PREFIXES Print the following list of words on the board, underlining the prefixes: *unfair, uncover, uneasy, refill, unsafe,* and *preheat.* Tell students that now it's their turn to read some words with prefixes.

Point to the word *unfair.* Ask: *What prefix, or word part, do the underlined letters usually stand for?* (un–) Ask: *What's this word part?* Scoop your finger under *un–* to signal students to respond. (un–) Then ask: *What's the next word part?* Scoop your finger under *fair* to signal students to respond. (fair) Point just to the left of *unfair* and say: *What's the whole word?* Pause for two seconds and then quickly sweep your finger under the whole word to signal students to respond. (unfair)

Follow the same procedure with the rest of the words on the list. Then have students read the entire list again. This time, have them read the whole word without first identifying the prefix. Provide additional practice, using the words *repay, unclear, prewash, unkind, untangle,* and *rename.*

painting teacher
covering speaking
waiting thankful

SUFFIXES Print the following list of words on the board, underlining the suffixes: *painting, covering, waiting, teacher, speaking,* and *thankful.* Tell students that now it's their turn to read words with suffixes.

Point to the word *painting.* Ask: *What suffix, or word part, do the underlined letters usually stand for?* (–ing) Ask: *What's this word part?* Scoop your finger under *paint* to signal students to respond. (paint) Then ask: *What's the next word part?* Scoop your finger under *–ing* to signal students to respond. (–ing) Point just to the left of *painting* and say: *What's the whole word?* Pause for two seconds and then quickly sweep your finger under the whole word to signal students to respond. (painting)

SEE ALSO . . .

LESSON MODELS

Word-Part Clues: Prefixes, p. 527

Word-Part Clues: Suffixes, p. 533

Follow the same procedure with the rest of the words on the list. Then have students read the entire list again. This time, have them read the whole word without first identifying the suffix. Provide additional practice, using the words *worker, sweeping, careful, matching, heating,* and *gardener.*

Apply to Connected Text

Provide opportunities for students to apply what they have learned about reading multisyllabic words with affixes. Have students find examples of multisyllabic words with affixes in reading program or content-area text. Ask them to pick two of the words and then show a classmate how to go about reading them.

OBSERVE & ASSESS

Questions for Observation	Benchmarks
(Point to the prefix un–.*)* What word part, or prefix, do these letters usually stand for?	Student can identify the prefix *un–* in isolation.
(Point to the suffix –ing.*)* What word part, or suffix, do these letters usually stand for?	Student can identify the suffix *–ing* in isolation.
(Point to the word unsafe.*)* What's this word?	Student can decode words with the prefix *un–*.
(Point to the word covering.*)* What's this word?	Student can decode words with the suffix *–ing*.

LESSON MODEL FOR

Reading Multisyllabic Words

Benchmarks

- ability to segment a multisyllabic word into parts
- ability to read multisyllabic words independently

Strategy Grade Level

- Grade 2 and above

Prerequisites

- Introducing Affixes, p. 304
- ability to pronounce in isolation affixes *dis–, ex–, pre–, re–, sub–, –tion*

Grouping

- whole class
- small group or pairs
- individual

Materials

- connected text

Flexible Strategy for Reading Big Words

Recent research supports a shift from rigid rules to a more flexible approach to the decoding of longer words. This sample lesson model is based on the Overt Strategy developed by Anita Archer, Mary Gleason, and Vicky Vachon (2006). In this strategy, students learn that they can be flexible in dividing a longer word into parts, or syllables, as long as they can ultimately make the word into a real word. The same model can be adapted and used to read other multisyllabic target words and to enhance multisyllabic word instruction in any commercial reading program.

Review Prefixes for Automaticity

Make a Prefix Recognition Grid, like the one shown below. Each of the five rows contains the same previously introduced prefixes in a different order. Use interactive whiteboard technology to display the grid. Tell students that they are going to practice reading prefixes. To warm up, point and sweep under each of the prefixes in the top row and say, for example: *This prefix is* pre–. Then ask: *What's the prefix?* (pre–) After the warm-up, say: *Now you are going to practice reading the prefixes. When I point to a prefix, read it aloud. Ready?* Then point to each prefix in order, starting with the top row and working down and then across each row. Review troublesome prefixes by pointing to them at random as students name them.

PREFIX RECOGNITION GRID

pre–	dis–	ex–	re–	sub–
sub–	ex–	pre–	dis–	re–
dis–	re–	sub–	ex–	pre–
re–	ex–	dis–	pre–	sub–
pre–	sub–	ex–	dis–	re–

FLEXIBLE STRATEGY FOR READING BIG WORDS

1. Circle the Prefixes and Suffixes
2. Underline the Vowels in the Uncircled Part(s) of the Word
3. Read the Word by Parts or Syllables
4. Read the Whole Word and Confirm Its Pronunciation

Teach/Model

Display the Flexible Strategy for Reading Big Words, such as the example shown above. Explain to students that you are going to show them how to use these steps to read multisyllabic words. Print the word *prevention* on the board.

1. Circle the Prefixes and Suffixes

Say: *Step 1 says to circle the prefixes and suffixes. Watch as I circle prefixes and suffixes in this word. Remember, prefixes are word parts that come at the beginning of words and suffixes are word parts that come at the end of words.* Circle *pre–* and say: *The prefix is* pre–. Point to *pre–* and ask: *What's the prefix?* (pre–) Circle *–tion* and say: *The suffix is* –tion. Point to *–tion* and ask: *What's the suffix?* (–tion)

2. Underline the Vowels in the Uncircled Part(s) of the Word

Say: *Step 2 says to underline the vowels in the uncircled parts of the word. Watch as I underline the vowels in the rest of the word—the part of the word that is not circled.* In the syllable *ven,* underline the *e*. Point to the *e* and say: *The vowel is* e. *The sound of this vowel is /ĕ/.* Point to the *e* and ask: *What's the sound?* (/ĕ/)

3. Read the Word by Parts or Syllables

Say: *Step 3 says to read the word by parts or syllables. Now I'll read the word part by part, or syllable by syllable.* Scoop your finger under the first syllable and say: */prē/.* Then scoop your finger under the second syllable and say: */ven/.* Finally, scoop your finger under the third syllable and say: */tion/.*

4. Read the Whole Word and Confirm Its Pronunciation

Say: *Step 4 says to read the whole word and confirm its pronunciation.* Point just to the left of *prevention* and say: *Now I'll read the whole word.* Quickly sweep your finger under the whole word and say: *prevention.* Ask: *Is this a real word that you recognize?* (yes) Say: *Yes, prevention is when you stop something from happening. For example, crime prevention is preventing crime from happening.* Follow the same procedure with the word *prescription.*

Guided Practice

Explain to students that now it's their turn to follow the steps of the strategy to read multisyllabic words. Print the word *prediction* on the board.

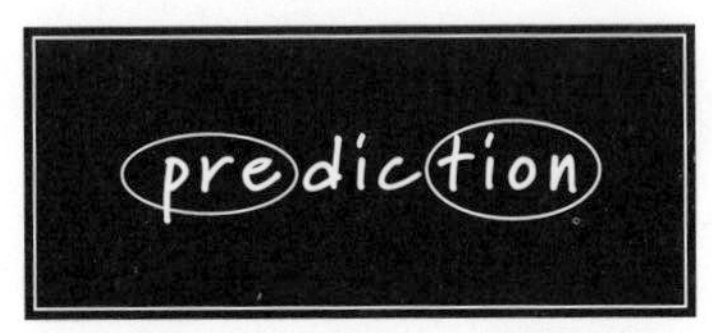

1. Circle the Prefixes and Suffixes

Say: *Step 1 says to circle the prefixes and suffixes.* Point to *prediction* and ask: *Does this word have a prefix?* (yes) *What's the prefix?* (pre–) *Does this word have a suffix?* (yes) *What's the suffix?* (–tion) Ask a volunteer to circle the prefix and suffix in *prediction.*

CORRECTIVE FEEDBACK If a student or students respond incorrectly, model the correct response for the entire group. For example, point under the prefix and say: *The prefix is* pre–. Then ask: *Everyone, what's the prefix?* (pre–)

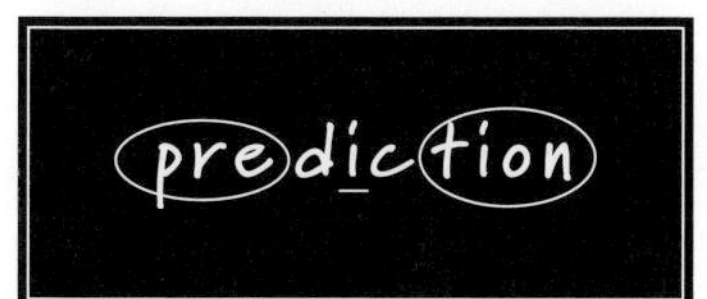

2. Underline the Vowels in the Uncircled Part(s) of the Word

Say: *Step 2 says to underline the vowels in the uncircled parts of the word.* Point to *prediction* and say: Pre– *and* –tion *are circled.* Ask: *What part of the word is not circled?* (dic) Ask: *Do you see a vowel in this part of the word?* (yes) *What is it?* (i) Ask a volunteer to underline the vowel. Point to the *i* and ask: *What's the sound?* (/i/)

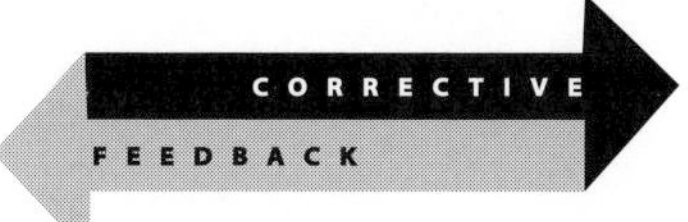

CORRECTIVE FEEDBACK If a student or students respond incorrectly, model the correct response for the entire group. For example, in the word *prediction,* point to the letter *i* and say: *The sound is /i/.* Then ask: *Everyone, what's the sound?* (/i/)

3. Read the Word by Parts or Syllables

Say: *Step 3 says to read the word by parts or syllables.* Say: *Now let's read the word part by part, or syllable by syllable.* Ask: *First part or syllable?* Scoop your finger under *pre–* to signal students to respond. (pre–) Ask: *Second part or syllable?* Scoop your finger under *dic* to signal students to respond. (dic) Ask: *Third part or syllable?* Scoop your finger under *–tion* to signal students to respond. (–tion)

CORRECTIVE FEEDBACK If a student or students respond incorrectly, model the correct response for the entire group. For example, point to *dic* and say: *The part or syllable is* dic. Ask: *Everyone, what's the part or syllable?* (dic) Say: *Yes,* dic. *Let's read all the parts again.*

4. Read the Whole Word and Confirm Its Pronunciation

Say: *Step 4 says to read the whole word and confirm its pronunciation.* Finally, point just to the left of *prediction* and ask: *What's the whole word?* Quickly sweep your finger under the whole word to signal students to respond. (prediction) Ask: *Is this a real word that you recognize?* (yes) Say: *Yes, when you make a prediction you say what you think might happen.*

CORRECTIVE FEEDBACK

CORRECTIVE FEEDBACK If a student or students don't recognize the word as it is pronounced, say: *Sometimes when you read a longer word, you don't pronounce it the right way and therefore it doesn't sound like a real word. You have to change the way you pronounce the word.* Point to the beginning of the target word and say, for example: *This word is pronounced* "prediction." *Say it with me.* Follow the same procedure with the words *distraction* and *reception.*

The letter pattern *-tion* is not truly a suffix. In a word ending in *-tion,* such as *interruption, t* is the final letter of the root word and *-ion* is the actual suffix. For decoding purposes, introducing *-tion* as a suffix is acceptable (Carnine et al. 2006).

Apply to Connected Text

Provide opportunities for students to apply what they have learned about reading multisyllabic words. Have students find examples of multisyllabic words in reading program or content area text. Ask them to pick one of the words and then show a classmate how to go about reading the word according to the steps in the Flexible Strategy for Reading Big Words.

Word Work: Dictation

This procedure is similar to the procedure for whole word dictation, but rather than spell each sound, students spell each syllable. Students will need a sheet of paper and a pencil.

1. Introduce the Word

Say: *Now we are going to practice spelling big words. We will spell each word one part or syllable at a time. The first word is* reflection. *I saw my reflection in the mirror.* Reflection. *What's the word?* (reflection)

2. Count the Parts or Syllables in the Word

Say: *Hold up one finger at a time while saying each part or syllable in* reflection *with me:* re•flec•tion. Ask: *How many parts or syllables in* reflection*?* (three) Ask: *What's the first part or syllable in* reflection*?* (re–) Ask: *What's the second part or syllable?* (flec) Ask: *What's the third part or syllable?* (–tion)

reflection

3. Spell Each Part or Syllable

Say: *The first part or syllable in* reflection *is* re–. *Think about the sounds in* re– *and then write the prefix on your papers.* Then say: *The second part or syllable in* reflection *is* flec. *Think about the sounds in* flec *and write the part or syllable on your papers.* Finally, say: *The third part or syllable in* reflection *is* –tion. *Think about how to spell* –tion *and then write the suffix on your papers.* Monitor students as they write each part or syllable, providing guidance as needed.

reflection

4. Compare and Correct

Print the word *reflection* on the board. Ask students to compare their spelling with yours. After giving them an opportunity to make corrections, say: *Now, let's say and spell the word together. First part or syllable?* (re–, r-e) *Second part or syllable?* (flec, f-l-e-c) *Third part or syllable?* (–tion, t-i-o-n) Repeat the same dictation procedure with the word *exception*.

OBSERVE & ASSESS

Question for Observation	Benchmark
(Point to a word.) Look at this word. Can you read the word by parts or syllables and then read the whole word?	Student can read multisyllabic words using the flexible strategy.

LESSON MODEL FOR

Reading and Writing Multisyllabic Words

Benchmarks

- ability to recognize a root word
- ability to decode words by morphemes, or word parts
- ability to recognize words in a word family

Strategy Grade Level

- Grade 2 and above

Prerequisites

- Introducing Affixes, p. 304
- ability to pronounce in isolation affixes *-al, -ed, in-, inter-, -ity, -ly-, multi-, -tion*

Grouping

- whole class
- small group or pairs
- individual

Materials

- none

Root Word Transformation Strategy

Many multisyllabic words are made up of word parts such as root words and affixes. The affixes often affect the pronunciation and usage of the root word. This sample lesson model is based the morphemic transformation strategy developed by John Shefelbine and Katherine Newman (2004). The same model can be adapted and used to introduce other multisyllabic words made up of word parts and to enhance multisyllabic word instruction in any commercial reading program.

Introduce Root Words

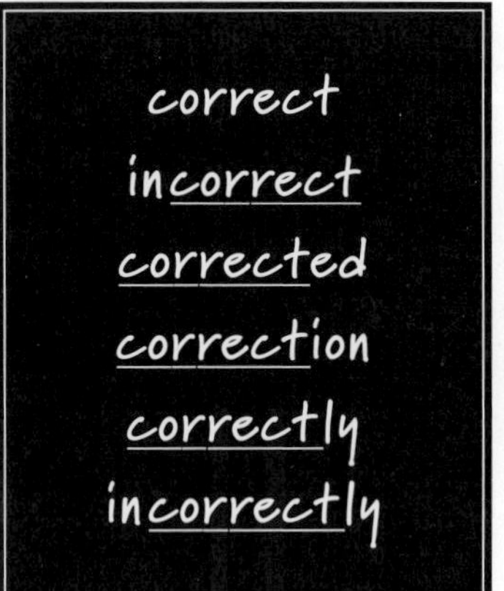

Explain to students that a root word is a single word that cannot be broken into smaller words or word parts. List the following words on the board: *correct, incorrect, corrected, correction, correctly,* and *incorrectly.* Point to *correct* and say: *The word* correct *is a single word that cannot be broken into smaller words or word parts; it is a root word. The rest of the words in the list contain the root word* correct. Underline *correct* in each of the words. Ask: *What is the common root word in each of these words?* (correct) Have students read the words aloud with you. Say: *Because these words have the same root word in common, they belong to the same word family.*

Teach/Model

Explain to students that you are going to show them how to form big words by adding word parts, such as prefixes and suffixes, to the same root word.

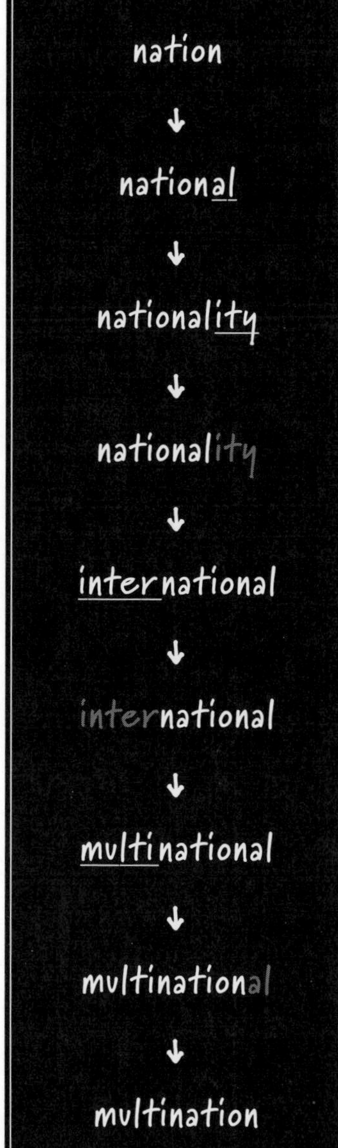

1. Introduce the Root Word

Print the word *nation* on the board and say: *This root word is* nation. Ask: *What's the root word?* Quickly sweep your finger under the whole word to signal students to respond. (nation) Say: *A nation is an individual country.*

2. Form Bigger Words

ADD Add *al* to *nation* to form *national.* Underline *al.* Then point to it and say: *This word part is* al. Point just to the left of the word and say: *Now I'll read the whole word.* Quickly sweep your finger under the whole word and say: *national.* Say: *Listen, the pronunciation of the vowel sound in the root word changed after I added* al. *We say* năational, *not* nātional.

ADD Add *ity* to *national* to form *nationality.* Underline *ity.* Then point to it and say: *This word part is* ity. Point just to the left of the word and say: *Now I'll read the whole word.* Quickly sweep your finger under the whole word and say: *nationality.*

ERASE Erase *ity* in *nationality.* Then add *inter* to *national* to form *international.* Underline *inter.* Then point to it and say: *This word part is* inter. Point just to the left of the word and say: *Now I'll read the whole word.* Quickly sweep your finger under the whole word and say: *international.*

ERASE Erase *inter* in *international.* Then add *multi* to form *multinational.* Underline *multi.* Then point to it and say: *This word part is* multi. Point just to the left of the word and say: *Now I'll read the whole word.* Quickly sweep your finger under the whole word and say: *multinational.*

ERASE Erase *al* in *multinational* to form *multination.* Underline *multi.* Then point to it and say: *This word part is* multi. Point just to the left of the word and say: *Now I'll read the whole word.* Quickly sweep your finger under the whole word and say: *multination*. Say: *Listen, the vowel sound in* nation *changed again when I removed the* al. *We say* multinātion, *not* multinătion.

nation
national
nationality
international
multinational
multination

3. Read Aloud the Word Family

Print the following words on the board: *nation, national, nationality, international, multinational,* and *multination.* Underline the root word *nation*. Say: *These words all have the same root word,* nation. *Therefore, we say that they belong to the same word family. I added word parts, such as prefixes and suffixes, to the root word* nation *to make bigger words.* Point to *nation* and ask: *What's the root word?* (nation) Say: *Let's read the rest of the words in the family.* Point just to the left of the word *national,* pause briefly, and then quickly sweep your finger under the whole word as you lead students in saying the word. Follow the same procedure with the rest of the words in the list.

Guided Practice

Explain to students that now it's their turn to read the bigger words formed by adding word parts, such as prefixes and suffixes, to the same root word.

1. Introduce the Root Word

Print the word *medic* on the board and say: *This root word is* medic. Ask: *What's the root word?* Quickly sweep your finger under the whole word to signal students to respond. (medic) Say: *A medic can be found working in a hospital or clinic.*

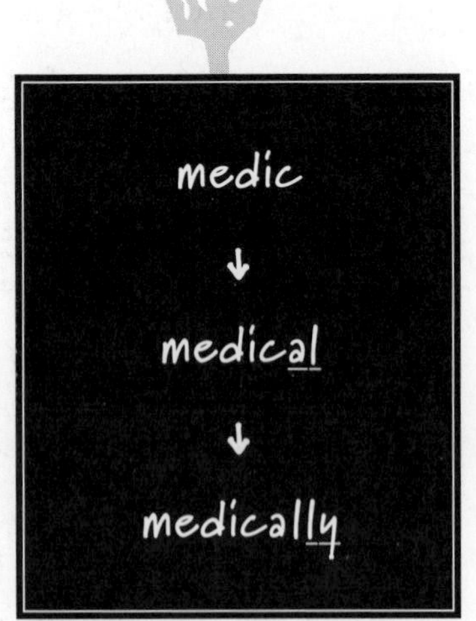

2. Form Bigger Words

ADD Add *al* to *medic* to form *medical.* Underline *al.* Then point to it and ask: *Word part?* (al) Point just to the left of the word and ask: *What's the word?* Quickly sweep your finger under the whole word to signal students to respond. (medical)

CORRECTIVE FEEDBACK
If a student responds incorrectly, stop immediately and model the correct response for the entire group.

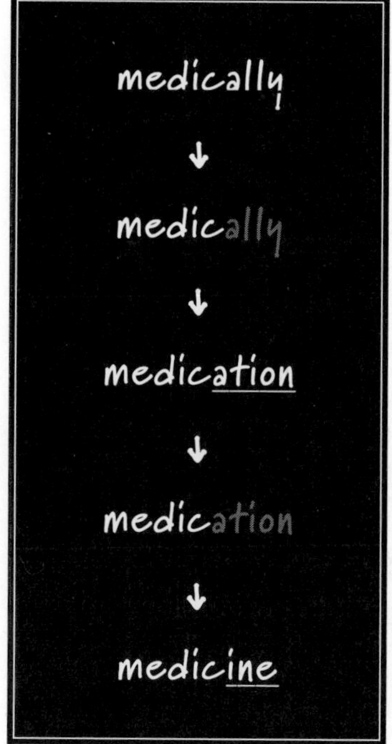

ADD Add *ly* to *medical* to form *medically.* Underline *ly.* Then point to it and ask: *Word part?* (ly) Point just to the left of the word and ask: *What's the word?* Quickly sweep your finger under the whole word to signal students to respond. (medically)

ERASE Erase *ally* in *medically.* Then add *ation* to *medic* to form *medication.* Underline *ation.* Then point to it and ask: *Word part?* (ation) Point just to the left of the word and ask: *What's the word?* Quickly sweep your finger under the whole word to signal students to respond. (medication)

ERASE Erase *ation* in *medication.* Then add *ine* to form *medicine.* Underline *ine.* Point to it and ask: *Word part?* (ine /ĭn/) Point just to the left of the word and ask: *What's the word? Be careful, there may be sound changes.* Quickly sweep your finger under the whole word to signal students to respond. (medicine)

CORRECTIVE FEEDBACK If a student or students pronounce the whole word incorrectly, stop immediately and model the correct response for the entire group. Ask: *Does this sound like a real word?* (no) Then, for example, say: *The* ine *in* medicine *is pronounced /ĭn/, not /īne/. The sound for consonant* c *has changed. When* c *is followed by* i, *it stands for the /s/ sound. We say /medisin/, not /medikin/, /medikine/, or /medisīne/. Say the word again with me:* medicine.

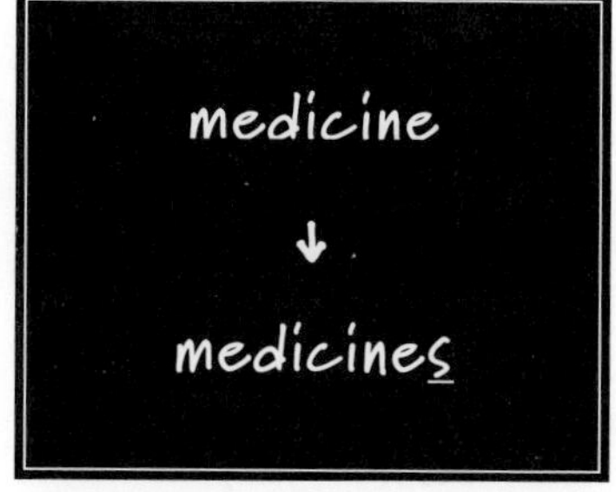

ADD Add *s* in *medicine* to form *medicines.* Underline the *s.* Point to it and ask: *Word part?* (s) Point just to the left of the word and ask: *What's the word?* Quickly sweep your finger under the whole word to signal students to respond. (medicines)

LESSON MODEL: Word Families, p. 524

3. Read Aloud the Word Family

Point to the list of words on the board and ask: *What do all these words have in common?* (The same root word *medic.*) Say: *Right. Word parts, such as prefixes and suffixes, were added to the same root word to make new words.* Point to *medic* and ask: *What's this word?* (medic) Say: *Now read aloud the rest of the words.* Then point just to the left of the next word *medical,* pause briefly, and then quickly sweep your finger under the whole word to signal students to respond. (medical) Follow the same procedure with the rest of the words in the list.

Word Work: Word Building

Print the following two-syllable root words on the board and have students identify them: *expect, depend, invent,* and *predict.* Challenge students to select a root word and create a list of as many words as they can by adding one or more affixes to the root word. For example, for the root word *depend* they might list the words *depended, dependable, dependent, independent,* and *independence.* When students are finished, have them compare their lists of word families.

Questions for Observation	Benchmarks
(Point to a list of words in the same word family.) Read the words.	Student can decode words using morphemic units.
(Point to a list of words in the same word family.) What root word is the same in all of the words?	Student can identify a common root word in a word family.

IV

SECTION IV

Reading Fluency

Introduction

READING FLUENCY

> As part of a developmental process of building decoding skills, fluency can form a bridge to reading comprehension.
>
> —PIKULSKI & CHARD, 2005

CCSS READING STANDARDS

Foundational Skills

Fluency

SEE ALSO . . .

Chapter 9: Fluency Assessment
Chapter 10: Fluency Instruction

The National Reading Panel (2000) found that an effective reading program must include instruction in reading fluency, a critical component of learning to read. Differences in reading fluency distinguish good readers from poor; a lack of reading fluency is a good predictor of reading comprehension problems (Stanovich 1991). Teachers can think of reading fluency as a bridge between the two major components of reading—decoding and comprehension. According to Rasinski (2004), "At one end of this bridge, fluency connects to accuracy and automaticity in decoding. At the other end, fluency connects to comprehension through prosody, or expressive interpretation." Automaticity is quick and effortless reading of words in or out of context (i.e., in connected text or as a list of words) (Ehri and McCormick 1998; Kuhn and Stahl 2003).

Reading fluency is complex and multifaceted. According to Hudson, Lane, and Pullen (2005), reading fluency is made up of at least three key elements: "*accurate* reading of connected text at a conversational *rate* with appropriate *prosody* or expression." Each of these elements—accuracy, rate, and prosody—has a clear connection to reading comprehension. Without accurate word reading, the reader will not have access to the author's intended meaning, and this can lead to misinterpretations of the text. Slow, laborious reading of the text taxes the reader's capacity to construct an ongoing interpretation of the passage. Poor prosody can lead to confusion through inappropriate or meaningless groupings of words, or through inappropriate applications of expression. At its heart, fluency instruction is focused on ensuring that word reading becomes automatic so that readers have sufficient cognitive resources to understand what they read. As LaBerge and Samuels (1974) noted, "A fluent reader decodes text automatically, and therefore can devote his/her attention to comprehending what is read."

Accuracy

Word-reading accuracy refers to the ability to recognize or decode words correctly. To achieve word-reading accuracy requires, first, a deep understanding of the alphabetic principle; second, the ability to blend sounds into words; and third, knowledge of a large number of high-frequency words (Ehri and McCormick 1998). These elements form the foundation for the automatic word reading that is necessary for fluent reading.

READING FLUENCY
the accurate reading of connected text at a conversational rate with appropriate prosody

RATE
how quickly and accurately a reader reads connected text

AUTOMATICITY
the quick and effortless reading of words in or out of context

Rate

Reading rate refers to how quickly and accurately one reads connected text. Rate is commonly measured as the number of words read correctly per minute (WCPM). How quickly, or automatically, readers can read individual words is almost as important as how accurately they can read them. In order to read at a fluent rate, a reader must be able to read a great number of the words with automaticity (Torgesen and Hudson 2006).

In reading, as with any complex activity, the demands on working memory decrease as automaticity increases (Sweller 1994; Sweller, Van Merriënboer, and Paas 1998). Decreasing the demands on working memory frees up cognitive resources that can be devoted to text comprehension (LaBerge and Samuels 1974). That is, when readers move quickly and smoothly through connected text, they can devote attention to grasping text meaning rather than figuring out the words. Conversely, readers who need to pay attention to decoding the words on the page cannot pay attention to comprehension at the same time. Consequently, they must switch attention rapidly back and forth between identifying individual words on the page and constructing meaning, which limits their ability to do either one well (Samuels 2006). This leads to the familiar situation of readers not understanding a passage they have just read.

> The development of automaticity in a skill or skills often reduces the load of the working memory by 90 percent.
>
> —SCHNEIDER, 2003

Prosody

PROSODY
the tonal and rhythmic aspects of spoken language

Prosody is defined as the rhythmic and tonal aspects of speech: the "music" of spoken language (Hudson et al. 2005). Prosody comprises a series of features including pitch (intonation), stress patterns (syllable prominence), and duration (length of time) that convey information above and beyond that provided by the actual words themselves (Allington 1983; Dowhower 1991; Schreiber 1980, 1991). Thus, prosodic reading includes appropriately chunking groups of words into phrases or meaningful units in accordance with the syntactic structure of the text (Kuhn and Stahl 2003). As such, it reflects an understanding of meaningful phrasing and syntax (Rasinski 2000).

When reading aloud with appropriate prosody, fluent oral reading sounds like spoken language (Stahl and Kuhn 2002). Though the exact relationship between prosody and reading comprehension is unclear (see Rasinski 2004; Breznitz 2006; Schwanenflugel et al. 2004), it appears to be an aspect of reading fluency worthy of attention. Oral models of fluent reading can help students see the relationship between appropriate prosody and the meaning of written text.

Fluency Influences

SEE ALSO . . .

Section II: Early Literacy
Section III: Decoding and Word Recognition
Section V: Vocabulary
Section VI: Comprehension

Several variables influence a student's fluent reading of a given text: a student's reading comprehension, the proportion of words a student recognizes instantaneously, a student's decoding speed and accuracy, a student's metacognitive abilities, the extent of a student's vocabulary knowledge or the size of a student's vocabulary, and whether or not the student is reading in a meaningful context. These factors will either impede or improve a student's fluent reading of a specific text (Torgesen and Hudson 2006).

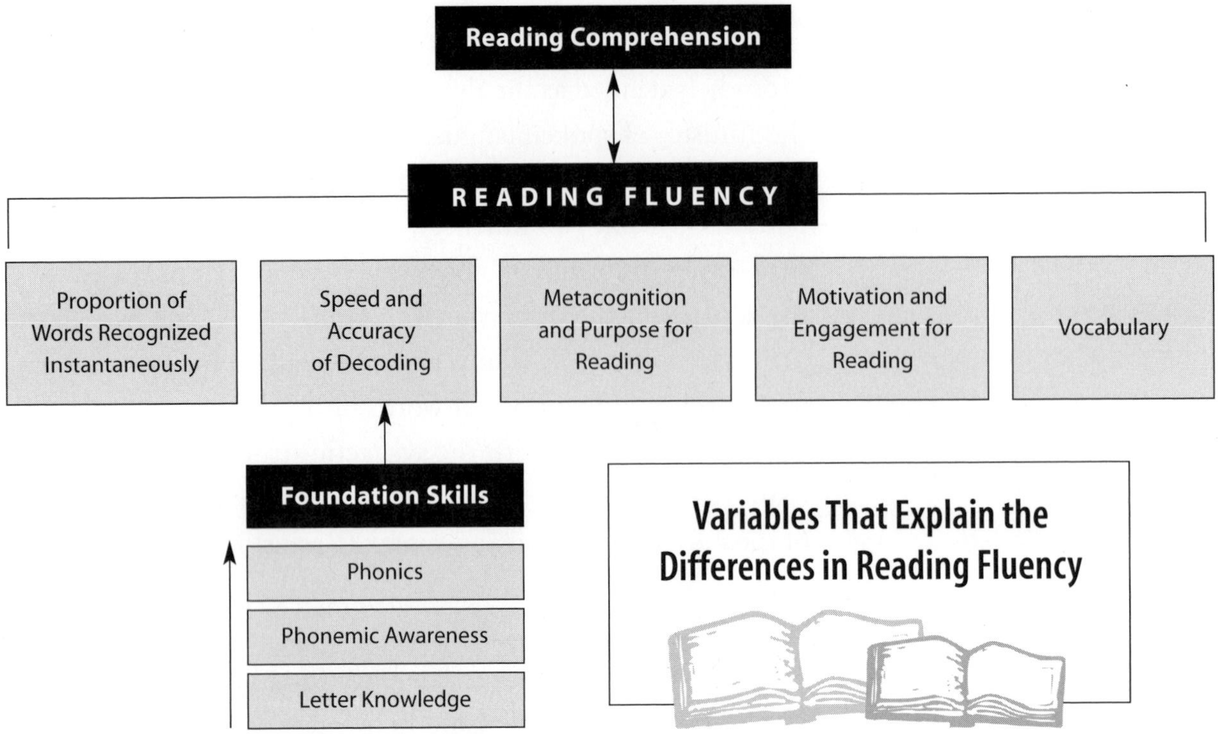

Reading Comprehension

READING FLUENCY

Proportion of Words Recognized Instantaneously

Speed and Accuracy of Decoding

Metacognition and Purpose for Reading

Motivation and Engagement for Reading

Vocabulary

Foundation Skills

Phonics

Phonemic Awareness

Letter Knowledge

Variables That Explain the Differences in Reading Fluency

> Fluency has been shown to have a reciprocal relationship with comprehension, with each fostering the other.
>
> —STECKER, ROSER & MARTINEZ, 1998

Reading Comprehension

While reading fluency aids reading comprehension, comprehension also plays a role in facilitating fluent reading, especially for beginning and struggling readers (Stanovich and Stanovich 1995; Pring and Snowling 1986). Students read words in a meaningful context faster than they read them out of context, such as in a word list (Jenkins et al. 2003).

Proportion of Words Recognized Instantaneously

This is the most important variable in explaining differences in reading fluency (Torgesen, Rashotte, and Alexander 2001). The process of figuring out an unfamiliar word, a word that is not known instantaneously, or by "sight," slows down a student's text reading rate.

Speed and Accuracy of Decoding

When words are not read instantaneously, or by "sight," they must be identified analytically, through decoding using either sound/spelling correspondences or chunks of words. When this process does not happen quickly and accurately, it will have a negative impact on reading fluency.

Metacognition and Purpose for Reading

SEE ALSO . . .

Metacognition, p. 615

Metacognition is being aware of one's thinking and in control of one's learning. It is a term that is generally associated with reading comprehension, but plays a role in reading fluency as well. Readers make many decisions about how to accomplish a reading task based on their purpose for reading a particular text. This self-regulation, or decision making, while reading is referred to as metacognitive control.

Reading purposes can range from studying for a test to savoring the style of a favorite author. Readers make conscious and unconscious decisions about how they approach a given reading task. When studying for a test, a student is likely to read at a slower rate than when reading a novel for pleasure. To avoid making mistakes when reading aloud, some students may unnecessarily slow their reading rate while others may sacrifice accuracy to read more quickly. The decisions students make as they regulate their reading affect their rate and accuracy.

Motivation and Engagement for Reading

SEE ALSO . . .

The Text, p. 611

When a student is reading a text that is not engaging or is not motivated to read a text, reading fluency is likely to suffer.

Vocabulary

SEE ALSO . . .

Extent of Word Knowledge, p. 409

Vocabulary Size, p. 410

Links Between Vocabulary and Comprehension, p. 414

Two aspects of vocabulary—size and accessibility—appear to influence reading fluency. First, a large vocabulary is helpful in decoding unfamiliar words; when a word is part of a student's oral vocabulary, the student can more easily decode and understand it (Kamil and Hiebert 2005). Second, fluency depends on how quickly known meanings can be accessed. If it takes a long time for a student to access the meaning of a known word, it is likely to slow down reading and cause fluency problems.

CHAPTER 9

Fluency Assessment

what? why? when? how?

what?

Fluency Assessment

> The comprehensive assessment of fluency must include measures of oral reading accuracy, rate of oral reading, and quality of oral reading.
>
> —PIKULSKI & CHARD, 2005

Because reading is so critical to success in and out of school and because many students struggle with fluent reading, fluency should be assessed often. Effective fluency assessments provide information that will guide instruction and improve student outcomes (Hosp, Hosp, and Howell 2007). Fluency assessment consists of listening to students read aloud and collecting information about their oral reading accuracy, rate, and prosody.

To measure students' progress and maximize teaching time, it is important to assess reading fluency reliably, validly, and efficiently. First, assessments should provide reliable, consistent scores no matter who is assessing the student or when the assessment is given. Second, they should be a valid, meaningful source of data for making instructional decisions. Finally, the assessments should be efficient in administration, scoring, and interpretation. As Tim Rasinski (2004) puts it, "Assessments should be as quick and easy to use as possible. If they are not, teachers may not find time to use them."

Fluency Acronyms

ORF oral reading fluency

CBM curriculum-based measurement

WCPM words correct per minute

Assessment of ORF: Rate and Accuracy

The combination of reading rate and accuracy is often referred to as oral reading fluency (ORF). Curriculum-based measurement (CBM) is the assessment tool that is most commonly used for measuring ORF. ORF is a good predictor of future reading performance. According to Hosp et al. (2007), "ORF CBM provides a reliable and valid way to (1) identify students who are at risk for reading failure, (2) identify which students

SEE ALSO . . .

Curriculum-Based Measurement (CBM), p. 12

CCSS READING STANDARDS

Foundational Skills

Fluency

Read with sufficient accuracy and fluency to support comprehension. (RF.1-5.4)

CBM data are used to assess whether students are growing satisfactorily as readers, whether they are at risk for reading failure, and whether their instruction should be modified.

—DENO & MARSTON, 2006

SEE ALSO . . .

ASSESSMENT MODELS
Assessment of ORF Rate and Accuracy, p. 340
Digital Graphing of ORF Scores, p. 349

are not making adequate progress given the instruction they are receiving, (3) identify students' instructional level, and (4) identify which students need additional diagnostic evaluation."

Extensive research shows that ORF CBM, as a measure of overall reading proficiency, plays a role in both screening and progress monitoring (e.g., Deno et al. 1983; Deno, Marston, and Mirkin 1982; Fuchs and Fuchs 1992; Fuchs et al. 2001; Fuchs, Fuchs, and Maxwell 1988). Screening assessments are conducted at the beginning of the school year to identify which students need help and which don't. These "first alert" measures are useful for determining the most appropriate starting point for instruction. Progress-monitoring assessments are used to identify students who are not making adequate progress according to a predetermined goal. They are also helpful for making instructional decisions.

Conducting an ORF CBM Assessment

In this quick and easy standardized approach to assessment, the teacher listens for one minute to a student who reads aloud from an unpracticed, grade-level passage. The teacher follows along in a copy of the passage and marks any errors the student makes. At the end of one minute, the teacher determines the student's ORF score by subtracting the number of errors from the total number of words read. The ORF scores are expressed as words correct per minute (WCPM). For example, if a student reads 72 words in one minute and makes 7 errors, the student has an ORF score of 65 WCPM. To monitor progress, the teacher can record a student's WCPM scores on a graph. The graph's visual form is helpful in facilitating the interpretation of the scores. By drawing in an aim line on the graph, the teacher can show the progress a student will need to make to achieve a predetermined goal.

ORF Performance Expectations

ORF norms and weekly growth rates are standards against which to compare students' performance. When a student's performance does not meet a particular standard, a teacher must find a way to fix the problem (Hosp et al. 2007).

SEE ALSO . . .

ASSESSMENT MODEL: Assessment of ORF Rate and Accuracy: Compare ORF Score to ORF Norms, p. 343

ORF Norms

One way to set standards for fluency performance is to compare students' ORF scores to the performance of others in their grade or at their instructional level. National norms provide a good indication of how students perform (Hosp et al. 2007). Oral Reading Fluency Norms, such as Hasbrouck and Tindal's (2006), have been collected over numerous years and from numerous sources. These norms represent the results of a one-minute timed sampling of students' oral reading of grade-level passages. They provide WCPM scores for students in Grades 1–8 during three different assessment time periods across a school year: fall, winter, and spring. For each grade level, the norms are listed as percentile scores: 90, 75, 50, 25, and 10. For example, a percentile score of 50 means that 50 percent of students received ORF scores equal to or lower than the number indicated.

To determine whether a student may be having difficulties with reading, the teacher can compare a student's WCPM score to the WCPM scores on ORF norms for the student's grade and time period of assessment; for example, Grade 2 in fall or Grade 7 in spring. Teachers can use these norms as benchmarks as they establish beginning-of-the-school-year baseline information about the reading fluency of their students. They can also refer to the norms during the school year as they work with students to increase their reading fluency (Osborn and Lehr 2003). The norms can help to indicate whether a student's fluency growth meets grade-level expectations or is increasing at a normal rate.

ORAL READING FLUENCY NORMS

Grades 1–8

Grade	Percentile	FALL WCPM	WINTER WCPM	SPRING WCPM
1	90		81	111
	75		47	82
	50		23	53
	25		12	28
	10		6	15
2	90	106	125	142
	75	79	100	117
	50	51	72	89
	25	25	42	61
	10	11	18	31
3	90	128	146	162
	75	99	120	137
	50	71	92	107
	25	44	62	78
	10	21	36	48
4	90	145	166	180
	75	119	139	152
	50	94	112	123
	25	68	87	98
	10	45	61	72
5	90	166	182	194
	75	139	156	168
	50	110	127	139
	25	85	99	109
	10	61	74	83
6	90	177	195	204
	75	153	167	177
	50	127	140	150
	25	98	111	122
	10	68	82	93
7	90	180	192	202
	75	156	165	177
	50	128	136	150
	25	102	109	123
	10	79	88	98
8	90	185	199	199
	75	161	173	177
	50	133	146	151
	25	106	115	124
	10	77	84	97

Hasbrouck and Tindal 2006.

ORF Facts

- **ORF scores increase most sharply in Grade 2.**
- **ORF scores increase at a constant rate in Grades 3 through 6.**
- **ORF scores in Grades 6, 7, and 8 show very little difference.**

According to Hasbrouck and Tindal (2006), an ORF score falling within the 10 words above or below the 50th percentile should be interpreted as within the normal, expected, and appropriate range for a student at that grade level at that time of the year. Using the data on the Oral Reading Fluency Norms table, which of the following student scores falls within the normal, expected, and appropriate range? (See Answer Key, p. 800.)

- A first-grade student who has a winter ORF score of 12 WCPM?
- A second-grade student who has a fall ORF score of 49 WCPM?
- A fourth-grade student who has a winter ORF score of 100 WCPM?
- A sixth-grade student who has a spring ORF score of 152 WCPM?

Diagnosis of Dysfluent Reading, p. 335

A WCPM score on an ORF assessment is just like a degree on a thermometer—a high temperature tells you that you have a fever, but not the cause of the fever or the treatment for it. An ORF score can indicate whether students are making good progress or are performing below expectations. However, like a temperature on a thermometer, an ORF score will not tell you why or what to do about it. For example, dysfluent readers may have the same low ORF score on the same grade-level passage for different reasons; one student may read accurately but slowly, while another may read inaccurately but quickly. To determine the particular problems leading to the poor ORF score, more diagnostic assessment is needed.

Weekly Growth Rates for ORF CBM: WCPM

Grade 1: 2 to 3 words

Grade 2: 1.5 to 2 words

Grade 3: 1 to 1.5 words

Grade 4: .85 to 1.1 words

Grade 5: .5 to .8 words

Grade 6: .3 to .65 words

Fuchs et al. 1993.

Weekly Growth Rates

It is important to know the rate of progress, or growth rate, a student is expected to make given typical instruction. Weekly growth rates indicate the average number of WCPM per week students are expected to gain in order to improve in reading. Fuchs et al. (1993) have determined reasonable to ambitious weekly growth rates for students in Grades 1–6.

SEE ALSO . . .

Comprehension Assessment: Response Formats, p. 701

ORF CBM and Upper-Grade Students

The demands of reading change as students move into the upper grades. In Grades 4 and above, text comprehension begins to depend more on content knowledge, vocabulary, and knowledge of expository text structures. Because of this, some researchers believe that Maze CBM may be a better predictor than ORF CBM of upper-grade students' future reading performance (Hosp et al. 2007). In Maze CBM, a student reads a passage silently instead of aloud. At about every seventh word, there is a group of three possible words for the student to choose from. The student has to choose the one word that makes the best sense, or belongs, in the sentence. According to Hosp et al. (2007), "Maze CBM appears to have a slightly better face validity than ORF for its relationship to comprehension."

Oral interpretation of text is more complex because it is more subjective than accuracy levels and reading rates.

—RASINSKI, 2004

Assessment of Prosodic Reading

Daane et al. (2005) suggest that "while rate and accuracy of oral reading are relatively straightforward characteristics both to observe and measure, it has proven more difficult to capture and measure the . . . 'ease' with which children read texts." Even though prosody, or the expressiveness of oral speech, is relatively difficult to measure reliably, it is often important to assess students' prosodic reading. To measure prosodic reading, the teacher listens to a student's oral reading of an independent-level passage and then compares the characteristics of the student's prosodic reading to a rating scale, or rubric.

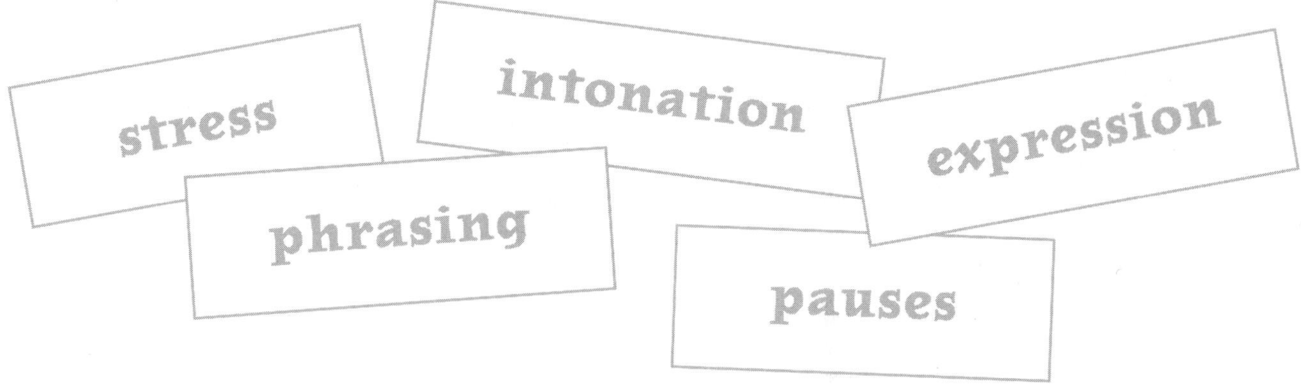

SEE ALSO . . .

ASSESSMENT MODEL: Assessment of Prosodic Reading, p. 355

This Prosody Assessment Rating Scale is based on a scale used in two reading fluency studies conducted as a part of the National Assessment of Educational Progress (Pinnell et al. 1995; Daane et al. 2005). Researchers used the original scale to evaluate the prosody of fourth-grade readers.

Prosody Assessment Rating Scale

Feature of Spoken Language	LEVEL 1 (NONPROSODIC)	LEVEL 2	LEVEL 3	LEVEL 4 (PROSODIC)
Stress	Equally stresses each word in a sentence	Equally stresses each word in a sentence or stresses the unimportant words in a sentence	Stresses the most important words in a sentence	Stresses all appropriate words in a sentence
Phrasing	Reads primarily word by word	Reads primarily in two-word phrases, but sometimes word by word	Reads primarily in three- or four-word phrases	Reads primarily in larger, meaningful phrases
	Often pauses after every word and within words	Often pauses within phrases	Often pauses between phrases, but occasionally pauses within them	Consistently pauses at the end of clauses and sentences
	Chunks words with no attention to author's syntax or does not chunk them at all	Chunks words with little attention to author's syntax	Often chunks words appropriately, preserving author's syntax	Consistently chunks words appropriately, preserving author's syntax
Intonation	Does not change pitch to reflect end marks	Occasionally changes pitch to reflect end marks	Often changes pitch to reflect end marks	Consistently changes pitch to reflect end marks
Expression	Reads in a monotone	Occasionally uses voice to reflect character's emotions or actions	Usually uses voice to reflect character's emotions or actions	Consistently uses voice to reflect character's emotions or actions
Pauses	Reads from one sentence to the next without pausing for punctuation	Pauses between sentences only when there is a period	Usually pauses at commas and end marks	Consistently pauses appropriately at all punctuation

Adapted from Daane et al. 2005; Dowhower 1991; Hudson, Lane, and Pullen 2005.

When children read too slowly or haltingly, the text devolves into a broken string of words and/or phrases; it's a struggle just to remember what's been read, much less extract its meaning.

—HASBROUCK, 2006

SEE ALSO . . .

Chapter 10: Fluency Instruction

Diagnosis of Dysfluent Reading

When fluency assessments show that a student is below the expected level of reading or not making sufficient progress, teachers must gather more in-depth information to determine the area of weakness that is causing the problem. Common causes of dysfluency include deficits in phonemic awareness, decoding, vocabulary, language syntax, and content knowledge. A "speed-accuracy trade-off" occurs when students either (1) slow down unnecessarily because they are overly concerned with accuracy or (2) make many mistakes in an attempt to read text quickly. The following informal checklist can guide teachers in identifying the possible causes of a student's dysfluent reading and, subsequently, in developing an effective instructional plan for the student.

Possible Causes of Dysfluency	
Is Reading Inaccurate? Does the student:	✓ have sufficient phonics knowledge and skills? ✓ have sufficient decoding skills—especially for multisyllabic word reading? ✓ recognize a large bank of high-frequency irregular words on sight? ✓ possess an average or greater oral vocabulary? ✓ know how to monitor his or her reading accuracy?
Is Reading Slow? Does the student:	✓ decode words sound by sound rather than by chunking? ✓ make several attempts before accurately decoding an unfamiliar word? ✓ lack automatic word recognition skills? ✓ have enough background knowledge to understand the text? ✓ make a "speed-accuracy trade-off"?
Is Reading Nonprosodic? Does the student:	✓ fail to notice or pause at punctuation? ✓ fail to pause at natural phrase boundaries? ✓ lack syntactic knowledge of English? ✓ lack expression in reading? ✓ focus too much on word identification?

why?

Fluency Assessment

The ability to measure students' levels of achievement and monitor their progress is key to successful fluency teaching.

—RASINSKI, 2004

Assessment of reading fluency is a good overall estimate of students' reading proficiency and a strong predictor of success in reading comprehension. Early identification of students who are not reading at the expected level or are not making sufficient progress is the key to preventing reading problems. Decades of research have validated the use of fluency-based measures for making essential instructional decisions (Hasbrouck and Tindal 2006). ORF assessment data can be used to place students in appropriate instructional groupings, identify students who are not making adequate progress, and monitor the progress of students who are reading below grade level and the effectiveness of their current instruction.

Research Findings . . .

The two best reasons for conducting ORF CBM are (1) that it is easy and time efficient to administer and score and (2) that it provides educators with information that can be used to inform instruction.

—HOSP ET AL., 2007

WCPM has been shown, in both theoretical and empirical research, to serve as an accurate and powerful indicator of overall reading competence, especially in its strong correlation with comprehension.

—HASBROUCK & TINDAL, 2006

[Oral reading fluency] correlates highly with other measures of reading proficiency, including teacher judgment, growth across grades, . . . and performance on formal and informal measures of reading, including measures of reading comprehension.

—ESPIN & FOEGEN, 1996

Teachers need to be able to gauge the effectiveness of their instruction in fluency; to do this, they need ways to assess student fluency validly and efficiently.

—RASINSKI, 2004

Suggested Reading . . .

The ABCs of CBM: A Practical Guide to Curriculum-Based Measurement (2007) by Michelle K. Hosp, John L. Hosp & Kenneth W. Howell. New York: Guilford.

Assessing Reading Fluency (2004) by Timothy Rasinski. Honolulu: Pacific Resources for Education and Learning.

A Focus on Fluency (2003) by Jean Osborn & Fran Lehr. Honolulu: Pacific Resources for Education and Learning.

What Research Has to Say About Fluency Instruction (2006) edited by S. Jay Samuels & Alan E. Farstrup. Newark, DE: International Reading Association.

when?

Fluency Assessment

A current unknown in adolescent literacy involves appropriate targets for reading fluency for students in middle and high school.

—TORGESEN ET AL., 2007

When to Assess

Generally, except for in Grade 1, screen students' oral reading fluency at the beginning of the school year or when students enter school. After that, monitor students' progress at least three times a year (fall, winter, spring). If a student's WCPM score is within plus or minus 10 WCPM of the 50th percentile on the ORF Norms table, or is more than 10 WCPM above the 50th percentile, a student is considered to be making adequate progress (Hasbrouck and Tindal 2006). For students who are not making adequate progress, progress monitoring should be more frequent, at least one or two times per month. When data from screening and progress monitoring assessments indicate that a student is reading well below the expected level, it may be necessary to administer a more diagnostic assessment to determine the student's specific area of weakness.

ORF CBM and Upper-Grade Students, p. 333

Older Struggling Readers

Individual differences in reading fluency contribute less to variations in reading comprehension at upper-grade levels than at elementary levels (Schatschneider et al. 2004). While the usefulness of using ORF to screen and monitor the progress of elementary students is well established through a large body of research, less is known about ORF and adolescent readers. What is known, however, is that the average levels of oral reading fluency stabilize at around 150 WCPM for students at the end of sixth, seventh, and eighth grades when reading grade-level text (Hasbrouck and Tindal 2006).

ORF CBM Assessment Guide		
Screening	Grade 1: All students	Middle of school year (winter)
	Grades 2–5: All students Grades 6–8: Students who are reading below expected grade level	Beginning of school year (fall)
Progress Monitoring	Grade 1: All students	Two times a year (winter, spring)
	Grades 2–5: All students Grades 6–8: Students who are reading below expected grade level	Three times a year (fall, winter, spring)
	Grades 1–8: Students who are reading below expected grade or goal level (Note: For students in Grades 6 and above who are reading below expected grade or goal level, Maze CBM may be more appropriate.)	At least one or two times per month

Purpose	✓ Fluency Assessment	Publisher
Screening	Test of Silent Contextual Reading Fluency (TOSCRF)	Pro-Ed
Screening Progress Monitoring	AIMSweb® Reading Curriculum-Based Measurement (R-CBM) ▸ Standard Oral Reading Fluency Assessment Passages	Pearson http://aimsweb.com
Screening Progress Monitoring	DIBELS® Next ▸ Dibels Oral Reading Fluency (DORF)	Sopris West http://dibels.org
Screening Progress Monitoring	CORE Literacy Library *Assessing Reading: Multiple Measures, 2nd Edition* ▸ MASI-R Oral Reading Fluency Measures	Arena Press
Screening Progress Monitoring Diagnostic	easy CBM™ ▸ Passage Fluency	Riverside Publishing http://easycbm.com

how?

Fluency Assessment

ASSESSMENT MODEL

Rate and Accuracy

Purposes

- screening
- progress monitoring

Strategy Grade Level

- Mid-Grade 1 and above

Grouping

- individual

Sample Text (Resources)

- "Weekend Campout" and "Weekend Campout" with word count
  Complexity Level: Grades 2–3

Activity Master (Resources)

- Student Progress Graph

Materials

- copy of "Weekend Campout"
- copy of "Weekend Campout" with word count
- timer
- red pen or pencil
- copy of Student Progress Graph
- pencil

Assessment of ORF Rate and Accuracy

A widely used curriculum-based measurement (CBM) procedure is the assessment of oral reading fluency (ORF), which targets two components of fluency: rate and accuracy. The ORF CBM approach serves as an index of the student's general reading achievement and answers three questions: (1) Is the student reading text quickly and accurately as compared with grade-level norms or other expectations? (2) Is the student making sufficient yearly progress? (3) Does the student's instruction need to be adjusted?

Using sample text to represent a standardized CBM grade-level passage, this sample assessment model provides an example of how to assess ORF rate and accuracy. The same model can be adapted and used with other appropriate grade-level passages. In an actual assessment, a student will read aloud for one minute from each of three unpracticed, grade-level passages.

Select Appropriate Text

When comparing student performance to grade-level expectations, use passages at the student's grade level—*not* at the student's actual reading level. For example, a fourth grader who reads at the third-grade level will read fourth-grade passages. Researchers recommend using standardized CBM passages for assessment because they have gone through a process of development and validation, are at a similar reading level across a grade level, and allow for comparisons across classrooms, schools, and districts (Hintze and Christ 2004). There should be about 250 words in each passage.

Listen to the Student Read

Set the timer for one minute. Ask a student to sit across from you or next to your nonwriting hand. Have a numbered copy of the sample text "Weekend Campout," the first of three passages, in front of you. The numbers indicate the cumulative line-by-line word count.

Give the student an unnumbered copy of the passage. Say: *I am going to check your reading today. I will use a timer to tell me how long you should read. When I say "Please begin," read aloud the first word in the passage and then continue reading across the line.* Demonstrate by pointing to the first word *The* and then sweeping your finger from left to right below the first line of text. Say: *Keep reading until I ask you to stop. Pay attention to what you are reading; I may ask you about it when you are done. If you get stuck, I'll tell you the word. The title of this passage is "Weekend Campout."* Ask: *Any questions?* After a short pause, say: *Please begin.* When the student reads the first word, start the timer. Following along on your numbered copy, use a red pen or pencil to keep track of student errors. See Fluency Scoring on the next page.

When the timer goes off, place a bracket (]) after the last word the student reads aloud. If the student is in the middle of a sentence when the time is up, allow the student to finish the sentence and then say "Stop." However, don't count any words read after the bracket.

Follow the same procedure to administer the next two grade-level passages.

Sources of Standardized ORF CBM Passages

- **AIMSweb® (Grades 1–8), http://www.aimsweb.com**
- **DIBELS® (Grades 1–6), Sopris West**
- **Edcheckup (Grades 1–6), http://www.edcheckup.com**

Weekend Campout

THE FRANCO FAMILY loves to be outdoors. They spend almost 10
every weekend camping. Fay Franco adores camping more 18
than anything. She will even pitch her tent in the backyard 29
just to sleep outside. 33
Fay has been to lots of campgrounds. Mar Vista Shores is her 45
favorite. The campsites are in the tall trees. Each spot has a beach view. 59
At Mar Vista Shores, noisy birdcalls wake Fay early. She hears 70
loud squawking and jumps up for breakfast. Then she packs a picnic. 82
Fay and her dad drive to the trailhead. It is the place where the hiking 97
trails start. They choose a path to take. Dad carries a daypack. It holds 111
a first aid kit, sweatshirts, food, and water. The path leads sharply 123
uphill to a waterfall. It is a steep climb! They hungrily devour their 136
lunch by the riverbank. From the rocks, Fay can watch the water 148
plummet over the cliff. 152
In the afternoon, Fay and her mom go to the seashore. Mom is a 166
rock hound. She hunts for neat-looking stones. Fay makes sandcastles. 177
Using wet sand, she builds high walls and towers. Sometimes she 188
pokes around the tide pools. She looks for crabs and starfish in the 201
rocks along the beach. 205
At dinnertime, the Franco family usually has a sunset cookout. 215
They light a campfire. They roast hotdogs. The sky 224
turns pink over the water. Nighttime falls. Fay 232
gets into her sleeping bag. She looks up to 241
see the stars twinkle overhead. 246
Fay thinks that weekend campouts 251
are almost perfect. The only flaw comes 258
when it is time to go home. 265

TEACHING READING SOURCEBOOK 708

Fluency Scoring

▸ NOT ERRORS	Student's Reading	Scoring Notes	Score
Correct Pronunciations Pronouncing a word correctly within the context of the sentence	*The path leads sharply uphill to a waterfall.*	The path leads sharply uphill to a waterfall.	8/8 words
Self-Corrections Self-correcting an error within three seconds	*The path went . . . leads sharply uphill to a waterfall.*	The path leads (SC) sharply uphill to a waterfall.	8/8 words
Insertions Adding a word	*The path leads very sharply uphill to a waterfall.*	The path leads ^very sharply uphill to a waterfall.	8/8 words
Repetitions Repeating a word or phrase	*The path . . . the path leads sharply . . . the path leads sharply uphill to a waterfall.*	The path leads sharply uphill to a waterfall.	8/8 words
Dialect or Accent Differences Using word pronunciations that vary due to dialect or accent	*Da path lead sharply uphill to a waterfall.*	The path leads sharply uphill to a waterfall.	8/8 words
▸ ERRORS	**Student's Reading**	**Scoring Notes**	**Score**
Mispronunciations Mispronouncing a word	*The path leads sharply uphill to a wiffle.*	The path leads sharply uphill to a ~~waterfall~~.	7/8 words
Mispronunciation of a Heteronym Saying *lĕads,* as in a lead pipe, instead of *lēads*	*The path leds sharply uphill to a waterfall.*	The path ~~leads~~ sharply uphill to a waterfall.	7/8 words
Omissions Leaving out a word	*The path leads uphill to a waterfall.*	The path leads ~~sharply~~ uphill to a waterfall.	7/8 words
Substitutions Substituting a different word, even if the word is semantically and syntactically correct	*The road leads directly uphill to a waterfall.*	The ~~path~~ leads ~~sharply~~ uphill to a waterfall.	6/8 words
Transpositions Reversing the order of words	*The path leads uphill sharply to a waterfall.*	The path leads ~~sharply~~ ~~uphill~~ to a waterfall.	6/8 words
Hesitations Hesitating or struggling with a word for more than three seconds so that teacher has to say the word	*The path leads . . . uphill to a . . .*	The path leads ~~sharply~~ uphill to a ~~waterfall~~.	6/8 words

THE FRANCO FAMILY loves to be outdoors. They spend almost 10
every weekend camping. Fay Franco adores camping more 18
than anything. She will even pitch her tent in the backyard 29
just to sleep outside. 33
Fay has been to lots of campgrounds. Mar Vista Shores is her 45
favorite. The campsites are in the tall trees. Each spot has a beach view. 59
At Mar Vista Shores, noisy birdcalls wake Fay early. She hears 70
loud squawking and jumps up for breakfast. Then she packs a picnic. 82
Fay and her dad drive to the trailhead. It is the place where the hiking 97
trails start. They choose a path to take. Dad carries a daypack. It holds 111
a first aid kit, sweatshirts, food, and water. The path leads sharply 123
uphill to a waterfall. It is a steep climb! They hungrily devour their 136
lunch by the riverbank. From the rocks, Fay can watch the water 148
plummet over the cliff. 152
In the afternoon, Fay and her mom go to the seashore. Mom is a 166
rock hound. She hunts for neat-looking stones. Fay makes sandcastles. 177
Using wet sand, she builds high walls and towers. Sometimes she 188
pokes around the tide pools. She looks for crabs and starfish in the 201
rocks along the beach. 205
At dinnertime, the Franco family usually has a sunset cookout. 215
They light a campfire. They roast hotdogs. The sky 224
turns pink over the water. Nighttime falls. Fay 232
gets into her sleeping bag. She looks up to 241
see the stars twinkle overhead. 246
Fay thinks that weekend campouts 251
are almost perfect. The only flaw comes 258
when it is time to go home. 265

TEACHING READING SOURCEBOOK • WEEKEND CAMPOUT 710

Calculate the ORF Score

ORF is expressed as "words correct per minute" (WCPM). To calculate the ORF score for each passage, first count the total number of words the student read and the number of errors the student made. Then subtract the errors from the total number of words read. For example, if a student reads 84 words in one minute and makes 2 errors, the ORF score is 82 WCPM.

[Total words read − errors = ORF score
84 − 2 = 82 WCPM]

After calculating the ORF score for each of the three passages, identify the highest score, the lowest score, and the median score—the score that is between the other two. For example, if the first passage is read at 82 WCPM, the second passage at 85 WCPM, and the third passage at 79 WCPM, the median score is 82 WCPM—82 is between 79 and 85 . Use this median score when interpreting the data and graphing a student's progress. If it is the student's very first assessment of the school year or other assessment period, the median score is referred to as the *baseline median score.*

If a student happens to read a whole passage in less than one minute (60 seconds), calculate a prorated score. For example, if a student read 140 words correct in 55 seconds, the prorated ORF score would be 153.

[60 seconds x 140 ÷ 55 seconds =
153 WCPM]

Compare ORF Score to ORF Norms

To determine whether a student may be having reading difficulties, compare the student's baseline median ORF score with the ORF norms from that student's grade level at the closest time period: fall, winter, or spring. See Oral Reading Fluency Norms, Grades 1–8, page 331.

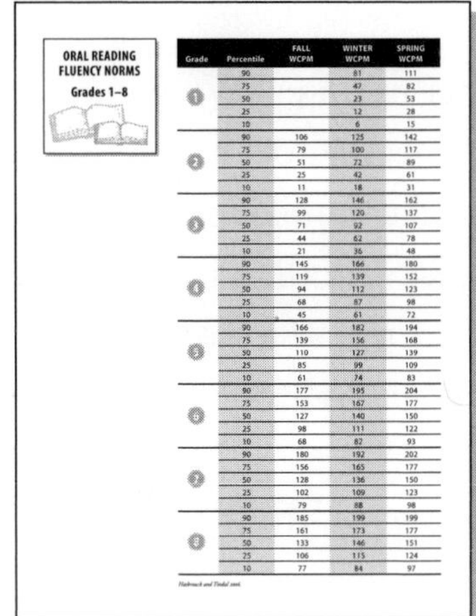

ORAL READING FLUENCY NORMS
Grades 1–8

Grade	Percentile	FALL WCPM	WINTER WCPM	SPRING WCPM
1	90		81	111
	75		47	82
	50		23	53
	25		12	28
	10		6	15
2	90	106	125	142
	75	79	100	117
	50	51	72	89
	25	25	42	61
	10	11	18	31
3	90	128	146	162
	75	99	120	137
	50	71	92	107
	25	44	62	78
	10	21	36	48
4	90	145	166	180
	75	119	139	152
	50	94	112	123
	25	68	87	98
	10	45	61	72
5	90	166	182	194
	75	139	156	168
	50	110	127	139
	25	85	99	109
	10	61	74	83
6	90	177	195	204
	75	153	167	177
	50	127	140	150
	25	98	111	122
	10	68	82	93
7	90	180	192	202
	75	156	165	177
	50	128	136	150
	25	102	109	123
	10	79	88	98
8	90	185	199	199
	75	161	173	177
	50	133	146	151
	25	106	115	124
	10	77	84	97

According to Hasbrouck and Tindal (2006), if a student's median ORF score is within plus or minus 10 WCPM of the 50th percentile on the Oral Reading Fluency Norms table, the student is considered to be meeting grade-level expectations in reading fluency. For example, if a sixth-grade student scores 118 WCPM in fall, the student is meeting grade-level expectations—118 WCPM is less than 10 WCPM below the 50th percentile score of 127 WCPM. But if a sixth-grade student scores 101 WCPM in fall, the student is failing to meet grade-level expectations—101 WCPM is more than 10 WCPM below the 50th percentile score of 127 WCPM.

A student who scores significantly below the 50th percentile should be further assessed using diagnostic tests that measure decoding skills and phonemic awareness before concluding that fluency alone is the problem. Once the specific reading skill weakness is identified, the student will need systematic instruction to improve underlying skills and increase reading fluency.

Record Student Data on the Progress Graph

The following student profile will be used to illustrate how to record and monitor student data on the progress graph.

Veronica is in sixth grade. On January 7 (Week 1), her baseline median ORF score was 82 WCPM, well below the 50th percentile score of 140 WCPM for winter on Hasbrouck and Tindal's Oral Reading Fluency Norms (2006). Since, according to these norms, Veronica's ORF score should be at least 150 WCPM in the spring, the teacher set Veronica's 12-week goal at 140 WCPM by March 24. Reaching this score in March would put Veronica solidly on the path to her ultimate target score of 150 WCPM at the end of the school year. Because her ORF score is well below grade-level expectations, the teacher is monitoring Veronica's progress every week.

SEE ALSO . . .

ASSESSMENT MODEL: For computer users, see also Digital Graphing of ORF Scores, p. 349

SEE ALSO . . .

LESSON MODEL: Timed Repeated Oral Reading, p. 374

To monitor student progress, it is essential to record student data in a visual form. Plotting the data points on a graph allows for both visual and numerical analysis of a student's level (score on a single occasion) and shows the amount of growth (change in scores over time).

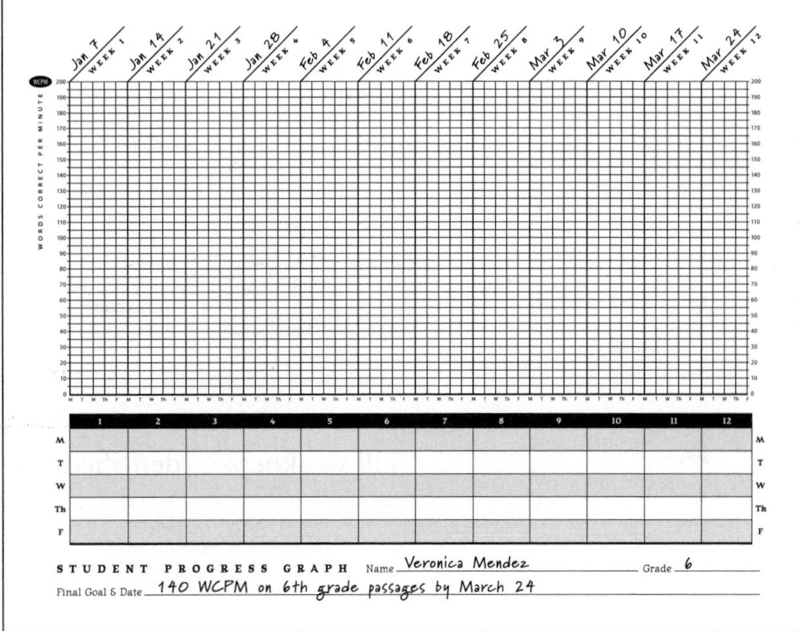

1. Enter Student Information

At the bottom of the Student Progress Graph, fill in the student's Name, Grade, and Final Goal & Date. On the diagonal lines labeled Week 1, Week 2, and so on at the top of the graph, enter Monday's date (month and day) for each of 12 consecutive weeks.

2. Enter and Plot Baseline Median Score

Starting on Monday of Week 1, enter the student's baseline median score below the graph in the corresponding box. Express the score as WCPM/errors. For example, on Monday of Week 1, Veronica read a total of 84 words and made 2 errors, so her teacher recorded 82/2 in the box. Next, plot the student's baseline median score. At the bottom of the graph, find the vertical line for the corresponding day of the week. (The lines for Mondays are in boldface.) Then follow that line straight up until you reach the horizontal line corresponding to the student's score. Make a dot, or data point, at the intersection of the two lines, or at the coordinates—for example, Monday of Week 1 and 82 WCPM.

Keeping track of the number of student errors is instructionally informative. A student who reads 82 WCPM with 10 errors has a different level of reading accuracy than a student who reads 82 WCPM with only 1 error.

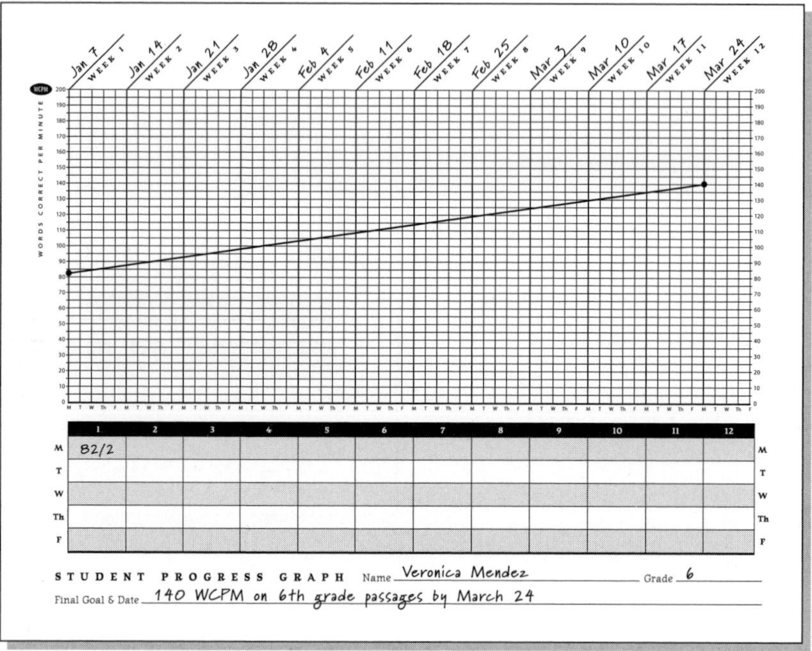

3. Set the Aim Line

Once a student's baseline median score has been plotted on the graph, plot the student's final goal, or target ORF score. Using a ruler, draw an aim line from the baseline median data point to the target ORF score data point. For example, Veronica's goal was 140 WCPM by March 24 (Week 12). So, on her Student Progress Graph the aim line goes from 82 WCPM (Week 1) to 140 WCPM (Week 12). The aim line shows the amount of growth needed for Veronica to reach her goal, or target ORF score, by a particular date.

4. Enter and Plot the Scores for Weeks 2–12

As the scores are collected, follow the procedure described in Step 2 to enter and plot ORF data for each of the remaining weeks. For example, Tuesday of Week 2 and 85 WCPM, Monday of Week 3 and 90 WCPM, and so on.

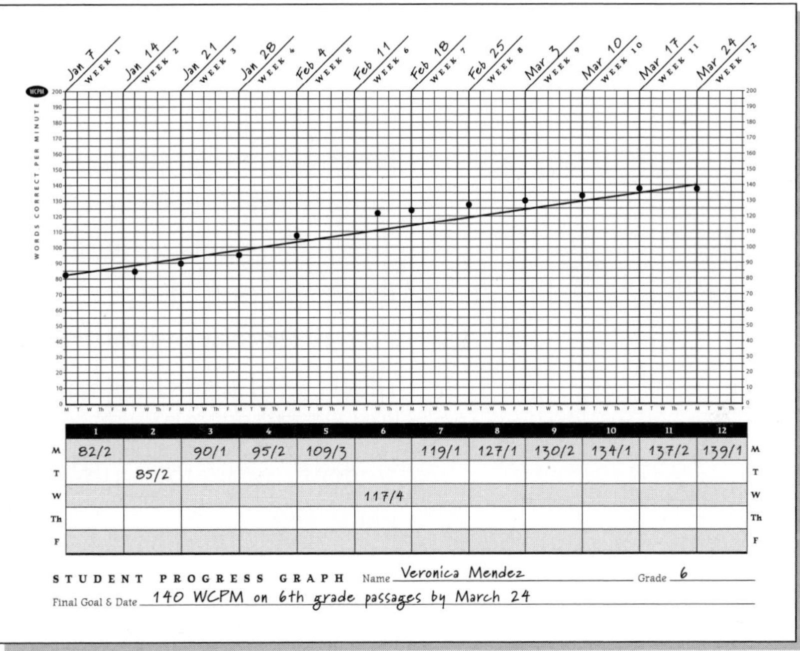

	1	2	3	4	5	6	7	8	9	10	11	12	
M	82/2		90/1	95/2	109/3		119/1	127/1	130/2	134/1	137/2	139/1	M
T		85/2											T
W						117/4							W
Th													Th
F													F

STUDENT PROGRESS GRAPH Name Veronica Mendez Grade 6

Final Goal & Date 140 WCPM on 6th grade passages by March 24

Monitor Student Progress

To determine whether the instruction the student is receiving is sufficiently intense or whether it needs to be adjusted, compare the student's ORF scores to the aim line. In general, a student is making adequate progress when the student's ORF scores are on or above the aim line. If the student has three ORF scores in a row that fall below the aim line, the student is not making adequate progress. For example, in Weeks 2, 3, and 4, Veronica's ORF scores fell below the aim line, and therefore the teacher adjusted Veronica's instruction. In Weeks 5 through 12, Veronica's ORF scores are on or above the aim line, indicating that she is making adequate progress and the instructional adjustment was successful.

Progress Monitoring and Response to Intervention (RtI)

ORF progress monitoring can also be used within the Response to Intervention (RtI) model for identifying students who may need intervention services and to monitor and document their responsiveness to the targeted intervention. If a student's baseline median ORF score is below grade level, use progressively less difficult passages to assess oral reading fluency until the student meets the target ORF score for a particular grade level. Start testing with three passages one-half to one grade level lower than the student's actual grade. Once the student's actual reading level is determined, assess the student at increasingly difficult levels of text until the student's grade-level fluency standards are reached. For example, for a seventh-grade student who is reading at a fourth-grade level, begin progress monitoring with fifth-grade text. When the student reaches the fifth-grade target score, change to sixth-grade text. When the student reaches the sixth-grade target score, change to seventh-grade text.

SEE ALSO . . .

Response to Intervention (RtI), p. 751

ASSESSMENT MODEL

ORF Data Recording

Purposes

- recording assessment data
- judging student progress

Strategy Grade Level

- Mid-Grade 1 and above

Prerequisite

- Assessment of ORF Rate and Accuracy, p. 340

Materials

- UW CBM Growth Calculator, http://www.fluentreader.org
- spreadsheet software program such as Excel® or Calc®

Digital Graphing of ORF Scores

The previous sample assessment model described how to use a paper graph for recording ORF data. This sample assessment model describes how to use a digital form of recording: the University of Washington (UW) CBM Growth Calculator developed by Joseph Jenkins and Gwen Sweeny. This digital graph is specifically designed to graph ORF data for progress monitoring and to record frequent (weekly or biweekly) assessment data. The Growth Calculator can be downloaded from http://www.fluentreader.org. To open it, you must have a spreadsheet program installed on your computer, such as Excel® or Calc®.

Collect Student ORF Data

Following the procedure described in the previous sample assessment model, Assessment of ORF Rate and Accuracy, listen to the student read aloud for one minute from each of three unpracticed, grade-level passages, calculate the student's ORF score, and compare the score to oral reading fluency norms.

Michael is in second grade. On September 8 (Week 0), his baseline median ORF score was 43 WCPM, below the 50th percentile score of 51 WCPM for fall on Hasbrouck and Tindal's Oral Reading Fluency Norms (2006). Since, according to these norms, Michael's ORF score should be at least 89 WCPM in the spring, the teacher set Michael's target ORF score at 80 WCPM by April 20 (Week 32). Reaching this score in April would put Michael solidly on the path to his ultimate target score of 89 WCPM at the end of the school year. Because his ORF score is below grade-level expectations, the teacher is monitoring Michael's progress by administering an ORF assessment every two weeks.

Growth Calculator Components

The Growth Calculator has three worksheets: Start Here, Sample Sheet, and PRF Template. The first worksheet is Start Here. It contains an explanation of how to use the Growth Calculator, including printing suggestions. The second worksheet is an annotated Sample Sheet. The Sample Sheet is divided into two parts: the data cells and the graph. The third worksheet is the PRF Template. For each student, create a copy of this template, or worksheet, and rename it using the student's name.

TEACHER NOTE

WRC (words read correctly) is the same as WCPM (words correct per minute).

DATA CELLS

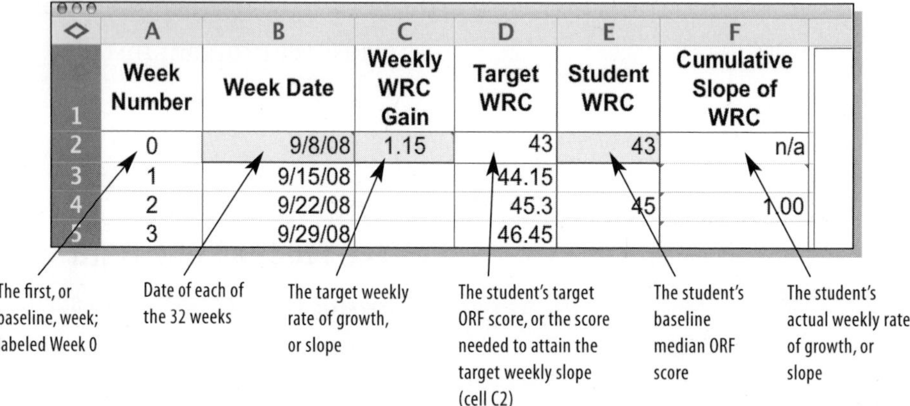

	A	B	C	D	E	F
1	Week Number	Week Date	Weekly WRC Gain	Target WRC	Student WRC	Cumulative Slope of WRC
2	0	9/8/08	1.15	43	43	n/a
3	1	9/15/08		44.15		
4	2	9/22/08		45.3	45	1.00
5	3	9/29/08		46.45		

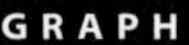
GRAPH

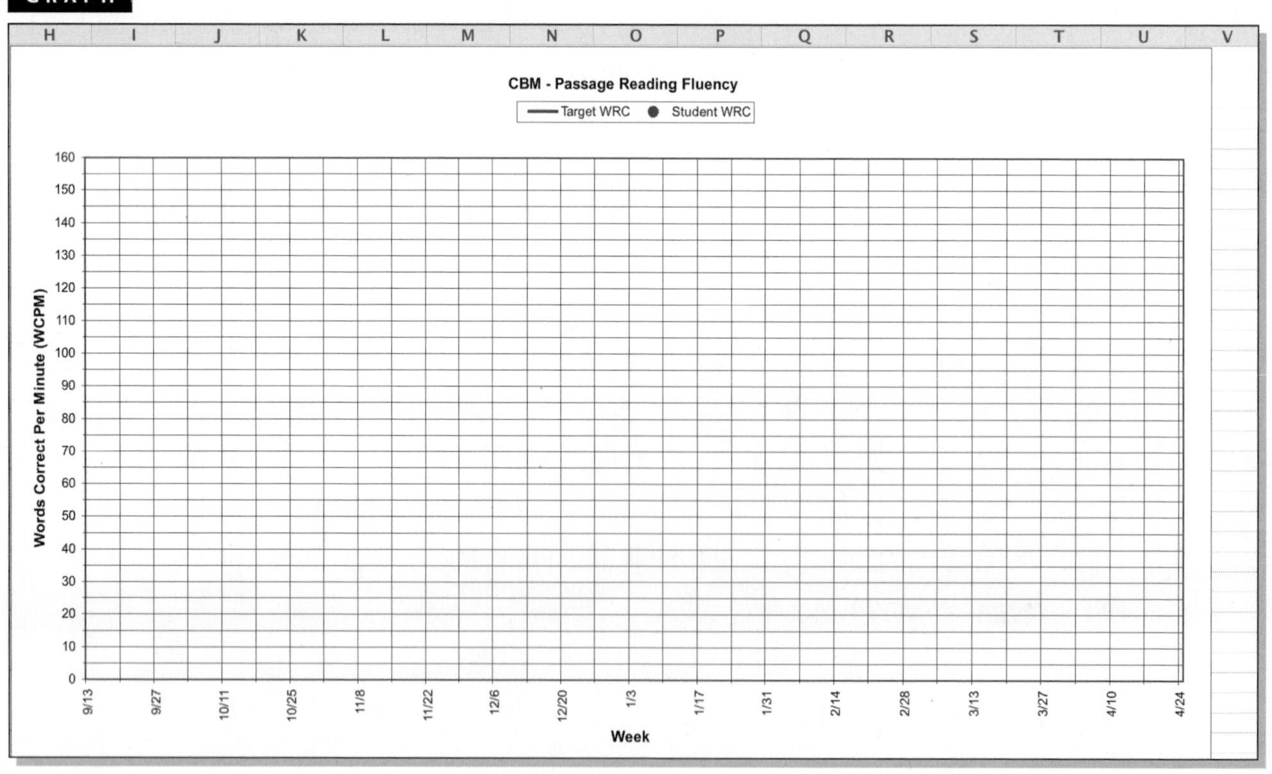

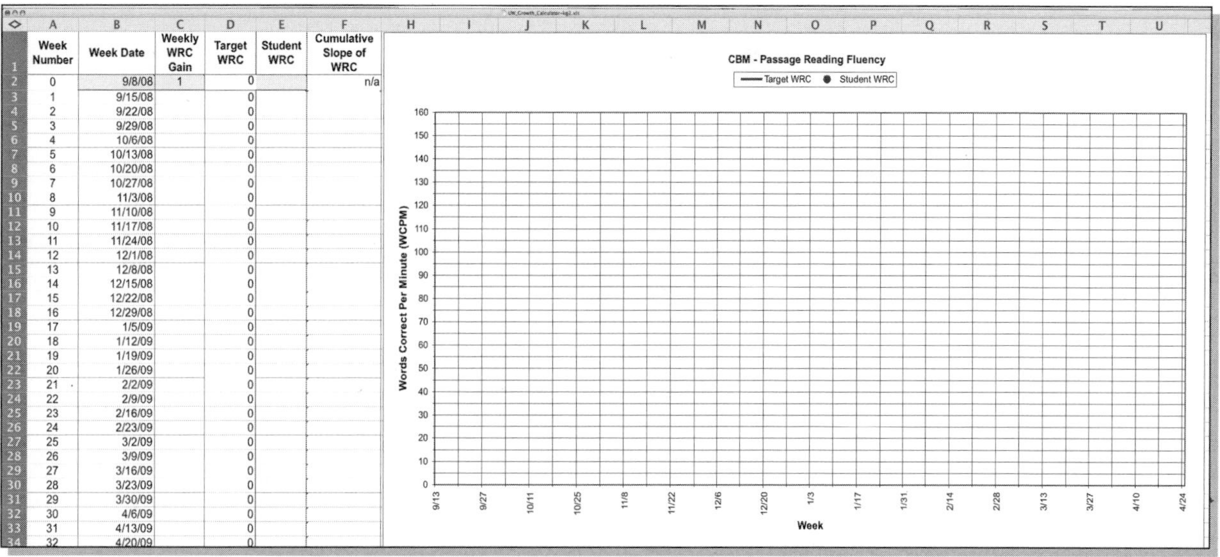

Week Number	Week Date	Weekly WRC Gain	Target WRC	Student WRC	Cumulative Slope of WRC
0	9/8/08	1	0		n/a
1	9/15/08		0		
2	9/22/08		0		
3	9/29/08		0		
4	10/6/08		0		
5	10/13/08		0		
6	10/20/08		0		
7	10/27/08		0		
8	11/3/08		0		
9	11/10/08		0		
10	11/17/08		0		
11	11/24/08		0		
12	12/1/08		0		
13	12/8/08		0		
14	12/15/08		0		
15	12/22/08		0		
16	12/29/08		0		
17	1/5/09		0		
18	1/12/09		0		
19	1/19/09		0		
20	1/26/09		0		
21	2/2/09		0		
22	2/9/09		0		
23	2/16/09		0		
24	2/23/09		0		
25	3/2/09		0		
26	3/9/09		0		
27	3/16/09		0		
28	3/23/09		0		
29	3/30/09		0		
30	4/6/09		0		
31	4/13/09		0		
32	4/20/09		0		

SLOPE

In CBM, slope indicates the weekly rate of growth. A positive slope value indicates the amount by which a student's reading fluency is getting better than it was. A negative slope value indicates the amount by which a student's reading fluency is getting worse than it was.

Enter Student Data

Begin by entering the student's information into the light-blue cells in Row 2, Week Date (cell B2), Weekly WRC Gain (cell C2), and Student WRC (cell E2). Data in columns A, D, and F are automatically generated by the program. An explanatory note is attached to each of the light-blue cells. You can read the note by moving your mouse over the cell.

1. Enter the Week Date

In light-blue cell B2, enter the Week Date, or the date of the student's initial, or baseline, assessment. For example, September 8, 2008, is the date of Michael's baseline assessment. The program automatically fills in the dates for the succeeding weeks.

2. Enter the Student's Target Weekly Rate of Growth

In light-blue cell C2, enter the Weekly WRC Gain, or the student's target weekly rate of growth, or target weekly slope. There are two methods for determining a student's target weekly rate of growth, or slope.

METHOD 1 In this method, the student's target weekly rate of growth, or slope, is determined by calculating how much weekly improvement a student needs to make to reach a target ORF score by a certain date. The target ORF score may be the 50th percentile of Hasbrouck and Tindal's Oral Reading Fluency Norms (2006) for a student's particular grade and time of year. For example, Michael's target ORF score is 80 WCPM and his baseline median ORF score is 43 WCPM. For Michael to reach his target in 32 weeks, his ORF score has to grow at least 1.15 words per week.

Use the following formula to calculate a student's target weekly rate of growth:

Target ORF score − baseline median ORF score ÷ number of weeks of instruction = target weekly rate of growth

80 WCPM − 43 WCPM ÷ 32 = 1.15 words per week

METHOD 2 This method is appropriate for working with students who are so far below grade-level expectations that it would be impossible for them to reach a target ORF score. In this method, the target weekly rate of growth, or slope, is determined by using research-based weekly growth rates for ORF. For example, according to Fuchs et al. (1993), Michael's target rate of growth would be 1.5 WCPM per week.

Weekly Growth Rates for ORF CBM: WCPM

Grade 1: 2 to 3 words

Grade 2: 1.5 to 2 words

Grade 3: 1 to 1.5 words

Grade 4: .85 to 1.1 words

Grade 5: .5 to .8 words

Grade 6: .3 to .65 words

Fuchs et al. 1993.

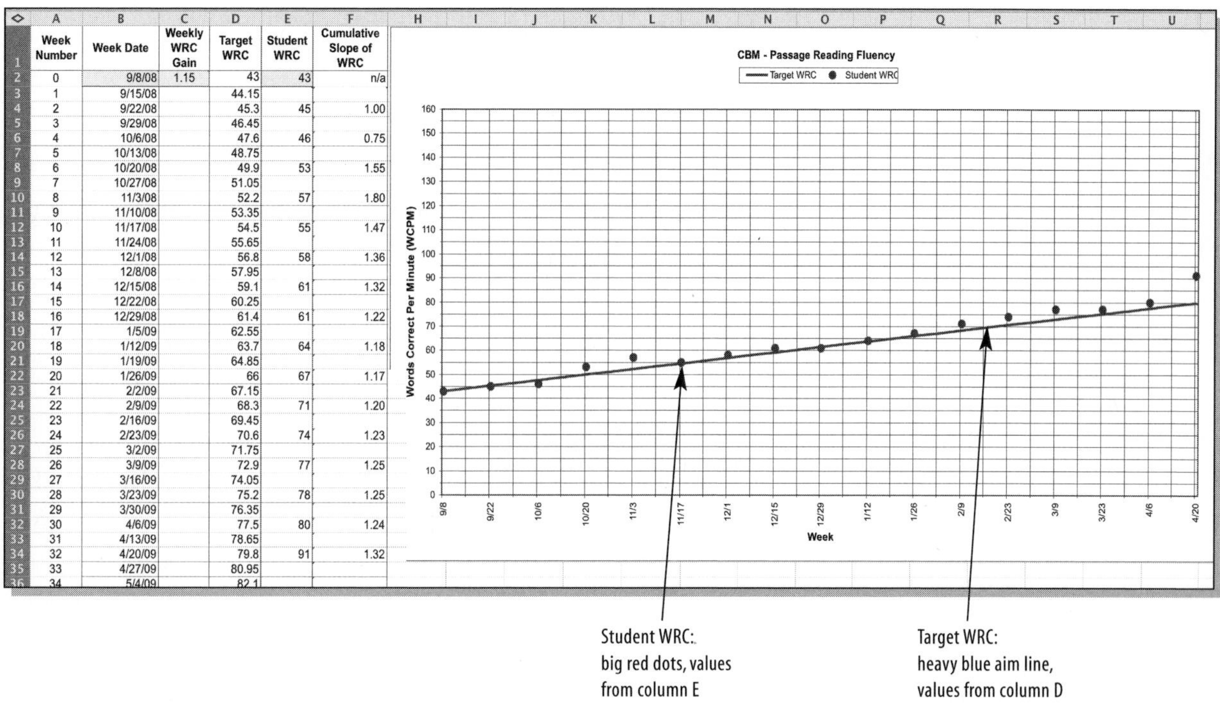

	A	B	C	D	E	F
1	Week Number	Week Date	Weekly WRC Gain	Target WRC	Student WRC	Cumulative Slope of WRC
2	0	9/8/08	1.15	43	43	n/a
3	1	9/15/08		44.15		
4	2	9/22/08		45.3	45	1.00
5	3	9/29/08		46.45		
6	4	10/6/08		47.6	46	0.75
7	5	10/13/08		48.75		
8	6	10/20/08		49.9	53	1.55
9	7	10/27/08		51.05		
10	8	11/3/08		52.2	57	1.80
11	9	11/10/08		53.35		
12	10	11/17/08		54.5	55	1.47
13	11	11/24/08		55.65		
14	12	12/1/08		56.8	58	1.36
15	13	12/8/08		57.95		
16	14	12/15/08		59.1	61	1.32
17	15	12/22/08		60.25		
18	16	12/29/08		61.4	61	1.22
19	17	1/5/09		62.55		
20	18	1/12/09		63.7	64	1.18
21	19	1/19/09		64.85		
22	20	1/26/09		66	67	1.17
23	21	2/2/09		67.15		
24	22	2/9/09		68.3	71	1.20
25	23	2/16/09		69.45		
26	24	2/23/09		70.6	74	1.23
27	25	3/2/09		71.75		
28	26	3/9/09		72.9	77	1.25
29	27	3/16/09		74.05		
30	28	3/23/09		75.2	78	1.25
31	29	3/30/09		76.35		
32	30	4/6/09		77.5	80	1.24
33	31	4/13/09		78.65		
34	32	4/20/09		79.8	91	1.32
35	33	4/27/09		80.95		
36	34	5/4/09		82.1		

3. Enter the Student's Baseline Median ORF Score

In light-blue cell E2, enter the Student WRC score, or the student's baseline median ORF score. Notice that after entering the score, a big red dot automatically appears on the graph on the 9/8 vertical axis next to 43 WCPM. In column D, the Student WRC scores, or the student's target ORF scores are then calculated automatically for each of the following weeks. Notice that the values from column D plot the heavy blue aim line that appears on the graph. When a larger number is entered in cell C2 the blue aim line gets steeper, and when a smaller number is entered the aim line gets more level.

4. Enter the Student's Successive ORF Scores

In column E, Student WRC, rows 3 through 32, enter the student's successive ORF scores for the corresponding weeks as they are collected.

	A	B	C	D	E	F
1	Week Number	Week Date	Weekly WRC Gain	Target WRC	Student WRC	Cumulative Slope of WRC
2	0	9/8/08	1.15	43	43	n/a
3	1	9/15/08		44.15		
4	2	9/22/08		45.3	45	1.00
5	3	9/29/08		46.45		
6	4	10/6/08		47.6	46	0.75
7	5	10/13/08		48.75		
8	6	10/20/08		49.9	53	1.55
9	7	10/27/08		51.05		
10	8	11/3/08		52.2	57	1.80
11	9	11/10/08		53.35		
12	10	11/17/08		54.5	55	1.47
13	11	11/24/08		55.65		
14	12	12/1/08		56.8	58	1.36
15	13	12/8/08		57.95		
16	14	12/15/08		59.1	61	1.32
17	15	12/22/08		60.25		
18						1.22

CBM - Passage Reading Fluency

Target WRC ● Student WRC

t Per Minute (WCPM)

160 150 140 130 120 110 100 90 80

DETAIL

C	F
Weekly WRC Gain	Cumulative Slope of WRC
1.15	n/a
	1.00
	0.75
	1.55
	1.80
	1.47
	1.36
	1.32
	1.22
	1.18
	1.17
	1.20
	1.23
	1.25
	1.25
	1.24
	1.32

Monitor Student Progress

There are two ways to determine whether the student is making sufficient progress. The first is by visually comparing the student's ORF scores (red dots) to the blue aim line. In general, a student is making enough progress when the student's ORF scores are on or above the aim line. If the student has three ORF scores in a row that fall below the aim line, the student is not making sufficient progress, indicating that instruction must be adjusted.

A second way to determine whether the student is making sufficient progress is to compare the student's actual weekly rate of growth, or slope (column F, Cumulative Slope of WRC), to the target weekly rate of growth, or slope (cell C2, Weekly WRC Gain). When the actual weekly rate of growth, or slope, is equal to or greater than the target weekly rate of growth, or slope, the student's growth is sufficient. For example, when the teacher compared Michael's actual weekly rates of growth, or slopes, in column F to his target weekly rate of growth, or slope, she found that in Weeks 6 through 32 Michael's actual weekly rate of growth, or slope, was greater than 1.15 WCPM. This indicated that Michael was making sufficient progress and was well on his way to ending the school year on target.

ASSESSMENT MODEL

Prosody

Purposes

- assess prosody of student reading
- determine instruction in one or more areas of prosody

Strategy Grade Level

- Grade 2 and above

Grouping

- individual

Sample Text (Resources)

- "Alaska Adventure" Complexity Level: Grades 4–5

Activity Master (Resources)

- Prosody Assessment Summary Form

Materials

- copies of "Alaska Adventure"
- copy of Prosody Assessment Summary Form

SEE ALSO . . .

Prosody Assessment Rating Scale, p. 334

Assessment of Prosodic Reading

Reading prosody is measured by listening to a student's oral reading of a passage. During a reading, a teacher or other evaluator listens to the reader's stress, phrasing, intonation, expression, and pauses and then compares these characteristics to the rating scale or rubric. According to Rasinski (2004), "since expression or interpretation of text is difficult to quantify, researchers have turned to rating scales or qualitative rubrics or to guide the assessment process and assign a grade or level." Using sample text to represent a passage at the student's independent reading level, this sample assessment model provides an example of how to assess prosody. The same model can be adapted and used with other appropriate independent-level passages.

Prepare to Assess

Select independent-level text that contains a sufficient variety of dialogue, emotion, description, punctuation, and sentence structures. It is difficult to expressively read an animal description or a narrative containing only declarative sentences. There should be about 200 words in each passage.

Before administering the assessment, become familiar with the four different levels of prosodic reading on the Prosody Assessment Rating Scale. Then review the assessment passage to be aware of the characteristics of prosodic reading to expect.

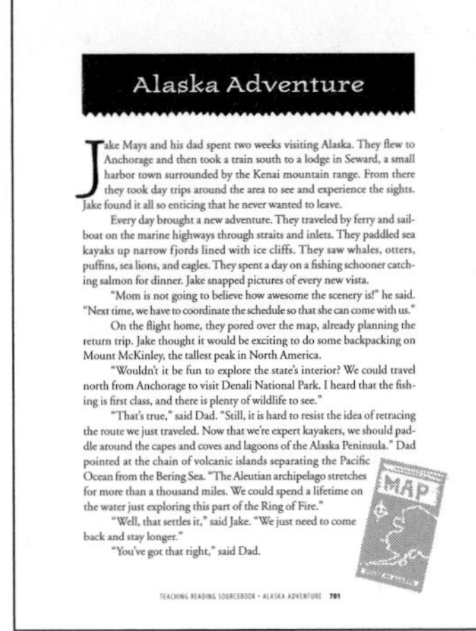

Alaska Adventure

Jake Mays and his dad spent two weeks visiting Alaska. They flew to Anchorage and then took a train south to a lodge in Seward, a small harbor town surrounded by the Kenai mountain range. From there they took day trips around the area to see and experience the sights. Jake found it all so enticing that he never wanted to leave.

Every day brought a new adventure. They traveled by ferry and sailboat on the marine highways through straits and inlets. They paddled sea kayaks up narrow fjords lined with ice cliffs. They saw whales, otters, puffins, sea lions, and eagles. They spent a day on a fishing schooner catching salmon for dinner. Jake snapped pictures of every new vista.

"Mom is not going to believe how awesome the scenery is!" he said. "Next time, we have to coordinate the schedule so that she can come with us."

On the flight home, they pored over the map, already planning the return trip. Jake thought it would be exciting to do some backpacking on Mount McKinley, the tallest peak in North America.

"Wouldn't it be fun to explore the state's interior? We could travel north from Anchorage to visit Denali National Park. I heard that the fishing is first class, and there is plenty of wildlife to see."

"That's true," said Dad. "Still, it is hard to resist the idea of retracing the route we just traveled. Now that we're expert kayakers, we should paddle around the capes and coves and lagoons of the Alaska Peninsula." Dad pointed at the chain of volcanic islands separating the Pacific Ocean from the Bering Sea. "The Aleutian archipelago stretches for more than a thousand miles. We could spend a lifetime on the water just exploring this part of the Ring of Fire."

"Well, that settles it," said Jake. "We just need to come back and stay longer."

"You've got that right," said Dad.

TEACHING READING SOURCEBOOK • ALASKA ADVENTURE 701

Listen to the Student Read

Ask a student to sit across from you or next to your nonwriting hand. Have a copy of "Alaska Adventure" in front of you. Say: *I'm going to ask you to read a passage aloud, and while you are reading I'm going to make some notes.* Give the student a copy of "Alaska Adventure." Say: *The title of this passage is "Alaska Adventure." When I say "Please begin," I'd like you to read the passage as if you are reading it to someone who has never heard it before. If you come to a word you don't know, try to figure it out. Do your best reading.* Ask: *Any questions?* After a short pause, say: *Please begin.* As you listen to the student read, on your copy of the passage circle any mispronounced words, underline words that are stressed, indicate the length of pauses, and make other additional notes or comments. For example:

STRESS Listen to how the student stresses, or emphasizes, various words. In a sentence, do all words receive equal stress or do only the most important words receive stress? Underline words that are stressed.

PHRASING Listen to the student's phrasing and indicate the length of the pauses between phrases. For a short pause, mark one front slash (/), and for a long pause, mark two front slashes (//).

INTONATION Note how the student uses end-mark punctuation to guide his or her intonation. Does the student's pitch rise for a question mark, get louder for an exclamation point, or dip for a comma?

EXPRESSION Note the student's expression when reading dialogue. Does the student use appropriate vocal tone to represent a character's mental state, such as excitement, sadness, fear, or confidence?

PAUSES Note whether the student pauses for punctuation, such as commas and end marks.

Record Observations on the Summary Form

Using your notes on the copy of the passage, fill in the student's Prosody Assessment Summary Form. Circle the score that best characterizes the student's reading prosody and then add relevant comments. A score of 1 or 2 indicates nonprosodic reading, or that the student has not yet achieved a minimum level of prosody for the grade or difficulty level of the passage. A score of 3 or 4 indicates prosodic reading.

Prosody Assessment Summary Form

Student Name *James Miller*
Teacher *Mr. Shepard* Grade *4*
Passage *Alaska Adventure* Date *Nov. 5, 2008*
Overall Score *3 transitioning to 4*

Circle the score that best captures the characteristics of the student's reading.
A score of 1 or 2 indicates nonprosodic reading, or that the student has not yet achieved a minimum level of prosody for the grade- or difficulty-level of the passage. A score of 3 or 4 indicates prosodic reading.

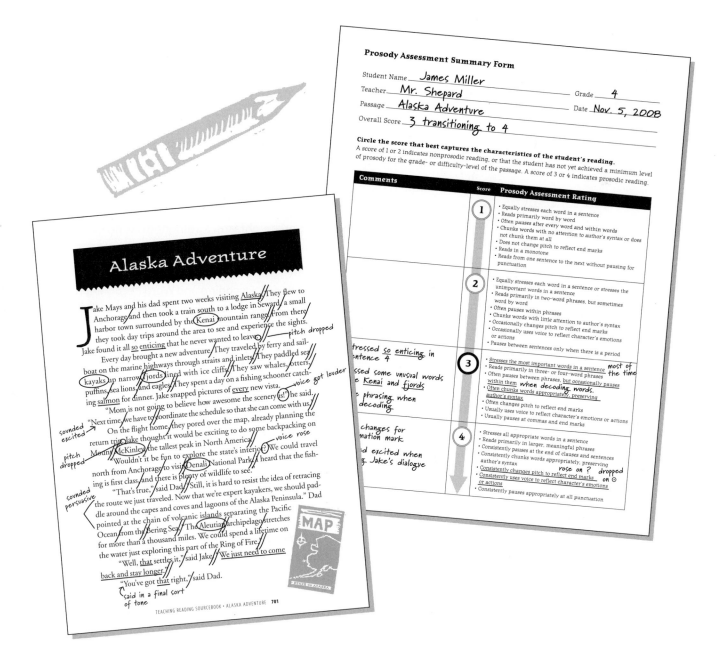

Comments	Score	Prosody Assessment Rating
	1	• Equally stresses each word in a sentence • Reads primarily word by word • Often pauses after every word and within words • Chunks words with no attention to author's syntax or does not chunk them at all • Does not change pitch to reflect end marks • Reads in a monotone • Reads from one sentence to the next without pausing for punctuation
	2	• Equally stresses each word in a sentence or stresses the unimportant words in a sentence • Reads primarily in two-word phrases, but sometimes word by word • Often pauses within phrases • Chunks words with little attention to author's syntax • Occasionally changes pitch to reflect end marks • Occasionally uses voice to reflect character's emotions or actions • Pauses between sentences only when there is a period
tressed so enticing in entence 4 *ssed some unusual words e Kenai and fjords* *phrasing when decoding*	(3)	• Stresses the most important words in a sentence *most of the time* • Reads primarily in three- or four-word phrases • Often pauses between phrases, but occasionally pauses within them *when decoding words.* • Often chunks words appropriately, preserving author's syntax • Often changes pitch to reflect end marks • Usually uses voice to reflect character's emotions or actions • Usually pauses at commas and end marks
changes for nation mark *d excited when Jake's dialogue*	4	• Stresses all appropriate words in a sentence • Reads primarily in larger, meaningful phrases • Consistently pauses at the end of clauses and sentences • Consistently chunks words appropriately, preserving author's syntax • Consistently changes pitch to reflect end marks *rose on ? dropped on ⊙* • Consistently uses voice to reflect character's emotions or actions • Consistently pauses appropriately at all punctuation

Alaska Adventure

Jake Mays and his dad spent two weeks visiting Alaska. They flew to Anchorage and then took a train south to a lodge in Seward, a small harbor town surrounded by the Kenai mountain range. From there they took day trips around the area to see and experience the sights. Jake found it all so enticing that he never wanted to leave. *— pitch dropped*

Every day brought a new adventure. They traveled by ferry and sailboat on the marine highways through straits and inlets. They paddled sea kayaks up narrow fjords lined with ice cliffs. They saw whales, otters, puffins, sea lions, and eagles. They spent a day on a fishing schooner catching salmon for dinner. Jake snapped pictures of every new vista.

"Mom is not going to believe how awesome the scenery is!" he said. *— voice got louder* "Next time, we have to coordinate the schedule so that she can come with us." *sounded excited*

On the flight home, they pored over the map, already planning the return trip. Jake thought it would be exciting to do some backpacking on Mount McKinley, the tallest peak in North America. *pitch dropped*

"Wouldn't it be fun to explore the state's interior? *— voice rose* We could travel north from Anchorage to visit Denali National Park. I heard that the fishing is first class, and there is plenty of wildlife to see."

"That's true," said Dad. "Still, it is hard to resist the idea of retracing the route we just traveled. Now that we're expert kayakers, we should paddle around the capes and coves and lagoons of the Alaska Peninsula." Dad pointed at the chain of volcanic islands separating the Pacific Ocean from the Bering Sea. "The Aleutian archipelago stretches for more than a thousand miles. We could spend a lifetime on the water just exploring this part of the Ring of Fire." *sounded persuasive*

"Well, that settles it," said Jake. "We just need to come back and stay longer."

"You've got that right," said Dad. *said in a final sort of tone*

MAP

STATE of ALASKA

TEACHING READING SOURCEBOOK • ALASKA ADVENTURE 701

Instructional Options for Nonprosodic Readers

The goal of any assessment is to determine a student's proficiency level and then to use the information to guide instruction. For nonprosodic readers, consider the following questions for interpretation and instructional options.

Questions for Interpretation	Instructional Options
Does the student's nonprosodic reading match the way he or she speaks?	A student cannot be expected to read at a different level of prosody than he or she speaks. Providing language instruction may be more appropriate than instruction in reading prosody.
Does the student equally stress each word in a sentence?	Have students practice placing the stress, or the emphasis, on different words in the same sentence. For example: • I am **so** happy. • **I** am so happy. • I am so **happy**.
Does the student read primarily word by word?	To group words into appropriate phrases, a student must first be able to automatically recognize the words. Providing instruction in decoding and word-reading accuracy and automaticity may improve a student's prosody. See Section III: Decoding and Word Recognition.
Does the student group words into appropriate phrases?	Provide instruction in recognizing phrase boundaries using phrase-cued text. See Lesson Model: Phrase-Cued Reading, p. 391.
Does the student use punctuation to guide intonation?	Provide contextualized instruction in the names and meanings of punctuation marks. Have students read the same sentence with different end punctuation. For example: • Visiting the public library is fun! • Visiting the public library is fun? • Visiting the public library is fun.
Does the student read in a monotone?	Use Readers Theatre to help develop a student's expression. See Lesson Model: Readers Theatre, p. 398.

CHAPTER 10

Fluency Instruction

what? why? when? how?

what?

Fluency Instruction

To develop fluency, we need teacher-directed lessons in which children spend the maximum amount of time engaged in reading connected text.

—STAHL & KUHN, 2002

Building reading fluency depends on more than just independent reading. Research shows that reading fluency instruction is a vital part of every reading program. Because practice develops fluency, it is important to ensure that every student has sufficient practice reading connected text at the right level. A variety of direct teaching methods provide increased opportunities for student practice with corrective feedback.

To develop fluency, students, with teacher assistance, must work on the three elements that indicate fluent reading: accuracy, rate, and prosody. These elements are intertwined, and working on one element often means simultaneously working on another. For example, an increase in accuracy will also improve reading rate. Likewise, an increase in rate is likely to improve prosody since students can now pay attention to the phrasing and meaning of the passage rather than focus attention on decoding individual words.

This chapter focuses primarily on fluency instruction in connected text. While regular- and irregular-word-reading accuracy and automaticity are important, they are primarily addressed in other sections of the Sourcebook. Instructional methods focused on connected text can be grouped into three main categories: independent silent reading, assisted reading, and repeated oral reading. In actual practice, these categories often overlap. A fourth category focuses on integrated fluency instruction.

SEE ALSO . . .

Chapter 6: Phonics

Chapter 7: Irregular Word Reading

Chapter 8: Multisyllabic Word Reading

CCSS READING STANDARDS

Foundational Skills

Fluency

Read with sufficient accuracy and fluency to support comprehension. (RF.1-5.4)

Independent Silent Reading

As Osborn and Lehr (2003) point out, "Independent silent reading encourages students to read extensively on their own, both in and out of the classroom, with minimal guidance and feedback." While research has not confirmed (or refuted) that independent silent reading improves either reading achievement or fluency, good readers typically read far more than poor readers during the school day (Allington 1983). Moreover, many poor readers become expert at looking as if they are reading when they really are not. Therefore, ample opportunities should be provided for all students, especially poor readers, to read connected text every day with adult feedback. In addition, students should be encouraged to read more outside school, either with a family member or on their own.

Methods for Building Fluency

Independent Silent Reading

Assisted Reading

Repeated Oral Reading

Integrated Fluency Instruction

Assisted Reading

One of the reasons students fail to read fluently is that they have not been exposed to models of fluent reading (Allington 1983). According to Blevins (2001), "students need many opportunities to hear text read. They need proficient fluency models; that is, they need to have a model voice in their heads to refer to as they monitor their own reading." By listening to good models of fluent reading, students learn how a reader's voice can help written text make sense (Kuhn and Stahl 2003).

Most assisted-reading methods initially provide students with a model of fluent reading (Osborn and Lehr 2003). Assisted reading can thus be defined as a set of instructional methods that provide support to students through the use of fluent models before or as they read (Kuhn and Stahl 2003). Methods of assisted reading take several forms, including teacher-assisted reading, peer-assisted reading, and audio-assisted reading. All such forms emphasize extensive practice as a means of improving students' fluency.

Assisted Reading

Teacher Assisted

Peer Assisted

Audio Assisted

Teacher-Assisted Reading

Any form of reading aloud to students provides them with a model for how words on a page turn into expressive phrases, sentences, and paragraphs. As Armbruster, Lehr, and Osborn (2001) point out, "By reading aloud effortlessly and with expression, a teacher can model how a fluent reader sounds during reading." Listening to an expressive reader shows students how reading, if done well, sounds and makes sense much like their speech. A critical element is that students see the words as they hear them being read.

Peer-Assisted Reading

In peer-assisted reading, paired students, or partners, take turns reading aloud to each other and providing corrective feedback. Usually, more-fluent readers are paired with less-fluent readers. According to Stahl and Heubach (2006), "partner reading provides an opportunity for students to read connected text within a socially supportive context." This context both motivates partners to read well and provides a supportive environment. Various forms of partner, or paired, reading have been found to produce significant gains in fluency (Eldredge 1990; Fuchs et al. 2007; Koskinen and Blum 1986; Topping 1987).

When poor readers in Grades 3 and 4 practiced reading basal stories with a recording, their oral reading fluency and comprehension improved as much as students who practiced the same materials with a teacher.

—SHANY & BIEMILLER, 1995

Audio-Assisted Reading

When reading with a recording as support, students follow along in their books as they hear a recording of a fluent reader read the book (Carbo 1981; Shany and Biemiller 1995). This can be done with a computer, a CD, or an audiotape. Because students will be working without adult support, it is important to make sure that the recorded text is at the student's independent reading level. It is also important to use a recording that is free from sound effects or music, has adequate prosody, and is slow enough for the dysfluent reader to keep up. If the recording is too fast for the student to keep up, the exercise turns into a listening session, which will not build reading fluency. Again, the critical element is that students see the words as they hear them being read.

Repeated oral reading substantially improves word recognition, speed, and accuracy as well as fluency.

—ARMBRUSTER ET AL., 2001

Repeated Oral Reading

In repeated oral reading, students read the same text repeatedly until a desired level of fluency is attained. Research has shown that repeated and monitored oral reading improves fluency and overall reading achievement. It provides the targeted, focused practice needed to improve all areas of reading fluency—accuracy, rate, and prosody—and is one of the most-studied methods for increasing reading fluency (e.g., Kuhn and Stahl 2003; Meyer and Felton 1999; National Reading Panel 2000).

The repeated readings technique (Samuels 1997) has many variations, including choral reading, audio-assisted reading, partner reading, and Readers Theatre—methods that involve rereading connected text to provide sufficient practice to build both automaticity and fluency. Some of these methods involve tracking WCPM scores. As Chard, Vaughn, and Tyler (2002) point out, "Repeated reading interventions for students with LD [learning disabilities] are associated with improvements in reading rate, accuracy, and comprehension." In short, practice is the key to building reading fluency.

SEE ALSO . . .

Choosing the Right Text, p. 367

Adaptations of Repeated Oral Reading

Repeated oral reading is very flexible and can be adapted in many ways to better fit into a reading program and meet individual student needs (Blum and Koskinen 1991). Here are some ways to adapt repeated oral readings after choosing the right text.

NUMBER OF REREADINGS The number of times a student reads a passage can vary in two ways: students read and reread text until a certain level of fluency is reached (e.g., until the student can read at 80 WCPM), or they can read text a set number of times (e.g., three or four times). If teachers have students read a text a set number of times, the most benefit can be obtained in three or four readings (Therrien 2004). The amount of improvement levels off after four readings, meaning

To become fluent readers, students need practice, practice, and more practice with reading.

—OSBORN & LEHR, 2003

that while students will continue to improve, improvement will decrease. If students read a text 10 times, they will not read 10 times better. Thus, it is better to switch students to a new text and begin the rereading again.

INSTRUCTIONAL GROUPINGS Teachers can group students engaged in repeated reading in a number of ways, such as individually with a teacher or another adult, in pairs, in a small group with a teacher, or in a large whole-class group.

PURPOSE FOR READING Students reading a text several times can devote each repetition to a different purpose. For example, they could read once to identify the motivations of a character, a second time to identify the setting, and a third to identify the solution or denouement. With expository text, students could read once to identify the main idea, a second time to identify three important ideas, and a third time to take notes.

SEE ALSO . . .

LESSON MODELS

Method for Reading Decodable Text, p. 235

Timed Repeated Oral Reading, p. 374

Partner Reading, p. 384

Phrase-Cued Reading, p. 391

Readers Theatre, p. 398

Methods of Repeated Oral Reading

Once teachers have used diagnostic assessment data to determine a student's area of weakness, they can match instructional methods to that student. Instructional methods designed to increase reading fluency vary both in their main focus (accuracy, rate, or prosody) and in their grouping strategies. Some methods are most appropriate for students reading individually with little support, other methods work well when used with same-level peers, and still others are most effective when students work with adults or more-capable peers who provide support and instruction. By choosing methods that provide more or less support or assistance and address a particular area of fluency, teachers can match their instruction to student needs.

From this basic form of repeated reading, a number of instructional procedures have emerged over the years. Some of the more widely used procedures include those in the following chart.

Research-Based Methods of Repeated Oral Reading

METHOD	DESCRIPTION	MAIN INSTRUCTIONAL FOCUS			TYPE OF ASSISTANCE			
		Accuracy	Rate	Prosody	Audio	Peer	Teacher/More Capable Reader	None
Timed Repeated Oral Reading Lesson Model: Timed Repeated Oral Reading, p. 374	In timed repeated oral reading, students work one on one with a teacher or partner to increase their automaticity in reading connected text. Students reread the same passage aloud until they can read it at a certain rate to meet a preset goal. The teacher times the student, provides corrective feedback, and graphs students' achievements.	X	X				X	
Self-Timed Repeated Oral Reading	In this variation of timed repeated oral reading, students independently practice reading a passage, time their own reading for one minute, record their score, and then read the passage again to try to beat the previous score.		X		X			X
Partner Reading Lesson Model: Partner Reading, p. 384	In partner reading, a pair of students takes turns reading aloud to each other. Students who are better readers are often paired with students who are less-able readers. The first student reads aloud a section of text while the second student follows along providing corrective feedback. The roles are then reversed.	X	X	X		X	X	
Phrase-Cued Reading Lesson Model: Phrase-Cued Reading, p. 391	In this method, phrase boundaries are marked in a text. Then the teacher provides instruction and modeling on how to read the text by appropriately chunking groups of words into phrases or meaningful units.			X			X	X
Readers Theatre Lesson Model: Readers Theatre, p. 398	In Readers Theatre, a small group rehearses and then performs a script. Performing the script for peers provides an authentic purpose for rereading the text.			X	X	X	X	
Radio Reading	A variation of Readers Theatre for older students, radio reading includes sound effects to make the performance sound like an old-time radio show.			X	X	X	X	
Choral Reading	Choral reading actively involves students as they read aloud in unison, as a whole class or small group, along with a teacher or more-capable reader. It can be used instead of traditional round-robin reading.	X		X		X	X	
Duet Reading	In duet reading, two students read aloud in unison.	X		X		X	X	
Echo Reading	In echo reading, a teacher or more-capable reader reads aloud a section of a text (e.g., a sentence, a paragraph, or a page) and students repeat the text section aloud as they point to the words they are reading.	X		X			X	
Reading with Recordings See Also ... Audio-Assisted Reading, p. 362	In this method, the student reads text aloud in synchronization with a recorded model, such as a software program, a CD, or an audiotape.	X		X	X			

FORI has demonstrated compellingly that fluency can be easily integrated into existing reading programs.

—RASINSKI & HOFFMAN, 2006

Integrated Fluency Instruction

Fluency-Oriented Reading Instruction (FORI) is an integrated approach to fluency instruction that combines repeated oral reading and teacher- and peer-assisted reading with independent silent reading (Stahl, Heubach, and Cramond 1997). The components of this three-part instructional program include the repeated reading of a selection from a core reading program, followed by independent silent reading practice at school and at home. FORI can be adapted and used with any core reading program, and there is good research evidence of its effectiveness with early elementary students. It has been used successfully with English-language learners to improve reading fluency and home-based reading practice (Morrow, Kuhn, and Schwanenflugel 2006).

Fluency-Oriented Reading Instruction (FORI)

	M	T	W	T	F
Reading a Selection from a Core Reading Program	Teacher Modeling	Repeated Reading			Text-Related Activities
	Teacher reads aloud and previews the selection.	Teacher-assisted choral reading	Teacher-assisted echo reading	Peer-assisted partner reading	Writing in response to reading
Free-Choice Independent Reading at School	Students independently read a book of their own choosing.				
Independent Reading at Home	Students read for 15–30 minutes in the book of their choosing.	Students read aloud the selection to a family member.	Students who need more practice read aloud the selection to a family member. Other students read for 15–30 minutes in the book of their choosing.		Students read for 15–30 minutes in the book of their choosing.

Based on Stahl and Heubach 2006; Kuhn and Schwanenflugel 2006.

Fluency develops as a result of many opportunities to practice reading with a high degree of success.

—ARMBRUSTER ET AL., 2001

SEE ALSO . . .

Decodable Text, p. 183

The Text, p. 610

Motivation and Engagement with Reading, p. 695

Choosing the Right Text

It is important to provide students with instruction and practice in fluency as they read connected text. The texts students read to develop fluency should be chosen carefully (Young and Bowers 1995). Criteria include text length, text genre, text content, and, most important, level of text difficulty.

Text Length and Genre

A general guideline is to use passages between 50 and 200 words in length, using shorter passages with beginning, slower readers and longer passages with better readers (Armbruster et al. 2001). Since most reading fluency instruction involves repeated readings, the passage should not be so long as to make multiple readings tedious. Passages should vary in genre; for example, use short stories, newspaper and magazine articles, biographies, informational text, songs, or poetry.

Text Content

Many struggling readers do not want to read a passage once, let alone several times; choosing the right passage can be the key to motivation. When choosing passages, teachers should consider whether the topic can hold the interest of the student. In addition, the more that words overlap between texts, the more transfer of fluent reading there is between them (Rashotte and Torgesen 1985). Therefore, teachers may want students to read texts that share a common theme-based vocabulary. For example, students reading a series of passages about rain forest animals might repeatedly encounter words such as *rain forest, canopy,* and *species.*

Level of Text Difficulty

A primary requirement for repeated oral reading is to make sure the text being read is at the correct level of difficulty for the student. For struggling readers, this text is often one or more grade levels below their actual grade. To increase fluency as quickly as possible for these students, the level of text difficulty should increase over time.

Levels of Text Difficulty		
Level of Difficulty	**Percent of Reading Accuracy**	**Appropriate for . . .**
INDEPENDENT LEVEL Relatively easy for the reader	95–100% (fewer than 5 errors per 100 words)	• Independent Reading • Choral or Duet Reading • Phrase-Cued Reading • Readers Theatre • Reading with Recordings • Timed Repeated Oral Reading
INSTRUCTIONAL LEVEL Challenging but manageable for the reader	90–94% (fewer than 10 errors per 100 words)	• Partner Reading • Teacher-Assisted Reading • Timed Repeated Oral Reading
FRUSTRATION LEVEL Difficult for the reader	Less than 90% (more than 10 errors per 100 words)	Not appropriate for fluency instruction

Based on Armbruster et al. 2001.

How to Determine the Level of Text Difficulty

To determine whether a particular text is at a student's independent, instructional, or frustration level, follow these steps:

STEP 1. Based on informal and formal assessment data, select a relatively short passage—of about 100 to 120 words—that seems to be at the student's reading level.

SEE ALSO . . .

Fluency Scoring, p. 342

STEP 2. Have the student read the first 100 words of the passage aloud. (The student could read more words, but it is easier to calculate the percentage if the student reads only 100 words.) As the student reads, keep track of errors: mispronunciations, omissions, substitutions, transpositions, and hesitations. If the student is having a great deal of difficulty, select an easier passage.

CCSS READING STANDARDS

Foundational Skills

Fluency

Read on-level text with purpose and understanding. (RF.1-5.4a)

Read on-level text orally with accuracy, appropriate rate, and expression on successive readings. (RF.1-5.4b)

STEP 3. Calculate the number of words read correctly by subtracting the number of student errors from the total number of words read. For example, if a student makes 3 errors when reading a 100-word passage, the number of words read correctly is 100 – 3, or 97.

STEP 4. Then calculate the percent of words read correctly, or the percent of accuracy. If the student reads 100 words, the number of correct words is the same as the percent of accuracy. For example, if a student reads 97 words correctly out of a 100-word passage, the accuracy level is 97 ÷ 100 = (.97), or 97%. If a student reads 112 words correctly out of a 120-word passage, the accuracy level is 112 ÷ 120 = (.93), or 93%.

STEP 5. Compare the student's accuracy level with the levels of text difficulty. For example, 97% accuracy means that the text is at the student's independent level (i.e., 95% to 100%).

Using the information on the Levels of Text Difficulty chart, choose the best answers. (See Answer Key, p. 800.)

Melvin read three passages with the following accuracy levels:

Passage One	**93% accuracy (93/100)**
Passage Two	**97% accuracy (97/100)**
Passage Three	**78% accuracy (78/100)**

Which passage is at Melvin's independent level? Instructional level? Frustration level?

Monica read three passages. Calculate the accuracy level for each.

Passage One	**100 words read with 14 errors**
Passage Two	**121 words read with 11 errors**
Passage Three	**115 words read with 6 errors**

Which passage is most appropriate for independent reading? For teacher-assisted reading? Not appropriate for fluency instruction?

why?

Fluency Instruction

> Students who are low in fluency may have difficulty getting the meaning of what they are reading.
>
> —NATIONAL READING PANEL, 2000

Accurate, automatic, and expressive reading is regarded by most educators as the mark of proficient reading. Yet many students fail to develop it. It is often assumed that if students can decode they will become fluent, but research has indicated that this is not necessarily so (Morrow, Kuhn, and Schwanenflugel 2006). According to Hudson, Lane, and Pullen (2005), "struggling readers may not gain reading fluency incidentally or automatically. In contrast to skilled readers, they often need direct instruction in how to read fluently and sufficient opportunities for intense, fluency-focused practice. . . ." Independent reading practice is thus not sufficient for many students to develop the level of reading fluency needed for proficient reading. One of the most compelling reasons to focus instructional efforts on students becoming fluent readers is the strong correlation between reading fluency and reading comprehension (Allington 1983; Johns 1993; Samuels 1988). Playing an important role in terms of a reader's ability to construct meaning from text, fluency has been shown to have a reciprocal relationship with comprehension (Stecker, Roser, and Martinez 1998). Because fluent readers do not have to concentrate fully on decoding, they can devote their attention to the meaning of the text.

Research Findings . . .

For students at all levels—but particularly for students at the beginning stages of learning to read—oral reading rate is strongly correlated with students' ability to comprehend both simple and complex text.

—TORGESEN & HUDSON, 2006

. . . while fluency in and of itself is not sufficient to ensure high levels of reading achievement, fluency is absolutely necessary for that achievement because it depends upon and typically reflects comprehension.

—PIKULSKI & CHARD, 2005

Although silent, independent reading may be a way to increase fluency and reading achievement, it should not be used in place of direct instruction in reading.

—ARMBRUSTER ET AL., 2001

Suggested Reading . . .

Building Fluency: Lessons and Strategies for Reading Success (2001) by Wiley Blevins. New York: Scholastic.

Fluency in the Classroom, 2nd Edition (2012) edited by Melanie R. Kuhn & Paula J. Schwanenflugel. New York: Guilford.

Fluency Instruction: Research-Based Best Practices (2006) edited by Timothy Rasinski, Camille Blachowicz & Kristin Lems. New York: Guilford.

Put Reading First: The Research Building Blocks for Teaching Children to Read, 3rd Edition (2006) by Bonnie Armbruster, Fran Lehr & Jean Osborn. Jessup, MD: National Institute for Literacy.

What Research Has to Say About Fluency Instruction (2006) edited by S. Jay Samuels & Alan E. Farstrup. Newark, DE: International Reading Association.

when?

Fluency Instruction

The development of oral reading fluency…is a gradually developing, complex skill.

—SPEECE & RITCHEY, 2005

Fluency Objectives

- **Decoding words accurately**
- **Recognizing words automatically**
- **Increasing reading rate while maintaining accuracy**
- **Reading with prosody**

When to Teach

Not every student needs instruction focused on building fluency. Assessment will determine which students need fluency instruction and then establish the students' particular area of weakness. Struggling readers may need to work on skills and knowledge that focus primarily on accuracy (e.g., word recognition), rate, prosody, or a combination of all three.

In Kindergarten through Grade 2, students should have daily opportunities to hear text read aloud in a fluent and expressive manner. In Grade 1, students should participate in the guided repeated oral readings of familiar texts. In Grade 2, students typically show a greater amount of growth in reading fluency. These students should have daily opportunities to repeatedly read text aloud with corrective feedback.

In Grades 3 through 5, reading fluency continues to contribute to overall reading comprehension along with vocabulary and background knowledge. As students shift to more difficult and complex texts, they still need daily practice reading aloud with corrective feedback.

Most students will not substantially increase their oral reading fluency rate and accuracy beyond Grade 6 (Torgesen et al. 2007). However, all students need ample amounts of reading practice in a wide range of texts to ensure that they do not fall

SEE ALSO . . .

Fluency Assessment, When to Assess, p. 338

behind. Ample practice is important, especially for struggling readers, because the number of unusual, content-specific words increases as students move into middle and high school.

To build a strong foundation for fluency in reading connected text, it is critical that students first develop accuracy and automaticity in recognizing letters, sound/spelling correspondences, and regular and irregular words. These components of word-reading accuracy, which are mainly covered in Section III: Decoding and Word Recognition, are included in the following chart.

When to Teach Fluency

TYPE OF INSTRUCTION	KINDERGARTEN	GRADE 1	GRADE 2	GRADES 3–5	GRADE 6 AND ABOVE
Letter Naming Fluency Chapter 4: Letter Knowledge	X	X			
Sound/Spelling Fluency Chapter 6: Phonics	X	X			
Regular Word Reading Automaticity Chapter 6: Phonics	X	X	X		
Irregular Word Reading Automaticity Chapter 7: Irregular Word Reading	X	X	X		
Multisyllabic Word Reading Automaticity Chapter 8: Multisyllabic Word Reading			X	X	X
Reading Decodable Text Chapter 6: Phonics	X	X	X		
Prosody—Phrasing		X	X	X	
Prosody—Expressiveness		X	X	X	
Reading Connected Text (Literary and Informational)		X	X	X	X
Modeled Fluent Reading	X	X	X	X	X
Independent Silent Reading	X	X	X	X	X

how? Fluency Instruction

LESSON MODEL FOR

Reading Fluency

Benchmarks

- ability to read fluently
- improvement in reading rate and accuracy

Strategy Grade Level

- Grade 2 and above

Prerequisite

- Assessment of ORF Rate and Accuracy, p. 340

Grouping

- individual

Sample Text (Resources)

- "BMX Bikes" and "BMX Bikes" with word count Complexity Level: Grade 2

Activity Master (Resources)

- Student Progress Graph

Materials

- copy of Student Progress Graph
- copy of "BMX Bikes"
- copy of "BMX Bikes" with word count
- timer, red pen or pencil

Timed Repeated Oral Reading

Timed repeated oral reading is an intervention strategy that is most appropriate for slow but accurate readers who need intense practice to increase their automaticity in reading connected text. While timed repeated oral reading is similar to the timed readings used to assess ORF rate and accuracy, it differs in several ways: (1) it is designed for struggling readers, not all students, (2) its purpose is to build a student's oral reading fluency, not to assess how well a student is meeting grade-level expectations, and (3) the text used is at a student's instructional or independent level, not grade level.

Therrien (2004) found that this strategy works better when the student reads to an adult rather than to a peer and when the student reads to reach a certain rate goal rather than a certain number of readings. To provide sufficient practice with enough continuity, timed repeated oral reading should take place at least three times a week with no more than one session per day.

In this sample lesson model, sample text is used to represent a passage at the student's instructional or independent reading level. The same model can be adapted and used with other passages—as long as the text is at the appropriate reading level.

Student Profile

Conrad is in third grade. While his reading is generally accurate, it is slow and choppy. On September 10, his baseline median ORF score on grade-level text was 17 WCPM, well below the 50th percentile score of 71 WCPM for fall on Hasbrouck and Tindal's Oral Reading Fluency Norms (2006). According to these norms, the 50th percentile score for winter is 92 WCPM. After determining that Conrad can independently read first-grade text with 97 percent accuracy at 62 WCPM, the teacher decided to set Conrad's final goal at 90 WCPM in mid-second-grade text by December 5.

Prepare

Using oral reading fluency (ORF) and diagnostic assessment data, identify the struggling readers who are likely to benefit from this technique.

Select Appropriate Text

SEE ALSO . . .

Choosing the Right Text, p. 367

The reading passages should be relatively short, between 100 and 250 words long at the student's instructional or independent reading level.

Enter Student Information on the Graph

SEE ALSO . . .

Enter the Student's Target Weekly Rate of Growth, p. 352, for more information about setting goals

Conrad's teacher has set a fairly ambitious final goal of increasing both text difficulty (early-first to mid-second grade) and rate (2.3 WCPM per week). Conrad is going to begin by reading early-first-grade text. His final goal is to read mid-second-grade text at 90 WCPM with no more than two errors by December 5—the end of Week 12. Having no more than two errors generally leads to 95 to 98 percent accuracy. This two-error limit applies to all the passages.

[90 WCPM − 62 WCPM = 28 WCPM ÷ 12 weeks = 2.3 WCPM per week]

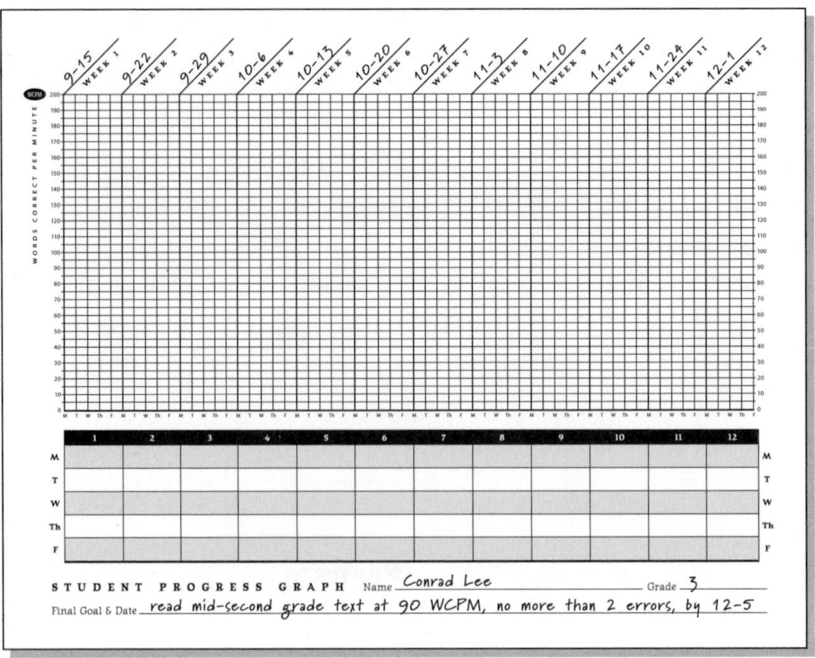

At the bottom of the Student Progress Graph, fill in the student's Name, Grade, and Final Goal & Date. On the diagonal lines labeled Week 1, Week 2, and so on at the top of the graph, enter Monday's date (month and day) for each of the 12 consecutive weeks.

BMX Bikes

BMX bikes should have 20-inch wheels. The bolts should be tight. Take off any lights, and take off the kickstand.

Bike height is from 10 to 13 inches. A short bike can go fast, but your feet can hit the ground on turns. A tall bike has room for turns, but it jerks at top speed.

Choose the size of the wheelbase for the way you ride. Short is good for ramp riding and jumping. Long is good for going down hills.

Hot bikes are made for cool moves. To pop a wheelie, pump hard on the pedals. Shift your weight to the back of the seat. Pull up on the front wheel. It will lift the wheel off of the ground. You will be able to ride for a long way with your front wheel up high.

Teach/Model—First Timed Reading

To introduce the first timed reading, say: *It is important to read smoothly and fluently, so it sounds like you are talking; it also helps readers to understand what they are reading. In this timed reading activity, you will read the same passage over and over until you can read it fluently at a certain rate. You also are going to learn to use a graph to keep a record of your reading improvement.*

Preview the Passage

Give the student the unnumbered copy of "BMX Bikes." Explain to the student that previewing a passage helps improve reading fluency. Then preview the text with the student. Say: *Please read the title of this passage.* Ask: *What's the title?* ("BMX Bikes")

If student is a very dysfluent reader who needs a great deal of support, model reading the passage aloud before asking the student to read it.

Ask: *What do you think this passage is about?* (Possible answer: *some kind of bike*) Say: *Now I'd like you to read aloud the passage. If you get stuck on a word, I'll help you to figure it out.* Monitor the student's reading and assist with decoding and word recognition as needed.

If the student needs assistance with more than 8 percent of the words (more than 11 of the 138 words in "BMX Bikes"), ask the student to read the whole passage one more time. If the student needs assistance with more than 10 percent of the words, select a less difficult passage.

BMX Bikes

BMX bikes should have 20-inch wheels. The bolts 8
should be tight. Take off any lights, and take off the kickstand. 20
Bike height is from 10 to 13 inches. A short bike can go 33
fast, but your feet can hit the ground on turns. A tall bike has 47
room for turns, but it jerks at top speed. 56
Choose the size of the wheelbase for the way you ride. 67
Short is good for ramp riding and jumping. Long is good for 79
going down hills. 82
Hot bikes are made for cool moves. To pop a wheelie, 93
pump hard on the pedals. Shift your weight to the back of the 106
seat. Pull up on the front wheel. It will lift the wheel off of the 121
ground. You will be able to ride for a long way with your front 135
wheel up high. 138

Listen to the Student Read

Set the timer for one minute. Ask a student to sit across from you or next to your nonwriting hand. Have a numbered copy of "BMX Bikes" in front of you. The numbers indicate the cumulative line-by-line word count. Say: *Doing your best reading, please read aloud this passage to me with expression and at a good even pace—a pace that isn't too slow or too fast. Start with the first word and read until the timer sounds. When you are ready, begin.*

When the student reads the first word, start the timer. Following along on your numbered copy, use a red pen or pencil to keep track of student errors. (See Fluency Scoring, p. 342.) When the timer goes off, place a bracket (]) after the last word the student reads aloud. When student finishes the sentence, say: *Great! You read really well.*

CORRECTIVE FEEDBACK

CORRECTIVE FEEDBACK If a student begins reading very quickly in a staccato and without expression, stop the student and have him or her start again. Say: *Remember that we aren't trying to read as fast as we can. We are trying to read the best that we can. Try it again, and don't forget to pay attention to what the passage is about. Ready, begin.*

Review Student Performance

Review the student's performance on the one-minute timed reading by providing positive feedback first. Say: *You did a great job reading. You read smoothly, carefully, and with expression. I was especially impressed with how you decoded the word* kickstand *so quickly and self-corrected the word* ground. Then provide corrective feedback on any word-reading errors the student made. Treat the errors as puzzles to be solved rather than big mistakes.

FOR ACCURACY Because errors negatively affect a WCPM score, it's important to correct a student's mistakes. Say: *Now let's correct your mistakes.* Point to *bolts.* Say: *This word is* bolts. Ask: *What's the word?* (bolts) Say: *Good. Now read the whole sentence again.* Have the student reread the sentence until he or she can accurately read it. Follow the same procedure for the word *jerks.*

FOR PROSODY If a student did not read with expression or correct phrasing, model correct prosody by reading one or two sentences aloud from the passage. Have the student repeat the sentences after you. If necessary, point out punctuation marks and explain how they cue proper expression.

Calculate the ORF Score

Tell the student that now you will show how to calculate his or her score. Explain that the score tells how many words the student read correctly per minute. To calculate the ORF score, first count the total number of words the student read and the number of errors the student made. Then subtract the errors from the total number of words read. Today Conrad read 62 words in one minute and made 2 errors, so his ORF score is 60 WCPM.

Total words read − errors = ORF score
62 − 2 = 60 WCPM

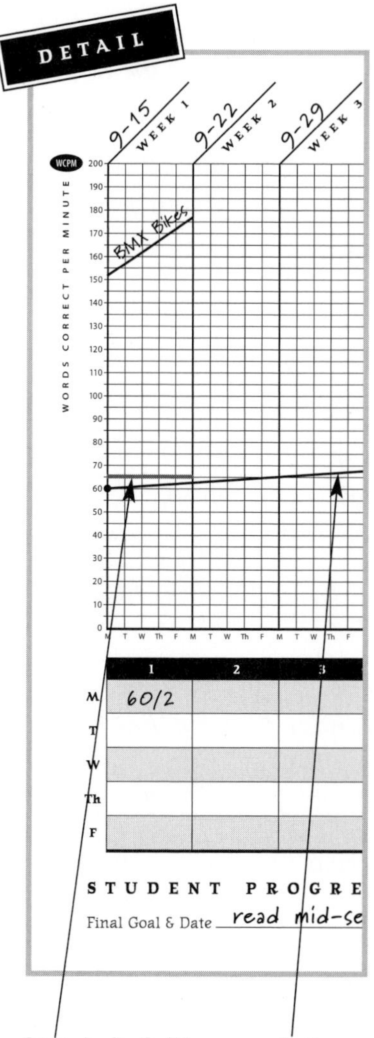

Passage Reading Goal Line

Aim Line

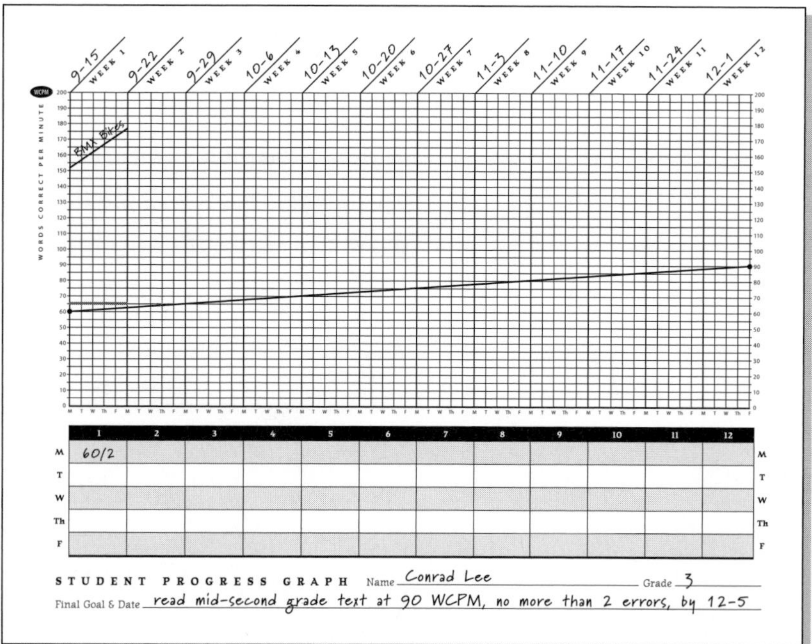

Introduce the Progress Graph and Enter Student Data

Once the student's ORF score is calculated, introduce the Student Progress Graph. Say: *This is a graph where we will keep track of your reading progress.* Point out the diagonal lines labeled Week 1, Week 2, and so on at the top of the graph and the abbreviations for the days of the week at the bottom of the graph. Explain that WCPM stands for "words correct per minute."

FINAL GOAL & DATE Point to the line labeled Final Goal & Date. Say: *See, here is where I wrote your final goal. Today you read a first-grade passage, "BMX Bikes," at 60 words correct per minute with 2 mistakes. Your final goal, by December 5, is to be reading a mid-second-grade passage at 90 words correct per minute with no more than 2 mistakes, or errors.*

ENTER AND PLOT SCORE Say: *In one minute, you read 62 words and made 2 mistakes. Your score is 60 words correct per minute, or 62 – 2. In the box for Monday of Week 1 below the graph, watch as I write the number of words you read correctly and the number of mistakes.* Write 60/2 in the box. *Now watch as I plot your score on the graph.* Put a dot on the coordinate for Monday, Week 1, and 60 WCPM as shown.

FINAL GOAL AND AIM LINE Say: *Today you scored 60 WCPM, but your final goal is to score 90 WCPM. On the graph I am going to draw a line, called an aim line, from your score today to your final goal. The aim line shows how much daily or weekly progress you need to make to meet your final goal.* Using a ruler, draw the student's aim line as indicated.

PASSAGE READING GOAL AND GOAL LINE Say: *Now we are going to set your "BMX Bikes" passage reading goal. You will read the passage as many times as it takes for you to reach the goal. I want you to try to improve your score each time you read, making no more than 2 mistakes. When you reach this passage reading goal, you get a new passage to read and a new goal. Each time you make your goal, we'll celebrate with something nice.*

A passage reading goal should be challenging but not too hard. Set the goal so the student will be reading at or just above the aim line within 5 to 7 repeated readings.

Say: *Look at the aim line. A passage reading goal should be a little bit above the aim line. For tomorrow, Tuesday, your aim line crosses at about 61 WCPM. Since 65 WCPM is a little above your aim line, your goal for "BMX Bikes" is to read 65 words correct per minute. Watch as I draw your passage reading goal line.* Across Week 1, draw a horizontal line at 65 WCPM.

Teach/Model—Repeated Timed Reading

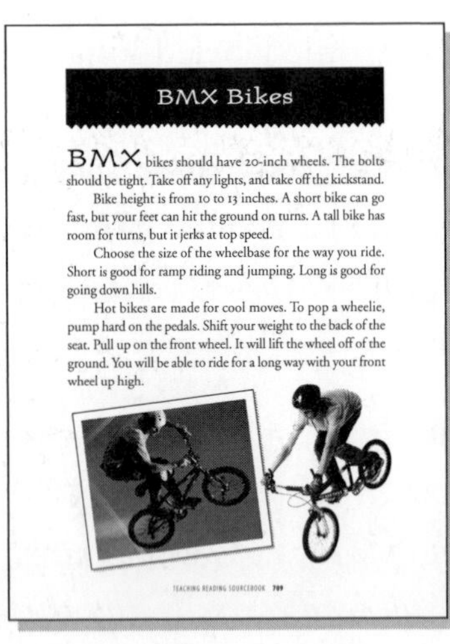

BMX Bikes

BMX bikes should have 20-inch wheels. The bolts should be tight. Take off any lights, and take off the kickstand.

Bike height is from 10 to 13 inches. A short bike can go fast, but your feet can hit the ground on turns. A tall bike has room for turns, but it jerks at top speed.

Choose the size of the wheelbase for the way you ride. Short is good for ramp riding and jumping. Long is good for going down hills.

Hot bikes are made for cool moves. To pop a wheelie, pump hard on the pedals. Shift your weight to the back of the seat. Pull up on the front wheel. It will lift the wheel off of the ground. You will be able to ride for a long way with your front wheel up high.

TEACHING READING SOURCEBOOK 709

Preview the Passage

Give the student an unnumbered copy of "BMX Bikes." Remind the student that previewing a passage helps improve reading fluency. Say: *This is the same passage you read yesterday.* Ask: *What's the title of this passage?* ("BMX Bikes") Say: *Please whisper-read the passage to yourself. If you get stuck on a word, ask me for help.*

Review Student Data and Set Goal for the Reading

Motivation is necessary for students to increase their reading fluency through practice and hard work. Having students monitor their progress and participate in setting goals for them-

If the student made a large number of errors on the first timed reading, ask: *How many mistakes did you make yesterday? How many fewer will you make today?*

selves supports motivation. Review the Student Progress Graph with the student. Say: *Look at yesterday's score. How many words correct per minute did you read?* (60 WCPM) Say: *How many mistakes did you make?* (2) Point to the passage reading goal line. Ask: *What's your goal for this passage?* (65 WCPM) *How far were you from the goal yesterday?* (5 words) Ask: *How many more words correct per minute do you think you can read today?* (3 more words) *With how many mistakes?* (no more than 2) *Good.* Say: *You'll need to read carefully because you have allowed yourself only 2 mistakes—the same as before. Let's see if you can reach your goal today.*

Listen to the Student Read and Review Student Performance

Follow the same procedure as in the First Timed Reading for listening to and then reviewing the student's performance.

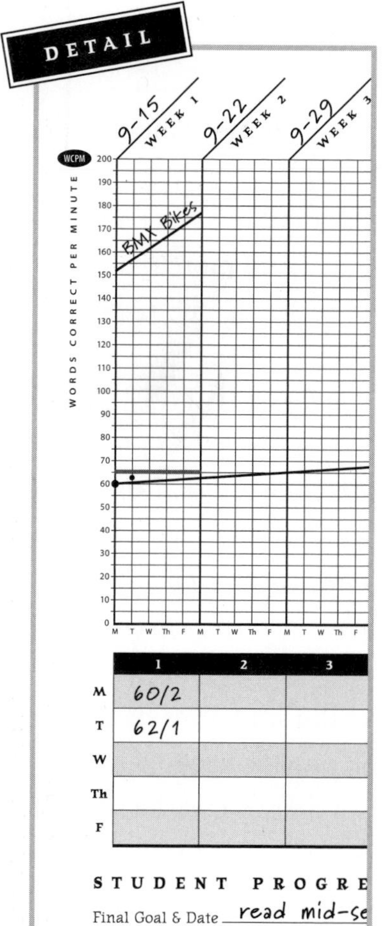

Calculate the ORF Score

To calculate the score, follow the procedure described in the First Timed Reading. Today Conrad read 63 words in one minute and made 1 error, so his ORF score is 62 WCPM.

Total words read − errors = ORF score
63 − 1 = 62 WCPM

Enter and Plot the ORF Score

Once the student's ORF score is calculated, enter and plot the score on the Student Progress Graph. Say: *Today you read 63 words and made 1 mistake. Your score is 62 words correct per minute, or 63 – 1. In the box for Tuesday of Week 1 below the graph, watch as I write the number of words you read correctly and the number of mistakes.* Write 62/1 in the box. *Now watch as I plot your score on the graph.* Put a dot on the coordinate for Tuesday, Week 1, and 62 WCPM as shown.

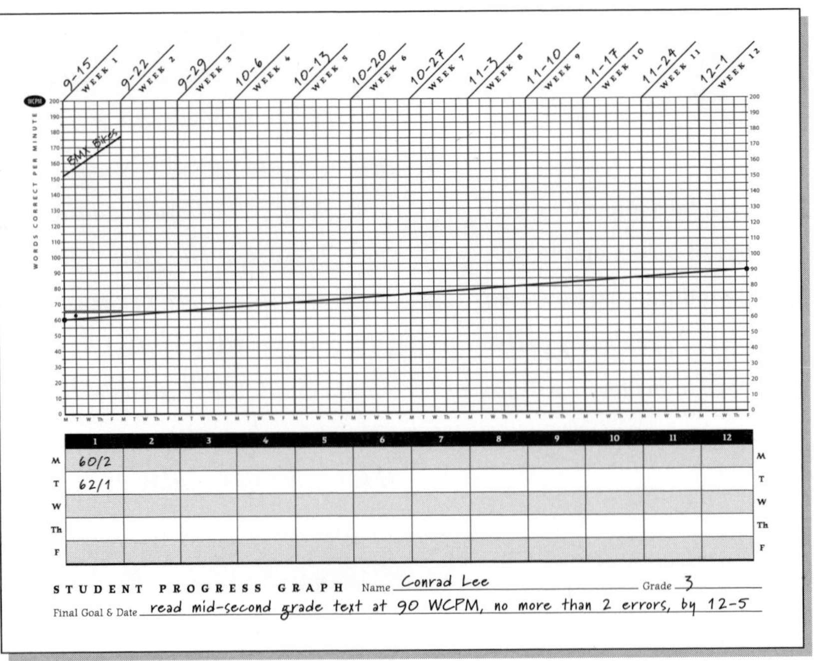

After six tries at reading the same passage, you may want to reevaluate the student's passage reading goal and independent reading level.

Determine Whether the Passage Reading Goal Was Met

This step is often called "making your goal" because the student is trying to reach the passage reading goal line marked on the graph. If a student's WCPM score is at or above the passage reading goal line and the student has made no more than two mistakes, the student has made his or her goal. Say: *On the graph, look at the passage reading goal line in relationship to the dot on the graph representing your score today of 62 WCPM.* Ask: *Is the dot above or below the goal line?* (below) Ask: *Did you make your goal?* (no) Ask: *Did you make more than 2 mistakes?* (no) Say: *Good. Your score is better today than it was yesterday, so you are closer to reaching your goal. With a little more effort, I'm sure you'll make it next time. You don't have much further to go.*

INTERVENTION STRATEGY If the student is having trouble meeting a passage reading goal, provide encouragement and support. As you provide support to the student, be sure to attribute reaching a goal to hard work—the idea that the student just needs to keep trying. For example, say: *Let's think about what you could do so that you would make your goal next time. You*

could practice the words you missed for homework, read the passage to a friend, or tell yourself to concentrate on not making so many mistakes next time. Ask: *What approach do you think will work best?* (Answers will vary.)

Celebrate and Move On

If the student makes his or her goal, then celebrate with the student. Provide forms of positive reinforcement that will help to keep the student's motivation high. For example, you can reward the student by adding his or her name to a special classroom list or allowing the student to participate in a special activity.

When the student makes the goal, he or she moves on to a new passage regardless of how many attempts it takes to make the goal—one reading or seven. At this point, make instructional decisions about the next repeated reading passage.

Instructional Decisions About the Next Repeated Reading Passage

Student Characteristics	Instructional Decision	Outcome
• The student accurately reads grade-level text at a slow rate.	• Do not change the difficulty level of the text. • Increase the passage reading goal (WCPM).	• The student reads the same level of text at a faster rate.
• The student accurately reads below-grade-level text at an average rate.	• Increase the difficulty level of the text. • Do not change the passage reading goal (WCPM).	• The student reads more difficult text at the same rate.
• The student accurately reads below-grade-level text at a slow rate.	• Increase the difficulty level of the text. • Increase the passage reading goal (WCPM).	• The student reads more difficult text at a faster rate.

LESSON MODEL FOR

Reading Fluency

Benchmarks

- ability to work productively with a partner
- ability to increase accuracy and rate in reading connected text

Strategy Grade Level

- Grades 2–6

Grouping

- pairs

Sample Text (Resources)

- "Marine Mammals" Complexity Level: Grades 4–5

Materials

- copies of "Marine Mammals"

Source

- *Peer-Assisted Learning Strategies: Reading Methods for Grades 2–6* (2008) by Douglas Fuchs, Lynn S. Fuchs, Patricia G. Mathes, and Deborah C. Simmons. Available from PAL's website, http://kc.vanderbilt.edu/pals.

SEE ALSO . . .

Choosing the Right Text, p. 367

Partner Reading

Partner reading is a motivational fluency-building technique for students who need more support than reading alone provides, but who need less support than a teacher or tutor provides. In this activity, every student in the class is paired with another student, and each pair consists of a higher- and a lower-performing student.

This sample lesson model is based on the Peer-Assisted Learning Strategies (PALS) program developed by Douglas and Lynn Fuchs and their colleagues at Vanderbilt University (Fuchs et al. 2007). In this sample lesson model, sample text is used to represent a passage at the student's instructional reading level. The same model can be adapted and used with other passages—as long as the text is at the appropriate reading level.

SET-UP PARTNER READING

Gather Student Data

ORAL READING FLUENCY Assess students' oral reading fluency (ORF). Use the same grade-level passage for each student's assessment in order to accurately compare the scores. If the same passage is not used, then it is unclear whether the differences in students' ORF scores are due to the student or to the passage. For more information, refer to Assessment of ORF Rate and Accuracy, p. 340.

INSTRUCTIONAL READING LEVEL Using grade-level standardized ORF passages, determine students' instructional reading level.

GRADE 3 • FALL

Student	Instructional Reading Level	ORF Score (WCPM)
Miguel	Grade 7	153
James	Grade 6	151
Sung Hee	Grade 5	125
Kim	Grade 4/5	100
Danielle	Grade 3	130
Roxanne	Grade 3	98
Kai	Grade 3	85
Britney	Grade 3	83
Jason	Grade 3	82
Tran	Grade 3	80
Michelle	Grade 3	77
Latoya	Grade 3	67
Justin	Grade 2	82
Kailey	Grade 2	65
Keela	Grade 2	59
Jonathan	Grade 2	56
Tiffany	Grade 1	48
Carl	Grade 1	45

Rank-Order Students

To determine partners, use assessment data to rank-order students according to their instructional reading level. Then record each student's ORF score.

Pair Students

Divide the rank-ordered classroom list in half. Then pair students in the higher-performing half with students in the lower-performing half. For example, Miguel, the top-ranked higher-performing student, would be paired with Tran, the top-ranked lower-performing student. Pair the remaining students using the same method.

Student Pairs	Higher Performing	Grade Level	Lower Performing	Grade Level
Pair A	Miguel	7	Tran	3
Pair B	James	6	Michelle	3
Pair C	Sung Hee	5	Latoya	3
Pair D	Kim	4/5	Justin	2
Pair E	Danielle	3	Kailey	2
Pair F	Roxanne	3	Keela	2
Pair G	Kai	3	Jonathan	2
Pair H	Britney	3	Tiffany	1
Pair I	Jason	3	Carl	1

ASSIGN PARTNERS Assign partners and then assign each pair the roles of first reader and second reader. Do not explain to students why they are assigned a particular role. The first readers are the stronger readers; second readers are the weaker readers. Tell partners that they will be working together for three or four weeks.

PARTNER SEATING ARRANGEMENTS There are two basic strategies for getting student partners together quickly and quietly. One strategy is to assign seats so that the partners sit next to each other during the whole time they are paired. Another is to designate one partner as the "mover" and the other partner as the "stayer." When the partner reading begins, the "movers" leave their seats and quietly move to sit with the "stayers."

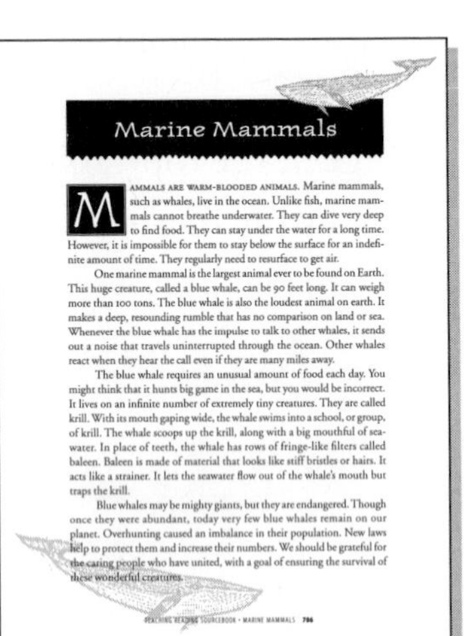

Marine Mammals

MAMMALS ARE WARM-BLOODED ANIMALS. Marine mammals, such as whales, live in the ocean. Unlike fish, marine mammals cannot breathe underwater. They can dive very deep to find food. They can stay under the water for a long time. However, it is impossible for them to stay below the surface for an indefinite amount of time. They regularly need to resurface to get air.

One marine mammal is the largest animal ever to be found on Earth. This huge creature, called a blue whale, can be 90 feet long. It can weigh more than 100 tons. The blue whale is also the loudest animal on earth. It makes a deep, resounding rumble that has no comparison on land or sea. Whenever the blue whale has the impulse to talk to other whales, it sends out a noise that travels uninterrupted through the ocean. Other whales react when they hear the call even if they are many miles away.

The blue whale requires an unusual amount of food each day. You might think that it hunts big game in the sea, but you would be incorrect. It lives on an infinite number of extremely tiny creatures. They are called krill. With its mouth gaping wide, the whale swims into a school, or group, of krill. The whale scoops up the krill, along with a big mouthful of seawater. In place of teeth, the whale has rows of fringe-like filters called baleen. Baleen is made of material that looks like stiff bristles or hairs. It acts like a strainer. It lets the seawater flow out of the whale's mouth but traps the krill.

Blue whales may be mighty giants, but they are endangered. Though once they were abundant, today very few blue whales remain on our planet. Overhunting caused an imbalance in their population. New laws help to protect them and increase their numbers. We should be grateful for the caring people who have united, with a goal of ensuring the survival of these wonderful creatures.

TEACHING READING SOURCEBOOK • MARINE MAMMALS

Select Appropriate Text

Provide reading material at the second, or weaker, reader's instructional reading level—no more than 10 errors per 100 words of text. Both members of a pair will read from the weaker reader's text. Choose from a wide range of reading materials, such as passages from core reading programs, content area textbooks, chapter books, decodable books, or magazines.

IMPLEMENT PARTNER READING

Direct Explanation

Explain to students that reading fluency is the ability to read accurately, quickly, and with good expression, and that fluent readers can pay better attention to the meaning of what they are reading. Tell them that they will be practicing reading fluency with a partner and that their partner will help to monitor their reading, provide help in figuring out hard words, and give general feedback on how they are doing. Say: *During partner reading, you will be either the first reader or the second reader. When you are not the reader, you are the coach. The job of the reader is to read accurately, quickly, and with good expression. The job of the coach is to listen for the reader's mistakes, help with hard words, and give feedback on how you are doing. First readers will read aloud a certain amount of text or for a certain amount of time while the second readers, or coaches, listen. Then partners will switch jobs and the second readers will read aloud a certain amount of text or for a certain amount of time while the first readers, or coaches, listen.*

1. Talk only to your partner.
2. Talk only about what you are reading.
3. Talk in a low voice.
4. Cooperate with your partner.
5. Try your best.

Teach/Model—Partner Behavior

Adams and Brown (2007) recommend introducing the partnerships as working relationships. Before students begin working together, model and explain the rules for partner behavior. Tell students that they will be working with the same partner for three or four weeks and that a partnership is a working relationship. Describe how coworkers have to cooperate, be polite, and treat each other with respect. Then discuss with students the Rules for Partner Behavior (Fuchs et al. 2007) shown above.

Kinds of Mistakes

- **Saying the Wrong Word**
- **Getting Stuck on a Word for More Than Four Seconds**
- **Skipping a Word**
- **Adding an Extra Word**

Fuchs et al. 2007.

Teach/Model—Identifying and Correcting Mistakes

Give explicit instructions on how coaches should monitor their partner's reading accuracy and provide corrective feedback. The following explanation of what coaches should say to readers when they make a mistake is based on Fuchs et al. 2007. Say: *When you are reading aloud, you will sometimes make a mistake. It's okay to make mistakes while reading—everyone does. Coaches are responsible for listening for and correcting any mistakes that their partner, the reader, may make.*

Distribute copies of the sample text "Marine Mammals" or a passage that is easy enough for all students to read accurately. Say: *There are special ways to fix mistakes. I will show you what to do when you're the coach and your partner, the reader, makes a mistake. There are four kinds of mistakes to listen for.*

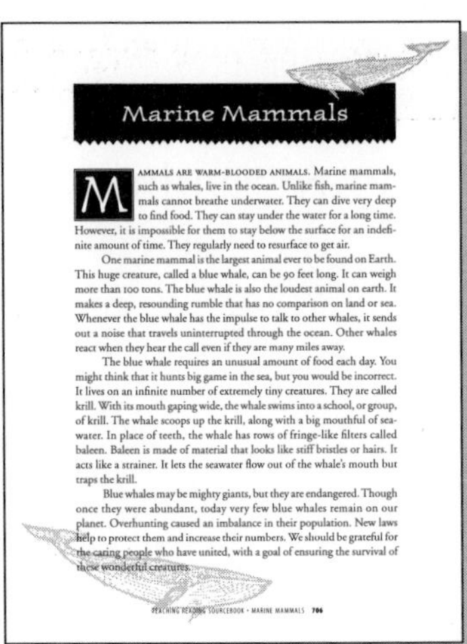

Marine Mammals

Mammals are warm-blooded animals. Marine mammals, such as whales, live in the ocean. Unlike fish, marine mammals cannot breathe underwater. They can dive very deep to find food. They can stay under the water for a long time. However, it is impossible for them to stay below the surface for an indefinite amount of time. They regularly need to resurface to get air.

One marine mammal is the largest animal ever to be found on Earth. This huge creature, called a blue whale, can be 90 feet long. It can weigh more than 100 tons. The blue whale is also the loudest animal on earth. It makes a deep, resounding rumble that has no comparison on land or sea. Whenever the blue whale has the impulse to talk to other whales, it sends out a noise that travels uninterrupted through the ocean. Other whales react when they hear the call even if they are many miles away.

The blue whale requires an unusual amount of food each day. You might think that it hunts big game in the sea, but you would be incorrect. It lives on an infinite number of extremely tiny creatures. They are called krill. With its mouth gaping wide, the whale swims into a school, or group, of krill. The whale scoops up the krill, along with a big mouthful of seawater. In place of teeth, the whale has rows of fringe-like filters called baleen. Baleen is made of material that looks like stiff bristles or hairs. It acts like a strainer. It lets the seawater flow out of the whale's mouth but traps the krill.

Blue whales may be mighty giants, but they are endangered. Though once they were abundant, today very few blue whales remain on our planet. Overhunting caused an imbalance in their population. New laws help to protect them and increase their numbers. We should be grateful for the caring people who have united, with a goal of ensuring the survival of these wonderful creatures.

TEACHING READING SOURCEBOOK • MARINE MAMMALS 706

Mammals are warm-blooded animals. Marine mammals, such as whales, live in the ocean. Unlike fish, marine mammals cannot breathe underwater. They can dive very deep to find food. They can stay under water for a long time. However, it is impossible for them to stay below the surface for an indefinite amount of time. They regularly need to resurface to get air.

MISTAKE—Saying the Wrong Word

Say: *One kind of mistake is when the reader says the wrong word, a word that is different from what is printed. Follow along as I read aloud the first sentence in "Marine Mammals." Listen for the word that I say wrong, or incorrectly. "Mammals are warm-blooded animules."* Ask: *What word did I say wrong, or incorrectly?* (animals) Repeat the procedure until students can identify this type of error.

CORRECTIVE FEEDBACK

CORRECTIVE FEEDBACK Explain to students that if the reader says the wrong word and doesn't self-correct within four seconds, the coach should immediately point to the word and say, for example, "Stop. You said the wrong word. The word is *animals*." Then the coach should ask, "What's the word?" (animals) Then the coach should say, "Good. Now read the sentence again." Say: *Let's practice. I'll be the reader and you'll be the coach. Follow along as I read aloud the second sentence. "Marine mammals, such as whales, live in the okan."* Coaches should follow the procedure described above to correct your pronunciation of the word *ocean*.

MISTAKE—Getting Stuck on a Word for More Than Four Seconds

Say: *Another kind of mistake is when the reader gets stuck on a word for more than four seconds. Follow along as I read aloud the second sentence. Count quietly to yourself to determine whether I figure out a word before four seconds. "Marine mammals, such as whales, live in the o . . . o . . . oc . . . oken . . . oseen . . . oshee.* Ask: *Did I get stuck on a word for more than four seconds?* (yes) Repeat the procedure until students can identify this type of error.

CORRECTIVE FEEDBACK

CORRECTIVE FEEDBACK Explain to students that if the reader gets stuck on a word for more than four seconds, the coach should immediately point to the word and say, for example, "The word is *ocean*." Then the coach should ask, "What's the word?" (ocean) Then the coach should say, "Good. Now read the sentence again." Say: *Let's practice. I'll be the reader and you'll be the coach. Follow along as I read aloud the sixth sentence. "However, it is impossible for them to stay below the surface for an ind . . . indee . . . infin . . . infit . . . amount of time."* Coaches should follow the procedure described above to identify the word *indefinite* for you.

MISTAKE—Skipping a Word

Say: *Another kind of mistake is when the reader skips a word. Follow along as I read aloud the third sentence. Listen for the word I skip, or leave out. "Unlike fish, marine mammals breathe underwater."* Ask: *What word did I skip?* (cannot) Repeat the procedure until students can identify this type of error.

CORRECTIVE FEEDBACK

CORRECTIVE FEEDBACK Explain to students that if the reader skips a word and doesn't self-correct, the coach should immediately say, for example, "Stop. You skipped a word. Read the sentence again." Say: *Let's practice. I'll be the reader and you'll be the coach. Follow along as I read aloud the fourth sentence. "They dive very deep to find food."* Coaches should follow the procedure described above to identify the word you skipped, the word *can.*

MISTAKE—Adding an Extra Word

Say: *Another kind of mistake is when the reader adds an extra word. Follow along as I read aloud the fifth sentence. Listen for the extra word that I added.* Read: *"They can stay under the water for a long time."* Ask: *What word did I add?* (the) Repeat the procedure until students can identify this type of error.

CORRECTIVE FEEDBACK Explain to students that if the reader adds an extra word and doesn't self-correct, the coach should immediately say, for example, "Stop. You added an extra word. Read the sentence again." Say: *Let's practice. I'll be the reader and you'll be the coach. Follow along as I read aloud the last sentence. "They regularly need to resurface to get some air."* Coaches should follow the procedure described above to identify the word you added, the word *some.*

For short passages, partners can switch roles after reading aloud one paragraph.
For longer passages or books, partners can switch roles after reading aloud for five minutes.

Practice Partner Reading

Have partners pair up and practice reading a short, one-or-two-page passage, such as "Marine Mammals," that is written at the second reader's instructional reading level. Generally, the first, or stronger, reader reads first to provide a model for the second, or weaker, reader.

Explain to students that you want them to partner-read the passage paragraph by paragraph. First readers will read aloud the first paragraph while the second readers, or coaches, will listen carefully and correct mistakes. Then partners will switch jobs and the second readers will read aloud the first paragraph while the first readers, or coaches, listen and correct mistakes. Partners should follow the same procedure with the remaining paragraphs in the passage. Monitor students as they practice partner reading. Point out any problems you observe and praise students for specific things done well.

LESSON MODEL FOR

Reading Fluency

Benchmarks

- ability to read with natural syntactic phrasing
- ability to read with expression

Strategy Grade Level

- Grade 2 and above

Grouping

- small group or pairs
- individual

Sample Text (Resources)

- "Alaska Adventure" and "Alaska Adventure" with phrase cues
  Complexity Level: Grades 4–5

Materials

- copies of "Alaska Adventure" with phrase cues
- copies of "Alaska Adventure"
- tape recorder (optional)

Phrase-Cued Reading

One of the characteristics of a fluent, proficient reader is the ability to read with appropriate phrasing—chunking words together into meaningful units. Dysfluent readers do not process text in meaningful phrases or chunks as they read. Their oral reading is characterized by staccato, word-by-word delivery that doesn't support comprehension.

A phrase-cued text is a passage in which phrase boundaries are explicitly marked or cued for the reader. Research supports the marking of phrase boundaries in printed text. O'Shea and Sindelar (1983) found that when first- through third-grade students read phrase-cued text, their reading comprehension increased. The effect was found for both good and poor readers but was especially pronounced for slow accurate readers. A review of research by Rasinski (1990) showed that marking phrase boundaries can improve students' reading comprehension, especially those whose knowledge of sentence structure (syntax) is not fully developed.

This sample lesson model is based on lesson cycles developed by Tim Rasinski (1994, 2003) and Wiley Blevins (2001). In this sample lesson model, sample text is used to represent an independent-level passage. The same model can be adapted and used with other passages—as long as the text is at students' appropriate level.

Introduce Phrasing

Using awkward phrasing, read a line from a nursery rhyme, such as "Jack Be Nimble." For example, read: *Jack be nimble Jack / be quick Jack / jumped over / the candlestick.* Ask: *Did you understand what I just read?* (no) Say: *That's right. When I read, I didn't group words in meaningful chunks.*

Say: *Now, I am going to read the same rhyme again. Listen to how I group the words. Jack be nimble / Jack be quick / Jack jumped over / the candlestick.* Ask: *Did you understand what I just read?* (yes) Say: *That's because this time I grouped words in meaningful chunks. Good readers read in chunks of words, or phrases. A phrase is a meaningful chunk of words. Phrases are read as separate units, with a pause in between each one.*

Phrase Cues

Short pause (/)

Longer pause (//)

Select and Mark the Text

Text passages should be relatively short, between 100 and 250 words in length, appropriate for reading aloud, and at students' independent reading level. Students should be able to read accurately at least 95 percent of the words in the passage; it is difficult to attend to appropriate phrasing while simultaneously decoding unfamiliar words. Begin instruction with passages having simple declarative sentences and short phrases. Then use passages with more complex sentence structures as students master the concept.

Alaska Adventure

Jake Mays and his dad/spent two weeks visiting Alaska.//They flew to Anchorage/and then took a train south/to a lodge in Seward,/a small harbor town/surrounded by the Kenai mountain range.//From there/they took day trips around the area/to see and experience the sights.//Jake found it all so enticing/that he never wanted to leave.//

Every day brought a new adventure.//They traveled by ferry and sailboat/on the marine highways/through straits and inlets.//They paddled sea kayaks/up narrow fjords/lined with ice cliffs.//They saw whales,/otters, puffins,/sea lions,/and eagles.//They spent a day/on a fishing schooner catching salmon for dinner.//Jake snapped pictures/of every new vista.//

"Mom is not going to believe how awesome the scenery is!" he said.// "Next time,/we have to coordinate the schedule/so that she can come with us."//

On the flight home,/they pored over the map,/already planning the return trip.//Jake thought it would be exciting/to do some backpacking/on Mount McKinley,/the tallest peak/in North America.//

"Wouldn't it be fun/to explore the state's interior?//We could travel north/from Anchorage/to visit Denali National Park.//I heard/that the fishing is first class,/and there is plenty of wildlife to see."//

"That's true,"/said Dad.//"Still,/it is hard to resist/the idea of retracing/the route we just traveled.//Now that we're expert kayakers,/we should paddle/around the capes and coves and lagoons/of the Alaska Peninsula."//

Dad pointed at the chain/of volcanic islands/separating the Pacific Ocean/from the Bering Sea.//"The Aleutian archipelago stretches/for more than a thousand miles.//We could spend a lifetime/on the water/just exploring this part of the Ring of Fire."//

"Well,/that settles it,"/said Jake.//"We just need/to come back/and stay longer."//

"You've got that right,"/said Dad.

MAP

STATE OF ALASKA

TEACHING READING SOURCEBOOK • ALASKA ADVENTURE 702

Using your intuitive sense of phrasing, on a copy of the passage mark appropriate phrase breaks. Mark short pauses, such as phrase boundaries within sentences, with one front slash (/), and longer pauses, such as at the end of sentences, with two front slashes (//).

Alaska Adventure

Jake Mays and his dad/spent two weeks visiting Alaska.//They flew to Anchorage/and then took a train south/to a lodge in Seward,/a small harbor town/surrounded by the Kenai mountain range.//From there/they took day trips around the area/to see and experience the sights.//Jake found it all so enticing/that he never wanted to leave.//

Every day brought a new adventure.//They traveled by ferry and sailboat/on the marine highways/through straits and inlets.//They paddled sea kayaks/up narrow fjords/lined with ice cliffs.//They saw whales,/otters, puffins,/sea lions,/and eagles.//They spent a day/on a fishing schooner catching salmon for dinner.//Jake snapped pictures/of every new vista.//

"Mom is not going to believe how awesome the scenery is!" he said.//"Next time,/we have to coordinate the schedule/so that she can come with us."//

On the flight home,/they pored over the map,/already planning the return trip.//Jake thought it would be exciting/to do some backpacking/on Mount McKinley,/the tallest peak/in North America.//

"Wouldn't it be fun/to explore the state's interior?//We could travel north/from Anchorage/to visit Denali National Park.//I heard/that the fishing is first class,/and there is plenty of wildlife to see."//

"That's true,"/said Dad.//"Still,/it is hard to resist/the idea of retracing/the route we just traveled.//Now that we're expert kayakers,/we should paddle/around the capes and coves and lagoons/of the Alaska Peninsula."//Dad pointed at the chain/of volcanic islands/separating the Pacific Ocean/from the Bering Sea.//"The Aleutian archipelago stretches/for more than a thousand miles.//We could spend a lifetime/on the water/just exploring this part of the Ring of Fire."//

"Well,/that settles it,"/said Jake.//"We just need/to come back/and stay longer."//

"You've got that right,"/said Dad.

MAP

TEACHING READING SOURCEBOOK • ALASKA ADVENTURE 702

Day 1—Model Reading Marked Text

Word by word in a monotone, say: *Good readers do not read word by word using one tone of voice.* Then with expression and appropriate phrasing, say: *Good readers read with expression in phrases, or meaningful chunks of words. Reading in phrases helps readers to understand what they are reading, even when reading to themselves.*

Preview the Text

Distribute copies of the phrase-cued text passage "Alaska Adventure." Say: *Previewing a passage before reading it can help us to understand it better. The title of this passage is "Alaska Adventure." Wow, it sure would be fun to go to Alaska. I've never been there. I wonder if I'm going to read about someone having an adventure on their trip to Alaska. I guess I'll read to find out.*

Jake Mays and his dad / spent two weeks visiting Alaska. // They flew to Anchorage / and then took a train south / to a lodge in Seward, / a small harbor town / surrounded by the Kenai mountain range. //

Explain the Marks

To explain the meaning of the single and double slashes, have students look at the first sentence in "Alaska Adventure." Tell them that the slashes are called phrase cues. Explain that although students may find phrase cues distracting at first, they will ultimately find them helpful in their oral reading. Tell students that one slash means to pause a little. Then read aloud the first sentence, slightly exaggerating the marked pauses between the phrases. Point out the period at the end of the first sentence followed by the double slashes. Then tell students that double slashes mean to pause longer than for a single slash. Say: *A period comes at the end of a sentence. Think about a period as a stop sign telling the reader to stop and pause for a moment.* Then read aloud the first two sentences, slightly exaggerating the marked pause between the sentences. In the second sentence, point out the comma followed by a single slash. Ask: *What does a single slash mean?* (to pause a little) Say: *The comma is followed by a single slash because a comma tells the reader to pause a little.* Then read aloud the second sentence, slightly exaggerating the marked pause after the comma.

"**Wouldn't it be fun / to explore the state's interior? //**

Now point out the question mark and the double slashes at the end of the first sentence in the fifth paragraph: "Wouldn't it be fun to explore the state's interior?" Say: *A question mark is like a period in that it comes at the end of a sentence. The double slashes after the question mark indicate that readers should pause longer. When asking a question, people usually raise their voice at the end of the sentence. I'll demonstrate.* Read aloud the sentence, slightly exaggerating the intonation.

Teacher Modeling

SEE ALSO . . .

Prosody, p. 323

Explain to students that when good readers read aloud, they read in phrases that sound like spoken language, which makes the text easier to understand. They embed intonation and expression that match the phrases. Then model reading the phrase-cued passage aloud as students follow along silently. Read with appropriate expression, emphasizing or slightly exaggerating the phrases.

"**Mom is not going to believe how awesome the scenery is!" he said. //**

After reading the passage, ask students for feedback on what they observed about your phrasing and expression. You also may wish to point out the first sentence of the third paragraph: "Mom is not going to believe how awesome the scenery is!" he said. Explain to students that the quotation marks indicate that the words are spoken by a character in a story. The reader says these words, or dialogue, in the character's voice, or as if the character is speaking. Also point out the exclamation mark at the end of the sentence. Tell students that an exclamation mark indicates that the sentence should be read with excitement.

Whole-Group Choral Reading

Now have students read aloud the phrase-cued text chorally. Say: *Now we will all read "Alaska Adventure" together. The slashes will help you see where the phrases are and when to pause. I'll read along with you. Ready, begin.* After reading, say: *That was terrific! Your reading matched the phrase cues. Tomorrow, we'll practice again.*

Alaska Adventure

Jake Mays and his dad/spent two weeks visiting Alaska.//They flew to Anchorage/and then took a train south/to a lodge in Seward,/a small harbor town/surrounded by the Kenai mountain range.//From there/they took day trips around the area/to see and experience the sights.//Jake found it all so enticing/that he never wanted to leave.//

Every day brought a new adventure.//They traveled by ferry and sailboat/on the marine highways/through straits and inlets.//They paddled sea kayaks/up narrow fjords/lined with ice cliffs.//They saw whales,/otters, puffins,/sea lions,/and eagles.//They spent a day/on a fishing schooner catching salmon for dinner.//Jake snapped pictures/of every new vista.//

"Mom is not going to believe how awesome the scenery is!" he said.//"Next time,/we have to coordinate the schedule/so that she can come with us."//

On the flight home,/they pored over the map,/already planning the return trip.//Jake thought it would be exciting/to do some backpacking/on Mount McKinley,/the tallest peak/in North America.//

"Wouldn't it be fun/to explore the state's interior?//We could travel north/from Anchorage/to visit Denali National Park.//I heard/that the fishing is first class,/and there is plenty of wildlife to see."//

"That's true,"/said Dad.//"Still,/it is hard to resist/the idea of retracing/the route we just traveled.//Now that we're expert kayakers,/we should paddle/around the capes and coves and lagoons/of the Alaska Peninsula."//Dad pointed at the chain/of volcanic islands/separating the Pacific Ocean/from the Bering Sea.//"The Aleutian archipelago stretches/for more than a thousand miles.//We could spend a lifetime/on the water/just exploring this part of the Ring of Fire."//

"Well,/that settles it,"/said Jake.//"We just need/to come back/and stay longer."//

"You've got that right,"/said Dad.

MAP

TEACHING READING SOURCEBOOK • ALASKA ADVENTURE 702

Day 2—Model and Practice with Marked Text

Teacher Modeling

Again model reading "Alaska Adventure" aloud as students follow along silently. Read with appropriate expression, slightly exaggerating the phrases. After reading the passage, ask students for feedback on what they observed about your phrasing and expression. For example, ask: *Did my reading match the phrase cues?* (Possible answers: *Yes, you paused at the slashes.*) Say: *That's right. My phrase-cued reading sounded like I was speaking.*

Whole-Group Choral Reading

FIRST TIME Have students chorally read aloud the phrase-cued passage. Say: *Now we will all read "Alaska Adventure" together. The slashes will help you see where the phrases are and when to pause. I'll read along with you. Ready, begin.* After reading, discuss a sentence that was particularly well read. Say: *I heard particularly good reading when you read this sentence. I heard you pause slightly at this phrase break and longer at that one.*

SECOND TIME Now ask students to chorally read the passage again. Tell them that this time they should pay close attention to the phrasing. After students read, ask: *Did your reading match the phrase cues this time? Did you read with expression? What sentences do you think you read particularly well?* (Answers will vary.)

SEE ALSO . . .

LESSON MODEL: Partner Reading, p. 384

Partner Reading

Have students practice reading aloud the phrase-cued passage with a partner. Explain to students that you want them to partner-read the passage paragraph by paragraph. First readers will read aloud the first paragraph while the second readers, or coaches, will listen carefully to see if the reader's phrasing matches the phrase cue. After the first reader reads the paragraph, the coach should provide positive feedback about the reader's phrasing. Then partners will switch jobs, and the second readers will read aloud the first paragraph while the first readers, or coaches, listen carefully for phrasing. Partners should follow the same procedure with the remaining paragraphs in the passage. Monitor the pairs and provide assistance as needed.

Alaska Adventure

Jake Mays and his dad/spent two weeks visiting Alaska.//They flew to Anchorage/and then took a train south/to a lodge in Seward,/a small harbor town/surrounded by the Kenai mountain range.//From there/they took day trips around the area/to see and experience the sights.//Jake found it all so enticing/that he never wanted to leave.//

Every day brought a new adventure.//They traveled by ferry and sailboat/on the marine highways/through straits and inlets.//They paddled sea kayaks/up narrow fjords/lined with ice cliffs.//They saw whales,/otters, puffins,/sea lions,/and eagles.//They spent a day/on a fishing schooner catching salmon for dinner.//Jake snapped pictures/of every new vista.//

"Mom is not going to believe how awesome the scenery is!" he said.// "Next time,/we have to coordinate the schedule/so that she can come with us."//

On the flight home,/they pored over the map,/already planning the return trip.//Jake thought it would be exciting/to do some backpacking/on Mount McKinley,/the tallest peak/in North America.//

"Wouldn't it be fun/to explore the state's interior?//We could travel north/from Anchorage/to visit Denali National Park.//I heard/that the fishing is first class,/and there is plenty of wildlife to see."//

"That's true,"/said Dad.//"Still,/it is hard to resist/the idea of retracing/the route we just traveled.//Now that we're expert kayakers,/we should paddle/around the capes and coves and lagoons/of the Alaska Peninsula."// Dad pointed at the chain/of volcanic islands/separating the Pacific Ocean/from the Bering Sea.//"The Aleutian archipelago stretches/for more than a thousand miles.//We could spend a lifetime/on the water/just exploring this part of the Ring of Fire."//

"Well,/that settles it,"/said Jake.//"We just need/to come back/and stay longer."//

"You've got that right,"/said Dad.

MAP

TEACHING READING SOURCEBOOK • ALASKA ADVENTURE 782

Day 3—Practice with Marked Text

Whole-Group Choral Reading

Have students chorally read aloud the phrase-cued passage. Say: *Now we will all read "Alaska Adventure" together. The slashes will help you see where the phrases are and when to pause. Ready, begin.* After reading, say: *That was terrific! What did you notice about your phrasing?* (It was good.) Ask: *What do you think made it good?* (Our reading matched the phrase cues.)

Individual or Partner Practice

Have students practice reading the passage again. They can choose to evaluate their reading of the passage by individually tape-recording themselves or by reading it to a partner. Monitor and assist students as needed.

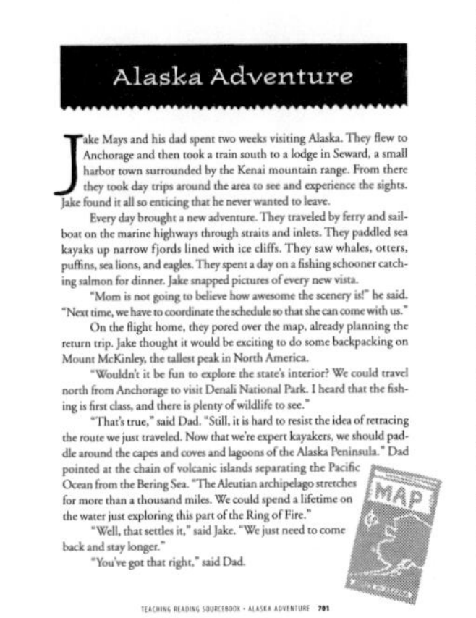

Alaska Adventure

Jake Mays and his dad spent two weeks visiting Alaska. They flew to Anchorage and then took a train south to a lodge in Seward, a small harbor town surrounded by the Kenai mountain range. From there they took day trips around the area to see and experience the sights. Jake found it all so enticing that he never wanted to leave.

Every day brought a new adventure. They traveled by ferry and sailboat on the marine highways through straits and inlets. They paddled sea kayaks up narrow fjords lined with ice cliffs. They saw whales, otters, puffins, sea lions, and eagles. They spent a day on a fishing schooner catching salmon for dinner. Jake snapped pictures of every new vista.

"Mom is not going to believe how awesome the scenery is!" he said. "Next time, we have to coordinate the schedule so that she can come with us."

On the flight home, they pored over the map, already planning the return trip. Jake thought it would be exciting to do some backpacking on Mount McKinley, the tallest peak in North America.

"Wouldn't it be fun to explore the state's interior? We could travel north from Anchorage to visit Denali National Park. I heard that the fishing is first class, and there is plenty of wildlife to see."

"That's true," said Dad. "Still, it is hard to resist the idea of retracing the route we just traveled. Now that we're expert kayakers, we should paddle around the capes and coves and lagoons of the Alaska Peninsula." Dad pointed at the chain of volcanic islands separating the Pacific Ocean from the Bering Sea. "The Aleutian archipelago stretches for more than a thousand miles. We could spend a lifetime on the water just exploring this part of the Ring of Fire."

"Well, that settles it," said Jake. "We just need to come back and stay longer."

"You've got that right," said Dad.

TEACHING READING SOURCEBOOK • ALASKA ADVENTURE 701

Day 4—Practice with Unmarked Text

Whole-Group Choral Reading

FIRST TIME Distribute unmarked copies of "Alaska Adventure." Point out that this version of "Alaska Adventure" doesn't have slashes to show where to pause for phrase breaks. Then have students chorally read aloud the unmarked passage along with you. Tell them to pay really close attention to reading in phrases.

SECOND TIME Now have students chorally read the unmarked passage on their own. After reading, ask: *What was it like reading without the slashes to help you? How was your phrasing? What part do you think you read particularly well?* (Answers will vary.)

Individual or Partner Practice

Have students practice reading the unmarked passage again. They can choose to evaluate their reading of the passage by individually tape-recording themselves or by reading it to a partner. Monitor and assist students as needed.

Day 5—Assess Phrase-Cued Reading

Meeting individually, listen to each student read aloud the unmarked passage. As you listen, use the phrasing section of the Prosody Assessment Rating Scale to assess the student.

SEE ALSO . . .

Prosody Assessment Rating Scale, p. 334

SEE ALSO . . .

LESSON MODEL: Assessment of Prosodic Reading, p. 355

If Score on Phrasing Section of Prosody Assessment Scale Is . . .	
Level 1 or 2	Continue phrase-cued text instruction with another passage with similar types of sentence structures.
Level 3	Continue phrase-cued text instruction with more passages with more difficult and varied sentence structures.
Level 4	Discontinue phrase-cued text instruction; continue to provide reminders and feedback about the student's phrasing.

LESSON MODEL FOR

Reading Fluency

Benchmarks

- ability to read aloud quickly and accurately
- ability to read aloud with prosody

Strategy Grade Level

- Grade 1 and above

Prerequisites

- Partner Reading, p. 384
- Phrase-Cued Reading, p. 391

Grouping

- small group

Sample Text (Resources)

- "TV Dinner" Complexity Level: Grades 3–4

Materials

- copies of "TV Dinner"
- highlighter markers
- recording of "TV Dinner"

Readers Theatre

Readers Theatre has been described as a "rehearsed group presentation of a script that is read aloud rather than memorized" (Flynn 2004). During this activity, emphasis is placed on prosodic reading (e.g., phrasing and expression) rather than props, costumes, or acting. There is limited research-based evidence on the effectiveness of Readers Theatre itself. None of the direct studies (e.g., Carrick 2000; Corcoran and Davis 2005; Keehn 2003; Millin and Rinehart 1999; Stayter and Allington 1991; Worthy and Prater 2002) have met the Department of Education's standard of peer-reviewed, published, randomized experimental evidence (Coalition for Evidence-Based Policy 2003).

Readers Theatre provides struggling readers with an authentic purpose, legitimate reason, and motivation for rereading text a number of times. As a form of repeated reading, a method that has strong research-based evidence of its effectiveness, Readers Theatre can help to improve students' oral reading fluency, that is, if there is a sufficient number of opportunities for students to reread the script. This sample lesson model is based on the cycle described by Millin and Rinehart (1999). In this lesson model, sample text is used to represent an independent-level script. The same model can be adapted and used with other scripts—as long as the text is at students' appropriate level.

Prepare

GROUP STUDENTS Depending on the number of characters in the script, form groups of students who read at about the same independent reading level. For "TV Dinner," there should be six students in each group.

SELECT THE SCRIPT Students should be able to read accurately at least 95 percent of the words in the script; it should be written at a group's independent reading level.

READERS THEATRE

Day 1:
Model & Practice

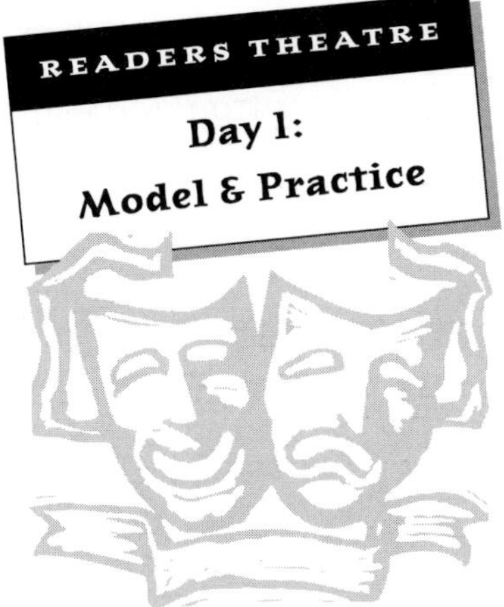

Teach/Model—Read Aloud and Discuss Story Elements

Tell students that they are going to practice reading and performing a script, using their voices to bring the characters to life. Explain that they won't have to memorize the script. Distribute a copy of the script to each student in the group. Read aloud the title and encourage students to make predictions about what a play called "TV Dinner" might be about. Then point to the list of characters and their descriptions: Madam Video, Cosmo, Dodo, Pauline, Henrietta, and Announcer. If students are unfamiliar with raccoons or guinea pigs, show pictures of them. Ask students to listen and follow along with you as you read the script aloud to model fluent, prosodic reading. When you read, use both your voice and facial expressions to communicate characters' feelings or emotions.

TV Dinner

BY THE SAN FRANCISCO MIME TROUPE

Characters
Announcer: a TV announcer
Madam Video: Video Central's evil empress
Cosmo and Dodo: two raccoons
Pauline: a twelve-year-old TV fanatic
Henrietta: Pauline's pet guinea pig

ANNOUNCER: Pauline watches too much TV. She's behind on homework, forgets to wash the dishes, and has no time to play with Henrietta, her pet guinea pig. One night Henrietta is "pignapped" by two raccoon servants of Madam Video. Pauline sets out to find her.

ANNOUNCER: The setting is Madam Video's control room at Video Central. The walls are lined with TV monitors. Cosmo and Dodo are playing around. Henrietta is strapped to a special chair. Madam Video enters the room.

MADAM: *(speaking to audience)* Hi, kids. What a glorious night for my experiment—full moon, low-lying fog. If my Video Visor invention works—which lets you watch more TV in less time—I'll rule the mind of every kid within reach of this tower. *(to Cosmo)* Have you found me a subject?

COSMO: A perfect subject, primed and ready, your coldness.

TEACHING READING SOURCEBOOK • TV DINNER 713

After reading, ask students to confirm their predictions about what the play was about and then lead a discussion focusing on character, setting, and plot. Ask questions such as: *What is the setting, or where does the story take place?* (Madam Video's control room at Video Central) *How does the story begin?* (Henrietta, Pauline's pet guinea pig, is pignapped by two raccoon servants of Madam Video, and Pauline sets out to find her.) *What happens next?* (Madam Video experiments on Henrietta to see if her new invention, the Video Visor, works. The Video Visor lets you watch more TV in less time.) *Then what happens?* (Pauline arrives and Madam experiments on her. She programs 30 minutes of commercials in 10 seconds.) *How does the story end?* (Madam's Video Visor works on Pauline. Madam is happy because she thinks she will be able to turn everyone into obedient slaves.) *Did you like the play? Why or why not? Who was your favorite character?* (Answers will vary.)

Teach/Model—Prosody and Punctuation

Direct students' attention to the following lines from the play and read them alone:

MADAM: You fools! You lazy bums! You, you—animals! I ask for a guinea pig to conduct my experiment and you bring me a . . . a . . .
COSMO: A guinea pig.
MADAM: I can't bear it. The experiment is ruined. It's worthless. You'll pay for this. I'm cutting you off. No TV.
COSMO: No TV? No, please, I can't stand it.

"No TV?"

First point out the pun on *guinea pig.* Say: *In this part of the script, there is a pun. A pun is a "clever use of a word with more than one meaning." As you know, a guinea pig is a small, furry animal. But there is another meaning for guinea pig. If you are used as a guinea pig in an experiment, it means that you are the first person used to test an experiment to see if it works. When Madam Video asked for a guinea pig to test her new invention, Cosmo and Dodo brought her Henrietta, a real guinea pig, instead of a test subject. Madam Video got really mad.*

Then explain to students that, when reading aloud, punctuation marks can indicate when to pause and when to raise or lower their voice. Point out the exclamation marks, the comma, the long dash, the three dots called ellipses, the periods, and the question mark. Tell students that you are going to read aloud the lines again and that you want them to pay attention to how the punctuation affects your reading.

Read aloud Madam's first line, putting as much anger and exasperation into your voice as possible and pausing appropriately. After reading, explain to students why the line was written that way. Explain that Madam was angry and that the punctuation

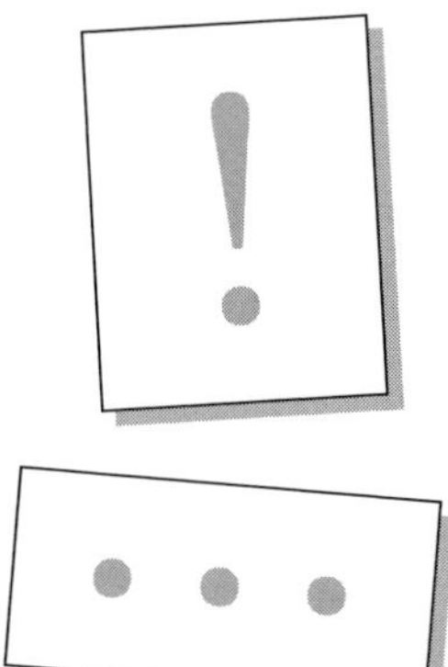

helped the author to show how she was feeling. Say: *The exclamation marks told me to read the first three sentences with strong feeling—Madam was really upset. In the second sentence, the comma told me to pause a little and the long dash told me to pause a little longer before emphasizing the word* animal *by saying it in a louder voice. In the fourth sentence, the groups of three dots, or ellipses, told me to pause some more to show that Madam is so mad she can hardly get the words out of her mouth or think of the right word to say. I've had that happen to me.* Read aloud Madam's line again. Then ask students to read it several times along with you. Call on volunteers to read aloud the line on their own.

Now read aloud Madam's second line, stopping appropriately at the end of each sentence. Say: *Periods are like stop signs telling the reader to stop and pause for a moment at the end of a sentence.* Read aloud Madam's second line again. Then ask students to read it several times along with you. Call on volunteers to read aloud the line on their own.

Finally, read aloud Cosmo's last line, raising your voice appropriately at the end of the question, pausing slightly for the commas, and stopping for the periods. Say: *The first sentence "No TV?" is a question. It ends in a question mark that tells me to raise my voice at the end of the sentence.* Ask students to practice asking Cosmo's question. Then read aloud Cosmo's second line again, pointing out the pauses for the commas and period. Then ask students to read it several times along with you. Call on volunteers to read aloud the line on their own.

SEE ALSO . . .

LESSON MODEL: Partner Reading, p. 384

Partner Practice

Pair students up for partner reading. Explain that you want them to read aloud the entire script. Readers will take turns by reading every other line. The first reader will read aloud the first line while the second reader listens. Then the second reader will read aloud the second line while the first reader listens. Then the first reader will read aloud the third line, and so on, until they get to the end of the script. When they get to the end, they should switch roles—the first reader becomes the second reader—and read the script again. While partners are reading, circulate among them to offer assistance in correctly pronouncing words, reading with feeling and emotion, and reading at an appropriate rate and volume.

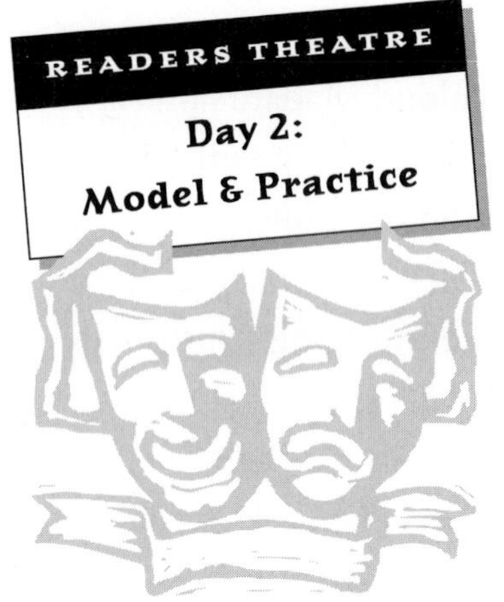

Listen to a Recording

Have students listen silently several times to an audio recording of "TV Dinner" while following along on their scripts. Then, individually or in a small group, have them read aloud along with the recording. Tell them to listen carefully to how punctuation signals expression, to how voices are used to show emotion, and to phrasing. Remind students that good readers read in meaningful chunks of words, or phrases, and that phrases are read as separate units, with a pause between each one.

Choose Parts

Assign a part to each student. Have students use a yellow highlighter to mark their part on a copy of the script.

Group Practice

Have students practice reading aloud the script again. Say: *This time, each student will read aloud his or her part in a regular voice while the rest of us whisper-read the lines. Let's try it. I'll be Madam. Everyone read along in a whisper while I read aloud.* Read aloud Madam's first lines with appropriate expression. When you finish, ask the student who is reading Cosmo's part to read aloud while the rest of the group whisper-reads. Then say: *Okay, now that we have the idea, please start again at the beginning. Who is reading Madam's part? Ready to read? Remember that if it isn't your part, whisper. Begin.* Monitor the group and provide assistance as needed.

SEE ALSO . . .

LESSON MODEL: Phrase-Cued Reading, p. 391

Individual Practice

Say: *I want you to practice reading your part again, this time individually. You have ten minutes. Remember to speak clearly and to pay close attention to your expression and phrasing.* Monitor students' reading as they practice. If needed, help students with phrasing by marking phrase boundaries on their script.

Group Practice

Listen again to the whole group as they read aloud the script. Say: *We are going to run through the entire script again with me as your audience. I am going to listen carefully to your phrasing and how you show the character's feelings with your voice. There should be a smooth transition from role to role. When the reader before you finishes his or her lines, start reading right away. Pay attention so you know when it's your turn.* As you listen, provide feedback, both positive and corrective, about phrasing, expression, and the transition from role to role.

Practice for Homework

For homework, have students take the script home and practice reading it aloud to members of their family.

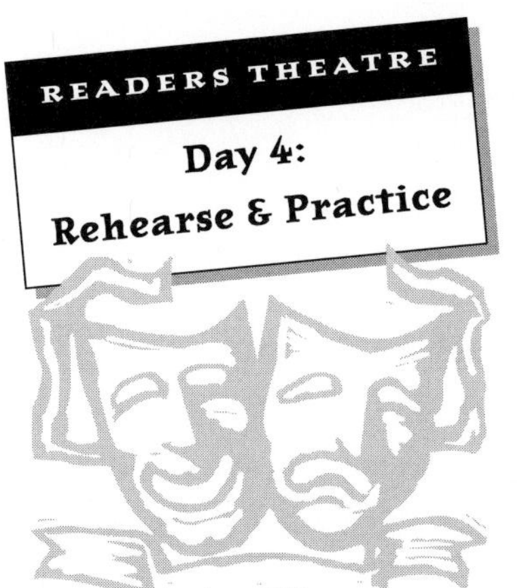

Rehearse the Script

Have students participate in a rehearsal of the script. Say: *Today we are going to rehearse the script. We are going to act like this is the real performance; I will not interrupt you while you're reading.* Listen to the rehearsal, noting any parts or lines that need additional practice. Then provide praise, support, and corrective feedback as indicated.

Individualized Practice

Have each student practice his or her part again. Assign students to a type of practice that provides the needed level of support. For students who need little feedback or help, have them practice with the recording. For students who need some support, have them practice with a partner. Students who need a great deal of support should practice with the teacher or another adult.

Practice for Homework

For homework, have students take the script home and practice reading their part aloud to members of their family.

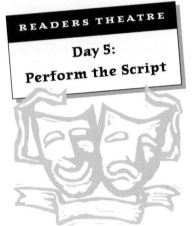

READERS THEATRE

Day 5: Perform the Script

Perform the Script

On the last day, have the group perform "TV Dinner" before an audience. The audience can be the rest of the class, a different class, the whole school, or parents. No costumes or props are needed. After the performance, students can take the script home for more repeated reading practice.

SECTION V

Vocabulary

Introduction

VOCABULARY

CCSS LANGUAGE STANDARDS

Vocabulary Acquisition and Use

CCSS READING STANDARDS

Literature • Informational Text

Craft and Structure

Interpret words and phrases as they are used in text. (CCR.4)

SEE ALSO . . .

Chapter 11: Specific Word Instruction

Chapter 12: Word-Learning Strategies

Chapter 13: Word Consciousness

Vocabulary is the knowledge of words and word meanings. As Steven Stahl (2005) puts it, "Vocabulary knowledge is knowledge; the knowledge of a word not only implies a definition, but also implies how that word fits into the world." Vocabulary knowledge is not something that can ever be fully mastered; it is something that expands and deepens over the course of a lifetime.

Instruction in vocabulary involves far more than looking up words in a dictionary and using the words in a sentence. Vocabulary is acquired incidentally through indirect exposure to words and intentionally through explicit instruction in specific words and word-learning strategies. According to Michael Graves (2000), there are four components of an effective vocabulary program: (1) wide or extensive independent reading to expand word knowledge, (2) instruction in specific words to enhance comprehension of texts containing those words, (3) instruction in independent word-learning strategies, and (4) word consciousness and word-play activities to motivate and enhance learning. This section covers the last three components.

Components of Effective Vocabulary Instruction

Incidental Vocabulary Learning	**Intentional Vocabulary Teaching**
Rich Oral Language Experiences **Wide Reading** Teacher Read-Alouds Independent Reading	**Specific Word Instruction** Rich and Robust Instruction of Words in Text **Word-Learning Strategies** Dictionary Use Morphemic Analysis Contextual Analysis Cognate Awareness (ELL)

Word Consciousness Adept Diction • Word Play • Word Origins

Vocabulary Forms

	RECEPTIVE	PRODUCTIVE
ORAL	**Listening** words we understand when others speak or read aloud to us	**Speaking** words we use when we talk to others
PRINT	**Reading** words we understand when we read them	**Writing** words we use when we write

Oral language development precedes and is the foundation for written language development . . . oral language is primary and written language builds on it.

—COMMON CORE STATE STANDARDS, 2010

CCSS

Forms of Vocabulary

There are various types, or forms, of vocabulary. Words themselves are encountered in two forms: oral and print. Oral vocabulary is the set of words for which students know the meanings when others speak or read aloud to them, or when they speak to others. Print vocabulary is the set of words for which students know the meanings when they read or write silently. In emergent readers, oral vocabulary is much larger than print vocabulary. As students become more literate, print vocabulary plays an increasingly larger role (Kamil and Hiebert 2005). Ultimately, print vocabulary is "much more extensive and diverse" than oral vocabulary (Hayes, Wolfer, and Wolfe 1996).

The knowledge of word meanings, or vocabulary, can also be divided according to whether it is receptive or productive. Receptive vocabulary is the set of words to which a student can assign some meaning when listening or reading. Productive vocabulary is the set of words students use frequently in their speaking and writing. Receptive vocabulary (listening or reading) is generally larger than productive vocabulary (speaking or writing) because people usually recognize more words than they regularly use.

Word learning is incremental; that is, it proceeds in a series of steps.

—GRAVES & WATTS-TAFFE, 2002

Extent of Word Knowledge

The extent of word knowledge has serious implications for how words are taught and how word knowledge is measured (Beck, McKeown, and Kucan 2002). According to Dale (1965), four levels can be used to describe the extent of a person's word knowledge: (1) have never seen or heard the word before, (2) have seen or heard the word before, but don't know what it means, (3) vaguely know the meaning of the word; can associate it with a concept or context, and (4) know the word well; can explain it and use it. As an unfamiliar word is encountered repeatedly over time, knowledge of the word grows and the word moves up the levels toward "know the word well." According to Graves and Watts-Taffe (2002), Dale's fourth level can be further divided into "having a full and precise meaning versus having a general meaning or using the word in writing versus only recognizing it when reading."

CONNECT TO THEORY

Using Dale's levels of word knowledge described above, analyze the extent of your knowledge about each of the words listed in the chart below.

	LEVELS OF WORD KNOWLEDGE			
	1	2	3	4
affix				
context				
dyslexia				
fricative				
mnemonic				
prosody				

Vocabulary Size

Estimates of student vocabulary size vary dramatically (Anderson and Freebody 1981). The variation occurs because of differences in the procedures used by vocabulary researchers and in the definition of what is counted as a distinct word (Anderson 1996). Researchers Nagy and Anderson (1984) and Biemiller (2005b) use different descriptive terms for what is counted as a distinct word.

WORD FAMILY
a group of words related in meaning

88,500 distinct word families in printed school English

40,000 word families known by Grade 12

ROOT WORD
a single word that cannot be broken into smaller words or parts

17,500 root word meanings in *The Living Word Vocabulary* (Grades K–12)

15,000 root word meanings known well by Grade 12

SEE ALSO . . .

Root Words and Word Families, p. 491

Nagy and Anderson (1984) attempted to resolve questions about the size of the vocabulary-learning task. Using a corpus of words gathered from school materials and textbooks (Carroll, Davies, and Richman 1971), they grouped related words into families by judging whether a student who knew the meaning of only one of the words in a family could infer the meanings of other related words in the family. For example, *sweet, sweetness,* and *sweetly* belong to the same word family. Compound words were judged in a similar way. From this analysis, Nagy and Anderson estimated that there are about 88,500 distinct word families in printed school English, and that an average twelfth grader probably knows about 40,000 of them.

While Nagy and Anderson (1984) count occurrences of word families, Biemiller (2005b) counts occurrences of root words. But since one word family is equivalent to one root word (and its related forms), the approach is essentially the same for both. Biemiller believes that when the meaning of a root word is known, derived words (i.e., other words in the word family) and compound words can probably be largely inferred from context while reading. According to Biemiller (2004), in Dale and O'Rourke's *The Living Word Vocabulary* (1981) there are about 17,500 root words known by students in Grade 12. Of these root words, they estimate that about 15,000 words are known well by a majority of students.

By the end of Grade 2, students know an average of about 6,000 root word meanings.

—BIEMILLER, 2005a

How Many Root Words Are Acquired per Year?

According to Biemiller (2005a), children through Grade 6 typically acquire about 800 to 1,000 root-word meanings per year. From age 1 through Grade 2, children gain an average of 860 root words per year, or about 2.4 words per day. From Grades 3 to 6, they gain an average of 1,000 root words per year, or about 2.8 root words per day. Biemiller's estimates are based on the known number of root words at each level of *The Living Word Vocabulary* (Dale and O'Rourke 1981).

Average Number of Root Words Acquired by Average Students

Age or Grade	Per Year	Per Week	Per Day
Ages 1–4	860	16.5	2.4
Grades K–2	860	16.5	2.4
Grades 3–6	1,000	19.2	2.8

Based on Biemiller 2005a.

Estimates of Cumulative Root-Word Knowledge

Age or Grade	Average Number of Root Words
End of Age 1	860
End of Age 2	1,720
End of Age 3	2,580
End of Age 4 (Pre-K)	3,440
End of Age 5 (K)	4,300
End of Grade 1	5,160
End of Grade 2	6,020
End of Grade 3	7,020
End of Grade 4	8,020
End of Grade 5	9,020
End of Grade 6	10,020

Based on Biemiller 2005a.

How Many Derived Words Are Acquired per Year?

A study by Anglin (1993) indicates that in Grade 1 the number of derived words (i.e., affixed or compound words) that students acquire is three times the number of root words. By Grade 5, the number of derived words and idioms increases to five times the number of root words.

Ratio of Root Words Acquired to Derived Words Acquired per Year

Grade	Root Words	Ratio	Derived Words
Grade 1	860	860 x 3	2,580
Grade 5	1,000	1,000 x 5	5,000

Based on Biemiller 2005a; Anglin 1993.

How Many Words Can Be Taught Directly?

When it comes to the number of root words or word families that can be taught in a school year, vocabulary researchers are basically in agreement. About 2 words per day, or 10 per week, can be taught directly.

Average Number of Root Words or Word Families That Can Be Taught Directly

Per School Week	Per School Year/180 days	Researcher
about 10	360 root words	Biemiller 2005a
about 8 to 10	about 400 word families	Beck et al. 2002
about 8 to 10	300 to 400 word families	Stahl et al. 1986

The Vocabulary Gap

Profound differences exist in vocabulary knowledge among learners. The word knowledge gap between groups of children begins before children enter school. This gap is too often not closed in later years. Hart and Risley (1995) found, for example, that three-year-olds from advantaged homes had oral vocabularies as much as five times larger than children from disadvantaged homes. Without intervention, this gap grows ever larger as students proceed through school.

Focusing vocabulary instruction on acquiring root words is an effective way to address the large number of words that students must learn each year.

—BIEMILLER & SLONIM, 2001

Biemiller (2005a) estimates that the bottom 25 percent of students begin Kindergarten with 1,000 fewer root-word meanings than average students. To make matters worse, these students who have the smallest vocabularies acquire only about 1.6 root words per day as compared with average students, who acquire about 2.4 root words per day. By the end of Grade 2, this results in a difference of about 2,000 words between average students and lower-quartile students. In fact, the number of root words known by a second grader in the lowest vocabulary quartile is about the same as the number of root words known by an average Kindergartener (Anglin 1993; Biemiller and Slonim 2001; Biemiller 2005a).

The Vocabulary Gap in Root-Word Knowledge

Grade	Average Student (at 2.4 root words per day)	Bottom 25% (at 1.6 root words per day)
End of Pre-K	3,440	2,440
End of K	4,300	3,016
End of Grade 1	5,160	3,592
End of Grade 2	6,020	4,168

To close the vocabulary gap in students who have impoverished vocabularies, vocabulary acquisition must be accelerated (Biemiller 2005b). According to Biemiller (2003, 2005a), "at the very least, it would seem desirable to prevent further decrements" by teaching at least two root-word meanings a day to students in Kindergarten through Grade 2. After Grade 2, all students, including those in the lowest quartile, apparently learn new root words at about the same rate (Biemiller and Slonim 2001). However, because of the initial vocabulary gap, if students in the lowest quartile are to ever "catch up" with their higher-level peers, they will need to learn words at an even faster rate—3.5 to 4 root words per school day (Biemiller 2003).

The importance of students acquiring a rich and varied vocabulary cannot be overstated.

—COMMON CORE STATE STANDARDS, 2010

Section III: Decoding and Word Recognition
Section IV: Reading Fluency
Section VI: Comprehension

Links Between Vocabulary and Comprehension

Vocabulary occupies an important position both in learning to read and in comprehending text: readers cannot understand text without knowing what most of the words mean (National Reading Panel 2000). According to Nagy (2005), "Of the many benefits of having a large vocabulary, none is more valuable than the positive contribution that vocabulary size makes to reading comprehension." To comprehend text, students require *both* fluent word recognition skills (i.e., decoding) and an average or greater vocabulary. According to Biemiller (2005b), "the presence of these two accomplishments does not guarantee a high level of reading comprehension, but the absence of *either* word recognition or adequate vocabulary ensures a low level of reading comprehension."

The Connecticut Longitudinal Study (Shaywitz et al. 1992) demonstrates that first-grade decoding ability (i.e., word recognition) is a major factor in reading comprehension, especially as students progress through the grades. Once a reader decodes a word, oral vocabulary plays a predominant part in reading comprehension. When beginning readers come to an unfamiliar word in text, they try to use the words they have heard—the words in their oral vocabularies—to make sense of the word in print. If the word is part of their oral vocabularies, readers can more easily and quickly decode and understand it (Kamil and Hiebert 2005).

For accomplished decoders, vocabulary knowledge probably plays more of a role in reading comprehension than word recognition skills (Biemiller 2005b). Cunningham and Stanovich (1997) found that first-grade orally tested vocabulary was predictive of eleventh-grade reading comprehension, whereas first-grade word recognition skills were not. From about third grade on, 95 percent of students can read more words than they can define or explain (Biemiller and Slonim 2001). The role of an early deficit in oral vocabulary thus becomes magnified.

Components of Vocabulary Instruction

The National Reading Panel (2000) concluded that there is no single research-based method for teaching vocabulary. From its analysis, the panel recommended using a variety of direct and indirect methods of vocabulary instruction.

Key to students' vocabulary development is building rich and flexible word knowledge.

—COMMON CORE STATE STANDARDS, 2010

CCSS

Intentional Teaching

Specific Word Instruction

- Selecting Words to Teach
- Rich and Robust Instruction

Word-Learning Strategies

- Dictionary Use
- Morphemic Analysis
- Cognate Awareness (ELL)
- Contextual Analysis

Intentional Vocabulary Teaching

According to the National Reading Panel (2000), explicit instruction of vocabulary is highly effective. To develop vocabulary intentionally, students should be explicitly taught both specific words and word-learning strategies. To deepen students' knowledge of word meanings, specific word instruction should be robust (Beck et al. 2002). Seeing vocabulary in rich contexts provided by authentic texts, rather than in isolated vocabulary drills, produces robust vocabulary learning (National Reading Panel 2000). Such instruction often does not begin with a definition, for the ability to give a definition is often the result of knowing what the word means. Rich and robust vocabulary instruction goes beyond definitional knowledge; it gets students actively engaged in using and thinking about word meanings and in creating relationships among words.

Research shows that there are more words to be learned than can be directly taught in even the most ambitious program of vocabulary instruction. Explicit instruction in word-learning strategies gives students tools for independently determining the meanings of unfamiliar words that have not been explicitly introduced in class. Since students encounter so many unfamiliar words in their reading, any help provided by such strategies can be useful.

Word-learning strategies include dictionary use, morphemic analysis, and contextual analysis. For ELLs whose language shares cognates with English, cognate awareness is also an important strategy. Dictionary use teaches students about multiple word meanings, as well as the importance of choosing the appropriate definition to fit the particular context. Morphemic analysis is the process of deriving a word's meaning by analyzing its meaningful parts, or morphemes. Such word parts include root words, prefixes, and suffixes. Contextual analysis involves inferring the meaning of an unfamiliar word by scrutinizing the text surrounding it. Instruction in contextual analysis generally involves teaching students to employ both generic and specific types of context clues.

Word Consciousness

Adept Diction

Word Play

Word Histories and Origins

Fostering Word Consciousness

A more general way to help students develop vocabulary is by fostering word consciousness, an awareness of and interest in words. Word consciousness is not an isolated component of vocabulary instruction; it needs to be taken into account each and every day (Scott and Nagy 2004). It can be developed at all times and in several ways: through encouraging adept diction, through word play, and through research on word origins or histories. According to Graves (2000), "If we can get students interested in playing with words and language, then we are at least halfway to the goal of creating the sort of word-conscious students who will make words a lifetime interest."

When students make multiple connections between a new word and their own experiences, they develop a nuanced and flexible understanding of the word they are learning.

—COMMON CORE STATE STANDARDS, 2010

CCSS

Multiple Exposures in Multiple Contexts

One principle of effective vocabulary learning is to provide multiple exposures to a word's meaning. There is great improvement in vocabulary when students encounter vocabulary words often (National Reading Panel 2000). According to Stahl (2005), students probably have to see a word more than once to place it firmly in their long-term memories. "This does *not* mean mere repetition or drill of the word," but seeing the word in different and multiple contexts. In other words, it is important that vocabulary instruction provide students with opportunities to encounter words repeatedly and in more than one context.

Findings of the National Reading Panel

Intentional instruction of vocabulary items is required for specific texts.

Repetition and multiple exposures to vocabulary items are important.

Learning in rich contexts is valuable for vocabulary learning.

Vocabulary tasks should be restructured as necessary.

Vocabulary learning should entail active engagement in learning tasks.

Computer technology can be used effectively to help teach vocabulary.

Vocabulary can be acquired through incidental learning.

How vocabulary is assessed and evaluated can have differential effects on instruction.

Dependence on a single vocabulary instructional method will not result in optimal learning.

Restructuring of Vocabulary Tasks

It is often assumed that when students do not learn new vocabulary words, they simply need to practice the words some more. Research has shown, however, that it is often the case that students simply do not understand the instructional task involved (National Reading Panel 2000). Rather than focus only on the words themselves, teachers should be certain that students fully understand the instructional tasks (Schwartz and Raphael 1985). The restructuring of learning materials or strategies in various ways often can lead to increased vocabulary acquisition, especially for low-achieving or at-risk students (National Reading Panel 2000). According to Kamil (2004), "once students know what is expected of them in a vocabulary task, they often learn rapidly."

Incidental Vocabulary Learning

The scientific research on vocabulary instruction reveals that most vocabulary is acquired incidentally through indirect exposure to words. Students can acquire vocabulary incidentally by engaging in rich oral-language experiences at home and at school, listening to books read aloud to them, and reading widely on their own. Reading volume is very important in terms of long-term vocabulary development (Cunningham and Stanovich 1998). Kamil and Hiebert (2005) reason that extensive reading gives students repeated or multiple exposures to words and is also one of the means by which students see vocabulary in rich contexts. Cunningham (2005) recommends providing structured read-aloud and discussion sessions and extending independent reading experiences outside school hours to encourage vocabulary growth in students.

Strategies for ELLs

Take Advantage of Students' First Language

Teach the Meaning of Basic Words

Review and Reinforcement

SEE ALSO . . .

English-Language Learners (ELLs), p. 17
English/Spanish Cognates, p. 64
Selecting Words for English-Language Learners (ELLs), p. 425
Word Tiers and Suggested Teaching Methods for ELLs, p. 426
Cognate Awareness, p. 496
Categories of Cognates in English and Spanish, p. 497

SEE ALSO . . .

LESSON MODELS
Introducing Function Words, p. 462
Vocabulary Hotshot Notebook, p. 601

Instruction for English-Language Learners (ELLs)

An increasing number of students come from homes in which English is not the primary language. From 1979 to 2003, the number of students who spoke English with difficulty increased by 124 percent (National Center for Education Statistics 2005). In 2003, students who spoke English with difficulty represented approximately 5 percent of the school population—up from 3 percent in 1979.

Not surprisingly, vocabulary development is especially important for English-language learners (ELLs). Poor vocabulary is a serious issue for these students (Calderón et al. 2005). ELLs who have deficits in their vocabulary are less able to comprehend text at grade level than their English-only (EO) peers (August et al. 2005). Findings indicate that research-based strategies used with EO students are also effective with ELLs, although the strategies must be adapted to strengths and needs of ELLs (Calderón et al. 2005).

Diane August and her colleagues (2005) suggest several strategies that appear to be especially valuable for building the vocabularies of ELLs. These strategies include taking advantage of students' first language if the language shares cognates with English, teaching the meaning of basic words, and providing sufficient review and reinforcement. Because English and Spanish share a large number of cognate pairs, the first instructional strategy is especially useful for Spanish-speaking ELLs. These students can draw on their cognate knowledge as a means of figuring out unfamiliar words in English. A second instructional strategy for ELLs is learning the meanings of basic words—words that most EO students already know. Basic words can be found on lists, such as the Dale-Chall List (Chall and Dale 1995). A third instructional strategy that ELLs particularly benefit from is review and reinforcement. These methods include read-alouds, teacher-directed activities, listening to audiotapes, activities to extend word use outside of the classroom, and parent involvement.

CHAPTER

11

Specific Word Instruction

what?
why?
when?
how?

what?

Specific Word Instruction

> Reading print and understanding words are two conditions needed for success in reading "grade-level" books.
>
> —BIEMILLER, 2005b

CCSS LANGUAGE STANDARDS

Vocabulary Acquisition and Use

Determine or clarify the meaning of unknown and multiple-meaning words and phrases. (CCR.4)

Demonstrate understanding of figurative language, word relationships, and nuances in word meanings. (CCR.5)

Acquire and use accurately a range of general academic and domain-specific words and phrases. (CCR.6)

CCSS READING STANDARDS

Literature • Informational Text

Craft and Structure

Interpret words and phrases as they are used in text. (CCR.4)

Explicit instruction has proven to be an effective way for students to acquire vocabulary knowledge (National Reading Panel 2000). Direct teaching of specific vocabulary words relevant to a given text can deepen students' knowledge of word meanings. The goal is to enable students to "use the instructed words in understanding a text containing those words and to recall the words well enough to use them in speech and writing" (Beck, McKeown, and Kucan 2002). Specific words can be directly introduced through teacher read-alouds or through independently read text.

According to reading researchers (Armbruster, Lehr, and Osborn 2001; Beck et al. 2002; National Reading Panel 2000; Stahl and Fairbanks 1986), specific word instruction should:

- focus on words that are contextualized in literature, important to the text, and useful to know in many situations;
- provide "rich," in-depth knowledge of word meanings—not just repeated definitions;
- provide clear, accessible explanations and examples of word meanings in various contexts, with opportunities for students to discuss, analyze, use, and compare the words in these contexts;
- provide multiple exposures to the words in more than one context;
- engage students in active, deep processing by getting them to use words in new contexts and to create associations among words.

Selecting Words to Teach

Though no formula or explicit list yet exists for selecting age-appropriate vocabulary for instruction, in the last few years several researchers have worked out strategies to identify such vocabulary. Isabel Beck and her colleagues (2002) have developed a systematic three-tier method for selecting vocabulary to teach. Margarita Calderón and her colleagues (2005) have modified Beck's tier system for English-language learners. Andrew Biemiller (2005a) and his colleagues are developing a sequenced list of words based on their findings that regardless of grade level, all students acquire words in roughly the same order.

All three tiers of words are vital to comprehension and vocabulary, although learning tier two and three words typically requires more deliberate effort.

—COMMON CORE STATE STANDARDS, 2010

CCSS

The Three-Tier System

Beck and McKeown (1985) have evolved a system, or algorithm, for selecting the words in a text best suited for direct explanation and focused instruction. In the system, a word is classified according to its level of utility, or tier (Beck et al. 2002). According to these researchers, a mature literate individual's vocabulary basically comprises three tiers of words: Tier-One words consist of basic words, such as *the, and, daddy,* and *food.* Except for English-language learners and students who are word impoverished, these words rarely require instruction in school. Tier-Two words occur frequently in language, are central to comprehension, and are understood by most mature language users. Tier-Two words are the best candidates for explicit instruction. Tier-Three words are low-frequency "specialized" words that are often limited to specific fields, domains of knowledge, or content areas such as social studies or science. Tier Threes should be taught only as they arise.

This concept of word tiers is not an exact science but a helpful guideline for choosing words for instructional attention. The boundaries between the tiers are not always clear cut. Thinking in terms of tiers is just a starting point—a way to frame the task of choosing candidate words for direct vocabulary instruction (Beck et al. 2002). This can be done by a process of elimination: first eliminate the Tier-One words, then the Tier-Three words, and you are likely to arrive at the Tier-Two words.

Guidelines for Using the Three-Tier System

TIER ONE

Ask Yourself . . .

- Is it a basic word whose meaning students are likely to know?
- Is it on the Dale-Chall List (Chall and Dale 1995)?

Examples: between, daddy, food, night, some, walk

Instructional Recommendation These words rarely require instruction, except for English-language learners and students who are word impoverished.

TIER TWO

Ask Yourself . . .

- Is it a word whose meaning students are unlikely to know?
- Is it a word that is generally useful—a "general-purpose word" that students are likely to encounter across a wide variety of domains?
- Can the meaning of the word be explained in everyday language, using words and concepts that are familiar to students?
- What is the word's instructional potential? Is its meaning necessary for comprehension of the text being read?

Examples: balcony, murmur, splendid

Instructional Recommendation These words are candidates for explicit instruction.

TIER THREE

Ask Yourself . . .

- Is it a word whose meaning students are unlikely to know?
- Is it a specialized word that does not appear frequently in written or oral language?
- Is the word specific to a particular content area or subject matter?

Examples: anthracite, mycelium, shoal

Instructional Recommendation These words are explained at point of contact or as the need arises.

Based on Beck et al. 2002; Biemiller 2004.

Categories of Word Knowledge (Average Second-Grade Student)		
Category of Word Knowledge	**Examples**	**Instructional Recommendation**
Words Known Well (known by more than 80 percent of students)	café, drop, fish, flood, spread, listen, loop, match, mask, swing, throat	No need to teach
Words Likely to Be Learned (known by 40 to 80 percent of students)	blab, cancel, distant, drama, possess, raw, shingle, tangle, thump, transfer	Teach
Word Unlikely to Be Learned (known by less than 40 percent of students)	abrasive, alias, cartilage, chaperone, destitute, franchise, junction, mammoth, polo, sequence, valor	Teach in upper grades

Based on Biemiller 2010.

Words are learned in approximately the same order.

—BIEMILLER, 2005a

Sequence of Word Acquisition

According to Andrew Biemiller (2005a), students acquire vocabulary in a relatively well-defined sequence that is ordered by vocabulary size rather than by grade level. For the most part, acquisition of a challenging word is built upon having the knowledge of certain more basic words first (Biemiller and Slonim 2001). For example, a word designated as Tier Two, such as *benevolent* or *leisurely,* may be too advanced in the sequence of word acquisition to be readily learned by a first- or second-grade student (Biemiller 2005b).

Within the sequence of word acquisition, students (regardless of their grade level) know certain word meanings well, partially know others, and are unlikely to learn some (Biemiller 2005a). Biemiller suggests focusing instruction on words that are partially known because they are "likely to be learned." Above is an example from his book *Words Worth Teaching.*

Sources

Dale-Chall List of 3,000 Words Known by Students in Grade 4

Readability Revisited: The New Dale-Chall Readability Formula (1995) by Jeanne S. Chall and Edgar Dale. Brookline, MA: Brookline Books.

Words Worth Teaching

Words Worth Teaching: Closing the Vocabulary Gap (2010) by Andrew Biemiller. Columbus, OH: SRA/McGraw-Hill.

According to Biemiller (2005a), selecting words to teach in the primary grades must take the sequence of word acquisition into account. To determine whether or not a word is likely to be known well by average first and second graders, Biemiller (2004) suggests referring to the Dale-Chall List (Chall and Dale 1995). If the word is on this list, it falls into the Tier One category—a basic word usually not a candidate for explicit instruction. Similarly, Biemiller's *Words Worth Teaching* (2010) contains root words that are likely to be known well by more than 80 percent of students in Grades K–2. In addition, it identifies the words that are likely to be learned—teachable words to be considered for instruction. However, when selecting words for Kindergarteners, students who are word impoverished, or English-language learners, it may be necessary to focus instruction in part on words that are likely to be known well.

From the second paragraph of "Marine Mammals" (p. 768), make a list of all the words that you believe could be good candidates (i.e., Tier Two) for specific word instruction. From the words you select, eliminate any words found on the Dale-Chall List (i.e., Tier One) and any specialized Tier-Three words. From the remaining words, select three target words. Explain your choice of words.

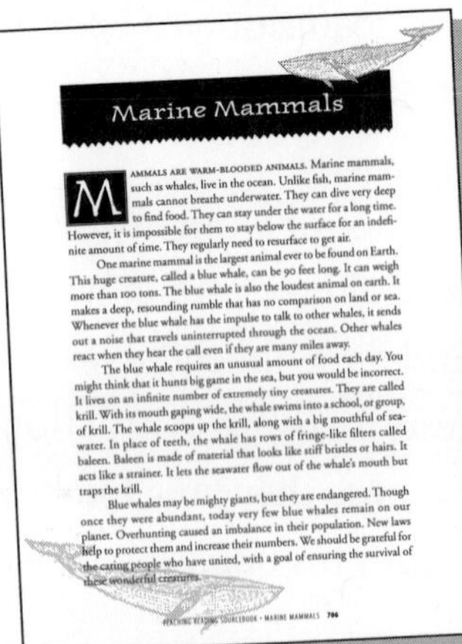

Marine Mammals

Mammals are warm-blooded animals. Marine mammals, such as whales, live in the ocean. Unlike fish, marine mammals cannot breathe underwater. They can dive very deep to find food. They can stay under the water for a long time. However, it is impossible for them to stay below the surface for an indefinite amount of time. They regularly need to resurface to get air.

One marine mammal is the largest animal ever to be found on Earth. This huge creature, called a blue whale, can be 90 feet long. It can weigh more than 100 tons. The blue whale is also the loudest animal on earth. It makes a deep, resounding rumble that has no comparison on land or sea. Whenever the blue whale has the impulse to talk to other whales, it sends out a noise that travels uninterrupted through the ocean. Other whales react when they hear the call even if they are many miles away.

The blue whale requires an unusual amount of food each day. You might think that it hunts big game in the sea, but you would be incorrect. It lives on an infinite number of extremely tiny creatures. They are called krill. With its mouth gaping wide, the whale swims into a school, or group, of krill. The whale scoops up the krill, along with a big mouthful of seawater. In place of teeth, the whale has rows of fringe-like filters called baleen. Baleen is made of material that looks like stiff bristles or hairs. It acts like a strainer. It lets the seawater flow out of the whale's mouth but traps the krill.

Blue whales may be mighty giants, but they are endangered. Though once they were abundant, today very few blue whales remain on our planet. Overhunting caused an imbalance in their population. New laws help to protect them and increase their numbers. We should be grateful for the caring people who have united, with a goal of ensuring the survival of these wonderful creatures.

Note: Dale-Chall List words found in second paragraph of "Marine Mammals": *animal, away, blue, call, called, creature, deep, Earth, feet, found, hear, huge, land, largest, long, loudest, many, miles, noise, ocean, one, sea, sends, talk, tons, travels, weigh, whale.*

Selecting Words for English-Language Learners (ELLs)

In developing a strategy for selecting words for English-language learners (ELLs), Margarita Calderón and her colleagues (2005) borrowed the tier system from Isabel Beck and her colleagues (2002) and then modified it. Using this modified set of criteria for ELLs sometimes results in reclassifying a word's previously designated tier. To guide instruction for ELLs, the modified criteria includes a word's

- concreteness (Is the word concrete or abstract? Can it be shown or demonstrated?)
- cognate status (Does the English word have a Spanish cognate?)
- depth of meaning (Does the word have multiple meanings?)
- utility (Is the meaning of the word key to understanding the selection?)

Even though English-only (EO) students are assumed to know most Tier-One words (e.g., words on the Dale-Chall List), this is not always the case for ELLs. For ELLs, these basic words may require explicit instruction. Basic words include both function and content words. Function words, such as *on, under, more, next,* and *some,* alert a reader to the structure of a sentence. Content words, such as *cottage* and *cousin,* carry information or meaning in text. There are two types of content words—words that are concrete and words that are abstract.

Teaching Spanish-speaking students to take advantage of their cognate knowledge can be a powerful tool (August et al. 2005). For ELLs whose first language shares cognates with English, a Tier-Two word that may be challenging for EO students could be considered Tier One for ELLs. Many less frequently used English words are cognates of more frequently used Spanish words; for example, *calabash* and *calabaza.*

CONCRETE WORDS
words that can be pictured, felt, or heard, such as *cottage, scalding,* or *shrill*

ABSTRACT WORDS
words that are difficult to demonstrate or picture, such as *cousin, democracy,* or *reluctant*

LESSON MODEL: Introducing Function Words, p. 462

COGNATES
words in two languages that share a similar spelling, pronunciation, and meaning

English/Spanish Cognates, p. 64
Cognate Awareness, p. 496

Word Tiers and Suggested Teaching Methods for ELLs

Word	EO Student	ELL	ELL Word Classification	ELL Suggested Teaching Method
shoes	Tier One	Tier One	Concrete word: meaning is known, but English label is unknown	Show a picture of the word
ring	Tier One	Tier Two	Concrete word: with multiple meanings	Show a picture of the word; discuss other meanings after reading
share	Tier One	Tier One	Abstract word	Briefly explain word meaning during reading of selection; translate
map	Tier One	Tier One	Cognate: high-frequency English word/high-frequency Spanish word (*map/mapa*)	No explanation; say English word and ask students to provide Spanish word
miles	Tier One	Tier Two	False cognate (the Spanish word *miles* means "thousands")	Point out and give the correct translation
shatter	Tier Two	Tier Two	Concrete word: not a cognate	May not need elaborate discussion
industrious	Tier Two	Tier One	Cognate: low-frequency English word/high-frequency Spanish word (*industrious/industrioso*)	May not need explanation
resist	Tier Two	Tier Two	Abstract word: not a cognate	Explicitly introduce
kayak	Tier Three	Tier Two	Concrete word: not a cognate	Show a picture of the word
calabash	Tier Three	Tier One	Cognate: low-frequency English word/high-frequency Spanish word (*calabash/calabaza*)	May not need explanation
baleen	Tier Three	Tier Two	Specialized word	Define in Spanish if simple English explanation cannot be given

Based on Calderón et al. 2005; Beck et al. 2002.

Rich and Robust Instruction

Effective vocabulary instruction creates rich knowledge of the meaning and uses of words—something that traditional dictionary definition approaches do not provide. This "robust" approach to vocabulary instruction involves not just direct explanation of the meanings of words, but also thought-provoking, playful, and interactive follow-up (Beck et al. 2002). As Beck et al. (2002) put it, robust instruction "offers rich information about words and their uses, provides frequent and varied opportunities for students to think about and use words, and enhances students' language comprehension and production."

Children in the primary grades are generally "preliterate"—they do not understand language in print as well as they understand oral language.

—BIEMILLER & BOOTE, 2006

Using Vocabulary Contextualized in Literature

According to the National Reading Panel (2000), vocabulary instruction should be incorporated into reading instruction, within the context of reading literary and informational text. Text provides a strong context within which to introduce target words. According to Beck et al. (2002), when words are introduced and explained in the context of a story, students learn word meanings in a situation that is familiar and provides "a rich example of the word's use." Students can learn word meanings from listening to adults read to them or by reading independently on their own.

SEE ALSO . . .

Read-Aloud Methods, p. 627

READ-ALOUD METHODS Explicit, teacher-directed vocabulary instruction can complement and enhance traditional storybook reading activities (Coyne et al. 2004). A story can provide a strong context within which to begin the word-meaning explanation. To this goal, Beck and McKeown (2001) developed Text Talk, a project aimed at capturing the benefits of teacher read-alouds. Text Talk has two main goals: (1) to enhance comprehension through interspersed open questions and (2) to enhance vocabulary development. In Text Talk, vocabulary is fully discussed *after* the reading of a story. During reading, the teacher may pause to briefly introduce each of the target words (Beck et al. 2002). The Direct Explanation Method developed

SEE ALSO . . .

LESSON MODELS

Text Talk: Read-Aloud Method, p. 436

Meaning Vocabulary: Direct Explanation Method, p. 443

Method for Independently Read Text, p. 453

Dialogic Reading: Picture Book Read-Aloud Method, p. 648

by Boote and Biemiller (2006) is appropriate for accelerating vocabulary acquisition in students who are not yet reading independently, have impoverished vocabularies, or need a boost. In this method, up to 25 "teachable" words are introduced over four separate readings of the same story. On the last day of the sequence, the words are cumulatively reviewed.

METHOD FOR INDEPENDENTLY READ TEXT Generally, the sequence for independently read text differs from the Text Talk read-aloud method in that target words are introduced *before* students read the selection. This helps make unfamiliar words available for students when they encounter them in their reading (Beck et al. 2002). In cases when a word is likely to affect comprehension, the most effective time to introduce its meaning may be at the moment the word is met in text. Introducing the meanings of target words as they are encountered during reading can be done simply and briefly by quickly explaining or defining the word in context.

Develop Word Meaning Through . . .

Student-Friendly Explanations

Teacher-Created Contexts

Active Engagement with Words

Introducing Specific Words

Providing word-meaning information is the first step in building word knowledge. To introduce words so that they take root in a student's vocabulary, keep in mind the following: (1) make word meanings explicit through student-friendly explanations, (2) incorporate teacher-created contexts as opposed to text-based contexts, and (3) get students actively engaged in discussing the word meanings right away (Beck et al. 2002).

STUDENT-FRIENDLY EXPLANATIONS Introduce new vocabulary to students by explaining a word's meaning rather than providing a dictionary definition for the word. To develop student-friendly explanations, follow two basic principles: (1) characterize the word and how it is typically used and (2) explain the meaning in everyday language—language that is accessible and meaningful to students (Beck et al. 2002). For example, a dictionary definition for the word *resist* such as "to

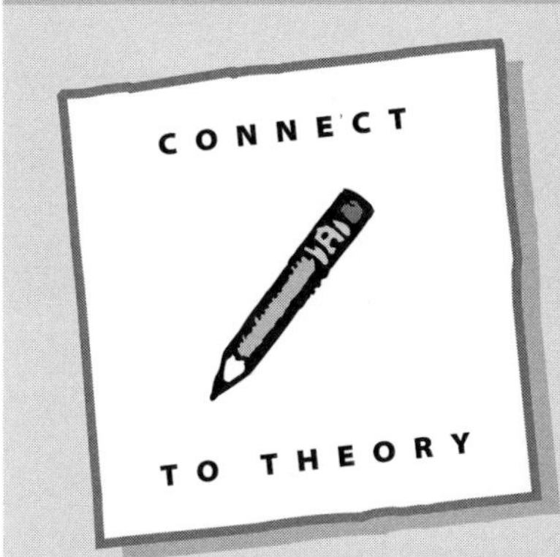

Create a student-friendly explanation for one of the target words you selected from the second paragraph of "Marine Mammals" **(p. 768)****. First look up the dictionary definition. Then develop your explanation using everyday, accessible language and words such as *something, someone,* or *describes.* For additional clarification, fold an example into your explanation. Finally, compare your explanation with the dictionary definition.**

> Dictionary definitions are not an effective vehicle for learning word meanings.
>
> —BECK ET AL., 2002

withstand the force or the effect of" is puzzling rather than helpful. To define *resist* in accessible language, try to frame the concept of resisting in student-friendly terms. Something like "when a person tries not to give in to something" is an example. Now consider whether that captures the full meaning of *resist.* In fact, it omits the idea of *resist* as putting up a struggle. To reflect that idea, we might alter or add to the definition to say "when a person struggles or fights not to give in to something."

TEACHER-CREATED CONTEXTS Sometimes a word's natural context—in text or literature—is not all that informative or helpful for deriving word meanings (Beck et al. 2002). For this reason, it is useful to intentionally create and develop instructional contexts that provide strong clues to a word's meaning. Instructional contexts are usually created by teachers, but can sometimes be found in commercial reading programs.

ACTIVE ENGAGEMENT WITH WORDS Provide short, playful, and lively opportunities for students to interact with words and process their meanings right away. This type of active engagement gives students repeated exposures to new words. Some examples of these interactions, using the word *interior,* are shown on the following page.

Active Engagement with Words	Target Word: interior
Questions	Jake thought it would be fun to explore the interior of Alaska. Why might you want to spend time in the interior of your state?
Example or Nonexample	Which one of these two sentences tells about the interior of Oregon? On their vacation, the family visited a lake in central Oregon. On their vacation, the family visited the beaches and coast of Oregon.
Finish the Idea	After a trip to the coast, we headed to the interior of the country because ________.
Have You Ever . . . ?	Can you describe a place you know about that is located in the interior of your state?
Choices	If what I say could be in the interior of a big island, say "center." If not, don't say anything. • a mountain • an ocean beach • a lighthouse • a small town

In-Depth Word Knowledge

Use the words

Explore facets of word meaning

Consider relationships among words

Developing In-Depth Word Knowledge

Providing students opportunities to process word meanings at a deeper, more complex level, rich instruction goes beyond definitional information to get students actively engaged in using new words and thinking about word meanings and creating relationships among words (Beck et al. 2002). This breadth and depth of information enables students to establish networks of connections between new words and known words (McKeown and Beck 2004).

Students should practice using a word to ensure that the word becomes an active part of their vocabulary, not just an isolated piece of information. For example, they can talk about situations the word would describe or they can consider instances

SEE ALSO . . .

LESSON MODELS

Concept Picture Sort, p. 467

Semantic Map, p. 470

Semantic Feature Analysis, p. 474

Possible Sentences, p. 478

Word Map, p. 481

Keyword Method, p. 484

Vocabulary Hotshot Notebook, p. 601

SEE ALSO . . .

Scaffolding, p. 625

when the word would be an appropriate choice. Students can respond to various characteristics of a word, explore the facets of its meaning, and apply the word's meaning in a variety of contexts. One commonly used way to reveal facets of a word's meaning is to have students differentiate between two descriptions of a target word.

Word knowledge is stored in networks of connected ideas, clustered in categories somewhat like a mental filing cabinet. Students should consider relationships among words—how word meanings interact. The more connections that can be built, the more opportunities there are to get at a word's meaning (Beck et al. 2002). Graphic organizers, such as maps, webs, and grids, show how words are related; they visually explore word relationships. They are a concrete way to process, reflect on, and integrate information and make categorical thinking visible. Using graphic organizers is an excellent method of helping students to visualize the abstractions of language. Therefore, they are an effective instructional strategy for English-language learners (Gersten and Baker 2001).

In a successful vocabulary program, words do not appear as part of a classroom exercise and then drop from sight.

—McKEOWN & BECK, 2004

Extending Word Use Beyond the Classroom

Ongoing instruction takes vocabulary learning beyond the classroom. It supports word ownership by students and produces deep and thorough word knowledge that is needed to affect comprehension. The more that students become aware of how words are used and where they are encountered outside class, the greater the chance that they will come to own them (McKeown and Beck 2004). There are many ways to make students conscious of target-word usage beyond the classroom. One of these methods is the Vocabulary Hotshot Notebook, which is described in Chapter 3: Word Consciousness.

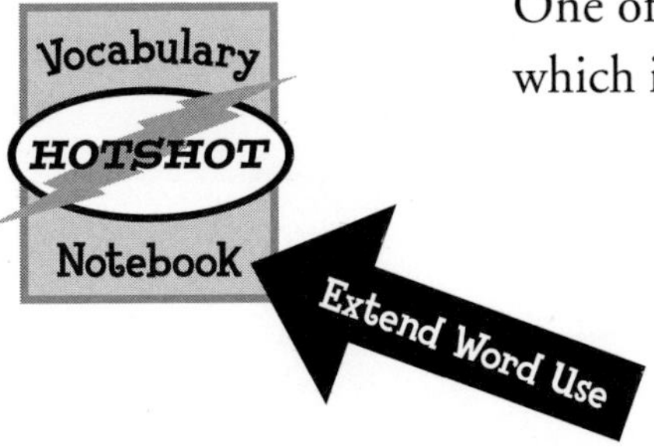

why? Specific Word Instruction

We use words to think; the more words we know, the finer our understanding is about the world.

—STAHL, 1999

According to the National Reading Panel (2000), explicit instruction in vocabulary can increase vocabulary learning and comprehension. Furthermore, vocabulary instruction should be incorporated into reading instruction. For vocabulary instruction to increase the comprehension of texts that contain unfamiliar words, it must be fairly intensive. This type of instruction provides students with a rich, in-depth knowledge of word meanings. Such in-depth knowledge can help students better understand what they are reading or hearing, and use words accurately. According to William Nagy (2005), "intensive or rich vocabulary instruction requires giving students information about what a word means and about how it is used, and providing them with opportunities to process this information deeply."

Research Findings . . .

Benefits in understanding text by applying letter-sound correspondences to printed material come about only if the target word is in the learner's oral vocabulary.

—NATIONAL READING PANEL, 2000

Preliminary evidence . . . suggests that as late as Grade 5, about 80 percent of words are learned as a result of direct explanation, either as a result of the child's request or instruction, usually by a teacher.

—BIEMILLER, 1999

People with more extensive vocabularies not only know more words but also know more about the words they know.

—CURTIS & GLASER, 1983

The first reason that vocabulary instruction often fails to produce measurable gains in reading comprehension is that much of the instruction does not produce a sufficient depth of word knowledge.

—NAGY, 1988

Suggested Reading . . .

Bringing Words to Life: Robust Vocabulary Instruction (2002) by Isabel L. Beck, Margaret G. McKeown & Linda Kucan. New York: Guilford.

Creating Robust Vocabulary: Frequently Asked Questions and Extended Examples (2008) by Isabel L. Beck, Margaret G. McKeown & Linda Kucan. New York: Guilford.

Meaningful Differences in the Everyday Experience of Young American Children (1995) by Betty Hart & Todd R. Risley. Baltimore, MD: Paul H. Brookes.

Put Reading First: The Research Building Blocks for Teaching Children to Read, 3rd Edition (2006) by Bonnie Armbruster, Fran Lehr & Jean Osborn. Jessup, MD: National Institute for Literacy.

Teaching and Learning Vocabulary: Bringing Scientific Research to Practice (2005) edited by Elfrieda H. Hiebert & Michael Kamil. Mahwah, NJ: Erlbaum.

Vocabulary Instruction: Research to Practice, 2nd Edition (2012) edited by Edward J. Kame'enui & James F. Baumann. New York: Guilford.

Words Worth Teaching: Closing the Vocabulary Gap (2010) by Andrew Biemiller. Columbus, OH: SRA/McGraw-Hill.

when?

Specific Word Instruction

> Vocabulary instruction should happen anytime and all the time.
>
> —MCKEOWN & BECK, 2004

When to Teach

It is important to begin direct instruction of specific words as early as possible, in either preschool or Kindergarten. Most of the vocabulary differences among students occur before Grade 3. By Grade 3, students with high vocabularies know thousands more word meanings than children who are experiencing delays in vocabulary development (Biemiller and Slonim 2001). Depending on the instructional situation, specific words can be introduced *before* reading, *during* reading, or *after* reading.

When to Directly Introduce Specific Words

Before Reading	During Reading	After Reading
Introduce target words	Briefly explain target words, as well as other words that may affect comprehension (Beck et al. 2002; Biemiller and Boote 2006)	Introduce (Beck et al. 2002) or review (Biemiller and Boote 2006) target words

Teacher Read-Alouds: During Reading, After Reading

Independently Read Text: Before Reading, During Reading

When to Assess and Intervene

The National Reading Panel (2000) suggests that a sound evaluation of a student's vocabulary be based on data from more than a single assessment. The more closely the assessment matches the instructional context, the more appropriate the conclusions about the instruction will be. Assessment that is

How Many Words to Directly Introduce?

Teacher Read-Alouds

KINDERGARTEN About three or four words per book at one or two books per week (Beck et al. 2002)

GRADE 1 About four or five words per book at one or two books per week (Beck et al. 2002)

GRADE 2 About five or six words per book at one or two books per week (Beck et al. 2002)

GRADES K–2 Up to 25 words per book at one book per week (Biemiller and Boote 2006)

Independently Read Text

GRADES 2–8 About eight to ten words per selection at one selection per week (Beck et al. 2002)

tied to instruction (e.g., the targeted words) will provide better information about students' specific learning. Standardized tests provide a global measure of vocabulary and may be used to provide a baseline.

Andrew Biemiller (2004) believes that the inability to readily assess vocabulary growth has been a major reason for lack of attention to vocabulary in the primary grades. Standardized vocabulary tests and his own Root Word Inventory (Biemiller and Slonim 2001) can be used as a baseline, but they are not usually feasible for classroom teachers. These tests usually take 10–15 minutes per student to administer. Biemiller thinks the best that teachers can do is to try to get a general idea of how well students know words. For example, students can raise their hand if they know a word and then tell what the word means.

Early, intensive intervention is especially critical for students who enter Kindergarten with impoverished oral vocabularies. Limited vocabulary knowledge places many students at risk for early failure in learning how to read and later failure in comprehending texts. Interventions that increase the effectiveness of storybook reading activities through explicit teaching of word meanings hold promise for decreasing the vocabulary differences among students in the primary grades (Coyne et al. 2004).

Purpose	✓ Vocabulary Assessment	Publisher
Screening	CORE Literacy Library *Assessing Reading: Multiple Measures, 2nd Edition* CORE Vocabulary Screening	Arena Press
Screening Progress Monitoring	Expressive One-Word Picture Vocabulary Test (EOWPVT-4) Receptive One-Word Picture Vocabulary Test (ROWPVT-4)	Academic Therapy Publications
Screening Progress Monitoring Diagnostic	easy CBM™ ▸ Vocabulary	Riverside Publishing http://easycbm.com

Specific Word Instruction

LESSON MODEL FOR

Contextualized Vocabulary

Benchmark

- ability to develop in-depth knowledge of word meanings

Strategy Grade Level

- Kindergarten – Grade 2

Grouping

- whole class
- small group or pairs

Sample Text (Resources)

- Read-Aloud—"Common Sense: An Anansi Tale"

Text Talk: Read-Aloud Method

This lesson model is based on Text Talk, a research-based method developed by Isabel Beck and Margaret McKeown and described in *Bringing Words to Life: Robust Vocabulary Instruction* (Beck et al. 2002). In Text Talk, text-specific vocabulary is extensively introduced after a story has been read aloud to students. Using sample text, this lesson model provides an example of how to introduce three previously selected target words. The same model can be adapted and used to enhance vocabulary instruction linked to the read-aloud stories and informational books in any commercial reading program.

Common Sense: An Anansi Tale

ANANSI, THE SPIDER, was full of mischief. He loved to play jokes and pull pranks on people. One day, he decided to collect all the common sense in the world. Everyone uses these little bits of good judgment every day. "If," Anansi thought, "I alone had all of this sensible information, I could sell it back to people when they needed it." Anansi imagined people lining up to pay him for answers to the simplest questions: *Anansi, what should I wear when it's cold outside? What should I do when I am hungry?*

"This is a brilliant scheme," thought Anansi. "I will have all the common sense in the world, and all the money in the world, too!"

So Anansi got a sack and started collecting common sense. *Brush your teeth to prevent cavities! Put your socks on before your shoes!* Anansi put them all in his sack.

The sack was soon bursting at the seams. "I need to find a better place to keep the common sense," thought Anansi. Just then he spied a calabash growing on a vine. It looked like a giant pumpkin. Anansi hollowed out the calabash. Then he stuffed all of the common sense inside and kept collecting.

When Anansi had gathered up ev
thought, "Now I just have to find a good

Anansi set off through the jungle
place. He dragged the calabash under f
through streams. He trudged from shrub
muddy trails and slid down steep hillsi
tallest tree in the jungle.

VOCABULARY HANDBOOK • COMMON SENS

"This is the perfect hiding place," he said. "The calabash will be safe and sound. No one would ever guess that I have hidden such a valuable treasure in such an unusual place."

Using a thick rope, Anansi tied the heavy calabash around his neck so that it dangled in front of him like a locket on a necklace. He started up the tree trunk, but climbing was hard. The calabash flopped and swayed. It banged Anansi's belly. It bruised his knees and elbows. The rope burned the back of his neck. But even though Anansi was aching and battered, he did not stop. The thought of getting rich kept him going.

As Anansi was struggling upward, he heard someone giggling below him. He looked down and saw a small boy leaning against the tree trunk.

Anansi called down to the boy. "What is so funny?" he asked.

"*You* are," said the boy. "Anyone with a pinch of common sense knows that it is easier to carry things on your back—especially if you are climbing a tree. How foolish can you get?"

The boy's words made Anansi furious! Anansi thought he had collected all the common sense in the world. How could he have missed the one piece he needed most? The thought made Anansi madder and madder. Finally
ung the calabash with all his

into a million pieces. The com-
ieces got caught in a breeze. The
mmon sense all over the world. And
eryone has a little bit of common
common sense to share. But, as you
all of it. It was Anansi who made it

OK • COMMON SENSE: AN ANANSI TALE 203

TEXT TALK FOR READ-ALOUDS

Target Words

mischief
waded
foolish

Point out to Spanish-speaking ELLs that *calabash* and *calabaza* are cognates.

Read the Story Aloud

Read aloud the sample text "Common Sense: An Anansi Tale." As you are reading, pause and give a brief explanation for each target word when you come to it, as well as for any words that are likely to affect comprehension. The explanations should not interrupt the flow of the story; target words will be fully explained after reading the story.

- At the target word *mischief,* stop and say: *Mischief means playing tricks on people.*
- At the Tier-Three word *calabash,* stop and say: *A calabash is like a big pumpkin. Have you ever carved a pumpkin on Halloween? You have to hollow out the pumpkin first.*
- At the target word *waded,* stop and say: *Wading is walking through water that is not deep, usually just at your ankles or knees or not higher than your waist.*
- At the target word *foolish,* stop and say: *A foolish person is someone who doesn't have good common sense.*

After Reading the Story

After reading the story, fully introduce the meanings of the target words, one word at a time.

TEXT TALK FOR READ-ALOUDS

Target Word

mischief

Introduce the Target Word

Contextualize the Word The context of the story provides a familiar situation within which to introduce the word. Say: *The story tells us that Anansi the spider is always up to some mischief.*

Say the Word Create a phonological representation of the word. Say: *Let's say the word together: mischief.* Ask: *What is the word?* (mischief)

Give a Student-Friendly Explanation Explain the word's meaning in everyday language—language that is clear and acces-

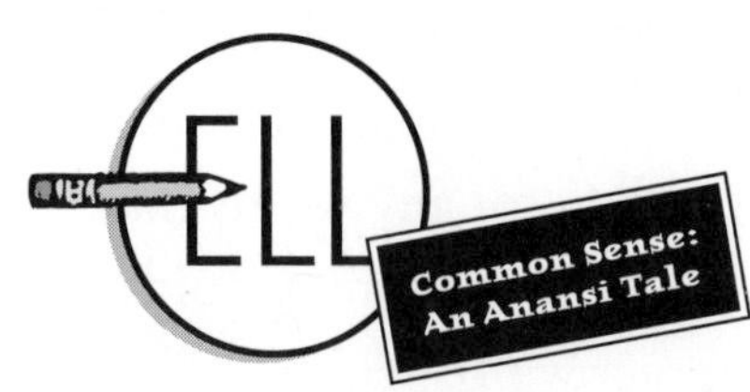

English/Spanish Cognates

brilliant • brillante
calabash • calabaza
furious • furioso
imagined • imaginó
information • información
jungle • jungla
million • millón
rich • rico
spied • espió
treasure • tesoro

False Cognates

scheme • esquema (diagram)
sensible • sensible (sensitive)

SEE ALSO . . .

Cognate Awareness, p. 496

sible to students. Say: *Mischief is behavior that is a little bit naughty—it's not really bad behavior. Someone who causes mischief likes to tease and play tricks.*

Provide a Different Context Show how the word can be used in a context different from the story context. Say: *When I found a plastic spider in my bed, I knew someone was up to mischief.*

Engage Actively with the Word Provide playful opportunities for students to interact with the word and process its meaning right away. Here are some examples:

FINISH THE IDEA Sentence starters require students to use and apply the meaning of a target word in a different context. Tell students that you are going to start a sentence and you want them to think of an ending. For example, say: *A puppy can get into a lot of mischief. Tell about some mischief a puppy might make. Try to use mischief when you tell about it. You can start out by saying, "My new puppy got into a lot of mischief when ______."*

CHOICES Making choices enables students to apply the meaning of a target word. Tell students that you are going to name some situations, and if a situation is an example of making mischief, they should say "mischief." If it isn't, they shouldn't say anything. For example, say:

- *Making "rabbit's ears" when someone is taking a picture* ("mischief")
- *Practicing the piano* (no response)
- *Jumping out and scaring someone* ("mischief")
- *Putting salt in the sugar bowl* ("mischief")

Say the Word Again Reinforce the word's meaning and phonological representation. Ask: *What is the word that describes behavior that is a little bit naughty?* (mischief)

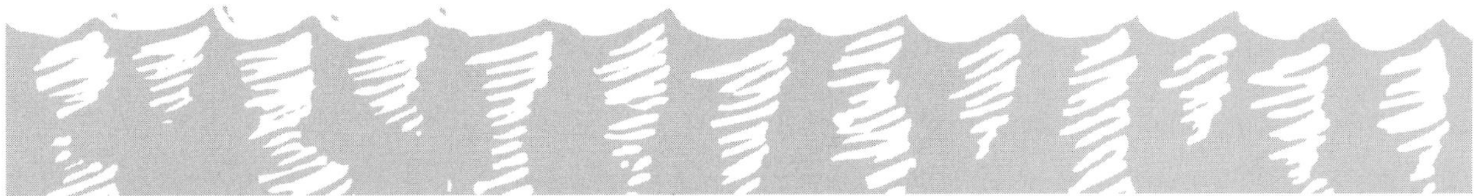

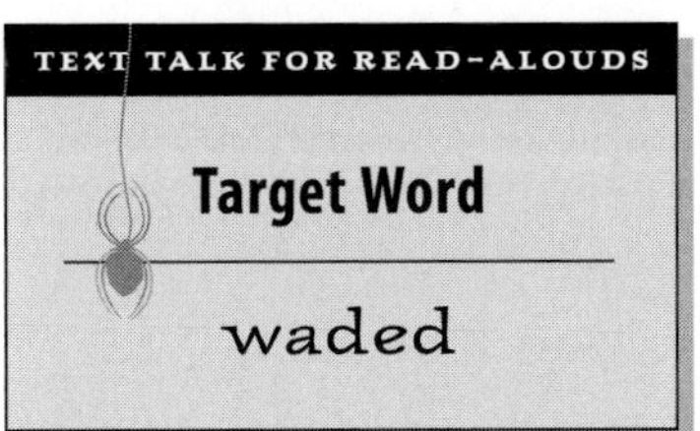

TEXT TALK FOR READ-ALOUDS
Target Word
waded

Introduce the Target Word

Contextualize the Word The context of the story provides a familiar situation within which to introduce the word. Say: *In the story, Anansi waded through streams.*

Say the Word Create a phonological representation of the word. Say: *Let's say the word together: waded.* Ask: *What is the word?* (waded)

Give a Student-Friendly Explanation Explain the word's meaning in everyday language—language that is clear and accessible to students. Say: *Wading has to do with walking through water or mud that is not deep. When you're wading, it is usually not too hard to move your legs to take a step forward.*

Provide a Different Context Show how the word can be used in a context different from the story context. Say: *Some kids like to wade in puddles after a heavy rain.*

Engage Actively with the Word Provide playful opportunities for students to interact with the word and process its meaning right away. Here are some examples:

QUESTIONS Ask questions that require students to apply the target word's meaning. Ask: *If you were hiking and had to cross a stream that had water in it up to your knees, what word would you use to describe how you walked across the stream?* (waded)

CHOICES Making choices enables students to apply the meaning of a target word. Tell students that you are going to name some places, and if a place is where someone could wade,

they should say "slish-slosh," the noise someone might make when wading. If it isn't, they shouldn't say anything. For example, say:

- *A supermarket* (no response)
- *A creek* ("slish-slosh")
- *A mud puddle* ("slish-slosh")
- *A hallway* (no response)

Say the Word Again Reinforce the word's meaning and phonological representation. Ask: *What is the word that describes walking through mud or water that is not deep?* (wading)

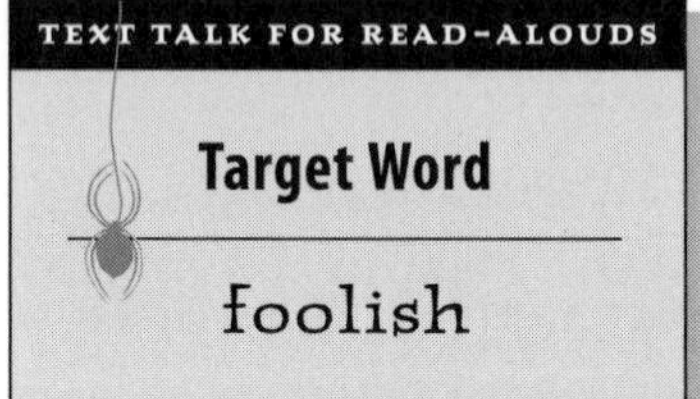

Introduce the Target Word

Contextualize the Word The context of the story provides a familiar situation within which to introduce the word. Say: *In the story, a boy tells Anansi he is very foolish to climb while carrying the calabash in front.*

Say the Word Create a phonological representation of the word. Say: *Let's say the word together: foolish.* Ask: *What is the word?* (foolish)

The word *foolish* is found on the Dale-Chall List (Chall and Dale 1995). Biemiller (2005a) considers *foolish* to be a word that is known well by average second graders.

Give a Student-Friendly Explanation Explain the word's meaning in everyday language—language that is clear and accessible to students. Say: *A foolish person is someone who doesn't use good common sense.*

Provide a Different Context Show how the word can be used in a context different from the story context. Say: *It is foolish to eat ice cream with a toothpick.*

Engage Actively with the Word Provide playful opportunities for students to interact with the word and process its meaning right away. Here are some examples:

FINISH THE IDEA Sentence starters require students to use and apply the meaning of a target word in a different context.

Tell students that you are going to start a sentence and you want them to think of an ending. For example, say: *I'd probably feel foolish if I got to school and realized that my shoes didn't match. Think of an example of being foolish. Try to use the word when you tell about it. You can start out by saying, "The most foolish thing I ever did was _______."*

CHOICES Making choices enables students to apply the meaning of a target word. Tell students that you are going to name situations, and if a situation is an example of acting foolish, they should say "tee-hee." If it isn't, they shouldn't say anything. For example, say:

- *Forgetting your jacket on a cold day* ("tee-hee")
- *Brushing your teeth* (no response)
- *Eating a lot of candy before dinner* ("tee-hee")
- *Studying for a spelling test* (no response)

Say the Word Again Reinforce the word's meaning and phonological representation. Ask: *What is the word that describes someone who doesn't have good common sense?* (foolish)

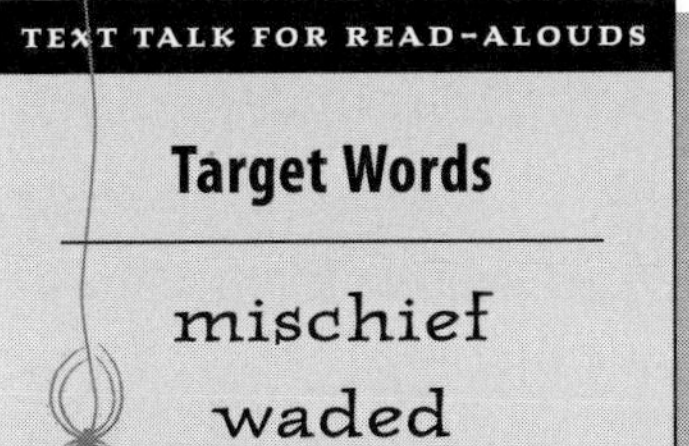

TEXT TALK FOR READ-ALOUDS
Target Words
mischief
waded
foolish

Bring the Target Words Together

After introducing the words one at a time, provide opportunities for students to use all the words together.

ONE QUESTION Using all the target words, develop one thought-provoking question and then challenge students to answer it. For example, ask: *What kind of mischief at the Pie Factory caused the foolish-looking workers to wade through a vat of banana cream?*

QUESTIONS: TWO CHOICES Develop a question in which students must choose the target word that best describes a particular situation. For example, ask: *If you went swimming alone at night, would it be foolish or wading?* (foolish)

QUESTIONS: ONE CONTEXT Using a single context, develop a question for each of the words. Have students answer the set of questions. In this example, the single context is a swimming pool. For example, ask: *What might be foolish to wear in a swimming pool? What mischief could you make if the pool lifeguard wasn't looking? If you had flippers on your feet, could you wade from the low end to the deep end of a swimming pool?*

QUESTIONS: SAME FORMAT Using a uniform format, develop a question for each of the words. Have students explain their answers. For example, ask: *If you are full of mischief, are you being naughty or nice? If you have to wade, would you be in deep water or a puddle? Is being foolish more like acting stupid or acting smart?*

PROMPTS Develop an open-ended discussion prompt for each of the words. Encourage students to respond creatively. For example, ask: *If identical twins wanted to get into some mischief, what could they do? If, after a big storm, your family has to wade to safety, what could have happened? If a friend refused to brush his teeth, what would you say to convince him that he was being foolish?*

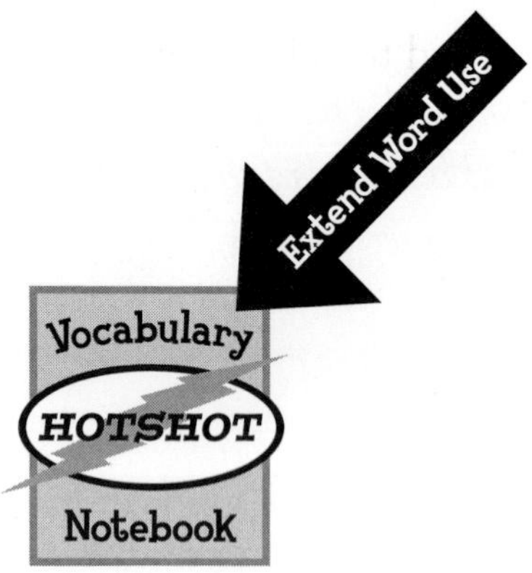

Extend Word Use Beyond the Classroom

Developing an in-depth, "rich," and permanent understanding of new vocabulary comes through multiple exposures in more than one context. There are many ways to keep students thinking about and using target words beyond the classroom. One of these methods is the Vocabulary Hotshot Notebook, which is described in Chapter 3: Word Consciousness.

LESSON MODEL: Vocabulary Hotshot Notebook, p. 601

LESSON MODEL FOR

Contextualized Vocabulary

Benchmarks

- ability to develop in-depth knowledge of many word meanings
- ability to improve story comprehension

Strategy Grade Level

- Pre-K – Grade 2

Grouping

- whole class
- small group or pairs
- individual

Sample Text (Resources)

- Read-Aloud—"Common Sense: An Anansi Tale"

Materials

- none

Meaning Vocabulary: Direct Explanation Method

This lesson model is based on a research-based method developed by Catherine Boote and Andrew Biemiller (Biemiller and Boote 2006; Boote 2006). It is especially appropriate for accelerating vocabulary acquisition in preliterate students who are not reading and/or decoding independently, have impoverished vocabularies, or need a boost. Using the direct explanation method, the teacher reads aloud a story four separate times over a three-day period, introducing up to 25 teachable words per selection. Other words are explained for comprehension only, all from the story context. On the fourth or last day of the sequence, the teachable words are cumulatively reviewed. Using sample text, this lesson model provides an example of how to introduce a large number of previously selected teachable words. The same model can be adapted and used to enhance vocabulary instruction linked to the read-aloud stories and informational books in any commercial reading program.

Select the Words

In this method, two types of words are introduced and explained: teachable words and comprehension words.

Teachable Words

Generally, teachable words are introduced and explained during the reading of a story and then reviewed. During the second, third, and fourth read-alouds, up to eight new teachable words are introduced. Teachable words are selected at the appropriate level from the Dale-Chall List of 3,000 Words Known by Students in Grade 4 (Chall and Dale 1995) and *Words Worth Teaching: Closing the Vocabulary Gap* (Biemiller 2010).

CONTINUED ▷

Although this method is appropriate for Kindergarteners, the sample text "Common Sense: An Anansi Tale" may be too difficult for them.

TEACHABLE TITLE WORDS Some teachable words are introduced before the first read-aloud. These are words whose meanings are crucial to the overall understanding of the story. Often, as in this sample text, the pretaught word is in the story title.

Comprehension Words

Some words are important to the comprehension of the text, but they are not identified as teachable words from the list of level-appropriate words in *Words Worth Teaching*. The meanings of these words are briefly explained for comprehension before each read-aloud; they are not reviewed afterward.

Common Sense: An Anansi Tale

ANANSI, THE SPIDER, was full of mischief. He loved to play jokes and pull pranks on people. One day, he decided to collect all the common sense in the world. Everyone uses these little bits of good judgment every day. "If," Anansi thought, "I alone had all of this sensible information, I could sell it back to people when they needed it." Anansi imagined people lining up to pay him for answers to the simplest questions: *Anansi, what should I wear when it's cold outside? What should I do when I am hungry?*

"This is a brilliant scheme," thought Anansi. "I will have all the common sense in the world, and all the money in the world, too!"

So Anansi got a sack and started collecting common sense. *Brush your teeth to prevent cavities! Put your socks on before your shoes!* Anansi put them all in his sack.

The sack was soon bursting at the seams. "I need to find a better place to keep the common sense," thought Anansi. Just then he spied a calabash growing on a vine. It looked like a giant pumpkin. Anansi hollowed out the calabash. Then he stuffed all of the common sense inside and kept collecting.

When Anansi had gathered up every bit of common sense, he thought, "Now I just have to find a good place to hide it."

Anansi set off through the jungle to find just the right hiding place. He dragged the calabash under ferns and over logs. He waded through streams. He trudged from shrub to bush to hedge. He hiked up muddy trails and slid down steep hillsides. Finally Anansi found the tallest tree in the jungle.

TEACHING READING SOURCEBOOK • COMMON SENSE: AN ANANSI TALE **710**

"This is the perfect hiding place," he said. "The calabash will be safe and sound. No one would ever guess that I have hidden such a valuable treasure in such an unusual place."

Using a thick rope, Anansi tied the heavy calabash around his neck so that it dangled in front of him like a locket on a necklace. He started up the tree trunk, but climbing was hard. The calabash flopped and swayed. It banged Anansi's belly. It bruised his knees and elbows. The rope burned the back of his neck. But even though Anansi was aching and battered, he did not stop. The thought of getting rich kept him going.

As Anansi was struggling upward, he heard someone giggling below him. He looked down and saw a small boy leaning against the tree trunk.

Anansi called down to the boy. "What is so funny?" he asked.

"*You* are," said the boy. "Anyone with a pinch of common sense knows that it is easier to carry things on your back—especially if you are climbing a tree. How foolish can you get?"

The boy's words made Anansi furious! Anansi thought he had collected all the common sense in the world. How could he have missed the one piece he needed most? The thought made Anansi madder and madder. Finally he lost his temper and swung the calabash with all his might against the tree trunk.

The calabash shattered into a million pieces. The common sense spilled out and pieces got caught in a breeze. The breeze blew little pieces of common sense all over the world. And that explains why today everyone has a little bit of common sense to use and a little bit of common sense to share. But, as you yourself know, nobody got all of it. It was Anansi who made it happen that way.

TEACHING READING SOURCEBOOK • COMMON SENSE: AN ANANSI TALE **711**

Glossary: Teachable Words for "Common Sense: An Anansi Tale"

▸ First Read-Aloud: Teachable Title Word

common sense	being able to make good decisions naturally

▸ Second Read-Aloud: Teachable Words

mischief	liking to have fun by playing tricks on people; playful misbehavior
judgment	making a decision after thinking carefully about something
sensible	showing good sense; a sensible person makes good decisions
information	knowing or learning facts about something
imagined (imagine)	to picture something in your mind
simplest (simple)	easy to understand
brilliant	very good, clever, or smart
scheme	a secret and sneaky plan

▸ Third Read-Aloud: Teachable Words

spied (spy)	to notice something
vine	a plant that climbs up or hangs down
stuffed (stuff)	to fill tightly or overfill something
waded (wade)	to walk through water that is not deep
trudged (trudge)	to walk slowly with heavy steps, usually because you are tired
hedge	a row of bushes along the edge of a garden, field, or road
steep	goes up very suddenly
valuable	very useful and important

VISUAL CLUE
Show a picture of a vine.

VISUAL CLUE
Demonstrate trudging.

VISUAL CLUE
Use your hand to show a sudden angle.

▸ Fourth Read-Aloud: Teachable Words

thick	big around and strong
dangled (dangle)	to hang or swing loosely from somewhere
swayed (sway)	to swing slowly from one side to the other
struggling (struggle)	to have a hard time with something; to try very hard to do something
foolish	not showing good common sense
temper	becoming angry very easily; angry feelings
might	power or strength
shattered (shatter)	to break into a lot of small pieces

DAY 1: FIRST READ-ALOUD

Before Reading

FIRST READ-ALOUD

Teachable Title Word

common sense

Introduce the Teachable Title Word

In this sample text "Common Sense: An Anansi Tale," the first teachable word or term, *common sense*, is found in the story title. Briefly introduce the term *common sense* before the first reading because the concept is crucial to overall understanding of the story. Say: *Today we are going to read a story called "Common Sense: An Anansi Tale." Having common sense means that you are able to make good decisions naturally. Making good decisions is not necessarily something you learn in school. For example, it is common sense to turn on a light when it gets too dark to read or to wear a coat when it is cold outside.*

FIRST READ-ALOUD

Comprehension Words

calabash
prank

Introduce the Comprehension Words

Now introduce the comprehension words *calabash* and *prank.* Say: *Knowing the meaning of* calabash *and* prank *will help you to understand the story. A calabash is like a big pumpkin. Some of you may know the Spanish word for* calabash—calabaza. *A prank is a silly trick done mostly for fun, like taping a "kick me" or "feed me" sign onto someone's back.*

To clarify meaning, it is often appropriate to use visual cues such as props, pictures, and pantomimes. For example, show a picture of a calabash.

Read the Story Aloud

Read the whole story aloud without pausing for word-meaning explanations. Students are unlikely to ask for word meanings while a story is being read (Biemiller and Boote 2006).

After Reading

Check Comprehension

Check students' understanding of the story by asking one or two comprehension questions. For example, ask:

- *Do you think Anansi makes good decisions in the story? Why or why not?*
- *If Anansi were a person, how would you describe him?*

The second read-aloud should take place on the same day as the first, either immediately following the first read-aloud or sometime later in the day.

If rereading the story immediately following the first read-aloud, you could briefly summarize the pages or paragraphs that do not have any teachable words in them. In your summary, avoid using any of the forthcoming teachable words.

Review the Teachable Title Word

Review the newly introduced teachable term by repeating its meaning and adding it to a story word list. For example, ask: *Do you remember the word combination* common sense? Print *common sense* on the first line of a story word list. Pointing to the term, ask: *Do you remember that having common sense means that you have a natural ability to make good decisions?* Display the story word list where it is highly visible to all students. Refer to the list whenever possible throughout the week.

DAY 1: SECOND READ-ALOUD

Before Reading

Introduce the Comprehension Words

SECOND READ-ALOUD

Comprehension Words

cavity
hollow out
safe and sound

Introduce the comprehension words *cavities, hollowed out,* and *safe and sound.* Say: *Knowing the meaning of* cavities *or* cavity *and* hollowed out *or* hollow out, *and* safe and sound *will help you to better understand the story. A cavity is a hole in a tooth. When you have a cavity in your tooth, you have to go to the dentist. If you hollow something out, you scoop out the inside part of it—like hollowing out a pumpkin on Halloween. Safe and sound means that something won't be touched, or nothing will happen to it.*

SECOND READ-ALOUD

Teachable Words

mischief
judgment
sensible
information
imagined (imagine)
simplest (simple)
brilliant
scheme

When possible, word-meaning explanations should be for the root words. Once the root words are explained, the derived words can be understood from context.

During Reading

Introduce the Teachable Words

Read the story aloud again. As you read the story, stop to introduce the first eight teachable words (paragraphs 1 and 2). To introduce each word, reread the sentence in which the word appears and then provide a brief student-friendly explanation to give meaning to the word. Try not to give meaning to a word by using an explanation that contains unknown words. Say: *We are going to read the Anansi story again, but this time as I read I am going to stop and explain some words that you might not know.* When you come to the first teachable word, *mischief*, reread the sentence: "*Anansi, the spider, was full of mischief.*" Then say: *Let me tell you that someone who is full of mischief likes to have fun by playing tricks on people. It's like playful misbehavior.* Then continue reading aloud, following the same procedure with the remaining seven words.

After Reading

Check Comprehension

Check students' understanding of the story by asking one or two comprehension questions. For example, ask:

- *Why does Anansi want all the common sense for himself?*
- *Where do we learn common sense?*

Review the Teachable Words

Review the eight newly introduced teachable words by repeating their meanings and adding them to the story word list. For example, ask: *Do you remember the word* mischief*?* On the story word list, print *mischief* below *common sense.* Pointing to *mischief*, ask: *Do you remember that mischief means playful misbehavior—like playing tricks on people?* Follow the same procedure with the remaining seven words. Display the story word list where it is highly visible to all students. Refer to the list whenever possible throughout the week.

DAY 2: THIRD READ-ALOUD

THIRD READ-ALOUD

Comprehension Words

bush
shrub

Before Reading

Introduce the Comprehension Words

Introduce the comprehension words *bush* and *shrub.* Say: *Knowing the meaning of* bush *and* scrub *will help you to better understand the story. A bush is a plant. It's like a very small tree. A shrub is a low bush.*

THIRD READ-ALOUD

Teachable Words

spied (spy)
vine
stuffed (stuff)
waded (wade)
trudged (trudge)
hedge
steep
valuable

During Reading

Introduce the Teachable Words

Read the story aloud again. As you read the story, stop to introduce the next eight teachable words (paragraphs 3 through 7). Say: *We are going to read the Anansi story again, but this time as I read I am going to stop and explain some other words that you might not know. I also want you to listen for the words we talked about yesterday.* When you come to the first new teachable word, *spied,* reread the sentence: *"Just then he spied a calabash growing on a vine."* Then say: *Let me tell you that in this story spied or spy means to notice something.* Then continue reading aloud, following the same procedure with the remaining seven words.

After Reading

Check Comprehension

Check students' understanding of the story by asking one or two comprehension questions. For example, ask:

- *What went wrong with Anansi's plan?*
- *Why do people have only some common sense?*

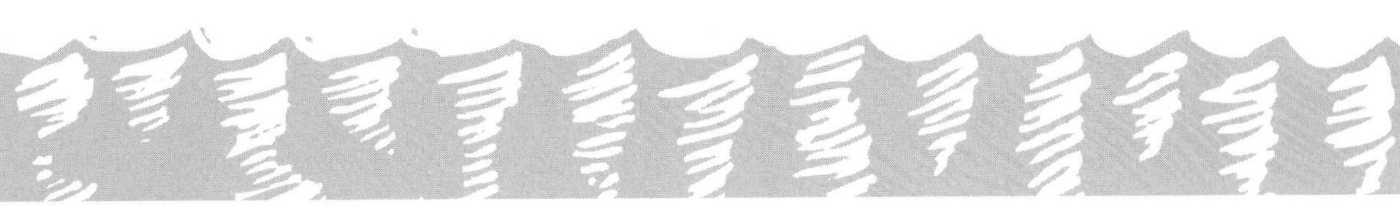

Review the Teachable Words

Review the eight newly introduced teachable words by repeating their meanings and adding them to the story word list. For example, ask: *Do you remember the word* spy*?* On the story word list, print *spy* below *scheme*. Pointing to *spy*, ask: *Do you remember that spy means to notice something?* Follow the same procedure with the remaining seven words. Display the story word list where it is highly visible to all students. Refer to the list whenever possible throughout the week.

DAY 3: FOURTH READ-ALOUD

FOURTH READ-ALOUD

Comprehension Words

locket
pinch

FOURTH READ-ALOUD

Teachable Words

thick
dangled (dangle)
swayed (sway)
struggling (struggle)
foolish
temper
might
shattered (shatter)

Before Reading

Introduce the Comprehension Words

Now introduce the comprehension words *locket* and *pinch*. Say: *Knowing the meaning of* locket *and* pinch *will help you to better understand the story. A locket is a small case that hangs from a necklace. A pinch is a very small amount of something, like salt, that you can hold between your thumb and first finger.*

During Reading

Introduce the Teachable Words

Read the story aloud again. As you read the story, stop to introduce the next eight teachable words (paragraphs 8 through 13). Say: *We are going to read the Anansi story again, but this time as I read I am going to stop and explain some more words that you might not know. I also want you to listen for the words we talked about yesterday.* When you come to the first teachable word, *thick,* reread the sentence: "*Using a thick rope, Anansi tied the heavy calabash around his neck so that it dangled in front of him like a locket on a necklace.*" Then say: *Let me tell you that thick describes something that is big around and strong—like a rope or a tree trunk.* Then continue reading aloud, following the same procedure with the remaining seven words.

After Reading

Check Comprehension

Check students' understanding of the story by asking one or two comprehension questions. For example, ask:

- *Do you think this is a true story? Why or why not?*

TEACHABLE WORDS

English/Spanish Cognates

brilliant • brillante

imagined • imaginó

information • información

spied • espió

False Cognates

scheme • esquema (diagram)

sensible • sensible (sensitive)

Review the Teachable Words

Review the eight newly introduced teachable words by repeating their meanings and adding them to the story word list. For example, ask: *Do you remember the word* thick? On the story word list, print *thick* below *valuable.* Pointing to *thick,* say: *Do you remember that thick describes something that is big around and strong?* Follow the same procedure with the remaining seven words. Display the story word list where it is highly visible to all students. Refer to the list whenever possible throughout the week.

DAY 4: CUMULATIVE REVIEW

On the last day of work with the story, cumulatively review the 25 teachable words using teacher-created, instructional context sentences. This time, have the students give the word meanings. Say: *Today I am not going to read the Anansi story again. Instead we are going to review the words on our story word list. I made up new sentences for the words.* Say each word and then read its new context sentence. For example, say: *Common sense . . . It's common sense to bring a towel to the beach.* Ask students to raise their hand if they know the meaning of *common sense.* Then ask a volunteer to give the meaning of the term. Follow the same procedure with the remaining 24 teachable words.

Keep track of the students who give meanings. Encourage all students to participate in the review.

Cumulative Review: Teachable Words

Word/Term	Teacher-Created Context Sentence
common sense	It's common sense to bring a towel to the beach.
mischief	The children were up to some mischief when they hid their mother's keys.
judgment	Cathy used good judgment when crossing the street.
sensible	Calling the doctor was a sensible thing to do.
information	Andy wrote the information on a piece of paper.
imagine	I can't imagine what life will be like 100 years from now.
simple	My homework was so simple that I did it in five minutes.
brilliant	Whoever thought of computers had a brilliant idea.
scheme	The police found out about the scheme to rob the bank.
spy	They did not spy any land from their spot on the ship.
vine	There is a long, curly vine growing in our backyard.
stuff	We had to stuff everything into our bags for the long trip.
wade	Bill likes to wade in the pond.
trudge	Last winter we had to trudge through deep snow.
hedge	Our neighbors have a hedge around their house.
steep	Those steep stairs are hard to climb.
valuable	The valuable new tool cost lots of money.
thick	The tree trunk was so thick that I couldn't put my arms around it.
dangle	My sisters like to dangle their legs over the edge of the pool.
sway	The branches of trees often sway in the wind.
struggle	Bad weather made it a struggle to get home on time.
foolish	Forgetting my warm jacket was a foolish thing to do.
temper	Jess lost his temper when someone accidentally hit him.
might	Linda tried with all her might but still could not push open the door.
shatter	If you hit the ball into a window, it will shatter the glass.

LESSON MODEL FOR

Contextualized Vocabulary

Benchmark

- ability to develop in-depth knowledge of word meanings

Strategy Grade Level

- Grade 2 and above

Grouping

- whole class
- small group or pairs

Sample Text (Resources)

- "Alaska Adventure" Complexity Level: Grades 4–5

Materials

- copies of "Alaska Adventure"

Method for Independently Read Text

This lesson model is based on research-based methods developed by Isabel Beck and her colleagues as described in *Bringing Words to Life: Robust Vocabulary Instruction* (Beck et al. 2002). Using sample text, this lesson model shows how to develop students' knowledge of four previously selected target words. The same model can be adapted and used to enhance contextualized vocabulary instruction in any commercial reading or content-area program.

Alaska Adventure

Jake Mays and his dad spent two weeks visiting Alaska. They flew to Anchorage and then took a train south to a lodge in Seward, a small harbor town surrounded by the Kenai mountain range. From there they took day trips around the area to see and experience the sights. Jake found it all so enticing that he never wanted to leave.

Every day brought a new adventure. They traveled by ferry and sailboat on the marine highways through straits and inlets. They paddled sea kayaks up narrow fjords lined with ice cliffs. They saw whales, otters, puffins, sea lions, and eagles. They spent a day on a fishing schooner catching salmon for dinner. Jake snapped pictures of every new vista.

"Mom is not going to believe how awesome the scenery is," he said. "Next time, we have to coordinate the schedule so that she can come with

On the flight home, they pored over the map, already plan
return trip. Jake thought it would be exciting to do some backpack
Mount McKinley, the tallest peak in North America.

"Wouldn't it be fun to explore the state's interior? We could
north from Anchorage to visit Denali National Park. I hea
ing is first class, and there is plenty of wildlife to see."

"That's true," said Dad. "Still, it is hard to resist the
the route we just traveled. Now that we're expert kayakers, we should
dle around the capes and coves and lagoons of the Alaska Peninsula."
pointed at the chain of volcanic islands separating the P
Ocean from the Bering Sea. "The Aleutian archipelago
for more than a thousand miles. We could spend a lif
the water just exploring this part of the Ring of Fire."

"Well, that settles it," said Jake. "We just
back and stay longer."

"You've got that right," said Dad.

VOCABULARY HANDBOOK • ALASKA ADVENTURE 201

INDEPENDENTLY READ TEXT

Target Words

vista
coordinate
interior
route

ALASKA

Before Reading the Selection

Before reading the selection, introduce the meanings of the target words, one at a time. Beck et al. (2002) suggest presenting the words "in ways that help them take root in students' vocabularies."

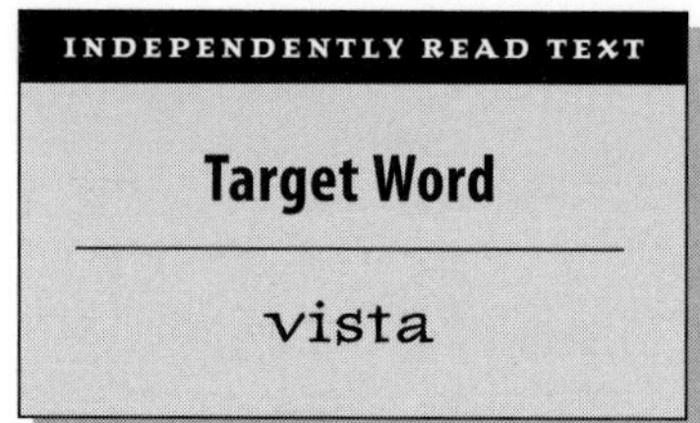

INDEPENDENTLY READ TEXT

Target Word

vista

Point out to Spanish-speaking ELLs that *vista* and *vista* are identically spelled cognates.

SEE ALSO . . .

Cognate Awareness, p. 496

Introduce the Target Word

Read and Pronounce the Word Print the word on the board and have students read and pronounce it. Say: *Let's say the word together: vista.* Ask: *What is the word?* (vista)

Give a Student-Friendly Explanation Explain the word's meaning in everyday language—language that is clear and accessible to students. Say: *A vista is a faraway scenic view, or a beautiful view from a high place.*

Provide a Different Context To ensure a clear, explicit concept of the word, develop a sentence with scaffolded questions. In your example, use the target word in a context that is similar to, but different from, the story context. For example, say: *Jake climbed to the top of a hill and took a picture of the beautiful vista that stretched out as far as he could see.* Then ask: *Why did Jake climb the hill? What could he see when he got to the top? So, what do you think vista means?*

Engage Actively with the Word Provide playful opportunities for students to interact with the word and process its meaning right away. Here are some examples:

QUESTIONS Ask questions that require students to apply the target word's meaning. Ask: *Where might you go to enjoy a scenic vista?*

FINISH THE IDEA Sentence starters require students to use and apply the meaning of a target word in a different context. Tell students that you are going to start a sentence and you want them to think of an ending. Say: *The vista stretched out to the horizon from where we stood on the* ________.

HAVE YOU EVER . . . ? To help students to understand that they have a place for the target word in their vocabularies, have them use the word to describe their own experiences. Ask: *Can you describe the most beautiful vista that you have ever seen? Where were you?*

INDEPENDENTLY READ TEXT

Target Word

coordinate

Introduce the Target Word

Read and Pronounce the Word Print the word on the board and have students read and pronounce it. Say: *Let's say the word together: coordinate.* Ask: *What is the word?* (coordinate)

Give a Student-Friendly Explanation Explain the word's meaning in everyday language—language that is clear and accessible to students. Say: *When you coordinate a plan, you match it up with someone else's.*

Point out to Spanish-speaking ELLs that *coordinate* and *coordinar* are cognates.

Provide a Different Context To ensure a clear, explicit concept of the word, develop a sentence with scaffolded questions. In your example, use the target word in a context that is similar to, but different from, the story context. For example, say: *Mom had to coordinate her work schedule to match Jake's school schedule so that she could get time off to travel to Alaska with him.* Then ask: *What did Mom want to do? What did she have to do to get time off? So, what do you think coordinate means?*

Engage Actively with the Word Provide playful opportunities for students to interact with the word and process its meaning right away. Here are some examples:

QUESTIONS Ask questions that require students to apply the target word's meaning. Ask: *How might you coordinate plans to visit a friend?*

FINISH THE IDEA Sentence starters require students to use and apply the meaning of a target word in a different context. Tell students that you are going to start a sentence and you want them to think of an ending. Say: *My sister and I tried to coordinate our after-school schedules because* ________.

HAVE YOU EVER . . . ? To help students to understand that they have a place for the target word in their vocabularies, have them use the word to describe their own experiences. Ask: *Can you describe a time when you should have, but did not, coordinate plans with someone? What happened?*

INDEPENDENTLY READ TEXT

Target Word

interior

Point out to Spanish-speaking ELLs that *interior* and *interior* are identically spelled cognates.

Introduce the Target Word

Read and Pronounce the Word Print the word on the board and have students read and pronounce it. Say: *Let's say the word together: interior.* Ask: *What is the word?* (interior)

Give a Student-Friendly Explanation Explain the word's meaning in everyday language—language that is clear and accessible to students. Say: *The interior of a state is the central area—the area that is away from the coast, state line, or border.*

Provide a Different Context To ensure a clear, explicit concept of the word, develop a sentence with scaffolded questions. In your example, use the target word in a context that is similar to, but different from, the story context. For example, say: *Jake wanted to travel inland to explore the interior of the state.* Then ask: *What did Jake want to explore? Where did he have to travel to do it? So, what do you think interior means?*

Engage Actively with the Word Provide playful opportunities for students to interact with the word and process its meaning right away. Here are some examples:

QUESTIONS Ask questions that require students to apply the target word's meaning. Ask: *Jake thought it would be fun to explore the interior of Alaska. Why might you want to spend time in the interior of your state?*

FINISH THE IDEA Sentence starters require students to use and apply the meaning of a target word in a different context. Tell students that you are going to start a sentence and you want them to think of an ending. Say: *After a trip to the coast, we headed to the interior of the country because* ______.

HAVE YOU EVER . . . ? To help students to understand that they have a place for the target word in their vocabularies, have them use the word to describe their own experiences. Ask: *Can you describe a place that you know about that is located in the interior of your state?*

INDEPENDENTLY READ TEXT

Target Word

route

Introduce the Target Word

Read and Pronounce the Word Print the word on the board and have students read and pronounce it. Say: *Let's say the word together: route.* Ask: *What is the word?* (route)

Give a Student-Friendly Explanation Explain the word's meaning in everyday language—language that is clear and accessible to students. Say: *A route is the way you travel to get from one place to another.*

Point out to Spanish-speaking ELLs that *route* and *ruta* are cognates.

Provide a Different Context To ensure a clear, explicit concept of the word, develop a sentence with scaffolded questions. In your example, use the target word in a context that is similar to, but different from, the story context. For example, say: *Dad looked at a map and found the best route to take around the Alaska Peninsula.* Then ask: *What kinds of things are shown on a map? What did Dad use the map for? So, what do you think route means?*

Engage Actively with the Word Provide playful opportunities for students to interact with the word and process its meaning right away. Here are some examples:

QUESTIONS Ask questions that require students to apply the target word's meaning. Ask: *Why might you take a different route to school?*

FINISH THE IDEA Sentence starters require students to use and apply the meaning of a target word in a different context. Tell students that you are going to start a sentence and you want them to think of an ending. Say: *We got lost when Dad took a new route from* _______.

HAVE YOU EVER . . . ? To help students to understand that they have a place for the target word in their vocabularies, have them use the word to describe their own experiences. Ask: *Can you describe the route that you usually take from home to school?*

Read the Selection

Provide copies of the selection "Alaska Adventure." Have students read the text independently, silently or aloud. When text is read aloud in class, stop and give a quick explanation of any target word that is likely to affect comprehension of the selection.

After Reading the Selection

Provide instructional activities that get students actively involved in using and thinking about word meanings.

INDEPENDENTLY READ TEXT

Target Words

vista
coordinate
interior
route

Develop In-Depth Knowledge of the Target Words

DISCUSSION PROMPTS Use story context as a basis for discussing word meanings with students. For example:

- Jake snapped pictures of every new *vista.* What kinds of things would you see in his photo album?
- What do Mom and Dad have to do to *coordinate* their work schedule and Jake's school schedule?
- What kinds of experiences might Jake have when he visits the *interior* of Alaska?
- Dad wants to retrace the *route* that he and Jake have already taken. Jake wants to see something new. Which route would you take if you had the choice?

Develop In-Depth Knowledge

EXAMPLES OR NONEXAMPLES Have students differentiate between two descriptions; one is an example of the target word, the other is a nonexample. Here are some models:

- If you think a sentence describes a vista, say "vista."

✓ From our campsite, we could see snow-covered mountains.
From our campsite, we could see the snack bar.

- If you think a sentence is an example of coordinate, say "coordinate."

✓ My team is going to meet at the park at exactly six o'clock.
No one told me where or when our team is going to meet.

- If you think a sentence tells about Oregon's interior, say "interior."

✓ On their vacation, the family visited a lake in central Oregon.
On their vacation, the family visited the coast of Oregon.

- If you think a sentence describes a route, say "route."

✓ Turn left where you see the big white house with the red barn.
We live next door to the big white house with the red barn.

JUXTAPOSITIONS Challenge students to answer a yes or no question containing two juxtaposed target words. For example:

- Could you *coordinate* plans to meet along a *route*? (yes)
- Could you find a beautiful *vista* in the *interior* of a state? (yes)

CHOICES Making choices enables students to apply the meaning of a target word. Tell students that you are going to name situations, and if a situation is an example of a vista, they should say "Wow!" If it isn't, they shouldn't say anything. For example:

- *Looking at a faraway view of a mountain peak* ("Wow!")
- *Looking at yourself in the mirror* (no response)
- *Looking at a bug through a magnifying glass* (no response)
- *Looking at the city from the top of a skyscraper* ("Wow!")

ELL Alaska Adventure

English/Spanish Cognates

adventure • aventura

archipelago • archipiélago

area • área

coordinate • coordinar

expert • experto

explore • explorar

interior • interior

islands • islas

lagoon • laguna

map • mapa

marine • marino

mountain • montaña

National Park • Parque Nacional

North America • Norteamérica

peninsula • peninsula

route • ruta

salmon • salmón

train • tren

visit • visitar

vista • vista

volcanic • volcánico

False Cognates

come • come (eats)

miles • miles (thousands)

MISSING WORDS As a group, read and discuss cloze sentences and agree on how to complete each one. For example:

- We set up a tripod so that we could photograph the ______ from the top of the hill. (vista)
- It took five phone calls for Mom to ______ the surprise party for Grandpa. (coordinate)
- You can explore the ______ by boat if you travel up the river. (interior)
- Make a map of the ______ we should take to bike from your house to the pool. (route)

TRUE/FALSE Provide 90 seconds for students to respond to true-false statements. For example:

- A vista gives you an up-close view. True or false? (false)
- It is hard to make plans unless you coordinate your schedule. True or false? (true)
- The interior of the country is close to the beach. True or false? (false)
- You can take more than one route to get from place to place. True or false? (true)

WORD ASSOCIATIONS After discussing the meanings of the target words, ask students to associate one of the words with a sentence or phrase. For example:

- Which word goes with a scenic view? (vista)
- Which word goes with a plan to meet Mom at the bus stop? (coordinate)
- Which word goes with central Montana? (interior)
- Which word goes with Highway 1 from Mexico to Canada? (route)

Assess Word Knowledge

Assess students' knowledge of the target words by giving them a multiple-choice quiz at the end of the week. Here is an example:

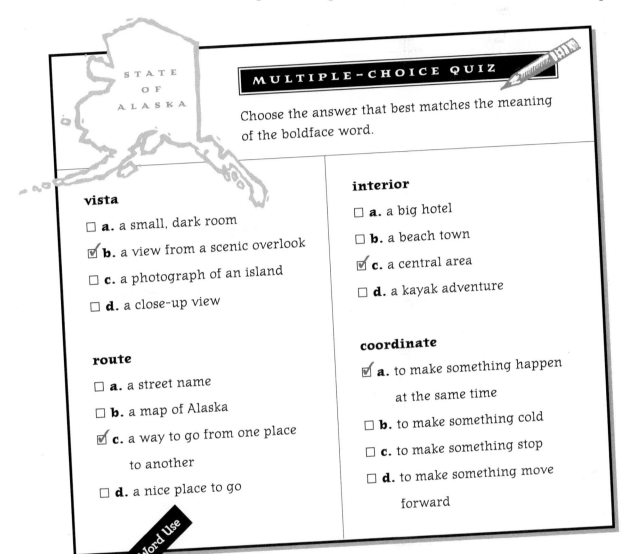

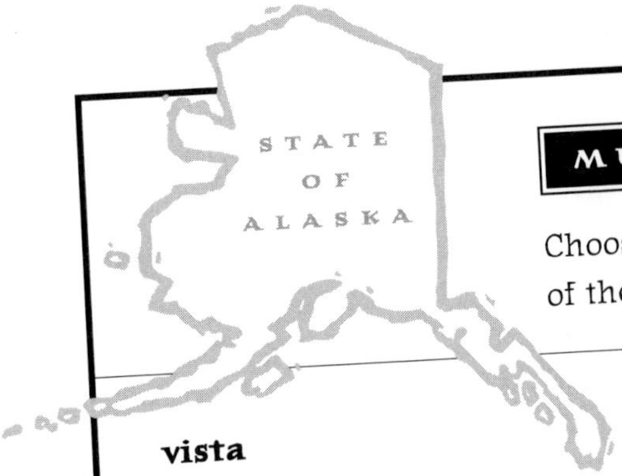

MULTIPLE-CHOICE QUIZ

Choose the answer that best matches the meaning of the boldface word.

vista

- ☐ **a.** a small, dark room
- ☑ **b.** a view from a scenic overlook
- ☐ **c.** a photograph of an island
- ☐ **d.** a close-up view

route

- ☐ **a.** a street name
- ☐ **b.** a map of Alaska
- ☑ **c.** a way to go from one place to another
- ☐ **d.** a nice place to go

interior

- ☐ **a.** a big hotel
- ☐ **b.** a beach town
- ☑ **c.** a central area
- ☐ **d.** a kayak adventure

coordinate

- ☑ **a.** to make something happen at the same time
- ☐ **b.** to make something cold
- ☐ **c.** to make something stop
- ☐ **d.** to make something move forward

Extend Word Use

LESSON MODEL: Vocabulary Hotshot Notebook, p. 601

Extend Word Use Beyond the Classroom

Developing an in-depth, "rich," and permanent understanding of new vocabulary comes through multiple exposures in more than one context. There are many ways to keep students thinking about and using target words beyond the classroom. One of these methods is the Vocabulary Hotshot Notebook, which is described in Chapter 3: Word Consciousness.

LESSON MODEL FOR

Basic Vocabulary

Benchmark

- ability to discriminate the meanings of the prepositions *on* and *under*

Strategy Grade Level

- Pre-K and above, as required

Prerequisite

- mastery of the words *book, desk, chair, pencil, fly, table*

Grouping

- whole class
- small group or pairs

Teaching Chart (Resources)

- Where Is the Fly?

Materials

- props: book, desk, chair, pencil
- PDF of Where Is the Fly?

FUNCTION WORDS

Target Word

on

Introducing Function Words

Function words alert a reader or speaker to the structure of the sentence; they are words that have syntactic function. Function words include articles (*a, an, the*), conjunctions (*and, but, or*), helping verbs (*been, should, will*), prepositions (*in, on, over*), and pronouns (*he, she, we*). Most English-only students learn function words in the first stages of language development (Stahl and Nagy 2000). ELLs, however, may be confused about function-word usage and meaning, and can benefit from explicit instruction (Anderson and Roit 1998). This sample lesson model targets the prepositions *on* and *under.* The same model can be adapted and used for introducing other function words.

Teach/Model

Tell students that they are going to learn a new word that they use often when they speak, read, and write. The word is *on.*

Introduce the Target Word

- Hold up a book. Ask: *What is this?* (a book)
- Point to a desk. Ask: *What is this?* (a desk)
- Put the book on the desk. Emphasizing the word *on,* say: *The book is* on *the desk.*
- Put the book on the floor under the desk. Say: *Is the book on the desk? No.*
- Hold the book under the desk. Say: *Is the book on the desk? No.*
- Put the book on the desk. Say: *Is the book on the desk? Yes, the book is on the desk.*
- Hold the book above the desk. Say: *Is the book on the desk? No.*
- Put the book on the desk. Say: *Is the book on the desk? Yes, the book is on the desk.*

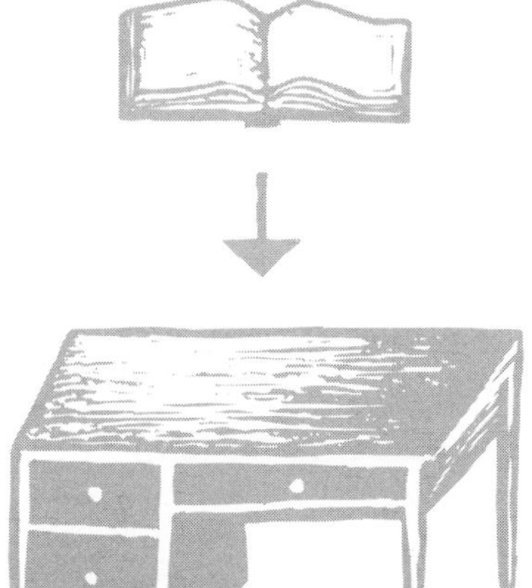

Guided Practice

- Put the book on the desk. Ask: *Is the book on the desk?* (yes)
- Put the book on the floor under the desk. Ask: *Is the book on the desk?* (no)
- Hold the book under the desk. Ask: *Is the book on the desk?* (no)
- Hold the book above the desk. Ask: *Is the book on the desk?* (no)
- Again put the book on the desk. Ask: *Is the book on the desk?* (yes)
- Say: *Say the whole sentence with me. The book is on the desk.*
- Say: *Now repeat the whole sentence by yourselves.* (The book is on the desk.)
- Point to the chair. Ask: *What is this?* (a chair)
- Hold up a pencil. Ask: *What is this?* (a pencil)

- Now put the pencil on the seat of the chair. Ask: *Is the pencil on the chair?* (yes)
- Put the pencil on the floor under the chair. Ask: *Is the pencil on the chair?* (no)
- Hold the pencil under the chair. Ask: *Is the pencil on the chair?* (no)
- Hold the pencil above the chair. Ask: *Is the pencil on the chair?* (no)
- Again put the pencil on the seat of the chair. Ask: *Is the pencil on the chair?* (yes)
- Say: *Say the whole sentence with me. The pencil is on the chair.*
- Say: *Now repeat the whole sentence by yourselves.* (The pencil is on the chair.)

CONTINUED ▷

Teach/Model

Tell students that they are going to learn a new word that they use often when they speak, read, and write. The word is *under.*

FUNCTION WORDS

Target Word

under

Introduce the Target Word

- Hold up a book. Ask: *What is this?* (a book)
- Point to a desk. Ask: *What is this?* (a desk)
- Put the book on the floor under the desk. Emphasizing the word *under,* say: *The book is* under *the desk.*
- Put the book on the desk. Say: *The book is on the desk.*
- Hold the book under the desk. Say: *The book is under the desk.*
- Put the pencil under the chair. Say: *The pencil is under the chair.*
- Put the pencil on the chair. Say: *The pencil is on the chair.*

Guided Practice

- Put the book under the desk. Ask: *Is the book under the desk?* (yes)
- Put the book on the desk. Ask: *Is the book under the desk?* (no)
- Put the book under the desk. Ask: *Is the book under the desk?* (yes)
- Say: *Say the whole sentence with me. The book is under the desk.*
- Say: *Now repeat the whole sentence by yourselves.* (The book is under the desk.)
- Put the pencil on the chair. Ask: *Is the pencil under the chair?* (no)
- Put the pencil under the chair. Ask: *Is the pencil under the chair?* (yes)
- Say: *Say the whole sentence with me. The pencil is under the chair.*
- Say: *Now repeat the whole sentence by yourselves.* (The pencil is under the chair.)

Guided Mixed Practice

Tell students that now they will practice using the words *on* and *under.*

FUNCTION WORDS

Target Words

on
under

Practice Using the Target Words—Set 1

- Put the book on the desk. Ask: *Is the book on the desk?* (yes) Say: *Now say the whole sentence.* (The book is on the desk.)
- Put the book under the desk. Ask: *Is the book on the desk?* (no) Ask: *Where is the book?* (The book is under the desk.)
- Again put the book on the desk. Ask: *Where is the book?* (on the desk) Say: *Now say the whole sentence.* (The book is on the desk.)
- Again put the book under the desk. Ask: *Where is the book now?* (under the desk) Say: *Now say the whole sentence.* (The book is under the desk.)
- Put the pencil on the seat of the chair. Ask: *Is the pencil on the chair?* (yes) Say: *Now say the whole sentence.* (The pencil is on the chair.)
- Put the pencil under the chair. Ask: *Is the pencil on the chair?* (no) Ask: *Where is the pencil?* (The pencil is under the chair.)
- Again put the pencil on the seat of the chair. Ask: *Where is the pencil?* (on the chair) Say: *Now say the whole sentence.* (The pencil is on the chair.)
- Again put the pencil under the chair. Ask: *Where is the pencil now?* (under the chair) Say: *Now say the whole sentence.* (The pencil is under the chair.)

CONTINUED ▷

FUNCTION WORDS

Target Words

on

under

SEE ALSO . . .

Chapter 7: Irregular Word Reading

Practice Using the Target Words—Set 2

Use interactive whiteboard technology to display Where Is the Fly?

- Say: *Look at the picture of flies and a table.*
- Point to a fly. Ask: *What is this?* (a fly)
- Point to the table. Ask: *What is this?* (a table)
- Say: *One of the flies is on the table.*
- Point to each fly and ask: *Is this fly on the table?* (Students answer yes or no.)
- Point to the fly that is on the table. Ask: *Where is this fly?* (on the table) Say: *Now say the whole sentence.* (The fly is on the table.)
- Say: *One of the flies is under the table.*
- Point to each fly and ask: *Is this fly under the table?* (Students answer yes or no.)
- Point to the fly that is under the table. Ask: *Where is this fly?* (under the table) Say: *Now say the whole sentence.* (The fly is under the table.)

Independent Practice

Using the models described above, have pairs of students practice identifying whether a book or pencil is on or under a classroom desk, table, or chair. The partners should take turns being "teacher" and "student."

LESSON MODEL FOR

Word Relationships

Benchmarks

- ability to classify grade-appropriate categories of words
- ability to identify and sort common words from within basic categories

Strategy Grade Level

- Kindergarten – Grade 1

Grouping

- whole class
- small group or pairs

Read-Aloud Text

- "A Lost Button" from *Frog and Toad Are Friends* (1970) by Arnold Lobel. New York: Scholastic.

Materials

- pictures of living and nonliving things
- old magazines
- scissors

Concept Picture Sort

Concept picture sorts provide primary students with an opportunity to classify and categorize, adding new information to their existing store of word knowledge. Providing a common frame of reference, read-alouds make great beginnings for concept sorts. This sample lesson model focuses on the differences between living and nonliving things. The same model can be adapted and used to enhance contextualized vocabulary instruction in any commercial reading or content-area program.

Prep Time

Divide a bulletin board into two sections.

Read the Story

Read aloud to students "A Lost Button" from *Frog and Toad Are Friends.* In the story, Toad loses a button and he and Frog, with the help of a sparrow and a raccoon, retrace their steps to try to find it.

Teach/Model

After reading the story, show a picture of Frog. Say: *Frog is a living thing because he grows and changes.* Post the picture of Frog in the left section of the bulletin board. Show a picture of Toad. Ask: *Is Toad a living thing or not a living thing?* (a living thing) Say: *That's right. Toad is a living thing because he grows and changes. I will post the picture of Toad near the picture of Frog. Frog and Toad are living things; they grow and change.* Show a picture of a button. Say: *A button is not a living thing because it does not grow or change.* Post the picture of the button in the right section of the bulletin board. Show a picture of a chair. Ask: *Is a chair a living thing or not a living thing?* (not

a living thing) Say: *That's right. A chair is not a living thing because it does not grow or change. I will post the picture of the chair near the picture of the button. A button and a chair are not living things; they do not grow or change.*

Guided Practice

Ask: *What are some other living things in the story?* (raccoon, sparrow, cattail, grass, tree) Show pictures of the other living things from the story and have students identify them. Ask: *What are some other not living things in the story?* (table, basket, spool, pincushion, needle) Show pictures of the other not living things from the story and have students identify them. Mix up the pictures. Then, using the following procedure, call on volunteers to add the pictures to the bulletin board in the appropriate category. For example, ask: *Is a table a living thing or not a living thing?* (not a living thing) *How do you know?* (It doesn't

Living Things
cattail
Frog
grass
raccoon
sparrow
Toad
tree

Not Living Things
basket
button
chair
needle
pincushion
spool
table

grow or change.) *Are you going to put the picture of the table under Frog or under the button?* (under the button) Say: *That's right. A table is not a living thing so it goes with the button.* Continue until all pictures have been sorted under the appropriate category.

Independent Practice

Distribute copies of old magazines and ask students to cut out pictures of two living things and two not living things. After students have had time to cut out the four pictures, ask them to put their pictures into two piles. In one pile, they put living things, such as frogs. In the other pile, they put not living things, such as buttons. Then call on volunteers to add their cutouts to the bulletin board. One volunteer at a time, for each picture, ask: *What is your picture? Is it a living thing or not a living thing? Does it belong with Frog or with the button?* When students have identified and matched the category, they add the picture to the bulletin board.

Extend Word Knowledge

Have students sort things within a category. For example, they can sort living things into categories of plants and animals. Explain that the group of living things has both plants and animals. Point out that animals are living things that can move from place to place and plants are living things that can't move.

Say: *I am going to name some living things that are posted on the bulletin board. If I name an animal, say "living animal." If I name a plant, say "living plant." Look at the picture of Frog. Frog can move. Is Frog a plant or an animal?* (animal) *That's right. Frog can jump. Look at the picture of a tree. A tree cannot move. Is a tree a plant or an animal?* (plant) *That's right. A tree stands still.* Continue by discussing the other pictures in the living category. As the categories are identified, move the pictures so that the plants and animals are grouped together.

LESSON MODEL FOR

Word Relationships

Benchmarks

- ability to classify words related to a specific concept
- ability to understand and use vocabulary related to specific content

Strategy Grade Level

- Grade 2 and above

Grouping

- whole class
- small group or pairs

Sample Text (Resources)

- "Alaska Adventure" Complexity Level: Grades 4–5

Materials

- Vocabulary Hotshot Notebooks

Point out to Spanish-speaking ELLs that *geography* and *geografía* are cognates.

Semantic Map

Word knowledge exists not as a list of discrete items but as networks of words clustered into categories (Beck et al. 2002). Semantic mapping, an activity for building connections between groups of semantically connected words, is highly flexible and adaptable to a number of different contexts. In semantic mapping, one concept or word is tied graphically to other related words. This sample lesson model focuses on vocabulary related to the study of geography. The same model can be adapted and used to enhance contextualized vocabulary instruction in any commercial reading or content-area program.

Introduce the Concept

Print the word *Geography* on the board and read it aloud. Tell students that the word *geography* comes from the Greek word *geographia,* which means "earth description." Remind them that geography is the study of the physical features of the earth's surface, such as mountains and rivers.

Brainstorm

Ask students to brainstorm a list of words related to the study of geography. As students brainstorm, list their suggestions on the board. For example, they might suggest terms such as *mountain, ocean, river, island,* or *volcano.* Then add words to the list from the sample text "Alaska Adventure," such as *strait, inlet, fjord, peninsula, peak,* and *archipelago.* If necessary, provide student-friendly explanations, such as the following:

- A *strait* is a narrow strip of water that joins two large bodies of water.
- An *inlet* is a narrow strip of water which goes from the ocean into the land.
- A *fjord* is an inlet with steep cliffs.

- A *peninsula* is a piece of land that sticks out and is almost completely surrounded by water.
- A *peak* is a mountain, or the top of a mountain.
- An *archipelago* is a group of many islands.

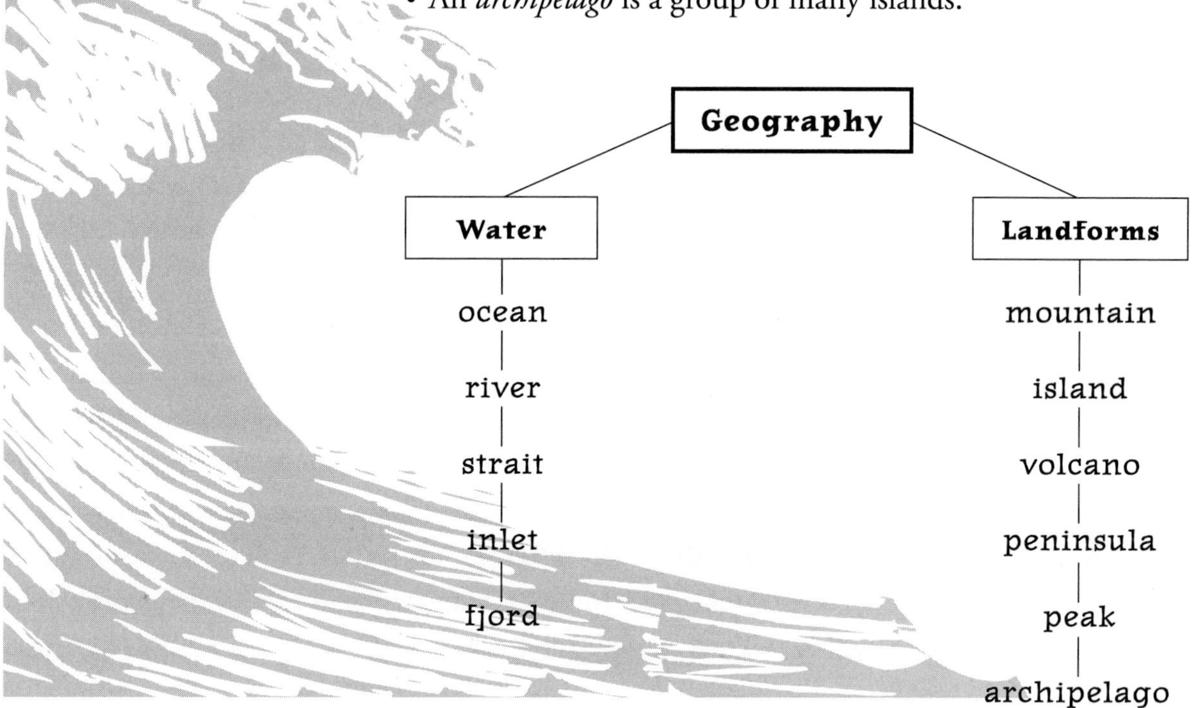

Make the Semantic Map

Tell students that making a semantic map can help them to understand relationships between words. Then have them use the brainstormed list of words to develop a map about geography. Tell students to look at the list of words. Say: *Let's group these words into categories. What do* ocean *and* river *have in common?* (They have to do with water.) Print the word *Water* on the board and draw a line connecting it to the word *Geography.* Next, ask students what other words they could add to this category. (Possible answers: *ocean, river, strait, inlet, fjord*) Add the words to the map. Say: *Can you group the remaining words into a category? What do* island *and* mountain *have in common?* (They are both landforms.) Print the word *Landforms* on the board and draw a line connecting it to the word *Geography.* Next, ask students what other words they could add to this category. (Possible answers: *mountain, island, volcano, peninsula, peak, archipelago*) Add the words to the map.

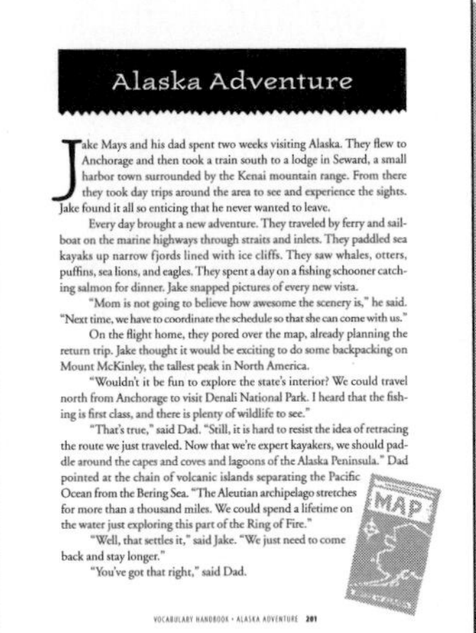

Alaska Adventure

Jake Mays and his dad spent two weeks visiting Alaska. They flew to Anchorage and then took a train south to a lodge in Seward, a small harbor town surrounded by the Kenai mountain range. From there they took day trips around the area to see and experience the sights. Jake found it all so enticing that he never wanted to leave.

Every day brought a new adventure. They traveled by ferry and sailboat on the marine highways through straits and inlets. They paddled sea kayaks up narrow fjords lined with ice cliffs. They saw whales, otters, puffins, sea lions, and eagles. They spent a day on a fishing schooner catching salmon for dinner. Jake snapped pictures of every new vista.

"Mom is not going to believe how awesome the scenery is," he said. "Next time, we have to coordinate the schedule so that she can come with us."

On the flight home, they pored over the map, already planning the return trip. Jake thought it would be exciting to do some backpacking on Mount McKinley, the tallest peak in North America.

"Wouldn't it be fun to explore the state's interior? We could travel north from Anchorage to visit Denali National Park. I heard that the fishing is first class, and there is plenty of wildlife to see."

"That's true," said Dad. "Still, it is hard to resist the idea of retracing the route we just traveled. Now that we're expert kayakers, we should paddle around the capes and coves and lagoons of the Alaska Peninsula." Dad pointed at the chain of volcanic islands separating the Pacific Ocean from the Bering Sea. "The Aleutian archipelago stretches for more than a thousand miles. We could spend a lifetime on the water just exploring this part of the Ring of Fire."

"Well, that settles it," said Jake. "We just need to come back and stay longer."

"You've got that right," said Dad.

VOCABULARY HANDBOOK • ALASKA ADVENTURE 201

Read the Selection

After completing the preliminary semantic map, have students read the sample text "Alaska Adventure." Students might read independently, read with a partner, or read the text aloud as a group.

Discuss the Selection and Revise the Map

After reading, ask students if there are any geography terms from the selection that could be added to the map. For example, students might suggest adding *lagoon, cove,* and *cape.* Explain the meaning of each term. Say: *A* lagoon *is a body of shallow water that is separated from the ocean by sand or rock.* Ask: *Where does* lagoon *go on the map?* (under *Water*) Add *lagoon* to the map. Say: *A* cove *is a small bay on the coast.* Ask: *Where does* cove *go on the map?* (under *Water*) Add *cove* to the map. Say: *A* cape *is a piece of land that sticks out into the ocean.* Ask: *Where does* cape *go on the map?* (under *Landforms*) Add *cape* to the map.

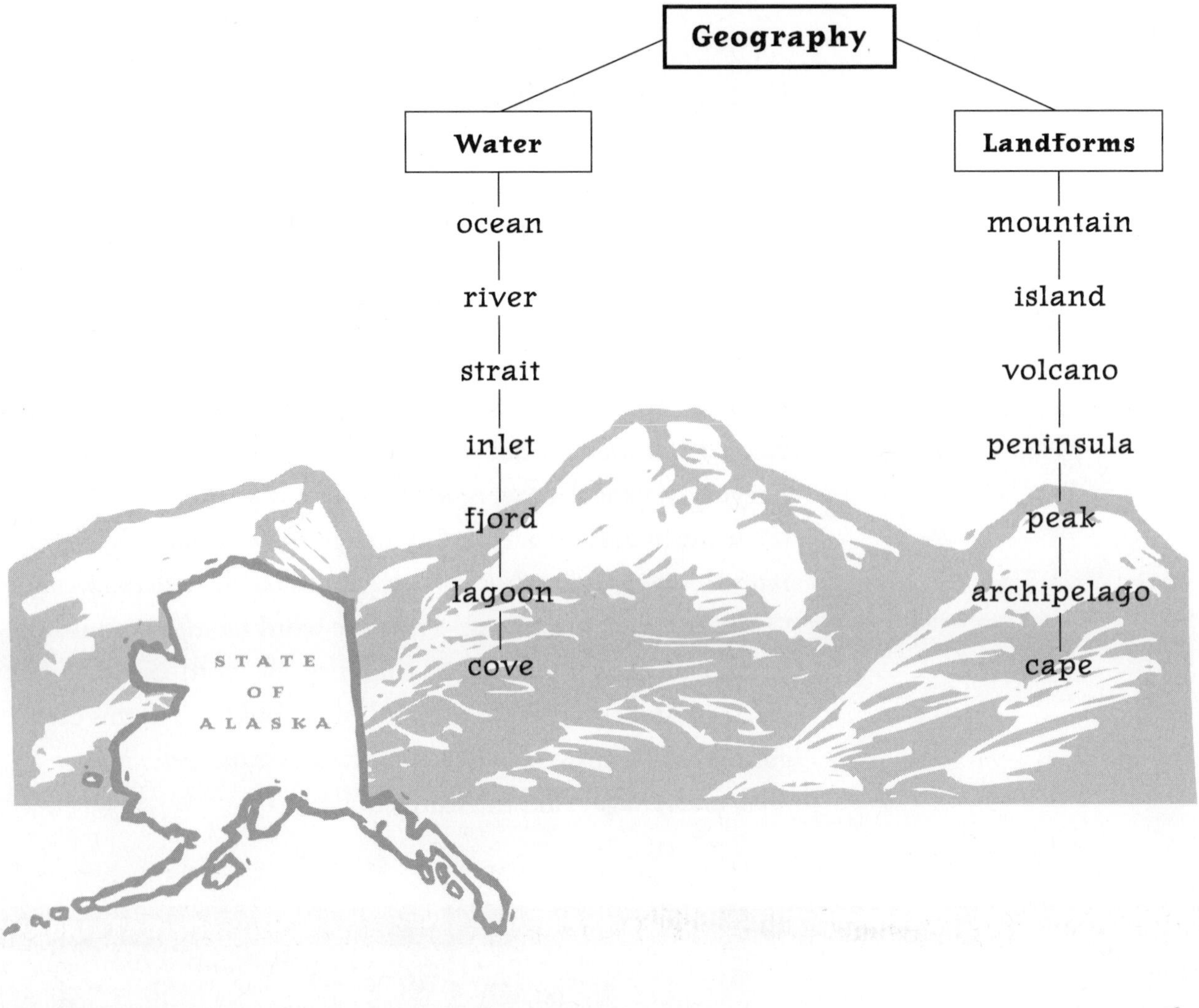

Geography

Water	**Landforms**
ocean	mountain
river	island
strait	volcano
inlet	peninsula
fjord	peak
lagoon	archipelago
cove	cape

STATE OF ALASKA

English/Spanish Cognates

archipelago • archipiélago
fjord • fiordo
island • isla
lagoon • laguna
mountain • montaña
ocean • océano
peak • pico
peninsula • península
strait • estrecho
volcano • volcán

Active Engagement

Engagement and discussion seem to be crucial to the effectiveness of semantic mapping (Stahl and Clark 1987). Provide situations in which students can interact with and discuss the words on the map. Here are some models:

Using the words on the map, have students respond to questions such as the following:

- If you wanted to tie up your boat for the night, would you look for a *strait* or a *cove*?
- If you wanted to go camping, would you pitch your tent in an *inlet* or on an *island*?
- If you wanted to go fishing, would you look for a *lagoon* or a *peninsula*?

Using the words on the map, have students respond to questions such as the following:

- How are a *cape* and a *peninsula* the same? How are they different?
- How are an *inlet* and a *fjord* the same? How are they different?
- Can an *island* have a *cape*? (Yes. A cape is a point of land.)
- Can a *peninsula* have a *lagoon*? (Yes. A peninsula is almost surrounded by water; part of the water could be separated by a ridge of rocks or sand to make a shallow pool.)
- What is the difference between a *peak* and a *volcano*? (A peak is the top of a mountain; a volcano is a peak that erupts.)

Have students use the words in the map to make up their own comparisons.

- Would you rather drive a car on a _______ or a _______?
- Would you use a boat to cross a _______ or a _______?
- If you wanted to enjoy the view, would you climb a _______ or a _______?

SEE ALSO . . .

LESSON MODEL: Vocabulary Hotshot Notebook, p. 601

LESSON MODEL FOR

Word Relationships

Benchmarks

- ability to categorize words
- ability to compare and contrast features of related words

Strategy Grade Level

- Grade 3 and above

Grouping

- whole class
- small group or pairs

Sample Text (Resources)

- "Alaska Adventure" Complexity Level: Grades 4–5

Materials

- dictionaries
- Vocabulary Hotshot Notebooks

Semantic Feature Analysis

Using a grid rather than a map format, semantic feature analysis is a systematic strategy for exploring and reinforcing vocabulary concepts through use of categorization. Helping students to understand the similarities and differences in related words, this strategy can be used before reading to develop vocabulary before or after reading to reinforce vocabulary (Readence 2004). This sample lesson model focuses on analyzing the category of boats. The same model can be adapted and used to enhance contextualized vocabulary instruction in any commercial reading or content-area program.

Select a Category

Select a category to be analyzed. For example, select the category of boats, which is tied to vocabulary in "Alaska Adventure." Tell students that they are going to construct a vocabulary grid that will help them learn the relationships between and among types of boats. On the board, begin a simple grid. Label the grid "Boats."

Add the Category Types

Encourage students to discuss what they know about boats. This may include the boats named in a reading selection such as the sample text "Alaska Adventure," their own boating experiences, or what they have seen on television or in the movies. It may be helpful to show photographs or illustrations of these types of boats. Then, with students' help, print the names of types of boats in the first column of the grid. For example: *ferry, sailboat, kayak, rowboat,* and *cruise ship.*

Add Features

With students' help, decide what features, or characteristics, of boats are to be explored. Start with only a few features and build on them later in the lesson. For this example, features to be examined are whether the boat uses oars, has a motor, has sails, or has an anchor. Across the top row of the grid, print features of boats.

BOATS	oars	motor	sails	anchor
ferry				
sailboat				
kayak				
rowboat				
cruise ship				

Show Feature Possession

Model how the grid can be used to show the features of each type of boat. Say: *If the boat has the feature, I'll write a plus sign. If it does not, I'll write a minus sign. For example, a ferry does not have oars and sails, but it does have a motor and an anchor.* Write a minus sign (–) under oars and sails and a plus sign (+) under motor and anchor. Continue by discussing the features of each boat, marking and discussing the grid as the students respond. Note that feature possession should reflect typical patterns. For example, a small sailboat does not have a motor, but larger sailboats usually do.

BOATS	oars	motor	sails	anchor
ferry	–	+	–	+
sailboat	–	+	+	+
kayak	+	–	–	–
rowboat	+	–	–	+
cruise ship	–	+	–	+

English/Spanish

+ plus sign • signo más

– minus sign • signo menos

Expand the Grid

Tell students that they are going to help you to expand the grid by adding more types and features. Then guide them in generating names for other types of boats as you add their suggestions to the grid. In our example, students suggest *schooner, tugboat,* and *canoe.* Next guide students in adding some new features, or characteristics, of boats to be analyzed. In our example, students suggest whether a boat has a mast or requires a crew. Help students to complete the grid by analyzing and then marking feature possession of the new types and features.

BOATS	oars	motor	sails	anchor	mast	crew
ferry	–	+	–	+	–	+
sailboat	–	+	+	+	+	+
kayak	+	–	–	–	–	–
rowboat	+	–	–	+	–	–
cruise ship	–	+	–	+	–	+
schooner	–	+	+	+	+	+
tugboat	–	+	–	+	–	+
canoe	+	–	–	–	–	–

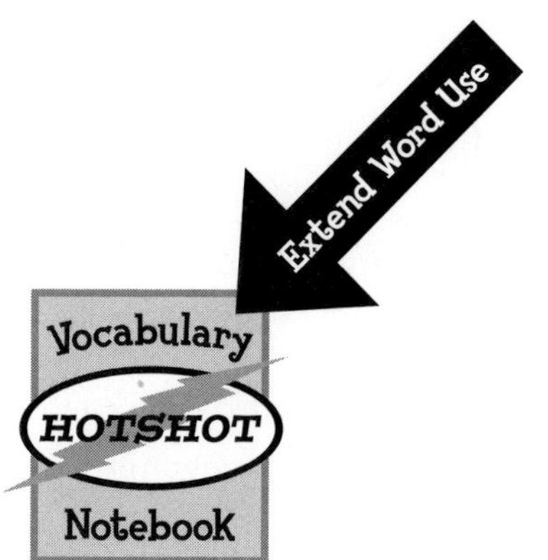

SEE ALSO . . .

LESSON MODEL: Vocabulary Hotshot Notebook, p. 601

Discuss and Explore the Grid

Discussion seems to be the key to this activity since there are many ambiguities, and discussion of these ambiguities seems to clarify the category, topic, or concept being analyzed (Stahl 1999). Exploring the feature grid is most effective when the students, rather than the teacher, make observations, point out connections, and note similarities and differences. In this final step, have students use the grid to compare and contrast types of boats by examining and discussing how they are related and yet unique. For instance, even though a kayak and a canoe are different, they share similar features. Schooners and sailboats are alike in that they both have masts, but a schooner has at least two masts while a sailboat has one.

Further exploration and expansion of the grid may continue, either independently or as a group, particularly as more distinct and discrete features of boats are identified in discussion. Students may also wish to research the category in order to identify specific types of boats, such as skiff or sloop, and explore distinct features, such as rigging and appointments.

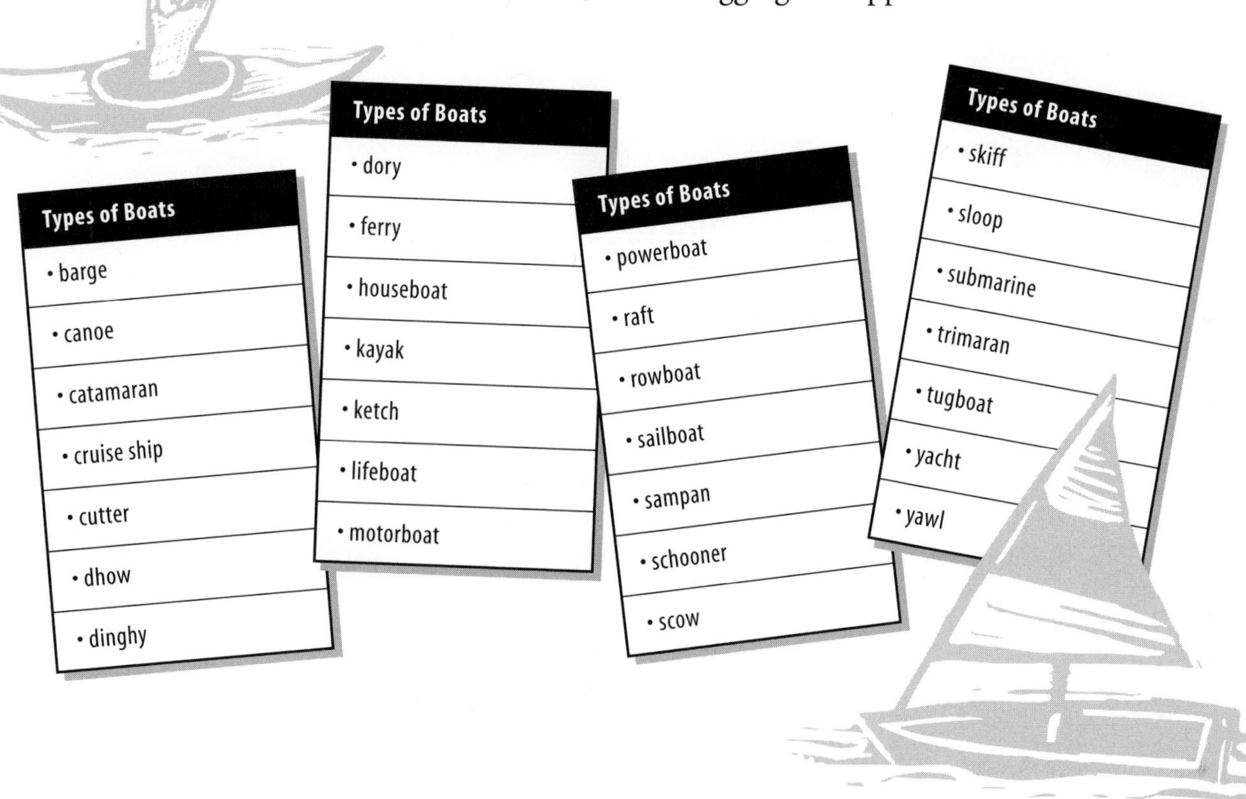

LESSON MODEL FOR

Word Relationships

Benchmark

- ability to acquire in-depth understanding of word meanings

Strategy Grade Level

- Grade 3 and above

Grouping

- whole class
- small group or pairs

Sample Text (Resources)

- "Studying the Sky"
  Complexity Level: Grades 3–4

POSSIBLE SENTENCES

Target Words

ancient
astronomer
constellation
galaxy
orbit
universe

Possible Sentences

Stahl and Kapinus (1991) found that the use of this prereading strategy significantly improved both students' recall of target word meanings and their comprehension of the selection containing those words. Since students have to use at least two words in each possible sentence, they are required to understand the relationship between the words. Through evaluation of sentence accuracy, students are forced to actively process semantic information about each word (Stahl 1999). This sample lesson model targets specific vocabulary found in "Studying the Sky," a short selection about astronomy. The same model can be adapted and used to enhance contextualized vocabulary instruction in any commercial reading or content-area program.

Select the Target Words

Select about six words from the sample text "Studying the Sky" that may be unknown to students, are central to the main idea of the selection, and are adequately defined by context within the selection. Then select about four words from the text that are likely to be known to students.

Introduce the Words

List the following words on the board:

ancient, astronomer, center, constellation,
galaxy, orbit, planet, stars, sun, universe

English/Spanish Cognates

ancient • anciano (elderly)
astronomer • astrónomo
constellation • constelación
galaxy • galaxia
orbit • órbita
universe • universo

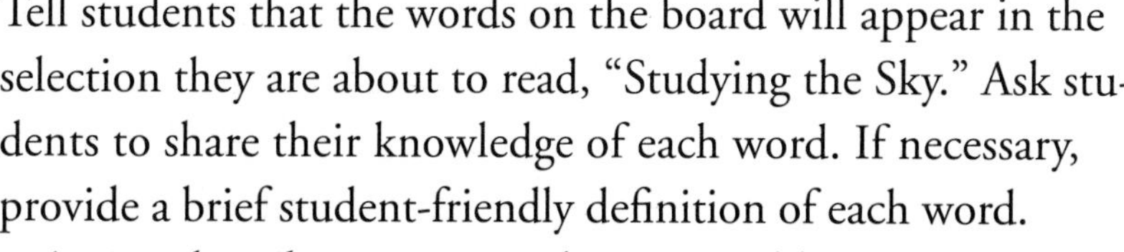

Tell students that the words on the board will appear in the selection they are about to read, "Studying the Sky." Ask students to share their knowledge of each word. If necessary, provide a brief student-friendly definition of each word.

- *Ancient* describes someone who is very old or something from a very long time ago.
- An *astronomer* is someone who studies planets and stars.
- A *constellation* is a group of stars visible from Earth. The stars create a shape that can be recognized and has a name, such as the Big Dipper.
- A *galaxy* is a group of billions of stars belonging to one star system. Earth is in the Milky Way galaxy.
- An *orbit* is a circular path that a heavenly body or satellite makes around another body in space.
- The *universe* is everything that exists, including all space and matter.

Write Possible Sentences

Next, have students work individually or in pairs to select two or three words from the list on the board. Tell them to make up one sentence that contains at least two of the words and that might appear in the selection they are about to read. Print the suggested sentences on the board and have them read aloud. Include both accurate and inaccurate statements without discussing them. For example, write the following sentences on the board:

Nine planets orbit around the sun.
A constellation is a great big galaxy.
An astronomer is someone who is ancient.
The sun is the center of the universe.

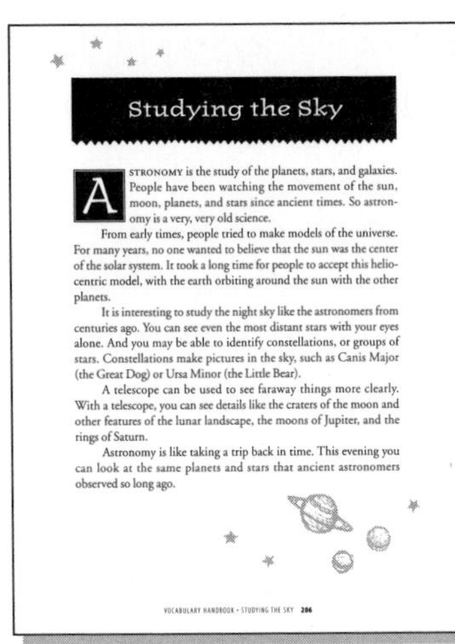

Studying the Sky

ASTRONOMY is the study of the planets, stars, and galaxies. People have been watching the movement of the sun, moon, planets, and stars since ancient times. So astronomy is a very, very old science.

From early times, people tried to make models of the universe. For many years, no one wanted to believe that the sun was the center of the solar system. It took a long time for people to accept this heliocentric model, with the earth orbiting around the sun with the other planets.

It is interesting to study the night sky like the astronomers from centuries ago. You can see even the most distant stars with your eyes alone. And you may be able to identify constellations, or groups of stars. Constellations make pictures in the sky, such as Canis Major (the Great Dog) or Ursa Minor (the Little Bear).

A telescope can be used to see faraway things more clearly. With a telescope, you can see details like the craters of the moon and other features of the lunar landscape, the moons of Jupiter, and the rings of Saturn.

Astronomy is like taking a trip back in time. This evening you can look at the same planets and stars that ancient astronomers observed so long ago.

VOCABULARY HANDBOOK • STUDYING THE SKY 206

Read the Selection

When students have finished contributing possible sentences using all the target words, have them read, independently or aloud, the selection "Studying the Sky."

Evaluate the Accuracy of the Possible Sentences

After students read the selection, go back and evaluate the accuracy of the possible sentences. Have students look again at the sentences on the board. Encourage them to discuss whether, based on their reading, each sentence is or is not accurate. If they determine that a sentence is accurate, place a checkmark beside it. If a sentence is inaccurate, help students to rewrite the sentence on the board to make an accurate statement. For example:

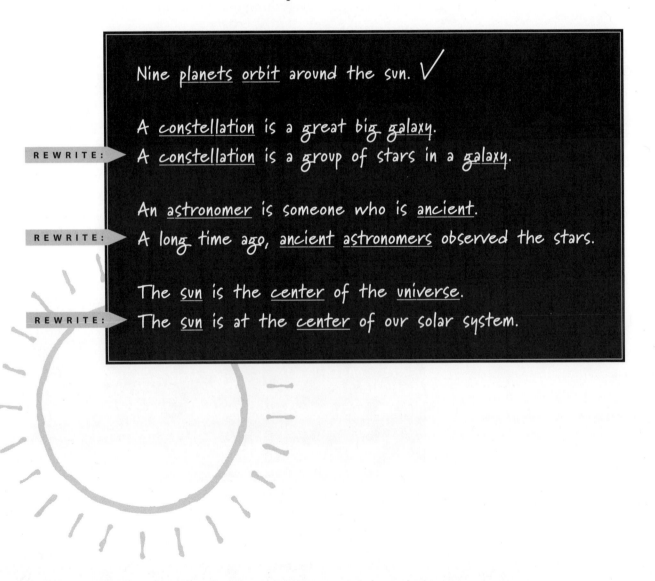

Nine planets orbit around the sun. ✓

A constellation is a great big galaxy.

REWRITE: A constellation is a group of stars in a galaxy.

An astronomer is someone who is ancient.

REWRITE: A long time ago, ancient astronomers observed the stars.

The sun is the center of the universe.

REWRITE: The sun is at the center of our solar system.

LESSON MODEL FOR

Word Relationships

Benchmark

- ability to acquire in-depth understanding of word meanings

Strategy Grade Level

- Grade 2 and above

Prerequisite

- knowing about antonyms and synonyms

Grouping

- whole class
- small group or pairs

Sample Text (Resources)

- "Alaska Adventure" Complexity Level: Grades 4–5

Activity Master (Resources)

- Word Map

Materials

- copies of Word Map
- Vocabulary Hotshot Notebooks

Word Map

Graphic organizers, such as this word map, help students to visualize how words connect to each other. They help restructure more difficult tasks. When students draw on their prior knowledge to make a concrete, graphic representation of a target word, they show how the word relates to other words and concepts. This sample lesson model targets specific vocabulary found in the sample text "Alaska Adventure." The same model can be adapted and used to enhance contextualized vocabulary instruction in any commercial reading or content-area program.

Teach/Model

Tell students that creating a word map can help them to understand how a new word is related to words and examples they already know. Remind students that in the selection "Alaska Adventure," Jack says, "Mom is not going to believe how awesome the scenery is." In other words, Jack thinks the scenery in Alaska is very impressive. Have students say "What awesome scenery!" in the way Jack would have said it. Tell students that *awesome* is a word that can mean "very impressive" or "very cool."

Then draw from students' experience by asking when they have used the word *awesome.* Ask: *How and when have you used the word* awesome*?* (Possible responses: *to express excitement, surprise, or joy*) Ask: *What are some examples of how you have used the word* awesome*?* (Possible responses: *Jack hit an awesome home run. Mom has an awesome new car.*)

SYNONYMS
words that are very close in meaning

ANTONYMS
words that are opposite or nearly opposite in meaning

On the board, print the target word *awesome* in the center box of a word map, as shown below. Say: *According to Jack, an example of something that is awesome is the scenery in Alaska.* Print *scenery in Alaska* in the example box of the map. Say: *An example of something that is not awesome, or a nonexample, could be a small parking lot.* Print *small parking lot* in the nonexample box of the map. Say: Impressive *is a word that means almost the same as* awesome. Impressive *could be used in place of the word* awesome. Print *impressive* in the synonym box of the map. Say: Ordinary *is a word that means the opposite of* awesome. Print *ordinary* in the antonym box of the map. When the word map is completed, have students discuss it and use the words on it in other contexts.

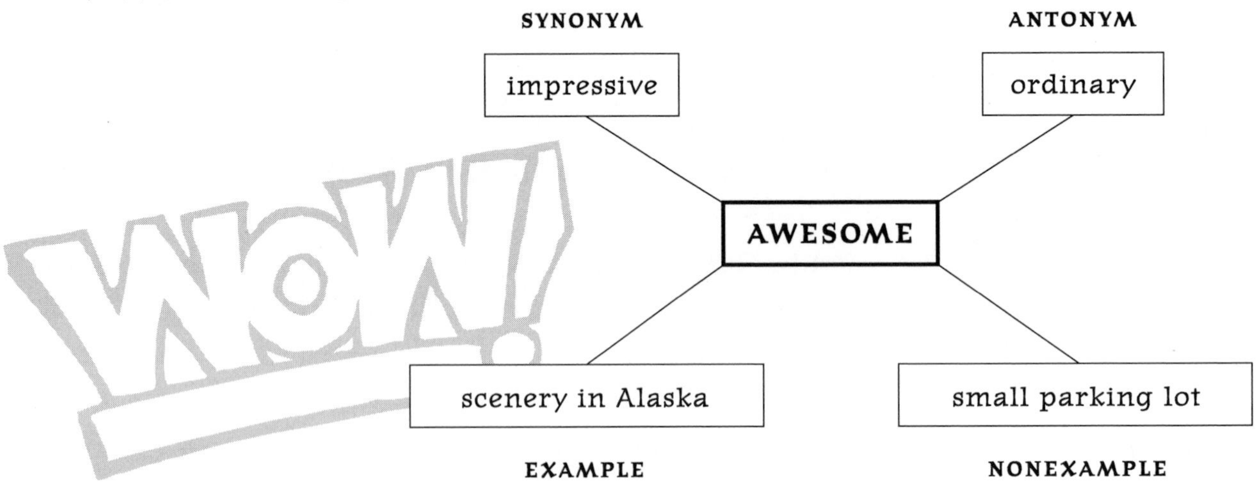

Guided Practice

Using the following activity, explore other examples and nonexamples of the word *awesome.* Say: *If the things or situations I describe are examples of something awesome, say "Wow!" If not, don't say anything.*

- a new pair of high-tech running shoes
- cleaning your room
- meeting the president of the United States
- an old pair of slippers
- a colorful rainbow

SEE ALSO . . .

Language Categories, p. 572

Next guide students in making a different word map for *awesome*. Say: *A colorful rainbow could be awesome.* Print *a colorful rainbow* in the example box of the map. Then ask: *What is the opposite of a colorful rainbow*? (Possible response: *a gray day*) Print students' responses in the nonexample box of the map. Continue by having students think of synonyms and antonyms. Say: *The word* impressive *has almost the same meaning as the word* awesome. Ask: *What other words mean almost the same as* awesome*?* (Possible responses: *amazing, exceptional, cool, extraordinary*) Print students' responses in the synonym box of the map. Say: *The word* ordinary *is one word that means the opposite of* awesome. Ask: *What other words mean the opposite of* awesome*?* (Possible responses: *dull, unexciting*) Print students' responses in the antonym box of the map. When the word map is completed, have students discuss it and use the words on it in other contexts.

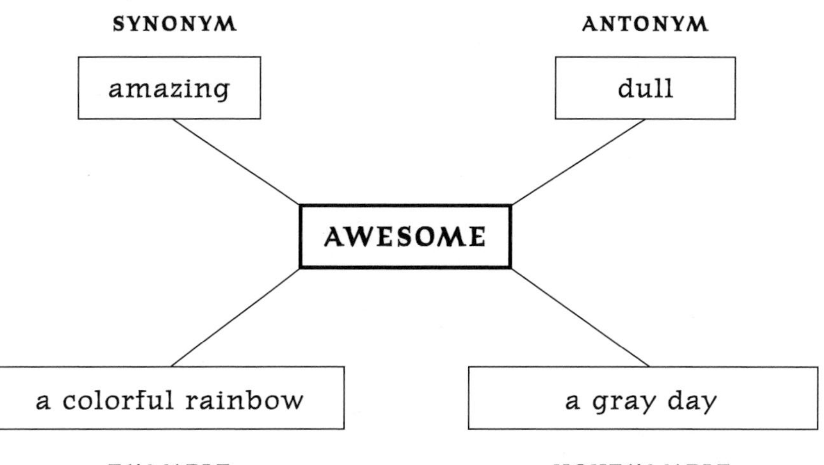

Extend Word Use

Vocabulary HOTSHOT Notebook

Independent Practice

Have students create their own Word Maps to explore other words they encounter in their reading. For example, students could complete a Word Map for the words *enticing, adventure,* or *interior* from "Alaska Adventure," or they can choose words from other books and stories. Invite volunteers to discuss the target words they have chosen, identify the synonyms and antonyms, and share their examples and nonexamples. Have them write sentences using the words on their maps.

SEE ALSO . . .

LESSON MODEL: Vocabulary Hotshot Notebook, p. 601

LESSON MODEL FOR

Word-Meaning Recall

Benchmark

- ability to remember word meanings

Strategy Grade Level

- Grade 3 and above

Grouping

- whole class
- small group or pairs
- individual

Sample Texts (Resources)

- "Alaska Adventure" Complexity Level: Grades 4–5
- "Studying the Sky" Complexity Level: Grades 3–4

Keyword Method

Mnemonic strategies are systematic procedures for enhancing memory. The word *mnemonic* comes from Mnemosyne, the name of Greek goddess of memory. The keyword method, a mnemonic strategy, has been shown to be effective with students who have learning difficulties and those who are at risk for educational failure (Mastropieri and Scruggs 1998). According to the National Reading Panel (2000), the keyword method may lead to significant improvement in students' recall of new vocabulary words. This sample lesson model targets two contextualized vocabulary words. The same model can be adapted and used to enhance recall of vocabulary words in any commercial reading or content-area program.

Direct Explanation

Explain to students that you are going to show them how to use the keyword method, a useful strategy for remembering the meanings of vocabulary words. Tell them you are going to model the strategy twice, using the words *archipelago* and *lunar*.

Teach/Model

1. Define the Target Word

Read aloud the following sentence from "Alaska Adventure." Then tell students that an *archipelago* is "a group of islands."

The Aleutian archipelago stretches for more than a thousand miles.

KEYWORD METHOD

Target Word
archipelago
Keyword
pelican

Point out to Spanish-speaking ELLs that *archipelago* and *archipiélago* are cognates.

2. Think of a Keyword for the Target Word

Say: *To help me remember the meaning of the word* archipelago, *a group of islands, I am going to think of another word, called a "keyword." The keyword is a word that sounds like* archipelago *and also is a word that can be easily pictured. My keyword for* archipelago *is* pelican. Pelican *sounds like* archipelago *and is the name of a water bird with a very large bill.*

3. Link the Keyword with the Meaning of the Target Word

Explain to students that the next step is to create an image of the keyword *pelican* and the meaning of the target word *archipelago* interacting in some way. Tell them it is important that the keyword and the meaning actually interact and are not simply presented in the same picture. On the board, sketch a picture of a pelican flying over a group of small islands. Say: *Look at the picture of the pelican flying over the group of islands.* Ask: Pelican *is the keyword for what word?* (archipelago) Say: *Yes,* archipelago. *To recall the meaning of the word* archipelago, *imagine a pelican flying over a group of small islands.*

4. Recall the Meaning of the Target Word

Tell students that when they see or hear the word *archipelago*, they should first think of its keyword and then try to remember the picture of the keyword and the meaning interacting. Ask: *What is the keyword for* archipelago*?* (pelican) *In the sketch, where was the pelican flying?* (over a group of islands) Say: *Right, over a group of islands.* Ask: *So what does* archipelago *mean?* (a group of islands)

KEYWORD METHOD

Target Word
lunar
Keyword
lonely

1. Define the Target Word

Read aloud the following sentence from "Studying the Sky." Then tell students that the word *lunar* means "of the moon."

> **With a telescope, you can see details like the craters of the moon and other features of the lunar landscape, the moons of Jupiter, and the rings of Saturn.**

Point out to Spanish-speaking ELLs that *lunar* and *lunar* are identically spelled cognates.

2. Think of a Keyword for the Target Word

Say: *To help me remember the meaning of the word* lunar, *"of the moon," I am going to think of a keyword. The keyword is a word that sounds like* lunar *and also is a word that can be easily pictured. My keyword for* lunar *is* lonely. Lonely *sounds like* lunar *and when I think of* lonely *I imagine someone sitting all alone.*

3. Link the Keyword with the Meaning of the Target Word

Explain to students that the next step is to create an image of the keyword *lonely* and the meaning of the target word *lunar* interacting in some way. On the board, sketch a picture of a wolf howling at the moon. Say: *Look at the picture of the lonely wolf howling at the moon.* Ask: Lonely *is the keyword for what word?* (lunar) Say: *Yes,* lunar. *To recall the meaning of the word* lunar, *imagine a lonely wolf howling at the moon.*

4. Recall the Meaning of the Target Word

Tell students that when they see or hear the word *lunar*, they should first think of its keyword and then try to remember the picture of the keyword and meaning interacting. Ask: *What is the keyword for* lunar? (lonely) *In the picture, what was the lonely wolf doing?* (howling at the moon) Say: *Right, howling at the moon.* Ask: *So what does* lunar *mean?* (of the moon)

CHAPTER

12

Word-Learning Strategies

what?
why?
when?
how?

what?

Word-Learning Strategies

If students have the task of learning tens of thousands of words and we can only teach them a few hundred words a year, then they have to do a lot of word learning on their own.

—GRAVES, 2000

SEE ALSO . . .

Monitoring Comprehension, p. 615

SEE ALSO . . .

LESSON MODELS

Using the Dictionary, p. 506

PAVE Procedure, p. 511

Concept of Definition Map, p. 516

Given the size of vocabularies they need, readers can and must improve their vocabularies independently. Independent word-learning strategies can help students to determine the meanings of unfamiliar words that have *not* been explicitly introduced to them. Knowledge of these types of strategies is generative; it transfers to the learning of new words (Nagy 2005). Directly teaching word-learning strategies, coupled with explicit instruction in specific words, can help students not only to increase their vocabularies, but also to become independent word learners (Baumann et al. 2003). According to the National Reading Panel (2000), effective word-learning strategies include:

- how to use dictionaries to confirm and deepen knowledge of word meanings;
- how to use morphemic (word-part) analysis to derive the meanings of words in text;
- how to use contextual analysis to infer the meanings of words in text.

Dictionary Use

Dictionary use is not as simple as it seems; students frequently have difficulty using the dictionary to define unfamiliar words (Miller and Gildea 1987). Traditionally, instruction in dictionary use has focused on mechanics—how to find an entry alphabetically, how to use guide words, how to separate words into syllables, how to use pronunciation keys—and on having

Student Dictionaries
Collins COBUILD New Student's Dictionary, 3rd Edition (2005). Glasgow, UK: HarperCollins.
Collins COBUILD School Dictionary of American English (2008). Boston: Heinle.
Heinle's Basic Newbury House Dictionary of American English, 2nd Edition (2004). Boston: Heinle.
Longman Dictionary of American English, 4th Edition (2008). Upper Saddle River, NJ: Pearson.

CCSS LANGUAGE STANDARDS

Vocabulary Acquisition and Use

Determine or clarify the meaning of unknown and multiple-meaning words and phrases. (CCR.4)

Demonstrate understanding of figurative language, word relationships, and nuances in word meanings. (CCR.5)

Acquire and use accurately a range of general academic and domain-specific words and phrases. (CCR.6)

CCSS READING STANDARDS

Literature • Informational Text

Craft and Structure

Interpret words and phrases as they are used in text. (CCR.4)

students use information from dictionary definitions to write sentences. Scott and Nagy (1997) contend that such instruction does not provide students with the guidance they need to make dictionary use an efficient, independent word-learning strategy.

Nonetheless, when used correctly, dictionaries are powerful aids to word understanding. Students can learn greatly from looking up a word and fully processing its definition (Jenkins and Dixon 1983). In fact, McKeown and her colleagues have found that the more students are exposed to definitions, the better they learn words (McKeown, Beck, Omanson, and Pople 1985).

The crucial point is that students should receive instruction in *how to use what they find in a dictionary entry.* They are then better able to translate the "cryptic and conventionalized content" of dictionary definitions into word knowledge they can use (Stahl and Nagy 2000). Teachers should model how to look up the meaning of an unfamiliar word, and how to choose the appropriate definition from an entry to make sure it fits a particular context. Students should be taught to use the dictionary not only when they come across a word they have never seen before, but also to further their knowledge of a word.

Types of Morphemes	
▸ **Free Morphemes** Can stand alone as words	Anglo-Saxon root words: *help, play, run*
▸ **Bound Morphemes** Cannot stand alone as words	Prefixes: *dis–, in–, re–, un–*
	Derivational suffixes: *–ful, –less, –ly*
	Inflectional suffixes: *–ed, –es, –ing, –s*
	Greek roots: *bio, graph, scope*
	Latin roots: *dict, ject, struct*

Morphemic Analysis

MORPHEMES
word-part clues; the meaningful parts of words

Morphemes, p. 42

LESSON MODELS
Compound Words, p. 521
Word Families, p. 524
Word-Part Clues: Prefixes, p. 527
Word-Part Clues: Suffixes, p. 533
Word-Part Clues: Roots, p. 537

The key instructional elements of morphemic analysis are morphemes, which include root or base words, Greek and Latin roots, and affixes (prefixes and suffixes). Morphemes are also referred to as word-part clues. There are two basic types of morphemes: free and bound. Free morphemes can stand alone as words; they do not have to be combined with other morphemes to make words. Anglo-Saxon root words are examples of free morphemes. Bound morphemes cannot stand alone; they must be attached to, or "bound" to, other morphemes to make words. Affixes (prefixes and suffixes) and Greek and Latin roots are examples of bound morphemes. By learning about morphemes, and the ways in which they contribute to the meaning of a word, students can build a foundation for independent word learning. Morphemic analysis can be an especially effective word-learning strategy for use with content-area text.

Explicit instruction in word-part clues (morphemes) typically involves teaching students the meanings of word parts, how to disassemble words into word parts, and how to reassemble the word parts to derive word meaning (Edwards et al. 2004;

Baumann et al. 2005). According to Biemiller (2005a), the meaning of unfamiliar affixed words can be derived when encountered if the meaning of the root words and affixes are known.

Root Words and Word Families

ROOT WORD
a single word that cannot be broken into smaller words or parts

WORD FAMILY
a group of words related in meaning

A root or base word is a single word that cannot be broken into smaller words or word parts. Root words are words from which many other words are formed. Knowing the meaning of one root word can provide a bridge to the meaning of other words related in meaning, or words belonging to a word family. Nagy and Anderson (1984) propose teaching word families, which include a root word and its derived forms. Their analysis of printed school English made clear that a large number of words that students encounter in reading are derivatives or inflections of familiar root words.

SEE ALSO . . .
LESSON MODELS
Compound Words, p. 521
Word Families, p. 524

Compound Words

An Anglo-Saxon compound word contains two free morphemes, or word parts. The meaning of some compound words is the same as the sum of its two parts; for example, *doghouse* and *bluebird.* Other compound words have a meaning that differs from the meaning of the sum of its two parts; for example, *butterfly* and *airline.*

Using Word-Part Clues to Derive Word Meaning

Step	Action	Example Word: disagreement
1	Look for the Root Word. *What does it mean?*	agree = to have the same opinion
2	Look for a Prefix. *What does it mean?*	dis = not or opposite
3	Look for a Suffix. *What does it mean?*	ment = state or quality of something
4	Put the Meanings of the Word Parts Together. *What is the meaning of the whole word?*	dis + agree + ment = state or quality of not having the same opinion

Based on Baumann et al. 2003, 2005.

Facts About Prefixes

Twenty prefixes account for 97 percent of the prefixed words in school reading materials

Four prefixes (*un–*, *re–*, *in–*, and *dis–*) account for 58 percent of all prefixed words

PREFIX
a word part added to the beginning of a root word that changes its meaning

SUFFIX
a word part added to the end of a root word that changes its meaning

LESSON MODELS
Word-Part Clues: Prefixes, p. 527
Word-Part Clues: Suffixes, p. 533

Prefixes

Affixes that come before root words are called prefixes. A prefix can alter the meaning of the root word to which it is "fixed," or attached. Graves (2004) gives several reasons why prefixes are particularly worth teaching and are well suited for instruction: (1) there is a relatively small number of prefixes, (2) prefixes are used in a large number of words, (3) prefixes tend to be consistently spelled, (4) prefixes are easy to identify because they occur at the beginning of words, and (5) prefixes usually have a clear lexical meaning.

Graves (2004) recommends that teachers provide explicit instruction in the most frequently used prefixes. White, Sowell, and Yanagihara (1989) suggest teaching prefixes in the order of their frequency, varying that order according to the demands of students' instructional texts. These researchers found that twenty prefixes account for about 97 percent of the prefixed words in printed school English. Four prefixes (*un–*, *re–*, *in–*, and *dis–*) account for about 58 percent of prefixed words.

Suffixes

Affixes that follow root words are called suffixes. A suffix can alter the meaning or function of the root word to which it is "fixed," or attached. There are two kinds of suffixes: inflectional and derivational. Inflectional suffixes (e.g., *–s*, *–es*, *–ed*, *–ing*) change the form of a word but not its speech part; these include verb forms, plurals, and comparatives and superlatives. Derivational suffixes (e.g., *–ful*, *–less*) are like prefixes in that they alter a root word's meaning. Inflectional suffixes are the most frequently occurring suffixes in school reading materials, while derivational suffixes appear in less than a quarter of all the words that contain suffixes (White et al. 1989). Even though derivational suffixes appear less frequently, researchers recommend that teachers do spend time directly teaching them (Edwards et al. 2004; Stahl 1999).

Most Frequent Prefixes, p. 44

Most Frequent Suffixes, p. 45

LIMITATIONS Morphemic analysis, though useful, does not always work. By only considering word-part clues, students may be misled about the true meaning of a word. White, Sowell, and Yanagihara (1989) pointed out some pitfalls: (1) some prefixes are not consistent in meaning (e.g., *in–* means both "not" and "in"), (2) sometimes the removal of what appears to be a prefix leaves no meaningful root word (e.g., *uncle*), and (3) sometimes the removal of what appears to be a prefix or a suffix leaves a word that is not obviously related in meaning to the whole word (e.g., *increase, bashful*).

Morphemic analysis does not always work. Using a student anthology or content-area textbook, look for words beginning with the letters *un, re, in,* or *dis.* From the group of words, select one example for each of the following four categories: (1) does not have a prefix and root word, (2) has a prefix and root word, (3) combined meanings of prefix and root word result in the meaning of the whole word, and (4) combined meanings of prefix and root word do not result in the meaning of the whole word. For an example, refer to the chart on page 532.

WORD-PART CLUE EVALUATION

WORD	Does Not Have Prefix and Root Word	Has Prefix and Root Word	Prefix + Root Word = Meaning	Prefix + Root Word ≠ Meaning

Common Greek and Latin Roots in English			
Root	**Meaning**	**Origin**	**Example**
astro	star	Greek	astronaut
aud	hear	Latin	audible
dict	say, tell	Latin	dictate
geo	earth	Greek	geology
graph	write, record	Greek	autograph
meter	measure	Greek	barometer
mit, miss	send	Latin	submit, mission
ology	study of	Greek	morphology
ped	foot	Latin	pedal
phon	sound	Greek	phonograph
port	carry	Latin	transport
spect	see	Latin	inspect
struct	build, form	Latin	construct
tele	from afar	Greek	telephone

SEE ALSO . . .

LESSON MODELS

Word-Part Clues: Roots, p. 537

Latin and Greek Number Words, p. 584

SEE ALSO . . .

Common Latin Roots, p. 46

Common Greek Roots, p. 47

Greek and Latin Roots

Greek and Latin roots are bound morphemes that cannot stand alone as words in English. Most Greek roots appear in combination with each other. For this reason, they are often called combining forms. Most Latin roots appear in combination with one or more affixes. Words of Greek and Latin origin are especially prevalent in English. About 60 percent of the words in English text are of Greek and Latin origin (Henry 1997). A relatively small number of Greek and Latin roots appear in hundreds of thousands of words (Henry 2003).

Latin-origin words used in science and technical fields account for a large number of English/Spanish cognates.

From the middle grades on, words with Greek and Latin roots form a large proportion of the new vocabulary that students encounter, primarily in their content-area textbooks. In English, Greek-based words tend to be related to math and science. Bear et al. (1996) suggest introducing Greek roots before Latin roots because their meaning is more apparent, or less abstract, than Latin roots. Stahl and Nagy (2000) believe that a distinction should be made between instructional time spent on Greek roots used in specialized scientific language and time spent on Latin roots whose meanings are more general-purpose.

Research on teaching roots is sparse; researchers and educators are divided as to whether it is profitable to teach them (Stahl and Nagy 2000). Researchers argue that a Latin root's meaning is not always strongly related to the meaning of a word containing the root. For example, knowing that Latin root *port* means "carry" may help with *portable* or *transport,* but probably does not help someone derive the meaning of *portico* or *portly.*

Select a Greek and Latin root from the chart on page 494. Beginning with the example word, brainstorm a list of at least five words that have the same root and also are related in meaning. Here are some examples:

- Greek root *astro* meaning "star": *astronaut, asterisk, asteroid, astrology, astronomy*
- Latin root *spect* meaning "see": *inspect, inspector, inspection, prospector, spectator*

Cognate Awareness

One method of building vocabulary among English-language learners whose language shares cognates with English is to capitalize on students' first-language knowledge (August et al. 2005). Cognates are words in two languages that share a similar spelling, pronunciation, and meaning. Students often can draw on their knowledge of words in their native language to figure out the meanings of cognates in English. Because of their common Latin and Greek roots, as well as the close connections between English and the Romance languages, English and Spanish share a large number of cognate pairs.

Second-language learners do not automatically recognize and make use of cognates (Nagy et al. 1993; Nagy 1988). Recent studies indicate that explicitly identifying cognates supports English-language acquisition for Spanish-speaking students (Carlo et al. 2004; Bravo, Hiebert, and Pearson 2005). When selecting cognates for instruction, it is important to focus on cognates that Spanish speakers are likely to know from their everyday Spanish use (Bravo, Hiebert, and Pearson 2005). These types of cognates include pairs that are high-frequency words in both English and Spanish (e.g., *animal/animal*) and pairs that have a high-frequency Spanish word and a low-frequency English word (e.g., *enfermo/infirm*). Dressler (2000) found that it is possible for Spanish-speaking students to make connections between cognates on the basis of sound alone. Thus, students who are not literate in Spanish but are orally proficient in the language can benefit from instruction in cognate awareness, as can students who are literate in Spanish.

English/Spanish cognates fall into several different categories: cognates that are spelled identically, cognates that are spelled nearly the same, cognates that are pronounced nearly the same, and false cognates. False cognates are pairs of words that are spelled identically or nearly the same in two languages but do not share the same meaning.

COGNATES
words in two languages that share a similar spelling, pronunciation, and meaning

FALSE COGNATES
pairs of words that are spelled the same or nearly the same in two languages but do not share the same meaning

English/Spanish Cognates, p. 64

Categories of Cognates in English and Spanish			
Category	**Definition**	**English**	**Spanish**
▸ **Cognates** have the same meaning	spelled identically	chocolate* doctor hotel	chocolate doctor hotel
	spelled nearly the same	class family music	clase familia música
	pronounced nearly the same	baby equal peace	bebé igual paz
▸ **False Cognates** have different meanings	spelled identically	pan pie red	pan (bread) pie (foot) red (net)
	spelled nearly the same	exit rope soap	éxito (success) ropa (clothing) sopa (soup)

*Based on Rodriguez 2001. *English word borrowed from Spanish*

You may be surprised how many English/Spanish cognates can be found in a typical text selection. Using the list below, identify cognates in the sample text "Marine Mammals" (p. 768); for example, *animals* and *animales.* Then consult an English/Spanish dictionary to make sure the meaning of the Spanish cognate has the same meaning as the English word in the text. (See Answer Key, p. 800.)

SPANISH WORDS: animales, marino, océano, imposible, aire, criatura, comparación, impulso, reaccionar, miles, número, grupo, filtros, material, gigantes, abundante, planeta, población, proteger

Students who are more skilled at reading and more knowledgeable about word meanings are those most able to learn word meanings from context.

—SCOTT, 2005

Contextual Analysis

Contextual analysis involves inferring the meaning of a word by scrutinizing surrounding text. Instruction in contextual analysis usually involves teaching students to identify and employ both generic and specific types of context clues. Research on the important role context plays in incidental word learning is compelling (Nagy and Scott 2000; Swanborn and de Glopper 1999). However, there is less information about whether teachers can enhance this "natural effect" through explicit instruction on how to employ context clues (Baumann et al. 2002). Kuhn and Stahl (1998) noted that the lack of research evidence about effective contextual analysis instruction is "disappointing." But since students encounter such an enormous number of words as they read, some researchers believe that even a small improvement in contextual analysis ability has the potential to produce substantial, long-term vocabulary growth (Nagy et al. 1985, 1987; Swanborn and de Glopper 1999).

SEE ALSO . . .

LESSON MODELS

Context Clues, p. 541

Introducing Types of Context Clues, p. 545

Applying Types of Context Clues, p. 551

CONTEXT CLUES
words or phrases that give readers hints or suggestions to the meaning of unfamiliar words

Types of Helpful Context Clues

Several studies suggest that simple practice in inferring word meanings from context may be just as effective as instruction in specific context-clue types (Kuhn and Stahl 1998). However, according to an analysis by Fukkink and de Glopper (1998), "clue instruction appears to be more effective than other instruction types or just practice." Baumann and his colleagues (2002, 2003, 2005) recommend instruction in five types of helpful context clues: definition, synonym, antonym, example, and general.

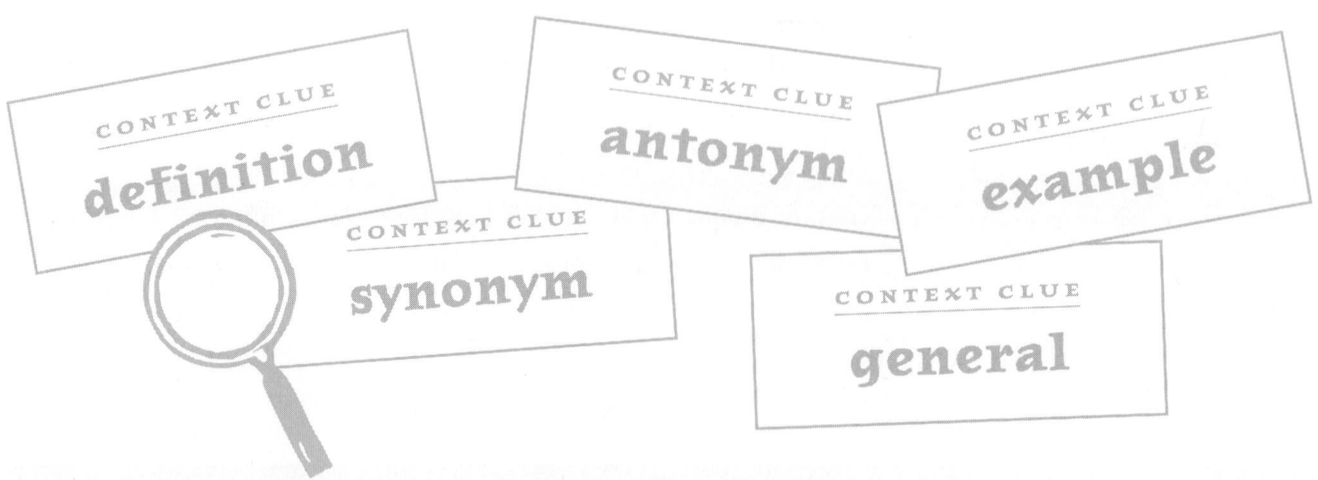

TYPES OF HELPFUL CONTEXT CLUES

Type	Description	Example Sentence
Definition	The author provides a direct definition of an unfamiliar word, right in the sentence. • SIGNAL WORDS: *is, are, means, refers to*	A conga *is* a barrel-shaped drum.
Appositive Definition	A type of definition clue. An appositive is a word or phrase that defines or explains an unfamiliar word that comes before it. • SIGNAL WORD: *or* • SIGNAL PUNCTUATION: set off by commas	At night you can see constellations, *or* groups of stars, in the sky.
Synonym	The author uses another word or phrase that is similar in meaning, or can be compared, to an unfamiliar word. • SIGNAL WORDS: *also, as, identical, like, likewise, resembling, same, similarly, too*	My dog Buck travels everywhere with me. My friend's canine buddy travels everywhere with him, *too*.
Antonym	The author uses another word or phrase that means about the opposite of, or is in contrast with, an unfamiliar word. • SIGNAL WORDS: *but, however, in contrast, instead of, on the other hand, though, unlike*	I thought the movie would be weird, *but* it turned out to be totally mundane.
Example	The author provides several words or ideas that are examples of an unfamiliar word. • SIGNAL WORDS: *for example, for instance, including, like, such as*	In science we are studying marine mammals *such as* whales, dolphins, and porpoises.
General	The author provides some nonspecific clues to the meaning of an unfamiliar word, often spread over several sentences.	Einstein rode his bike everywhere. He thought driving a car was way too complicated.

Based on Baumann et al. 2003, 2005.

CCSS READING STANDARDS

Foundational Skills

Fluency

Use context to confirm or self-correct word recognition and understanding, rereading as necessary. 1-5. [RF.1-5.4c]

Unhelpful Context Clues

One of the problems in teaching contextual analysis is that it does not always work; sometimes the context does not provide enough clues to determine a word's meaning (Edwards et al. 2004). Many naturally occurring written contexts found in literature and expository texts are not all that informative for inferring word meanings; they are not equally rich and are sometimes unreliable (Beck et al. 2002). It is important to inform students that there are limits to contextual analysis. Beck and her colleagues (2002) describe two types of unhelpful context clues: misdirective and nondirective. They explain that unhelpful contexts are not in themselves wrong or a misuse of language. The context surrounding an unfamiliar word may communicate the author's ideas well, but provide no help in inferring the meaning of the word.

UNHELPFUL CONTEXT CLUES

Type	Description	Example Sentence
Misdirective	These clues seem to direct the reader to an incorrect meaning for the word.	"She looks so happy and beautiful in her party dress," said Jim maliciously.
Nondirective	These clues seem to be of no assistance in directing the reader toward any particular meaning for the word; the unfamiliar word could have a number of inferable meanings.	When I answered the phone, I heard my sister's agitated voice.

Based on Baumann et al. 2002.

Context clues can be either helpful or unhelpful. Using a student anthology or content-area textbook, look for words that may be unfamiliar to students. From target-word context, find one example of each type of context clue. For each context sentence or sentences, identify the target word by underlining it in blue; the signal words and signal punctuation by underlining them in red; and the context clues by underlining them in green.

CONTEXT CLUES

Type of Context Clue	Target Word	Context Sentence or Sentences
• Definition		
• Appositive Definition		
• Synonym		
• Antonym		
• Example		
• General		
• Misdirective		
• Nondirective		

When morphemic and contextual analysis instruction is provided in combination, the effects appear to be just as powerful as when it is provided in isolation.

—BAUMANN ET AL., 2002

LESSON MODELS

Introducing The Vocabulary Strategy, p. 555

Practicing The Vocabulary Strategy, p. 562

CSR (Collaborative Strategic Reading), p. 720

Combined Morphemic and Contextual Analysis

In recent studies, James Baumann and his colleagues (2003, 2005) explored the effectiveness of teaching middle-grade students (Grades 4–8) to use morphemic and contextual analysis in tandem. The studies' primary instructional strategy was called the Vocabulary Rule, an integrated approach that combines the use of context clues and word-part clues. The researchers concluded that students can be taught to use word-part and context clues to learn vocabulary independently and that combined instruction is just as effective as separate instruction (Baumann et al. 2005).

The Vocabulary Strategy chart below is based upon Baumann's combined approach. The five steps take students through a complete process that integrates three previously learned strategies: using context clues to infer a word's meaning, using word-part clues to derive a word's meaning, and using the dictionary to confirm a word's meaning.

THE VOCABULARY STRATEGY

To figure out the meaning of an unfamiliar word that you come across while reading:

1. **Look for Context Clues** in the Words, Phrases, and Sentences Surrounding the Unfamiliar Word
2. **Look for Word-Part Clues** Within the Unfamiliar Word
   A. Try to Break the Word into Parts. (If you can't, skip to Step 3.)
   B. Look at the Root Word. What does it mean?
   C. Look at the Prefix. What does it mean?
   D. Look at the Suffix. What does it mean?
   E. Put the Meanings of the Word Parts Together. What is the meaning of the whole word?
3. **Guess the Word's Meaning** (Use Steps 1 and 2.)
4. **Try Out Your Meaning in the Original Sentence** to Check Whether or Not It Makes Sense in Context
5. **Use the Dictionary**, if Necessary, to Confirm Your Meaning

Based on Baumann et al. 2003, 2005.

why?

Word-Learning Strategies

Students learn words independently when they are taught strategies for determining the meanings of words by analyzing morphemic and contextual clues.

—EDWARDS ET AL., 2004

There are many more words to be learned than can be directly taught in even the most ambitious program of vocabulary instruction. Even when instruction in specific words is as robust as possible, students still need to learn much of their vocabulary independently (Graves et al. 2004). A great deal of research now supports direct instruction in word-learning strategies as one of the components of a comprehensive vocabulary program (National Reading Panel 2000). While the research has not yet proven the efficacy of these word-learning strategies in all cases or over long periods, it has shown that such strategies are generally effective in that they help students determine the meaning of many unfamiliar words encountered in their reading (Baumann et al. 2002, 2003).

Two widely used methods of helping students learn to deal with unfamiliar words on their own are contextual and morphemic analysis. According to Nagy (1988), "there is no doubt that skilled word learners use context and their knowledge of prefixes, roots, and suffixes to deal effectively with new words." Therefore, readers who are skillful in applying morphemic and contextual analysis have the potential to independently acquire the meanings of many unfamiliar words.

Research Findings . . .

Instruction in morphemic and contextual analysis provides an important complement to a vocabulary program that includes instruction in specific words as well as independent reading and word play and word consciousness activities.

—BAUMANN ET AL., 2003

More than 60% of the new words that readers encounter have relatively transparent morphological structure—that is, they can be broken down into [meaningful] parts.

—NAGY ET AL., 1989

For every word a child learns, we estimate that there are an average of one to three additional related words that should also be understandable to the child, the exact number depending on how well the child is able to utilize context and morphology to induce meaning.

—NAGY & ANDERSON, 1984

Teaching people to learn better from context can be a highly effective way of enhancing vocabulary development.

—STERNBERG, 1987

Suggested Reading . . .

Teaching and Learning Vocabulary: Bringing Scientific Research to Practice (2005) edited by Elfrieda H. Hiebert & Michael Kamil. New York: Routledge.

Teaching Vocabulary in All Classrooms, 4th Edition (2009) by Camille Blachowicz & Peter J. Fisher. Boston: Allyn & Bacon.

Teaching Word Meanings (2006) by Steven A. Stahl & William E. Nagy. Mahwah, NJ: Erlbaum.

The Vocabulary Book: Learning & Instruction (2006) by Michael F. Graves. New York: Teacher's College Press.

Vocabulary Instruction: Research to Practice, 2nd Edition (2012) edited by Edward J. Kame'enui & James F. Baumann. New York: Guilford.

What Research Has to Say About Vocabulary Instruction (2008) edited by Alan E. Farstrup & Jay Samuels. Newark, DE: International Reading Association.

when?

Word-Learning Strategies

> Teaching word-learning strategies will take a lot of time during initial instruction.
>
> —GRAVES, 2000

SEE ALSO . . .

CORE Literacy Library

Assessing Reading: Multiple Measures, 2nd Edition

When to Teach

Effective word-learning strategy instruction should provide students with sufficient opportunities to "internalize the strategies and receive the support required to apply them across multiple contexts over time" (Baumann et al. 2005). On the other hand, it is important not to dedicate inordinate amounts of time to such lessons. Graves (2000) suggests that middle-grade students spend two to four hours a week in *initial* word-learning strategy instruction—about three weeks out of the year. The average amount of instructional time for the whole school year would be about 20 minutes per week.

Based on word frequency data, some researchers recommend that instruction in morphemic analysis may be appropriate for students from about fourth grade on (Nagy, Diakidoy, and Anderson 1993; White, Power, and White 1989). However, as early as second grade, teachers may begin instruction in compound words, word families, and simple prefixes and suffixes.

New vocabulary can be acquired through the skillful use of context clues in reading and listening. Beginning in Kindergarten, when reading aloud, the teacher can model the use of context clues to determine the meaning of unfamiliar words or concepts. In Grades 2 and 3, students learn how to use context clues in independently read text. In Grades 4 and above, students learn about the types of context clues and their uses.

Sequence of Instruction

Contextual Analysis

Context clues in read-alouds

Context clues in independently read text

Types of context clues: definition, synonym, antonym, example, general

Morphemic Analysis

Compound words

Prefixes and derivational suffixes with Anglo-Saxon root words

Greek roots

Latin roots

Greek and Latin roots plus affixes

When to Assess and Intervene

The National Reading Panel (2000) suggests that a sound evaluation is based on data from more than a single vocabulary assessment. The more closely the assessment matches the instructional context, the more appropriate the conclusions about the instruction will be. Assessment that is tied to instruction will provide better information about students' specific learning.

According to Blachowicz and Fisher (2002), what is central to the assessment of word-learning strategies is a process, such as thinking aloud or self-evaluation, that reveals the students' metacognitive thinking. For example, teachers can ask students to "Say out loud the thinking you were doing as you figured out the meanings of the words" (Baumann et al. 2002). Simple alternative, authentic assessment formats also can be useful, and the multiple-choice format of most standardized tests also provides a global measure of vocabulary and may be used as a baseline.

Purpose	✓ Norm-Referenced Vocabulary Assessment	Publisher
Diagnostic	Gates-MacGinitie Reading Tests, 4th Edition (GMRT)	Riverside Publishing
Diagnostic	Peabody Picture Vocabulary Test, 4th Edition (PPVT-4)	Pearson
Diagnostic	Stanford Diagnostic Reading Test, 4th Edition (SDRT-4)	Pearson
Diagnostic	Woodcock Reading Mastery Tests, 3rd Edition (WRMT™-III)	Pearson

how?

Word-Learning Strategies

LESSON MODEL FOR

Dictionary Use

Benchmark

- ability to effectively use the dictionary to determine the precise meaning of words

Strategy Grade Level

- Grade 2 and above

Prerequisite

- knowing how to locate words in a dictionary

Grouping

- whole class
- small group or pairs

Sample Texts (Resources)

- "Weekend Campout" Complexity Level: Grades 2–3
- "Percussion Instruments" Complexity Level: Grades 4–5

Materials

- dictionaries
- PDF of "Weekend Campout"
- PDF of "Percussion Instruments"
- Vocabulary Hotshot Notebooks

Using the Dictionary

Since students frequently have difficulty using the dictionary to find definitions of unknown words, they need to be taught how to work effectively with a tool that they will use throughout their school years and that many adults use almost daily (Graves et al. 2004; Miller and Gildea 1987). This sample lesson model can be adapted and used to enhance vocabulary instruction in any commercial reading or content-area program.

Direct Explanation

Tell students that they are going to be learning how to use a dictionary to define, clarify, and confirm the meaning of unfamiliar words. Explain that it is worthwhile to learn how to find the correct definition in the dictionary and that using the dictionary isn't always as simple as it may seem.

Say: *You don't just use a dictionary to look up a word you've never seen or heard of before. Often you look up a word that you think you already know but whose actual meaning you want to discover. Sometimes you know what a word means but you want to get a more exact definition. Sometimes you are not exactly sure what a word means and you want to confirm that you are using it correctly. Wondering about words is a good start when it comes to using a dictionary. Anytime you use a word and think, "Does that word mean what I think it means?" you can reach for a dictionary and find out.*

Guidelines for Using the Dictionary

The first entry that you find for a word might not be the one you are looking for. Make sure you have found and read all the entries for a word.

When you find the right entry, read all the different meanings, or definitions, that the dictionary gives for the word. Do not just read part of the entry.

Choose the dictionary meaning that best matches the context in which the word is used. One meaning will make sense, or fit better, than any other.

Weekend Campout

THE FRANCO FAMILY loves to be outdoors. They spend almost every weekend camping. Fay Franco adores camping more than anything. She will even pitch her tent in the backyard just to sleep outside.

Fay has been to lots of campgrounds. Mar Vista Shores is her favorite. The campsites are in the tall trees. Each spot has a beach view.

At Mar Vista Shores, noisy birdcalls wake Fay early. She hears loud squawking and jumps up for breakfast. Then she packs a picnic. Fay and her dad drive to the trailhead. It is the place where the hiking trails start. They choose a path to take. Dad carries a daypack. It holds a first aid kit, sweatshirts, food, and water. The path leads sharply uphill to a waterfall. It is a steep climb! They hungrily devour their lunch by the riverbank. From the rocks, Fay can watch the water plummet over the cliff.

In the afternoon, Fay and her mom go to the seashore. Mom is a rock hound. She hunts for neat-looking stones. Fay makes sandcastles. Using wet sand, she builds high walls and towers. Sometimes she pokes around the tide pools. She looks for crabs and starfish in the rocks along the beach.

At dinnertime, the Franco family usually has a sunset cookout. They light a campfire. They roast hotdogs. The sky turns pink over the water. Nighttime falls. Fay gets into her sleeping bag. She looks up to see the stars twinkle overhead.

Fay thinks that weekend campouts are almost perfect. The only flaw comes when it is time to go home.

VOCABULARY HANDBOOK • WEEKEND CAMPOUT 207

Display Guidelines for Using the Dictionary, such as the example shown above. Discuss the guidelines aloud, explaining each one of the points. Make sure that students understand the kinds of information they can derive from a dictionary definition.

Teach/Model

Use interactive whiteboard technology to display "Weekend Campout." Underline the word *pitch* in the fourth sentence. Tell students that you are going to show them how to use a dictionary to determine the meaning of the word *pitch.* Explain that they might have a feel for what the word *pitch* means without being exactly sure. Then read aloud the following sentence:

DICTIONARY USE

Target Word

pitch

She will even pitch her tent in the backyard just to sleep outside.

Have students look up the word *pitch* in the dictionary; a possible dictionary entry appears below.

> [1]**pitch** /pich/ *vb* **1 :** to throw a baseball to a batter **2 :** to set up and fix firmly in the ground **3 :** to fall or plunge forward with force
> [2]**pitch** *n* **1 :** a throw or toss **2 :** amount of slope **3 :** highness or lowness of a sound
> [3]**pitch** *n* **1 :** a dark, sticky substance that is made from tar **2 :** resin from pine trees

Instruction related to dictionary definitions should be simple and direct and involve children in analyzing dictionary definitions in the course of vocabulary instruction.

—STAHL, 2005

Read All the Entries

Refer to the first guideline. Ask students how many dictionary entries there are for the word *pitch.* (In the example given here, there are three.) Have students read all the entries and choose the one that seems to fit the meaning they are looking for. (In the example given here, it is the first entry.)

Read All the Different Meanings in an Entry

Refer to the second guideline. Ask students how many different meanings, or definitions, they find in the first entry. (Answers will vary depending on what dictionary is used. In the example given here, there are three meanings in the first entry.) Then invite a volunteer to read all three meanings in the first entry. Remind students not to stop when they come to the meaning they think they are looking for but to read the whole entry all the way through.

Choose the Meaning that Makes Sense

Now refer to the third guideline. Tell students to choose a definition for *pitch* from the first entry that they think makes sense in the context of the original sentence. For example, say: *In the sentence, I don't think that* pitch *has anything to do with throwing a baseball. I don't think she would throw a baseball at the tent in the backyard.* Continue with the other choices, talking through the reasoning that goes into eliminating the definitions that will not work. Then guide students to conclude that the meaning "to set up and fix firmly in the ground" is the correct meaning for *pitch.* Now have them try out the dictionary meaning they selected in the original sentence to confirm whether or not it makes sense. Say: *In the sentence, I am going to substitute* set up *for the word* pitch *to see if it makes sense. "She will even set up her tent in the backyard just to sleep outside." Yes, that makes sense.*

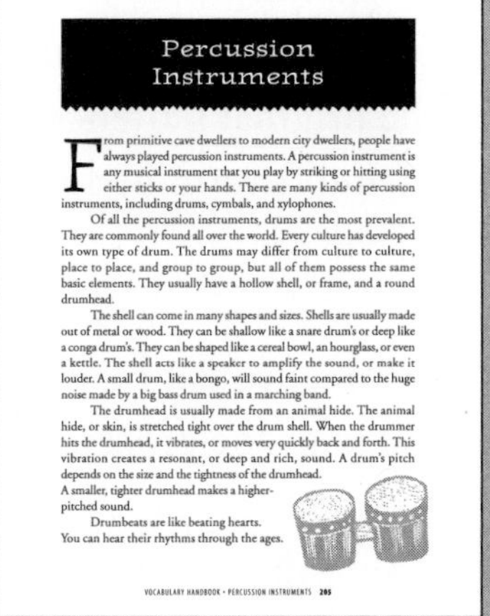

Percussion Instruments

From primitive cave dwellers to modern city dwellers, people have always played percussion instruments. A percussion instrument is any musical instrument that you play by striking or hitting using either sticks or your hands. There are many kinds of percussion instruments, including drums, cymbals, and xylophones.

Of all the percussion instruments, drums are the most prevalent. They are commonly found all over the world. Every culture has developed its own type of drum. The drums may differ from culture to culture, place to place, and group to group, but all of them possess the same basic elements. They usually have a hollow shell, or frame, and a round drumhead.

The shell can come in many shapes and sizes. Shells are usually made out of metal or wood. They can be shallow like a snare drum's or deep like a conga drum's. They can be shaped like a cereal bowl, an hourglass, or even a kettle. The shell acts like a speaker to amplify the sound, or make it louder. A small drum, like a bongo, will sound faint compared to the huge noise made by a big bass drum used in a marching band.

The drumhead is usually made from an animal hide. The animal hide, or skin, is stretched tight over the drum shell. When the drummer hits the drumhead, it vibrates, or moves very quickly back and forth. This vibration creates a resonant, or deep and rich, sound. A drum's pitch depends on the size and the tightness of the drumhead. A smaller, tighter drumhead makes a higher-pitched sound.

Drumbeats are like beating hearts. You can hear their rhythms through the ages.

VOCABULARY HANDBOOK • PERCUSSION INSTRUMENTS 205

DICTIONARY USE

Target Word

pitch

Guided Practice

Use interactive whiteboard technology to display "Percussion Instruments." Underline the word *pitch* in the fourth paragraph. Then read aloud the following sentence:

> **A drum's <u>pitch</u> depends on the size and tightness of the drumhead.**

Tell students that in this sentence the word *pitch* is used in a different context than it was used in "Weekend Campout." Then guide students to use the same dictionary entries to determine the meaning of the word *pitch* in this sentence. Remind students to refer to the Guidelines for Using the Dictionary. When students have analyzed all of the possible entries and definitions, discuss which meaning best fits. Then have students substitute the dictionary meaning they selected in the original sentence. For example, in this sentence "a drum's throw" doesn't make sense, but "a drum's highness or lowness of sound" does make sense.

Percussion Instruments

From primitive cave dwellers to modern city dwellers, people have always played percussion instruments. A percussion instrument is any musical instrument that you play by striking or hitting using either sticks or your hands. There are many kinds of percussion instruments, including drums, cymbals, and xylophones.

Of all the percussion instruments, drums are the most prevalent. They are commonly found all over the world. Every culture has developed its own type of drum. The drums may differ from culture to culture, place to place, and group to group, but all of them possess the same basic elements. They usually have a hollow shell, or frame, and a round drumhead.

The shell can come in many shapes and sizes. Shells are usually made out of metal or wood. They can be shallow like a snare drum's or deep like a conga drum's. They can be shaped like a cereal bowl, an hourglass, or even a kettle. The shell acts like a speaker to amplify the sound, or make it louder. A small drum, like a bongo, will sound faint compared to the huge noise made by a big bass drum used in a marching band.

The drumhead is usually made from an animal hide. The animal hide, or skin, is stretched tight over the drum shell. When the drummer hits the drumhead, it vibrates, or moves very quickly back and forth. This vibration creates a resonant, or deep and rich, sound. A drum's pitch depends on the size and the tightness of the drumhead. A smaller, tighter drumhead makes a higher-pitched sound.

Drumbeats are like beating hearts. You can hear their rhythms through the ages.

VOCABULARY HANDBOOK • PERCUSSION INSTRUMENTS 205

Independent Practice

Continue to display "Percussion Instruments." Point to and underline the word *faint.* Then read aloud the following sentence:

> **A small drum, like a bongo, will sound faint compared to the huge noise made by a big bass drum used in a marching band.**

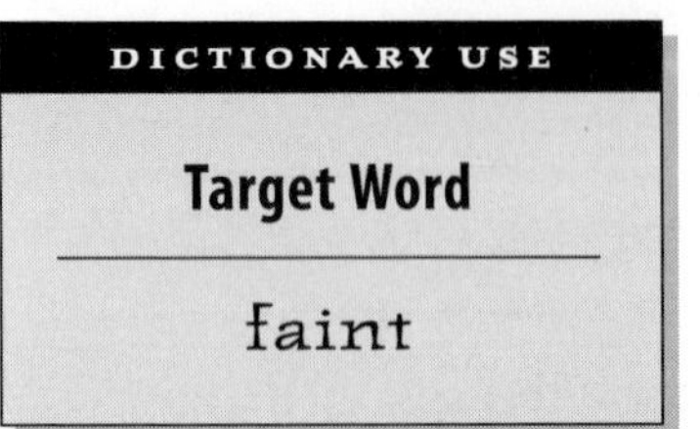

Have students refer to the Guidelines for Using the Dictionary as they find the appropriate dictionary definition for *faint.* (Possible response: *something that is not strong*) Remind students to choose the meaning that makes sense in the context of the sentence and to confirm their choice by substituting the dictionary definition they selected in the original sentence. After students have looked up the word and determined its meaning, encourage volunteers to model the process.

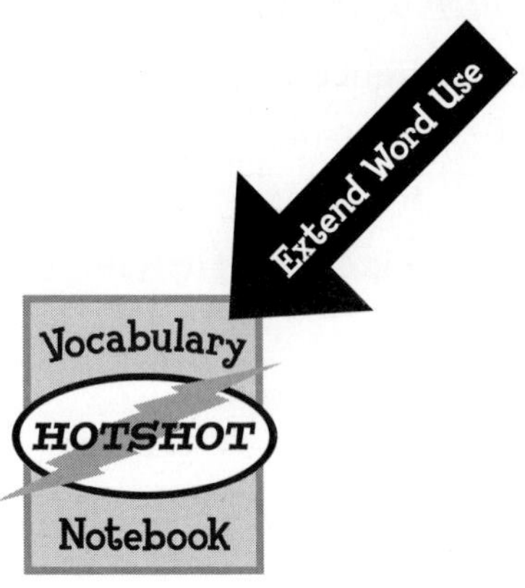

Encourage students to use the dictionary on a regular basis so that they become comfortable with it and with the procedure for finding word meanings. Invite students to share information they come across when they are learning about unfamiliar words or when they are verifying meanings for words that are familiar but not precisely known.

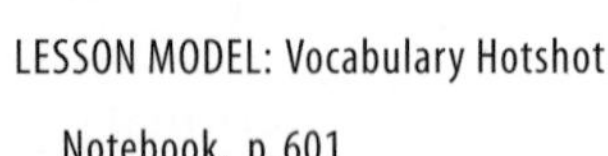

SEE ALSO . . .

LESSON MODEL: Vocabulary Hotshot Notebook, p. 601

LESSON MODEL FOR

Dictionary Use

Benchmarks

- ability to use the dictionary to verify a word's meaning
- ability to use context to predict a word's meaning

Strategy Grade Level

- Grade 3 and above

Grouping

- whole class
- small group or pairs

Prerequisite

- Using the Dictionary

Sample Text (Resources)

- "Alaska Adventure" Complexity Level: Grades 4–5

Activity Master (Resources)

- PAVE Map

Materials

- PDF and copies of PAVE Map
- dictionaries
- Vocabulary Hotshot Notebooks

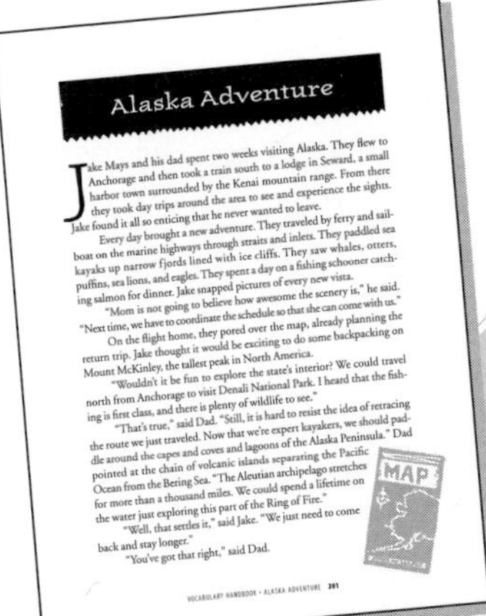

Alaska Adventure

Jake Mays and his dad spent two weeks visiting Alaska. They flew to Anchorage and then took a train south to a lodge in Seward, a small harbor town surrounded by the Kenai mountain range. From there they took day trips around the area to see and experience the sights. Jake found it all so enticing that he never wanted to leave.

Every day brought a new adventure. They traveled by ferry and sailboat on the marine highways through straits and inlets. They paddled sea kayaks up narrow fjords lined with ice cliffs. They saw whales, otters, puffins, sea lions, and eagles. They spent a day on a fishing schooner catching salmon for dinner. Jake snapped pictures of every new vista.

"Mom is not going to believe how awesome the scenery is," he said. "Next time, we have to coordinate the schedule so that she can come with us."

On the flight home, they pored over the map, already planning the return trip. Jake thought it would be exciting to do some backpacking on Mount McKinley, the tallest peak in North America.

"Wouldn't it be fun to explore the state's interior? We could travel north from Anchorage to visit Denali National Park. I heard that the fishing is first class, and there is plenty of wildlife to see."

"That's true," said Dad. "Still, it is hard to resist the idea of retracing the route we just traveled. Now that we're expert kayakers, we should paddle around the capes and coves and lagoons of the Alaska Peninsula." Dad pointed at the chain of volcanic islands separating the Pacific Ocean from the Bering Sea. "The Aleutian archipelago stretches for more than a thousand miles. We could spend a lifetime on the water just exploring this part of the Ring of Fire."

"Well, that settles it," said Jake. "We just need to come back and stay longer."

"You've got that right," said Dad.

VOCABULARY HANDBOOK • ALASKA ADVENTURE 281

PAVE Procedure

Developed by Bannon et al. (1990), PAVE stands for the components of this strategy: prediction, association, verification, and evaluation. In the PAVE Procedure, students predict a word's meaning using sentence context, verify its meaning by consulting the dictionary, evaluate the word's predicted meaning, and associate the word's meaning to an image (Blachowicz and Fisher 2002). This sample lesson model targets specific vocabulary found in "Alaska Adventure." The same model can be adapted and used to enhance vocabulary instruction in any commercial reading or content-area program.

Direct Explanation

Tell students that they are going to learn how to complete a PAVE Map. To complete the PAVE Map, they will use sentence context and a dictionary to confirm a target word's predicted definition. Explain that knowing how to follow the PAVE Procedure may help them to determine the appropriate meaning of an unfamiliar word.

Teach/Model

Read aloud the sample text "Alaska Adventure." Then use interactive whiteboard technology to display the PAVE Map. Tell students that you are going to take them through a step-by-step procedure for completing a PAVE Map for the word *vista*. Then model the procedure described on the following pages.

PAVE MAP

1 Context Sentence:
Jake snapped pictures of every new vista.

2 Target Word: vista

3 Predicted Meaning: nice view

4 Sentence Using Word's Predicted Meaning:
From our motel room, we can see a vista of the parking lot.

5 Word's Dictionary Definition: a distant view from a high place

6 Revised Sentence Using Verified Definition:
From the scenic overlook, there is a spectacular vista of snow-covered mountains that goes on as far as the eye can see.

7

Word Image

PAVE PROCEDURE

Target Word

vista

Point out to Spanish-speaking students that *vista* and *vista* are identically spelled cognates.

1. Copy the Context Sentence

On the map, point to and read aloud Step 1, Context Sentence. Say: *I'm going to find and copy the context sentence in which the word* vista *appears.* On the PAVE Map, print the sentence "Jake snapped pictures of every new vista." and read it aloud. Say: *In "Alaska Adventure," this is the context sentence in which the word* vista *appears.*

2. Print the Target Word

On the map, point to and read aloud Step 2, Target Word. Say: *Next, I'm going to print the target word* vista *on the map.* On the map, print the word *vista.* Then say: *Let's say the word together:* vista.

3. Predict the Word's Meaning

On the map, point to and read aloud Step 3, Predicted Meaning. Tell students that next you are going to use sentence context

to predict the meaning of the word *vista.* Say: *I predict that* vista *means "nice view" because in the sentence, Jack is taking pictures. People like to take pictures of nice views.* Print the predicted meaning on the map.

4. Write a Sentence Using the Word's Predicted Meaning

On the map, point to and read aloud Step 4, Sentence Using Word's Predicted Meaning. Say: *Now I'll make up a sentence using my predicted meaning of the word* vista*—"nice view." Here is my sentence: "From our motel room, we can see a vista of the parking lot."* Print the sentence on the map.

5. Use the Dictionary to Verify the Word's Meaning

On the map, point to and read aloud Step 5, Word's Dictionary Definition. Say: *Now, I am going to use a dictionary to verify my predicted meaning of the word* vista. *I've got to be sure to choose a definition that makes sense in the context of the sentence in which the word is used. First, I am going to check all definitions and find the one that is closest in meaning.* Read aloud the following sample dictionary entry:

> **vista 1.** A beautiful, distant view from a high place. **2.** A mental picture of a series of events in the past or future.

Say: *It looks like the first definition of* vista, *"a beautiful, distant view from a high place," is the one I should use. In my predicted definition, I thought* vista *meant "nice view." But to be more precise, a vista is more than a nice view. It is a distant view from a high place. I think a scenic overlook or the top of a mountain would be a good place to see a vista. I am going to write the dictionary definition for* vista *on the map.* On the map, write the definition, "a beautiful, distant view from a high place."

CONTINUED ▷

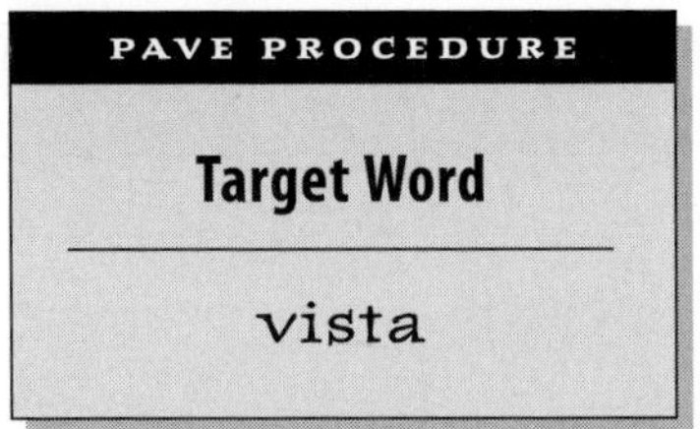

6. Revise the Sentence Using the Word's Verified Definition

On the map, point to and read aloud Step 6, Revised Sentence Using Verified Definition. Tell students that now you will revise your original sentence. Say: *Now I'm going to revise my original sentence so it has the sense of looking out from a high place to a view in the distance. Can you picture me at a scenic overlook looking out over hundreds of miles to a range of snow-capped mountains?* On the map, write a revised sentence using the dictionary definition. For example, "From the scenic overlook, there is a spectacular vista of snow-covered mountains that goes on as far as the eye can see."

7. Draw a Picture to Associate the Word's Meaning

On the map, point to and read aloud Step 7, Word Image. Tell students that drawing a picture, or image, of a word may help them to remember its meaning. On the map, make a quick sketch of a snow-covered mountain peak as seen from a distance. Say: *This image will help me to remember that a vista has to do with a distant view from a high place.*

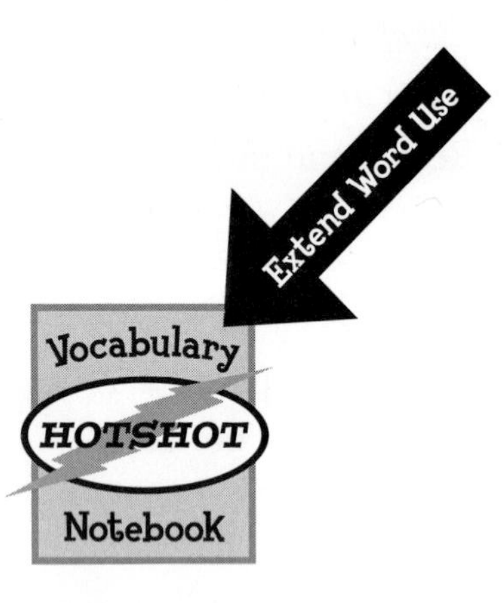

SEE ALSO . . .

LESSON MODEL: Vocabulary Hotshot Notebook, p. 601

Guided Practice

Give students each a copy of the PAVE Map. Choosing a possibly unfamiliar target word from a reading or content-area textbook, guide students through the steps of the PAVE Procedure as described above. This time, as you model filling in the PAVE Map, have students follow along by copying what you write onto their copies of the map. Encourage students to complete Steps 6 and 7 on their own, developing revised sentences and sketching their own word images.

PAVE MAP

1 Context Sentence:

They had come to a stream which twisted and tumbled between high rocky banks, and Christopher Robin saw at once how dangerous it was. "It's just the place," he explained, "for an Ambush."
"What sort of bush?" whispered Pooh to Piglet.

2 Target Word: ambush

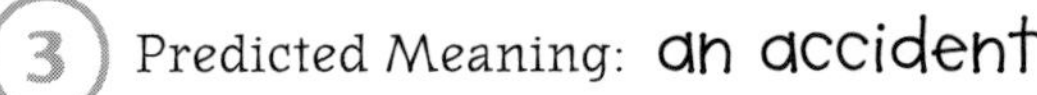

3 Predicted Meaning: an accident

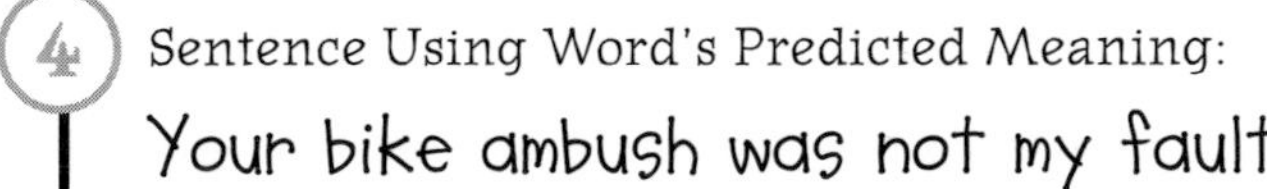

4 Sentence Using Word's Predicted Meaning:
Your bike ambush was not my fault.

7 "Boo!"

Word Image

5 Word's Dictionary Definition: a surprise attack made from a hiding place

6 Revised Sentence Using Verified Definition:
They hid in the thick grass until it was time for the ambush.

PAVE PROCEDURE

Target Word

ambush

Independent Practice

Give students each another copy of the PAVE Map. Ask them to choose an unfamiliar word from a selection or book they are reading and complete a PAVE Map for the word.

An example of a completed PAVE Map for the target word *ambush* in an excerpt from *Winnie the Pooh* by A. A. Milne is shown above. You may wish to ask volunteers to present their word to the rest of the class. Here is an example of a student presentation: *The target word was* ambush. *It was in this sentence: "It's just the place," he explained, "for an Ambush." I predicted that* ambush *meant "accident." From the dictionary, I found out that it means "a surprise attack made from a hiding place." So, the original sentence meant that this was just the place for a surprise attack. The sentence I wrote was: "They hid in the thick grass until it was time for the ambush." To remember the meaning of the word, I drew a picture of a bush saying, "Boo!"*

LESSON MODEL FOR

Dictionary Use

Benchmarks

- ability to complete a Concept of Definition Map
- ability to recognize and write a good dictionary definition

Strategy Grade Level

- Grade 3 and above

Grouping

- whole class
- small group

Sample Texts (Resources)

- "Percussion Instruments" Complexity Level: Grades 4–5
- "Marine Mammals" Complexity Level: Grades 4–5

Activity Master (Resources)

- Concept of Definition Map

Materials

- copies of "Percussion Instruments"
- PDF and copies of Concept of Definition Map
- copies of "Marine Mammals"
- dictionaries and other references
- Vocabulary Hotshot Notebooks

Concept of Definition Map

According to Schwartz and Raphael (1985), a Concept of Definition Map can help students to develop a clear, concrete idea of what "knowing" a word really means. A Concept of Definition Map includes the three elements of a good definition: (1) the overarching category to which the word belongs: What is it? (2) the important features or characteristics of the word or concept: What is it like? and (3) specific examples: What are some examples? This sample lesson model works best with nouns. The same model can be adapted and used to enhance vocabulary instruction in any commercial reading or content-area program.

Direct Explanation

Tell students that knowing the parts of a good definition will help them to analyze whether or not they "really know" the full meaning of a word or concept. Explain that completing a Concept of Definition Map will help them to understand the three elements of a good definition: the general category to which the word belongs, the defining features or characteristics of the word, and some examples of the word.

Teach/Model

Give students copies of the sample text "Percussion Instruments" and then read aloud the selection. Use interactive whiteboard technology to display the Concept of Definition Map. Print the word *drum* in the center box of the map. Tell students that using information about drums from the selection will help them learn about the parts of a dictionary definition.

Complete the Map

WHAT IS IT? Point to the heading What Is It? and ask a volunteer to read it aloud. Say: *A definition usually identifies the general category to which the word belongs. According to the text,*

CONCEPT OF DEFINITION MAP

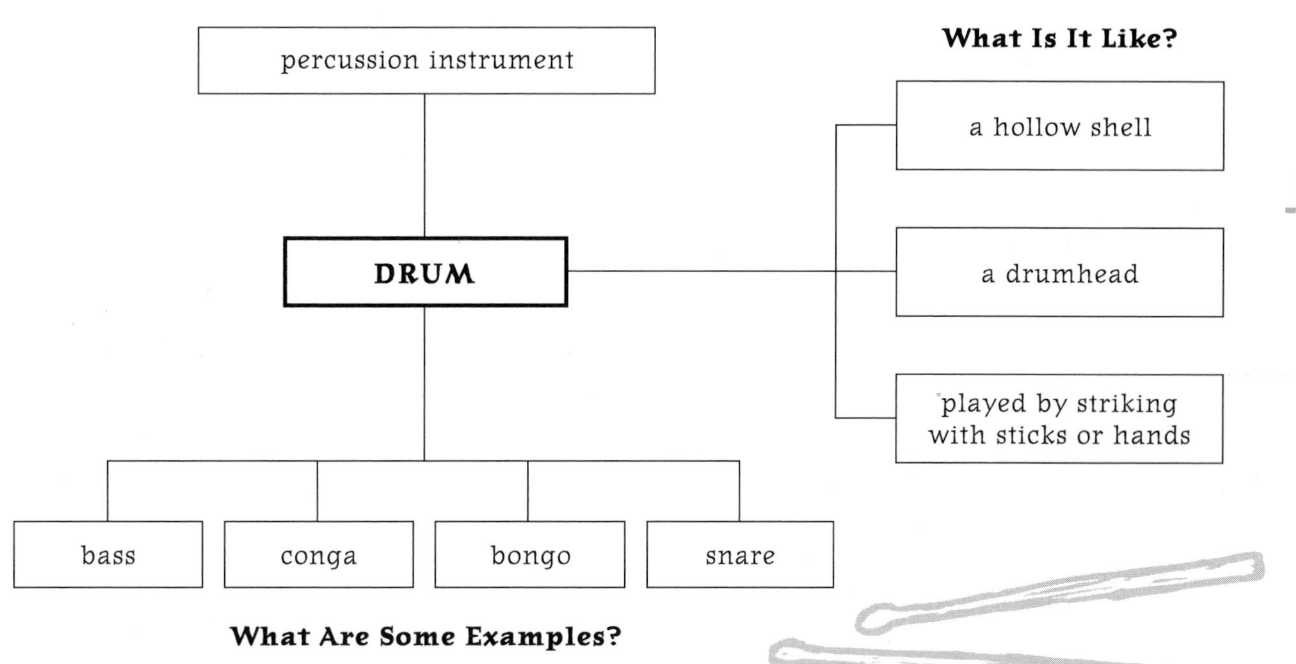

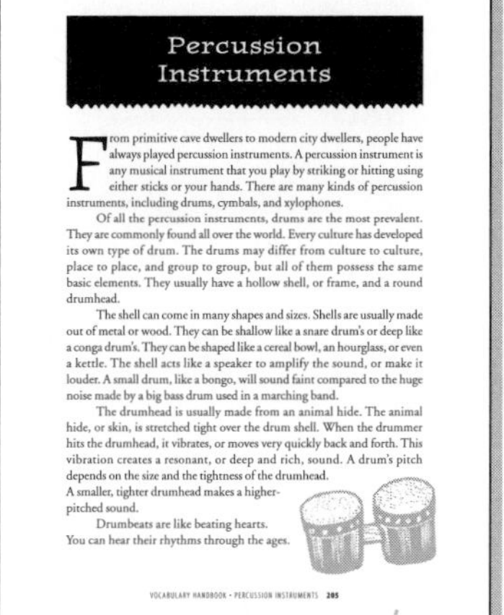

Percussion Instruments

From primitive cave dwellers to modern city dwellers, people have always played percussion instruments. A percussion instrument is any musical instrument that you play by striking or hitting using either sticks or your hands. There are many kinds of percussion instruments, including drums, cymbals, and xylophones.

Of all the percussion instruments, drums are the most prevalent. They are commonly found all over the world. Every culture has developed its own type of drum. The drums may differ from culture to culture, place to place, and group to group, but all of them possess the same basic elements. They usually have a hollow shell, or frame, and a round drumhead.

The shell can come in many shapes and sizes. Shells are usually made out of metal or wood. They can be shallow like a snare drum's or deep like a conga drum's. They can be shaped like a cereal bowl, an hourglass, or even a kettle. The shell acts like a speaker to amplify the sound, or make it louder. A small drum, like a bongo, will sound faint compared to the huge noise made by a big bass drum used in a marching band.

The drumhead is usually made from an animal hide. The animal hide, or skin, is stretched tight over the drum shell. When the drummer hits the drumhead, it vibrates, or moves very quickly back and forth. This vibration creates a resonant, or deep and rich, sound. A drum's pitch depends on the size and the tightness of the drumhead. A smaller, tighter drumhead makes a higher-pitched sound.

Drumbeats are like beating hearts. You can hear their rhythms through the ages.

VOCABULARY HANDBOOK • PERCUSSION INSTRUMENTS 205

a drum is a percussion instrument. I am going to print percussion instrument *in the box under What Is It?* Print the words *percussion instrument* in the box.

WHAT IS IT LIKE? Point to the heading What Is It Like? and ask a volunteer to read it aloud. Say: *A good definition usually includes important defining features or characteristics that show how the word is different from other members of its category. According to the selection, the features or characteristics of a drum include a hollow shell and a drumhead, played by striking with sticks or hands. I am going to print these features in the boxes below the heading What Is It Like?* Print the three features in boxes below the heading.

WHAT ARE SOME EXAMPLES? Point to the heading What Are Some Examples? and ask a volunteer to read it aloud. Say: *A definition sometimes gives examples of the word. The selection* *names the following kinds or types of drums: snare, conga, bongo, and bass. I am going to print the names of these drums in the boxes above the heading What Are Some Examples?* Print the names of the drums in boxes above the heading.

Use the Map to Write a Definition

Parts of a Dictionary Definition
category What Is It?
features What Is It Like?
examples What Are Some Examples?

Point out that a dictionary definition often follows the same structure as the parts of the map. A dictionary definition specifies the category to which a word belongs (What Is It?), its important features or characteristics (What Is It Like?), and some examples or types (What Are Some Examples?).

Display the following incomplete sentences and read them aloud by saying: *A drum is a blank. It has blank, blank, and blank. Some types of drums are blank, blank, and blank.*

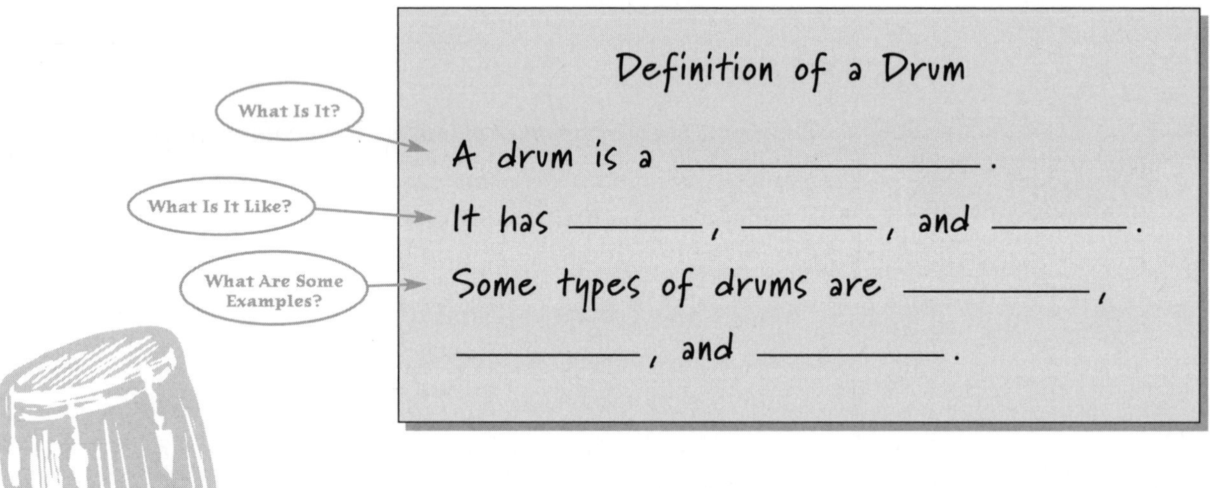

Definition of a Drum
What Is It?
A drum is a ________.
What Is It Like?
It has ______, ______, and ______.
What Are Some Examples?
Some types of drums are ______, ______, and ______.

Have students use the three categories of information (What Is It? What Is It Like? What Are Some Examples?) on the map to fill in the blanks and create a comprehensive definition of a drum. For example: *A drum is a percussion instrument. It has a hollow shell, a drumhead, and is played by striking with sticks or hands. Some types of drums are bass, conga, bongo, and snare.*

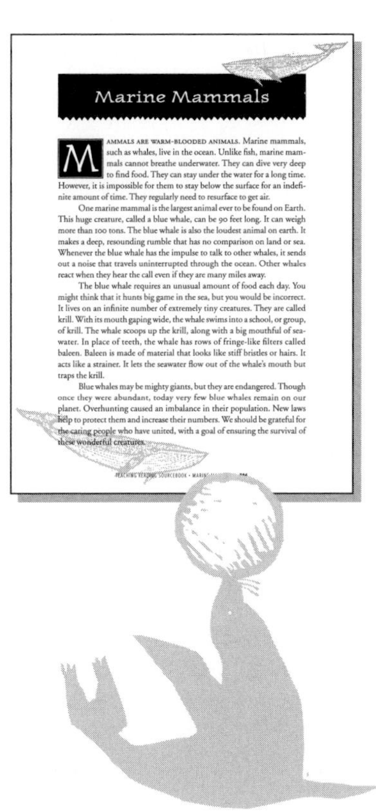

Marine Mammals

MAMMALS ARE WARM-BLOODED ANIMALS. Marine mammals, such as whales, live in the ocean. Unlike fish, marine mammals cannot breathe underwater. They can dive very deep to find food. They can stay under the water for a long time. However, it is impossible for them to stay below the surface for an indefinite amount of time. They regularly need to resurface to get air.

One marine mammal is the largest animal ever to be found on Earth. This huge creature, called a blue whale, can be 90 feet long. It can weigh more than 100 tons. The blue whale is also the loudest animal on earth. It makes a deep, resounding rumble that has no comparison on land or sea. Whenever the blue whale has the impulse to talk to other whales, it sends out a noise that travels uninterrupted through the ocean. Other whales react when they hear the call even if they are many miles away.

The blue whale requires an unusual amount of food each day. You might think that it hunts big game in the sea, but you would be incorrect. It lives on an infinite number of extremely tiny creatures. They are called krill. With its mouth gaping wide, the whale swims into a school, or group, of krill. The whale scoops up the krill, along with a big mouthful of seawater. In place of teeth, the whale has rows of fringe-like filters called baleen. Baleen is made of material that looks like stiff bristles or hairs. It acts like a strainer. It lets the seawater flow out of the whale's mouth but traps the krill.

Blue whales may be mighty giants, but they are endangered. Though once they were abundant, today very few blue whales remain on our planet. Overhunting caused an imbalance in their population. New laws help to protect them and increase their numbers. We should be grateful for the caring people who have united, with a goal of ensuring the survival of these wonderful creatures.

Guided Practice

Give students copies of "Marine Mammals" and then read aloud the selection. Ask: *How many of you think you know what marine mammals are? Can you tell me the general category to which marine mammals belong? Can you name any important characteristics of marine mammals? Can you name any examples of marine mammals?* Tell students that they are going to discover what they really know about marine mammals by filling in a Concept of Definition Map.

Give students copies of the Concept of Definition Map. Then use interactive whiteboard technology to display the map. Print the words *marine mammal* in the center box of the map and direct students to do the same. Ask students to reread the first sentence. Ask: *To what general category does a marine mammal belong?* (warm-blooded animal) Print *warm-blooded animal* in the box under the heading What Is It? and direct

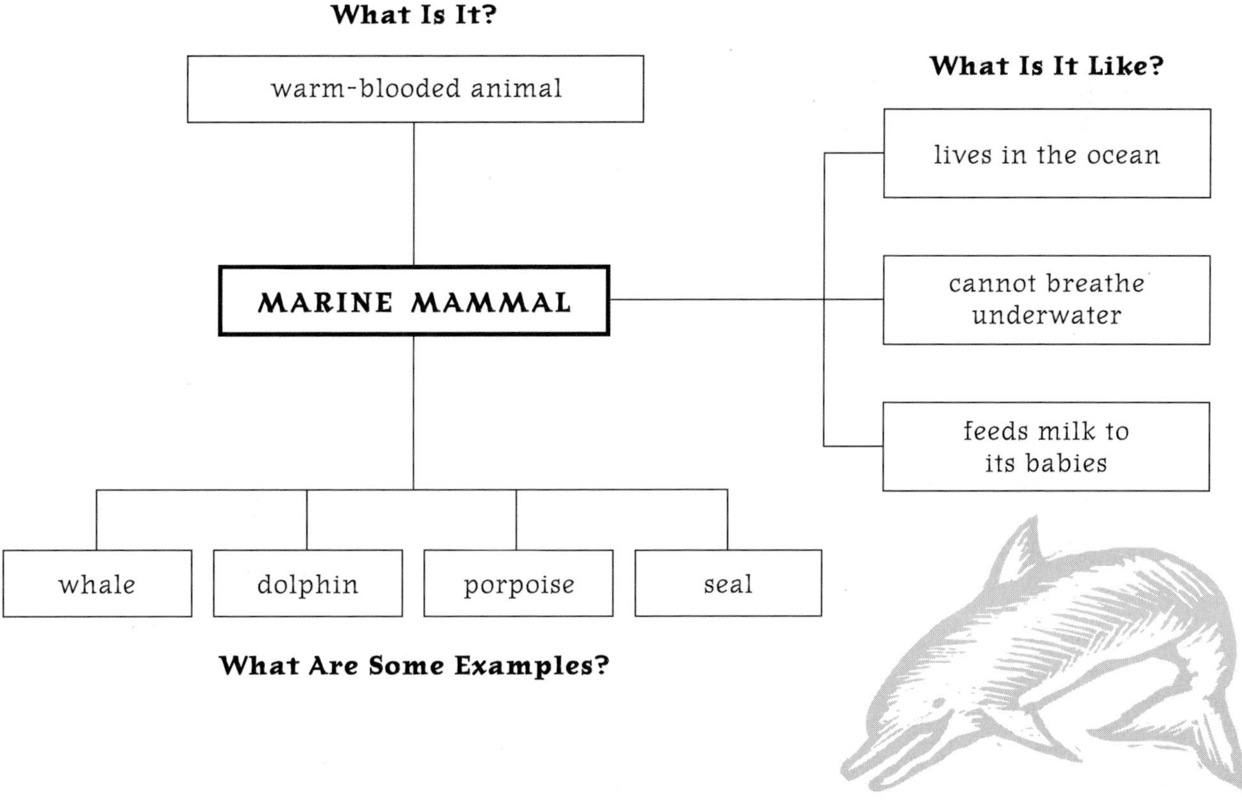

students to do the same. Ask: *According to the selection, what are important characteristics of a marine mammal?* (Possible responses: *lives in the ocean, cannot breathe underwater*) Print *lives in the ocean* and *cannot breathe underwater* in two of the boxes under the heading What Is It Like? and direct students to do the same. Ask: *What is one type of marine mammal?* (a whale) Print *whale* in one of the boxes above the heading What Are Some Examples? and direct students to do the same.

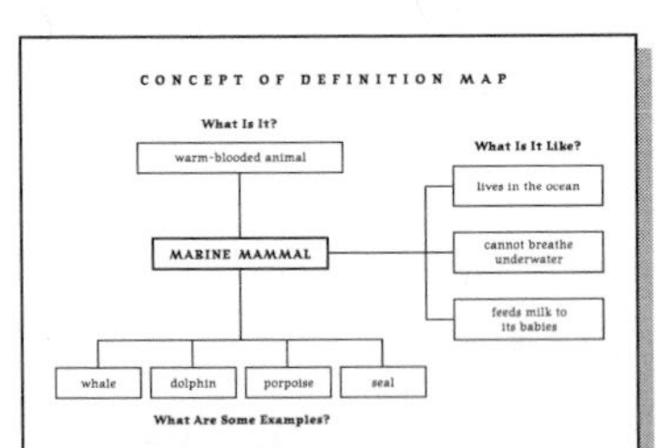

Point out to students that the map for marine mammals is incomplete. To complete the map, they need to fill in one more box under What Is It Like? and to provide three more examples above the heading What Are Some Examples? Ask students to use a dictionary or other reference materials to complete the map. Students might suggest adding *feeds milk to its babies* under What Is It Like? and the examples *dolphins, porpoises,* and *seals.* After students have completed their maps, have them use the information on the map to write a definition of a marine mammal. For example: *A marine mammal is a warm-blooded animal. It lives in the ocean, cannot breathe underwater, and feeds milk to its babies. Some examples of a marine mammal are whales, dolphins, porpoises, and seals.*

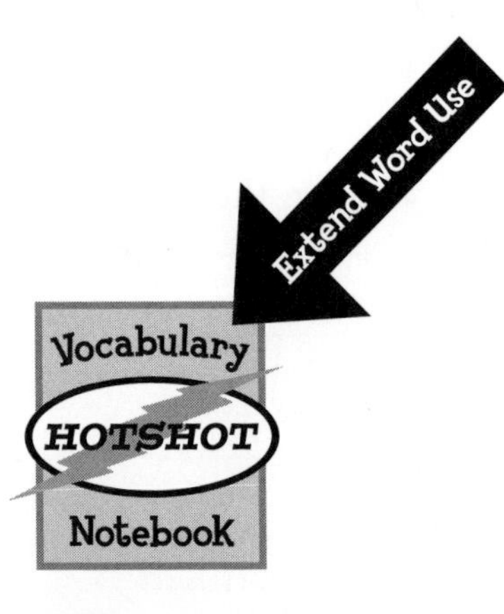

Give students opportunities to share their maps and definitions, describe the process they used, and tell if what they know now about marine mammals differs from what they knew before.

SEE ALSO . . .

LESSON MODEL: Vocabulary Hotshot Notebook, p. 601

Independent Practice

Provide students with another copy of the Concept of Definition Map so that they can explore other words or concepts they encounter in their reading. For example, students can choose words from authentic literature or content-area texts. Invite volunteers to discuss why they chose a particular target word and then share their maps and definitions.

LESSON MODEL FOR

Morphemic Analysis

Benchmark

- ability to use individual words in a compound word to derive its meaning

Strategy Grade Level

- Grade 2

Grouping

- whole class
- small group or pairs

Sample Text (Resources)

- "Weekend Campout" Complexity Level: Grades 2–3

Materials

- clip art pictures: a shoe and a shoebox
- word cards *shoe, box, bee, hive, class, room, dog, house, fire, wood, home, work, rain, coat, wrist, watch*
- PDF of "Weekend Campout"
- dictionaries
- Vocabulary Hotshot Notebooks

Compound Words

The meaning of some compound words can be derived from the meanings of the two smaller words that comprise them: for example, *doghouse* and *bluebird.* Other compound words have a meaning that differs from the meaning of the two smaller words: for example, the word *butterfly.* This sample lesson model can be adapted and used to enhance vocabulary instruction in any commercial reading or content-area program.

Direct Explanation

Tell students that *shoebox* is a compound word—a word made up of two smaller words. Display the word cards *shoe* and *box* and have students read them aloud. Next, push or set the cards together to form the word *shoebox.* Have students say the new word and provide a simple definition; for example, "a box for shoes." Say: *The word* shoebox *is made up of two smaller words that can each stand alone. Knowing the meaning of each of the words in a compound word can help you figure out the meaning of the whole word.*

Teach/Model

Using interactive whiteboard technology, display the picture of a shoe. Say: *This is a shoe.* Print the word *shoe* below the picture. Remove the picture of the shoe and display the picture of a shoebox. Say: *This is a box.* Print the word *box* below the picture. Now show the picture of the shoe again. Move, or drag, the shoe inside the shoebox. Say: *Now, we have a shoebox.* Ask: *What is a shoebox?* (a box for shoes) Print the word *shoebox,* and say: *Now we have shoebox.*

Read the following sentences aloud, asking students to suggest the compound word that completes each sentence.

- A box for shoes is a ________________. (shoebox)
- A fish that is gold is a ________________. (goldfish)
- A boat that sails is a ________________. (sailboat)
- A bird that is blue is a ________________. (bluebird)

Display the following word cards in random order: *bee, hive, class, room, dog, house, fire, wood, home, work, rain, coat, wrist, watch.* Read the words aloud with students. Point out that each word has a meaning of its own, and that each can be used as part of a compound word. Have students suggest compound words that can be made from two of the word cards; as they suggest them, slide the two word cards together. Then invite volunteers to take turns making up incomplete sentences (like the ones above) for their classmates to complete. For example, they might suggest: *A house for a dog is a* ______________.

Some compound words have a meaning that differs from the meaning of the two smaller words. Point out to students examples of these words, such as *butterfly* and *hotdog*.

Guided Practice

Use interactive whiteboard technology to display "Weekend Campout." Read the selection aloud, as students follow along with you. Then circle the following compound words: *weekend, backyard, campgrounds,* and *campsites.* Say: *These words are compound words. Sometimes you can figure out the meaning of a compound word if you know the meaning of the two smaller words.* Ask: *What are the two smaller words that make up the compound word* weekend*?* (*week* and *end*) Ask: *Based upon the meaning of the two smaller words, what is the meaning of* weekend*?* (the end of the week) Follow the same procedure for the other three words.

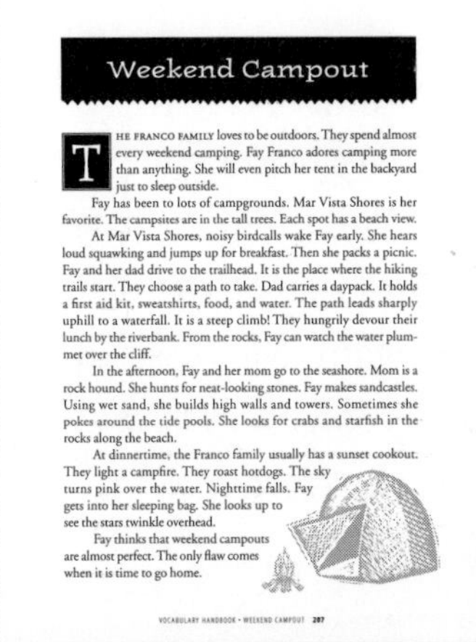

Weekend Campout

THE FRANCO FAMILY loves to be outdoors. They spend almost every weekend camping. Fay Franco adores camping more than anything. She will even pitch her tent in the backyard just to sleep outside.

Fay has been to lots of campgrounds. Mar Vista Shores is her favorite. The campsites are in the tall trees. Each spot has a beach view.

At Mar Vista Shores, noisy birdcalls wake Fay early. She hears loud squawking and jumps up for breakfast. Then she packs a picnic. Fay and her dad drive to the trailhead. It is the place where the hiking trails start. They choose a path to take. Dad carries a daypack. It holds a first aid kit, sweatshirts, food, and water. The path leads sharply uphill to a waterfall. It is a steep climb! They hungrily devour their lunch by the riverbank. From the rocks, Fay can watch the water plummet over the cliff.

In the afternoon, Fay and her mom go to the seashore. Mom is a rock hound. She hunts for neat-looking stones. Fay makes sandcastles. Using wet sand, she builds high walls and towers. Sometimes she pokes around the tide pools. She looks for crabs and starfish in the rocks along the beach.

At dinnertime, the Franco family usually has a sunset cookout. They light a campfire. They roast hotdogs. The sky turns pink over the water. Nighttime falls. Fay gets into her sleeping bag. She looks up to see the stars twinkle overhead.

Fay thinks that weekend campouts are almost perfect. The only flaw comes when it is time to go home.

VOCABULARY HANDBOOK • WEEKEND CAMPOUT 287

Compound Words	
weekend • end of a week	campgrounds • grounds on which to camp
backyard • yard in the back	campsites • sites or places on which to camp

Compound Words
birdcalls • calls of birds
breakfast • breaking the fast
trailhead • head of the trail
daypack • backpack for during the day
sweatshirts • shirts for sweat
uphill • up the hill
waterfall • place where water falls
riverbank • bank of a river
afternoon • after 12 o'clock noon
seashore • shore of the sea
sandcastles • castles made of sand
starfish • sea animal shaped like a star
dinnertime • time for dinner
sunset • setting of the sun
cookout • cooking food outdoors
campfire • fire built by campers
nighttime • time when it is night
overhead • over or above your head
weekend • end of the week
campouts • outdoor camping

Now circle the compound words *outdoors* and *outside.* Ask: *What are the two smaller words that make up the compound word* outdoors*?* (*out* and *doors*) Say: *The meaning of the compound word* outdoors *is different from the meaning of the two smaller words.* Outdoors *actually means "outside or in the open air," not "doors that go out." The same is true for* outside, *which actually means "in the open air."*

Independent Practice

Have pairs of students go through the remaining three paragraphs, finding and circling the compound words *birdcalls, breakfast, trailhead, daypack, sweatshirts, uphill, waterfall, riverbank, afternoon, seashore, sandcastles, starfish, dinnertime, sunset, cookout, campfire, hotdogs, nighttime, into, overhead, weekend,* and *campouts.* Remind students that some compound words have a meaning that differs from the meaning of the two smaller words, such as the words *hotdogs* and *into.* Then ask pairs to make a chart, like the one shown below, and use it to list each compound word, the two smaller words that make up the compound, and the meaning of the compound derived from the two smaller words. When students have finished, call on pairs to share information about the compound words they have found and listed on their charts.

COMPOUND WORD EVALUATION

Compound Word	Two Smaller Words	Meaning
trailhead	trail + head	the head of the trail

LESSON MODEL FOR

Morphemic Analysis

Benchmark

- ability to use concept of word families to derive the meanings of unfamiliar words

Strategy Grade Level

- Grade 2 and above

Prerequisite

- ability to identify root words

Grouping

- whole class
- small group or pairs

Materials

- dictionaries
- Vocabulary Hotshot Notebooks

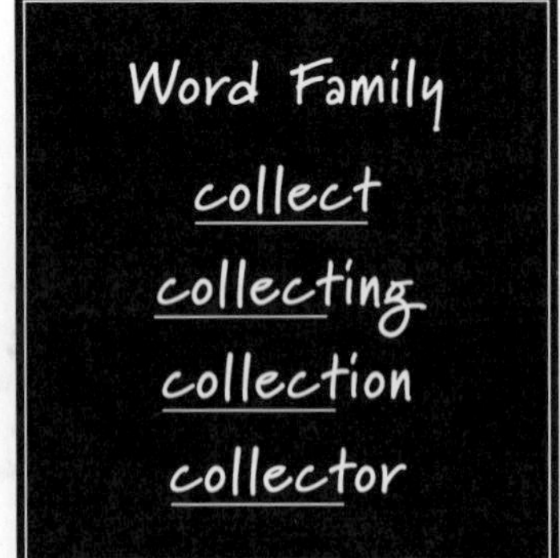

Word Families

According to Nagy and Anderson (1984), a word family is a group of words related in meaning. For example, the words *add, addition, additive,* and *adding* belong to the same word family. Since words in a family all share the same root word, students who know the meaning of one of the words in a family can guess or infer the meanings of the others. This sample lesson model focuses on using knowledge about root words and word families to derive the meanings of unfamiliar words. The same model can be adapted and used to enhance vocabulary instruction in any commercial reading or content-area program.

Direct Explanation

Remind students that a root word is a single word that cannot be broken into smaller words or parts. Tell them that they can sometimes figure out the meaning of an unfamiliar word if they know the meaning of its root word. Explain that a group of words that has the same root word is called a word family and that words belonging to the same word family have related meanings. Point out to students that the word family *runner, running,* and *rerun* share the same root word, *run.* Explain to students that knowing about root words and word families can help them to figure out the meanings of unfamiliar words encountered in their reading.

Teach/Model

Print the word family *collect, collecting, collection,* and *collector* on the board and read it aloud. Say: *These words all belong to the same word family.* Collect, collecting, collection, *and* collector *all are formed from the root word* collect. Underline the root word *collect* in the words. Say: *If you collect things, you bring them together from several places. A collector is someone who finds things and brings them together, and a collection is a group of different but related things, such as a CD collection. I'm going to make up some sentences using words that share the root word* collect*: My friend likes collecting things. He is a collector of South American stamps. He keeps his collection in his desk.* Ask students to brainstorm different kinds of collections or collectors that they know about.

Guided Practice

Remind students that word families are words that share the same root word. Then print the following sentences on the board:

HONEST

An honest person is someone who always tells the truth and does not cheat or break the law.

> Honestly, none of my friends are dishonest people. Honesty is something that I greatly respect. In my honest opinion, you cannot trust everyone.

> Word Family
> honestly
> dishonest
> honesty
> honest

Read the sentences aloud. Ask: *Which words have the same root word?* (honestly, dishonest, honesty, honest) Say: *That's right, the words* honestly, dishonest, honesty, *and* honest *belong to the same word family.* Ask: *What is the root word?* (honest) Print the word family on the board and ask a volunteer to underline the root word *honest.* Then call on volunteers to explain the meaning of the root word *honest* and how the meanings of the other words in the family are closely related. For example, ask:

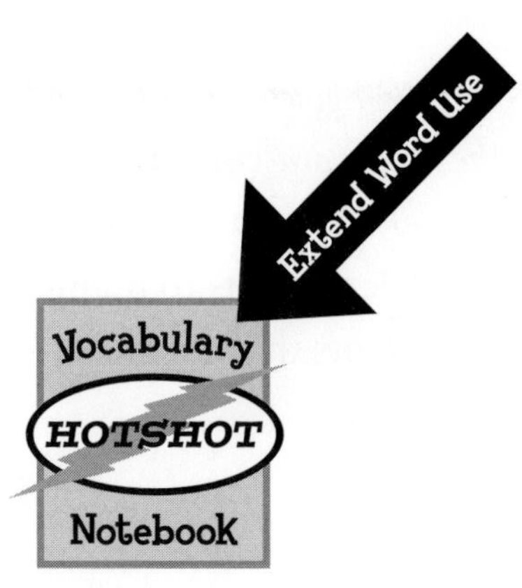

LESSON MODEL: Vocabulary Hotshot Notebook, p. 601

What are some examples of honesty? What are some examples of a lack of honesty, or dishonesty? (Answers will vary.) Then have students write sentences using words belonging to the *honest* word family. Provide an opportunity for students to share their sentences with the class.

Independent Practice

Challenge students to a Word Family Marathon. Give students 15 minutes to look through textbooks and other reading materials for words that are formed from root words. Have them make a list of the words on a worksheet, such as the one shown below. Then, for each word that they find, ask them to identify the root word and then brainstorm or use a dictionary to identify other words in the family. Have students each share one entry and explain how the meaning of the root word relates to the meaning of the other words in the family.

WORD FAMILY MARATHON

Word I Found	Root Word of Word I Found	Other Words in Family
disagree	agree	agreeable, agreeing, agrees, agreed, agreement

LESSON MODEL FOR

Morphemic Analysis

Benchmarks

- ability to identify the meaning of frequently used prefixes
- ability to derive word meanings from word-part clues

Strategy Grade Level

- Grade 2 and above

Prerequisite

- Introducing Affixes, p. 304

Grouping

- whole class
- small group or pairs
- individual

Sample Text (Resources)

- "Marine Mammals" Complexity Level: Grades 4–5

Materials

- chart paper
- PDF of "Marine Mammals"
- Vocabulary Hotshot Notebooks

Word-Part Clues: Prefixes

Graves (2004) defines prefixes as "elements that are attached to full English words." He suggests that beginning instruction in prefixes be restricted to common prefixes attached to Anglo-Saxon root words. Baumann et al. (2005) found that introducing affixes in groups or families helped students learn, recall, and apply them well. This sample lesson model targets prefixes *un–*, *in–*, and *im–*, or the "Not" Prefix Family. The same model can be adapted and used to enhance vocabulary instruction in any commercial reading or content-area program.

Direct Explanation

Remind students that a root word is a single word that cannot be broken into smaller words or word parts and that a prefix is a word part added to the beginning of a root word that changes its meaning. Explain to students that since many root words have prefixes, it is useful to know how to look for and use these word parts to figure out the meanings of words. Caution them, however, that while this strategy is often useful, there are occasions when it does not work at all.

Teach/Model

Print the following information about the "Not" Prefix Family on the board:

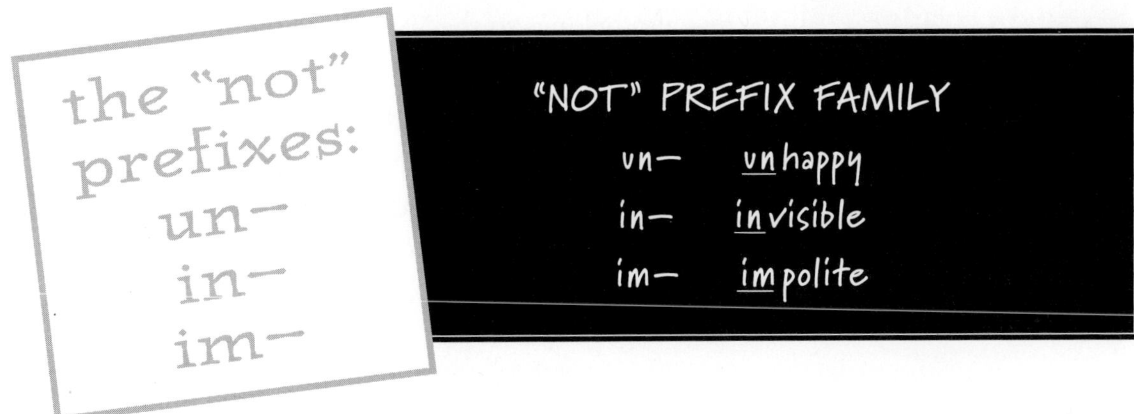

the "not" prefixes:
un–
in–
im–
"NOT" PREFIX FAMILY
un– unhappy
in– invisible
im– impolite

Explain to students that families of prefixes have meanings in common. The prefixes *un–, in–,* and *im–* belong to the "Not" Prefix Family because they share the meaning of "not." Point out that *unhappy* means "not happy," *invisible* means "not visible," and *impolite* means "not polite."

PREFIXES

un/certain
un/fair
un/wise

Print the words *uncertain, unfair,* and *unwise* on the board and read them aloud. Say: *These words all begin with the prefix* un–, *a prefix belonging to the "Not" Prefix Family.* Point to the word *uncertain.* Say: *I'm going to show you how to use word-part clues to figure out what this word means. First I'll break the word into parts: prefix and root word.* Draw a slash between *un* and *certain.* Say: Uncertain *has two parts, the prefix* un– *and the root word* certain. *The root word* certain *means "sure." The prefix* un– *means "not." Now I'll put the meanings of the word parts together to get the meaning of the whole word. If* un– *means "not" and* certain *means "sure," then* uncertain *must mean "not sure" or "not certain."* Ask: *Who can tell me something they are uncertain about?* (Answers will vary.) Follow the same procedure for *unfair* and *unwise.*

PREFIXES

in/active
in/complete
in/justice

Next print the words *inactive, incomplete,* and *injustice* on the board and read them aloud. Then follow the same teaching procedure as described above, pointing out that the prefix *in–* also belongs to the "Not" Prefix Family.

Finally, print the words *imperfect, immature,* and *improper* on the board and read them aloud. Then follow the same teaching procedure as described above, pointing out that the prefix *im–* also belongs to the "Not" Prefix Family.

POINT OUT LIMITATIONS Explain to students that they must be careful when using this word-part clue strategy because it does not always work. Point out that sometimes the removal of letters that appear to be a prefix leaves no meaningful root word. Then provide the following three examples:

Print the word *uncle* on the board and read it aloud. Draw a slash between *un* and *cle* and then cover up the letters *un.* Say: *When I cover up the letters* un *in* uncle, *I am left with* cle, *which is not a meaningful root word. The letters* u *and* n *at the beginning of* uncle *do not function as a prefix.*

in/dex

Print the word *index* on the board and read it aloud. Draw a slash between *in* and *dex* and then cover up the letters *in.* Say: *When I cover up the letters* in *in* index, *I am left with* dex, *which is not a meaningful root word. The letters* i *and* n *at the beginning of* index *do not function as a prefix.*

im/agine

Print the word *imagine* on the board and read it aloud. Draw a slash between *im* and *agine* and then cover up the letters *im.* Say: *When I cover up the letters* im *in* imagine, *I am left with* agine, *which is not a meaningful root word. The letters* i *and* m *at the beginning of* imagine *do not function as a prefix.*

un/easy

Now provide students with a different type of example. Print the word *uneasy* on the board and read it aloud. Draw a slash between *un* and *easy.* Say: *Sometimes, the combined meanings of a prefix and a root word do not help you to figure out the meaning of a whole word.* Uneasy *has two parts, the prefix* un– *and the root word* easy. *The prefix* un– *means "not." A common meaning of* easy *is "simple or effortless." But* uneasy *doesn't mean "not simple"; it actually means "uncomfortable or anxious." In this case, combining the meanings of the prefix* un– *and a common meaning of the root word* easy *doesn't result in the meaning of the whole word.*

The most common meaning of the word *easy* is "simple or effortless." Removing the suffix –*y* from *easy* leaves the root word *ease. Ease* can be defined as "the state of feeling comfortable."

WORD-PART CLUE EVALUATION

WORD	Does Not Have Prefix and Root Word	Has Prefix and Root Word	Prefix + Root Word = Meaning	Prefix + Root Word ≠ Meaning
unlike		un + like	not like	
impossible		im + possible	not possible	
indefinite		in + definite	not definite, unlimited	
uninterrupted		un + interrupted	not interrupted	
under	un + der			
impulse		im + pulse		sudden urge

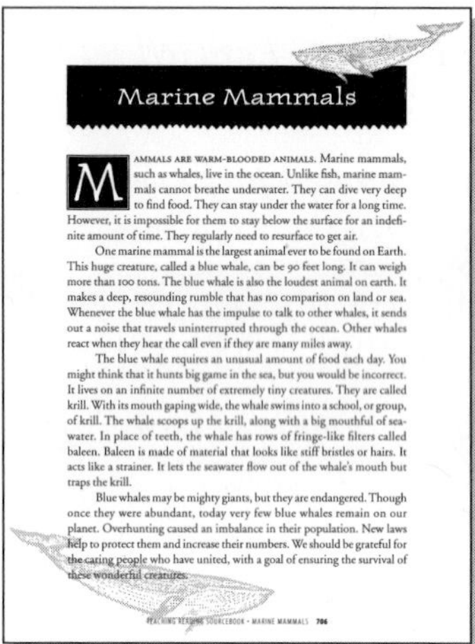

Marine Mammals

Mammals are warm-blooded animals. Marine mammals, such as whales, live in the ocean. Unlike fish, marine mammals cannot breathe underwater. They can dive very deep to find food. They can stay under the water for a long time. However, it is impossible for them to stay below the surface for an indefinite amount of time. They regularly need to resurface to get air.

One marine mammal is the largest animal ever to be found on Earth. This huge creature, called a blue whale, can be 90 feet long. It can weigh more than 100 tons. The blue whale is also the loudest animal on earth. It makes a deep, resounding rumble that has no comparison on land or sea. Whenever the blue whale has the impulse to talk to other whales, it sends out a noise that travels uninterrupted through the ocean. Other whales react when they hear the call even if they are many miles away.

The blue whale requires an unusual amount of food each day. You might think that it hunts big game in the sea, but you would be incorrect. It lives on an infinite number of extremely tiny creatures. They are called krill. With its mouth gaping wide, the whale swims into a school, or group, of krill. The whale scoops up the krill, along with a big mouthful of seawater. In place of teeth, the whale has rows of fringe-like filters called baleen. Baleen is made of material that looks like stiff bristles or hairs. It acts like a strainer. It lets the seawater flow out of the whale's mouth but traps the krill.

Blue whales may be mighty giants, but they are endangered. Though once they were abundant, today very few blue whales remain on our planet. Overhunting caused an imbalance in their population. New laws help to protect them and increase their numbers. We should be grateful for the caring people who have united, with a goal of ensuring the survival of these wonderful creatures.

TEACHING READING SOURCEBOOK • MARINE MAMMALS 706

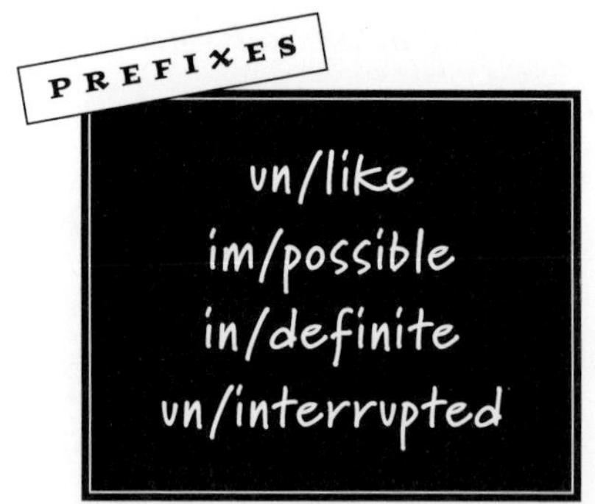

Guided Practice

Tell students that they are going to practice looking for words that appear to begin with "Not" Family Prefixes *un–, in–,* and *im–,* along with evaluating whether or not the letter groups are really prefixes and, if they are, whether or not using word-part clues is helpful in figuring out the meaning of the whole word. On chart paper, make a five-column Word-Part Clue Evaluation chart, such as the one shown above. Then read aloud and explain each of the column headings.

Use interactive whiteboard technology to display "Marine Mammals" and ask a volunteer to read aloud the first two paragraphs of the selection. Then guide students to identify the words in the sentences that may belong to the "Not" Prefix Family. On the chart, record the words *unlike, impossible, indefinite, uninterrupted, under,* and *impulse.* Next tell students that they are going to use the Word-Part Clue Evaluation chart to help them to analyze each of the listed words.

Point to the word *unlike* in the first paragraph of the selection. Say: *The word* unlike *begins with the letters* un, *which could be a prefix, so I'm going to try to break* unlike *into parts. I see the*

English/Spanish Cognates
impossible • imposible
impulse • impulso

root word like *and the prefix* un–, *so I'm going to print* un + like *in the third column of the chart under the heading Has Prefix and Root Word. Now I'll combine the meanings of the prefix* un– *and the root word* like. *I think* unlike *means "not like." To confirm, I'll substitute my meaning in the sentence: Not like fish, marine mammals can breathe underwater. Yes, "not like" makes sense. I'll print* not like *in the fourth column under the heading Prefix + Root Word = Meaning.*

Follow the same procedure for the words *impossible, indefinite,* and *uninterrupted.* All have prefixes and root words that are meaningful, so for these words the strategy works.

LIMITATIONS

un/der

LIMITATIONS Next, point to the word *under* in the first paragraph. Say: *The word* under *begins with the letters* un, *which could be a prefix, so I'm going to try to break the word into parts.* Ask: *Is* der *a meaningful word?* (no) *Do the letters* un *at the beginning of* under *function as a prefix?* (no) Say: *I'm going to print* un + der *in the second column of the chart under the heading Does Not Have Prefix and Root Word, to show that* under *does not have a prefix and a root word.*

im/pulse

Now point to the word *impulse* in the second paragraph. Say: *The word* impulse *begins with the letters* im, *which could be a prefix, so I'm going to try to break the word into parts. I see the root word* pulse, *so I'm going to print* im + pulse *in the third column under the heading Has Prefix and Root Word. Now I'll combine the meanings of the prefix* im– *and the root word* pulse. *The word* pulse *means "a regular beat," and the prefix* im– *means "not."* Ask: *When you combine these two meanings, what do you get?* ("not a regular beat") Say: *Right, I'm going to try out this meaning in the sentence: "Whenever the blue whale has not a regular beat to talk to other whales . . ."* Ask: *Does this meaning make sense in the sentence?* (no) Say: *That's right, the word* impulse *actually means "a sudden urge." Let's try this meaning in the sentence: "Whenever the blue whale has a sudden urge to talk to other*

Impulse **is a derivate of the word *impel. Impel* means "to be driven to do something."**

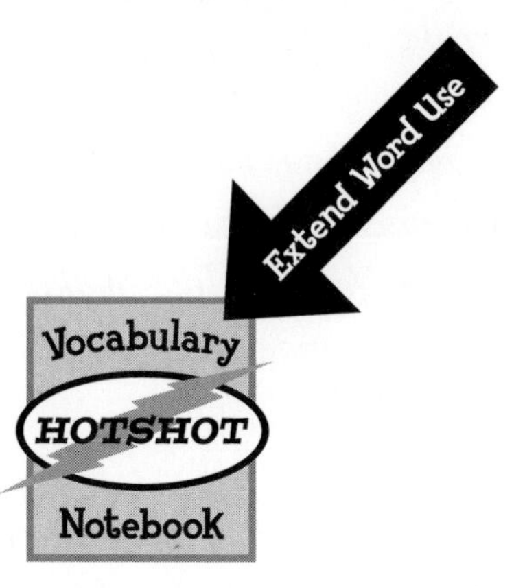

LESSON MODEL: Vocabulary Hotshot Notebook, p. 601

whales . . ." That makes sense! In this case, combining the meanings of the prefix im– *and the root word* pulse *did not result in the meaning of the whole word. For* impulse, *I'm going to print the phrase* sudden urge *in the last column under the heading Prefix + Root Word ≠ Meaning.*

Independent Practice

Have students make a five-column chart, such as the one shown below. Have them copy the headings from the Word-Part Clue Evaluation chart onto their papers. Tell them that they are going to use the chart to finish the evaluation of possible prefixed words in "Marine Mammals." After students have completed their analysis, go over what they have found as a group. Encourage students to share their data and their rationale.

WORD-PART CLUE EVALUATION

WORD	Does Not Have Prefix and Root Word	Has Prefix and Root Word	Prefix + Root Word = Meaning	Prefix + Root Word ≠ Meaning
unusual		un + usual	not usual	
incorrect		in + correct	not correct	
infinite		in + finite	not finite, not limited	
imbalance		im + balance	not balanced, not equal in importance	
increase		in + crease		to become greater in number
united	un + ited			

LESSON MODEL FOR

Morphemic Analysis

Benchmarks

- ability to identify the meaning of derivational suffixes
- ability to derive word meanings from word-part clues

Strategy Grade Level

- Grade 2 and above

Prerequisite

- Introducing Affixes, p. 304

Grouping

- whole class
- small group or pairs
- individual

Sample Text (Resources)

- "Marine Mammals" Complexity Level: Grades 4–5

Materials

- chart paper
- PDF of "Marine Mammals"
- Vocabulary Hotshot Notebooks

SUFFIXES

cheer/ful
peace/ful
truth/ful
use/ful

Word-Part Clues: Suffixes

Researchers recommend that teachers spend time teaching derivational suffixes because, like prefixes, they are fairly regular in meaning and can lead to vocabulary expansion (Edwards et al. 2004). Common derivational suffixes include *–able, –ful, –less, –ness,* and *–or.* This sample lesson model targets the derivational suffix *–ful,* which is stable and obvious in meaning and thus easy for students to understand and apply to words. The same model can be adapted and used to enhance vocabulary instruction in any commercial reading or content-area program.

Direct Explanation

Remind students that a root word is a single word that cannot be broken into smaller words or word parts and that a suffix is a word part added to the end of a root word that changes its meaning. Explain to students that since many root words have suffixes, it is useful to know how to look for and use these word parts to figure out the meanings of words. Caution them, however, that while this strategy is often useful, there are occasions when it does not work at all.

Teach/Model

Print the words *cheerful, peaceful, truthful,* and *useful* on the board and read them aloud. Say: *These words all end with the suffix* –ful, *which means "full of."*

Point to the word *cheerful.* Say: *I'm going to show you how to use word-part clues to figure out what this word means. First I'll break the word into parts: root word and suffix.* Draw a slash between *cheer* and *ful.* Say: Cheerful *has two parts, the root word* cheer *and the suffix* –ful. *The root word* cheer *means "joy." The suffix* –ful *means "full of." Now I'll put the meanings of the word parts together to get the meaning of the whole word. If* cheer *means "joy" and* –ful *means "full of," then* cheerful *must mean "full of joy."* Ask: *Who can tell me why someone might be cheerful?* (Answers will vary.) Follow the same procedure for *peaceful, truthful,* and *useful.*

POINT OUT LIMITATIONS Explain to students that they must be careful when using this strategy because it does not always work. Print the word *bashful* on the board and read it aloud. Draw a slash between *bash* and *ful.* Say: *Sometimes a root word is not obviously related in meaning to the whole word.* Say: Bashful *has two parts, the root word* bash *and the suffix* –ful. *The root word* bash *means "to smash something really hard." The suffix* –ful *means "full of." But the word* bashful *does not mean "full of a hard smash"; it actually means "uneasy in the presence of others." In this case, combining the meanings of the root word* bash *and the suffix* –ful *does not result in the meaning of the whole word.*

In *bashful*, the root word *bash* actually comes from the word *abash* which means "to make somebody feel ashamed, embarrassed, or uncomfortable."

Guided Practice

Tell students that they are going to practice looking for words that end with the suffix *–ful,* along with evaluating whether or not using word-part clues is helpful in figuring out the meaning of the whole word. On chart paper, make a four-column Word-Part Clue Evaluation chart, such as the one shown below. Then read aloud and explain each of the column headings.

WORD-PART CLUE EVALUATION

WORD	Has Root Word and Suffix	Root Word + Suffix = Meaning	Root Word + Suffix ≠ Meaning
mouthful	mouth + ful	a full mouth	
wonderful	wonder + ful	full of wonder	
grateful	grate + ful		wanting to thank someone

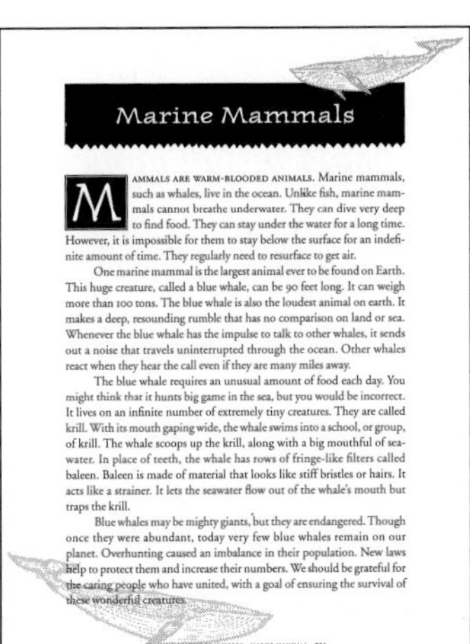

Marine Mammals

MAMMALS ARE WARM-BLOODED ANIMALS. Marine mammals, such as whales, live in the ocean. Unlike fish, marine mammals cannot breathe underwater. They can dive very deep to find food. They can stay under the water for a long time. However, it is impossible for them to stay below the surface for an indefinite amount of time. They regularly need to resurface to get air.

One marine mammal is the largest animal ever to be found on Earth. This huge creature, called a blue whale, can be 90 feet long. It can weigh more than 100 tons. The blue whale is also the loudest animal on earth. It makes a deep, resounding rumble that has no comparison on land or sea. Whenever the blue whale has the impulse to talk to other whales, it sends out a noise that travels uninterrupted through the ocean. Other whales react when they hear the call even if they are many miles away.

The blue whale requires an unusual amount of food each day. You might think that it hunts big game in the sea, but you would be incorrect. It lives on an infinite number of extremely tiny creatures. They are called krill. With its mouth gaping wide, the whale swims into a school, or group, of krill. The whale scoops up the krill, along with a big mouthful of seawater. In place of teeth, the whale has rows of fringe-like filters called baleen. Baleen is made of material that looks like stiff bristles or hairs. It acts like a strainer. It lets the seawater flow out of the whale's mouth but traps the krill.

Blue whales may be mighty giants, but they are endangered. Though once they were abundant, today very few blue whales remain on our planet. Overhunting caused an imbalance in their population. New laws help to protect them and increase their numbers. We should be grateful for the caring people who have united, with a goal of ensuring the survival of these wonderful creatures.

TEACHING READING SOURCEBOOK • MARINE MAMMALS 706

Use interactive whiteboard technology to display "Marine Mammals" and ask a volunteer to read aloud the last two paragraphs of the selection. Then guide students to identify the words in the sentences that contain the suffix *–ful.* On the chart, record the words *mouthful, wonderful,* and *grateful.* Next, tell students that they are going to use the Word-Part Clue Evaluation chart to help them to analyze each of the listed words.

Point to the word *mouthful* in the third paragraph of the selection. Say: *The word* mouthful *ends with the letters* ful, *which could be a suffix, so I'm going to try to break* mouthful *into parts.* Ask: *Who can tell me the root word?* (mouth) *Who can tell me the suffix?* (ful) *The word* mouthful *has a root word and a suffix, so I am going to print* mouth + ful *in the second column of the chart under the heading Has Root Word and Suffix.* Say: *The suffix* –ful *can mean "full."* Ask: *When you combine the meanings of* mouth *and* –ful, *what do you get?* ("a full mouth") Say: *Right, I'm going to try the meaning in the sentence: "The whale scoops up the krill, along with a full mouth of sea water." That makes sense. So I'm going to print the phrase* a full mouth *in the third column under the heading Root Word + Suffix = Meaning.* Follow the same procedure for the word *wonderful* in the fourth paragraph of the selection.

CONTINUED ▷

LIMITATIONS Now point to the word *grateful* in the fourth paragraph. Say: *The word* grateful *ends with the letters* ful, *which could be a suffix, so I'm going to try to break* grateful *into parts. I see the root word* grate, *so I'm going to print* grate + ful *in the second column under the heading Has Root Word and Suffix. Now I'll combine the meanings of the root word and the suffix.* Ask: *What is a meaning of the root word* grate*?* ("a metal grid, like the one on a barbecue") *What is the meaning of the suffix* –ful*?* ("full of") Ask: *When you put together these two meanings, what do you get?* ("full of metal grid") Say: *Right, I'm going to try out this meaning in the sentence: "We should be full of metal grid for the caring people. . . ."* Ask: *Does this meaning make sense in the sentence?* (no) Say: *That's right, the word* grateful *actually means "wanting to thank someone." Let's try this meaning in the sentence: "We should want to thank the caring people. . . ." That makes sense! In this case, combining the meanings of the root word* grate *and the suffix* –ful *did not result in the meaning of the whole word. For* grateful, *I'm going to print the phrase* wanting to thank someone *in the last column under the heading Root Word + Prefix ≠ Meaning.*

The *grate* in *grateful* actually comes from the Latin root *grat* which means "thanks."

Independent Practice

Have students fold lined sheets of paper lengthwise into fourths and then copy onto their paper the headings from the Word-Part Clue Evaluation chart. Tell students that they are going to use the chart to record and analyze words that end with the suffix *–ful.* Then direct them to look through their textbooks for words that end in the suffix *–ful.* After students have finished finding words and evaluating them, have the group share the words they have found along with their evaluations.

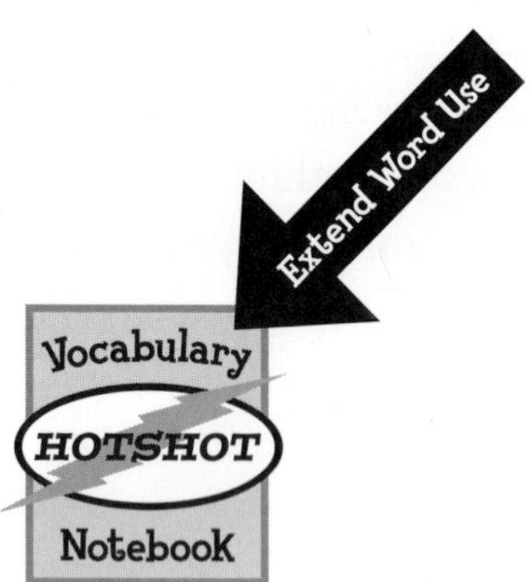

SEE ALSO . . .

LESSON MODEL: Vocabulary Hotshot Notebook, p. 601

LESSON MODEL FOR

Morphemic Analysis

Benchmark

- ability to use knowledge of Greek roots to derive the meaning of unfamiliar words

Strategy Grade Level

- Grade 4 and above

Grouping

- whole class
- small group or pairs

Sample Text (Resources)

- "Studying the Sky" Complexity Level: Grades 3–4

Activity Master (Resources)

- Word-Part Web

Materials

- PDF and copies of Word-Part Web
- PDF of "Studying the Sky"
- dictionaries
- Vocabulary Hotshot Notebooks

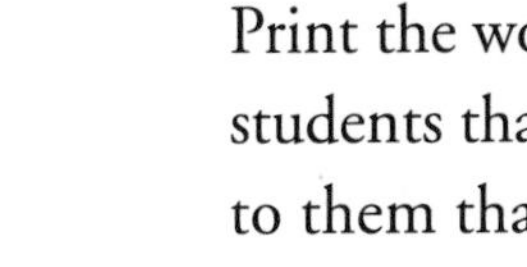

tele + phone = telephone

Word-Part Clues: Roots

Students should understand that Greek and Latin roots are important meaning elements within words. It is useful to select roots from texts students are reading, choosing those that are most likely to occur again. Generally, Greek roots are introduced before Latin roots because their meanings are more apparent and the way in which they combine with other elements is more understandable. This sample lesson model focuses on knowledge of Greek roots to derive the meanings of unfamiliar words. The same model can be adapted and used to enhance vocabulary instruction in any commercial reading or content-area program.

Direct Explanation

Tell students that roots are word parts that come from the Greek and Latin languages. Explain that the difference between a root word and a root is that a root word, such as *play,* can stand alone as a word in English, but a root, such as *tele,* is not a word in English. Tell students that knowing about Greek roots can help them to figure out the meanings of unfamiliar words.

Teach/Model

Print the word *telephone* on the board and read it aloud. Tell students that they all know what a telephone is. Then explain to them that they may not know that the word *telephone* is made up of two Greek roots: *tele* and *phone.* Underline *tele* in *telephone.* Tell students that the Greek root *tele* means "distant or far away." Then print the following mathematical sentence on the board and read it aloud: *tele + phone = telephone.*

Say: *The other Greek root in* telephone *is* phone*; it means "sound." So if* tele *means "distant" and* phone *means "sound," the word* telephone *literally means "distant sound."* Ask: *Can anyone tell* *me how this literal meaning of the word* telephone *relates to the real-life function of a telephone?* (Possible response: *A telephone is equipment that is used to talk to someone in another, usually distant, place.*)

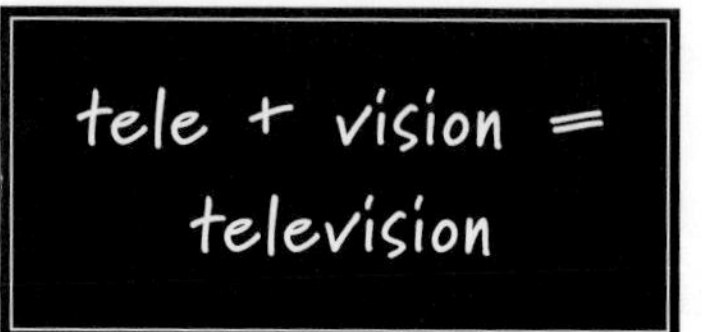

Next, print the word *television* on the board. Explain that the word *television* is made up of the root *tele* and the word *vision.* Underline *tele* in *televison.* Then print the following mathematical sentence on the board and read it aloud: *tele + vision = television.*

Point out to Spanish-speaking ELLs that *television* and *televisión* are identically spelled cognates.

Say: Vision *is not a word of Greek origin. You may already know the meaning of the word* vision—*it has to do with "the ability to see something." So if* tele *means "distant," the word* television *literally means "distant vision."* Ask: *Can anyone tell me how this literal meaning of the word* television *relates to the real-life function of television?* (Possible response: *Television is a system of sending pictures, and sounds, over a distance so people can see them on a television set.*)

Use interactive whiteboard technology to display the Word-Part Web. Say: *I am going to begin a Word-Part Web for* tele. Print the word part *tele* in the middle oval. Say: *The words* telephone *and* television *both contain the root* tele. Then print these words in the web, as shown on the facing page.

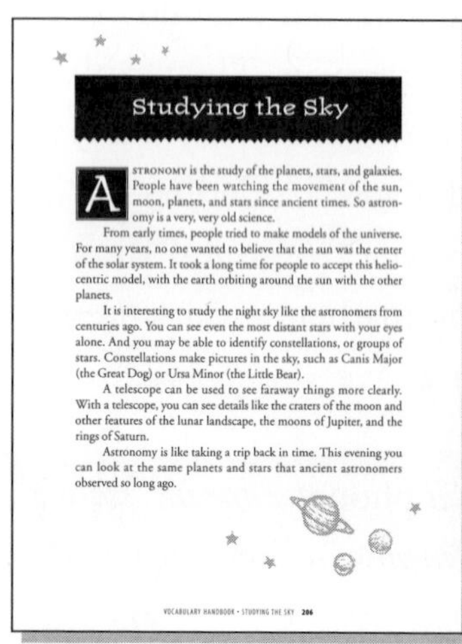

Studying the Sky

ASTRONOMY is the study of the planets, stars, and galaxies. People have been watching the movement of the sun, moon, planets, and stars since ancient times. So astronomy is a very, very old science.

From early times, people tried to make models of the universe. For many years, no one wanted to believe that the sun was the center of the solar system. It took a long time for people to accept this heliocentric model, with the earth orbiting around the sun with the other planets.

It is interesting to study the night sky like the astronomers from centuries ago. You can see even the most distant stars with your eyes alone. And you may be able to identify constellations, or groups of stars. Constellations make pictures in the sky, such as Canis Major (the Great Dog) or Ursa Minor (the Little Bear).

A telescope can be used to see faraway things more clearly. With a telescope, you can see details like the craters of the moon and other features of the lunar landscape, the moons of Jupiter, and the rings of Saturn.

Astronomy is like taking a trip back in time. This evening you can look at the same planets and stars that ancient astronomers observed so long ago.

VOCABULARY HANDBOOK • STUDYING THE SKY 206

Guided Practice

Use interactive whiteboard technology to display "Studying the Sky," highlighting the following sentence and underlining the word *telescope.*

A telescope can be used to see faraway things more clearly.

Print the word *telescope* on the board, underlining *tele.* Point to *tele* and ask: *What is the meaning of the root* tele*?* (distant or far away). Cover up *tele* and ask: *If I cover up* tele, *what is left?* (scope) Ask: *Who can print on the board a mathematical sentence for the word* telescope*?* Then ask a volunteer to read the mathematical sentence aloud: *tele + scope = telescope.*

English/Spanish Cognates

telegram • telegrama

telephone • teléfono

telescope • telescopio

Say: Scope *is another Greek root. It means "to view or to look at."* Ask: *So if* tele *means "distant or far away" and* scope *means "to view or look at," what is the literal meaning of the word* telescope*?* (Possible response: *to view or look at from a distance*) Ask: *Can anyone tell me how the literal meaning of the word* telescope *relates to the real-life function of a telescope?* (Possible response: *A telescope is an instrument that makes distant things seem larger and nearer when you look through it.*)

SEE ALSO . . .

Common Greek and Latin Roots in English, p. 494

Display the partially completed Word-Part Web and say: *I am going to add the word* telescope *to our Word-Part Web.* Ask: *Can anyone think of another word having the word root* tele *that we could add to the web?* (Possible responses: *telecast, telegram, telesales*) Add students' suggestions to the web.

WORD-PART WEB

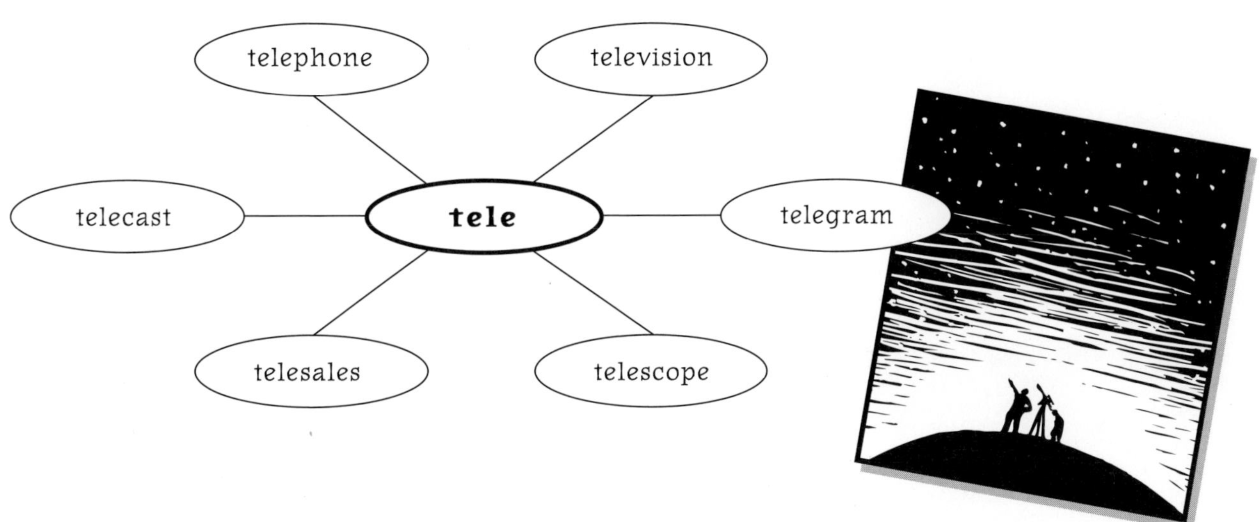

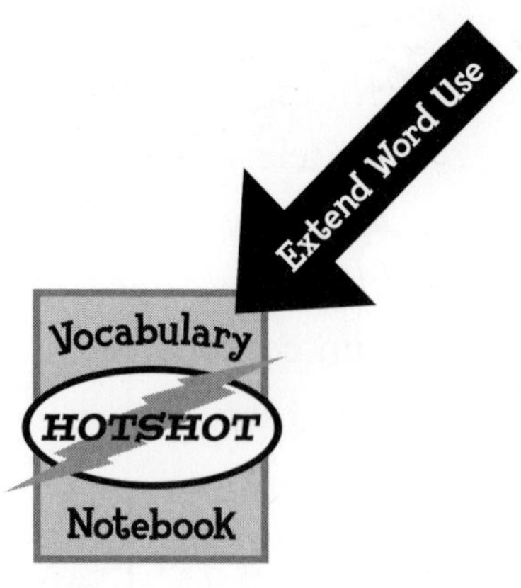

LESSON MODEL: Vocabulary Hotshot Notebook, p. 601

English/Spanish Cognates

chronoscope • cronoscopio
horoscope • horóscopo
kaleidoscope • caleidoscopio
microscope • microscopio
periscope • periscopio
stethoscope • estetoscopio

Independent Practice

Remind students that the Greek root *scope,* as in *telescope,* means "to view or to look at." Provide a copy of the Word-Part Web to pairs of students and ask them to construct a web for *scope.* Tell them that they should begin by printing the root *scope* in the center oval. Students should brainstorm and then record in the web all the words they can think of that have the root *scope* in them. (For example, *stethoscope, microscope, periscope, horoscope, kaleidoscope, chronoscope.*) After completing their webs, students should look up the definition of each unfamiliar word in the dictionary, explain the meaning of each word, and then tell how the root *scope* relates to that meaning.

WORD-PART WEB

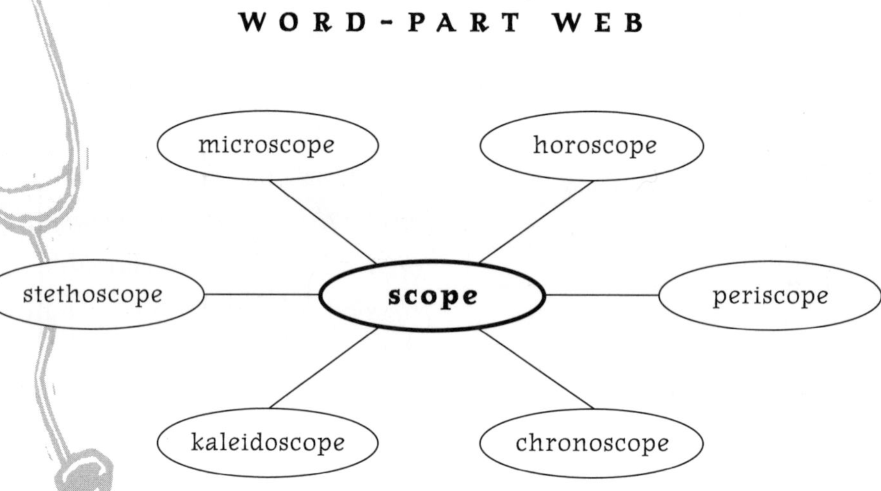

LESSON MODEL FOR

Contextual Analysis

Benchmark

- ability to use contextual analysis to infer word meanings

Strategy Grade Level

- Grade 2 and above

Grouping

- whole class
- small group or pairs
- individual

Sample Text (Resources)

- "Weekend Campout" Complexity Level: Grades 2–3

Materials

- chart paper
- PDF of "Weekend Campout"
- dictionaries
- Vocabulary Hotshot Notebooks

Context Clues

Directly teaching students how to use context clues to determine word meanings seems to be a logical—and critical—component of vocabulary instruction. Because students encounter such an enormous number of words as they read, even a small improvement in their ability to infer the meanings of unfamiliar words can result in a large number of words learned (Fukkink and de Glopper 1998). This sample lesson model can be adapted and used to enhance vocabulary instruction in any commercial reading or content-area program.

Direct Explanation

Explain to students that context clues are words or phrases that give readers clues or ideas to the meaning of other words. Tell students that knowing about context clues may help to determine the meanings of unfamiliar words they may come across in their reading. Then print the following cloze sentence on the board and read it aloud: *They just delivered the sausage and cheese ________ that we ordered.*

They just delivered the sausage and cheese ________ that we ordered.

Ask: *Who can guess the missing word in this sentence?* (pizza) *How did you know?* (Possible responses: *Pizzas come with sausage and cheese. Most pizza parlors deliver pizzas.*) *That's right. You just used the context clues in the sentence to correctly choose the missing word. The word* pizza *makes sense in the sentence:* They just delivered the sausage and cheese pizza that we ordered.

USING CONTEXT CLUES

When you come across an unfamiliar word in your reading:

1. Look for words or phrases that may be clues, or hints, to the word's meaning.
2. First, look for clues in the sentence that contains the word. Then, if you need to, look for clues in the sentences that come before or after.
3. Using the context clues, try to determine the meaning of the unfamiliar word.
4. Try out meaning in the original sentence, to check whether or not it makes sense.

When she fell off her bike, Nancy got a bruise on her knee that quickly turned black and blue.

Teach/Model

Display a copy of the Using Context Clues chart. Read the four steps aloud, briefly discussing each step. Tell students that much of the time they can use context clues to determine the meaning of an unfamiliar word in their reading.

Now print the following sentence on the board and read it aloud: *When she fell off her bike, Nancy got a bruise on her knee that quickly turned black and blue.*

Say: *I'm not sure about the meaning of the word* bruise. *I'm going to look for clues to help me determine its meaning. In the sentence, it says that Nancy fell off her bike. Nancy could have gotten hurt. I hurt myself the last time I fell off my bike. Maybe a bruise has something to do with being hurt.* Black and blue *is a really helpful clue. I know that if you are bumped really hard, an area of your skin will turn black and blue. I think a bruise is a black-and-blue mark on your skin that you get from being hurt. I'm going to try my meaning in the sentence to see how it works:* When she fell off her bike, Nancy got a black-and-blue mark on her knee. *That makes sense!*

> When I answered the phone, I heard my sister's <u>agitated</u> voice.

POINT OUT LIMITATIONS Say: *We were easily able to figure out the meaning of the word* bruise *using the context clues in the sentence. However, sometimes context doesn't help much. Some sentences don't provide enough information about the meaning of an unfamiliar word.* Print the following sentence on the board and read it aloud: *When I answered the phone, I heard my sister's agitated voice.*

Say: *This is an example of unhelpful context clues. I'm not sure about the meaning of* agitated *in this sentence, and I can't find any context clues to help me:* answered, phone, *and* voice *don't really help me. A number of possible meanings could make sense in this sentence, including "loud," "tiny," "quiet," "excited," "soft," "smooth," "frantic," or "boring," but the meaning of* agitated *is "very worried or upset." So, in this case, there are no context clues to help me.*

THE FRANCO FAMILY loves to be outdoors. They spend almost every weekend camping. Fay Franco adores camping more than anything. She will even pitch her tent in the backyard just to sleep outside.

Fay has been to lots of campgrounds. Mar Vista Shores is her favorite. The campsites are in the tall trees. Each spot has a beach view.

At Mar Vista Shores, noisy birdcalls wake Fay early. She hears loud squawking and jumps up for breakfast. Then she packs a picnic. Fay and her dad drive to the trailhead. It is the place where the hiking trails start. They choose a path to take. Dad carries a daypack. It holds a first aid kit, sweatshirts, food, and water. The path leads sharply uphill to a waterfall. It is a steep climb! They hungrily devour their lunch by the riverbank. From the rocks, Fay can watch the water plummet over the cliff.

In the afternoon, Fay and her mom go to the seashore. Mom is a rock hound. She hunts for neat-looking stones. Fay makes sandcastles. Using wet sand, she builds high walls and towers. Sometimes she pokes around the tide pools. She looks for crabs and starfish in the rocks along the beach.

At dinnertime, the Franco family usually has a sunset cookout. They light a campfire. They roast hotdogs. The sky turns pink over the water. Nighttime falls. Fay gets into her sleeping bag. She looks up to see the stars twinkle overhead.

Fay thinks that weekend campouts are almost perfect. The only flaw comes when it is time to go home.

VOCABULARY HANDBOOK • WEEKEND CAMPOUT 207

Guided Practice

Tell students that you are going to show them how to use context clues to figure out the meaning of an unfamiliar word that they may encounter in their reading. Use interactive whiteboard technology to display "Weekend Campout." Then ask a volunteer to read aloud the following sentences:

> **The path leads sharply uphill to a waterfall. It is a <u>steep</u> climb!**

Underline the word *steep* in blue. Say: *I'm not sure about the meaning of the word* steep. *So I am going to ask you to help me look for clues to its meaning.* Ask: *Can anyone find a context clue in the second sentence?* (*Climb* may be a clue.) Underline the word *climb* in green. Ask: *Does the word* climb *provide enough information for you to figure out the meaning of* steep? (no) *Where can you look if you need more clues?* (in the first sentence) *Are there any context clues in the first sentence?* (sharply, uphill)

Underline the words *sharply* and *uphill* in green. Say: *Let's put together the clues that we found and try to determine a meaning for* steep. *When you climb, you go upward or uphill. A steep climb may be one that goes up a hill that has a sharp slant, or is almost straight up and down.* Steep *may mean something like "a slant that is almost straight up and down." You've got to be in good shape to climb a steep hill.* Ask: *Who wants to try our meaning for* steep *in the sentence to see if it fits?* (It is an almost straight-up-and-down climb!) Say: *That makes sense, so for now we'll assume that* steep *refers to the up-and-down slant of a hill.*

Independent Practice

In "Weekend Campout," underline the words *devour* and *plummet* in blue. Ask a volunteer to read aloud the next two sentences:

> **They hungrily devour their lunch by the riverbank. From the rocks, Fay can watch the water plummet over the cliff.**

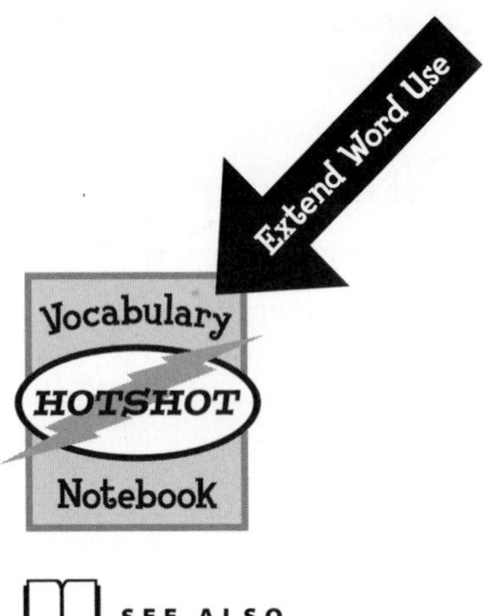

SEE ALSO . . .

LESSON MODEL: Vocabulary Hotshot Notebook, p. 601

Ask pairs of students to follow the steps on the Using Context Clues chart to figure out the meanings for *devour* and *plummet.* Have them share their context clues, meanings, and the process they used to arrive at the meanings. Then have them look up the words in a dictionary to confirm the meanings. (Possible meanings: Devour *means "to eat quickly and eagerly."* Plummet *means "to drop steeply and suddenly downward."*)

LESSON MODEL FOR

Contextual Analysis

Benchmarks

- ability to recognize types of semantic context clues
- ability to use context clues to infer word meanings

Strategy Grade Level

- Grade 4 and above

Prerequisite

- Context Clues, p. 541

Grouping

- whole class
- small group or pairs
- individual

Teaching Chart (Resources)

- Types of Helpful Context Clues

Materials

- copies of Types of Helpful Context Clues chart

DEFINITION CLUES

Target Word

conga

Introducing Types of Context Clues

Instruction in specific types of context clues is an effective approach for teaching students to use context to infer word meanings (Fukkink and de Glopper 1998). Baumann and his colleagues (2002, 2003) recommend teaching five types of context clues: definition, synonym, antonym, example, and general. This sample lesson model can be adapted and used to enhance vocabulary instruction in any commercial reading or content-area program.

Direct Explanation

Tell students that they can sometimes use context clues to figure out the meaning of an unfamiliar word they come across in their reading. Remind them that context clues are the words, phrases, and sentences surrounding an unfamiliar word that can give hints or clues to its meaning. Caution students that although these clues can prove to be helpful, they can sometimes be misleading.

Teach/Model

Give students copies of the Types of Helpful Context Clues chart. Briefly go over the chart, identifying the types of context clues and discussing the example for each one. Tell students that they should refer to the chart as they learn more about the five different types of context clues.

Definition Context Clues

Explain to students that in a definition clue the author provides the reader with the specific definition, or meaning, of a word right in the sentence. Point out that words such as *are, is, means,* and *refers to* can signal that a definition clue may follow. Then display the following sentences:

ELL
English-Language Learner

English/Spanish Cognate

conga • conga

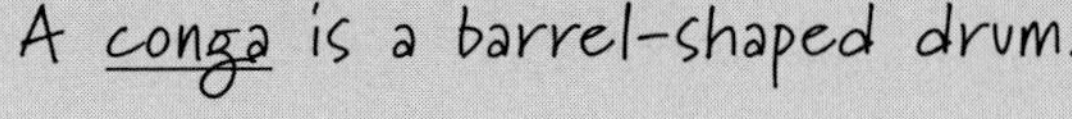
A conga is a barrel-shaped drum.

At night you can see constellations, or groups of stars, in the sky.

Read aloud the first sentence. Say: *I'm going to look for a context clue to help me understand the meaning of the word* conga. Underline *conga* in blue. Say: *In the sentence, I see the word* is. *The word* is *can signal a definition context clue.* Underline *is* in red. Say: *The phrase* a barrel-shaped drum *follows the word* is. Underline the context clue in green. Say: *A conga is a barrel-shaped drum. The author has given a definition context clue.*

TYPES OF HELPFUL CONTEXT CLUES

Type	Description	Example Sentence
Definition	The author provides a direct definition of an unfamiliar word, right in the sentence. • SIGNAL WORDS: *is, are, means, refers to*	A conga *is* a barrel-shaped drum.
Appositive Definition	A type of definition clue. An appositive is a word or phrase that defines or explains an unfamiliar word that comes before it. • SIGNAL WORD: *or* • SIGNAL PUNCTUATION: set off by commas	At night you can see constellations, *or* groups of stars, in the sky.
Synonym	The author uses another word or phrase that is similar in meaning, or can be compared, to an unfamiliar word. • SIGNAL WORDS: *also, as, identical, like, likewise, resembling, same, similarly, too*	My dog Buck travels everywhere with me. My friend's canine buddy travels everywhere with him, *too*.
Antonym	The author uses another word or phrase that means about the opposite of, or is in contrast with, an unfamiliar word. • SIGNAL WORDS: *but, however, in contrast, instead of, on the other hand, though, unlike*	I thought the movie would be weird, *but* it turned out to be totally mundane.
Example	The author provides several words or ideas that are examples of an unfamiliar word. • SIGNAL WORDS: *for example, for instance, including, like, such as*	In science we are studying marine mammals *such as* whales, dolphins, and porpoises.
General	The author provides some nonspecific clues to the meaning of an unfamiliar word, often spread over several sentences.	Einstein rode his bike everywhere. He thought driving a car was way too complicated.

Based on Baumann et al. 2003, 2005.

APPOSITIVE DEFINITION CLUE Explain to students that sometimes a definition clue is set off in a sentence by commas, and that this type of definition clue is called an appositive definition clue. Tell them that an appositive is a word or phrase that defines or explains a word that comes before it. Point out that appositives may include a signal word such as *or.*

English/Spanish Cognate

constellation • constelación

Read aloud the second sentence. Say: *I'm going to look for a context clue to help me understand the meaning of the word* constellations. Underline *constellations* in blue. Say: *In the middle of the sentence, following the word* constellations, *there is a phrase set off by commas. Commas and the word* or *can signal an appositive definition clue.* Underline the commas and the word *or* in red. Say: *The phrase* or groups of stars *is an appositive definition clue.* Underline the appositive definition clue in green. Say: *A constellation is a group of stars. The author has given an appositive definition clue.*

Synonym Context Clues

Remind students that a synonym is a word that has the same, or almost the same, meaning as another word. Explain that in a synonym context clue the author uses a familiar word or phrase in a sentence or nearby sentence that is similar in meaning, or can be compared, to the word they are trying to understand. Point out that words such as *also, as, identical, like, resembling, same, similarly,* and *too* can signal a synonym context clue. Then display the following sentences:

English/Spanish Cognate

canine • canino

> My dog Buck travels everywhere with me. My friend's canine buddy travels everywhere with him, too.

Read aloud the two sentences. Say: *I'm going to look for a context clue to help me understand the meaning of the word* canine. Underline *canine* in blue. Say: *At the end of the second sentence, I see the word* too. Too *can signal a synonym context clue.* Underline *too* in red. Say: *The first sentence tells about a dog, my dog Buck, who travels everywhere with me. The next sentence tells about my friend's canine buddy who travels everywhere with him. I know the word* buddy *means "friend" and that a dog is often called "man's best friend." So I'm going to guess that the word* canine *has something to do with dogs.* Dog *is a synonym context clue for* canine. Underline *dog* in green. Say: *The word* canine *means "relating to a dog." The author has given a synonym context clue.*

Antonym Context Clues

Remind students that an antonym is a word or phrase that means the opposite of another word. Explain that in an antonym context clue the author uses a familiar word or phrase in a sentence or nearby sentence that is the opposite in meaning to, or can be contrasted with, the word they are trying to understand. Point out to students that words such as *but, however, in contrast, instead of, on the other hand, though,* and *unlike* can signal an antonym context clue. Then display the following sentence:

> I thought the movie would be weird, but it turned out to be totally <u>mundane</u>.

Read the sentence aloud. Say: *I'm going to look for a context clue to help me understand the meaning of the word* mundane. Underline *mundane* in blue. Say: *In the middle of the sentence, I see the word* but. *The word* but *can signal an antonym context clue.* Underline *but* in red. Say: *I think the word* weird *may mean the opposite of* mundane. Underline *weird* in green. Say:

Everybody knows that weird *means "strange or unusual." Something that is the opposite of* weird *is something that is ordinary or commonplace. So I'm going to guess that the word* mundane *means "ordinary." In the sentence, I'm going to substitute the word* ordinary *for the word* mundane*: "I thought the movie would be weird, but it turned out to be totally ordinary." That makes sense! The author has given an antonym context clue.*

Example Context Clues

Explain to students that in an example context clue the author names things in the sentence or nearby sentences that belong to the same category as, or are examples of, the word they are trying to understand. Point out that words such as *for example, for instance, including, like,* and *such as* can signal an example context clue. Then display the following sentence:

> In science we are studying marine mammals such as whales, dolphins, and porpoises.

Read aloud the sentence. Say: *I'm going to look for a context clue to help me understand the meaning of the term* marine mammals. Underline *marine mammals* in blue. Say: *In the sentence, I see the words* such as. Such as *can signal an example context clue.* Underline *such as* in red. Say: *In the sentence, I see a familiar animal name. A whale is one example of a marine mammal. Dolphins and porpoises are other examples.* Underline the example context clues in green. Say: *The author has provided example context clues.*

General Context Clues

Remind students that the context in which an unfamiliar word appears often—but not always—contains specific clues to the word's meaning. Explain that sometimes the author provides only general context clues to the meaning of an unfamiliar word, and that these clues are often spread over several sentences or a paragraph. In this case, students can use details in the words or sentences surrounding the unfamiliar word, along with their prior knowledge and experience, to infer the meaning of the unfamiliar word. Then display the following sentences:

> Einstein rode his bike everywhere.
> He thought driving a car was way too complicated.

English/Spanish Cognate

complicated • complicado

Read aloud the two sentences. Say: *I'm going to look for general context clues to help me understand the meaning of the word* complicated. Underline *complicated* in blue. Say: *To ride a bicycle, you have to know how to pedal, brake, and steer. A bike doesn't have a motor. To drive a car, though, you need to know how to fill it with gas, how to back up and park, and what to do if it breaks down. It's a lot harder to drive a car than a bike. I think* complicated *has something to do with being hard to do. In the sentence, I'm going to substitute the word* hard *for the word* complicated*: "He thought driving a car was way too hard." That makes sense. Now, I'm going to check the dictionary to be sure. According to the dictionary, something that is complicated has many parts and is therefore difficult to understand. Hard to do and difficult to understand are close in meaning. The author has given only general context clues. So using what I knew about driving helped me to figure out the meaning of the word* complicated.

LESSON MODEL FOR

Contextual Analysis

Benchmarks

- ability to recognize types of semantic context clues
- ability to use context clues to infer word meanings

Strategy Grade Level

- Grade 4 and above

Prerequisite

- Introducing Types of Context Clues, p. 545

Grouping

- whole class
- small group or pairs
- individual

Sample Text (Resources)

- "Percussion Instruments" Complexity Level: Grades 4–5

Teaching Chart (Resources)

- Types of Helpful Context Clues

Materials

- PDF of "Percussion Instruments"
- lined paper
- Vocabulary Hotshot Notebooks

Applying Types of Context Clues

This is the second part of the Types of Context Clues lesson model. These sample lesson models can be used to enhance vocabulary instruction in any commercial reading or content-area program.

Direct Explanation

Tell students that they are going to practice using what they know about types of context clues to figure out the meanings of some possibly unfamiliar words. Remind students that they may find it useful to refer to the Types of Helpful Context Clues chart.

Guided Practice

Use interactive whiteboard technology to display the first page of "Percussion Instruments," underlining the following target words in blue: *percussion instrument, percussion instruments, prevalent,* and *differ.*

A percussion instrument is any musical instrument that you play by striking or hitting using either sticks or your hands. There are many kinds of percussion instruments, including drums, cymbals, and xylophones. Of all the percussion instruments, drums are the most prevalent. They are commonly found all over the world. The drums may differ from culture to culture, place to place, and group to group, but all of them possess the same basic elements.

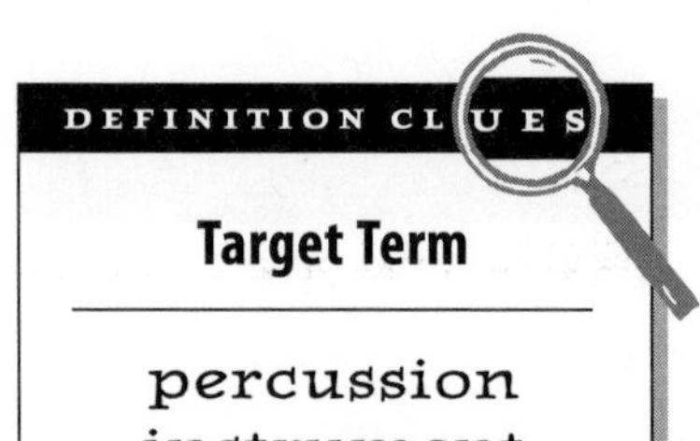

A percussion instrument is any musical instrument that you play by striking or hitting using either sticks or your hands.

After asking a volunteer to read aloud the first sentence, say: *Let's try to figure out the meaning of the term* percussion instrument. Ask: *Are there any signal words in the sentence?* (yes, *is*) Underline *is* in red. Ask: *What type of context clue might we look for?* (definition clue) Say: *Right.* Ask: *What is a percussion instrument?* ("any musical instrument that you play by striking or hitting using either sticks or your hands") Underline the definition clue in green. Ask: *Where did you find the definition context clue?* (right in the sentence) Now ask a volunteer to read aloud the second sentence:

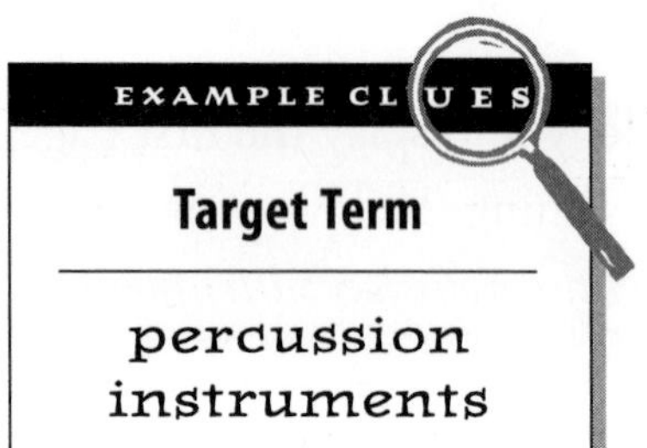

There are many kinds of percussion instruments, including drums, cymbals, and xylophones.

Say: *This sentence tells us more about percussion instruments.* Ask: *Is there a signal word in the sentence?* (yes, *including*) Underline *including* in red. Ask: *What type of context clue might we look for?* (example clue) Say: *Right.* Ask: *Does the sentence give some examples of percussion instruments?* (yes, *drums, cymbals,* and *xylophones*) Underline the example clues in green. Say: *That's right.* Drums, cymbals, *and* xylophones *are examples of percussion instruments.* Now ask a volunteer to read aloud the next two sentences:

English/Spanish Cognates

percussion • percusión

instruments • instrumentos

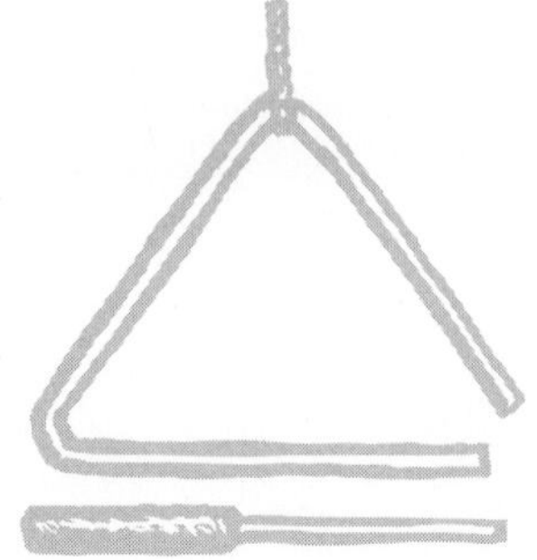

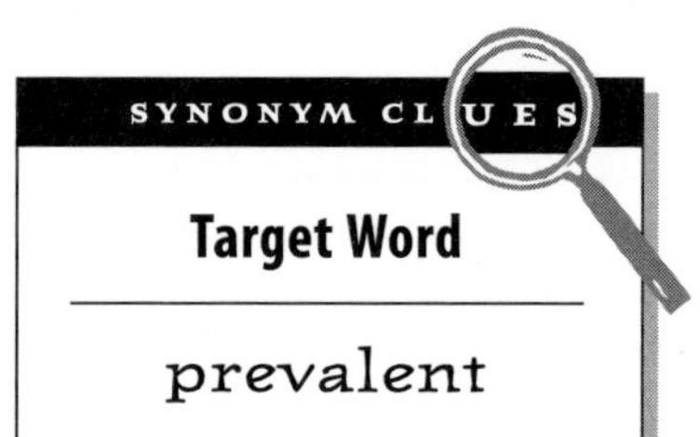

Of all the percussion instruments, drums are the most prevalent. They are commonly found all over the world.

Say: *The unfamiliar word in the first sentence is* prevalent. Ask: *Can you find a signal word in these sentences?* (no) Say: *That's right, there are not always signal words to help us.* Ask: *Can you find a word or phrase in either one of the sentences that could be a synonym context clue?* (yes, *commonly found*) Underline the synonym clue in green. Say: *Yes,* prevalent *and* commonly found *have similar meanings.* Prevalent *means "very common."* Ask: *Who can substitute* very common *for* the most prevalent *to see if it makes sense?* Have the volunteer make the substitution and repeat the sentences. Now ask a volunteer to read aloud the next sentence:

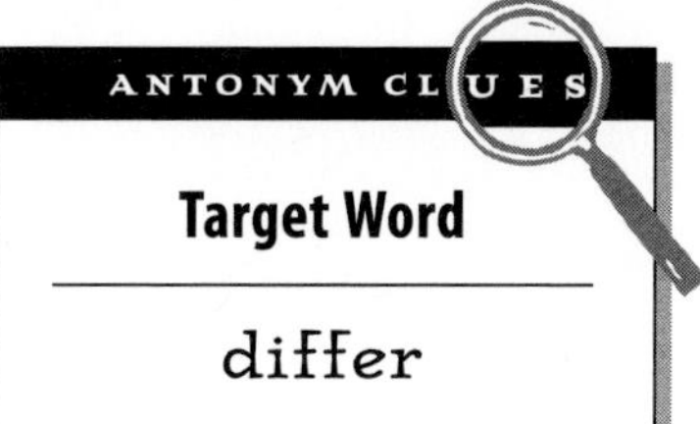

The drums may differ from culture to culture, place to place, and group to group, but all of them possess the same basic elements.

Say: *The unfamiliar word in the sentence is* differ. Ask: *Can you find a signal word in the sentence?* (yes, *but*) Underline *but* in red. Ask: *What kind of context clue might we look for?* (an antonym clue) Ask: *Can you find a word or phrase in the sentence that may mean the opposite of* differ*?* (yes, *same*) Underline the antonym clue in green. Ask: *Why did you choose* same*?* (Possible response: Differ *reminds me of the word* different *and I know that* same *and* different *are opposites.*) Say: *Right, if things differ, it means that they are "not like each other." The word* differ *means almost the opposite of the word* same. Ask: *Who can substitute the phrase* are not like each other *for the phrase* may differ *to see if it makes sense?* Have the volunteer make the substitution and repeat the sentence.

CONTEXT CLUE EVALUATION

Unfamiliar Word	Signal Word or Punctuation	Context Clue	Type of Context Clue
amplify	or, comma	make it louder	appositive, definition
faint	compared to	huge noise	antonym
hide	or, commas	skin	synonym
vibrates	or	moves very quickly back and forth	definition
resonant	or, commas	deep and rich	synonym
rhythms	none	beating hearts	general

English/Spanish Cognates

amplify • amplificar

vibrate • vibrar

resonant • resonante

rhythms • ritmos

LESSON MODEL: Vocabulary Hotshot Notebook, p. 601

Independent Practice

In "Percussion Instruments," underline the following target words in blue: *amplify, faint, hide, vibrates, resonant,* and *rhythms.* Tell students that they are going to practice using different types of context clues to figure out the meaning of the underlined words.

Then have students fold lined paper lengthwise in fourths and copy onto their papers the headings from the Context Clue Evaluation chart shown above. Have students work in pairs to complete the chart. After students have completed their analysis, go over what they have found together. Encourage students to think aloud as they share their process, choices, and rationale. An example of a completed chart is shown above.

LESSON MODEL FOR

Combined Morphemic & Contextual Analysis

Benchmark

- ability to use a combination of contextual and morphemic analysis to figure out word meanings

Strategy Grade Level

- Grade 4 and above

Prerequisites

- Word-Part Clues: Prefixes, p. 527
- Word-Part Clues: Suffixes, p. 533
- Context Clues, p. 541
- Introducing Types of Context Clues, p. 545

Grouping

- whole class
- small group or pairs
- individual

Teaching Charts (Resources)

- The Vocabulary Strategy
- Types of Helpful Context Clues

Materials

- chart paper
- dictionaries
- Vocabulary Hotshot Notebooks

Introducing The Vocabulary Strategy

The Vocabulary Strategy is an adaptation of the Vocabulary Rule, a teaching strategy employed in two recent studies by Baumann et al. (2002, 2003, 2005). When encountering unfamiliar words in their reading, students can expand their vocabularies by knowing when to use contextual analysis (e.g., context clues), when to use morphemic analysis (e.g., word-part clues), and when to use both strategies in combination. The Vocabulary Strategy is presented in two parts: introducing the strategy and practicing the strategy. These sample lesson models can be used to enhance vocabulary instruction in any commercial reading or content-area program.

Direct Explanation

Remind students of the word-part and context-clue strategies they have already learned. Display a copy of The Vocabulary Strategy chart on the following page. Explain to students that The Vocabulary Strategy is a strategy for figuring out the meaning of an unfamiliar word by using context and word-part clues in combination. Then read the five steps of the strategy aloud, briefly explaining how each step functions. Point out to students that sometimes The Vocabulary Strategy cannot be fully applied—the surrounding text does not always contain useful context clues and some words cannot be divided into smaller parts.

THE VOCABULARY STRATEGY

To figure out the meaning of an unfamiliar word that you come across while reading:

1. **Look for Context Clues** in the Words, Phrases, and Sentences Surrounding the Unfamiliar Word
2. **Look for Word-Part Clues** Within the Unfamiliar Word
   A. Try to Break the Word into Parts. (If you can't, skip to Step 3.)
   B. Look at the Root Word. What does it mean?
   C. Look at the Prefix. What does it mean?
   D. Look at the Suffix. What does it mean?
   E. Put the Meanings of the Word Parts Together. What is the meaning of the whole word?
3. **Guess the Word's Meaning** (Use Steps 1 and 2.)
4. **Try Out Your Meaning in the Original Sentence** to Check Whether or Not It Makes Sense in Context
5. **Use the Dictionary**, if Necessary, to Confirm Your Meaning

Based on Baumann et al. 2003, 2005.

VOCABULARY STRATEGY

Target Words

cramped
uncomfortable
trudged

Print the following social-studies text excerpt on chart paper, and ask a volunteer to read it aloud. Tell students that today they will learn how to use The Vocabulary Strategy to figure out the meanings of the words *cramped, uncomfortable,* and *trudged.*

A wagon train on the move could be one mile long and one mile wide. Bumping along inside a cramped wagon was a hard and uncomfortable way to travel. Pioneers often trudged beside the wagons instead. Consequently, most people walked slowly all the way to Oregon—nearly two thousand miles.

VOCABULARY STRATEGY

Target Word

uncomfortable

A wagon train on the move could be one mile long and one mile wide. Bumping along inside a cramped wagon was a hard and <u>uncomfortable</u> way to travel.

Teach/Model—Context and Word-Part Clues

1. Look for Context Clues

In the excerpt, point to the word *uncomfortable*. Say: *I'm going to use The Vocabulary Strategy to figure out the meaning of* uncomfortable. *Step 1 says to look for context clues. I'm going to read the words, phrases, and sentences surrounding* uncomfortable *to see if I can find any context clues.* Read aloud the second sentence. Say: *The phrase* bumping along *and the word* hard *may be context clues. Riding down a bumpy road really bothers me; it can be rough on your body.* Hard *means "very difficult." I wonder if* uncomfortable *describes how it feels when something is rough or bothersome to your body.*

2A. Look for Word-Part Clues—Try to Break the Word into Parts

Say: *Now we are going to look for word-part clues. Step 2A tells me to try to break the word into parts. I see that I can break* uncomfortable *into three word parts: prefix* un–, *root word* comfort, *and suffix* –able. *If I can figure out what the parts mean and then put the word back together, I will get the meaning of the whole word.*

2B. Look for Word-Part Clues—Look at the Root Word

Say: *Step 2B says to look at the root word of* uncomfortable. *The root word is a single word that cannot be broken into smaller words or parts. The root word of* uncomfortable *is* comfort. *I think that* comfort *means "when your body feels relaxed"—such as the way it feels when you are napping on a pile of fluffy pillows.*

CONTINUED ▷

VOCABULARY STRATEGY

Target Word

uncomfortable

un/comfort/able

ROOT WORD
a single word that cannot be broken into smaller words or parts

PREFIX
a word part added to the beginning of a root word that changes its meaning

SUFFIX
a word part added to the end of a root word that changes its meaning

2C. Look for Word-Part Clues—Look at the Prefix

Say: *Step 2C says to look at the prefix.* Say: *I see the prefix* un–. *The prefix* un– *means "not or opposite of." If I put the prefix* un– *and the root word* comfort *together, I get the word* uncomfort. Uncomfort *may mean "when your body doesn't feel relaxed."*

2D. Look for Word-Part Clues—Look at the Suffix

Say: *Step 2D says to look at the suffix.* Say: *I see the suffix* –able. *The suffix* –able *means "able to or can be done."*

2E. Look for Word-Part Clues—Put the Meanings of the Word Parts Together

Say: *Step 2E says to put the meanings of the root word and any prefix or suffix together to build the meaning of the whole word. If* un– *means "not," and* comfort *means "when your body feels relaxed,"* uncomfort *means "when your body does not feel relaxed." Then, if* –able *means "able to," then* uncomfortable *may mean "when your body is not able to feel relaxed."*

3. Guess the Word's Meaning

Say: *Now let's go to Step 3. It says to use what I inferred from context clues in Step 1 and what I derived from word-part clues in Step 2 to guess, or speculate about, the meaning of* uncomfortable. *I think that* uncomfortable *might mean "not very relaxing, or rough on my body."*

4. Try Out Your Meaning in the Original Sentence

Say: *Now let's go to Step 4. It tells me to try out my meaning in the original sentence, to see whether or not it makes sense in context. I am going to substitute* not very relaxing, or rough on my body *for the word* uncomfortable. *"Bumping along inside a cramped wagon was a hard and not very relaxing, or rough on my body way to travel." Yes, that makes sense. Your body can't be relaxed when it is being bumped up and down.*

5. Use the Dictionary

Say: *Step 5 tells me to use the dictionary to confirm the meaning of* uncomfortable. Say: *The dictionary says that* uncomfortable *means "feeling a lack of or not providing physical comfort." My guess based on context clues and word-part clues was close.*

Conclude by saying: *Each step of The Vocabulary Strategy helps us to get closer to the meaning of an unfamiliar word. Together, the five steps of The Vocabulary Strategy helped us understand the meaning of the word* uncomfortable.

VOCABULARY STRATEGY

Target Word

trudged

Pioneers often trudged beside the wagons instead. Consequently, most people walked slowly all the way to Oregon—nearly two thousand miles.

Teach/Model—Context Clues Only

Tell students that sometimes they have to skip steps of The Vocabulary Strategy, as in the next example, where there are no word-part clues to rely on.

1. Look for Context Clues

Display the Types of Helpful Context Clues chart. Say: *I am going to use this chart to help me to figure out the meaning of* trudged. *Step 1 of The Vocabulary Strategy tells me to look for context clues.* Say: *I can't find any context clues in the third sentence "Pioneers often trudged beside the wagons instead," so I am going to look for clues in the next sentence, "Consequently, most people walked slowly all the way to Oregon—nearly two thousand miles." I think I may have found a synonym clue for* trudged, *the phrase "walked slowly."* Trudged *might mean almost the same as "walked slowly."*

CONTINUED ▷

VOCABULARY STRATEGY

Target Word

trudged

2A. Look for Word-Part Clues—Try to Break the Word into Parts

Say: *Now let's go to Step 2. Step 2A says to try to break the word into parts. In* trudged, *I see the ending* –ed, *which tells me that the word is in the past tense, but I don't see a meaningful prefix or suffix. So I'll skip down to Step 3.*

3. Guess the Word's Meaning

Say: *Step 3 says to use the context clues I found in Step 1 to guess the meaning of the word. I think trudging may be a way of walking—walking slowly.*

4. Try Out Your Meaning in the Original Sentence

Point out to Spanish-speaking ELLs that *pioneer* and *pionero* are cognates.

Say: *Now let's go to Step 4. It tells me to try out my meaning in the original sentence, to see whether or not it makes sense in context. I am going to substitute* walked slowly *for* trudged. *"Pioneers often walked slowly beside the wagons instead." In other words, instead of riding in the wagons, the pioneers walked slowly beside them. That makes sense.*

5. Use the Dictionary

Say: *Step 5 tells me to use the dictionary to confirm the meaning of* trudged. *The dictionary says that* to trudge *is "to walk with slow, heavy steps." My guess from the use of context was close, but I didn't get the part about "heavy steps." That make sense. The pioneers must have been really tired. I walk that way when I'm tired, especially at the end of a long hike.*

VOCABULARY STRATEGY

Target Word

cramped

Bumping along inside a cramped wagon was a hard and uncomfortable way to travel.

Teach/Model—Nondirective Context Clues Only

Tell students that The Vocabulary Strategy doesn't always work well. Sometimes a word has no word-part clues and the context clues are limited. In those cases, the best you can do is to make a general guess about what a word means.

1. Look for Context Clues

Say: *I am going to try to use The Vocabulary Strategy to figure out the meaning of the word* cramped. *Step 1 tells me to look for context clues. I can tell that* cramped *is an adjective that describes the word* wagon, *but I can't really find any other context clues that help me to guess what it means. With such limited context, there are a number of possible meanings for the word* cramped *that would make sense in the sentence. The words* closed, little, hot, *and* old *are all adjectives that could describe the wagon.*

2A. Look for Word-Part Clues—Try to Break the Word into Parts

Say: *Now let's go to Step 2 of The Vocabulary Strategy. Step 2A says to try to break the word into parts. In* cramped, *I see the ending* –ed, *which tells me that the word is in the past tense, but I don't see a meaningful prefix or suffix. I'll have to skip down to Step 5 and look up* cramped *in the dictionary.*

Remember this lesson model is presented in two parts. The second part, Practicing The Vocabulary Strategy, begins on page 562.

5. Use the Dictionary

Say: *Step 5 tells me to use the dictionary. The dictionary says that* cramped *means "uncomfortably small or overcrowded." That makes sense. The pioneers were uncomfortable because they were crowded into too small a space. The wagons must have been tightly packed with family possessions; the wagons were too small for all the things the pioneers had to bring with them.*

LESSON MODEL FOR

Combined Morphemic & Contextual Analysis

Benchmark

- ability to use a combination of contextual and morphemic analysis to figure out word meanings

Strategy Grade Level

- Grade 4 and above

Prerequisites

- Introducing The Vocabulary Strategy, p. 555

Grouping

- whole class
- small group or pairs
- individual

Activity Master (Resources)

- The Vocabulary Strategy Worksheet

Teaching Charts (Resources)

- The Vocabulary Strategy
- Types of Helpful Context Clues

Materials

- chart paper
- PDF and copies of The Vocabulary Strategy Worksheet
- dictionaries
- Vocabulary Hotshot Notebooks

Practicing The Vocabulary Strategy

This is the second part of The Vocabulary Strategy lesson. These sample lesson models can be used to enhance vocabulary instruction in any commercial reading or content-area program.

Direct Explanation

Display a copy of The Vocabulary Strategy chart and the Types of Helpful Context Clues chart. Print the following science text excerpt on chart paper, and ask a volunteer to read it aloud.

> **The blue whale is the loudest animal on earth. The noise it makes is incomparable on land or sea; it is one of a kind. Whenever the blue whale wants to talk to other whales, it sends out a long, deep rumble. Whales many miles away can hear the sound.**

VOCABULARY STRATEGY

Target Words

incomparable
rumble

Give students two copies of The Vocabulary Strategy Worksheet. Tell them that today they will learn how to use The Vocabulary Strategy and The Vocabulary Strategy Worksheet to figure out the meanings of the words *incomparable* and *rumble.* Explain that you are going to guide them through the procedure for filling out the worksheet, helping them to apply the five steps of The Vocabulary Strategy.

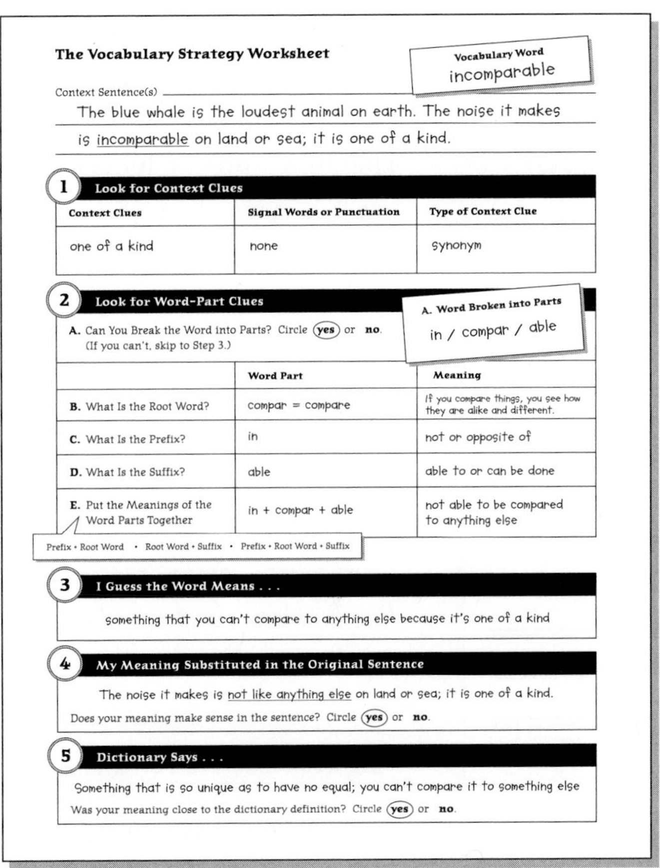

The Vocabulary Strategy Worksheet

Vocabulary Word: incomparable

Context Sentence(s): The blue whale is the loudest animal on earth. The noise it makes is incomparable on land or sea; it is one of a kind.

1 Look for Context Clues

Context Clues	Signal Words or Punctuation	Type of Context Clue
one of a kind	none	synonym

2 Look for Word-Part Clues

A. Can You Break the Word into Parts? Circle (yes) or no. (If you can't, skip to Step 3.)

A. Word Broken into Parts: in / compar / able

	Word Part	Meaning
B. What Is the Root Word?	compar = compare	If you compare things, you see how they are alike and different.
C. What Is the Prefix?	in	not or opposite of
D. What Is the Suffix?	able	able to or can be done
E. Put the Meanings of the Word Parts Together	in + compar + able	not able to be compared to anything else

Prefix • Root Word • Root Word • Suffix • Prefix • Root Word • Suffix

3 I Guess the Word Means . . .

something that you can't compare to anything else because it's one of a kind

4 My Meaning Substituted in the Original Sentence

The noise it makes is not like anything else on land or sea; it is one of a kind.

Does your meaning make sense in the sentence? Circle (yes) or no.

5 Dictionary Says . . .

Something that is so unique as to have no equal; you can't compare it to something else

Was your meaning close to the dictionary definition? Circle (yes) or no.

Point out to Spanish-speaking ELLs that *incomparable* and *incomparable* are identically spelled cognates.

Guided Practice—Context and Word-Part Clues

Use interactive whiteboard technology to display The Vocabulary Strategy Worksheet. Say: *We are going to fill in this worksheet together. I will model on my worksheet, and you will copy what I write onto your worksheets. For the first example, we are going to figure out the meaning of the word* incomparable. On the worksheet, print *incomparable* in the box labeled Vocabulary Word and then copy the first two sentences of the excerpt—the context sentences. Have students do the same.

1. Look for Context Clues

Say: *Step 1 says to look for context clues in the words, phrases, and sentences surrounding* incomparable. Ask: *Can anyone find any context clues for* incomparable? (Possible answer: *one of a kind*) Say: *I am going to print the context clues in the box labeled Context Clues, and you should do the same.* Ask: *Do you see any*

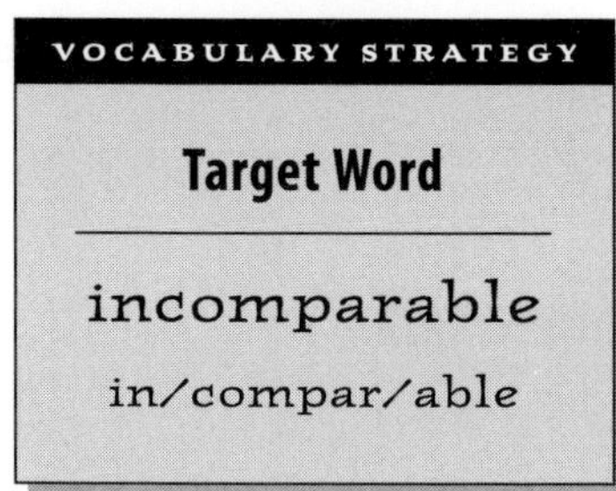

The Vocabulary Strategy Worksheet

Vocabulary Word: incomparable

Context Sentence(s): The blue whale is the loudest animal on earth. The noise it makes is incomparable on land or sea; it is one of a kind.

1 Look for Context Clues

Context Clues	Signal Words or Punctuation	Type of Context Clue
one of a kind	none	synonym

2 Look for Word-Part Clues

A. Can You Break the Word into Parts? Circle yes or no. (If you can't, skip to Step 3.)

A. Word Broken into Parts: in / compar / able

	Word Part	Meaning
B. What Is the Root Word?	compar = compare	If you compare things, you see how they are alike and different.
C. What Is the Prefix?	in	not or opposite of
D. What Is the Suffix?	able	able to or can be done
E. Put the Meanings of the Word Parts Together	in + compar + able	not able to be compared to anything else

Prefix + Root Word · Root Word + Suffix · Prefix + Root Word + Suffix

3 I Guess the Word Means . . .

something that you can't compare to anything else because it's one of a kind

4 My Meaning Substituted in the Original Sentence

The noise it makes is not like anything else on land or sea; it is one of a kind.

Does your meaning make sense in the sentence? Circle yes or no.

5 Dictionary Says . . .

Something that is so unique as to have no equal; you can't compare it to something else

Was your meaning close to the dictionary definition? Circle yes or no.

signal words or punctuation that might indicate the type of context clues we found? (no) *Let's print* none *in the box labeled Signal Words or Punctuation.* Now have students look at the Types of Helpful Context Clues chart. Ask: *What type of context clue did you find?* (synonym) Say: *Let's print* synonym *in the box labeled Type of Context Clue.*

2A. Look for Word-Part Clues—Can You Break the Word into Parts?

Have students look at Step 2A: Look for Word-Part Clues. Ask: *Can you break the word* incomparable *into parts?* (yes) Say: *Let's circle* yes *on the worksheet and break* incomparable *into three word parts—prefix, root word, and suffix—by drawing a slanted line between the parts. Let's print* in/compar/able *in the box labeled Word Broken into Parts.*

2B. Look for Word-Part Clues—What Is the Root Word?

Say: *Now we are going to look at each of the word parts in* incomparable. Ask: *What is the root word?* (compare) *That's right. On the worksheet, let's print* compare *in the box next to Root Word.* Ask: *Who knows what* compare *means?* (Possible answer: *If you compare things, you see how they are alike and how they are different.*) *Let's print the meaning on our worksheets.*

2C. Look for Word-Part Clues—What Is the Prefix?

Say: *Now let's look at the prefix.* Ask: *What is the prefix?* (in–) *On the worksheet, let's print* in– *next to Prefix.* Ask: *What is the meaning of the prefix* in–? (not or opposite of) Say: *That's right. Let's print the meaning on our worksheets.*

2D. Look for Word-Part Clues—What Is the Suffix?

Have students look at the suffix. Ask: *What is the suffix?* (–able) *On the worksheet, let's print* –able *next to Suffix.* Ask: *What is the meaning of the suffix* –able? (able to or can be done) Say: *That's right. Let's print the meaning on our worksheets.*

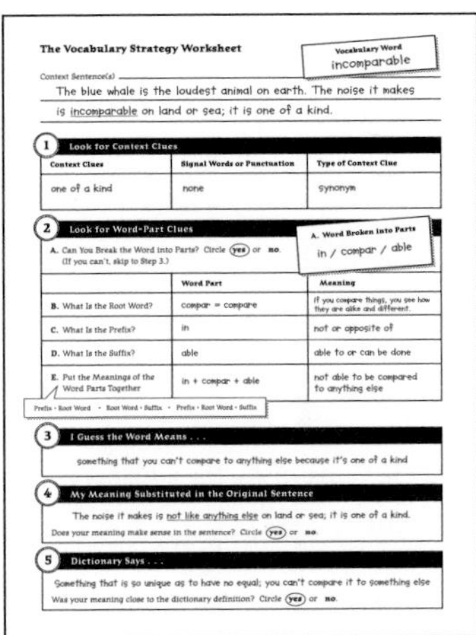

The Vocabulary Strategy Worksheet

Vocabulary Word: incomparable

Context Sentence(s): The blue whale is the loudest animal on earth. The noise it makes is incomparable on land or sea; it is one of a kind.

1 Look for Context Clues

Context Clues	Signal Words or Punctuation	Type of Context Clue
one of a kind	none	synonym

2 Look for Word-Part Clues

A. Can You Break the Word into Parts? Circle (yes) or no. (If you can't, skip to Step 3.)

A. Word Broken into Parts: in / compar / able

	Word Part	Meaning
B. What Is the Root Word?	compar = compare	If you compare things, you see how they are alike and different.
C. What Is the Prefix?	in	not or opposite of
D. What Is the Suffix?	able	able to or can be done
E. Put the Meanings of the Word Parts Together	in + compar + able	not able to be compared to anything else

Prefix + Root Word • Root Word + Suffix • Prefix + Root Word + Suffix

3 I Guess the Word Means . . .

something that you can't compare to anything else because it's one of a kind

4 My Meaning Substituted in the Original Sentence

The noise it makes is not like anything else on land or sea; it is one of a kind.

Does your meaning make sense in the sentence? Circle (yes) or no.

5 Dictionary Says . . .

Something that is so unique as to have no equal; you can't compare it to something else

Was your meaning close to the dictionary definition? Circle (yes) or no.

2E. Look for Word-Part Clues— Put the Meanings of the Word Parts Together

Say: *Now we're going to build the meaning of the whole word by putting the meanings of the three word parts together: prefix plus root word plus suffix.* Have students print the whole word *incomparable* on the worksheet. Ask: *Using the meanings of all of the word parts, what is the meaning of* incomparable? (not able to be compared to anything else) Say: *That's good. Let's print this meaning on our worksheets.*

3. I Guess the Word Means . . .

Have students go to Step 3. Say: *In Step 3 we use both context clues and word-part clues to guess what the unfamiliar word means.* Ask: *In your own words, who can tell me what* incomparable *means?* (something so unusual it is not like anything else) Say: *That's a good guess. Let's print that meaning on our worksheets.*

4. My Meaning Substituted in the Original Sentence

Direct students to Step 4. Say: *Now we are going to substitute our meaning in the original sentence.* Ask: *Who can say the sentence aloud, replacing* incomparable *with our meaning?* (The noise it makes is not like anything else on land or sea; it is one of a kind.) Say: *On our worksheets, let's print the original sentence, substituting our meaning for* incomparable. Ask: *Does the meaning we guessed make sense in the sentence?* (yes) *Let's circle* yes.

5. Dictionary Says . . .

Direct students to Step 5. Ask: *Who wants to look up* incomparable *in the dictionary?* (The dictionary definition says that *incomparable* is "something that is so unique as to have no equal.") Ask: *Was our meaning close to the dictionary definition?* (yes) *Let's circle* yes *on the worksheet.*

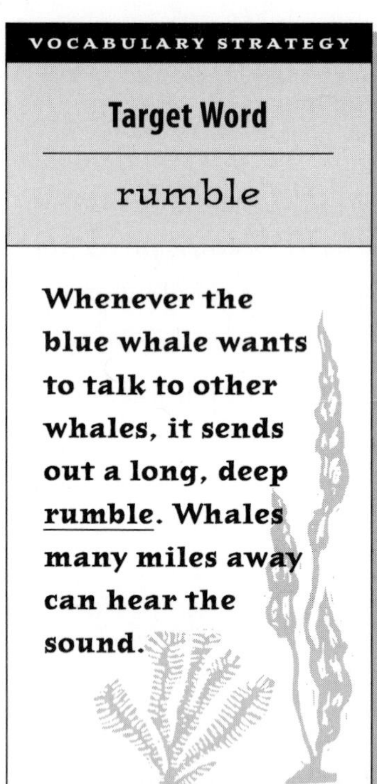

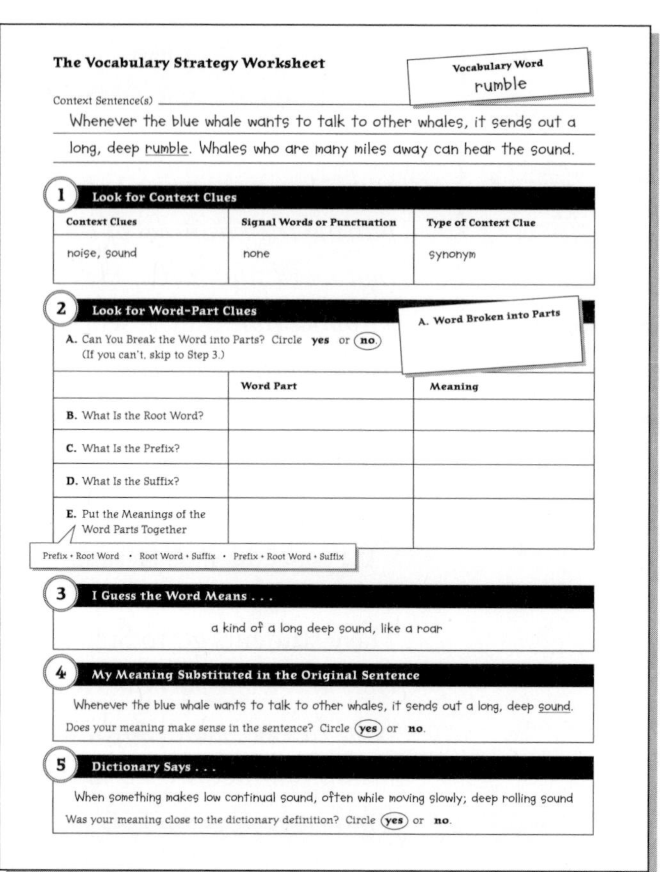

The Vocabulary Strategy Worksheet

Vocabulary Word: rumble

Context Sentence(s): Whenever the blue whale wants to talk to other whales, it sends out a long, deep rumble. Whales who are many miles away can hear the sound.

1 Look for Context Clues

Context Clues	Signal Words or Punctuation	Type of Context Clue
noise, sound	none	synonym

2 Look for Word-Part Clues

A. Can You Break the Word into Parts? Circle yes or (no)
(If you can't, skip to Step 3.)

A. Word Broken into Parts

	Word Part	Meaning
B. What Is the Root Word?		
C. What Is the Prefix?		
D. What Is the Suffix?		
E. Put the Meanings of the Word Parts Together		

Prefix • Root Word • Root Word • Suffix • Prefix • Root Word • Suffix

3 I Guess the Word Means . . .

a kind of a long deep sound, like a roar

4 My Meaning Substituted in the Original Sentence

Whenever the blue whale wants to talk to other whales, it sends out a long, deep sound.
Does your meaning make sense in the sentence? Circle (yes) or no.

5 Dictionary Says . . .

When something makes low continual sound, often while moving slowly; deep rolling sound
Was your meaning close to the dictionary definition? Circle (yes) or no.

Guided Practice—Context Clues Only

Use interactive whiteboard technology to display The Vocabulary Strategy Worksheet. Say: *For the next example, we are going to focus on figuring out the meaning of the word* rumble. *I will model on my worksheet, and you will copy what I write onto your worksheets.* On the top of the worksheet, print the vocabulary word and the last two sentences of the excerpt. Have students do the same. Then ask a volunteer to read the sentences aloud. Tell students that sometimes they have to skip steps of The Vocabulary Strategy when there are no word-part clues to rely on.

1. Look for Context Clues

Ask: *Can anyone find any context clues for the word* rumble*?* (Possible answers: *noise, sound*) Say: *Let's print the context clues for* rumble *on our worksheets.* Ask: *Do you see any signal words*

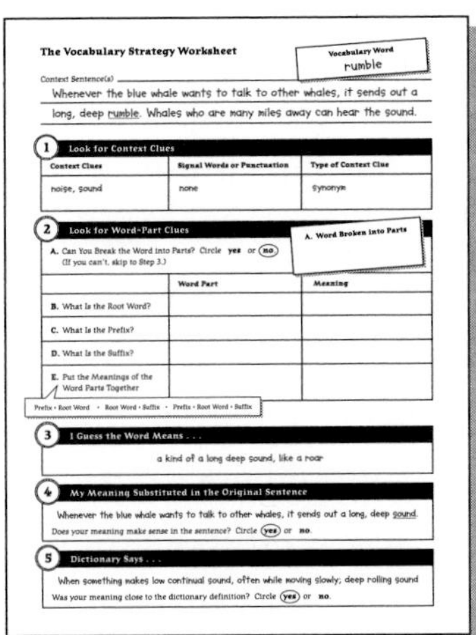

The Vocabulary Strategy Worksheet

Vocabulary Word: rumble

Context Sentence(s): Whenever the blue whale wants to talk to other whales, it sends out a long, deep rumble. Whales who are many miles away can hear the sound.

1 Look for Context Clues

Context Clues	Signal Words or Punctuation	Type of Context Clue
noise, sound	none	synonym

2 Look for Word-Part Clues

A. Can You Break the Word into Parts? Circle yes or (no) (If you can't, skip to Step 3.)

A. Word Broken into Parts

	Word Part	Meaning
B. What Is the Root Word?		
C. What Is the Prefix?		
D. What Is the Suffix?		
E. Put the Meanings of the Word Parts Together		

Prefix + Root Word • Root Word + Suffix • Prefix + Root Word + Suffix

3 I Guess the Word Means . . .

a kind of a long deep sound, like a roar

4 My Meaning Substituted in the Original Sentence

Whenever the blue whale wants to talk to other whales, it sends out a long, deep sound.

Does your meaning make sense in the sentence? Circle (yes) or no.

5 Dictionary Says . . .

When something makes low continual sound, often while moving slowly; deep rolling sound

Was your meaning close to the dictionary definition? Circle (yes) or no.

or punctuation that might indicate the type of context clues we found? (no) *Let's print* none *in the box labeled Signal Words or Punctuation. Now let's look at the Types of Helpful Context Clues chart.* Ask: *What types of context clues did you find?* (synonym) Say: *Let's print* synonym *in the box labeled Type of Context Clue.*

2A. Look for Word-Part Clues—Can You Break the Word into Parts?

Say: *Now let's go to Step 2A. Can we break the word* rumble *into word parts?* (no) Say: *That's right, the word* rumble *is a single word that can't be broken into parts. Let's circle* no *and skip down to Step 3.*

3. I Guess the Word Means . . .

Say: *Step 3 tells us to use the context clues to guess what we think* rumble *means.* Ask: *In your own words, who can tell me what* rumble *means?* (a kind of long, deep sound, like a roar) Say: *That's a good guess. Let's print that meaning on our worksheets.*

4. My Meaning Substituted in the Original Sentence

Direct students to Step 4. Ask: *Who can read the sentence aloud, replacing* rumble *with our meaning?* (Whenever the blue whale wants to talk to other whales, it sends out a long, deep sound.) Say: *On our worksheets, let's print the original sentence, substituting our meaning for* rumble. Ask: *Does the meaning we guessed make sense in the sentence?* (yes) *Let's circle* yes.

5. Dictionary Says . . .

Have students go to Step 5. Ask: *Who wants to look up* rumble *in the dictionary to confirm our meaning?* (The dictionary says that rumble is "a low continual, or deep, rolling sound, often while moving slowly.") Ask: *Was our meaning close to the dictionary definition?* (yes) *Let's circle* yes *on our worksheets.*

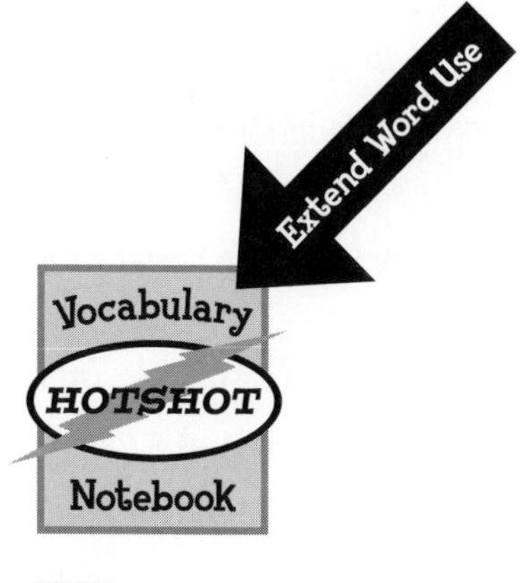

SEE ALSO . . .

LESSON MODEL: Vocabulary Hotshot Notebook, p. 601

Independent Practice

Ask a volunteer to review the steps of The Vocabulary Strategy and how the strategy was used to figure out the meanings of *incomparable* and *rumble.* Select two words from a selection in students' social studies or science textbook. Print the words on the board. Then ask students to independently read the selection and apply The Vocabulary Strategy to figure out the words. Make sure students understand that they should use a separate worksheet for each targeted word. You may want to help students begin the assignment by going through the beginning steps with them.

When students have completed their worksheets, have them share their results as a group. Try to have them explain which strategy they found more useful, if they found the combination of both context clues and word-part clues more useful than either one alone, and if so, why.

CHAPTER

13

Word Consciousness

what?
why?
when?
how?

what?

Word Consciousness

Students who are word conscious are aware of the words around them—those they read and hear and those they write and speak.

—GRAVES & WATTS-TAFFE, 2002

Word consciousness can be defined simply as interest in and awareness of words (Anderson and Nagy 1992; Graves and Watts-Taffe 2002). According to Scott and Nagy (2004), "students need to become conscious of how words work and ways they can use them." Students who have developed word consciousness use words skillfully; they appreciate the subtleties of word meaning. More than that, word-conscious students are curious about language, like to play with words, and enjoy investigating the origins and histories of words.

Word Consciousness . . .

- **Awareness of words**
- **Enjoyment of words**
- **Playing with words**
- **Interest in words**
- **Appreciation of words**
- **Satisfaction in using words well**

Scott and Nagy (2004) believe that rather than treating it as an isolated component of vocabulary instruction "teachers need to take word consciousness into account throughout each and every day." One way to accomplish this is by building a classroom "rich with words" (Beck, McKeown, and Kucan 2002). A word-rich classroom environment is a place filled with all types of word resources, such as dictionaries, thesauruses, word walls, crossword puzzles, Scrabble and other word games, literature, poetry books, and word-play and joke books. It is a place that fosters the development of word consciousness.

Adept Diction

ADEPT DICTION
the skillful use of words in speech and writing

A word-rich environment supports the use of *adept diction*—"the skillful use of words in speech and writing" (Graves 2000). Teachers can model adept diction in their own choice of words, point out skillful use of words in the texts students are reading,

CCSS LANGUAGE STANDARDS

Vocabulary Acquisition and Use

Determine or clarify the meaning of unknown and multiple-meaning words and phrases. (CCR.4)

Demonstrate understanding of figurative language, word relationships, and nuances in word meanings. (CCR.5)

Acquire and use accurately a range of general academic and domain-specific words and phrases. (CCR.6

CCSS READING STANDARDS

Literature • Informational Text

Craft and Structure

Interpret words and phrases as they are used in text. (CCR.4)

Fostering Word Consciousness

Adept Diction
- in teacher's use of language
- in reading texts
- in student's speech and writing
- beyond the classroom

Word Play

Word Histories and Origins

Responding Through Writing, p. 630

and encourage students to expand the range of word choices in their own speech and writing (Graves 2000; Beck et al. 2002; Graves and Watts-Taffe 2002; Scott and Nagy 2004).

Teachers who deliberately use skillful language that intrigues and challenges students can set the tone for the classroom and motivate students to expand their verbal horizons and use more precise language. This type of modeling can become a natural part of the classroom conversation. For example, teachers can use the word *procrastinator* to describe a student who puts off doing assignments until the last minute, or say "please *refrain* from talking" to ask students to be quiet.

The texts students are reading offer another opportunity for recognizing skillful diction. Accomplished authors use precise and colorful words in their writing. In well-written literature, students can look for and collect "gifts of words," or phrases the author employed to paint a particularly vivid picture or to add texture or tone to the writing. Group discussion about these phrases (e.g., metaphors, similes, and descriptive language) provides an opportunity to talk about skillful choice of words, word meaning, and the author's use of language (Scott and Nagy 2004).

Precision in word choice plays a fundamental role in effective writing. Students should be encouraged to employ adept diction in their own writing. According to Scott and Nagy (2004), "In writing, unlike in conversation, word choice is one of the most important, if not the most important, tool for expressive power." Encouraging adroit word usage involves creating contexts in which students can experiment with new words (Graves and Watts-Taffe 2002). During writing conferences, a teacher might urge students to rethink word choices in an effort to make their writing more vivid, precise, or suitable for a particular audience (Graves 2000).

Being a word-conscious teacher is the best way to promote word consciousness among students.

—LANE & ALLEN, 2010

Extend Word Use

Vocabulary HOTSHOT Notebook

SEE ALSO . . .

LESSON MODEL: Vocabulary Hotshot Notebook, p. 601

McKeown and Beck (2004) describe a successful vocabulary program as one in which "words do not appear as part of a classroom exercise and then drop from sight." They strongly suggest motivating students to take their vocabulary learning into the outside world: "The more students discover how words are used and where they appear outside the class, the greater the chance that they will really use the words in their own speaking and writing, and come to own them." Through nurturing this link between school and the outside world, vocabulary learning becomes less an isolated classroom-based activity.

To motivate students, teachers can reward them when they find—either hearing or seeing—the same words outside school that have been introduced as target words in school. For this purpose, Beck, Perfetti, and McKeown (1982) created a device they called a Word Wizard Chart. Teachers recorded target words on the chart and then challenged students to find these words in sources outside school, such as in books and newspapers, on the radio or television, on billboards, or in conversations. When students brought their sightings back to school, they earned points. The points were recorded next to each student's name on the chart in the classroom. Every few weeks, the teacher added up the points and gave students achievement awards.

Language Categories

Category	Word Origin	Definition	Examples
Synonyms	Greek, "same name"	Words that are very close in meaning	*happy/glad*
Antonyms	Greek, "opposite name"	Words that are opposite or nearly opposite in meaning	*up/down* *hot/cold*
Homographs	Greek, "same writing"	Words that are spelled the same but have different meanings and different origins	*bark* (tree covering) *bark* (sound a dog makes)

SEE ALSO . . .

LESSON MODELS

Word Map, p. 481

Antonym Scales, p. 588

Web Word Web, p. 592

Poetry as Word Play, p. 598

Language Categories

- **Synonyms**
- **Antonyms**
- **Homographs**

Alerting students to the ways that language is categorized contributes to adept diction. Being aware of relationships among words, such as synonyms, antonyms, and homographs, helps students to make finer distinctions in their word choices. *Synonyms* are words that are "very close in meaning." According to Templeton (1997), "When students study the fine gradations of meaning that separate synonyms, they learn progressively finer conceptual distinctions." These distinctions involve knowing both the denotations and connotations words can have. *Denotation* refers to the literal meaning of a word; for example, "not physically strong" is the denotative meaning of the word *weak. Connotation* refers to the feeling associated with a word. A word can have a positive, negative, or neutral connotation; for example, *weak* has a negative connotation when it means "lack of strength of character." Sometimes connotation is the difference in meaning between two synonyms.

DENOTATION
the literal meaning of a word

CONNOTATION
the feeling associated with a word

Antonyms are words that are "opposite or nearly opposite in meaning." There are different types of antonym relationships. Polar, or complementary, antonyms have no middle ground. These antonym pairs either are mutually exclusive (e.g., girl and boy) or undo the meaning of each other (e.g., right and wrong). Scalar, or gradable, antonym pairs allow for gradations of meaning between them (e.g., happy and sad). Scalar antonyms can be useful for teaching analogies.

Homographs are "two or more words that are spelled the same but have different meanings and different origins." For example, *jam* ("a spread made from fruit boiled with sugar"), *jam* ("to push something into a tight space"), and *jam* ("to play music in an improvised way") are homographs. Homographs are often used in puns that play on the ambiguity of the words. For example, the pun "Time flies like a bird; fruit flies like melon" capitalizes on two different homograph pairs: *flies* (the verb) and *flies* (the insects), and *like* (the preposition) and *like* (the verb).

A good metaphor implies an intuitive perception of the similarity of the dissimilar.

—ARISTOTLE

SEE ALSO . . .

LESSON MODELS

Animal Idioms, p. 580

Five-Senses Simile Web, p. 595

Knowledge of terms such as antonym, synonym, and homograph is part of word consciousness, as is the ability to deal with figures of speech (Scott and Nagy 2004). *Figurative language* uses figures of speech that enable speakers and writers to express ideas in fresh, new ways. The most common figures of speech are similes, metaphors, and idioms. A simile is a comparison that is explicitly signaled by the word *like* or *as.* The term simile comes from the Latin root *similes,* meaning "like." Metaphors are comparisons that are not explicitly signaled by *like* or *as.* Coming from the Greek roots *meta,* meaning "over," and *phor,* meaning "carry," metaphors "carry over" a comparison or contrast with one object, event, or person to another object, event, or person. An idiom is a phrase or expression in which the entire meaning is different from the usual meanings of the individual words within it. Learning about idioms is useful in the vocabulary development of all students, but especially for ELLs, who often focus on the literal meanings of words. For example, "to cut the mustard," if taken literally, would not convey its true meaning: to do a capable job.

Figurative Language

Figure of Speech	Word Origin	Definition	Examples
Simile	Latin, "like"	A comparison of two things that are not the same by using the word *like* or *as*	*as easy as pie* *float like a butterfly*
Metaphor	Greek, "carry over"	A comparison of two things that are not the same without using the word *like* or *as*	*My friend is a walking encyclopedia.*
Idiom		An expression that cannot be understood by the meanings of the individual words within it	*to cut the mustard* *to be in a pickle*

Categories of Word Play

EXPRESSIONS

proverbs
out of sight, out of mind

slang
junk food

NAMES

eponyms (after a person)
watt (after James Watt)

toponyms (after a place)
sardines (after the island of Sardinia)

WORD FORMATIONS

acronyms
ZIP (Zone Improvement Plan)

portmanteaus
motel (motor + hotel)

WORD GAMES

hink pinks
angry father—mad dad

puns
Time flies like a bird; fruit flies like melon.

riddles
How can you make a baby buggy?
(tickle his toes)

Tom Swifties
"Let's hurry," said Tom swiftly.

tongue twisters
She sells seashells by the seashore.

WORD MANIPULATIONS

anagrams
(formed by rearranging the letters of another word)
read—dear

palindromes
(read the same forward and backward)
mom, radar

Based on Johnson 2001.

Word play is sporting with the medium as medium.... It plays on sense and imagery to create the humor and nonsense of unusual connections.

—MOFFETT & WAGNER, 1992

Word Play

Research shows that word and language play can stimulate students' natural interest in and curiosity about language, help improve reading and vocabulary development, reveal the structures of language, and foster independent learning (Blachowicz and Fisher 2004; Johnson, Johnson, and Schlichting 2004; Graves 2000). Word play is "a playful attitude toward words in particular and language in general" (Graves 2000). It engages students in active, social learning, builds on children's natural curiosity about language, and provides the motivation to continue improving their language skills. Word play is accomplished through the manipulation of meanings, arrangements, sounds, spellings, and various other aspects of words (Johnson et al. 2004). Johnson (2001) organized types of word

LESSON MODELS
Animal Idioms, p. 580
Latin and Greek Number Words, p. 584
Poetry as Word Play, p. 598

play into categories such as names, expressions, word formations, word games, and word manipulations, as shown on the previous page.

Literature can be used to engage students in word play. Books in which plays on words are an important part of the story's humor lend themselves to raising word consciousness. Authors such as Dr. Seuss and Jack Prelutsky intentionally and strategically construct and play around with words so as to engage children in playful and humorous interactions with language (Johnson et al. 2004).

Try your hand at creating a Tom Swifty. A Tom Swifty is a type of word play named after Tom Swift, the fictional character featured in a series of adventure books published from 1910 to 1935. In book dialogue, Tom rarely said anything without a qualifying adverb; for example, "Tom said eagerly" or "Tom said jokingly." All Tom Swifties follow the same basic pattern: what Tom said and how Tom said it. In a true Tom Swifty, the adverb relates both properly and punningly to Tom's spoken words. Here are some examples:

"And that's another plus for you," said Tom positively.
"My pencil is dull," said Tom pointlessly.

LESSON MODELS
Latin and Greek Number Words, p. 584
Web Word Web, p. 592

Word Histories and Origins

Words, like living things, have histories that change over time. Knowing about the histories of words can help instill in students a greater consciousness and appreciation of them. Each word—along with its word parts—has a story behind it, which tells why the word has come to mean what it does. New words are coined to represent new ideas or objects: *Internet, cyberspace, 'hood.* Old words can be applied to new situations:

Greek
Specialized words used mostly in science and technology. *astronaut, geology, automatic, barometer, phonograph, telephone*
Latin
Longer, more sophisticated words used in formal contexts, such as content-area texts and literature. *audible, dictate, pedal, transport, inspect, construct*
Anglo-Saxon
Short, everyday words used frequently in ordinary conversation and beginning reading texts. *house, happy, play, boy, girl*

Layers of the English Language

bug, mouse, monitor, crash, drive. In addition, many words that were common in past years now have different or expanded meanings, or have become obsolete. *Bad* now means "good"; *cool* means "acceptable." *Gee whiz* and *jeepers* are hardly ever heard today.

Curiosity about words includes learning about their origins, too. The structure and origins of English words come primarily from Anglo-Saxon, Latin, and Greek (Henry 2003). The Anglo-Saxon layer is characterized by short, everyday words used frequently in ordinary conversation and beginning reading texts. The Latin layer consists of longer, more sophisticated words used in formal contexts such as content-area textbooks and literature. Latin is the basis for the Romance languages, including French, Italian, Portuguese, Romanian, and Spanish, all of which have contributed words to English. The Greek layer contains specialized words used mostly in science and technology. During the Renaissance, Greek words entered English by the thousands to meet the needs of scholars and scientists.

Sorting words is one way to internalize what you have learned about the layers of the English language. Using the Layers of the English Language chart above and the chart of Common Greek and Latin Roots in English on p. 494, sort the following words according to their origin: Anglo-Saxon, Latin, or Greek. (See Answer Key, p. 800.)

WORD SORT: telephoto, table, respectful, predict, phonogram, pedestrian, micrometer, made, instructor, geocentric, export, branch, book, grapheme, audit, astrology, airplane, after, omit

why?

Word Consciousness

A huge step toward fostering word consciousness comes from simply recognizing that we want to make students consciously aware of words and their importance.

—GRAVES, 2000

Word consciousness forms the basis for a continuing love of words and language that students can carry with them beyond their school years (Anderson and Nagy 1992; Graves and Watts-Taffe 2002). According to Scott and Nagy (2004), one aspect of word consciousness, adept diction, is essential for sustained vocabulary growth. Skillful word choice enhances the ability to communicate ideas; it is essential to effective writing. Moreover, reflecting upon and paying attention to an author's choice of words contributes to reading comprehension. Word play, another aspect of word consciousness, helps students become more aware of the structure and rules of language. Understanding word play is a metacognitive act, or a conscious thought process. Word play also requires metalinguistic awareness, the ability to reflect on and manipulate units of language (Scott and Nagy 2004).

Providing an environment rich with words and word play can be especially helpful for word-deprived students. Blachowicz and Fisher (2002) found that students struggling with reading "almost universally" had not played word games either at home or at school, and that "When we invited them to do so, they often become animated and motivated learners."

Research Findings . . .

Word consciousness is crucial to learners' success in expanding the breadth and depth of students' word knowledge over the course of their lifetimes.

—GRAVES & WATTS-TAFFE, 2002

To effectively promote vocabulary growth, teachers must aim to help students develop vocabulary knowledge that is generative*—the kind of knowledge that will transfer to and enhance the acquisition of other words as well. Word consciousness is an aspect of generative vocabulary knowledge.*

—SCOTT & NAGY, 2004

Children learn best when they have strong personal interest and are actively and interactively involved with learning. . . . It is important that we incorporate word and language play activities in the classroom to stimulate, sustain, and recapture that natural interest.

—JOHNSON, JOHNSON & SCHLICHTING, 2004

Suggested Reading . . .

Bringing Words to Life: Robust Vocabulary Instruction (2002) by Isabel L. Beck, Margaret G. McKeown & Linda Kucan. New York: Guilford.

Teaching Vocabulary in All Classrooms, 4th Edition (2009) by Camille Blachowicz & Peter J. Fisher. Boston: Allyn & Bacon.

Teaching Word Meanings (2006) by Steven A. Stahl & William E. Nagy. Mahwah, NJ: Erlbaum.

The Vocabulary Book: Learning & Instruction (2006) by Michael F. Graves. New York: Teacher's College Press.

Vocabulary Instruction: Research to Practice, 2nd Edition (2012) edited by Edward J. Kame'enui & James F. Baumann. New York: Guilford.

The Vocabulary Teacher's Book of Lists (2004) by Edward Bernard Fry. San Francisco: Jossey-Bass.

how? Word Consciousness

LESSON MODEL FOR

Word Consciousness

Benchmarks

- ability to interpret literal and figurative meanings of idioms
- ability to research origins of idioms

Strategy Grade Level

- Kindergarten and above

Grouping

- whole class
- small group or pairs

Materials

- small plastic toy horses
- drawing paper
- crayons or markers
- dictionaries

Source

- *Scholastic Dictionary of Idioms* (2006) by Marvin Terban. New York: Scholastic.

Animal Idioms

An idiom is a phrase or expression in which the entire meaning is different from the usual meanings of the individual words within it. Idioms are fun to work with because they are part of everyday vocabulary. Students enjoy working with figurative meanings, as well as imagining possible literal meanings for the expressions. They also enjoy finding out about the origins of idiomatic expressions, some of which are very old. Introducing idioms by topic can make them easier for students to remember. This sample lesson model focuses on introducing idioms that make use of animals or animal comparisons.

Explanation

Tell students that an idiom is an expression that cannot be fully understood by the meanings of the individual words that are contained within it. The meaning of the whole idiom has little, often nothing, to do with the meanings of the words taken one by one. Point out to students that idioms are often used in writing or speech to make expression more colorful and that some of the most colorful English idioms make use of animals or animal comparisons. Explain that many idioms have interesting origins that may not make literal sense to us today, but made perfectly good sense during the times in which they were coined.

ANIMAL IDIOMS

Target Idioms

to hold your horses

to be raining cats and dogs

Tell students that the expression “to hold your horses” is an idiom. Demonstrate its literal meaning by holding a bunch of small plastic toy horses in your hand. Tell students that when someone tells you “to hold your horses” it would be silly to think that they wanted you to hold a bunch of horses in your hand. The whole expression “to hold your horses” actually means “to slow down, wait a minute, or be more patient.” For example, if you were impatiently waiting for your sister to get off the phone, your sister might say to you, “Hold your horses. I’ll be off the phone in a minute!”

Learning about idioms can be particularly helpful for ELLs because the gap between the literal meaning of individual words and the intended meaning of the expression often causes trouble in translation.

Tell students that “to be raining cats and dogs” is another idiom. Ask students whether, if someone said it’s “raining cats and dogs,” they would expect to look up and see animals falling from the sky. Then explain to them that “raining cats and dogs” is used to describe when it’s raining really heavily or really hard. Ask volunteers to describe a time they remember when it was “raining cats and dogs.”

Ask students to draw pictures of the literal meaning of either “to hold your horses” or “to be raining cats and dogs.” Then have them take turns showing their illustration and using the idiom correctly in a context sentence.

ANIMAL IDIOMS

Target Idiom

to let the cat out of the bag

Animal Idioms
• to have ants in your pants
• to take the bull by the horns
• to let the cat out of the bag
• to have the cat get your tongue
• to be raining cats and dogs
• the straw that broke the camel's back
• to have a cow
• to wait until the cows come home
• to be in the doghouse
• to let sleeping dogs lie
• to be in a fine kettle of fish
• to seem a little fishy
• to live high on the hog
• to look a gift horse in the mouth
• to eat like a horse
• to hear it straight from the horse's mouth
• to hold your horses
• to put the cart before the horse
• to change horses in midstream
• to be a wolf in sheep's clothing

Collaborative Practice

Tell students that they are going to work together in groups to make a drawing of an animal idiom's literal meaning and then act out its real, or figurative, meaning. They will see if the drawings and skits they make provide enough information for their classmates to figure out what the idiom really means. To begin, select a group of three students to demonstrate the activity. Tell this group that their idiom is "to let the cat out of the bag" and that this idiom means "to give away a secret."

Divide the group tasks as follows: One student will draw the idiom the way it would look if it meant literally what it said: by drawing a sketch of a cat leaping out of a paper bag. This student labels the drawing with the idiom, "to let the cat out of the bag." The other two students develop a brief skit about the figurative meaning of the idiom: "to give away a secret." For example, they could develop a simple scene where someone finds out about a surprise birthday party, because a brother or sister gives it away beforehand. The last line could be: "You let the cat out of the bag."

When the group is finished, have them show the idiom's literal meaning in the drawing, and then act out its figurative meaning in the skit. Have the group challenge their classmates to guess the idiom's figurative, or intended, meaning and then correctly use the idiom in a sentence: *Nancy let the cat out of the bag when she told Nick about the surprise birthday party.*

When the whole class has understood how this activity works, assign a different animal idiom, with its figurative meaning, to other groups of students. Each group then works out its plan for making the drawing and acting out the skit. Have the groups take turns demonstrating their idioms to the class, so the class can guess the idiom's figurative meaning and use it in a sentence.

Other Idioms

- to be in a pickle
- to beat around the bush
- to bite off more than you can chew
- to burn your bridges
- to catch someone red-handed
- to cost an arm and a leg
- to cut corners
- to get up on the wrong side of the bed
- to have a chip on your shoulder
- to have something up your sleeve
- to know the ropes
- to make ends meet
- to pay through the nose
- to pull strings
- to see eye to eye
- to shoot the breeze
- to spill the beans
- to stick your neck out
- to take a rain check
- to touch something with a ten-foot pole
- to turn over a new leaf
- to wear your heart on your sleeve

Extend Word Knowledge

Students in intermediate grades will enjoy extending the idiom activity outlined above by searching out idiom origins. For example, "to hold your horses" is from the 1800s in America, a time before automobiles. If a carriage driver was letting his team of horses go too fast, he was told to "hold his horses." By pulling back on the horses' reins, the driver could slow the horses to a stop. It is believed that "raining cats and dogs" may have come from Norse mythology in which dogs were associated with windy storms and cats were associated with rain. Today the idiom "to let the cat out of the bag" has nothing to do with a cat or a bag, but hundreds of years ago it actually did. When buying a pig at a farmers' market, a favorite trick of a dishonest merchant was to put a worthless cat into your bag instead of a costly pig. You might not find out about the trick until you got home and let the cat out of the bag.

To research the origin of a particular idiom, students can use a book like the *Scholastic Dictionary of Idioms,* if it is available. If not, have them make use of online resources for idioms, which are many and varied. Show them how to Google the idiom, in quotes, and add the word origins after it to find numerous references. After completing the research, a group can share their idiom's literal and figurative meaning with the class. Then the group can develop and sketch and act out the idiom's original meaning, challenging the class to explain the origin of the idiom, as well as how the idiom's original meaning relates to its currently used figurative meaning.

LESSON MODEL FOR

Word Consciousness

Benchmark

- ability to understand Latin and Greek number prefixes

Strategy Grade Level

- Grade 4 and above

Grouping

- whole class
- small group or pairs
- individual

Materials

- dictionaries

SEE ALSO . . .

LESSON MODEL: Word-Part Clues: Prefixes, p. 527

Latin and Greek Number Words

Latin and Greek number morphemes are often called prefixes because they appear at the beginning of words (Henry 2003). Teaching Latin- and Greek-based number words is useful because these words appear over and over in upper-grade math and science textbooks. This sample lesson model focuses on becoming aware of and then playing with number prefixes and number words.

Explanation

Remind students that a prefix is a word part added to the beginning of a root word that changes its meaning. Tell students that many English words begin with number prefixes from Latin or Greek. It is important to know these prefixes because related number words appear over and over, especially in math and science textbooks. Explain that in this lesson they are going to have a little bit of fun with number prefixes.

Explain that Latin number prefixes are found at the beginning of words in categories such as groups of musicians (*tet* as in *quartet*), multiples of something (*uple* as in *quadruple*), number of sides of something (*lateral* as in *quadrilateral*), number of years between two events (*ennial* as in *quadrennial*), and words for large numbers (*illion* as in *quadrillion*). Then point out that Greek number prefixes are found at the beginning of words in categories such as the number of sides of plane figures (*gon* as in *pentagon*), number of faces of solid figures (*hedron* as in *pentahedron*), number of angles (*angle* as in *pentangle*), and number of events in an athletic competition (*athlon* as in *pentathlon*).

Display a Number Prefixes chart, such as the one shown on the facing page. Go over the Latin and Greek prefixes for each numeral and the related words they can form. Make sure to explain to students the meaning of each of the related words.

Number Prefixes			
Numeral	**Latin**	**Greek**	**Related Words**
1	uni–	mono–	unicycle, monotone
2	bi–, duo–	di–	bilingual, duet, dichotomy
3	tri–	tri–	triangle, trilateral, triple
4	quad–	tetra–	quadruple, tetrahedron
5	quint–	penta–	quintuplet, pentagon
6	sex–	hex–	sextuplet, hexagon
7	sept–	hept–	septet, heptagon
8	octa–	octo–	octagonal, octopus
9	non–, nove–	ennea–	nonagon, novena, ennead
10	deci–	dec–, deca–	decimal, decade, decathlon
100	cent–	hect–	centennial, hectogram
1,000	milli–	kilo–	millipede, kilobyte
10,000		myria–	myriad
1,000,000		mega–	megabyte, megawatt
1,000,000,000		giga–	gigabyte, gigahertz

Guided Practice

Now print the words *unicycle, bicycle,* and *tricycle* on the board. Ask students to use the Number Prefixes chart to answer the following questions:

- How many wheels does a unicycle have? (*one*) What is the number prefix? (*uni–*) Draw one wheel next to the word *unicycle.*
- How many wheels does a bicycle have? (*two*) What is the number prefix? (*bi–*) Draw two wheels next to the word *bicycle.*
- How many wheels does a tricycle have? (*three*) What is the number prefix? (*tri–*) Draw three wheels next to the word *tricycle.*

Latin Number Words
athletic events: biathlon, triathlon, tetrathlon, pentathlon, heptathlon, decathlon
groups of musicians: duet, trio, quartet, quintet, sextet, septet, octet, nonet, dectet
multiples: triple, quadruple, quintuple, sextuple, septuple, octuple, nonuple, decuple

Greek Number Words
sides of plane figures: triangle, tetragon, pentagon, hexagon, heptagon, octagon, enneagon, nonagon, decagon
years between events: biennial, triennial, quadrennial, quinquennial, centennial

Now ask students to use the Number Prefixes chart to answer the following category-related questions:

- If eight people sing in an octet, how many people sing in a quartet? (*four*) In a septet? (*seven*)
- If three countries make a trilateral agreement, how many countries would be involved in a bilateral agreement? (*two*)
- If a triangle has three angles, how many angles in a quadrangle? (*four*)
- If a pentagon has five sides, how many sides in an octagon? (*eight*) In a hexagon? (*six*)
- If a decathlon has ten athletic events, how many events are there in a triathlon? (*three*) In a biathlon? (*two*)
- If a centennial is the one-hundredth-year anniversary, what is a bicentennial? (*a two-hundredth-year anniversary*)
- If a megawatt is a million watts of electricity, what is a kilowatt? (*one thousand watts*)

Collaborative Practice

QUESTION MASTER GAME Prepare students by telling them that today they will get to be the "question master"—the person who makes up questions and asks others to find the answers. The question master uses the Number Prefixes chart to make up questions for the rest of the class to answer. Then the rest of the class tries to answer the questions. For example, the question master might ask:

- If two computers are for sale at the same price—one with 50 megabytes of memory, and one with 50 gigabytes—which one would you buy? (*50 gigabytes*) Why? (*You get more for the same price.*)
- How many kilobytes are in a gigabyte? (*one million*)

- Would it be faster to count the legs on a bug called a millipede or on a bug called a centipede? (*a centipede*) Why? (*fewer number of legs*)

Allow as many students as possible to play the role of question master. Students will probably need time to prepare questions. To facilitate the process, you might want to have students work in groups of two or three.

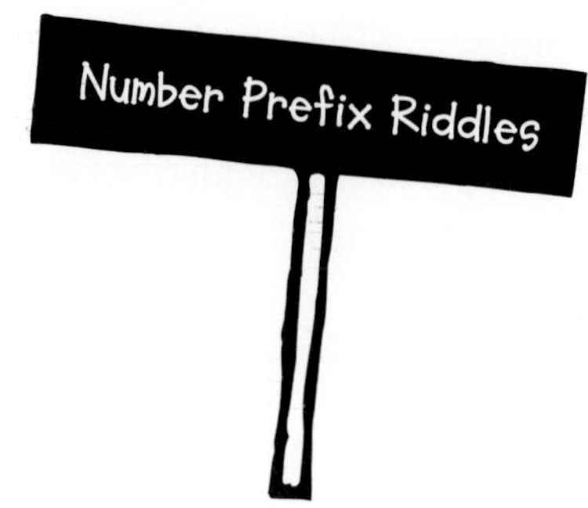

NUMBER PREFIX RIDDLES Students can also use number prefixes to create riddles. In this case, the answers to the riddles are made-up words that contain number prefixes. The made-up words are usually plays on real words. To begin, have students work in pairs or groups of three. Tell them that each group is to try to make up one or more riddles using made-up words they create with number prefixes. They then ask the class to answer them. To conclude, they will put the best riddles together to make a class book of number riddles.

To give students the idea, write two or more of these examples on the board:

- What do you call a four-armed octopus? (*a quadropus*)
- What would you call a cycle that had one million wheels? (*a megacycle*)
- An announcer said, "Barry Bonds just hit another quadruple." What is the usual baseball name for a quadruple? (*a home run*)

When students have made up their own riddles, have them present the riddles to the class to figure out. The class can vote on the most original, funniest, and hardest riddle. They can also decide on which riddles can go in the number riddle book.

LESSON MODEL FOR

Word Consciousness

Benchmarks

- ability to identify complementary and gradable antonym pairs
- ability to scale antonyms

Strategy Grade Level

- Grade 4 and above

Prerequisite

- knowing about antonyms

Grouping

- whole class
- small group or pairs

Materials

- dictionaries and thesauruses

Antonym Scales

Opposites, or antonyms, are among the first word relationships children learn; for example, soon after children learn the meaning of *up,* they learn the meaning of *down.* In this sample lesson model, students are introduced to two kinds of antonyms: complementary and gradable. Once they see the difference between the two types, students focus on gradable antonyms, learning how to arrange words in a scale, or semantic gradient. Antonym scales help students to see and express the degrees of meaning between gradable antonym pairs. They also serve to enhance students' adept diction, or skillful use of words.

Explanation

Remind students that antonyms are words that are "opposite or nearly opposite in meaning." For example, the opposite of *top* is *bottom*; the opposite of *hot* is *cold*; the opposite of *yes* is *no.* Then tell students that there are two types of antonyms. The first type is called *complementary.* These are words, like *up* and *down,* that express an either/or relationship. An elevator is either going *up* or *down*; there's no in-between movement. Then explain that the second type is called *gradable.* These are antonyms, like *hot* and *cold,* that form opposite ends of a continual scale. Point out that we can name many other temperatures between hot and cold, such as *cool* or *warm.* To illustrate both types, print these examples on the board:

> Complementary Antonyms: push/pull, dead/alive, off/on, sink/float, right/wrong, absent/present
>
> Gradable Antonyms: ugly/beautiful, best/worst, dark/light, fast/slow, good/bad, hot/cold

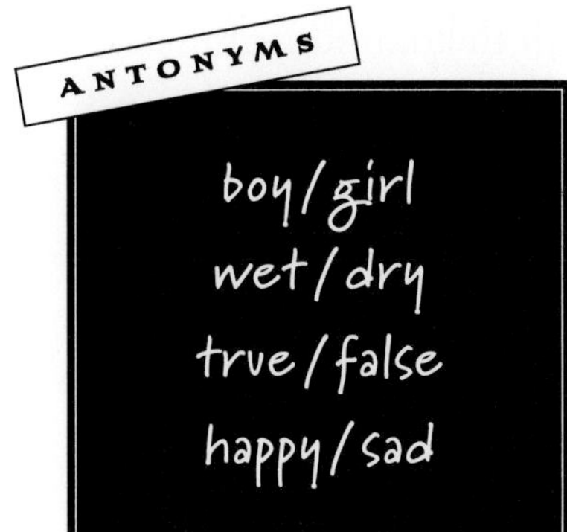

ANTONYMS
boy/girl
wet/dry
true/false
happy/sad

Guided Practice

Print several antonym pairs on the board and have the class decide whether each pair is complementary or gradable. For example: *boy/girl, true/false* (complementary); *wet/dry, happy/sad* (gradable). Students may need help in thinking some of these through.

Now invite students to think of other complementary antonym pairs to add to those they have identified above. Remind them that in complementary pairs, if one exists, the other cannot. You can also point out that, usually, thinking of one automatically brings up the other. If students have trouble, you can help by naming the first element in the following pairs—*send/receive, give/take, married/single, sink/float, remember/forget*—and having them say the other.

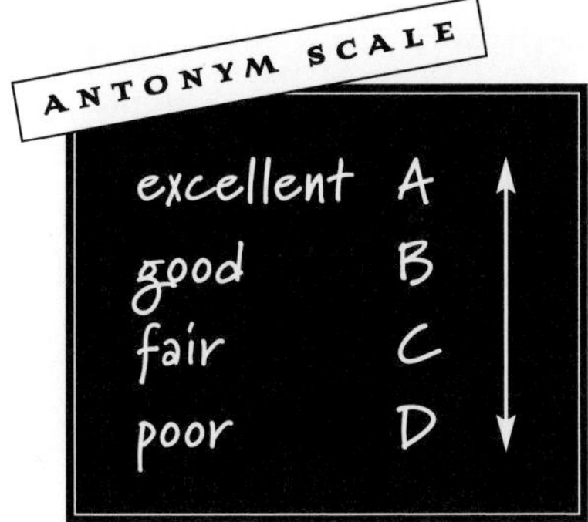

ANTONYM SCALE
excellent A
good B
fair C
poor D

Explain to students that they are going to use gradable antonyms to make an antonym scale. Tell them they are familiar with this type of scale from school: grades given for schoolwork form a scale, from A to D—from excellent at best to poor at worst—or whatever your grading scale happens to be. To illustrate this point, on the board draw an antonym scale like the one shown at left. Discuss the scale. Then ask students where they think terms such as *terrific, fantastic,* and *okay* would go on the scale. (Answers may vary.) Point out that gradable antonyms all have in-between terms that can be placed on a scale like this.

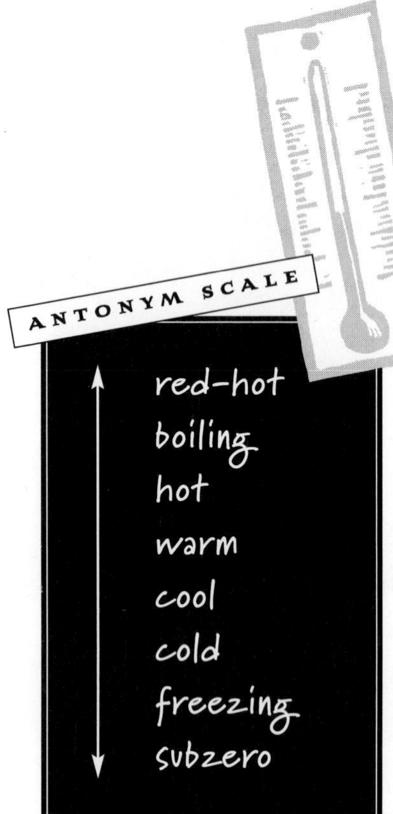

Collaborative Practice

Now tell students that they are going to work in pairs to make their own antonym scale. The scale is about temperature and it goes from *red-hot* to *subzero.* Then print the following words on the board in random order: *boiling, warm, hot, cool, red-hot, cold, subzero, freezing.*

Ask the class to tell you which is the word for the absolute hottest. (*red-hot*) Which is the word for the absolute coldest? (*subzero*) Then go through the list with them, finding the next hottest (*boiling*) and so on, placing the words in order according to their degree of hot or cold in the temperature scale. The order from top to bottom should be: *red-hot, boiling, hot, warm, cool, cold, freezing, subzero.*

When the temperature scale is completed, tell students that you have another scale for them to do on their own. This scale is about appearance and it goes from *hideous* to *magnificent.* Print the following words on the board in random order: *hideous, gorgeous, ugly, attractive, beautiful, plain, magnificent, repulsive.*

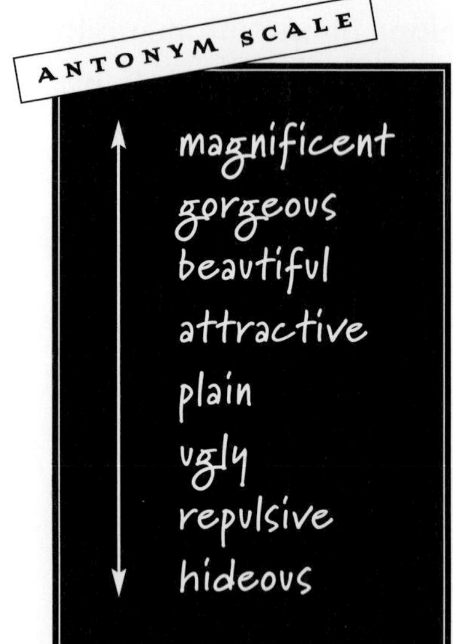

Tell students they are to arrange the words in order from *hideous* to *magnificent.* Have students work in pairs to make their scale. Point out that they can consult a dictionary or a thesaurus to help them arrange the words. When they have completed their scales, have students present their ordered scale and say why they chose *beautiful* over *attractive* or *magnificent* over *gorgeous.* The order from top to bottom could be: *magnificent, gorgeous, beautiful, attractive, plain, ugly, repulsive, hideous.* Ask if there are other terms to describe appearance that would fit on this scale.

Independent Practice

Print the following gradable antonym pairs on the board: *dark/light, big/small, early/late, easy/difficult, fancy/plain, fast/slow, rich/poor.* Have pairs of students pick a gradable antonym pair from the list and make a scale on their own. If they prefer, they can select their own gradable antonym pair. Tell the pairs to arrange the words from one extreme to the other to show degrees of meaning. Remind them that they do not necessarily have to start with either of the words they've chosen—there may be more extreme words for both ends. For example, *hot/cold* only describes the scale; *red-hot* and *boiling* are both more extreme than *hot.* Remind them also that different people start in different ways. Though most begin with the most extreme pair and fill in the middle terms, others begin in the middle with *warm* and work to both extremes, *boiling* and *subzero.*

When pairs have completed their scales, have them present the scales to the rest of the class. Ask pairs to justify the order they chose and also describe how they went about their task: choosing the most extreme ends first and filling in the middle, or starting in the middle and moving to the extremes, or some other way.

Extend Word Knowledge

Some verbally adept students might also enjoy deciding which is the most appropriate antonym for any given word. For example, given the words *tall, little, big, short, small,* and *large,* students might enjoy discussing why they think the best choices are *tall/short, big/little,* and *large/small,* but not *large/little* or *big/short.* Similarly, why does *good/terrible* not express antonym opposition as well as *good/bad* or *excellent/terrible*? Other difficulties might arise with what are called "near opposites," like *giant/dwarf, shout/whisper, town/country,* and *work/play.*

LESSON MODEL FOR

Word Consciousness

Benchmarks

- ability to use modern homographs
- ability to understand that word meanings evolve and change over time

Strategy Grade Level

- Grade 3 and above

Prerequisite

- knowing about homographs

Grouping

- whole class
- small group or pairs
- individual

Materials

- dictionaries

Web Word Web

Semantic webs, or word webs, make word meanings and word relationships visible. By putting word meanings into graphic form, word webs display the variety of meanings a word can have, and show the semantic relatedness of target words to other words and concepts.

In English, the oldest, most common words seem to have developed varied meanings over time. These words with identical spelling but a variety of meanings are called homographs. Word webs can help students—especially English-language learners—in sorting out these varied and changing meanings of common words. The sample lesson model utilizes a word web for focusing students' attention on modern uses for the word *web,* as in the World Wide Web.

Explanation

Tell students that language changes over time. New words are created to represent new ideas and new inventions. In the case of computer terminology, many old words have been given new meanings. One example is the word *mouse.* Until recently, the word *mouse* commonly meant "a small furry rodent with a long tail," but now the word *mouse* also describes "a small handheld device that plugs into a computer."

Remind students that they have previously learned about homographs and that homographs are words that are spelled the same but have different meanings and different origins. Point out that *mouse* the animal and *mouse* the computer device are homographs. Ask students to make quick pencil sketches illustrating the two meanings for *mouse.* After comparing their sketches, ask students if they can guess how the computer mouse got its name. (Possible response: *They have similar shapes and the cord looks like a long tail.*)

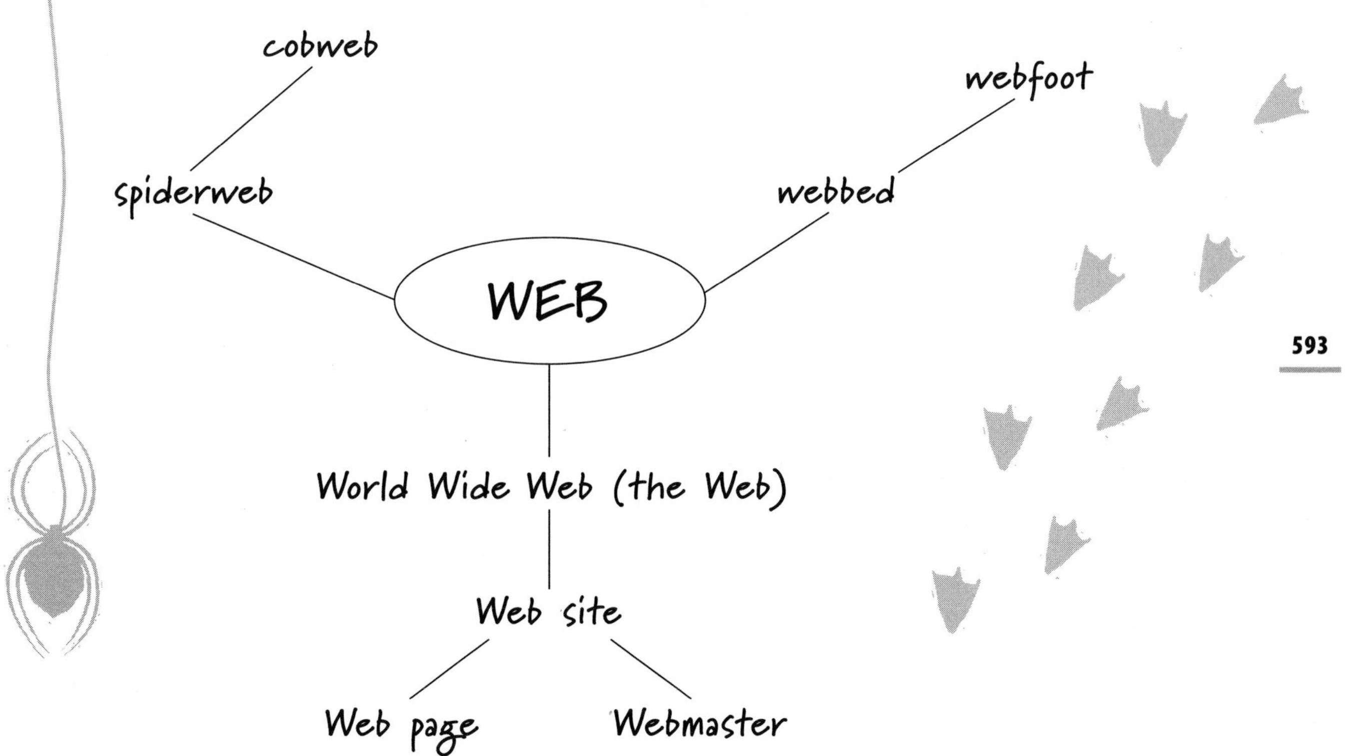

WORD WEB

Target Word

web

Guided Practice

Tell students that another common word that has a new high-tech meaning is *web.* Explain to students that they are going to help you to make a *word web* and that a word web is a drawing that shows how words can be related in meaning. To begin, print the word *web* in the center of the board. Have students brainstorm the various meanings for the word *web.* For each new meaning draw a connecting line from the center to the printed meaning. From each new meaning draw further lines to related words extending from the new word. This creates a word web with multiple connections for the word *web,* as shown above.

When the word web is completed, point out to students that it shows not only the older meanings of *web,* but also its newer meanings. Take the time to discuss each meaning and its connections. For example, from the meaning of *web* as a "delicate woven structure" comes *spiderweb* with all its connecting threads, which is related to *cobweb,* a spiderweb covered with

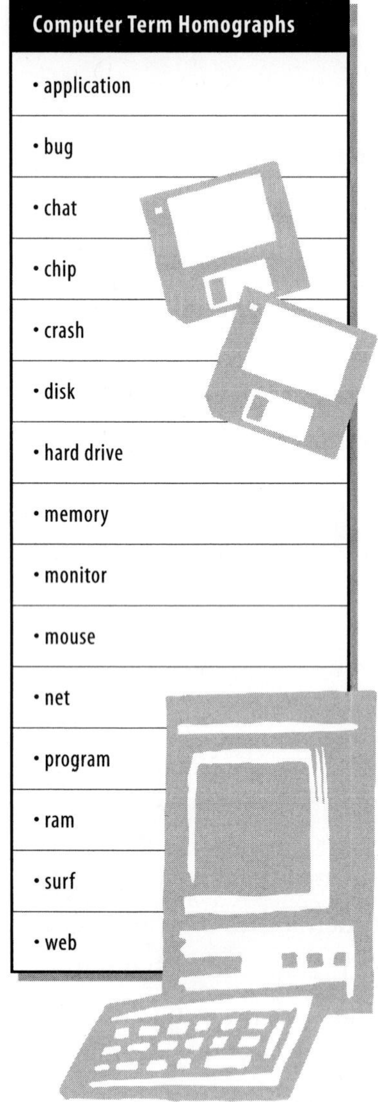

dust. For *webbed,* "a membrane of skin joining the digits of an animal's foot," name animals with webbed feet, such as ducks. Point out that the *World Wide Web* is often just called the *Web.* The World Wide Web is part of the Internet, a complex network. From the *World Wide Web* comes the related term *Web site,* "a group of related pages on the Web," and from *Web site,* the related terms *Web page,* "one page of information on a Web site," and *Webmaster,* "a person responsible for the creation or maintenance of a Web site." Have students discuss the meanings and relationships of all these words. Then invite students to suggest other words to add to the word web, such as *Web browser, Webcam,* or *Webcast.* Discuss the meaning and placement of each of the words.

Finally, you may wish to ask students if they can imagine why the *World Wide Web* is called a *web* in the first place. (Possible response: *It's a virtual space where you make connections to other people and places; from those connections arise still further connections, as in a spider's web or a fishnet or the word web they are creating.*)

Extend Word Knowledge

To extend the web activity, have students brainstorm a list of other computer terms that are homographs; for example, *application, bug, chat, chip, crash, disk, hard drive, memory, monitor, net, program, ram,* or *surf.* Then have pairs of students choose one term and make their own word webs. Tell them they may consult a dictionary to find more meanings for their target word.

When they have completed their webs, students can share their work with the rest of the class and discuss the connections they have discovered. Allow others in the class to help by adding connections that may have been missed. You may wish to display the webs on a classroom bulletin board.

LESSON MODEL FOR

Word Consciousness

Benchmarks

- ability to use adept diction
- ability to write similes

Strategy Grade Level

- Grade 2 and above

Prerequisite

- knowing about similes and synonyms

Grouping

- whole class

Activity Master (Resources)

- Five-Senses Simile Web

Materials

- PDF and copies of Five-Senses Simile Web
- chart paper

Five-Senses Simile Web

Engaging all the senses helps students in the production of many types of figurative language, especially similes. The Five-Senses Simile Web, based on the research of Graves and Watts-Taffe (2002), does this in a graphic way. Using words they have read or otherwise encountered, students construct simile webs by drawing lines from the target word to descriptions on how the word relates to each of the five senses. They try to describe how an abstract word smells, tastes, looks, sounds, and feels. This sample lesson model gives students a new and enjoyable way to engage with words as they learn about the sensory comparisons used widely in similes.

Explanation

Remind students that a simile is a comparison of two unlike things using the word *as* or *like.* Tell students that they are going to use the five senses to create a simile web for *boredom.* Begin by asking volunteers to explain what they think *boredom* means. Accept any reasonable answers, such as "If you are bored, you feel tired and impatient because you are not interested in something or because you have nothing to do."

Guided Practice

Use interactive whiteboard technology to display the Five-Senses Simile Web. Print the word *boredom* in the center. Now ask students to link *boredom* to specific sensory images. Ask them to imagine what the word *boredom* smells like, tastes like, feels like, sounds like, and looks like. Use their responses to fill in the simile web. The web should look something like the one on the following page, with sample responses shown.

FIVE-SENSES SIMILE WEB

Target Word

boredom

FIVE-SENSES SIMILE WEB

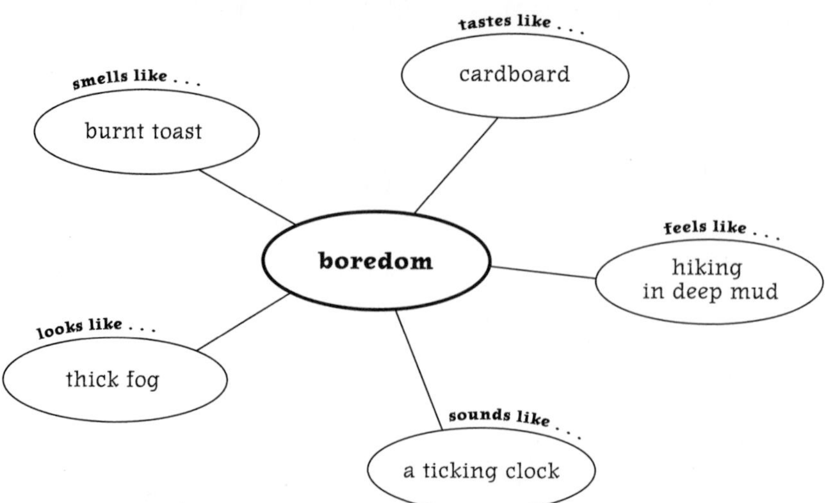

Boredom

Boredom smells like . . .
Burnt toast
Water

Boredom tastes like . . .
Cardboard
Dry grass

Boredom looks like . . .
Thick fog
A rainy day

Boredom sounds like . . .
A ticking clock
Silence

Boredom feels like . . .
Hiking in deep mud
Being alone

Now have students elaborate on their ideas by revising their suggested similes, encouraging thoughtful, unusual, or offbeat suggestions. That is, on the simile web replace some of the image words with synonyms. For example, *hiking* under "feels like" could be changed to *slogging*. *Thick fog* under "looks like" could be changed to *soupy fog*. Emphasize that the more vivid and precise their sense images are, the better the picture is that students create for themselves and for their readers.

Collaborative Practice

Tell students that poets use sensory images regularly. Have the class dictate a collaborative poem about boredom, with each student contributing a simile for each of the five senses. Write the collaborative poem on chart paper and have students take turns reading it aloud.

Written Practice

Students in intermediate grades can be asked to make their own simile webs for more complex words. For example, a web can be constructed for the word *anticipation*. Begin by asking for volunteers to explain what they think *anticipation* means. Accept any reasonable answers, such as "If you anticipate something pleasant or exciting that is going to happen, you look forward to it with pleasure."

FIVE-SENSES SIMILE WEB

Target Word

anticipation

Give each student a copy of the Five-Senses Simile Web. Then use interactive whiteboard technology to display the web. Print the word *anticipation* in the center of the web and have students do the same. Now ask students to imagine what the word *anticipation* smells like, tastes like, feels like, sounds like, and looks like. As a group, fill in the first sense, "smells like." Then have students complete the web on their own, finding a sensory association for each of the remaining senses. Point out to students that they can make their sensory similes more colorful by carefully choosing the most precise words.

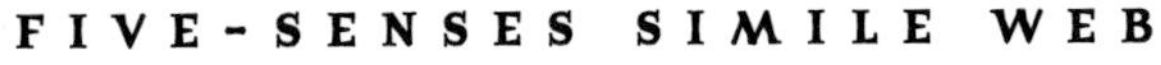
FIVE-SENSES SIMILE WEB

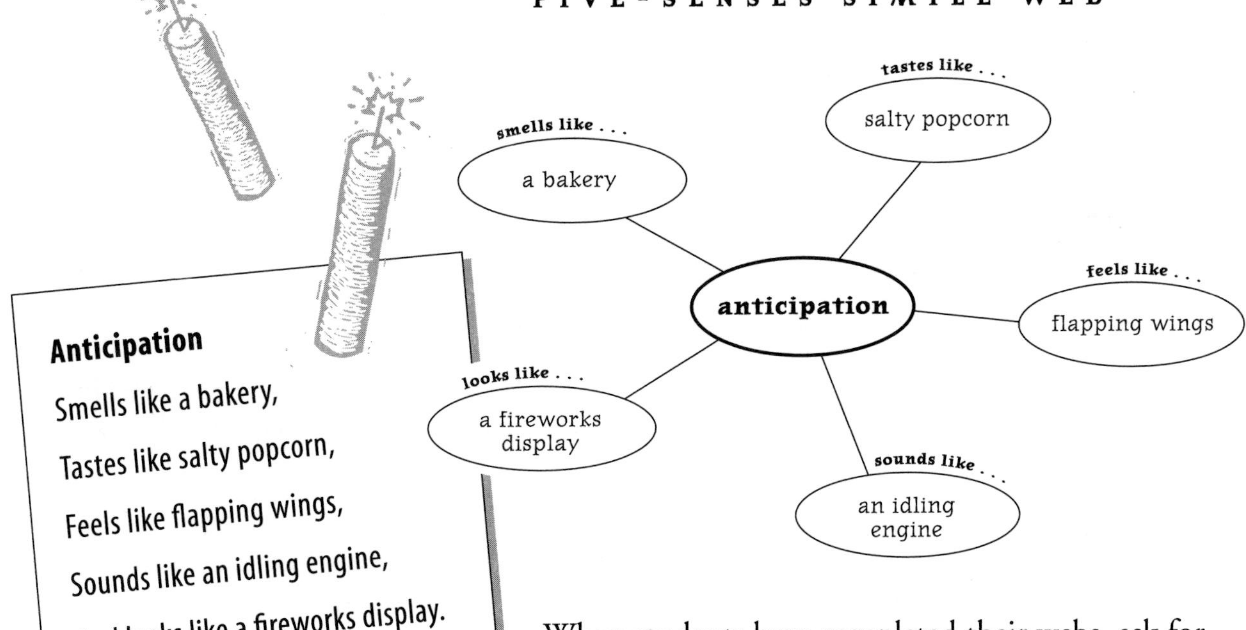
smells like . . .
a bakery
tastes like . . .
salty popcorn
anticipation
feels like . . .
flapping wings
looks like . . .
a fireworks display
sounds like . . .
an idling engine
Anticipation
Smells like a bakery,
Tastes like salty popcorn,
Feels like flapping wings,
Sounds like an idling engine,
And looks like a fireworks display.

When students have completed their webs, ask for volunteers to share their responses for each sensory mode. Make sure all students understand that they are seeking to expand their understanding of the word *anticipation* by imagining how it would be interpreted by each of their senses.

Then ask students to use their *anticipation* simile webs to write poems. When they have finished, students can read their poems aloud to the class. Discuss with them how using the senses helps to enlarge the idea of what a word means, and how its meaning can best be conveyed to others.

LESSON MODEL FOR

Word Consciousness

Benchmarks

- ability to use adept diction in writing
- ability to use synonyms and antonyms
- ability to write diamante and cinquain poems

Strategy Grade Level

- Grade 3 and above

Prerequisite

- knowing about antonyms, synonyms, and syllables

Grouping

- whole class
- small group or pairs

Materials

- dictionaries

Poetry as Word Play

Writing poetry is well suited for word play. Poets are, after all, writers whose use of words is both skillful and playful. Students can also play with words and find that they wind up with poems. One effective way to introduce students to this type of word play is to engage them in writing poetry. This sample lesson model focuses on two poetic forms: diamantes and cinquains. A diamante is a diamond-shaped poem with seven lines. It can be used to explore either antonyms or synonyms. A cinquain has five lines, with each line having a specific number of syllables.

Diamante Poems

Tell students that a diamante is a seven-line poem in the shape of a diamond. In a diamante, each line uses specific kinds of words, such as adjectives or *–ing* words. Explain that diamantes are created using either antonym pairs or synonym pairs. On a handout, provide an example of an antonym diamante poem and information about its structural form, as shown below and on the facing page.

ANTONYM DIAMANTE Read the antonym diamante poem aloud. Then explain the form of a diamante to students by comparing this diamante with the chart showing its structural form. Explain that the words in the first and last lines are antonyms, and then point out the different parts of speech in each line. Discuss Line 4, the middle of the poem, and explain how it provides a transition between the antonyms in Lines 1 and 7.

Asleep
Comfy, cozy
Slumbering, snuggling, dreaming
Night, rest, dawn, shine
Blinking, yawning, stretching
Alive, alert
Awake

Antonym Diamante Poem

STRUCTURAL FORM OF AN ANTONYM DIAMANTE POEM	
LINE 1:	Antonym 1
LINE 2:	Two adjectives describing Antonym 1
LINE 3:	Three *–ing* words describing Antonym 1
LINE 4:	Two nouns related to Antonym 1; two nouns related to Antonym 2
LINE 5:	Three *–ing* words describing Antonym 2
LINE 6:	Two adjectives describing Antonym 2
LINE 7:	Antonym 2

Now ask students to write their own antonym diamante poems. First have them brainstorm a list of antonym pairs, such as *asleep* and *awake.* Write the list on the board and ask students to choose an antonym pair to use in the development of their poem. Tell students to begin by filling in Line 1 with one of the antonyms in the pair (Antonym 1) and Line 7 with the other antonym in the pair (Antonym 2). Encourage students to consult a dictionary or thesaurus for help in selecting words. When students have finished writing, encourage them to share their antonym diamante poems with the class.

Synonym Diamante Poem

Ocean
Endless, blue
Sparkling, shifting, drifting
Whitecaps, swells, tides, waves
Rising, splashing, crashing
Powerful, ceaseless
Sea

SYNONYM DIAMANTE Now challenge students to write their own synonym diamante poems. Explain that a synonym diamante follows the same structural form as an antonym diamante, except that Lines 1 and 7 are synonyms and in Line 4 the four nouns relate to both Synonym 1 and Synonym 2.

STRUCTURAL FORM OF A CINQUAIN POEM	
LINE 1:	Two syllables–a one-word subject, a noun
LINE 2:	Four syllables–two adjectives describing the subject
LINE 3:	Six syllables–three *-ing* words describing the subject
LINE 4:	Eight syllables–a descriptive phrase about the subject
LINE 5:	Two syllables–a synonym for the subject, a noun

Cinquain Poems

Baby Duck

Duckling
Yellow, downy
Waddling, dunking, splashing
A baby bird in the water
Quacker

Football

Lineman
Bull-necked, slammer
Rising, charging, tackling
Sunday nightmare of quarterbacks
Trencher

Cinquain Poems

Tell students that a cinquain is a five-line poem describing a person, place, or thing. Point out that the word *cinq* means "five" in French and that the five lines of a cinquain have two, four, six, eight, and two syllables, respectively. In addition, most lines have a specific number of words.

On a handout, provide examples of a cinquain poem and information about its structural form, as shown on this page. Read the cinquain poems aloud. Then count their lines and the number of syllables in each line. Explain the form of a cinquain poem to students by comparing it with the chart showing its structural form.

Now have students choose topics and write cinquains of their own. To help them in this exercise, you may wish to have students work in pairs or groups of three. Make clear that they may have to experiment with several word choices before finding those that fit. This is part of the "play" of poetry. Some students may have trouble limiting the syllables. If so, have them write cinquains following the internal structure only, focusing on word choice and descriptive requirements rather than the exact syllabication for each line.

LESSON MODEL FOR

Word Consciousness

Benchmarks

- ability to keep track of target vocabulary words
- ability to extend word use beyond the classroom

Strategy Grade Level

- Grade 2 and above

Grouping

- whole class
- small group or pairs
- individual

Sample Text (Resources)

- "Alaska Adventure" Complexity Level: Grades 4–5

Activity Master (Resources)

- Vocabulary Hotshot Notebook Page

Materials

- PDF and copies of Vocabulary Hotshot Notebook Page
- three-ring binders
- three-hole punched paper
- Vocabulary Hotshot Scoreboard
- dictionaries

Vocabulary HOTSHOT

Vocabulary Hotshot Notebook

Developing an in-depth and permanent understanding of new vocabulary comes through frequent encounters and use. Research makes clear that students do not own the new words they learn after only one exposure. Rather, it takes repeated reinforcement with a new word for a student to be able to use it confidently in speech or writing (Beck et al. 2002).

One way to ensure ongoing vocabulary learning is for students to keep a personal vocabulary notebook (McKeown and Beck 2004). Another way is by using devices such as a Word Wizard Chart (Beck et al. 1982). The Vocabulary Hotshot Notebook combines these two methods. Designed to motivate student interest in words, it provides a place and an opportunity for students not only to record target words, but also to keep track of these new words as they encounter them in the outside world. It is also a motivational activity in which students earn points for seeing, hearing, or using the target words in places outside the classroom. This sample lesson model can be adapted and used to enhance vocabulary instruction in any commercial reading or content-area program.

How to Make a Vocabulary Hotshot Notebook

1. Using three-hole punched paper and two-sided copying, make eight copies of the Vocabulary Hotshot Notebook Page per student (i.e., four sheets of paper, for 16 words).
2. Put the pages into a three-ring binder for each student.

CONTINUED ▷

Explanation

Distribute the Vocabulary Hotshot Notebooks to students. Explain to students that they will use their Vocabulary Hotshot Notebooks to keep track of new vocabulary words introduced in class and to make the new words their own. After entering the new vocabulary words in their notebooks, students will be on the lookout for the words in places and sources both inside and outside school: in other books, on signs, on bulletin boards, in newspapers and magazines, on the radio or on television, on billboards, or in conversations. Tell students that they will earn points for recording these encounters in their notebooks, and that the encounters can be with the word itself or a word in the same family. The goal is to earn enough notebook points in two weeks to become a Vocabulary Hotshot.

LEVELS OF ACHIEVEMENT Prepare a Vocabulary Hotshot Scoreboard, such as the one shown below. Referring to the scoreboard, explain the levels of achievement to students. Tell them that there are three categories of winners: Hotshots, Big Shots, and Little Shots. They must earn 40 points to be a Hotshot, 30 points to be a Big Shot, and 20 points to be a Little Shot. At the end of two weeks, students' names will be recorded on the scoreboard according to the number of notebook points they earned.

Vocabulary HOTSHOT Scoreboard	Hotshots 40 points	Big Shots 30 points	Little Shots 20 points
	Billy	Anna	Jimmy
	Linda	Jamal	Barbara
	Marco	Ricardo	Matt
	Kenesha	Patricia	Sandy
	Isabel	Lin Yeng	Simon

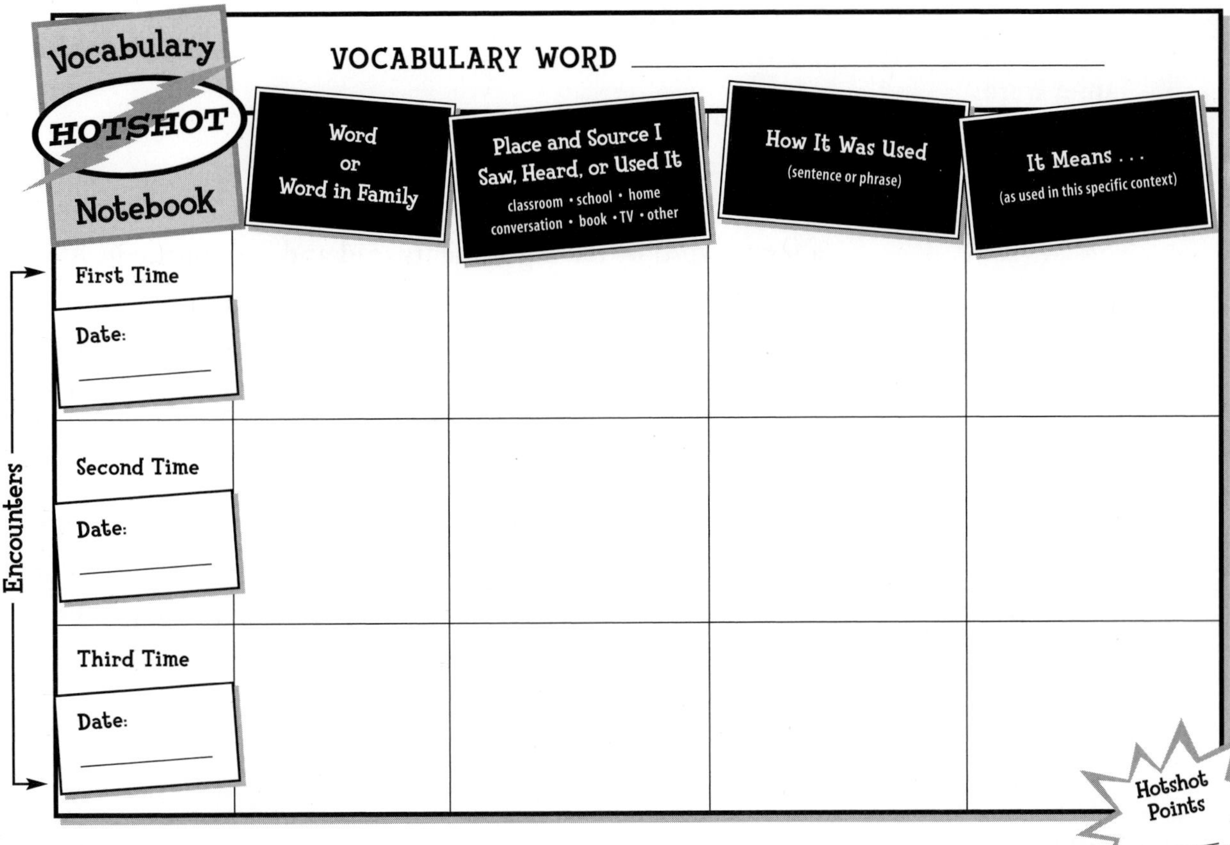

Vocabulary HOTSHOT Notebook

VOCABULARY WORD ____________

Encounters	Word or Word in Family	Place and Source I Saw, Heard, or Used It classroom • school • home conversation • book • TV • other	How It Was Used (sentence or phrase)	It Means . . . (as used in this specific context)
First Time Date: ______				
Second Time Date: ______				
Third Time Date: ______				

Hotshot Points ______

Levels of Achievement

Hotshot ☆ 40 points

Big Shot ☆ 30 points

Little Shot ☆ 20 points

NOTEBOOK POINT SYSTEM Use interactive whiteboard technology to display the Vocabulary Hotshot Notebook Page. Point out that there is a separate fill-in entry form for each new word and that there are two forms on each notebook page. Then describe the notebook point system. Tell students that they get one point for accurately completing a First Time, Second Time, or Third Time row of requested information. They can earn three points for each word. In one week, at eight words per week, they can earn a total of 24 points. In two weeks, they can earn a total of 48 points. Out of the possible 48 points, they will need 40 points to become a Vocabulary Hotshot. Explain that the First Time row will be completed as a group in class when a new word is introduced, so that all students can easily earn at least 16 points.

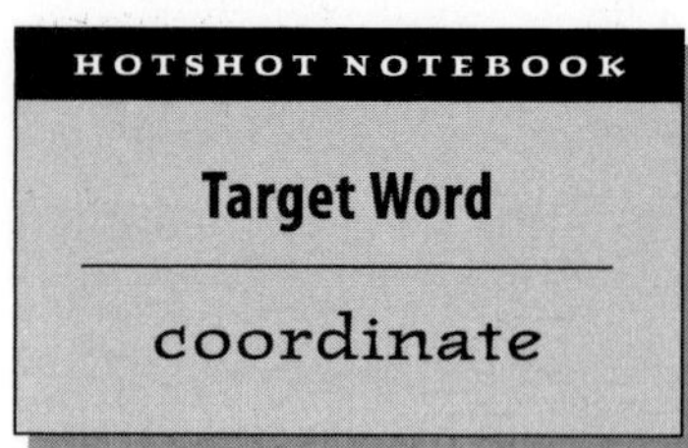

HOTSHOT NOTEBOOK

Target Word

coordinate

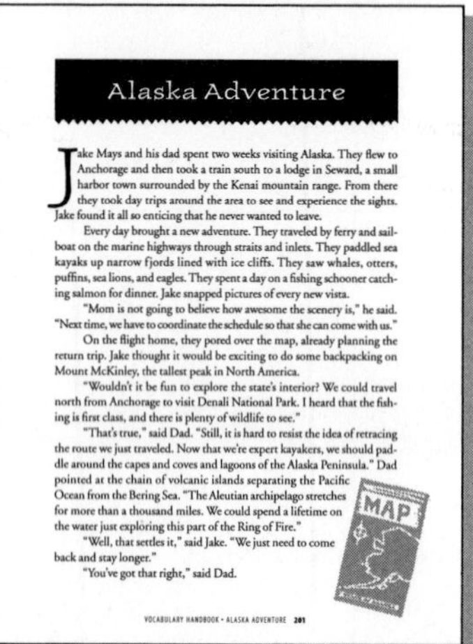

Alaska Adventure

Jake Mays and his dad spent two weeks visiting Alaska. They flew to Anchorage and then took a train south to a lodge in Seward, a small harbor town surrounded by the Kenai mountain range. From there they took day trips around the area to see and experience the sights. Jake found it all so enticing that he never wanted to leave.

Every day brought a new adventure. They traveled by ferry and sailboat on the marine highways through straits and inlets. They paddled sea kayaks up narrow fjords lined with ice cliffs. They saw whales, otters, puffins, sea lions, and eagles. They spent a day on a fishing schooner catching salmon for dinner. Jake snapped pictures of every new vista.

"Mom is not going to believe how awesome the scenery is," he said. "Next time, we have to coordinate the schedule so that she can come with us."

On the flight home, they pored over the map, already planning the return trip. Jake thought it would be exciting to do some backpacking on Mount McKinley, the tallest peak in North America.

"Wouldn't it be fun to explore the state's interior? We could travel north from Anchorage to visit Denali National Park. I heard that the fishing is first class, and there is plenty of wildlife to see."

"That's true," said Dad. "Still, it is hard to resist the idea of retracing the route we just traveled. Now that we're expert kayakers, we should paddle around the capes and coves and lagoons of the Alaska Peninsula." Dad pointed at the chain of volcanic islands separating the Pacific Ocean from the Bering Sea. "The Aleutian archipelago stretches for more than a thousand miles. We could spend a lifetime on the water just exploring this part of the Ring of Fire."

"Well, that settles it," said Jake. "We just need to come back and stay longer."

"You've got that right," said Dad.

VOCABULARY HANDBOOK • ALASKA ADVENTURE 201

Teach/Model

Before Reading the Selection

Before reading an independently read text selection, introduce a target word by having students read and pronounce it. After repeating the word with you, students can record the word in their Vocabulary Hotshot Notebooks. For this sample lesson model, the word *coordinate* is used, a target word from the sample text "Alaska Adventure."

VOCABULARY WORD Continue displaying the Vocabulary Hotshot Notebook Page. Point to and read aloud the top line: Vocabulary Word. Tell students that you are going to print the new vocabulary word *coordinate* on the line labeled Vocabulary Word and that they should do the same.

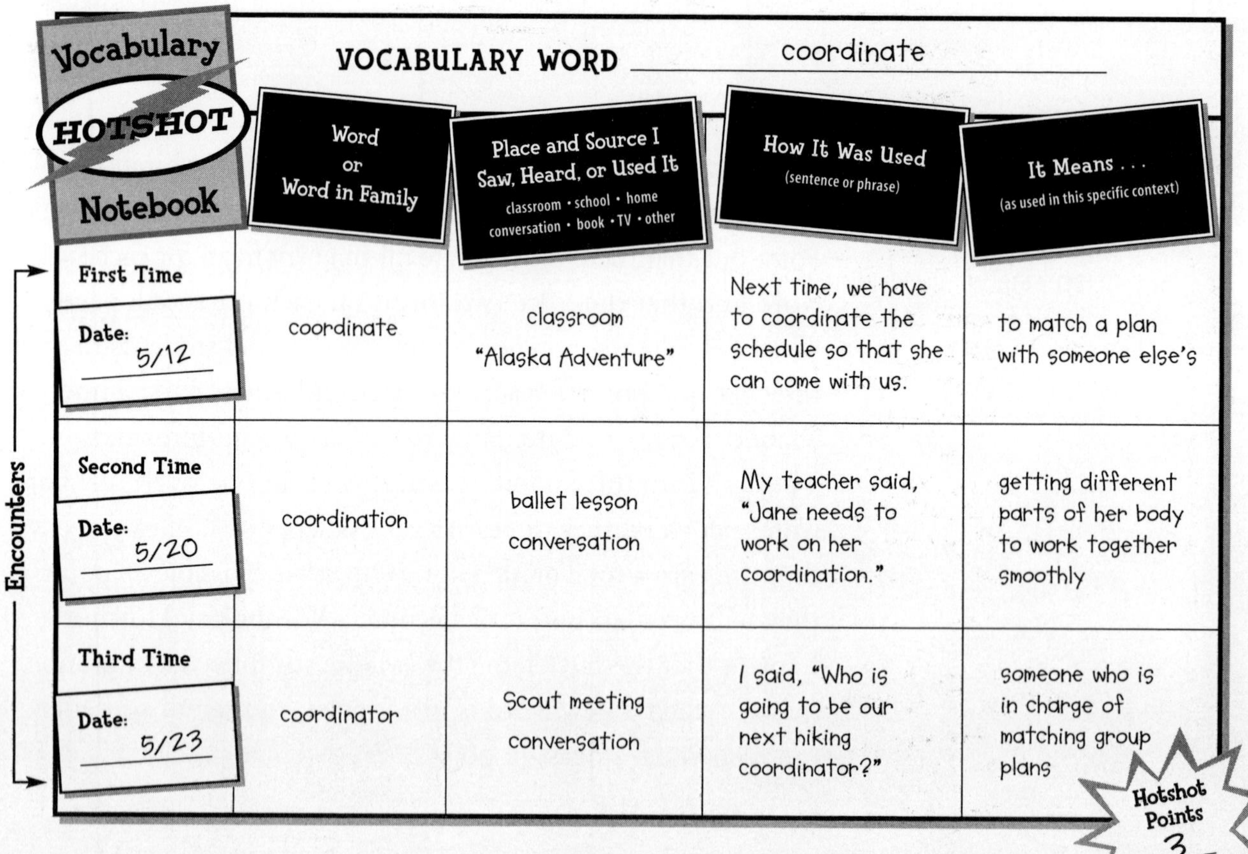

Vocabulary HOTSHOT Notebook

VOCABULARY WORD coordinate

Encounters	Word or Word in Family	Place and Source I Saw, Heard, or Used It (classroom • school • home conversation • book • TV • other)	How It Was Used (sentence or phrase)	It Means . . . (as used in this specific context)
First Time Date: 5/12	coordinate	classroom "Alaska Adventure"	Next time, we have to coordinate the schedule so that she can come with us.	to match a plan with someone else's
Second Time Date: 5/20	coordination	ballet lesson conversation	My teacher said, "Jane needs to work on her coordination."	getting different parts of her body to work together smoothly
Third Time Date: 5/23	coordinator	Scout meeting conversation	I said, "Who is going to be our next hiking coordinator?"	someone who is in charge of matching group plans

Hotshot Points 3

After Reading the Selection

COORDINATE
to match a plan with someone else's

After providing a student-friendly explanation for *coordinate,* tell students that they will add to their Notebooks what they now know about the word. Point to and read aloud the first column: First Time and Date, Second Time and Date, and Third Time and Date. Explain to students that each entry form has a place for three encounters with the word or a word in the same family. Tell students that the First Time row is where they will record information about a new word introduced in class.

WORD OR WORD IN FAMILY Tell students that you are going to show them how to fill in the First Time row. Print today's date in the space labeled Date and then print the word *coordinate* in the first row of the column labeled Word or Word in Family. Have students do the same. Remind students that a group of words that has the same root word is called a word family and that words that belong to the same word family are related in meaning. Point out that the words *coordination, coordinated,* and *coordinator* all belong to the same word family as *coordinate.*

PLACE AND SOURCE I SAW, HEARD, OR USED IT Point to and read aloud the next column heading. Explain to students that in this column they will record the place they saw, heard, or used a word; for example, in class, in the school cafeteria, on the street, at home, or at a movie theater. They will also record the source; for example, a book, a magazine, a Web page, a billboard, a TV show, a radio program, or a conversation. Tell them that for the word *coordinate,* the place they read it is in the classroom and the source is a selection called "Alaska Adventure." Print *classroom* and *"Alaska Adventure"* in the first row of the third column and have students do the same.

HOTSHOT NOTEBOOK

Target Word

coordinate

Next time, we have to coordinate the schedule so that she can come with us.

HOW IT WAS USED Point to and read aloud the next column heading. Explain that this column is for recording the actual sentence or phrase in which the word was used. In "Alaska Adventure," *coordinate* was used in the following sentence: "Next time, we have to coordinate the schedule so that she can come with us." Tell students that in the first row of the fourth column you are going to write the sentence in which *coordinate* occurred and that they should do the same.

IT MEANS . . . Point to and read aloud the next column heading. Remind students that they have discussed the meaning of *coordinate* and that now they will explain the meaning in their own words. If they want to, students can use a dictionary to confirm their meaning. Then print "to match a plan with someone else's" in the first row of the fifth column and have students do the same.

Point to and read aloud Hotshot Points. Conclude by telling students that now they have filled in the whole First Time row and that for this they will each earn one point. Points will be counted every two weeks.

VARIATION Students can use the Vocabulary Hotshot Notebook to record words they discover on their own—words encountered in independent reading or words heard outside the classroom—that they find particularly fascinating or interesting.

Extend Word Knowledge

Using an example such as the one shown above, display a completed entry for the word *coordinate.* Point out to students that for *coordinate* there are still two more rows to be filled in and that this is the real challenge. Tell students that the Second Time and Third Time rows are where they should record seeing, hearing, or using the word *coordinate,* or words related to *coordinate.* Explain that for second and third encounters students can also get points for practicing the word: using it either in conversation or in their written work. Emphasize that with many words, the meaning and the way it was used will differ on the second and third encounters, depending on the context in which the word was used. They cannot simply fill in the same information automatically for each encounter. Then go over the sample entries in the Second Time and Third Time rows, making sure that students understand the procedure.

SECTION VI

Comprehension

Introduction

COMPREHENSION

SEE ALSO . . .

Chapter 14: Literary Text

Chapter 15: Informational Text

Comprehension is often viewed as "the essence of reading" (Durkin 1993). It involves interacting with text, using intentional thinking to construct meaning. The RAND Reading Study Group (RRSG 2002) defines reading comprehension as "the process of simultaneously extracting and constructing meaning through interaction and involvement with written language." Harris and Hodges (1995) refer to it as "the construction of the meaning of a written text through a reciprocal interchange of ideas between the reader and the message in a particular text." Perfetti (1985) simply calls it "thinking guided by print."

Fundamentals of Comprehension

Reading comprehension consists of three interrelated elements—the text that is to be comprehended, the reader who is doing the comprehension, and the activity and related tasks in which comprehension is a part—all set within a larger social and cultural context that shapes and is shaped by the reader (RRSG 2002).

The Reader

To match texts to readers, the characteristics of the reader must be taken into consideration. Each reader brings to the act of reading a unique set of competencies that affect comprehension. These competencies vary not only from reader to reader, but also within an individual, depending on the text and the activity. Reader competencies include reading fluency, vocabulary knowledge, general world knowledge, knowledge of specific comprehension strategies, and motivational factors such as interest in the content or self-efficacy as a reader (RRSG 2002).

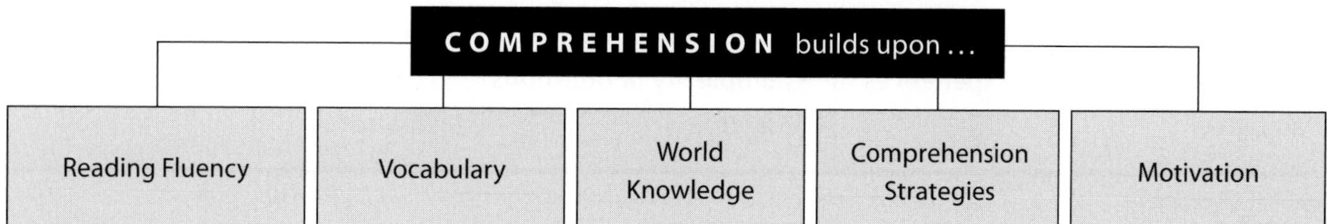

CCSS READING STANDARDS

Literature • Informational Text

Range of Reading and Level of Text Complexity

Read and comprehend complex literary and informational texts independently and proficiently. (CCR.10)

SEE ALSO . . .

Considerate Texts, p. 686

The Text

One of the key requirements of the Common Core State Standards for Reading (NGA and CCSSO 2010) is that all students must be able to comprehend texts of steadily increasing complexity as they progress through school. Text is any printed or electronic form of connected written language. Most texts fall into one of two broad categories—literary and informational. Literary text includes stories, dramas, and poetry. Informational text includes literary nonfiction and historical, scientific, and technical texts. Texts can be easy or difficult to understand, depending on factors inherent in the text, on relationship between the text and the knowledge and abilities of the reader, and on the activities or tasks in which the reader is engaged (RRSG 2002). The Common Core model for measuring text complexity consists of three equally important, interrelated components: qualitative measures of text complexity, quantitative measures of text complexity, and reader and task considerations.

Common Core State Standard's Model for Measuring Text Complexity

COMPONENT	DIMENSIONS OR VARIABLES		HOW BEST MEASURED?
Qualitative Measures of Text	• Levels of Meaning or Purpose • Structure • Language Conventionality and Clarity • World Knowledge Demands		By an attentive human reader
Quantitative Measures of Text	• Readability formulas (word length or frequency, sentence length, text cohesion)		By computer software tools
Reader & Task Considerations Matching texts to particular readers and tasks	READER • Motivation • Knowledge • Experiences	TASK • Purpose for reading • Complexity of task itself • Complexity of questions asked	By educators employing their professional judgment, experience, and knowledge of their students and the subject matter

NGA and CCSSO 2010.

Qualitative Measures of Text Complexity

LITERARY TEXT

DIMENSION		EASY →	DIFFICULT
Levels of Meaning		Single and literal levels of meaning which are explicitly stated	Multiple levels of complex meaning which may be ambiguous
Structure	Narrative Structure	Simple, explicit, and conventional	Complex, implicit, and unconventional
	Narration	No shifts in point of view	Many shifts in point of view
	Order of Events	Chronological or sequential	Frequent shifts in time and sequence; use of flashback
Language	Conventionality Clarity	Easy-to-understand, literal, clear, contemporary, familiar, conversational	Generally unfamiliar figurative, ambiguous, ironic, archaic, or overly academic
World Knowledge Demands	Life Experiences	Simple, single theme; everyday experiences that are common to most readers; single perspective presented	Complex, multiple themes; experiences that are uncommon to most readers; multiple perspectives presented
	Cultural/Literary Knowledge	Common, everyday cultural/literary knowledge required	Extensive depth of cultural/literary knowledge required
	Intertextuality	No references or allusions to other texts and/or cultural elements	Many references or allusions to other texts and/or cultural elements

INFORMATIONAL TEXT

DIMENSION		EASY →	DIFFICULT
Purpose		Explicitly stated purpose or main idea	Implicit purpose or main idea which may be hidden or obscure
Structure	Organization	Simple; explicit connections between ideas; conforms to the conventions of the genre	Highly complex; implicit connections between ideas; conforms to the conventions of a specific content area
	Text Features	If used, are helpful, but not essential, to understanding the text	If used, are essential to understanding the text
	Graphics	If used, are helpful, but not essential, to understanding the text	If used, are essential to understanding the text; may provide information not conveyed in the text
Language	Conventionality Clarity	Easy-to-understand literal, clear, contemporary, familiar, conversational language	Generally unfamiliar figurative, ambiguous, ironic, archaic, content-specific, or overly academic language
World Knowledge Demands	Content-Area Knowledge	Only everyday, practical knowledge required	Extensive, specialized content-area knowledge required
	Intertextuality	No references to or citations of other texts or outside ideas	Many references to or citations of other texts or outside ideas

Based on NGA and CCSSO 2010.

Being able to read complex text independently and proficiently is essential for high achievement in college and the workplace....

—COMMON CORE STATE STANDARDS, 2010

Engaged Readers

- **Want to read**
- **Enjoy learning**
- **Believe in their ability to read**
- **Seek to understand**
- **Work to improve their skills**
- **Accept new challenges**
- **Have high self-efficacy**
- **Find satisfaction in successful reading**

Guthrie and Wigfield 2000.

Motivation and Engagement with Reading, p. 695

The Activity and Related Tasks

The activity of reading includes three task-related variables: one or more *purposes,* a set of *processes* for reading the text, and the *outcomes* of performing the activity (RRSG 2002). Setting a purpose for reading—that is, identifying the reading task—is a critical part of instruction (Blanton, Wood, and Moorman 1990). Reading purposes can range from learning information for a test to understanding the rules for a game, to savoring the style of a favorite author, or to locating the answer to a puzzling question. Once the purpose is set, the reader applies a range of processes—from decoding to higher-level thinking skills—to achieve it. Each purpose may require a unique type of reading. For example, readers approach text differently when they are scanning for information, studying for a test, or enjoying the feeling of a poem. The intended outcomes of reading are also part of the activity. Outcomes of reading a text may include increased content knowledge, a solution to a real-world problem, and/or reading engagement. Guthrie et al. (2004) describe *reading engagement* as "interaction with text that is simultaneously motivated and strategic."

The Context

The larger social and cultural context in which reading occurs shapes (and is shaped by) the interrelated elements of reader, text, and activity (RRSG 2002). Most reading activities occur in the context of classroom instruction. Instructional decisions a teacher makes—from groupings to presentation—can crucially impact the reading experience (Almasi 2003). In turn, students bring to the classroom their own capacities and understandings about reading, developed through their experiences in their homes and neighborhoods (Snow and Sweet 2003). Literacy is considered a cultural activity, both because it is learned through social interactions and because different cultural groups interpret the world and communicate information in different ways (RRSG 2002).

BEFORE READING

- Set a goal.
- Preview the text.
- Predict what the text will say.

DURING READING

- Read sequentially, skimming some parts, focusing on others.
- Reread some sections.
- Make notes.
- Tune in to main ideas and ideas related to goal.
- Check and adapt predictions.
- Monitor and repair comprehension.
- Connect to world knowledge to make inferences.
- Paraphrase/summarize passages.
- Respond to and evaluate text.

AFTER READING

- Reread selectively.
- Summarize.
- Reflect.
- Think about how information might be used in the future.

Pressley 2002a; Pressley and Afflerbach 1995.

What Good Readers Do

Recent innovations in comprehension instruction have been built on a foundation of what good readers do. The effective reading processes, or strategies, of good readers can be explicitly taught, and doing so improves comprehension (National Reading Panel 2000). By observing how good readers read, research over the last two decades has revealed that reading comprehension is not an automatic or passive process, but one that is highly interactive and planned. Pressley and Afflerbach (1995) have developed a description of the wide range of strategies that good readers use before, during, and after reading.

BEFORE READING Before reading, good readers set a goal for what they hope to gain from the text. They often look over the text to note the structure and may skim for a general idea of content. They use this information to predict what the text will tell them and whether it is likely to meet their goals.

DURING READING During reading, good readers approach text intentionally—skimming, concentrating, rereading, or making notes. They also monitor comprehension as they read: they notice whether they generally understand the text, whether their predictions were correct, and whether the text is relevant to their purpose. They note problems with unknown words or confusing text. When something is confusing, they use repair strategies such as rereading a section to find something they've missed, reading on for further information, or making inferences using their own knowledge to fill in the gaps. Good readers also evaluate and ask questions about what they are reading. They may judge how well the text is written or decide whether they believe the information.

AFTER READING After reading, good readers sometimes reread selectively to focus on a particular part of a text. They often summarize what they've read and think about ways they might use the information they've learned.

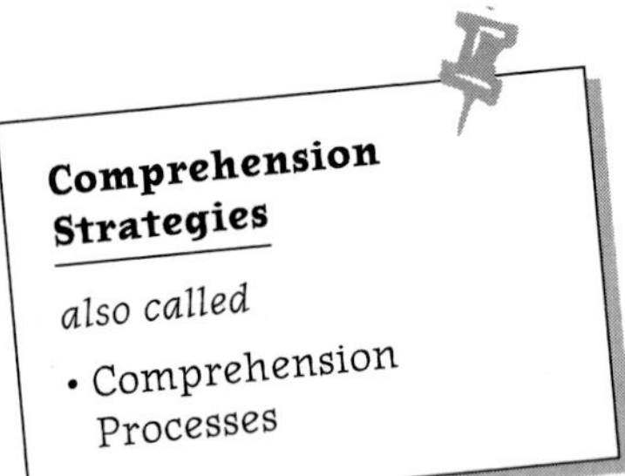

CCSS READING STANDARDS

Literature • Informational Text

Key Ideas and Details

Read closely to determine what text says explicitly and to make logical inferences from it. (CCR.1)

Comprehension Strategies

The "good readers" research indicates that skilled reading involves conscious application of *comprehension strategies.* Comprehension strategies are conscious plans that readers apply and adapt to make sense of text and get the most out of what they read. Comprehension strategy instruction aims to help students become active readers in control of their own comprehension (Pressley, El-Dinary et al. 1992). Key strategies to teach include monitoring comprehension, connecting to world knowledge, predicting, recognizing text structure, asking questions, answering questions, constructing mental images, and summarizing (National Reading Panel 2000; Duke and Pearson 2002; Pressley 2002a). As students interact with different texts, they can learn to become aware of their comprehension, and then to choose and apply the appropriate strategies as tools.

Comprehension Strategies	
Monitoring Comprehension	Being actively aware of whether one is, or is not, understanding the text and then dealing with problems as they arise
Connecting to World Knowledge	Linking knowledge that stems from previous experiences with ideas in the text
Predicting	Making an informed guess about what will come next in a reading, based on world knowledge and clues from the text
Recognizing Text Structure	Identifying the way text is organized
Asking Questions	Asking oneself questions about the text being read
Answering Questions	Finding and using information from text to answer teacher questions
Constructing Mental Images	Forming mental pictures in one's head as one reads
Summarizing	Distilling information into a concise, synthesized form

METACOGNITION "thinking about thinking"	
Metacognitive Knowledge Awareness of one's thinking and learning "How do I learn?"	**Metacognitive Control** Self-regulation of thinking and learning "How can I learn better?"

Reading strategies should work in the service of reading comprehension ... and assist students in building knowledge from texts.

—COLMAN & PIMENTEL, 2012

Effective use of strategies is driven by students' *metacognition.* Metacognition is "the knowledge and control we have of our own cognitive [i.e., thought] processes" (Baker 2002). It has two key aspects. *Metacognitive knowledge* is students' awareness of how they are thinking and learning as they work on a task. *Metacognitive control* is students' ability to self-regulate—that is, to adapt their learning approaches to accomplish a task. Instruction in metacognition forms the foundation for comprehension strategies instruction. Effective use of all other strategies requires reflecting on, monitoring, and regulating one's own thinking processes.

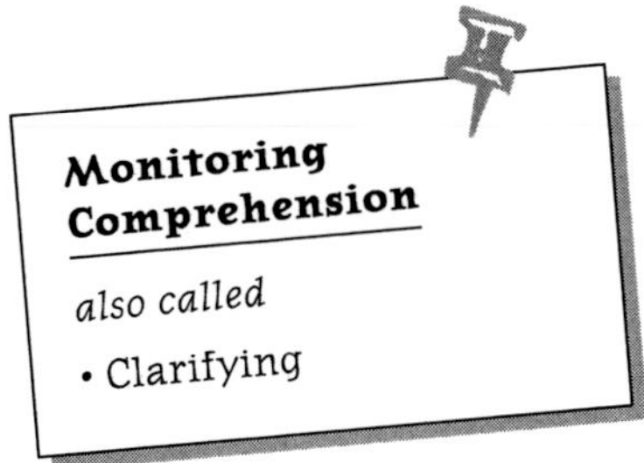

Monitoring Comprehension

Monitoring comprehension involves being actively aware of whether one is understanding the text and dealing with problems as they arise. A critical challenge in comprehension is that many students—particularly struggling adolescent readers—not only fail to understand what they read, but also remain unaware of their failure (Gersten et al. 2001; Brown 2002). Struggling readers often have the "illusion of comprehension"—believing that if they can decode the words, they have understood the text (RRSG 2002). In contrast, good readers know when they are confused (Baker and Brown 1984). Thus, instruction aimed at improving comprehension teaches students to become aware of when they fail to understand a text, and to use learned strategies to resolve comprehension failures.

SEE ALSO . . .

Monitoring Comprehension, pp. 639, 688

CCSS READING STANDARDS

Literature • Informational Text

Craft and Structure

Interpret words and phrases as they are used in text. (CCR.4)

Chapter 12: Word-Learning Strategies

Effective comprehension monitoring is a form of "self-listening" that includes students' noticing what they *do* understand, identifying what they *do not* understand, and using appropriate "fix-up" strategies to resolve problems or confusion (Taylor and Frye 1992). Anderson (1980) explained the process of monitoring as "the clicks of comprehension and the clunks of comprehension failure." When reading is running smoothly, it *clicks* along, like a train rolling down the track, until the reader hits a *clunk.* A clunk is something that impedes the reading process. Almasi (2003) points out that there are two types of clunks: (1) *word clunks,* when a student cannot recognize a word, and (2) *meaning clunks,* when a student doesn't understand a word, sentence, or passage. Word clunks can be resolved using decoding and other word recognition strategies. Meaning clunks can be resolved by using vocabulary and comprehension strategies in conjunction with fix-up strategies.

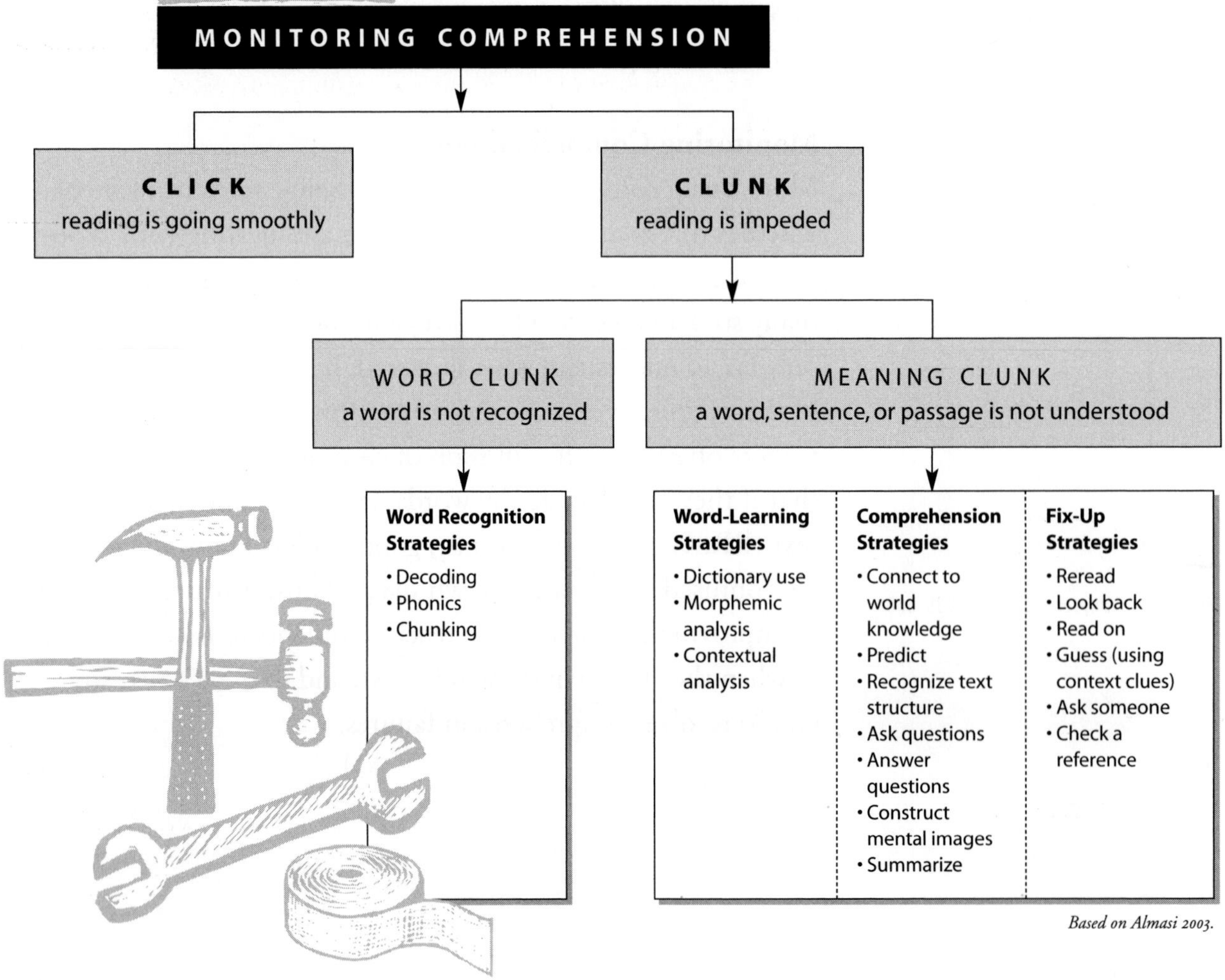

MONITORING COMPREHENSION

CLICK
reading is going smoothly

CLUNK
reading is impeded

WORD CLUNK
a word is not recognized

MEANING CLUNK
a word, sentence, or passage is not understood

Word Recognition Strategies	Word-Learning Strategies	Comprehension Strategies	Fix-Up Strategies
• Decoding • Phonics • Chunking	• Dictionary use • Morphemic analysis • Contextual analysis	• Connect to world knowledge • Predict • Recognize text structure • Ask questions • Answer questions • Construct mental images • Summarize	• Reread • Look back • Read on • Guess (using context clues) • Ask someone • Check a reference

Based on Almasi 2003.

Monitoring is fundamental to reading comprehension, and it has a reciprocal relationship with all other comprehension strategies. That is, monitoring guides the reader in applying each of the other strategies. In turn, each strategy serves as a tool that aids in both building and monitoring comprehension.

The Role Monitoring Plays in Applying the Other Strategies

To monitor when...	Students do this...
Connecting to World Knowledge	• Check whether the text is consistent with background knowledge and experiences. • Check whether the background knowledge activated is relevant to the text.
Predicting	• Confirm predictions while reading. • Adapt predictions based on new information in text.
Recognizing Text Structure	• Identify parts of the text that represent text structure elements. • Seek clarification when information seems inconsistent with the expected text structure.
Asking Questions	• Adapt questions when encountering new information in the text. • See if they can answer their own questions.
Answering Questions	• Note whether they are able to find adequate answers to teacher-directed questions.
Constructing Mental Images	• Confirm whether the text matches their image. • Adapt visualizations based on text descriptions.
Summarizing	• Evaluate the summary to see if it reflects understanding of the text.

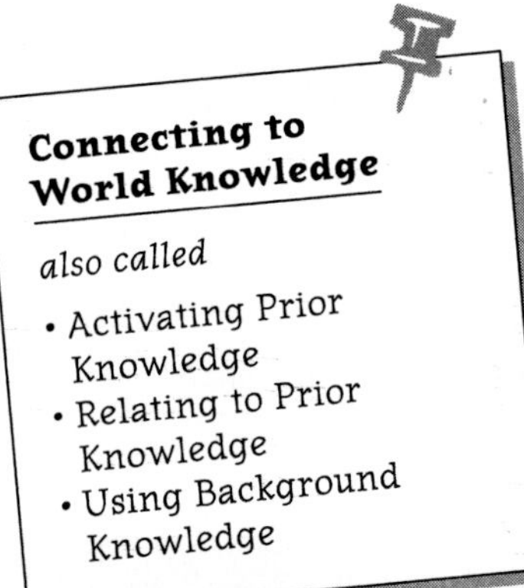

Connecting to
World Knowledge
also called
• Activating Prior Knowledge
• Relating to Prior Knowledge
• Using Background Knowledge

Connecting to World Knowledge, pp. 640, 689

SCHEMA
a mental network of knowledge structures

Connecting to World Knowledge

Connecting to world knowledge is linking knowledge from previous experiences with ideas in the text. Anderson and Pearson's (1984) research showed that what readers knew about the topic of a text before reading it had a huge impact on the messages they took away from reading. Some educators assert that the best way to improve students' comprehension is to build their knowledge base by focusing reading instruction primarily on content (Hirsch 1987, 2006). Reading widely and deeply can help students to master reading skills and to acquire world knowledge that helps them construct meaning (New Standards Primary Literacy Committee 1999). While reading, students encounter words and concepts that will form the foundation for future learning.

The role of the reader's world knowledge in comprehension is best understood through Anderson and Pearson's (1984) *schema theory* of how knowledge is organized. Schema theory suggests that the mind stores information in a network of knowledge structures called *schemas* (or schemata). As good readers see topics in a text, they access their schema (i.e., what they know) for the topic. Each schema is connected to many related schemas, so once a schema is activated, the reader has access to a whole network of information to support understanding the text at hand. In turn, new information from the text gets linked into existing schemas, making the information easier to understand and recall. A schema web is one way to show a schema.

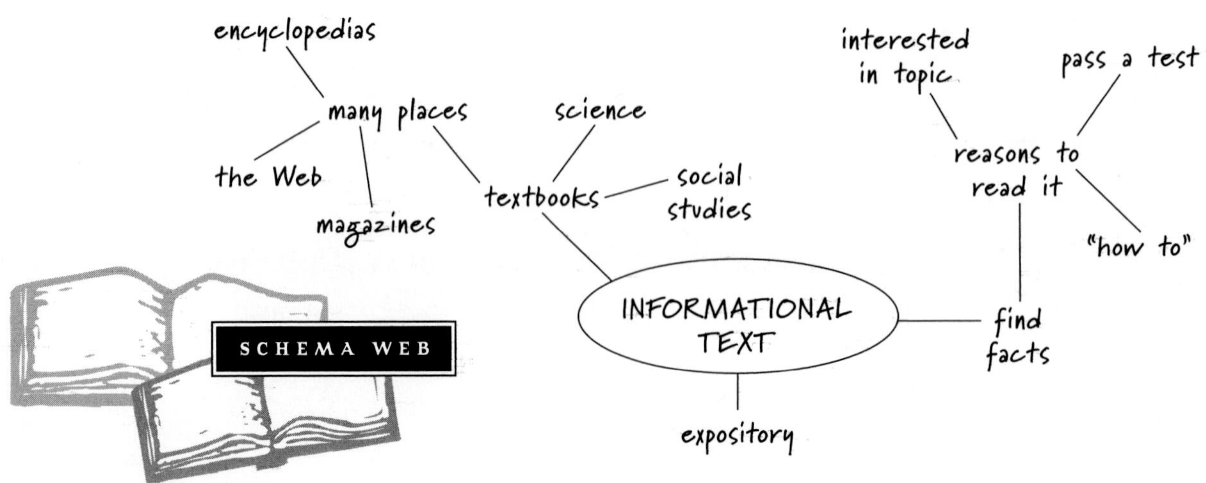

SCHEMA WEB

The next chapter in this section is about literary text. Tap into your available schema for literary text and create a web to show it.

A strong knowledge base alone may not be enough to improve comprehension; having world knowledge is only half the battle (Pressley and Block 2002). First, readers often fail to automatically apply what they know to make sense of what they're reading (Pressley, El-Dinary et al. 1992). Second, when students do use world knowledge, they frequently tap into experiences that are irrelevant to the text, sending them off on tangents that impair comprehension (Pressley and Block 2002). Therefore, it is imperative to teach students how to use their background knowledge appropriately, by assessing how the new information fits with, expands upon, or changes what they already know.

Predicting, pp. 640, 689

Predicting

Predicting is making an informed guess about what will come next in a reading, based on world knowledge and clues from the text. A prediction is a hypothesis to test while reading—a guess about what will happen or what information will be presented. When readers make predictions, they set up expectations based on their experience and knowledge of similar situations. Those expectations set a purpose for reading and motivate them to read on. Good readers make predictions about what they will read, read to confirm those predictions, and revise or make new predictions as they continue to read (Pressley and Afflerbach 1995). Before reading, predicting helps focus students' thinking; while reading, predicting helps guide students' reading (Almasi 2003). After reading, students review and evaluate the predictions they generated. This important aspect of predicting also improves students' recall of the text.

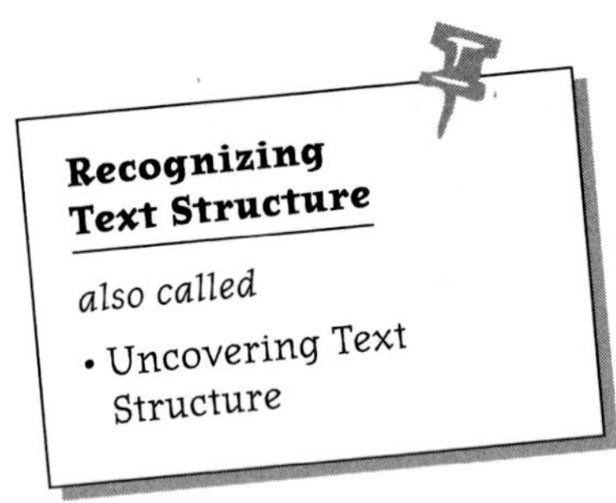

Recognizing Story Structure, p. 636
Recognizing Informational Text Structures, p. 687

Recognizing Text Structure

Recognizing text structure is identifying the way text is organized—uncovering its organizational logic. Text structures reflect the meaningful connections among the ideas in the text. Students who struggle to comprehend text often lack awareness of text structure (Williams 2005). Recognizing text structure can guide readers in identifying key information and improve students' recall of what they have read (Klingner, Vaughn, and Boardman 2007). Different types of text are organized in different ways. Literary text typically follows a single pattern, often called story structure or story grammar. Story structure includes the elements of setting, characters, plot, and theme. Informational, or expository, text follows a variety of structures, including description, compare-contrast, cause-effect, problem/solution, and time order. Because of its varying structures and because it more often deals with unfamiliar content, expository text is often more difficult to comprehend (Kucan and Beck 1997).

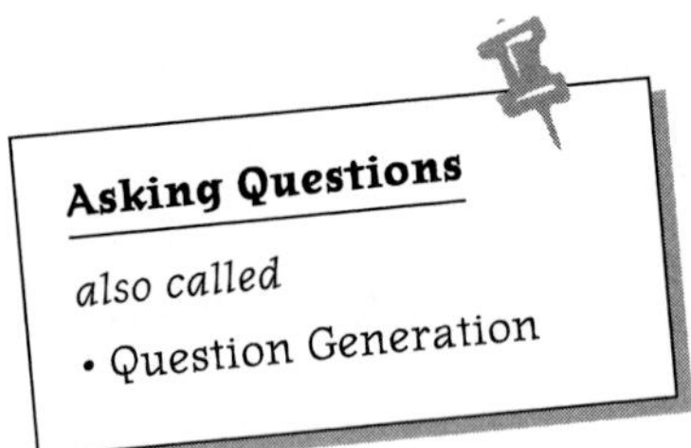

Asking Questions, pp. 637, 690

Asking Questions

Active readers ask themselves questions about the text being read. Generating questions engages readers with the text, as students are motivated by their own queries rather than just those of the teacher (National Reading Panel 2000). Asking questions also serves as a form of self-assessment (Ciardiello 1998). Teaching students to ask themselves questions and look for answers helps in both building and monitoring comprehension.

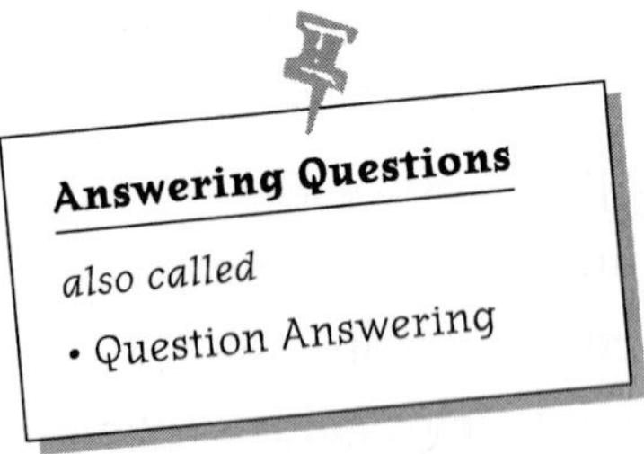

Answering Questions, pp. 639, 691

Answering Questions

In addition to asking their own questions, students need to be able to find answers to teachers' questions. Question-answering strategies encourage students to better answer questions and, as a result, to learn more as they read (Armbruster, Lehr, and Osborn 2001). Such strategies include knowing how to locate information to answer questions. Answers to questions may be found in the text itself or other reference materials or may come from students' own world knowledge.

Types of Teacher Questions

Type	Definition	Example
LITERAL	Questions for which the answer appears directly in the text	What is the definition of schema?
INFERENTIAL	Questions for which the answer is implied, although not explicitly stated in one place in the text	How can students' schemas for a topic help them understand what they read?
APPLIED	Questions for which a reader must integrate text information with evaluative thinking to construct an answer	What elements would you include in your personal schema of good reading comprehension?
STRATEGIC	Questions that prompt students to apply comprehension strategies to make meaning	Where on the page could you find the definition of schema? What do you imagine as you read about how schemas work? How do your reading experiences affect what elements you include in your schema of good reading?

Based on Fordham 2006.

CCSS READING STANDARDS

Literature • Informational Text

Key Ideas and Details

Ask and answer questions to demonstrate understanding of key details in a text. (RL.K-3.1; RI.K-3.1)

Teacher questions are a means to build students' comprehension strategy processes and to assess students' understanding. They are only one aspect of comprehension strategies instruction and should not be solely relied upon (Pressley et al. 1998). Different types of teacher questions stimulate different types of student thinking. One reliable finding is that higher-level questioning is consistently related to higher levels of student growth in reading comprehension (Taylor et al. 2003). Thus, the quality of students' thinking or answers can depend on the types of questions teachers are asking. Fordham (2006) recommends that teachers ask "strategic questions"—questions that prompt students to apply comprehension strategies to make meaning and foster metacognition. In a review of many research studies, Pressley, Wood et al. (1992) found that, to be effective, teacher questions must require both deep processing of the information and relating it to prior knowledge.

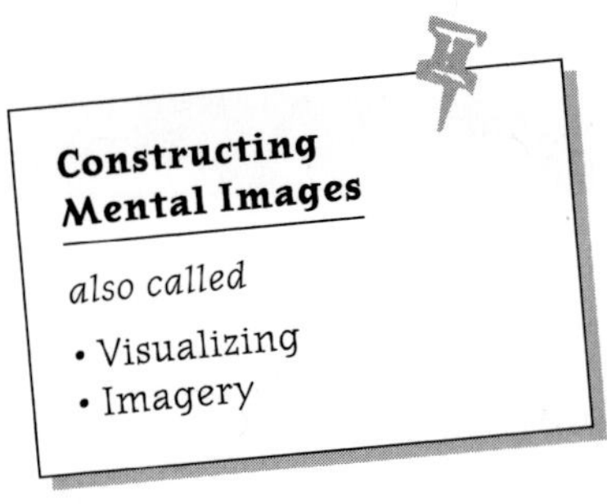

Constructing Mental Images, pp. 640, 692

Constructing Mental Images

Constructing mental images is a strategy of making a mental image, or picture, to represent the text content. Research has consistently shown that constructing mental images increases comprehension. One possible reason is that imagery promotes active processing of text; that is, it requires the reader to construct meaningful images that link text information with prior knowledge (Chan, Cole, and Morris 1990). Images also can provide a structure for organizing and remembering text (Gambrell and Koskinen 2002). If one considers verbal and nonverbal memory as separate interconnected systems, images can serve as mental "pegs" on which verbal information from text is hooked (Sadoski and Paivio 1994). These pegs store information in the brain in a way that makes it easier to retrieve.

In some cases, readers are guided by visuals provided with the text (illustrations, photographs, graphic organizers). In other cases, they rely solely on the text itself, imagining what is described in words. Good readers often automatically visualize what is happening in text as they read, whereas poor readers do not. Students who don't automatically construct mental images can be taught to do so, improving their comprehension (Gambrell and Koskinen 2002).

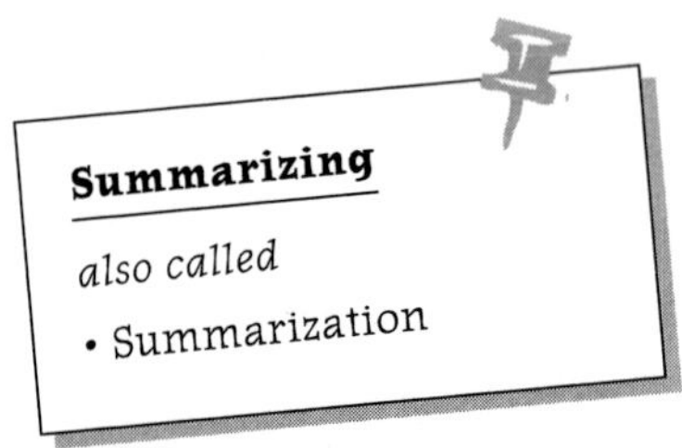

Summarizing, pp. 641, 693

Summarizing

Harris and Hodges (1995) define a summary as a "brief statement that contains the essential ideas of a longer passage or selection." Skill in summarization can make students more aware of the way a text is structured and how ideas are related (National Reading Panel 2000). Summarizing requires students to distill information into a concise, synthesized form and then to restate the information. This involves analyzing the text at a fairly deep level (Marzano, Pickering, and Pollock 2001). Students who struggle with reading comprehension have much difficulty with summarizing (Klingner et al. 2007).

Multiple-Strategy Instruction Programs

also called

- Comprehension Instructional Frameworks
- Combined Instructional Frameworks
- Comprehension Routines
- Multiple-Strategy Packages
- Multicomponent Approaches

Multiple-Strategy Instruction Programs

It takes a whole repertoire of strategies, not just a single strategy, to read well. Effective readers are able to choose and adapt strategies as a particular text or reading activity demands (Afflerbach 2002). Almasi (2003) uses the analogy of a "cognitive toolbox." When readers realize that something has gone wrong, they can reach into their cognitive toolbox to select a tool or strategy that will help resolve the difficulty. Thus, it is critical to teach students when to use particular strategies and how to use several strategies in coordination (Pressley 2000b). In fact, the National Reading Panel (2000) regards the need for multiple comprehension strategies instruction as its most important finding. Rather than teaching strategies or skills in isolation, multiple-strategy instruction programs teach students flexible ways to apply a repertoire of comprehension strategies (Liang and Dole 2006; RRSG 2002). Each program offers a unique packaging of strategies and a unique way of teaching the strategies.

Comprehension strategies often work together as a whole. For example, when you make predictions, you may rely on clues from the layout of the text. Your world knowledge of individual topics may further suggest how and why the ideas fit together. Quickly scan the upcoming headings and subheadings of this introduction. Use your world knowledge along with the text structure to make some predictions about what you are going to learn. As you read, note whether the text matched your predictions or presented something different. This verification process is a form of comprehension monitoring.

MAKING AND VERIFYING PREDICTIONS

What is my prediction?	Did the text verify my prediction?	If not, what was the difference?
I think I'm going to learn about a special kind of strategy called an explicit comprehension strategy.	No.	I learned an explicit way to teach comprehension strategies.

> The explicitness with which teachers teach comprehension strategies makes a difference in learner outcomes, especially for low-achieving students.
>
> —RRSG, 2002

SEE ALSO . . .

What Good Readers Do, p. 613

Explicit Comprehension Strategies Instruction

Research indicates that strong readers often use comprehension strategies automatically when they read, whereas poor readers often do not. Janice Almasi (2003) identifies five characteristics of "good strategy users" that are essential for proficient reading. She further asserts that when students do not use strategies, it is because one or more of these essential characteristics is not in place. Explicit instruction helps students develop these characteristics to internalize and self-regulate comprehension strategies (National Reading Panel 2000; RRSG 2002). Given explicit instruction, students should be able to transfer and apply comprehension strategies to their independent reading (Griffin, Malone, and Kame'enui 1995; Pressley et al. 1989).

Characteristics of Good Strategy Users: Implications for Instruction

Good Strategy Users:	Good Comprehension Strategies Instruction:
possess extensive content knowledge.	builds students' knowledge base through providing rich, meaningful content.
are motivated to use strategies.	builds students' confidence in the usefulness of strategies and in their ability to use them.
possess strong metacognition.	develops student metacognition so students are aware of when they need to use strategies.
are able to analyze reading tasks and goals.	teaches students why, when, and how to use a variety of strategies.
possess a variety of strategies, used in coordination.	teaches students how to choose and apply appropriate strategies for diverse texts and tasks.

Based on Almasi 2003.

Model of Explicit Strategy Instruction		
Step	**Teacher Role**	**Student Role**
Direct Explanation	Explain to students what the strategy is, how to use it, why the strategy helps comprehension, and when to apply it.	Attend to teacher explanations. Understand what the strategy is and why it helps.
Modeling	Model or demonstrate how to apply the strategy, usually by thinking aloud while reading a text.	Observe how the strategy works and how to apply it.
Guided Practice	Guide and assist students as they begin to apply the strategy. Provide feedback about students' use of the strategy and its effectiveness.	Practice using the strategy. Think aloud while reading, and discuss strategy use. Respond to feedback, adapting strategy use if needed.
Independent Practice	Assess the need for further support or reminders. Monitor students' strategy use as they transfer what they have learned to new tasks.	Apply the strategy independently and transfer it to a variety of new situations.

Duke and Pearson 2002; Armbruster et al. 2001.

SCAFFOLDING
gradually releasing to students the responsibility for strategy use

Scaffolding

One of the most important techniques of explicit instruction is *scaffolding*—a process of shifting responsibility for learning from the teacher to the students. Graves, Watts, and Graves (1994) define scaffolding as "a temporary supportive structure that teachers create to help a student or a group of students to accomplish a task that they could not complete alone." Pressley's (2002b) description explains the scaffolding metaphor and its educational meaning:

> The scaffolding of a building under construction provides support when the new building cannot stand on its own. As the new structure is completed and becomes freestanding, the scaffolding is removed. So it is with scaffolded adult–child academic interactions. The adult carefully monitors when enough instructional input has been provided to permit the child to make progress toward an academic goal, and thus the adult provides support only when the child needs it.

> Scaffolds enable all students to experience rather than avoid the complexity of text.
>
> —COLMAN & PIMENTEL, 2012

Gradual and careful fading of scaffolding is paramount to comprehension strategies instruction. Both the teacher and students have responsibilities at each phase of instruction, with the bulk of responsibility shifting from teacher to student over time (RRSG 2002). Scaffolding in the Model of Explicit Instruction shows how instruction is scaffolded to gradually build student independence. From top to bottom, the graphic indicates the progression of the shift from teacher responsibility to student responsibility. Informal assessment of students' strategy use often identifies the need for additional support as indicated. This scaffolded support may take the form of additional explanation, modeling, guidance, or feedback. Instructional tools for scaffolding can include graphic organizers, prompts, cooperative learning, and read-aloud methods.

Scaffolding in the Model of Explicit Instruction

Based on El-Dinary 1993; Bergman 1992; Duke and Pearson 2002; Pearson and Gallagher 1983.

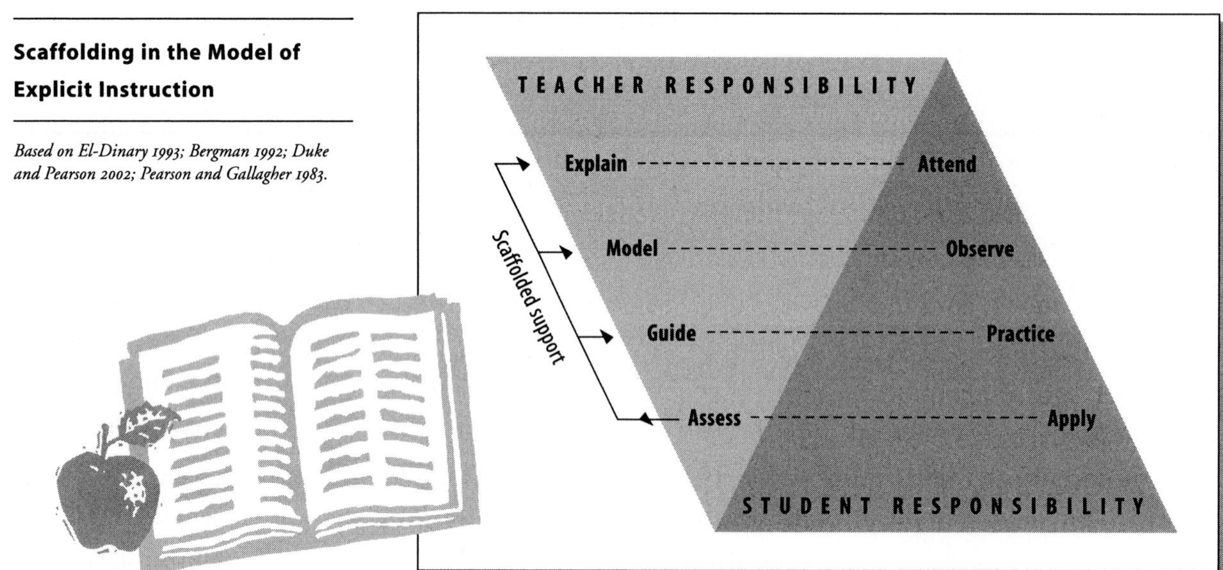

Scaffolding Tools

Graphic Organizers

Prompts

Cooperative Learning

Read-Aloud Methods

GRAPHIC ORGANIZERS A graphic organizer is a visual representation of knowledge that structures information to demonstrate relationships. Graphic organizers—such as story maps, diagrams, and charts—illustrate concepts and interrelationships among concepts in a text (Armbruster et al. 2001). Such graphic organizers are particularly useful for teaching complex strategies such as summarization and recognizing text structure.

PROMPTS Prompts are verbal or nonverbal cues that encourage strategy use. Early in instruction, verbal prompts may be more structured; for example, "This is a very descriptive paragraph. It seems like a good place to visualize." As instruction progresses, prompts encourage self-regulation; for example, "What strategy could you choose to help you figure that out?" Nonverbal prompts might include hand gestures that represent strategy names (Block 2004).

Cooperative Learning
also called
• Collaborative Learning Structures
• Peer-Mediated Instruction

COOPERATIVE LEARNING In cooperative learning, students work together as partners or in small groups on a clearly defined task such as helping each other learn, choose, and apply comprehension strategies (Lehr and Osborn 2005). Some of the benefits of cooperative learning are improvement in students' motivation, ability to work collaboratively, and opportunities to experience other approaches to understanding (Alvermann and Eakle 2003). A key finding of the RRSG report (2002) is that "teachers who give students choices, challenging tasks, and collaborative learning structures increase their motivation to read and comprehend text."

> A systematic approach to reading aloud can yield important academic benefits for children.
>
> —LANE & WRIGHT, 2007

Read-Aloud Methods, p. 427

READ-ALOUD METHODS Effective read-alouds encourage students to actively engage with the text—relating it to their knowledge and experiences, making and checking predictions, and asking questions (Lane and Wright 2007). Both beginning readers and older struggling readers are often challenged by the fact that, though they can handle complex content, their decoding and word recognition skills limit their ability to read complex text (Beck and McKeown 2001; Fisher and Frey 2004). For such readers, listening to text read aloud provides access to a wide range of complex text that they would be unable to read for themselves. Even students who can read independently continue to benefit from listening to, responding to, and analyzing literature that is read to them.

Students who meet the Standards actively seek the wide, deep, and thoughtful engagement with high-quality literary and informational texts . . . .

—COMMON CORE STATE STANDARDS, 2010

Contextualized Instruction

Comprehension strategies instruction should occur in the context of reading carefully selected texts rather than in isolation. Toward the goal of providing plenty of guided opportunities for students to think about and interpret text, Torgesen (2007) recommends the following practices:

- Present strategies as tools for building comprehension rather than as "ends in themselves."
- Keep the focus on constructing the meaning of text rather than on the strategies themselves.
- Focus on thinking about the text itself rather than on thinking about how to process the text.
- Spend the most time on collaborative, scaffolded application and less time on early explicit descriptions.

Close Reading

Rereading

"Reading with a Pencil"

Noticing Confusing Parts

Discussing the Text

Answering Text-Dependent Questions

Lapp, Frey, and Fisher 2012.

To be effective for developing comprehension, texts need to be "conceptually challenging enough to require grappling with ideas and taking an active stance toward constructing meaning" (Beck and McKeown 2001). Texts must also appeal to students' interests to maintain their attention and promote proficient reading. Research shows that students reading high-interest texts can often surpass their typical reading levels, whereas students reading low-interest texts tend to perform below capacity, even with text at their level (Snow 2003).

Research with adolescents who appear to be struggling readers also has shown that they are often quite literate with alternate forms of text, such as comic books and text messages (Alvermann 2001; RRSG 2002). At-risk students may be particularly engaged by digital text such as that found on the Internet (Alvermann and Eakle 2003). In fact, even adolescents considered at risk of dropping out of high school proved highly capable when reading digital texts (O'Brien 2001). These high-interest texts are relevant to students' lives and meet their varied interests and therefore can help them to become lifelong readers (Alvermann and Eakle 2003).

Reader Response

SEE ALSO . . .

Reader Response, pp. 642, 694

READER RESPONSE meaning-making through personal response and reflection

Comprehension is not simply a matter of one reader understanding one text in one way. Reader response approaches stem from the work of Louise Rosenblatt (1978, 1995), who suggested that meaning is constructed through the interaction between the reader and the text—it does not come solely from the reader or solely from the text. In her classic work, she showed that readers' interpretations, reactions, and emotional responses to text had an impact on the meaning they constructed from it, that is, on their comprehension. Not only will different readers respond to a text in different ways, but also several readers in collaboration often will produce meanings that no single reader could. In a reader response approach to comprehension, such differences are acknowledged and even encouraged as portals to deeper understanding. Discussion and writing can be effective ways to foster reader response.

> Opportunities to engage in text-based discussions over time can have a general impact on reading comprehension.
>
> —TORGESEN ET AL., 2007

Discussion-Oriented Instruction

Participation in open, sustained discussions of reading content increases students' ability to think about and learn from text (Torgesen et al. 2007). Both student-directed and teacher-directed text discussions can be effective before, during, and after reading. Discussions that take place while reading may be even more effective than discussions after students have read on their own (Sandora, Beck, and McKeown 1999). Student-led discussion groups can engage students with text and help them become confident and eager readers (Raphael, Kehus, and Damphousse 2001). Teacher-directed discussions can pose higher-order questions to help students focus their thinking about text at a deeper level. Dialogue in which teachers and students share both their comprehension strategies and their personal responses also can help students understand and interpret text (Pressley 2000b).

Writing Stances for Responding to Text	
Writing Stance	**Writing Objective**
WRITING INTO	• Access world knowledge. • Raise questions and set purposes for reading. • Foster word consciousness. • Make connections between self and text.
WRITING THROUGH	• Chart information. • Identify important information, supporting details, and plot points. • Explore characters, setting, and other literary elements.
WRITING OUT	• Reflect and respond. • Give personal, creative, and/or critical responses. • Make connections between text and self, other texts, and theme. • Explore text concepts.

Based on Raphael et al. 2004.

Expressing opinions and interpretations in writing helps readers organize their thoughts about a text.

—LEHR & OSBORN, 2005

Responding Through Writing

Responding to literature through writing can improve students' comprehension for two reasons: (1) Reading and writing both involve constructing meaning. For students to express opinions and interpretations in writing, they must organize their thoughts about the text. (2) Writing gives students insight into literary "tools of the trade" such as style, word choice, precision, and organization. When students understand these tools as writers, they can better appreciate and understand them as readers (Lehr and Osborn 2005).

The act of putting words down on paper "pushes students' thinking beyond casual reflection" (Raphael, Pardo, and Highfield 2002). Raphael et al. (2004) suggest three writing stances for responding to text—writing into, writing through, and writing out. As students write *into, through,* and *out* of their texts, they learn to see writing as a tool that can serve many functions: to reflect on reading, to gather and organize information, to practice literary forms, and to share ideas with others.

The relationship between English-language learners' syntactic knowledge of English and their text comprehension ...may intersect with their vocabulary knowledge, background knowledge, and second-language oral proficiency.

—GARCÍA, 2003

SEE ALSO . . .

English-Language Learners (ELLs), p. 17

Instruction for English-Language Learners (ELLs)

For English-language learners, reading comprehension is closely tied to oral English proficiency (August and Shanahan 2006). ELLs often have adequate word-level skills, such as decoding and word recognition, to allow them to attain levels of performance equal to those of native English speakers. However, this is not the case for text-level skills—reading comprehension and writing (August and Shanahan 2006). Since ELLs' reading comprehension is often hampered by their proficiency in English, it is useful to promote their language production and vocabulary acquisition, while simultaneously working on comprehension skills (Francis et al. 2006).

According to Torgesen et al. (2007), "much of what we know about effective comprehension instruction for native English speakers is theoretically justifiable for ELLs and likely to be effective." Effective comprehension instruction for ELLs and their classmates must be explicit and direct and must actively engage students in monitoring their use of strategies during the comprehension process (Francis et al. 2006).

With ELL students, it is particularly important to emphasize transferring strategies from their native language to English. ELLs who are able readers in their primary language often have developed several comprehension strategies that they can transfer to reading in English (Garcia 2003). Rather than reteach literate ELL students comprehension strategies that they already use in their native language, it is more productive to teach them how to apply their existing strategies to English-language texts.

CHAPTER 14

Literary Text

what? Literary Text

Types of Literary Texts

STORIES

- Adventures
- Fables
- Fairy tales
- Fantasies
- Folktales
- Legends
- Myths
- Novels
- Realistic fiction
- Science fiction
- Short stories
- Tall tales

DRAMA

POETRY

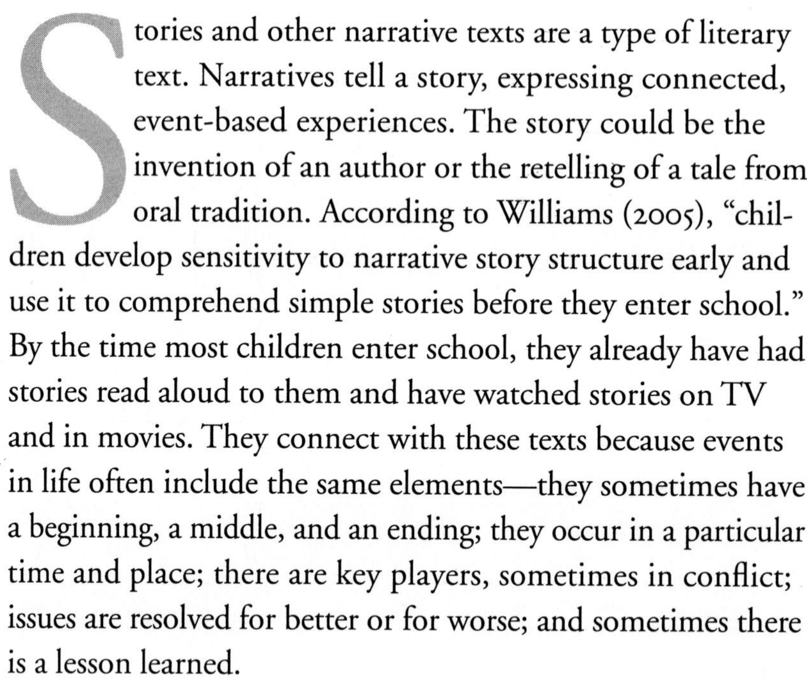

Stories and other narrative texts are a type of literary text. Narratives tell a story, expressing connected, event-based experiences. The story could be the invention of an author or the retelling of a tale from oral tradition. According to Williams (2005), "children develop sensitivity to narrative story structure early and use it to comprehend simple stories before they enter school." By the time most children enter school, they already have had stories read aloud to them and have watched stories on TV and in movies. They connect with these texts because events in life often include the same elements—they sometimes have a beginning, a middle, and an ending; they occur in a particular time and place; there are key players, sometimes in conflict; issues are resolved for better or for worse; and sometimes there is a lesson learned.

Story Structure

Story structure pertains to how stories and their plots are systematically organized into a predictable format. Knowing about story structure provides a framework that helps students to discover what is most relevant for understanding a story (Williams 2002). Most narratives are organized around a set of elements, sometimes referred to as *story grammar* (Mandler 1987). Story elements include setting, characters, plot, and theme. Stories often begin by describing the setting and characters, then indicating a particular problem faced by one of the characters. Then the story explains how the problem is solved, concluding by showing how the characters were affected by the events.

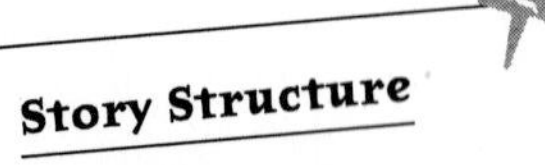

Story Structure

also called

- Story Elements
- Story Grammar
- Narrative Text Structure

CCSS READING STANDARDS

Literature

Key Ideas and Details

Ask and answer questions to demonstrate understanding of key details in a text. (RL.K-3.1)

Describe characters, settings, and events in a story. (RL.K-4.3)

Craft and Structure

Describe the overall structure of a story. (RL.2.5)

The Text, p. 610

Setting

The setting of a story tells *when* and *where* the story takes place. Some stories have specific settings, while others take place at some indefinite time (e.g., the future) or in some indefinite place (e.g., an unnamed country). The setting also can change within a story—moving back (flashback) or jumping ahead (flash-forward) before returning to the main time frame of the story.

Characters

Characters are the people, animals, or creatures in a story. The main character, also known as the *protagonist*, moves the action forward, sometimes by acting against a villain or rival, the *antagonist.* To understand a character, readers must be able to tap into characterization techniques: what the author states directly about the character; what the character says, does, and thinks; and how other story characters react and respond to the character. The main character's motivation—sometimes explicit, sometimes implied—drives the plot.

Plot

The plot of a story tells what happened and gives the story a beginning, a middle, and an ending. It is the sum of a series of events. In general, the components of a narrative plot include

- the *problem* a character faces—the *conflict*;
- the sequence of *events* that happens as the character attempts to solve the problem;
- the *outcome*, or *resolution*, of the attempts to solve the problem.

Theme

The theme is the big idea that the author wants the reader to take away from reading the story. Williams (2002) explains that a theme "expresses a relationship among story elements and comments on that relationship in some way." The theme can be expressed as a lesson or an observation that is generalized beyond the specifics of the story plot.

SEE ALSO . . .

Comprehension Strategies, p. 614

Comprehension Strategies

Recognizing Story Structure

Asking Questions

Answering Questions

Monitoring Comprehension

Connecting to World Knowledge

Predicting

Constructing Mental Images

Summarizing/Retelling

SEE ALSO . . .

LESSON MODEL: Story Structure, p. 651

Strategy Application

Story-structure knowledge drives the application of comprehension strategies to narratives. When reading narratives, good readers use their knowledge of story elements to ask and answer questions, monitor story comprehension, predict and preview, connect to world knowledge, construct mental images, and summarize or retell. Thus, recognizing the elements of story structure is a prerequisite to effective strategy use.

Recognizing Story Structure

Explicit instruction on story structure enhances students' memory and recall of narratives, with even greater benefits for struggling readers (National Reading Panel 2000). Being aware of story structure is an aid in summarizing; it helps students identify which parts of the story to attend to the most. Story structure can be taught through question answering and asking strategies and through graphic organizers called story maps. A story map is a visual representation of a story "based on a logical organization of events and ideas of central importance to the story and their interrelationships" (Beck and McKeown 2006). Used *before* reading, a story map enhances students' ability to predict and set purposes for reading; used *while* reading, it serves to focus attention and help the reader monitor incoming information and compare it to earlier predictions (Almasi 2003). During story reading, a set of basic questions, or prompts, can help students to identify story elements and use this information to fill in a story map. On the story map, students can record the setting, characters, problem, events that happen as the character tries to solve the problem, outcome, and theme of the story as they unfold over time.

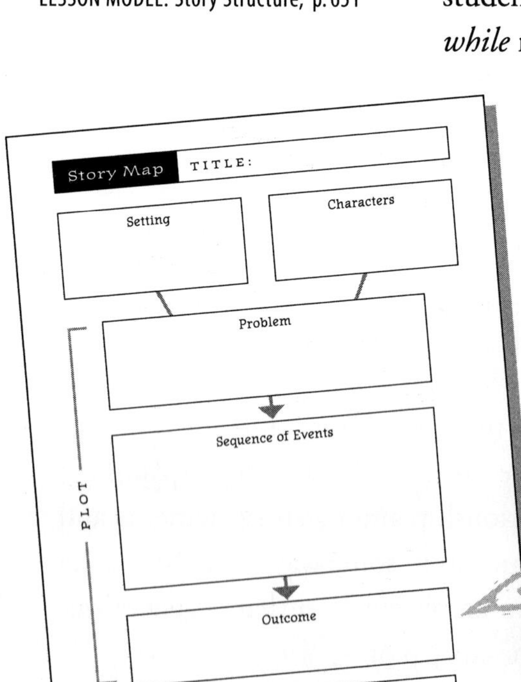

Asking Questions

Asking questions of text can serve as an organizational guide to story structure, promote active reading, and help students identify important information (Mandler and Johnson 1977; RRSG 2002). Students need instruction in how to pose effective questions. Initially, the teacher's questions provide support—serving as models of the types of questions students can ask themselves while reading. With guidance, students can begin to ask such questions on their own.

Story Structure Questions

STORY ELEMENT	QUESTION *(bulleted items indicate higher-level questions)*
Setting	Where and when does the story take place?
Characters	Who is the story about? • Who is the main character, or protagonist? • What is the character's physical description? • What are the character's personality traits?
Problem	What is the problem the character faces? What does the character want to do? • What tough decisions does the character face? • Is there a struggle for survival against a force of nature? • What motive, or reason, does the character have for resolving the problem?
Sequence of Events	What does the main character do about the problem? What happens as the character tries to solve the problem?
Outcome	How does the story turn out? Does the character solve the problem? • What is the resolution, or final attempt that solves or fails to solve the problem? • Does the story end in a twist, or an unexpected complication that occurs and causes an unexpected resolution of the problem?
Theme	What lesson does the main character learn? What lesson did you learn from the story? What is the moral of the story? • What is the author trying to tell the reader?

PLOT

Sample Question for "Common Sense: An Anansi Tale" (p. 765)

BLOOM'S TAXONOMY

Level of Thinking	Definition	Thinking Processes Involved	Possible Question Frames	Sample Question
1. KNOWLEDGE	Recognizing or recalling literal information	arrange, define, duplicate, label, list, memorize, name, recognize, recall, repeat	Who ___? What ___? When ___? Where ___? How ___?	Where did Anansi stuff the common sense?
2. COMPREHENSION	Constructing meaning from text	classify, describe, discuss, explain, infer, interpret, paraphrase, restate, review, summarize	Can you retell ___? Can you explain ___? What did ___ look like? What kind of character was ___? Why did ___?	Can you explain why no one has all the common sense?
3. APPLICATION	Applying text content to a new situation	apply, choose, demonstrate, dramatize, illustrate, practice, schedule, sketch, solve, use	How is ___ an example of ___? How is ___ related to ___? Why is ___ significant? Can you organize ___ to show ___? How could ___?	How could Anansi have used better common sense when hiding the calabash?
4. ANALYSIS	Breaking down ideas into their parts to show how they are related	analyze, appraise, categorize, compare, contrast, differentiate, distinguish, examine, question, test	What is the structure of ___? What steps did ___? How does ___ compare or contrast with ___? What evidence can you list for ___? What motives did ___ have for ___?	What steps did Anansi take to hide the common sense?
5. SYNTHESIS	Combining different ideas to create an original work	assemble, compose, construct, create, design, develop, formulate, organize, propose, write	What would you ___? How could you adapt/expand ___? What might happen if you ___? What solutions would you suggest for ___? If you were ___?	If you were Anansi, what would you have done with the common sense? Draw a picture or act it out.
6. EVALUATION	Judging value or effectiveness, based on some criteria or standards	appraise, argue, assess, defend, estimate, judge, rate, select, support, evaluate	How effective was ___? Do you think ___? What is the most important ___? How would you decide about ___? Do you agree ___?	Do you think Anansi would be a good friend? Why or why not?

Based on Bloom 1956; Otero, Leon, and Graesser 2002; RRSG 2002.

1. Knowledge
3. Application
5. Synthesis
2. Comprehension
4. Analysis
6. Evaluation

Answering Questions

In addition to asking and answering their own questions about story structure, students can answer teacher-directed questions. Questions that spark a full range of thinking skills encourage a deeper level of comprehension. Bloom (1956) developed a taxonomy to classify levels of thinking in learning, which can guide teachers in developing questions, from low level to high level, which can be applied to text (RRSG 2002).

Bloom's Taxonomy suggests a range of possible text-based questions. Using "The Case of the Blue Carbuncle" (p. 762), develop a sample question for each level of Bloom's Taxonomy. (See Answer Key, p. 800.)

Questions for Self-Monitoring

- **Do I have a sense of when and where the story takes place?**
- **Have I identified the main character?**
- **Do I understand the problem?**
- **Am I following the plot?**
- **Did I figure out how the problem was resolved?**
- **Do I understand the lesson of the story?**

Monitoring Comprehension

Knowledge of story structure drives comprehension monitoring for narratives. Monitoring comprehension involves noting how well one's understanding of a story is progressing. Students can ask themselves questions to check their understanding of story elements.

THINK-ALOUDS A think-aloud involves saying what you are thinking while you read. Both teacher and student think-alouds can strengthen comprehension (Duke and Pearson 2002; Kucan and Beck 1997; Bereiter and Bird 1985; Silven and Vauras 1992). When teachers think aloud, they model how to monitor comprehension. When students think aloud, they can better self-monitor their own comprehension (Baumann, Seifert-Kessel, and Jones 1992). They can identify parts of the story that don't make sense, and then describe how they are using strategies to repair comprehension.

Mature comprehension involves generalization beyond the story characters and events to real-life people and events.

—WILLIAMS, 2005

Connecting to World Knowledge

Integrating story information with previous life experiences enables students to understand, feel, value, and retain the depth of an author's meaning. Guiding students to connect a story with other stories they have read also can broaden and deepen their literary understanding (Block and Pressley 2003). Teacher guidance in helping students stay focused on relevant prior knowledge is particularly important for the success of connecting to world knowledge (Dole et al. 1991).

Questions for Predicting

- **Does the title provide a clue to what the story will be about?**
- **What do you know about the author?**
- **What does the opening artwork suggest about the setting? The characters?**
- **Is the text likely to be fiction or nonfiction?**

Predicting

Narratives with predictable story plots or repetitive phrases are excellent for developing students' ability to predict (Block and Pressley 2003). Based on world knowledge and story structure, good readers make informed predictions before and during reading. Predicting before reading, or previewing, helps students to focus their attention while reading. Teachers can guide prediction through questions that apply what students know about story structure (Neuman 1988).

Constructing Mental Images

Using mental imagery, or "making pictures in your mind," can help students to understand what a story is about (Gambrell and Koskinen 2002). Through explicit instruction, students can learn to picture authors' descriptions as a way to build and monitor their comprehension. It is easy to imagine concrete text, such as the sentence *He looked down and saw a small boy leaning against the tree trunk.* For more abstract or unfamiliar ideas, good readers create their own images. When reading the sentence *The sack was soon bursting at the seams,* readers can form their own ideas about what the sack looked like. Sometimes readers must adapt their mental images as they encounter new information in the text. If the author later writes *The worn-out leather sack was about to fall apart,* readers might need to change their original vision of the sack.

Poor readers do not spontaneously employ mental imagery as a comprehension strategy.

—GAMBRELL & KOSKINEN, 2002

CCSS READING STANDARDS

Literature

Key Ideas and Details

Retell, determine theme, and/or summarize a story. (RL.K-5.2)

SEE ALSO . . .

LESSON MODELS

Story Structure, p. 651

Strategies for Summarizing, p. 711

Summarizing

Summarizing, an important skill for students to master, focuses on story elements. Teachers can use a series of story structure questions, sometimes called a narrative summary frame, to elicit important story information. Students use the answers to the questions to guide them in summarizing a story.

Summarizing often takes the form of retelling—restating the events of a story (Klingner et al. 2007). Teachers can use retelling to assess comprehension and to guide students toward a deeper understanding of a story. As readers become more competent, their retellings become more sophisticated (Brown and Cambourne 1987). Jill Hansen (2004) advocates a developmental approach to retelling instruction. At each developmental level, teachers guide students toward the next, deeper level.

EMERGENT LEVEL

- Focus on event listing and sequencing.
- Introduce basic story elements.

EARLY FLUENT LEVEL

- Help students apply the basic story elements in oral and written retellings.
- Introduce identifying main events that lead the main character from the problem to the outcome.
- Model and guide retelling events in sequence and integrating story elements, using story maps.

FLUENT LEVEL

- Introduce plot summary—retelling key events in chronological order.
- Practice to refine sequencing and story elements in retellings.

Although students benefit from retelling with teacher guidance, they can quickly move on to retell stories to one another. Paired retelling sessions are even more effective if they are interactive, with the listener providing feedback. A Retelling Feedback Form could be used to support paired retellings.

RETELLING FEEDBACK FORM

Did my partner tell about . . .	
✓ The setting?	yes or no
✓ The characters?	yes or no
✓ The problem?	yes or no
✓ The attempts to solve the problem?	yes or no
✓ The outcome?	yes or no
✓ The story events in the correct order?	yes or no
✓ The best part of the retelling was . . .	

Transactional Theories Behind Transactional Strategies Instruction (TSI)

Field	Basic Idea
LITERATURE *(Rosenblatt 1978)*	Meaning is found not in the text alone, nor in the reader's mind alone, but is constructed in a transaction between the reader and text.
LITERACY *(Bleich 1978; Bloome 1988; Morrow 1990)*	As students discuss what they read, they build a group interpretation that is different from what any single reader would have developed alone.
COGNITIVE PSYCHOLOGY *(Vygotsky 1978; Wood, Bruner, and Ross 1976)*	As groups work on tasks together, over time, individuals begin to internalize the processes of the group.
DEVELOPMENTAL PSYCHOLOGY *(Bell 1968; Bjorkland 1989; Sameroff 1975)*	Children's actions impact the behaviors of adults in their world. Group activities are determined jointly by participants as they interact with a task.
ORGANIZATIONAL PSYCHOLOGY *(Hutchins 1991)*	When groups solve problems, they produce solutions that no one individual in the group would have produced .

Based on Pressley and Wharton-McDonald 1998.

Multiple-Strategy Instruction Program: TSI

Transactional Strategies Instruction (TSI) is a research-validated, multiple-strategy instruction approach developed by Michael Pressley and colleagues (Pressley, El-Dinary et al. 1992). In TSI, understanding the text shares equal weight with learning the coordinated use of comprehension strategies. TSI emphasizes collaborative discussion among learners, with metacognition, motivation, and reader response as the focus of instruction (Brown et al. 1996). TSI is named for diverse theories from several fields—all of which include the concept of "transactions." It embodies the full range of transactions—between reader and text, between readers, and between reader and teacher.

LESSON MODEL: TSI (Transactional Strategies Instruction), p. 659

CCSS READING STANDARDS

Literature • Informational Text

Key Ideas and Details

Read closely to determine what text says explicitly. (CCR.1)

Reader Response

Reader response refers to how readers interact with stories and form personal responses that influence their interpretations (Rosenblatt 1978). Two ways to enhance reader interactions with stories are through discussion and writing.

SEE ALSO . . .

LESSON MODELS

Dialogic Reading: Picture Book Read-Aloud Method, p. 648

Book Club: Writing in Response to Literature, p. 677

QtA (Questioning the Author), p. 733

Students who meet the Standards readily undertake the close, attentive reading that is at the heart of understanding and enjoying complex works of literature.

—COMMON CORE STATE STANDARDS, 2010

CCSS

DISCUSSION-ORIENTED INSTRUCTION Discussion supports students in the process of developing meaning. When groups read and discuss text together, interpretations emerge that would not be available to a person analyzing text alone (Morrow 1990). Both teacher-directed and student-directed discussions can help students understand and interpret literature. Teachers may pose open-ended queries to engage students in interacting with the text and conversing about it (Beck and McKeown 2006). For narratives, such queries may include the following: *How do things look for the character now? How is the author making you feel right now about these characters?* Student-directed discussion groups, such as book clubs, also can be engaging, as students learn to direct the course of their own thoughtful conversations about text (Raphael et al. 2001).

WRITING IN RESPONSE TO LITERATURE Research has shown that such writing–reading connections can support and improve students' comprehension (Torgesen et al. 2007). Written responses can enhance students' interactions with texts before, during, and after reading. The Book Club program (Raphael et al. 2001, 2004) contains a strong writing component that emphasizes three categories of written response to literature: personal, creative, and critical.

Responses to Literature Through Writing

Response	Draws On	Description	Writing Examples
PERSONAL	Emotion	Sharing personal stories Valuing text	• Journal entry • Personal essay
CREATIVE	Imagination	Engaging with text Engaging with author	• Poem inspired by theme • Dialogue based on text
CRITICAL	Evaluation	Analyzing text	• Paragraph critiquing literary element • Essay about author's message

Based on Raphael et al. 2001.

why? Literary Text

Through extensive reading of stories ... students gain literary and cultural knowledge as well as familiarity with various text structures and elements.

—COMMON CORE STATE STANDARDS, 2010

CCSS

Teaching students to identify and represent story structure improves their comprehension of narratives, a type of literary text (RRSG 2002). It also enhances students' memory and recall of text and helps them organize and write stories (Short and Ryan 1984; Fitzgerald and Teasley 1986). One reason that students' understanding of text structure supports reading comprehension is that structures are common across texts (Coyne et al. 2007). Being aware of the "samenesses" across texts allows students to consider authors' messages in a broader context of literature and the world (Carnine and Kinder 1985). Knowing about story structure elements gives students a frame of reference for processing and remembering story information (Dickson, Simmons, and Kame'enui 1998). Story structure elements provide the framework for applying comprehension strategies to most literary text (Pearson and Fielding 1991; Graesser, Golding, and Long 1991).

Research Findings . . .

Through extensive reading of stories . . . , students gain literary and cultural knowledge as well as familiarity with various text structures and elements.

—COMMON CORE STATE STANDARDS, 2010

Instruction of the content and organization of stories improves story comprehension, measured by the ability of the reader to answer questions and recall what was read.

—NATIONAL READING PANEL, 2000

Helping students to recognize the structure inherent in text—and match it to their own cognitive structures—will help them understand and produce not only text but also spoken discourse.

—WILLIAMS, 2005

Story structure instruction shows positive effects for a wide range of students, from kindergarten to the intermediate grades to high school to special populations, and to students identified as struggling readers.

—DUKE & PEARSON, 2002

Suggested Reading . . .

Comprehension Instruction: Research-Based Best Practices, 2nd Edition (2008) edited by Cathy Collins Block & Sherri R. Paris. New York: Guilford.

A Focus on Comprehension (2005) by Fran Lehr & Jean Osborn. Honolulu: Pacific Resources for Education and Learning.

Improving Reading Comprehension in Kindergarten Through 3rd Grade: A Practical Guide (2010) by Timothy Shanahan, Kim Callison, Christine Carriere, Nell Duke, David Pearson, Christopher Schatschneider & Joe Torgesen. Washington, DC: U.S. Department of Education.

Teaching Reading Comprehension to Students with Learning Disabilities (2007) by Janette K. Klingner, Sharon Vaughn & Alison Boardman. New York: Guilford.

Teaching Strategic Processes in Reading (2003) by Janice F. Almasi. New York: Guilford.

Text Complexity: Raising Rigor in Reading (2012) by Douglas Fisher, Nancy Frey & Diane Lapp. Newark, DE: International Reading Association.

when?

Literary Text

> Explicit comprehension strategies instruction should begin in the primary grades and continue through high school.
>
> —RRSG, 2002

Story Complexity Factors

Number of characters

Number of plots, goals, and subgoals

Number of attempts by the characters to achieve the goals

Explicitness of story elements

Amount of background knowledge required

Length of story

Readability of story

Carnine et al. 2006.

SEE ALSO . . .

When to Assess and Intervene, p. 700

When to Teach

Comprehension instruction should begin as soon as students start to interact with text and should continue through high school (Duke and Pearson 2002; Pressley and Block 2002; RRSG 2002). Effective teaching balances explicit comprehension strategies instruction with the literary experience of a story. For students as young as preschoolers, storybook read-alouds provide opportunities for modeling and practicing strategies applications (Lane and Wright 2007). When students begin to read stories on their own, they learn to apply comprehension strategies in tandem with decoding and word-level strategies. As they progress through the grades, students apply strategies to increasingly complex stories (Carnine et al. 2006). Thus, many adolescent literacy researchers advocate explicit comprehension strategies instruction, particularly for struggling readers (Brown 2002; Alvermann and Eakle 2003; Fisher and Frey 2004; Raphael et al. 2001).

When to Assess and Intervene

Comprehension instruction should be accompanied by reliable assessment aligned with instruction (Lehr and Osborn 2005). Yet, according to researchers (RRSG 2002; Spear-Swerling 2006; Klingner et al. 2007), most traditional assessments are inadequate in several ways in that they: (1) often confuse comprehension with vocabulary, background knowledge, word reading ability, and other reading skills, (2) fail to represent the complexity of comprehension, based on current understandings, and (3) do not distinguish specific processes that underlie comprehension problems, or explain why a student is struggling. Therefore, traditional assessments should be combined with teachers' ongoing informal assessment of students' comprehension and strategy use. Retellings, student think-alouds, and other process-focused measures may serve as useful tools for diagnosing and remediating comprehension problems. Think-aloud protocols, in particular, are among the most significant advances in comprehension assessment tools, making comprehension processes more visible (Pearson and Hamm 2005; Pressley and Hilden 2005).

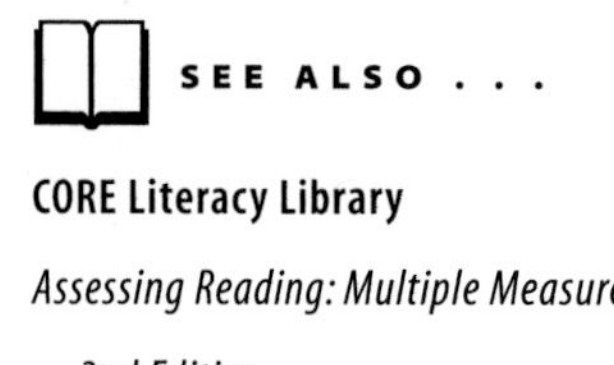

CORE Literacy Library
Assessing Reading: Multiple Measures, 2nd Edition

When to Apply Comprehension Strategies in Literary Text

STRATEGY	BEFORE READING: To orient students to the story and task	DURING READING: To build an understanding of the story	AFTER READING: To check whether students understood the story
Recognizing Story Structure	Use story elements as a framework for reading.	Identify story elements as they appear in the text.	Use story elements to check understanding of the story.
Predicting	Generate predictions about the story.	Verify, adapt, and add predictions about the story.	Review accuracy of predictions.
Monitoring Comprehension	Keep in mind that the goal of reading is to understand the story.	Note if the story is making sense, and use fix-up strategies as needed.	Reflect on what the story was about and whether it made sense.
Connecting to World Knowledge	Preview text to connect it with prior knowledge.	Use knowledge/experiences to make sense of the story.	Connect the story to life experiences and other reading.
Asking Questions	Generate questions about what will happen.	Ask questions to clarify confusing story elements.	Ask higher-order questions to extend story understanding.
Answering Questions	Answer questions about the title and illustrations.	Answer questions about the plot and other story elements.	Answer higher-order questions to extend learning.
Constructing Mental Images	Create a mental picture based on the story title.	Visualize ongoing story events.	Visualize the overall story (a "mental movie").
Summarizing/ Retelling	Plan to be able to retell or summarize the story.	Build partial retellings as the story progresses.	Retell or summarize the story, orally or in writing.

how? Literary Text

LESSON MODEL FOR

Listening Comprehension

Benchmarks

- ability to actively engage in storybook reading
- ability to participate in conversations about a story
- ability to answer meaningful questions about a story
- ability to actively process story content
- ability to attend to story structure elements
- ability to respond to the complexities of text

Strategy Grade Level

- Pre-K – Grade 1

Grouping

- small group

Read-Aloud Text

- an illustrated version of "The Three Little Pigs"

Materials

- none

Dialogic Reading: Picture Book Read-Aloud Method

Created by Grover Whitehurst and colleagues (1988), dialogic reading is an interactive read-aloud method that fosters student engagement during read-alouds. In this scaffolded approach, students become the teller of the story; the teacher becomes the listener, the questioner, and the audience, guiding students as they read a story multiple times (Whitehurst 1992). Dialogic reading has proved to have a positive effect on oral language development (Zevenbergen and Whitehurst 2003). Although there are no direct research data, this method of reading aloud also can support comprehension by building awareness of story structure, fostering engagement, and incorporating the active, strategic processing of text. According to Doyle and Bramwell (2006), "dialogic reading gives teachers a structure in which to ask meaningful questions that begin a conversation about what is happening in the story and help students comprehend the story."

Dialogic reading gives students access to books before they can read them independently. It is most commonly used with Pre-Kindergarteners but is suitable for older students as well (Lane and Wright 2007). Virtually all picture books are appropriate for dialogic reading; the best books have rich, detailed illustrations and are tied to students' interests. A small-group setting is ideal for this method. Students who are read to in a small group demonstrate better story comprehension than students who are read to as a whole class (Morrow and Smith 1990).

Types of Prompting (CROWD)

During dialogic reading, the teacher prompts students with questions that encourage them to actively engage with the story. The technique utilizes five types of prompts, or teacher questions: Completion, Recall, Open-Ended, Wh–, and Distancing (CROWD). Recall and distancing prompts are more difficult for students than completion, open-ended, and wh– prompts.

Dialogic Reading Prompts (CROWD)

Prompt	Description	Examples
C COMPLETION	Fill-in-the-blank prompts used primarily with rhyming or predictable stories • Support comprehension by building prediction abilities	• Not by the hair of my chinny-chin-_____. (chin) • Then I'll huff and I'll puff and I'll blow your house _____. (in)
R RECALL	Questions about specific details from the story • Support comprehension by building story sequencing and retelling abilities	• Can you remember what happened to the first and second little pigs? (The wolf ate them.) • Can you remember which pig made the strongest house? (the third little pig)
O OPEN-ENDED	Questions/statements that encourage a response to story illustrations in the student's own words • Support comprehension by providing opportunities for personal interpretation	• Tell me what's happening in this picture. • What do you see on this page?
W WH–	Questions that begin with *who, what, when, where,* or *why* • Support comprehension by directing attention to story elements	• What is the first little pig building? (a house) • Look at the picture. What's the wolf doing? (knocking)
D DISTANCING	Questions that form a bridge between stories and the real world by relating the pictures and words in the story to experiences outside the story • Support comprehension by encouraging connections to world knowledge	• Do you know anyone who builds houses? What kinds of things do they do? • Have you ever seen a real pig or wolf? Tell me what you know about them.

PEER Sequence

Technique		Description	Example
P	PROMPT	Using the five types of prompts (CROWD), ask students to respond to the story.	Point to the illustration and ask: *What's the first little pig building?* (house)
E	EVALUATE	Evaluate, or affirm, a student's response.	Say: *That's right.*
E	EXPAND	Expand a student's response by adding information to it.	Say: *The little pig is building a straw house.*
R	REPEAT	Have the student repeat your expanded response.	Ask: *Can you say that?* (The little pig is building a straw house.)

If a student cannot answer your prompt, answer the prompt yourself. Then ask the student to repeat the answer.

Interactive Instructional Sequence (PEER)

Students can learn most from stories when they are actively involved in the reading experience. In dialogic reading, the teacher helps students become tellers of a story using an interactive instructional sequence called the PEER sequence: Prompt, Evaluate, Expand, Repeat. The PEER sequence encourages students to say more about their understanding of the story. It is through this sequence that students "become the teller of the story."

Scaffolding Techniques

Dialogic reading relies on repeated readings of a story or book. Each time a story is read, do less and less reading of the written words and leave more to students. Take a gamelike, turn-taking approach to using the method. For example, read aloud one page and then ask students to "read" the next. Taking turns helps to keep students' interest level high, making the whole reading experience fun and engaging.

LESSON MODEL FOR

Recognizing Story Structure

Benchmarks

- ability to ask and answer questions about story structure elements
- ability to fill in a story map
- ability to identify the theme of a story
- ability to apply a story's theme to real life

Strategy Grade Level

- Grade 2 and above

Grouping

- whole class
- small group or pairs

Prerequisite

- ability to answer basic literal comprehension questions

Sample Text (Resources)

- "Common Sense: An Anansi Tale" Complexity Level: Grades 2–3

Activity Master (Resources)

- Story Map

Materials

- PDF and copies of Story Map
- copies of "Common Sense: An Anansi Tale"

Story Structure

This sample lesson model is based in part on the steps of Theme Scheme, a theme-identification program developed by Joanna Williams (2002, 2005). Theme Scheme teaches students to ask and answer questions about story structure elements with an emphasis on theme—a particularly challenging concept for struggling students to grasp (Williams 1993). However, unlike Theme Scheme, this lesson model incorporates instruction in story maps. Research has shown that when readers are taught to record story structure elements on a story map while reading, their comprehension is enhanced (Idol 1987).

In this lesson model, sample text is used to represent a selection at the student's independent reading level. The same model can be adapted and used to enhance comprehension instruction for literary text in any commercial reading or language arts program—as long as the text is at the appropriate level.

Direct Explanation

Use interactive whiteboard technology to display the Story Map. Tell students that certain parts of stories are almost always there. These parts are called story structure elements. Explain that using a story map when listening to or reading stories will help them to focus on story elements and to understand and remember the story better. Pointing to the corresponding box on the Story Map, explain each of the following story elements.

SETTING Say: *This box is where you print the story setting. The setting of a story is when and where the story takes place.*

CHARACTERS Say: *This box is where you print the names of the characters. Characters are the people, animals, or creatures in a story.*

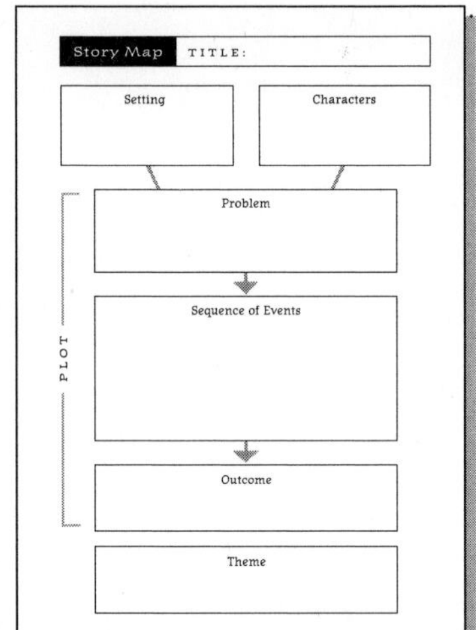

PLOT Pointing to the bracket labeled Plot, say: *The plot tells what happened and gives the story a beginning, a middle, and an ending. The bracket indicates that the plot has three parts—a problem, a sequence of events, and an outcome.*

PROBLEM Say: *This box is where you print the character's problem. The main characters in a story always have a problem, or something that they want to do. The problem is usually presented at the beginning and continues through the middle of a story.*

SEQUENCE OF EVENTS Say: *This box is where you print the sequence of events. These are the things that happen as the character attempts to solve the problem; they usually happen in the middle of a story.*

OUTCOME Say: *This box is where you print the outcome of the story, or how the story turns out. The outcome is almost always at the end of the story.*

THEME Say: *This box is where you print the theme. The theme of a story is the message that the author wants the reader to take away from reading the story; it is the lesson or observation the story is intended to teach. Identifying a theme is like digging for treasure—sometimes the theme is discovered easily and other times it is not. After we read the story, we will learn more about identifying the theme.*

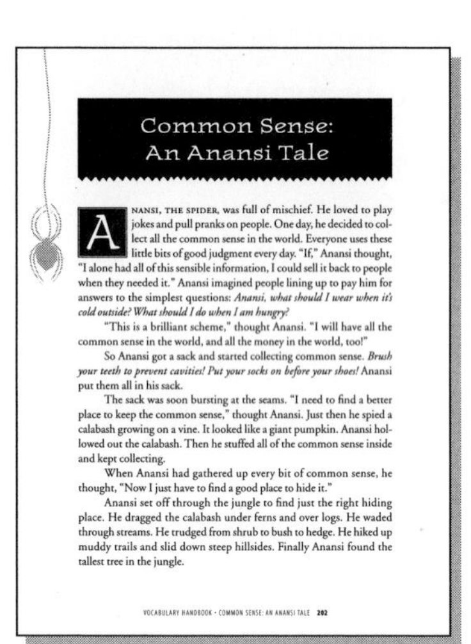

Common Sense: An Anansi Tale

ANANSI, THE SPIDER, was full of mischief. He loved to play jokes and pull pranks on people. One day, he decided to collect all the common sense in the world. Everyone uses these little bits of good judgment every day. "If," Anansi thought, "I alone had all of this sensible information, I could sell it back to people when they needed it." Anansi imagined people lining up to pay him for answers to the simplest questions: *Anansi, what should I wear when it's cold outside? What should I do when I am hungry?*

"This is a brilliant scheme," thought Anansi. "I will have all the common sense in the world, and all the money in the world, too!"

So Anansi got a sack and started collecting common sense. *Brush your teeth to prevent cavities! Put your socks on before your shoes!* Anansi put them all in his sack.

The sack was soon bursting at the seams. "I need to find a better place to keep the common sense," thought Anansi. Just then he spied a calabash growing on a vine. It looked like a giant pumpkin. Anansi hollowed out the calabash. Then he stuffed all of the common sense inside and kept collecting.

When Anansi had gathered up every bit of common sense, he thought, "Now I just have to find a good place to hide it."

Anansi set off through the jungle to find just the right hiding place. He dragged the calabash under ferns and over logs. He waded through streams. He trudged from shrub to bush to hedge. He hiked up muddy trails and slid down steep hillsides. Finally Anansi found the tallest tree in the jungle.

VOCABULARY HANDBOOK • COMMON SENSE: AN ANANSI TALE 202

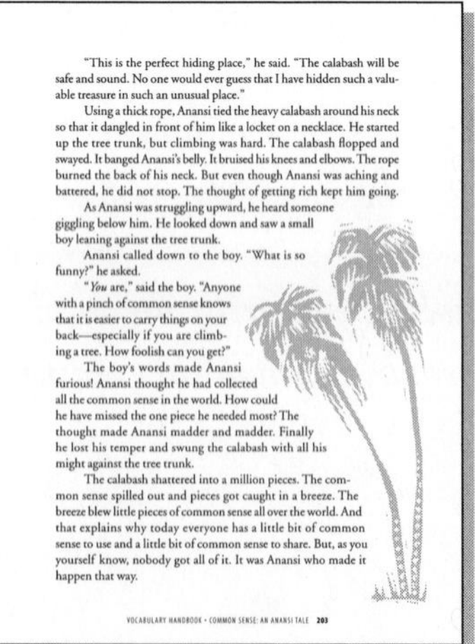

"This is the perfect hiding place," he said. "The calabash will be safe and sound. No one would ever guess that I have hidden such a valuable treasure in such an unusual place."

Using a thick rope, Anansi tied the heavy calabash around his neck so that it dangled in front of him like a locket on a necklace. He started up the tree trunk, but climbing was hard. The calabash flopped and swayed. It banged Anansi's belly. It bruised his knees and elbows. The rope burned the back of his neck. But even though Anansi was aching and battered, he did not stop. The thought of getting rich kept him going.

As Anansi was struggling upward, he heard someone giggling below him. He looked down and saw a small boy leaning against the tree trunk.

Anansi called down to the boy. "What is so funny?" he asked.

"*You* are," said the boy. "Anyone with a pinch of common sense knows that it is easier to carry things on your back—especially if you are climbing a tree. How foolish can you get?"

The boy's words made Anansi furious! Anansi thought he had collected all the common sense in the world. How could he have missed the one piece he needed most? The thought made Anansi madder and madder. Finally he lost his temper and swung the calabash with all his might against the tree trunk.

The calabash shattered into a million pieces. The common sense spilled out and pieces got caught in a breeze. The breeze blew little pieces of common sense all over the world. And that explains why today everyone has a little bit of common sense to use and a little bit of common sense to share. But, as you yourself know, nobody got all of it. It was Anansi who made it happen that way.

VOCABULARY HANDBOOK • COMMON SENSE: AN ANANSI TALE 203

Introduce the Story

Tell students that they are going to read a story called "Common Sense: An Anansi Tale." Say: *Before we read, let me share a little background about this folktale. Anansi the spider is a West African folk hero known for his cleverness. Anansi loves to plan and scheme, trying to outsmart everyone. Sometimes, Anansi comes up with a clever plan and finds smart solutions to puzzling problems. Other times, he winds up causing lots of mischief.*

STORY STRUCTURE QUESTIONS	
Setting	Where and when does the story take place?
Characters	Who is the story about?
Problem	What is the problem the character faces? What does the character want to do?
Sequence of Events	What does the main character do about the problem? What happens as the character tries to solve the problem?
Outcome	How does the story turn out? Does the character solve the problem?
Theme	What lesson does the main character learn? What lesson did you learn from the story?

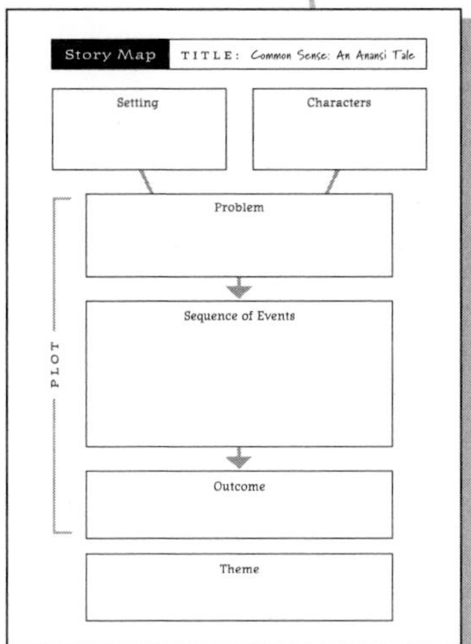

Teach/Model

Use interactive whiteboard technology to display the Story Map. Nearby display a copy of the Story Structure Questions teaching chart, such as the example shown above. Tell students that they are going to learn how to use the story structure questions to guide them in filling out the corresponding boxes on the Story Map. Then give students copies of the Story Map and "Common Sense: An Anansi Tale." Say: *Together we are going to read the Anansi tale and fill in a story map. I will model asking the questions and filling in my story map, and you will record information on your own story maps. Let's start by reading the title of the story.* Ask a volunteer to read aloud the title. Say: *The title of this story is "Common Sense: An Anansi Tale."* Then print the title in the box labeled Title on the Story Map and have students do the same.

You may want to read the story aloud while students follow along in their text.

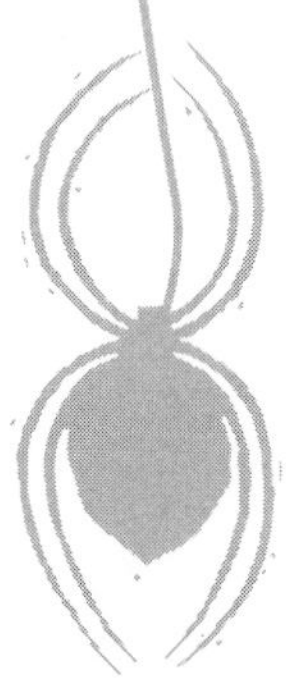

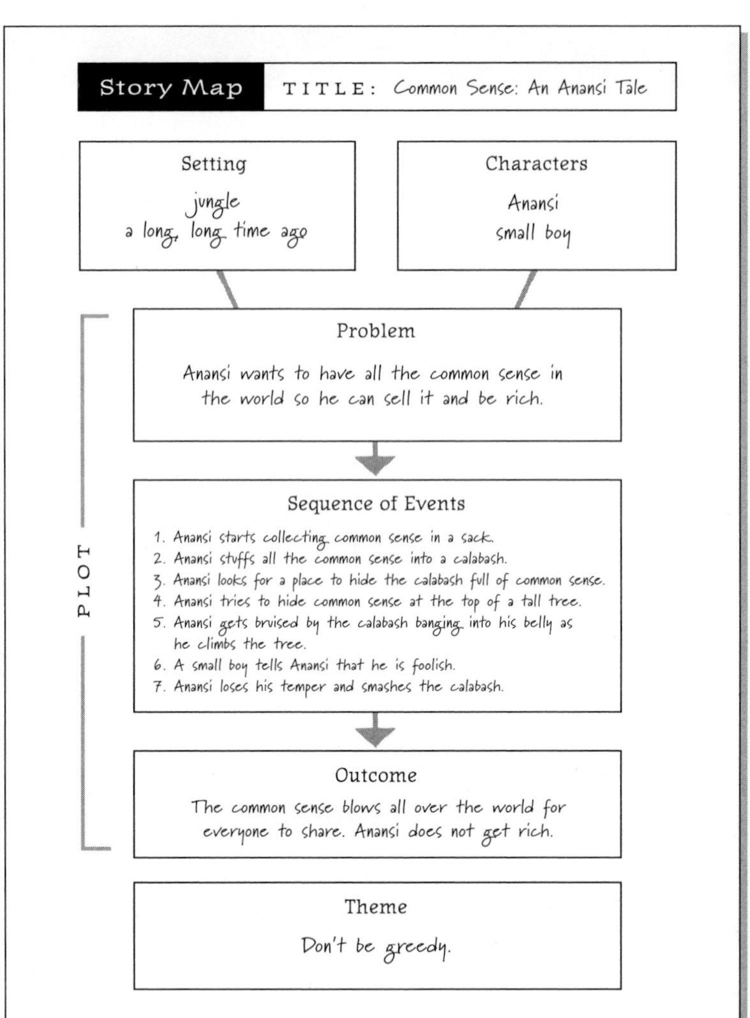

Story Setting, Characters, Plot

Tell students that as they read the story they will be looking for the setting, characters, and plot. Explain that these story elements won't necessarily appear in order, so they have to be on the lookout. Remind them that the plot includes the problem, sequence of events, and outcome.

CHARACTER Say: *The title of this story tells us that the story will be about Anansi. Anansi is the main character.* Point to the corresponding question on the Story Structure Questions chart and ask a volunteer to read it aloud. Ask: *Who is the story about?* (Anansi) Say: *I am going to print Anansi's name in the box labeled Characters on the Story Map, and you should do the same.*

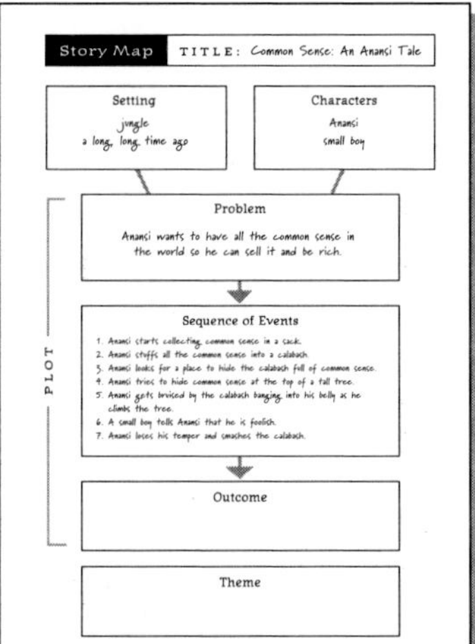

PROBLEM Ask a volunteer to read as other students follow along in their text. After reading paragraphs 1 and 2, stop the reader and say: *Now I think we have some information about Anansi's problem.* Point to the corresponding questions on the Story Structure Questions chart and ask a volunteer to read them aloud. Ask: *What is the problem Anansi faces? What is he trying to do?* (Possible response: *He wants to have all the common sense in the world so he can be rich.*) Say: *We can add this information to the Story Map. I am going to print Anansi's problem in the box labeled Problem, and you should do the same using your own words.*

EVENT 1 Ask a new volunteer to read aloud as other students follow along in their text. After reading paragraph 3, stop the reader and say: *So, this part of the story begins to tell about the things that happen as Anansi tries to solve his problem.* Point to the corresponding questions on the Story Structure Questions chart and ask a volunteer to read them aloud. Ask: *What is the first thing that Anansi does to solve his problem?* (Possible response: *Anansi starts collecting the common sense in a sack.*) Say: *I am going to print the first thing that Anansi does in the box labeled Sequence of Events on the Story Map, and you should do the same.* Follow the same procedure for paragraphs 4 through 8.

EVENT 2 After reading paragraph 4, stop the reader and ask: *What is the next thing that Anansi does?* (Possible response: *Anansi stuffs the common sense into a calabash.*)

EVENT 3 After reading paragraph 5, stop the reader and ask: *What is the next thing that Anansi does?* (Possible response: *Anansi looks for a place to hide the calabash full of common sense.*)

SETTING After reading paragraph 6, stop the reader and say: *This paragraph tells about the story setting.* Point to the corresponding question on the Story Structure Questions chart and ask a volunteer to read it aloud. Ask: *Where does the story take place?* (the jungle) Print the information in the box labeled Setting on the Story Map and have students do the same. Ask: *Do we know when the story takes place?* (no) Say: *The author doesn't tell us when the story takes place, so we can leave that infor-*

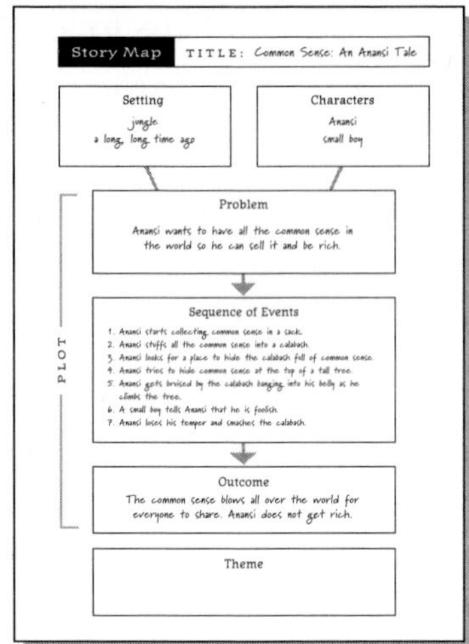

Story Map TITLE: Common Sense: An Anansi Tale

Setting
jungle
a long, long time ago

Characters
Anansi
small boy

PLOT

Problem
Anansi wants to have all the common sense in the world so he can sell it and be rich.

Sequence of Events
1. Anansi starts collecting common sense in a sack.
2. Anansi stuffs all the common sense into a calabash.
3. Anansi looks for a place to hide the calabash full of common sense.
4. Anansi tries to hide common sense at the top of a tall tree.
5. Anansi gets bruised by the calabash banging into his belly as he climbs the tree.
6. A small boy tells Anansi that he is foolish.
7. Anansi loses his temper and smashes the calabash.

Outcome
The common sense blows all over the world for everyone to share. Anansi does not get rich.

Theme

mation out or we can make our best guess. I'm thinking that if this is a folktale it is probably supposed to be happening a long, long time ago. I'm going to put that in my story map with a question mark next to it, and you can do the same.

EVENTS 4 AND 5 After reading paragraphs 7 and 8, stop the reader and ask: *What's the next thing that Anansi does?* (Possible response: *First, Anansi tries to hide the calabash at the top of the tallest tree and then he gets bruised by the calabash banging into his belly as he climbs the tree.*)

EVENT 6 After reading paragraphs 9 through 11, stop the reader and ask: *What's the next thing that happens?* (Possible response: *A small boy tells Anansi that he is foolish because he is carrying the calabash in the front.*)

CHARACTERS After reading paragraph 9, stop the reader and say: *This paragraph names another character in the story.* Ask: *Who's the other character?* (a small boy) Print the information in the box labeled Characters on the Story Map and have students do the same.

EVENT 7 After reading paragraph 12, stop the reader and ask: *What's the next thing that happens?* (Possible response: *Anansi loses his temper and smashes the calabash.)*

OUTCOME After reading paragraph 13, stop the reader and say: *This paragraph tells the outcome of the story.* Point to the corresponding questions on the Story Structure Questions chart and ask a volunteer to read them aloud. Ask: *How does the story turn out? Does the character solve the problem?* (Possible response: *A breeze blows common sense all over the world for everyone to share. Anansi does not get rich.*) Print the information in the box labeled Outcome on the Story Map and have students do the same.

SETTING Point out the phrase "that explains why everyone today." Ask: *Does this give us any additional information about the setting?* Note that this phrase suggests that the story happened a long time ago. Erase the question mark next to *a long, long time ago* in the box labeled Setting on the Story Map and have students do the same.

At this point, the story maps will be filled in, except for the theme. Have students work individually or in pairs to develop an oral retelling of the story, using their completed story maps.

Story Theme

Continue displaying the Story Map. Print the Theme Identification Questions on the board. Say: *Now our story map is complete except for the theme. Remember how I said that finding the theme is sometimes like digging for treasure? Now I'm going to show you how to identify the theme of the Anansi story by asking and answering three questions.*

Read aloud the first question: *Was the outcome of the story good or bad? Explain why.* Say: *I'm going to say the outcome was bad because it was bad for Anansi, and he was the main character in the story. The reason it was bad for Anansi is that he wanted to keep all of the common sense, but instead he lost it all.*

Read aloud the next question: *What lesson does the main character learn?* Say: *To answer this question, I am going to complete the following sentence: The main character learned that he or she should/shouldn't _______. Here is my complete sentence: Anansi learned that he should not have been so greedy and that he should not have tried to keep all the common sense for himself.*

Read aloud the last question: *What lesson did you learn from the story?* Say: *To answer this question, I am going to complete the following sentence: We should/shouldn't _______. Here is my complete sentence: We shouldn't be greedy.*

Say: *So, this story teaches us a lesson about greed. Someone who is greedy wants more of something than is necessary or fair. Because Anansi was greedy—and foolish, he ended up losing what he wanted instead of gaining it. The theme of the story is: Don't be greedy.* Ask: *What is the theme of the story?* (Don't be greedy.) Say: *Now I am going to print the theme in the box labeled Theme on the Story Map, and you should do the same.*

THEME IDENTIFICATION QUESTIONS

1. Was the outcome of the story good or bad? Explain why.

2. What lesson does the main character learn? (The main character learned that he or she should/shouldn't ______.)

3. What lesson did you learn from the story? (We should/shouldn't ______.)

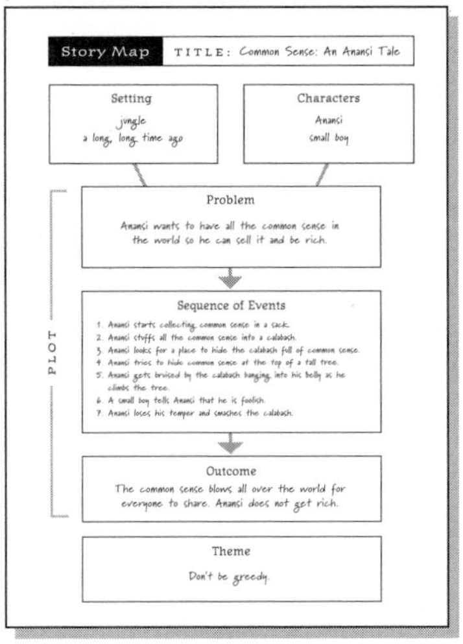

Story Map TITLE: Common Sense: An Anansi Tale

Setting: jungle; a long, long time ago

Characters: Anansi; small boy

PLOT

Problem: Anansi wants to have all the common sense in the world so he can sell it and be rich.

Sequence of Events
1. Anansi starts collecting common sense in a sack.
2. Anansi stuffs all the common sense into a calabash.
3. Anansi looks for a place to hide the calabash full of common sense.
4. Anansi tries to hide common sense at the top of a tall tree.
5. Anansi gets bruised by the calabash banging into his belly as he climbs the tree.
6. A small boy tells Anansi that he is foolish.
7. Anansi loses his temper and smashes the calabash.

Outcome: The common sense blows all over the world for everyone to share. Anansi does not get rich.

Theme: Don't be greedy.

Guided Practice: Theme Transfer

After students identify the theme, have them transfer and apply the generalized theme—to other stories and to real-life experiences. Explain to students that thinking about how the theme applies to other situations can help them better understand and remember the theme.

Other Stories

Have students read or read aloud a short fable with a similar theme, such as the story of King Midas. Have them fill in the Story Map, using the story structure questions as scaffolds. Ask students to answer the theme identification questions to find the theme, following the same procedure as described above. Say: *Today we learned about using a story map to show the parts of a story, and we learned how to identify the theme of a story.* Ask: *What's a theme?* (the lesson of a story) Ask: *What is the theme of the Anansi and Midas stories?* (Don't be greedy.) Point out that the stories had the same or similar theme(s).

Real-Life Experiences

Say: *Remember that the theme of a story is supposed to teach us a lesson. One good way to learn the lesson is to think about how it applies or connects to your own life.* Then have students share their experiences with greed; for example, getting sick after eating the biggest slice of birthday cake. Use the following discussion prompts, as needed:

- How does the theme apply to your life?
- Tell about a time when you or someone you know learned the same lesson.
- Why is the lesson important to learn?
- Describe some situations in which the lesson would apply.

LESSON MODEL FOR

Multiple-Strategy Instruction

Benchmark

- ability to coordinate a repertoire of strategies to guide comprehension

Strategy Grade Level

- Grade 2 and above

Prerequisites

- Story Structure, p. 651
- knowing how to use the strategies individually
- familiarity with Think-Pair-Share

Grouping

- small group

Sample Text (Resources)

- "The Case of the Blue Carbuncle" Complexity Level: Grades 4–5

Activity Master (Resources)

- Predictions Worksheet

Materials

- PDF of Predictions Worksheet
- copies of "The Case of the Blue Carbuncle"

TSI (Transactional Strategies Instruction)

This sample lesson model offers a snapshot of Transactional Strategies Instruction (TSI), a multiple-strategy instruction approach developed by Michael Pressley and colleagues (Pressley, El-Dinary et al. 1992). Through teacher-student dialogue while reading, TSI emphasizes coordinated use of strategies to help students to build and monitor comprehension. Strategies are first introduced individually, following the model for explicit instruction. Over time, responsibility for strategy choices shifts from the teacher to the students. TSI has proven effective for a range of struggling readers, from primary-grade students to adolescents (Gaskins and Elliot 1991; Brown et al. 1996).

This lesson model differs somewhat from the original TSI; it is, however, consistent with TSI's emphasis on knowing where and when to use particular strategies. In this lesson model, sample text is used to represent a selection at students' independent reading level. The same model can be adapted and used to enhance comprehension instruction for literary or informational text in any commercial reading or content-area program—as long as the text is at the appropriate level.

Review: Comprehension Strategies

Display a copy of the Comprehension Strategies and Questions teaching chart, such as the example shown on the following page. Remind students that using comprehension strategies can help them understand and remember what they read. Point out that they have used each of these strategies individually, and they have had some practice in choosing which strategy to use. Review the chart with students. For each strategy, review the description and then call on students to read aloud the questions they can ask to help them in applying the strategy.

Comprehension Strategies and Questions	
STRATEGY	**QUESTIONS I CAN ASK**
Monitor Comprehension Stop periodically and check to make sure that you understand the text.	• Does this make sense? • What fix-up strategy can I use to figure it out? **FIX-UP STRATEGIES** **• Reread** **• Look back** **• Read on** **• Guess (using context clues)** **• Ask someone** **• Check a reference**
Connect to World Knowledge Draw on your background knowledge and experience to help you understand the text.	• Connect: What do I already know about this? Have I had a similar experience? • Verify: Is what I know really related to the text? • Decide: Is what I know helping me to understand the text?
Predict Make informed guesses about what you think will happen in the text.	• Predict: What do I think will happen next? What makes me think so? • Verify: Does the text support my prediction? • Decide: Was my prediction accurate? Do I need to change it?
Construct Mental Images Make pictures of the text in your mind as you read.	• Visualize: What does this (person, place, thing) look like? What makes me think so? • Verify: Does the text support my image? • Decide: Was my image accurate? Do I need to change it?
Ask Questions Ask yourself questions about the text to keep involved in your reading.	• What am I curious about? • What do I want to know more about?
Summarize Use what you know about story structure to identify important story information. Then shrink this information and put it into your own words.	• Where and when does the story take place? (setting) • Who is the story about? (characters) • What is the problem the character faces? (problem) • What happens as the character tries to solve the problem? (sequence of events) • How does the story turn out? Does the character solve the problem? (outcome) • What lesson did you learn from the story? (theme)

Direct Explanation

Explain to students that good readers use a variety of strategies to help them make sense of the text and get the most out of what they read. Tell them that you are going to show them how strategies can work together smoothly, in coordination, and how to choose the one that works the best in each situation.

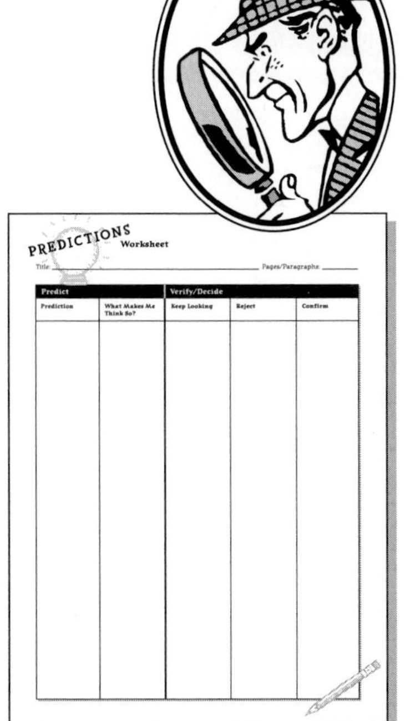

Use interactive whiteboard technology to display the Predictions Worksheet. Say: *Good readers make predictions about what they are reading. Predictions are based on evidence in the text and what you already know. The Predictions Worksheet can help you to keep track of your predictions as you read.* Pointing to the corresponding headings on the Predictions Worksheet, say: *The Worksheet has two big divisions: Predict and Verify/Decide. To predict, you make a prediction and then give evidence about what makes you think so. Verifying and deciding work together. As you read, you verify a prediction by looking for evidence in the text. When you find some possible evidence in the text, you can decide if you need to keep looking for more conclusive evidence, to reject a former prediction if it was wrong, or to confirm a former prediction if it was right. It's a cycle—predict, verify, decide.*

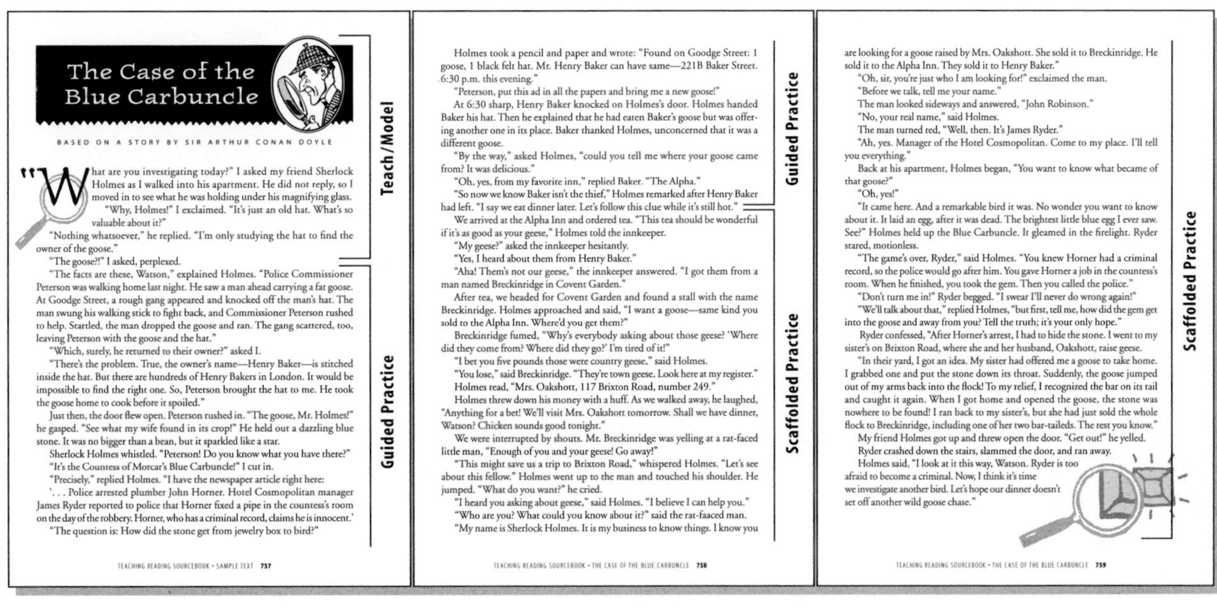

The Case of the Blue Carbuncle

BASED ON A STORY BY SIR ARTHUR CONAN DOYLE

Teach/Model

"What are you investigating today?" I asked my friend Sherlock Holmes as I walked into his apartment. He did not reply, so I moved in to see what he was holding under his magnifying glass.

"Why, Holmes!" I exclaimed. "It's just an old hat. What's so valuable about it?"

"Nothing whatsoever," he replied. "I'm only studying the hat to find the owner of the goose."

"The goose?!" I asked, perplexed.

Guided Practice

"The facts are these, Watson," explained Holmes. "Police Commissioner Peterson was walking home last night. He saw a man ahead carrying a fat goose. At Goodge Street, a rough gang appeared and knocked off the man's hat. The man swung his walking stick to fight back, and Commissioner Peterson rushed to help. Startled, the man dropped the goose and ran. The gang scattered, too, leaving Peterson with the goose and the hat."

"Which, surely, he returned to their owner?" asked I.

"There's the problem. True, the owner's name—Henry Baker—is stitched inside the hat. But there are hundreds of Henry Bakers in London. It would be impossible to find the right one. So, Peterson brought the hat to me. He took the goose home to cook before it spoiled."

Just then, the door flew open. Peterson rushed in. "The goose, Mr. Holmes!" he gasped. "See what my wife found in its crop!" He held out a dazzling blue stone. It was no bigger than a bean, but it sparkled like a star.

Sherlock Holmes whistled. "Peterson! Do you know what you have there?"

"It's the Countess of Morcar's Blue Carbuncle!" I cut in.

"Precisely," replied Holmes. "I have the newspaper article right here:

'. . . Police arrested plumber John Horner. Hotel Cosmopolitan manager James Ryder reported to police that Horner fixed a pipe in the countess's room on the day of the robbery. Horner, who has a criminal record, claims he is innocent.'

"The question is: How did the stone get from jewelry box to bird?"

TEACHING READING SOURCEBOOK • SAMPLE TEXT 757

Guided Practice

Holmes took a pencil and paper and wrote: "Found on Goodge Street: 1 goose, 1 black felt hat. Mr. Henry Baker can have same—221B Baker Street. 6:30 p.m. this evening."

"Peterson, put this ad in all the papers and bring me a new goose!"

At 6:30 sharp, Henry Baker knocked on Holmes's door. Holmes handed Baker his hat. Then he explained that he had eaten Baker's goose but was offering another one in its place. Baker thanked Holmes, unconcerned that it was a different goose.

"By the way," asked Holmes, "could you tell me where your goose came from? It was delicious."

"Oh, yes, from my favorite inn," replied Baker. "The Alpha."

"So now we know Baker isn't the thief," Holmes remarked after Henry Baker had left. "I say we eat dinner later. Let's follow this clue while it's still hot."

Scaffolded Practice

We arrived at the Alpha Inn and ordered tea. "This tea should be wonderful if it's as good as your geese," Holmes told the innkeeper.

"My geese?" asked the innkeeper hesitantly.

"Yes, I heard about them from Henry Baker."

"Aha! Them's not our geese," the innkeeper answered. "I got them from a man named Breckinridge in Covent Garden."

After tea, we headed for Covent Garden and found a stall with the name Breckinridge. Holmes approached and said, "I want a goose—same kind you sold to the Alpha Inn. Where'd you get them?"

Breckinridge fumed, "Why's everybody asking about those geese? 'Where did they come from? Where did they go?' I'm tired of it!"

"I bet you five pounds those were country geese," said Holmes.

"You lose," said Breckinridge. "They're town geese. Look here at my register."

Holmes read, "Mrs. Oakshott, 117 Brixton Road, number 249."

Holmes threw down his money with a huff. As we walked away, he laughed, "Anything for a bet! We'll visit Mrs. Oakshott tomorrow. Shall we have dinner, Watson? Chicken sounds good tonight."

We were interrupted by shouts. Mr. Breckinridge was yelling at a rat-faced little man, "Enough of you and your geese! Go away!"

"This might save us a trip to Brixton Road," whispered Holmes. "Let's see about this fellow." Holmes went up to the man and touched his shoulder. He jumped. "What do you want?" he cried.

"I heard you asking about geese," said Holmes. "I believe I can help you."

"Who are you? What could you know about it?" said the rat-faaced man.

"My name is Sherlock Holmes. It is my business to know things. I know you

TEACHING READING SOURCEBOOK • THE CASE OF THE BLUE CARBUNCLE 758

Scaffolded Practice

are looking for a goose raised by Mrs. Oakshott. She sold it to Breckinridge. He sold it to the Alpha Inn. They sold it to Henry Baker."

"Oh, sir, you're just who I am looking for!" exclaimed the man.

"Before we talk, tell me your name."

The man looked sideways and answered, "John Robinson."

"No, your real name," said Holmes.

The man turned red, "Well, then. It's James Ryder."

"Ah, yes. Manager of the Hotel Cosmopolitan. Come to my place. I'll tell you everything."

Back at his apartment, Holmes began, "You want to know what became of that goose?"

"Oh, yes!"

"It came here. And a remarkable bird it was. No wonder you want to know about it. It laid an egg, after it was dead. The brightest little blue egg I ever saw. See?" Holmes held up the Blue Carbuncle. It gleamed in the firelight. Ryder stared, motionless.

"The game's over, Ryder," said Holmes. "You knew Horner had a criminal record, so the police would go after him. You gave Horner a job in the countess's room. When he finished, you took the gem. Then you called the police."

"Don't turn me in!" Ryder begged. "I swear I'll never do wrong again!"

"We'll talk about that," replied Holmes, "but first, tell me, how did the gem get into the goose and away from you? Tell the truth; it's your only hope."

Ryder confessed, "After Horner's arrest, I had to hide the stone. I went to my sister's on Brixton Road, where she and her husband, Oakshott, raise geese.

"In their yard, I got an idea. My sister had offered me a goose to take home. I grabbed one and put the stone down its throat. Suddenly, the goose jumped out of my arms back into the flock! To my relief, I recognized the bar on its tail and caught it again. When I got home and opened the goose, the stone was nowhere to be found! I ran back to my sister's, but she had just sold the whole flock to Breckinridge, including one of her two bar-taileds. The rest you know."

My friend Holmes got up and threw open the door. "Get out!" he yelled.

Ryder crashed down the stairs, slammed the door, and ran away.

Holmes said, "I look at it this way, Watson. Ryder is too afraid to become a criminal. Now, I think it's time we investigate another bird. Let's hope our dinner doesn't set off another wild goose chase."

TEACHING READING SOURCEBOOK • THE CASE OF THE BLUE CARBUNCLE 759

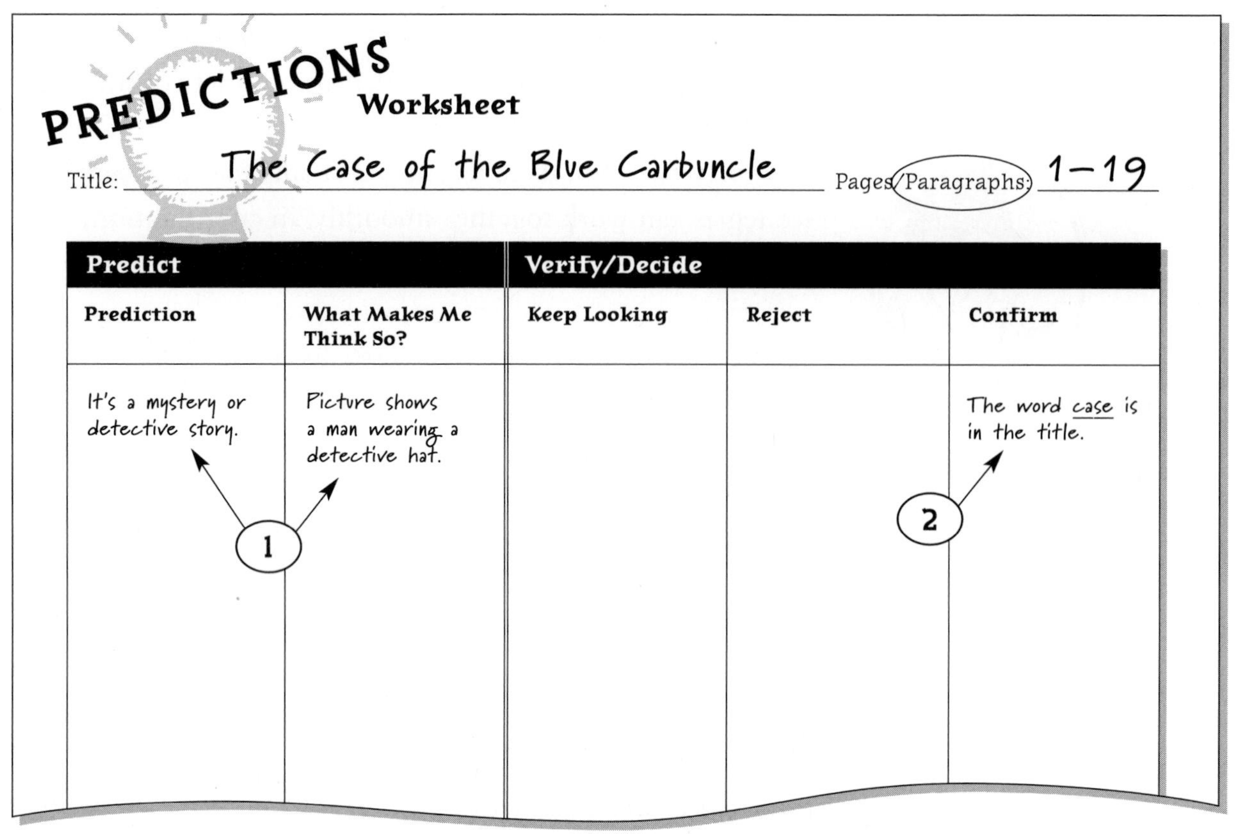

PREDICTIONS Worksheet

Title: The Case of the Blue Carbuncle Pages/Paragraphs: 1–19

Predict		Verify/Decide		
Prediction	**What Makes Me Think So?**	**Keep Looking**	**Reject**	**Confirm**
It's a mystery or detective story. (1)	Picture shows a man wearing a detective hat. (1)			The word <u>case</u> is in the title. (2)

Teach/Model: Preview the Story

Continue displaying the Comprehension Strategies chart and the Predictions Worksheet. Distribute copies of "The Case of the Blue Carbuncle" to the group. Say: *I'm going to think aloud to show you how to use the strategies in coordination. Each time I use a strategy, I will point to it on the Comprehension Strategies chart. As I read, I will record information on the Predictions Worksheet.*

(1) **THINK ALOUD** *Good readers make connections between what they already know and what they are reading. The first thing I see on the page is a picture. Using my world knowledge, I think this man is a detective. I remember an old movie in which a detective wore a hat like that. It looks like he's studying something pretty closely, which is something detectives do. So, I'm going to predict that this is a mystery or detective story. On the Predictions Worksheet, I'm going to print my first prediction and what makes me think so.*
✦ CONNECT TO WORLD KNOWLEDGE, PREDICT

THINK ALOUD

2 **THINK ALOUD** *Now I'm going to read the title of the story. The title is "The Case of the Blue Carbuncle." The word* case *in the title typically relates to a mystery, or to a crime. I think that's good enough evidence to confirm my prediction about this being a mystery. On the Predictions Worksheet, I am going to print my evidence under Confirm.* ✦ PREDICT

THINK ALOUD *Good readers constantly monitor, or check, their comprehension. There is a word in the title that is new to me. I have no idea what a carbuncle is. I don't even know enough to make a good guess. I only know that this one is blue. I believe I'll read on to see if I can find story clues to help me figure out what this word means. Reading on, or reading ahead for more information, is a fix-up strategy. As I read, I'm also going to ask myself, "What's a carbuncle?" Right now, I'm applying a variety of strategies.* ✦ MONITOR COMPREHENSION, ASK QUESTIONS

THINK ALOUD

Teachable Moment: Mystery Genre

THINK ALOUD *Since I'm pretty sure this is a mystery, I'm going to stop and connect to what I know about mysteries. The setting for a mystery is often the scene of a crime or a detective's office. The characters typically include detectives and suspects. The problem is a mysterious event—a crime to be solved or an unexplained occurrence. The sequence of events involves a series of clues that give hints about motives (or reasons) and opportunities for various characters to commit the crime. Some clues are helpful, and some are not. Misleading clues are called red herrings—they are meant to throw the reader offtrack and give the mystery more exciting twists and turns. The outcome of the story is typically the solution to the mystery. I'm going to use what I know about mysteries to help me make sense of this story. I know a mystery is confusing at the beginning, revealing information little by little as the plot progresses.* ✦ CONNECT TO WORLD KNOWLEDGE, SUMMARIZE

Teachable moments—introducing, reviewing, and suggesting strategies based on students' immediate needs—are effective tools for responsive instruction (Pressley, El-Dinary et al. 1992).

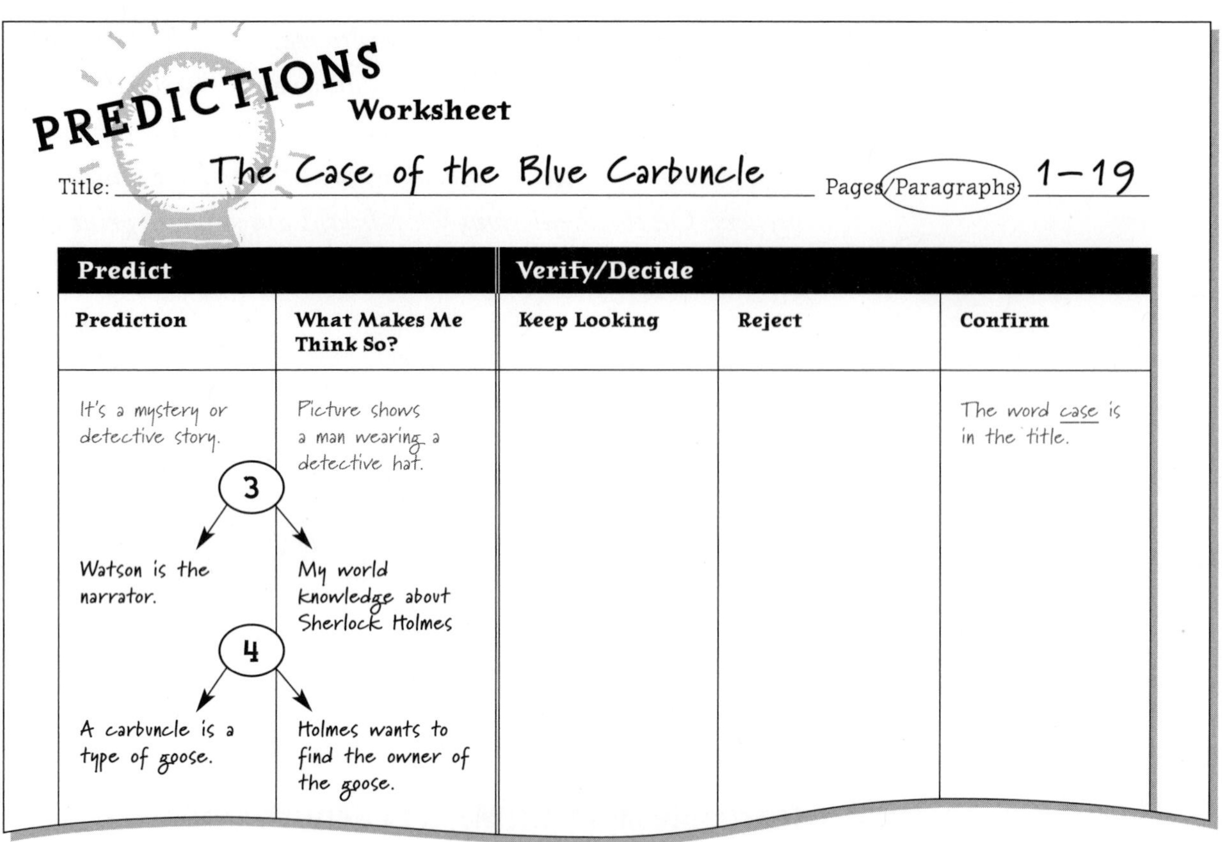

PREDICTIONS Worksheet

Title: The Case of the Blue Carbuncle Pages/(Paragraphs) 1–19

Predict		Verify/Decide		
Prediction	**What Makes Me Think So?**	**Keep Looking**	**Reject**	**Confirm**
It's a mystery or detective story.	Picture shows a man wearing a detective hat.			The word case is in the title.
(3) Watson is the narrator.	My world knowledge about Sherlock Holmes			
(4) A carbuncle is a type of goose.	Holmes wants to find the owner of the goose.			

Teach/Model: Read the Story Aloud

Read the story aloud to students as they follow along in their texts. Stop to model strategy use as indicated. As you apply each strategy, refer to it on the Comprehension Strategies chart. Continue recording information on the Prediction Worksheet.

"What are you investigating today?" I asked my friend Sherlock Holmes as I walked into his apartment. He did not reply, so I moved in to see what he was holding under his magnifying glass.

THINK ALOUD

(3) THINK ALOUD *Sherlock Holmes—that's a famous name. My world knowledge is that he is a fictional character, so I know for sure this mystery is fiction. I also know that Sherlock Holmes has a sidekick named Dr. Watson. Since the first quote here says, "I asked my friend Sherlock Holmes," I predict that the narrator is Watson. On the Predictions Worksheet, I'm going to print my second prediction and what makes me think so.* ✦ CONNECT TO WORLD KNOWLEDGE, PREDICT

THINK ALOUD *Good readers ask themselves questions as they read to better understand the story. So, now I'm asking myself, "What is Holmes looking at with his magnifying glass?"* ✦ ASK QUESTIONS

"Why, Holmes!" I exclaimed. "It's just an old hat. What's so valuable about it?"

THINK ALOUD *That answered my question—he's studying an old hat. Good readers picture in their minds what is happening as they read. I'm visualizing Sherlock Holmes with this big, round magnifying glass, carefully studying an old, beat-up hat. What makes me think so? Well, I got that image from different descriptions in the text. My mental image is helping me get a sense of the setting and characters, and especially this scene. I'm thinking it must have looked pretty funny to Watson. From my world knowledge about Sherlock Holmes, I think he often does unusual things like this.* ✦ CONSTRUCT MENTAL IMAGES, CONNECT TO WORLD KNOWLEDGE

"Nothing whatsoever," he replied. "I'm only studying the hat to find the owner of the goose."

"The goose?!" I asked, perplexed.

4 **THINK ALOUD** *Okay, I can see the author's starting to set up the mysterious event, which is the problem in a mystery. I think my world knowledge about mysteries definitely is going to help me understand this story. I think the mysterious event has something to do with this goose, and somehow this old hat is involved. Like Sherlock's friend, the narrator, I'm asking, "What does the hat have to do with the mystery?" I still have no idea what a carbuncle is. I'm going to predict that maybe it's a type of goose. What makes me think so is that Holmes wants to find the owner of the goose.* On the Predictions Worksheet, record your predictions and what makes you think so. ✦ CONNECT TO WORLD KNOWLEDGE, ASK QUESTIONS, PREDICT, SUMMARIZE

The dictionary defines a carbuncle as a "red precious stone." It has been speculated that Sherlock Holmes was somewhat color-blind.

PREDICTIONS Worksheet

Title: The Case of the Blue Carbuncle Pages/Paragraphs 1–19

Predict		Verify/Decide		
Prediction	**What Makes Me Think So?**	**Keep Looking**	**Reject**	**Confirm**
It's a mystery or detective story.	Picture shows a man wearing a detective hat.			The word case is in the title.
Watson is the narrator.	My world knowledge about Sherlock Holmes		(5)	"The facts are these, Watson."
A carbuncle is a type of goose.	Holmes wants to find the owner of the goose.	A man dropped the goose and ran. (6)		

THINK ALOUD

THINK ALOUD *I think this would be a good place to stop and summarize what has happened in the story so far. It may help me to better understand the story. What is the problem the character faces? Here is my summary so far: Sherlock Holmes is trying to find the owner of a goose. Somehow an old hat is a clue.*
✦ SUMMARIZE

Say: *Notice that already I've used a few strategies. During my think-alouds, I jumped around using all kinds of different strategies to understand the text. These are strategies that good readers use automatically. When I'm reading, I use the same strategies. I just use them really quickly, in my brain. My reading is smooth.*

Student think-alouds serve a twofold purpose, providing peer modeling of strategies and helping teachers assess comprehension and strategies application.

Guided Practice

Have students chorally read the next part of the story, stopping to coach students as indicated. As you coach students to apply a particular strategy, refer to the strategy name on the Comprehension Strategies chart. Whenever the group reaches a confusing part, coach students by asking: *What can we do to figure that out?* Then encourage them to choose a fix-up strategy. Say: *We're going to read aloud the story together, and I will stop once in a while and coach you to use strategies. I want you to respond by thinking aloud.*

"The facts are these, Watson," explained Holmes.

(5) Ask: *Based on what we've just read, can we confirm the prediction about who the narrator is?* (Possible response: *Yes, I think this confirms that Watson is the narrator. The dialogue indicates that Holmes is speaking to Watson.*) On the Predictions Worksheet, record this new evidence under Confirm. ✦ PREDICT

"Police Commissioner Peterson was walking home last night. He saw a man ahead carrying a fat goose. At Goodge Street, a rough gang appeared and knocked off the man's hat. The man swung his walking stick to fight back, and Commissioner Peterson rushed to help. Startled, the man dropped the goose and ran. The gang scattered, too, leaving Peterson with the goose and the hat."

(6) Ask: *Based on what we've just read, can we verify our prediction about the carbuncle being a type of goose?* (Possible response: *It doesn't say for sure, but since the man dropped the goose and ran, maybe he stole the goose. So, maybe the goose is the blue carbuncle, and the mystery is finding the man who stole it.*) Say: *There is still not enough information to confirm or reject this prediction, so we need to keep looking. But since we have some evidence related to the prediction, we should add it to the worksheet.* On the Predictions Worksheet, record this new evidence under Keep Looking. ✦ PREDICT

Think-Pair-Share: A Cooperative Learning Technique

- **THINK: Work alone to develop a response.**
- **PAIR: Work with a peer to discuss and refine the response.**
- **SHARE: Communicate the response to the whole class.**

McTighe and Lyman 1988.

Ask: *How many of you know what a police commissioner is?* Say: *Since some of you are unsure, let's try using a fix-up strategy. Let's ask someone.* Ask: *Does anyone know what it is?* (Possible response: *I've heard of Commissioner Gordon from* Batman. *He's the guy in charge of the police.*) Say: *Good. You connected to your world knowledge. Peterson is a high-ranking police officer.* ✦ MONITOR COMPREHENSION, CONNECT TO WORLD KNOWLEDGE

Say: *This paragraph is action packed. Constructing a mental image may be helpful in understanding the sequence of events. Let's do a think-pair-share: first picture the events in the order they happened, then describe your mental movie to a partner and work with the partner to refine it, and finally share it with the whole class. There are no right or wrong mental images as long as they are supported by the text.* ✦ CONSTRUCT MENTAL IMAGES

PREDICTIONS Worksheet

Title: The Case of the Blue Carbuncle Pages/(Paragraphs) 1–19

Predict		Verify/Decide		
Prediction	**What Makes Me Think So?**	**Keep Looking**	**Reject**	**Confirm**
It's a mystery or detective story.	Picture shows a man wearing a detective hat.			The word case is in the title.
Watson is the narrator.	My world knowledge about Sherlock Holmes			"The facts are these, Watson."
A carbuncle is a type of goose.	Holmes wants to find the owner of the goose.	A man dropped the goose and ran.		
(7) Henry Baker stole the goose.	He ran away when the police came.			

Ask: *Using your mental image, can anyone sum up what happened in this scene?* (Possible response: *A man was walking down the street carrying a goose when some mean people came up and knocked off his hat. The man started to fight back. When the police officer ran to help him, everybody ran away, so the officer was left with the hat and the goose.*) ✦ SUMMARIZE

"Which, surely, he returned to their owner?" asked I.

"There's the problem. True, the owner's name—Henry Baker—is stitched inside the hat. But there are hundreds of Henry Bakers in London. It would be impossible to find the right one. So, Peterson brought the hat to me. He took the goose home to cook before it spoiled."

7 Ask: *Where does the story take place?* (London) Say: *Who is Peterson, again? Looking back is a good fix-up strategy to use when you are confused about who's who.* Have students look back to identify Peterson as the police commissioner. Ask: *Would anyone like to ask a question?* (Possible responses: *What does Henry Baker have to do with the story? Why did he run when the police came?*) Say: *We could make a prediction about that. Can anyone make a prediction?* (Possible response: *Henry Baker stole the goose and that's why he ran away.*) On the Predictions Worksheet, record students' predictions and what makes them think so. ✦ SUMMARIZE, MONITOR COMPREHENSION, ASK QUESTIONS, PREDICT

Just then, the door flew open. Peterson rushed in. "The goose, Mr. Holmes!" he gasped. "See what my wife found in its crop!"

SEE ALSO . . .

LESSON MODEL: Using the Dictionary, p. 506

Say: *I'm not sure what a goose's crop is. Does anyone else wonder what it is? Let's choose a fix-up strategy. How about checking a reference, such as the dictionary?* Call on a student to use the Guidelines for Using the Dictionary (p. 507) to define, clarify, and confirm the meaning of *crop.* (a pouch in a bird's throat where food is stored for digestion) Say: *Now that we know what a* crop *is, let's reread the last sentence together. Reread is a good fix-up strategy to use to get back in the flow of reading after you were stuck.* ✦ MONITOR COMPREHENSION

PREDICTIONS Worksheet

Title: The Case of the Blue Carbuncle Pages/(Paragraphs) 1–19

Predict		**Verify/Decide**		
Prediction	**What Makes Me Think So?**	**Keep Looking**	**Reject**	**Confirm**
It's a mystery or detective story.	Picture shows a man wearing a detective hat.			The word case is in the title.
Watson is the narrator.	My world knowledge about Sherlock Holmes			"The facts are these, Watson."
A carbuncle is a type of goose.	Holmes wants to find the owner of the goose.	A man dropped the goose and ran.	(8) The blue carbuncle is the stone found inside the goose.	
Henry Baker stole the goose.	He ran away when the police came.			
(9) The goose swallowed the carbuncle.	(9) The carbuncle was inside the goose's crop (throat).			
(10) Henry Baker stole the carbuncle.	(10) The stone was inside the goose he dropped.			
(10) John Horner stole the carbuncle.	(10) He was in the countess's room on the day of the robbery. He has a criminal record.			

He held out a dazzling blue stone. It was no bigger than a bean, but it sparkled like a star. Sherlock Holmes whistled. "Peterson! Do you know what you have there?"

"It's the Countess of Morcar's blue carbuncle!" I cut in.

(8) Ask: *What do we need to do about our earlier prediction about the carbuncle?* (Possible response: *Reject the prediction that the carbuncle is a goose.* On the Predictions Worksheet, record the evidence under Reject. ✦ PREDICT, MONITOR COMPREHENSION

(9) Ask: *Are you curious about anything so far in the story? Do you have a question about it?* (Possible response: *How did a stone get inside a goose?*) *Can you make a prediction?* (Possible response: *The goose swallowed the carbuncle.*) On the Predictions Worksheet, record students' predictions and what makes them think so. ✦ ASK QUESTIONS, PREDICT

"Precisely," replied Holmes. "I have the newspaper article right here:

'. . . Police arrested plumber John Horner. Hotel Cosmopolitan manager James Ryder reported to police that Horner fixed a pipe in the countess's room on the day of the robbery. Horner, who has a criminal record, claims he is innocent.'

"The question is: How did the stone get from jewelry box to bird?"

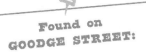

Holmes took a pencil and paper and wrote: "Found on Goodge Street: 1 goose, 1 black felt hat. Mr. Henry Baker can have same—221B Baker Street. 6:30 p.m. this evening."

"Peterson, put this ad in all the papers and bring me a new goose!"

Found on
GOODGE STREET:

1 goose, 1 black felt hat. Mr. Henry Baker can have same—221B Baker Street. 6:30 p.m. this evening.

(10) Ask: *Can anyone sum up the problem, or the mysterious event?* (Possible response: *Holmes needs to figure out who stole the blue carbuncle and how it got inside the goose.*) Ask: *Does anyone have a prediction about who stole the blue carbuncle?* (Possible responses: *Henry Baker or John Horner*) On the Predictions Worksheet, record students' predictions and what makes them think so. ✦ SUMMARIZE, PREDICT

PREDICTIONS Worksheet

Title: The Case of the Blue Carbuncle Pages/Paragraphs 1–19

Predict		Verify/Decide		
Prediction	**What Makes Me Think So?**	**Keep Looking**	**Reject**	**Confirm**
It's a mystery or detective story.	Picture shows a man wearing a detective hat.			The word case is in the title.
Watson is the narrator.	My world knowledge about Sherlock Holmes			"The facts are these, Watson."
A carbuncle is a type of goose.	Holmes wants to find the owner of the goose.	A man dropped the goose and ran.	The blue carbuncle is the stone found inside the goose.	
Henry Baker stole the goose.	He ran away when the police came.		Baker came to Holmes's apartment. He wouldn't have risked it if he had stolen the goose.	
The goose swallowed the carbuncle.	The carbuncle was inside the goose's crop (throat).			
Henry Baker stole the carbuncle.	The stone was inside the goose he dropped.	He responded to the ad that said he could get the goose and hat back.	He doesn't care that Holmes gives him a different goose.	
John Horner stole the carbuncle.	He was in the countess's room on the day of the robbery. He has a criminal record.			

11

12

At 6:30 sharp, Henry Baker knocked on Holmes's door.

(11) Ask: *So, what do you think about the fact that Henry Baker responded to the ad?* (Possible responses: *Well, if he stole the blue carbuncle, he would definitely want to get the goose back. He probably didn't steal the goose, though—if the goose were stolen, he probably wouldn't have risked coming to Holmes's apartment to get it.*) Ask: *So, what do we need to do with our predictions?* (Possible responses: *We can reject the prediction that Baker stole the goose. We need to keep looking to see if Baker stole the carbuncle.*) On the Predictions Worksheet, record the new evidence under Keep Looking and Reject, respectively. ✦ PREDICT

Holmes handed Baker his hat. Then he explained that he had eaten Baker's goose but was offering another one in its place. Baker thanked Holmes, unconcerned that it was a different goose.

"By the way," asked Holmes, "could you tell me where your goose came from? It was delicious."

"Oh, yes, from my favorite inn," replied Baker. "The Alpha."

"So now we know Henry Baker isn't the thief," Holmes remarked after Henry Baker had left. "I say we eat dinner later. Let's follow this clue while it's still hot."

(12) Ask: *What do you think here? How does Holmes know that Baker isn't the thief?* (Possible response: *Henry Baker doesn't care that Holmes gives him a different goose.*) On the Predictions Worksheet, record the new evidence under Reject. ✦ PREDICT

Say: *Remember that in a mystery, the author hopes to surprise you in the end. So, the author will often try to trick you with clues that throw you offtrack—those red herrings we talked about. So, when we read this mystery, we will probably change a lot of our predictions along the way. The clue about Henry Baker being the thief is a red herring.*

Open-Ended Prompts

Does anyone want to think aloud here?

What do you think about this?

Do you have any ideas here?

Anyone want to use a strategy?

Was there anything you didn't understand?

Do you need to choose a fix-up strategy?

Scaffolded Practice

Continue choral-reading the rest of the story. When students appear surprised, curious, or confused, stop reading and have students respond to an open-ended prompt. Student responses should be in a think-aloud form and include identification of the strategy used. Refer students to the Comprehension Strategies teaching chart if they have difficulty. If students make or verify predictions, record the information on the Predictions Worksheet. For new predictions, you may need to use a second worksheet.

Possible Student Think-Aloud Responses

Paragraph	Student Think-Aloud	Strategies Used
21	I wonder why the innkeeper responded hesitantly. I'll predict that he stole the carbuncle.	Ask Questions / Predict
24	I'm going to connect to my world knowledge. I think Covent Garden is a farmers' market. We go to the farmers' market every Saturday. I can visualize what Covent Garden may look like.	Connect to World Knowledge Construct Mental Images
25	I wonder why Breckinridge got angry when Holmes asked about buying a goose. Maybe he's the one who stole the carbuncle? I'll make a prediction.	Ask Questions / Predict Monitor Comprehension
28	I wonder if Mrs. Oakshott has anything to do with the robbery. Maybe she stole the carbuncle?	Ask Questions / Predict Monitor Comprehension
31	I need to choose a fix-up strategy. I can't remember what Brixton Road has to do with the story. (Mrs. Oakshott lives on Brixton Road.)	Monitor Comprehension
33	I'm going to picture in my mind what the rat-faced little man looked like.	Construct Mental Images
39	I wonder if James Ryder, the rat-faced man, was the one who stole the carbuncle. He lied to Holmes about his real name. I know that people who are guilty often tell lies to cover up the truth.	Predict Connect to World Knowledge
43	Why is Holmes talking about a blue egg? I don't get it. I need to choose a fix-up strategy. I think I'll reread the paragraph. (Holmes is using a metaphor. The blue egg is the blue carbuncle.)	Ask Questions Monitor Comprehension
44	I need to choose a fix-up strategy. I can't remember what Horner has to do with the story. I guess I'll look back. (Horner fixed the pipe in the countess's room on the day of the robbery.)	Monitor Comprehension
45	I'm going to connect to my world knowledge. I think Ryder was lying when he said he'd "never do wrong again." He just didn't want to get arrested.	Connect to World Knowledge
48	I'm going to make a mental movie to help me better understand how the geese got mixed up.	Construct Mental Images
51	Maybe Ryder really meant he'd never do wrong again. Holmes says Ryder is too afraid to become a criminal. Sometimes getting caught is enough of a lesson.	Connect to World Knowledge

PREDICTIONS Worksheet

Title: The Case of the Blue Carbuncle Pages/(Paragraphs) 20–51

Predict		Verify/Decide		
Prediction	**What Makes Me Think So?**	**Keep Looking**	**Reject**	**Confirm**
The innkeeper stole the carbuncle.	Baker got the goose at the Alpha Inn.	The innkeeper hesitates to answer Holmes's question about the geese.	The innkeeper was just confused about what geese Holmes was talking about. He did not ask about where the goose was now.	
Breckinridge stole the carbuncle.	The goose came from a meat seller named Breckinridge.	Breckinridge is angry when Holmes asks about the geese.	He's just angry because people keep bothering him for information about the geese.	
Mrs. Oakshott stole the carbuncle.	She raised the goose.		She is Ryder's sister. He put the stone in the goose.	
The rat-faced man stole the carbuncle.	The rat-faced man asks Breckinridge about the geese.	He acts nervous, looking sideways. He lies about his name. He is the manager of the hotel.		Ryder, the rat-faced man, confesses to the crime.

After-Reading Wrap-Up

Conclude the lesson by discussing the story outcome, the author's craft, predictions, and strategy use.

DISCUSS THE OUTCOME Point out that the outcome of the story is the solution to the mystery. Ask students to identify the outcome. (Possible response: *Ryder, the hotel manager, stole the stone and tried to "frame," or blame it on, the plumber.*)

DISCUSS THE AUTHOR'S CRAFT Ask a volunteer to reread the last paragraph. Point out that this paragraph contains puns and an idiom. Remind students that a pun is a type of word play and an idiom is an expression in which the entire meaning is different from the usual meanings of the individual words within it. Guide students to look back in the text for clues to the meaning of the pun "investigate another bird." (Possible response: *Holmes is referring to eating his chicken dinner.*) Explain to students that "wild goose chase" is both a pun and an idiom. Literally, Holmes and Watson went on a search about a wild goose. The idiomatic expression means "a useless or hopeless search for something that doesn't exist or can't be found." Point out what Sherlock Holmes is famous for—solving the most "impossible" mysteries.

SEE ALSO . . .

LESSON MODEL: Animal Idioms, p. 580

DISCUSS PREDICTIONS Review the completed Predictions Worksheet. Tell students that reviewing the predictions can help them to summarize the story. Discuss which of the predictions were confirmed and which were rejected. Point out that even a carefully made prediction may end up having to be rejected, especially when the author is trying to create twists in the plot. Explain that rejecting a prediction indicates that one is paying attention to and is involved in the story—something that good readers do.

DISCUSS STRATEGY USE Have students identify the strategies they used. Discuss with students how using a variety of strategies in coordination helped them to better understand and enjoy the story.

LESSON MODEL FOR

Reader Response

Benchmark

- ability to identify and write personal, creative, and critical responses to literature

Strategy Grade Level

- Grade 3 and above

Grouping

- whole class

Prerequisite

- knowledge of literary devices

Sample Text (Resourcces)

- "The Case of the Blue Carbuncle" Complexity Level: Grades 4–5

Activity Master (Resources)

- Tripod Response Sheet

Materials

- PDF and copies of Tripod Response Sheet
- copies of Tripod Response Sheet with writing prompts

Source

- *Book Club: A Literature-Based Curriculum, 2nd Edition* (2002) by Taffy E. Raphael, Laura S. Pardo, and Kathy Highfield. Lawrence, MA: Small Planet Communications.

Book Club: Writing in Response to Literature

Students need instruction and support to develop their skills in using writing as a tool for reflecting on reading. This sample lesson model is based on the writing strand of the Book Club program (Raphael et al. 2002; Raphael et al. 2001). Book Club provides instruction in three categories, or angles, of written response to literature: personal, creative, and critical. Response options in these three categories help students to focus their writing and provide a structure for responding to reading from different angles. They also serve as the focus of student Book Club discussions.

This sample lesson model would be most appropriate after students have gained some familiarity with a variety of response options, or writing prompts. The same model can be adapted and used to enhance instruction for literary text in any commercial reading or language arts program—as long as the text is at the appropriate level. In this model, sample text is used to represent a story at the student's independent reading level.

Direct Explanation: Angles of Written Response

Use interactive whiteboard technology to display the Tripod Response Sheet. Explain to students that writing is one way to respond to what they have read. Then point out that the Tripod Response Sheet is divided into sections and that this format allows them to display three different angles of written response on a single page. One section focuses on personal response, or connecting the story to their own lives and feelings; another on creative response, or using their imaginations to engage with the story; and another on critical response, or analyzing the text and the author's craft.

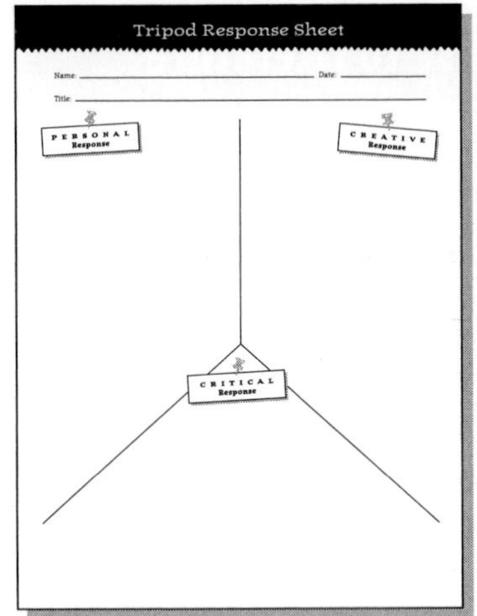

Angles of Written Response

- **Personal**
- **Creative**
- **Critical**

PERSONAL RESPONSE Point to the heading Personal Response. Explain to students that stories not only entertain us and introduce us to interesting new people, places, and ideas, but they also can help us better understand ourselves. Good readers make connections between a story and their own lives to understand the story more deeply. Suggest that as students read, they ask themselves whether the events in the book remind them of events or experiences in their own lives. They can write about their real life event and how it was similar to the event in the book. Personal response options encourage students to relate text to their lives through writing. These responses can also include sharing feelings brought out by the text.

CREATIVE RESPONSE Point to the heading Creative Response. Explain to students that when they respond creatively, they are using their imaginations to explore ideas in text. This includes engaging creatively with the text by putting themselves in a situation or altering a text event. For example, students respond creatively when they speculate "What if . . ." —changing events or characters in ways that affect the outcome of the story. Students can also engage creatively with the author by imagining themselves as author. When students write a creative response, they can apply the author's ideas and issues in new ways or to new situations.

CRITICAL RESPONSE Point to the heading Critical Response. Explain to students that when they respond critically, they are analyzing aspects of the literary work. Tell students that authors reveal information about characters, situations, and theme in a variety of ways. Some of the most important ways are through dialogue, point of view, voice, imagery, or foreshadowing. These literary techniques are what we call the author's craft. When students write a critical response, they can analyze the author's use of a specific literary technique and explain whether it was effective or ineffective. They can also identify the author's purpose for writing the text and then assess how well the author met that purpose. Or they can describe the impact the story had on them as readers, such as changing their beliefs or feelings about an issue, and explain how the author created that impact. Point out to students that as they become familiar with elements of the author's craft, they can begin to identify text features specific to an author across texts. They can also compare the literary techniques of different authors.

Guided Practice: Tripod Response Sheet

Using response options, or writing prompts, such as the ones shown on this and the following page, create a Tripod Response Sheet for "The Case of the Blue Carbuncle." After reading the mystery, give each student a copy of the Tripod Response Sheet with writing prompts and a blank Tripod Response Sheet. Explain to students that you're going to guide them in using the Tripod Response Sheet to respond to "The Case of the Blue Carbuncle" from three different angles: personal, creative, and critical. After choosing a writing prompt for each angle, they will write their response in the corresponding section of the blank Tripod Response Sheet. Tell students that later they will get together in small groups to share and discuss their written responses.

- Describe how this story reminds you of another story you've read or seen.
- Describe what you have in common with a character or event in the story.
- Choose the character in the story that you'd most like to meet. Explain why.
- Write about a time when you were involved in solving a mystery.
- Write about any emotions you experienced when reading the story and why the story made you feel that way.

PERSONAL RESPONSE Say: *First let's focus on personal responses. Personal responses include sharing experiences and feelings, placing yourself in a story situation, or comparing yourself to story characters.* Point to the first writing prompt and read it aloud: *Describe how this story reminds you of another story you've read or seen.* Ask: *Why is this categorized as a personal response?* (Possible response: *It relates the story to something I've already experienced, something familiar.*) Brainstorm ideas about the kinds of things students could write in response to this prompt. Explain that the best way to organize this personal response is to describe something in the story and then tell what it reminds them of. For example, they could compare and contrast "The Case of the Blue Carbuncle" with another mystery they've read or seen. Follow the same procedure with the remaining prompts.

- Write a diary entry from the point of view of a different story character.
- Write a different ending to the story.
- Write a Readers Theatre script based on the story.
- Write a letter of advice to one of the characters in the story.
- Write a newspaper article about an event in the story.

- Interpret what the dialogue reveals about each character.
- Critique the author's skillful choice of words.
- Record the words and actions that give clues to events that happen later in the story.
- Analyze the story's point of view and voice and discuss whether this is effective.
- Discuss the author's purpose in writing the story and whether it achieves this purpose.

CREATIVE RESPONSE Say: *Now let's focus on creative responses. Creative responses include using your imagination to explore ideas in a story and to create new works based on the story.* Point to the first writing prompt and read it aloud: *Write a diary entry from the point of view of a different story character.* Ask: *Why is this categorized as a creative response?* (Possible response: *It's creating a new work based on ideas or elements in the story.*) Brainstorm ideas about the kinds of things students could write in response to this prompt. Explain that the best way to develop this creative response is to identify who is telling the story, choose a different character to be the narrator, and think about that character's perspective on the story events. Follow the same procedure with the remaining prompts.

CRITICAL RESPONSE Say: *Now let's focus on critical responses. Critical responses include analyzing whether the author did a good job writing the text.* Point to the first writing prompt and read it aloud: *Interpret what the dialogue reveals about each character.* Ask: *Why is this categorized as a critical response?* (Possible response: *It has to do with the author's use of dialogue as a literary technique, or part of the author's craft.*) Brainstorm ideas about the kinds of things students could write in response to this prompt. Explain that the best way to develop this critical response is to first read the dialogue aloud and then to think about what the words reveal about the characters' personalities, feelings, and points of view. Follow the same procedure with the remaining prompts.

Have students select a writing prompt for each angle of response. Then have them write their responses on the blank Tripod Response Sheet.

CHAPTER 15

Informational Text

what? why? when? how?

what? Informational Text

Types of Informational Texts

- Assembly instructions
- Autobiographies
- Biographies
- Brochures
- Catalogs
- Digital sources
- Directions
- Encyclopedias
- Forms
- Historical texts
- Literary nonfiction
- Magazine articles
- News articles
- Recipes
- Repair manuals
- Scientific texts
- Signs
- Technical texts
- Textbooks
- Web sites

CCSS READING STANDARDS

Informational Text

Key Ideas and Details

Ask and answer questions to demonstrate understanding of key details in a text. (RI.K-3.1)

Determine the main idea of a text; summarize the text. (RI.3-4.2)

Craft and Structure

Describe the overall structure in a text. (RI.4.5)

Informational, or expository, text communicates facts about the natural or social world (Duke 2006). It can be found in a wide range of genres and formats, from content-area textbooks to cookbooks to Internet Web sites. Informational text tends to be more complex, diverse, and challenging than literary text (RRSG 2002). Reading and understanding informational text involves more abstract thinking than does reading and understanding the typical story. Readers must compare and contrast ideas, recognize complex causality, synthesize information, and evaluate solutions proposed for problems.

In content-area reading, "the priority of instructing for reading comprehension must be balanced with the priority of teaching the content area itself" (RRSG 2002). Just as it is important to integrate informational texts into language arts instruction, so it is important to integrate comprehension instruction into content-area teaching, particularly for adolescents (Sadler 2001; Alvermann and Eakle 2003; Fisher and Frey 2004). Doing so can improve both the learning of content and comprehension abilities. Torgesen et al. (2007) make the following recommendations for improving adolescent literacy instruction in the content areas: (1) provide explicit comprehension strategies instruction throughout the school day, (2) include plenty of open, sustained discussion of reading content, (3) hold high standards for text, conversation, questions, and vocabulary, (4) build motivation and engagement with reading, and (5) teach essential content knowledge.

Informational Text Structures and Signal Words		
Text Structure	**Signal Words or Phrases**	**Sample Topic Sentences**
DESCRIPTION Explains, defines, or illustrates a concept or topic	for example, for instance, main parts, such as, this particular	A flowering tree has four main parts: roots, stems, leaves, and flowers. Each part has several elements, each with a distinct function. For example, the roots include ...
COMPARE-CONTRAST Presents similarities and differences between two or more objects, places, events, or ideas	*compare:* like, alike, just as, similar, both, also, too *contrast:* unlike, differ, but, in contrast, on the other hand, however	Although both literary and informational texts are useful for building reading comprehension, these types of text differ in several ways.
CAUSE-EFFECT Presents the reasons an event happened and its results	because, due to, since, therefore, so, as a result, consequently, lead to, this is why, the reason, result in, consequences	Higher fuel prices can result in a variety of consequences ...
PROBLEM/SOLUTION Poses a problem and suggests possible solutions	*problem:* problem, question, the trouble *solution:* solution, answer, in response	Loss of trees poses a problem for the environment by increasing levels of carbon dioxide in the atmosphere. In response, there are several actions one can take.
TIME ORDER (SEQUENCE) Groups ideas by order or time	first, next, then, afterward, later, last, finally, now, after, before, stages, steps	The development of a butterfly follows four distinct stages. First, ...

SEE ALSO ...

The Text, p. 610

Recognizing Informational Text Structure, p. 687

Informational Text Structure

Informational text is organized, or structured, in a specific way to guide readers in identifying key information and making connections among ideas. Informational texts use a limited number of organizational structures, including description, compare-contrast, cause-effect, problem/solution, and time order. Each of these informational text structures is associated with a set of signal words that can indicate the underlying organization. For example, texts using the compare-contrast structure include words such as *like, similar, in contrast.* When readers come across these words while reading, it can help them identify that the text is comparing or contrasting.

Graphic Organizers

Because they are concrete representations, graphic organizers provide a means for students to (1) record information about underlying text structures, (2) see how concepts fit within text structures, (3) focus on the most important ideas in the text, (4) examine relationships among text concepts, (5) recall key text information, and (6) write well-organized summaries (Armbruster et al. 2001; Trabasso and Bouchard 2002).

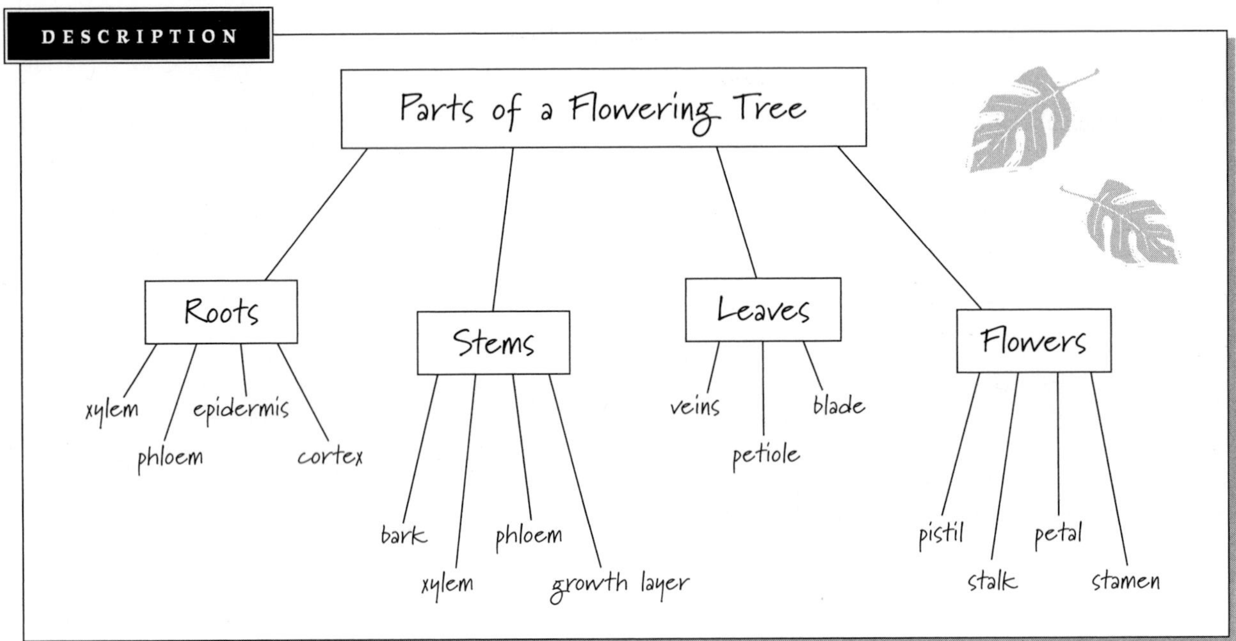

COMPARE-CONTRAST

	TYPE OF TEXT	
ATTRIBUTE	LITERARY	INFORMATIONAL
Instructional usefulness	Building reading comprehension	Building reading comprehension
Major purposes	To entertain To teach a moral lesson	To inform To teach a procedure
Where found	Storybooks Magazines Novels Comic books	Textbooks Magazines Recipes Manuals

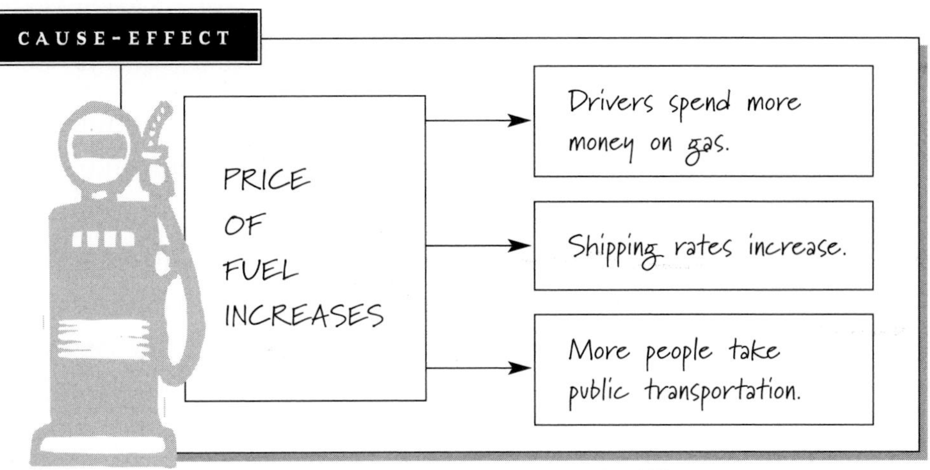
CAUSE-EFFECT
PRICE OF FUEL INCREASES
Drivers spend more money on gas.
Shipping rates increase.
More people take public transportation.

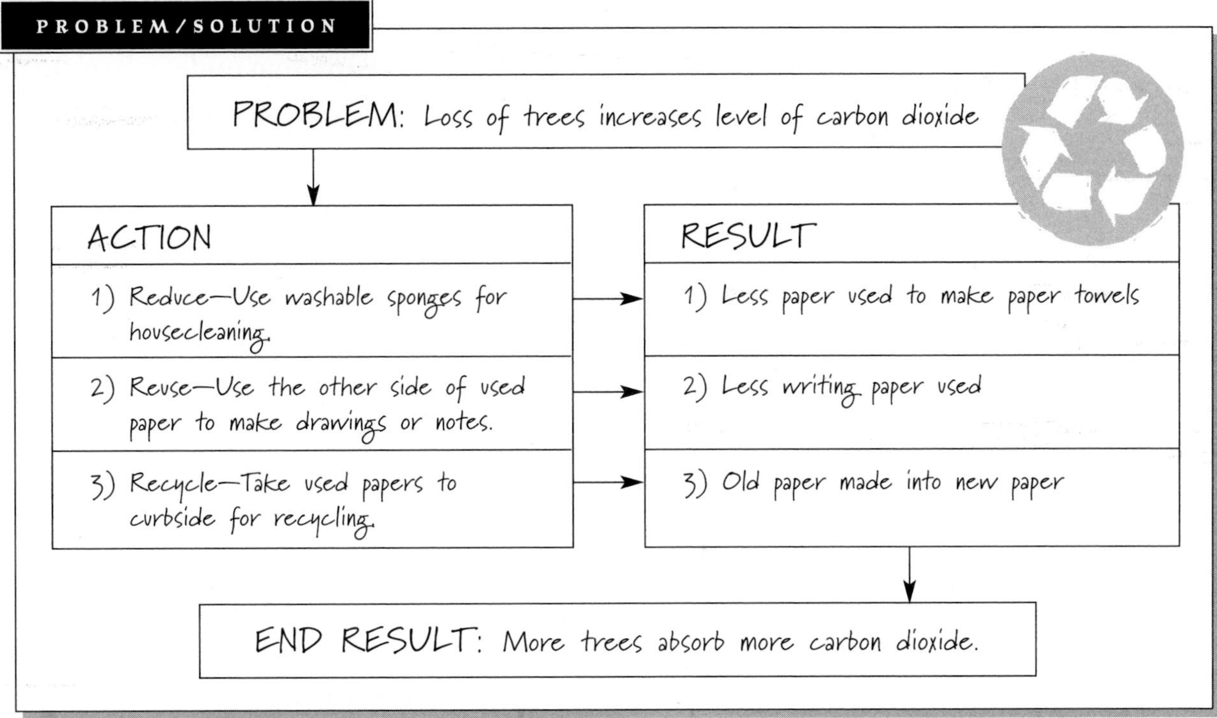
PROBLEM/SOLUTION
PROBLEM: Loss of trees increases level of carbon dioxide
ACTION
1) Reduce—Use washable sponges for housecleaning.
2) Reuse—Use the other side of used paper to make drawings or notes.
3) Recycle—Take used papers to curbside for recycling.
RESULT
1) Less paper used to make paper towels
2) Less writing paper used
3) Old paper made into new paper
END RESULT: More trees absorb more carbon dioxide.

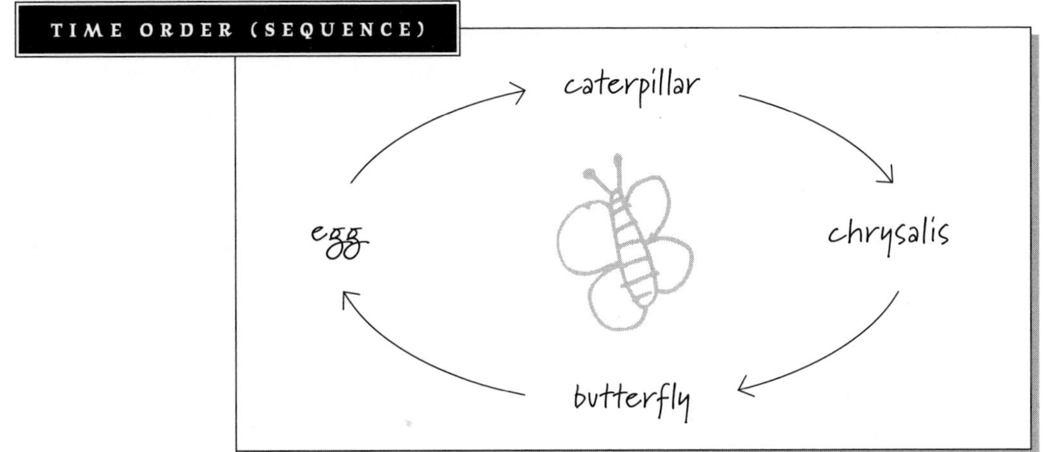
TIME ORDER (SEQUENCE)
caterpillar
chrysalis
butterfly
egg

SEE ALSO . . .

The Text, p. 610

A considerate text is a text that facilitates comprehension and learning from reading.

—ARMBRUSTER, 1996

Considerate Texts

Considerate texts facilitate comprehension and learning. In contrast, inconsiderate texts can be more difficult for students to comprehend. The idea of considerate texts applies mostly to informational text whose main purpose is to help the reader acquire new information. Three overlapping features characterize and help define considerate text: structural cues, coherence, and audience appropriateness (Armbruster 1996).

Structural Cues

The more apparent the text structure is to the reader, the higher the probability that the reader will learn from reading. Structural cues are aspects of text that suggest, indicate, or emphasize its structure. They can function as a map or outline of the main ideas in the text, alerting readers to the important idea(s). These cues include introductions, summaries, and glossaries as well as graphic features such as chapter titles, headings, sidebars, charts and tables, type font, type style, bulleted or numbered lists, and the use of icons.

Coherence

Coherence refers to clarity of writing, that is, logically and clearly explaining events and ideas in text. Several features characterize coherence: (1) main ideas that are explicitly stated and located in prominent places, (2) information limited to that which supports the development of the main idea, (3) a logical ordering of events and ideas, (4) the use of signal words to clarify the relationships between events and ideas, (5) the use of precise terms rather than ambiguous pronouns, and (6) smooth transitions between topics (Armbruster 1996).

Audience Appropriateness

Considerate texts build on the existing world knowledge that readers are likely to have. Audience appropriateness is the extent to which the text matches this knowledge. Conceptual density, or the number of new concepts introduced per unit of text, influences audience appropriateness. The denser the conceptual load, the more difficult the text (Kintsch and Keenan 1973).

SEE ALSO . . .

Comprehension Strategies, p. 614

Comprehension Strategies

Recognizing Informational Text Structures

Monitoring Comprehension

Connecting to World Knowledge

Predicting

Asking Questions

Answering Questions

Constructing Mental Images

Summarizing

SEE ALSO . . .

The Text, p. 610

Informational Text Structures and Signal Words, p. 683

Graphic Organizers, p. 684

> Almost any approach to teaching the structure of informational text improves both comprehension and recall of key text information.
>
> —DUKE & PEARSON, 2002

Strategy Application

All comprehension strategies are applicable to informational text. With informational texts, reading purposes and tasks often drive the selection and application of comprehension strategies (Blanton, Wood, and Moorman 1990). Particularly when comprehension instruction is tied to content-area learning, it is important to read with a purpose in mind (Neufeld 2005). Whenever possible, informational reading instruction should be done in meaningful contexts and for authentic purposes—that is, for the kinds of reasons that would engage a student outside the school context (Dreher 2002; Guthrie and Ozgungor 2002; Duke 2006). The RAND Reading Study Group (RRSG 2002) asserts that when comprehension strategies are closely linked with knowledge in a content area, students are more likely to learn the strategies fully, perceive strategies as valuable tools, and use them in new learning situations.

Recognizing Informational Text Structures

Learning the text structures and clues for identifying them can improve students' comprehension and recall of informational text (Duke and Pearson 2002; Taylor and Beach 1984). Understanding a text's organizational structure can also help students summarize text by helping them locate and keep track of important information to include in a summary.

The ability to recognize informational text structures can be developed through the use of signal words, physical features, and graphic organizers (Williams 2005; Williams and Stafford 2005). Students can learn to detect signal words that distinguish particular text structures. They can also note text features, such as headings, sidebars, boldface type, and tables, that cue the overall organization of text. Students can create graphic organizers to demonstrate how text is constructed, to lay out relevant information, and to make order out of text.

 SEE ALSO . . .

Motivation and Engagement with Reading, p. 695

CCSS READING STANDARDS

Literature • Informational Text

Key Ideas and Details

Read closely to determine what text says explicitly. (CCR.1)

Monitoring Comprehension

Particularly when reading to learn new information, students must be actively aware of whether they understand the text and must deal with comprehension problems as they arise. Strategic monitoring requires metacognitive awareness, which includes knowledge about ourselves, the tasks we face, and the strategies we use (Garner 1987). Locating information is frequently the purpose or task one faces when reading informational texts. Therefore, monitoring one's reading of informational text includes strategies that guide students in the processes of searching, scanning, and skimming (Duke 2006; Dreher 2002). Dreher (2002) developed a model that outlines characteristics of an efficient text search, along with monitoring questions to guide each step in the search process (see also Guthrie and Mosenthal 1987).

Text-Search Model: Reading to Locate Information

Search Process	Description	Questions for Monitoring Text Search Tasks
Goal Formation	Set one's own goal or figure out what to do with an assigned task.	Exactly what information do I need?
Category Selection	Determine what categories will lead to the target information. May use index, table of contents, headings.	How should I approach this material? How is this material organized? What are the available features?
Information Extraction	Distinguish useful from irrelevant information.	Is the information I need located here? Does the information here make sense?
Integration	Integrate information in ongoing synthesis between prior knowledge and goal-relevant information.	Do I need to combine this information with other material that I have located or already know?
Recycling	Assess whether more information is needed. Continue through previous components until goal is met.	Do I have all the information that I need? If not, I should continue searching.

Based on Dreher 2002.

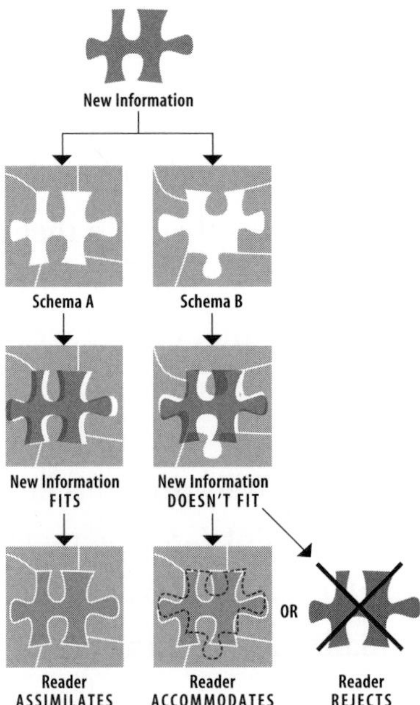

Connecting to World Knowledge

Students learn new information from text by linking it with knowledge that stems from their previous experiences. Readers' world knowledge shapes the way they perceive information in text (Anderson and Pearson 1984). When readers' world knowledge matches what is presented in the text, they assimilate the new information—connecting it readily into their existing schema for the topic. In contrast, when their world knowledge conflicts with information presented in the text, either readers accommodate by modifying their schema to fit the new information or they reject the information and maintain their previous understanding (Pardo 2004). Particularly in the content areas, such as science, students may tap into world knowledge that is either inaccurate or irrelevant to the text (Pressley and Block 2002). To avoid being distracted or led astray, students need teacher guidance when connecting their world knowledge with informational text.

K-W-L

Step 1: What I Know
(accessing what students know)

Step 2: What I Want to Find Out
(identifying what students want to learn)

Step 3: What I Learned
(noting what students learned from the text)

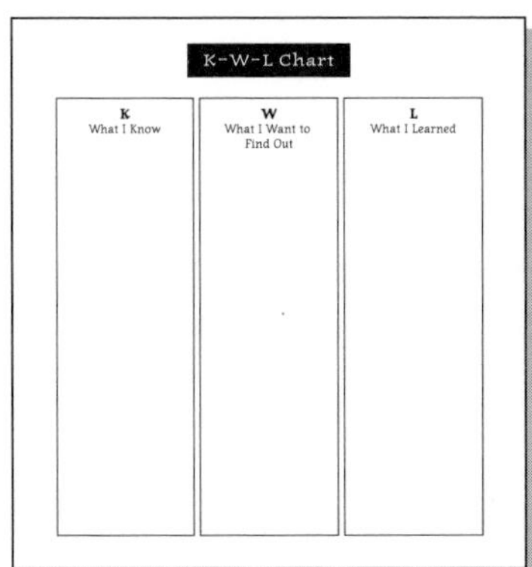

K-W-L The K-W-L procedure (Ogle 1986) is a frequently used technique for tapping into students' world knowledge. The procedure involves three steps: (1) accessing what students know, (2) identifying what students want to learn, and (3) noting what students learned from the text.

Predicting

A prereading skim of the text often results in an informed guess—based on world knowledge and clues in the text—about what is going to be covered. Students make predictions about informational text based on scanning structural cues that indicate its organization. As students preview the layout of the text, headings, and graphic organizers, they use their knowledge of such cues to predict the purpose of the text as a whole, as well as the functions of various parts of the text (Block 2004). Previewing in this way organizes students' thinking, preparing them to learn the information presented in text.

Most of the required reading in college and workforce training programs is informational in structure and challenging in content.

—COMMON CORE STATE STANDARDS, 2010

SEE ALSO . . .

Types of Teacher Questions, p. 621

Bloom's Taxonomy, p. 638

Asking Questions

Asking oneself questions about the text being read is a particularly useful strategy for learning technical information (Allison and Shrigley 1986; Graesser and Person 1994). Students need instruction in how to ask higher-level questions that help them learn from informational text. *Elaborative interrogation* is a complex name for a simple questioning strategy that encourages students to generate hypotheses as a way to remember facts (Wood, Pressley, and Winne 1990). Upon encountering a new fact in text, students simply ask themselves, "Why does this fact make sense?" Asking "why" serves as a form of *interrogation* (questioning) that helps students to *elaborate* on (expand or explain) text information, thus personalizing it and making it easier to remember. Elaborative interrogation is particularly useful with concept-dense content, such as math and science texts, and it has consistently and greatly improved text recall (Pressley 2000a).

Practice using elaborative interrogation to learn facts about brain geography. As you read the excerpt, stop and ask yourself "why" questions, then try to answer them. Even if your answer isn't technically accurate, it can help you remember the information by forming connections with your world knowledge. Here is a possible "why" question and answer for the first fact: *Why does it make sense that the two sides of the brain are called hemispheres?* (Possible answer: *A sphere is a ball shape, like a circle; the prefix* hemi- *means "half." The two sides of the brain are like half-circles.*) (See Answer Key, p. 800.)

The brain is made up of two mirror-image sides, or hemispheres. Each hemisphere of the brain is divided into four lobes, or sections: frontal, parietal, temporal, and occipital. The left hemisphere of the brain is associated with speech, language processing, and reading.

Questions and tasks should require thinking about the text carefully and finding evidence in the text itself to support the response.

—COLMAN & PIMENTEL, 2012

SEE ALSO . . .

LESSON MODEL: QAR (Question-Answer Relationships), p. 702

Answering Questions

One type of question-answering instruction focuses on developing students' understanding of question-answer relationships (Raphael and Pearson 1985). The Question-Answer Relationships (QAR) framework developed by Taffy Raphael (1986) clarifies for students how they can approach the task of reading texts and answering questions. QAR is based on the idea that a three-way relationship exists among the type of question, the text to which it refers, and the reader's prior knowledge (Pearson and Johnson 1978). The vocabulary of QAR—Right There, Think and Search, On My Own, and Author and Me—provides teachers and students with a shared language for talking about these relationships and improving questioning practices (Raphael and Au 2005).

Question-Answer Relationships (QAR)

In the Text	In My Head
RIGHT THERE (literal) The answer to the question is "right there" in one sentence; the question and answer have the same wording.	ON MY OWN (inferential and evaluative) The answer to the question comes entirely from students' world knowledge.
THINK AND SEARCH (literal) The answer to the question requires searching across the text; the question and answer have different wordings.	AUTHOR AND ME (inferential) The answer to the question comes from understanding the text in conjunction with students' world knowledge.

Based on Raphael 1982, 1986.

Constructing Mental Images

Constructing mental images has proved to be an effective strategy for comprehending complex informational text. Readers can create pictures of the author's words in their minds as they read, depicting the content of the text. As the text provides new information, the readers' images also change. Gambrell and Bales (1986) found that by making mental images of informational passages, students were able to detect when information was incomplete or inconsistent, and thus were able to determine when they needed further clarification. While reading a passage aloud to students, teachers can model the thinking process involved in mental imagery. These think-aloud activities can help students to learn how to visualize independently. Here is an example:

The nervous system is a network of cells called neurons, which transmit information in the form of electrical signals.

THINK ALOUD

THINK ALOUD *I'm picturing all of these round cells smooshed together, and I'm imagining sparks coming out of the cells, moving through one cell to the next one.*

When a nerve impulse reaches the synapse at the end of a neuron, it cannot pass directly to the next one.

THINK ALOUD

THINK ALOUD *Okay, I need to change my picture because now I read that there's this synapse thing at the end and the impulse doesn't pass directly. So, now I'm picturing the cells having little tentacles at one end, which is how I'm imagining the synapse. I need to read on to get some more information for my mental picture.*

Practice modeling the strategy of constructing mental images by developing a think-aloud for each of the remaining sentences in the passage about the nervous system. Remember to adapt your mental image as new information is presented in the text. (See Answer Key, p. 800.)

Instead, it triggers the neuron to release a chemical neurotransmitter that drifts across the gap between the two neurons. On reaching the other side, it fits into a tailor-made receptor on the surface of the target neuron, like a key in a lock. This docking process converts the chemical signal back into an electrical nerve impulse.

SEE ALSO . . .

LESSON MODELS

Strategies for Summarizing, p. 711

CSR (Collaborative Strategic Reading), p. 720

SEE ALSO . . .

Informational Text Structure, p. 683

Recognizing Informational Text Structures, p. 687

Summarizing

Being aware of the explicit structure of informational text is an aid in summarizing it. There is more than one research-based approach to summarizing informational text. In the paragraph shrinking approach demonstrated by Fuchs et al. (2007), students first identify the most important information about a paragraph, or the main idea. They then shrink this information into one main-idea statement of 10 words or less. In Collaborative Strategic Reading (CSR), this process is called getting the gist (Klinger et al. 2007). In the rule-based approach developed by Brown, Campione, and Day (1981), students follow a set of rules or steps to produce a summary: (1) substitute a more general term for a list of specific terms; (2) delete redundant information, (3) delete information that is not absolutely necessary, or central, to overall meaning; and (4) select or create a topic sentence. Once students have developed summaries, or main-idea statements, for individual paragraphs, they combine them to make a final summary of the whole passage.

LESSON MODEL: CSR (Collaborative Strategic Reading), p. 720

CSR Strategies

- **Preview**
- **Click and Clunk**
- **Get the Gist**
- **Wrap Up**

Klingner et al. 2001.

Multiple-Strategy Instruction Program: CSR

Instruction in multiple, coordinated reading comprehension strategies improves literacy (Biancarosa and Snow 2006). Collaborative Strategic Reading (CSR) is a research-validated program in which students learn to use comprehension strategies that support their understanding of informational text (Klingner et al. 2001). The development of CSR was influenced significantly by Reciprocal Teaching (Palincsar and Brown 1984) and Transactional Strategies Instruction (Pressley, El-Dinary et al. 1992). According to Klingner et al. (2007), CSR provides an "independent way to interact with grade-level textbooks and learn important content." CSR encourages students to self-monitor their comprehension by using a set of four comprehension strategies.

Reader Response

Even when reading factual text, readers use their existing knowledge and experiences to respond to the information and to the author's point of view or biases. Responding to informational text in personal ways allows students to deepen their learning from a reading, building further connections between the text and their own lives. Discussion-oriented instruction and writing for content-area learning are two ways to enhance reader interactions with informational text.

Discussion-Oriented Instruction

LESSON MODEL: QtA (Questioning the Author), p. 733

Directed discussion can focus students' attention on text content and ideas. The Questioning the Author (QtA) approach, developed by Isabel Beck and Margaret McKeown (2006), uses teacher-posed queries during reading to keep text discussion flowing as students build understanding of a text. Queries are designed to engage students in a way that helps them uncover the author's intent and meaning. Emphasizing the fallibility of the author, QtA teaches students to question what they read, to think, to probe, to associate, and to critique.

SEE ALSO . . .

LESSON MODEL: Book Club: Writing in Response to Literature, p. 677

Writing for Content-Area Learning

In content-area instruction, students are often expected to write about what they read. Thus, writing is a particularly important form of response to informational text. Nell Duke (2006) emphasizes the importance of having students make reading/writing connections with informational text by studying authors' writing styles,writing reviews of texts, making improvements to existing texts, and producing their own informational texts.

Engaged reading is the primary pathway toward the competencies and expertise needed for achievement.

—GUTHRIE, 2005–6

Motivation and Engagement with Reading

Engaged readers are strongly motivated to learn from what they are reading—taking satisfaction in successful reading, believing in their reading skills, and persisting in the face of difficulty. They are knowledge-driven, gaining conceptual understanding of science through reading. They are socially interactive, interacting with other students to learn. They are strategic, possessing a variety of cognitive comprehension strategies for learning from texts (Guthrie 2005–6). When students are engaged with text, they are also more likely to use a variety of effortful strategies to gain understanding (Guthrie et al. 2004).

SEE ALSO . . .

LESSON MODEL: CORI (Concept-Oriented Reading Instruction), p. 739

Concept-Oriented Reading Instruction (CORI), developed by John Guthrie and his colleagues (Guthrie et al. 1998), integrates literacy instruction with content-area instruction, particularly in science or social studies. CORI is one of the few approaches in which understanding the content and learning the process (i.e., comprehension strategies) share equal weight (Liang and Dole 2006). According to John Guthrie (2005–6), students' growth in reading comprehension is substantially influenced by their amount of engaged reading. Therefore, CORI's primary aim is to increase students' reading engagement. McPeake and Guthrie (2007) have identified the five instructional practices that enhance motivation for and engagement with reading. These motivational practices are relevance, choice, collaboration, success, and conceptual theme.

Engaged Readers

- **Motivated**
- **Knowledge-driven**
- **Socially interactive**
- **Strategic**

McPeake and Guthrie 2007.

Challenges of Web-Based Text
• seeing less of the text at once
• having little control over the timing or speed of text presentation
• navigating hyperlinks, scrolling, accessing files, computer skills
• dealing with lack of linearity and clear beginning and ending
• choosing among multiple paths through a body of text
• identifying useful links
• evaluating the relevance of linked information
• being distracted by intriguing but irrelevant links
• integrating text with multimedia
• getting a sense of the text overall
• comprehending difficult text (often several grade levels higher than intended audience)
• reading critically, judging accuracy, and assessing credibility

Alvermann and Eakle 2003; Kim and Kamil 2003; Spires and Estes 2002.

Web-Based Text

Web-based text offers both opportunities and challenges for instruction (RRSG 2002). Readers can follow links to definitions, background, or more detailed explanations to support comprehension (Kim and Kamil 2003; RRSG 2002). Research has shown that when students lack world knowledge about a topic, they often learn more easily from Web-based text than from printed text, as long as options for navigation and browsing are limited (Mayer 1997; Shin, Schallert, and Savenye 1994). Electronic text also can be more engaging than traditional text, especially for struggling readers (Alvermann and Eakle 2003). For example, O'Brien (1998, 2001) found that even adolescents identified as "at risk" of dropping out of high school were highly literate with electronic texts.

Instruction for Reading on the Web

Reading on the Web requires specialized strategy applications. The additional complexities and distractions of Web-based text create the need for further strategic support. Through explicit instruction, students can learn to adapt and transfer their strategies to meet these challenges.

Dodge (1997) developed a method for maximizing students' efficient use of the Web. This method, called WebQuest, poses an open-ended problem that students solve using Internet resources (Spires and Estes 2002). Providing key Internet links to students, the WebQuest organizes the learning task and prevents endless searching for information. Small-group collaboration provides opportunities for students to work together to construct meaning. Incorporating Web resources at varying levels of difficulty and readability gives all students a chance to participate and contribute.

Strategy Application in Web-Based Text		
Strategy	**In addition to being able to . . .**	**Web readers must . . .**
Recognizing Text Structure	identify the way text is organized	switch quickly and adeptly among various text structures
Monitoring Comprehension	be actively aware of whether text is making sense	determine the relevance of volumes of information in layers of potentially distracting links
Connecting to World Knowledge	connect previous experiences with ideas in the text	draw from previous experiences of navigating Web sites and search engines
Predicting	make informed guesses about what will come next	make predictions about the most relevant links and how to move through text to find information
Asking Questions	ask themselves questions about the text being read	condense questions into keywords that are most likely to lead to relevant links
Answering Questions	find and use information from text to answer teacher questions	identify the most promising and accessible resources for answering questions, which may include Web browsers, search engines, etc.
Constructing Mental Images	create their own mental pictures	learn to use, evaluate, and integrate the many visuals on the Web—such as video clips, photographs, clip art, and charts
Summarizing	summarize information found in a single text	synthesize information gathered from a whole Web site or several Web sites

Based on Eagleton and Dobler 2007.

http://www

why?

Informational Text

Informational literacy is central to success, and even survival, in advanced schooling, the workplace, and the community.

—DUKE, 2000b

Informational text has gained increasing importance in early reading instruction. Reading informational text serves several functions for young readers: it builds content knowledge and vocabulary; capitalizes on students' interests, curiosities, and experiences; presents opportunities for students to develop areas of expertise; prepares students for the type of texts they will read most frequently as adults; supports students in both answering and raising questions; and serves as a tool for both solving and posing problems (Duke 2004, 2006).

Students' success or failure in school is closely tied to their ability to comprehend informational text. As students progress through school, understanding informational text becomes both more essential and more challenging. Informational text increasingly becomes the source of students' new knowledge and information. The demands of learning from text also increase as text becomes more complicated in middle and high school. In addition to informational text found in books and articles, students frequently must access information via the Web and other multimedia sources. To improve their level of reading proficiency—or just to maintain it—students must become more advanced in both the range and the flexibility of their reading comprehension strategies (Duke and Pearson 2002).

Research Findings . . .

Achieving success in subject areas ranging from social studies to science requires that students be able to comprehend the texts of such subjects.

—NEUFELD, 2005

Middle- and high-school students spend most of their time in content-area classes and must learn to read expository, informational, content-area texts with greater proficiency.

—TORGESEN ET AL., 2007

Informational text can be a vehicle to gain, work through, and communicate knowledge about the . . . world, a vehicle to inspire and attract students to literacy.

—DUKE, 2000b

Suggested Reading . . .

Comprehension Instruction: Research-Based Practices, 2nd Edition (2008) edited by Cathy Collins Block & Sherri R. Paris. New York: Guilford.

Effective Instruction for Adolescent Struggling Readers (2008) by Alison Gould Boardman & Colleagues. Portsmouth, NH: RMC Research Corporation, Center on Instruction.

Improving Reading Comprehension in Kindergarten Through 3rd Grade: A Practical Guide (2010) by Timothy Shanahan, Kim Callison, Christine Carriere, Nell Duke, David Pearson, Christopher Schatschneider & Joe Torgesen. Washington, DC: U.S. Department of Education.

Teaching Reading Comprehension to Students with Learning Difficulties (2007) by Janette K. Klingner, Sharon Vaughn & Alison Boardman. New York: Guilford.

Text Complexity: Raising Rigor in Reading (2012) by Douglas Fisher, Nancy Frey & Diane Lapp. Newark, DE: International Reading Association.

What Content-Area Teachers Should Know About Adolescent Literacy (2007) by the National Institute for Literacy. Jessup, MD: National Institute for Literacy.

when? Informational Text

> Providing more experience with informational texts in the early grades may help to mitigate the substantial difficulty many students have with this form of text in later schooling.
>
> —DUKE, 2000b

When to Teach

Primary-grade students need increased instructional time with informational text (Duke 2004). Because of their natural curiosity, young children often prefer age-appropriate informational texts such as dinosaur encyclopedias and bug books (Block 2004; Duke 2006). Students who have had informational text read aloud to them are more likely to select this type of text for independent reading (Dreher and Dromsky 2000). Listening to informational text can also build knowledge, especially when combined with other ways of learning (Anderson and Guthrie 1999). After Grade 3, reading content-area informational texts becomes increasingly important in helping students expand their knowledge of science, social studies, mathematics, and other subjects (Torgesen et al. 2007). It is critical to balance and integrate explicit comprehension strategies instruction with an emphasis on the content of the text at hand.

SEE ALSO . . .

When to Assess and Intervene, p. 646

When to Assess and Intervene

No single test captures the complexity of comprehension; the best way to assess reading comprehension is with a combination of measures (RRSG 2002). Tests of reading comprehension vary according to response format, or how students demonstrate understanding of what they have read (Spear-Swerling 2006). Response formats may include cloze, Maze CBM, open-ended and multiple-choice question answering, retelling, and thinking aloud. Regardless of format, it is important that comprehension assessment texts be at students' instructional level of difficulty—at least a 90 percent rate of accuracy (Klingner et al. 2007).

Particularly for diagnostic purposes, it is necessary to assess comprehension processes as well as outcomes (RRSG 2002). For example, assessments should examine students' ability to use comprehension strategies appropriately to understand text (Lehr and Osborn 2005). When assessment reveals that students are either misusing or not using a specific strategy, the teacher can respond with instructional support. Students' own comprehension monitoring also serves as a form of self-assessment of both comprehension and strategies use (Afflerbach 2002).

SEE ALSO . . .

CORE Literacy Library

Assessing Reading: Multiple Measures, 2nd Edition

Comprehension Assessment: Response Formats	
Cloze	Students fill in blanks in a passage by choosing, from a bank of suggested words, the one word that best completes the sentence. EXAMPLE: The rooster _______ at the break of dawn.
Maze CBM	Students choose the one out of three possible words that makes the best sense in the sentence. EXAMPLE: Can you (jump, hit, sneeze) the ball to me?
Open-Ended	Students construct oral or written responses to questions about a passage.
Multiple-Choice	Students select the best response to a question about a passage.
Retelling	Students are prompted to orally retell or reconstruct what they remember about a passage.
Think Aloud	Students talk about their thinking as they read a passage, responding periodically to teacher prompts.

Based on Spear-Swerling 2006; Klingner et al. 2007; Hosp, Hosp, and Howell 2007; Lehr and Osborn 2005.

how? **Informational Text**

LESSON MODEL FOR

Question Answering

Benchmarks

- ability to answer factual, inferential, and evaluative questions
- ability to identify factual, inferential, and evaluative questions
- ability to use background knowledge to answer questions

Strategy Grade Level

- Grade 3 and above

Grouping

- whole class
- small group or pairs

Sample Text (Resources)

- "Albert Einstein Asks a Question" Complexity Level: Grades 3–4

Activity Master (Resources)

- QAR Worksheet

Materials

- PDF and copies of "Albert Einstein Asks a Question"
- PDF and copies of QAR Worksheet

QAR (Question-Answer Relationships)

According to the National Reading Panel (2000), teaching students strategies for answering questions is an important part of comprehension instruction. QAR is a research-based method and language framework developed by Taffy Raphael (1986) for enhancing students' ability to talk about and answer comprehension questions. Applicable to both literary and informational texts, QAR helps students understand that answers come from one of two main sources of information: In the Text and In My Head. These sources are further divided into four QAR categories: Right There, Think and Search, On My Own, and Author and Me. This language of QAR is introduced through analyzing the differences between questions with answer sources in the text and those with answer sources coming from students' own background knowledge or experiences (Raphael and Au 2005).

In this sample lesson model, sample text is used to represent a selection at students' independent reading level. The same model can be adapted and used to enhance comprehension instruction for literary or informational text in any commercial reading or content-area program—as long as the text is at the appropriate level.

Question-Answer Relationships (QAR)	
IN THE TEXT	**IN MY HEAD**
Right There The answer to the question is "right there" in one sentence; the question and answer have the same wording.	**On My Own** The answer to the question comes entirely from students' world knowledge.
Think and Search The answer to the question requires searching across the text; the question and answer have different wordings.	**Author and Me** The answer to the question comes from understanding the text in conjunction with students' world knowledge.

Based on Raphael 1982, 1986.

Introduce QAR

Display a Question-Answer Relationships (QAR) teaching chart, such as the example shown above. Cover the chart, except for the title and the first row. Explain to students that they can use QAR, or Question-Answer Relationships, whenever they need to answer questions about what they are reading. Point out that the QAR strategy for answering questions has its own language. Then point to the headings In the Text and In My Head. Tell students that there are two main places to find the answer to a question. Explain that one place to find an answer is in what they are reading, or In the Text. The other place to find an answer is from what they already know or have experienced, or In My Head.

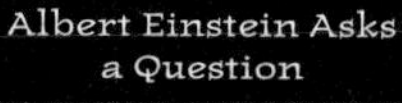

Albert Einstein Asks a Question

BY JOHN ROSS

ALBERT EINSTEIN was born in Ulm, Germany, in 1879. When he was five, he was sick in bed for a time. His father gave him a compass. "But why does the needle always point north?" asked the boy. "I don't know why," his dad confessed. Later, the young Einstein studied the subject and found out the answer. And he never stopped asking questions after that. "The most important thing is to keep asking questions," Einstein would always tell young people who wanted to become scientists.

Einstein did not do well in school. His teachers said he was slow to learn. "Albert will never amount to very much," said the principal. But Einstein's mind wasn't slow. It was really working much faster than the school principal could ever have imagined. He wanted to know how everything worked. He thought a lot about space and time. He thought a lot about energy. He thought about atoms and how all the energy inside them could explode outward. He thought about how light travels in waves. He wondered what would happen to a person if he or she traveled at the speed of light, and he guessed that person would never grow old.

Einstein's scientific theories forever changed our understanding of the world. He called his ideas "theories" or "thought experiments." He tested his experiments by making pictures in his mind and using his imagination like a laboratory. These thought experiments were so hard to explain that sometimes only a few people in the whole world could understand what Einstein was thinking. Einstein's most famous theory

TEACHING READING SOURCEBOOK • SAMPLE TEXT 753

Use interactive whiteboard technology to display the first page of "Albert Einstein Asks a Question." Read aloud the first paragraph. Then ask: *When Einstein was sick, what did his father give him?* (a compass) Ask: *How did you know the answer to this question?* (Possible response: *It was in what I read, or In the Text.*) Ask: *Why would you give a gift to someone who was sick?* (Possible response: *To make the person feel better.*) Ask: *How did you know the answer to this question?* (Possible response: *It came from my experience, or In My Head.*) Tell students that they have just uncovered the two main places to look for answers to questions: In the Text or In My Head.

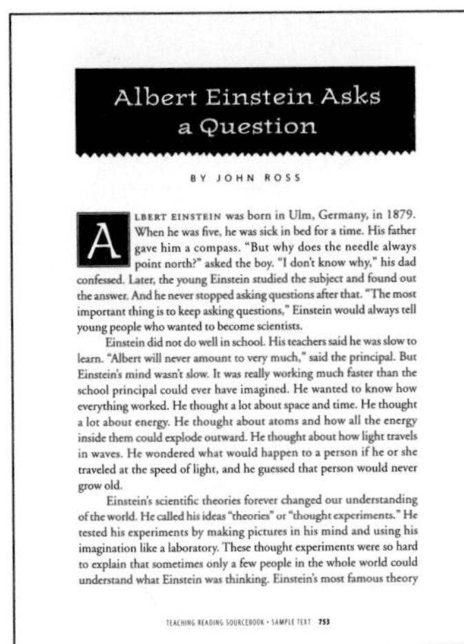

Albert Einstein Asks a Question

BY JOHN ROSS

ALBERT EINSTEIN was born in Ulm, Germany, in 1879. When he was five, he was sick in bed for a time. His father gave him a compass. "But why does the needle always point north?" asked the boy. "I don't know why," his dad confessed. Later, the young Einstein studied the subject and found out the answer. And he never stopped asking questions after that. "The most important thing is to keep asking questions," Einstein would always tell young people who wanted to become scientists.

Einstein did not do well in school. His teachers said he was slow to learn. "Albert will never amount to very much," said the principal. But Einstein's mind wasn't slow. It was really working much faster than the school principal could ever have imagined. He wanted to know how everything worked. He thought a lot about space and time. He thought a lot about energy. He thought about atoms and how all the energy inside them could explode outward. He thought about how light travels in waves. He wondered what would happen to a person if he or she traveled at the speed of light, and he guessed that person would never grow old.

Einstein's scientific theories forever changed our understanding of the world. He called his ideas "theories" or "thought experiments." He tested his experiments by making pictures in his mind and using his imagination like a laboratory. These thought experiments were so hard to explain that sometimes only a few people in the whole world could understand what Einstein was thinking. Einstein's most famous theory

TEACHING READING SOURCEBOOK • SAMPLE TEXT 753

Teach/Model

When students have a clear picture of the differences between the two main QAR categories, In the Text and In My Head, present the subcategories. First introduce In the Text QARs: Right There and Think and Search. Then introduce In My Head QARs: On My Own and Author and Me.

In the Text QARs

Continue displaying the first page of "Albert Einstein Asks a Question" and the Question-Answer Relationships (QAR) teaching chart. Uncover the left side of the teaching chart, revealing the two categories of In the Text QARs. Explain to students that there are two different types of In the Text QARs, Right There and Think and Search.

IN THE TEXT

- Right There
- Think and Search

Read aloud the first two paragraphs of the sample text. Then print the following pair of questions on the board: *What did Einstein tell young people who wanted to become scientists? What topics did Albert like to think about?* Tell students that you are going to model how to use QAR to find the answers to these In the Text questions.

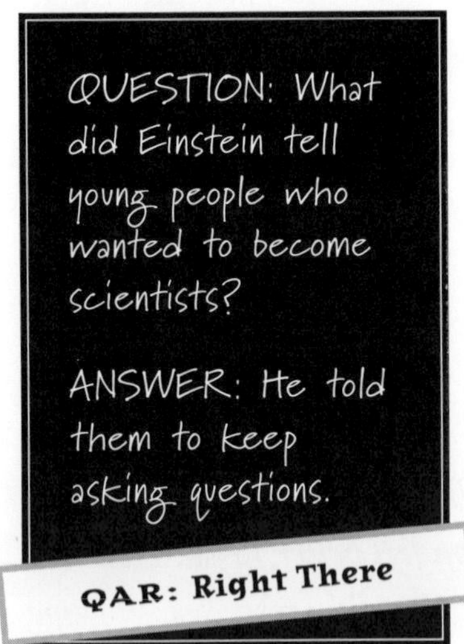

Ask the first question: *What did Einstein tell young people who wanted to become scientists?* Say: *The answer to this question is in the text. First, I'm going to look for words in the text that match the words in the question.* Circle the words *tell young people* and *scientists.* Say: *Now I'm going to scan the same sentence these words appear in to see if I can find the answer.* Circle the words *keep asking questions.* Say: *This is the answer to the question. Einstein told young people who wanted to be scientists to keep asking questions.* On the board, print the answer below the question. Say: *This is a Right There QAR. The words from the question and words that answer the question are right there, all in one sentence. The answer is easy to find.* Below the answer, print the QAR, Right There.

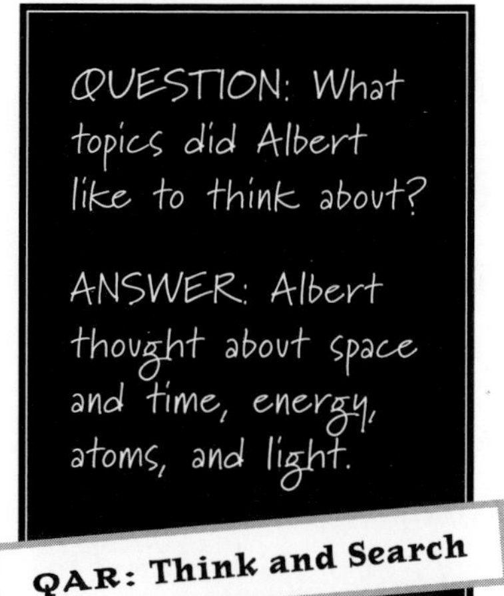
QUESTION: What topics did Albert like to think about?
ANSWER: Albert thought about space and time, energy, atoms, and light.
QAR: Think and Search

Now ask the second question: *What topics did Albert think about a lot?* Say: *The answer to this question is also in the text, but I may have to look a little harder. First, I'm going to look for words in the text that match the words in the question. In the second paragraph, the word* thought *is repeated four times.* Circle the word *thought* each time it appears. Say: *Now I'm going to reread the four sentences. Maybe I'll find the topics that Albert thought about. Yes, here they are.* Circle the words *space and time, energy, atoms,* and *light.* Say: *The answer is Albert thought about space and time, energy, atoms, and light.* On the board, print the answer below the question. Say: *This is a Think and Search QAR. To answer this question I had to search for information in different parts of the text, think about the information I found, and then combine the information into one answer. The answer was in the text but not all in one place. I had to think and search.* Below the answer, print the QAR, Think and Search.

Have students use the pair of questions and answers to compare the two categories of In the Text QARs. Ask: *How were the two questions the same?* (They were both In the Text answers.) Ask: *How were they different?* (The first answer was found in one place, in one sentence. The second answer was found in more than one place, in four different sentences of the paragraph.)

In My Head QARs

In My Head

- On My Own
- Author and Me

Continue displaying the first page of "Albert Einstein Asks a Question" and the Question-Answer Relationships (QAR) teaching chart. Now uncover the rest of the teaching chart, revealing the two categories of In My Head QARs. Explain to students that there are also two different types of In My Head QARs, On My Own and Author and Me.

If necessary, ask students to reread silently the first two paragraphs of the sample text. Then print the following pair of questions on the board: *Have you ever misjudged someone's ability? Tell about it. How did the gift of the compass change Einstein's*

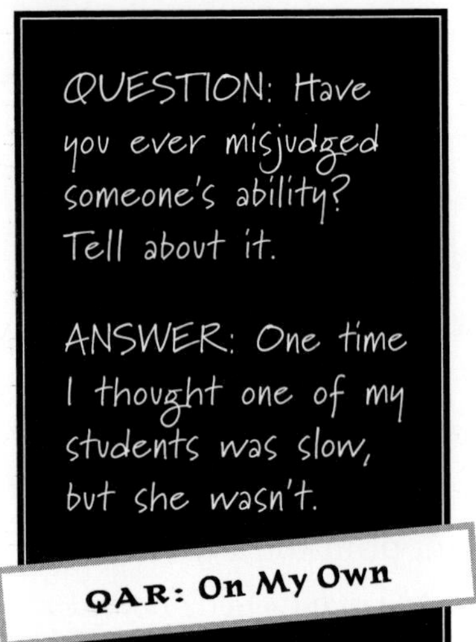
QUESTION: Have you ever misjudged someone's ability? Tell about it.
ANSWER: One time I thought one of my students was slow, but she wasn't.
QAR: On My Own

life? Tell students that you are going to model how to use QAR to find the answers to these two In My Head questions.

Ask the first question: *Have you ever misjudged someone's ability? Tell about it.* Say: *This is a question I can answer on my own without ever reading the text. The answer is found In My Head. It is completely based on what I remember from my own experience as a teacher. I remember one time I had a student who never seemed to be paying attention. Foolishly, I assumed she was slow. One day, I noticed that she was a talented artist. I had misjudged her.* On the board, print the answer below the question. Say: *So, I found the answer to this question in my head from my own experience, without needing any information from the text. I answered it on my own.* Below the answer, print the QAR, On My Own.

QUESTION: How did the gift of the compass change Einstein's life?

ANSWER: It caused him to ask a question and then search for its answer. It led him to become interested in science.

QAR: Author and Me

Ask the second question: *How did the gift of the compass change Einstein's life?* Say: *Well, I could answer the first question based entirely on my experience, but to answer this one I need to have read the text. First, I will look for words in the text that match the words in the question.* In the first paragraph, circle the word *compass.* Say: *Oh, right here it says that Einstein asked a question about the compass and then studied the subject and found out the answer. I remember that Einstein told young people who wanted to become scientists that they should keep asking questions. I know that looking for the answers to questions is part of the scientific method. So I'm going to combine what I already know about science with something the author says in the text to come up with the answer. I think the gift of the compass caused Einstein to ask a question and then search for its answer, which may have led him to become interested in science.* On the board, print the answer below the question. Say: *I couldn't have answered this question without reading the text, but, on the other hand, the author didn't provide all of the information I needed. My answer came from both the author and me.* Below the answer, print the QAR, Author and Me.

Albert Einstein Asks a Question

BY JOHN ROSS

LBERT EINSTEIN was born in Ulm, Germany, in 1879. When he was five, he was sick in bed for a time. His father gave him a compass. "But why does the needle always point north?" asked the boy. "I don't know why," his dad confessed. Later, the young Einstein studied the subject and found out the answer. And he never stopped asking questions after that. "The most important thing is to keep asking questions," Einstein would always tell young people who wanted to become scientists.

Einstein did not do well in school. His teachers said he was slow to learn. "Albert will never amount to very much," said the principal. But Einstein's mind wasn't slow. It was really working much faster than the school principal could ever have imagined. He wanted to know how everything worked. He thought a lot about space and time. He thought a lot about energy. He thought about atoms and how all the energy inside them could explode outward. He thought about how light travels in waves. He wondered what would happen to a person if he or she traveled at the speed of light, and he guessed that person would never grow old.

Einstein's scientific theories forever changed our understanding of the world. He called his ideas "theories" or "thought experiments." He tested his experiments by making pictures in his mind and using his imagination like a laboratory. These thought experiments were so hard to explain that sometimes only a few people in the whole world could understand what Einstein was thinking. Einstein's most famous theory

TEACHING READING SOURCEBOOK • SAMPLE TEXT 753

is the theory of relativity. This is how he explained the theory of relativity: "If you sit with a pretty girl for an hour, it seems like only a minute. But if you sit on a hot stove for a minute, it seems like an hour. That's relativity."

In 1933, Albert Einstein fled Germany and went to the United States. From then until his death in 1955, he taught at Princeton University in New Jersey. There, he enjoyed sailing, playing the violin, putting together jigsaw puzzles, and building houses from playing cards. Einstein rode his bicycle everywhere; he thought driving was way too complicated.

When Einstein wanted to think, he often went for a walk. He usually wore a long overcoat and a black hat on top of his wild white hair (which was always uncombed). He would bring a notepad with him, to take notes on his "thought experiments." Sometimes he would get so lost in his own thoughts that he would get lost for real. Einstein would have to ask neighbors for directions home.

When this famous scientist died at the age of 76, he left his brain to science. Scientists wanted to see if it was different from the average human brain. Nothing unusual turned up—until quite recently. In June 1999, a research team from Canada announced that Einstein's brain is fifteen percent wider than normal in one particular area. This area seems to have something to do with mathematical thinking. Maybe having a wider area *caused* Einstein to be a math genius. Maybe having a wider area is the *result* of Einstein's being a math genius. Or maybe this larger area doesn't mean either of these things. Hmmm. Maybe it has to do with asking all those questions.

TEACHING READING SOURCEBOOK • ALBERT EINSTEIN ASKS A QUESTION 754

Guided Practice

Print four questions, such as the ones shown on the following page, on the QAR Worksheet. Use interactive whiteboard technology to display the worksheet. Distribute copies of "Albert Einstein Asks a Question." Read aloud paragraphs 3 and 4 of the selection as students follow along.

1 Read aloud the first question: *What is Einstein's most famous theory?* Ask: *Where do you think you will find the answer to this question, in the text or in your head?* (in the text) Say: *Yes, this sounds like information that will be in the text. Now you need to see if the answer is right there or if you will need to think and search.* Ask: *Are there any words in the text that match the words in the question?* (yes, *famous theory*) Have students circle the words on their copies of the selection. Ask: *Can you find the answer to the question in the same sentence?* (yes) Ask: *So, what category of QAR is this?* (Right There) On the worksheet, print the QAR in the corresponding space. Ask: *What is the answer?* (Einstein's most famous theory is the theory of relativity.) On the worksheet, print the answer in the corresponding space. Ask: *How do you know that it was his most famous theory?* (It says so in the text; the answer is right there in one sentence.) Say: *The answer to this question is right there. You found all the information you needed in one sentence.*

2 Read aloud the second question: *What types of experiments do scientists do?* Ask: *Where do you think you will find the answer to this question, in the text or in your head?* (in my head) Say: *Yes, it sounds like information you may already know.* Ask: *Will you also need information from the text, or can you answer the question on your own?* (on my own) Say: *Yes, this is a question you can answer on your own without ever reading the text.* Ask: *So, what category of QAR is this?* (On My Own) On the worksheet, print the QAR. Say: *Yes, the answer to this question is based entirely on your own background knowledge.* Ask: *Now that you know this is*

QAR (Question-Answer Relationships) Worksheet

Title: Albert Einstein Asks a Question Pages/(Paragraphs): 3 and 4

Question	Answer	QAR
1 What is Einstein's most famous theory?	His most famous theory is the theory of relativity.	Right There
2 What types of experiments do scientists do?	Scientists do experiments by mixing things in test tubes, then keeping track of what happens.	On My Own
3 Based on Einstein's simple description of relativity, can you provide a similar example of relativity in your life?	When I play a video game, an hour seems like a minute. But when I have to stay after school, a minute seems like an hour.	Author and Me
4 How did Einstein travel around Princeton, New Jersey?	Einstein rode around on his bike.	Think and Search

an On My Own QAR, what answer would you give for this question? (Possible response: *Scientists do experiments by mixing things in test tubes, then keeping track of what happens.*) On the worksheet, record the answer.

3 Read aloud the third question: *Based on Einstein's simple description of relativity, can you provide a similar example of relativity in your life?* Ask: *Where do you think you will find the answer to this question, in the text or in your head?* (Possible response: *Both. I need an example from my life—that's from me, but first I need to understand Einstein's description of relativity—that's from the author.*) Ask: *So, what category of QAR do you think this is?* (Author and Me) On the worksheet, print the QAR. Say: *Great, so you know that before you can connect your experiences you will need to find some information from the text.* Ask: *Are there any*

Guidelines for Effective Questioning

- **Use clear phrasing.**
- **Avoid multiple-part questions.**
- **Allow greater response time before you comment.**
- **Listen carefully to students' responses.**
- **Provide tactful modeling of correct grammar.**
- **Encourage students to elaborate.**
- **Create a supportive atmosphere.**

words in the text that match the words in the question? (relativity) Have students circle the word on their copies of the selection. Say: *So, now you can answer this question by seeing how the author explains Einstein's theory of relativity and then connecting it with your own experience.* Ask: *Who can answer this question?* (Possible response: *When I play a video game, an hour seems like a minute. But when I have to stay after school, a minute seems like an hour.*) On the worksheet, record the answer. Say: *Figuring out that this was an Author and Me QAR helped you know where to find the information you needed to answer the question—you needed some information from the text and some from your own experiences.*

4 Read aloud the fourth question: *How did Einstein travel around Princeton, New Jersey?* Ask: *Where do you think you will find the answer to this question, in the text or in your head?* (in the text) Say: *Now you need to see if the answer is right there or if you will need to think and search.* Ask: *Are there any words in the text that match the words in the question?* (Princeton, New Jersey) Have students circle the words. Ask: *Is the answer to the question in the same place?* (no) Say: *Right, to answer this question you have to look for information in different parts of the text, and then combine the information into one answer.* Ask: *So what category of QAR is this?* (Think and Search) On the worksheet, print the QAR. Say: *So now you know you will have to search across parts of the text to find the answer. When you think you've found the answer, circle the words.* Ask: *Who can answer this question?* (Einstein rode around on his bike.) On the worksheet, record the answer. Ask: *Where did you find the answer?* (In the last sentence of the same paragraph it says that Einstein rode his bike.) Say: *Figuring out that this was a Think and Search QAR helped you know where you needed to look to find the answer. To answer this question, you needed to combine information from different parts of the paragraph.*

Collaborative Practice

Print the questions shown below on a copy of the QAR Worksheet. Then make copies of the worksheet and give them to students. Have pairs of students read paragraphs 5 and 6 of the selection. Ask students to work together to fill in the worksheet. Have them identify the QARs and the answers. Support students as needed. If necessary, help them locate text information to support their answers or articulate information from their experiences. When the worksheets are completed, call on pairs of students to share and explain their QARs and answers.

QAR (Question-Answer Relationships) Worksheet Q A R

Title: Albert Einstein Asks a Question Pages/(Paragraphs): 5 and 6

Question	Answer	QAR
What does it mean to be a genius?	Being a genius means you are way smarter than most people. Being a genius means you know a lot about a specific area or topic.	On My Own
Why did Einstein carry a notepad when he went for a walk?	To take notes on his thought experiments.	Right There
What did scientists discover about the area of Einstein's brain that has to do with mathematical thinking?	The area of Einstein's brain that has to do with mathematical thinking is 15% wider than normal.	Think and Search
Which explanation about Einstein's brain makes the most sense to you, and why?	• I think the mathematical part of Einstein's brain became larger because he used it so much—like exercise for the brain. The text shows that he did a lot of thinking. • I think Einstein was a math genius because that part of his brain was already larger. The text shows he was already a scientific thinker at age five.	Author and Me

LESSON MODEL FOR

Summarizing

Benchmarks

- ability to identify the main idea of a paragraph
- ability to summarize a series of paragraphs

Strategy Grade Level

- Paragraph Shrinking Grades 2 and above
- Rule-Based Summary Strategy Grades 4 and above

Grouping

- whole class
- small group or pairs
- individual

Prerequisite

- knowing how to identify a topic sentence

Sample Text (Resources)

- "The Greenhouse Effect" Complexity Level: Grades 6–8

Materials

- copies of "The Greenhouse Effect"

Strategies for Summarizing

Summarizing involves sifting through information, identifying what is important, and then synthesizing and restating that information. Research emphasizes the importance of breaking down the process of summarizing into a structure that students can easily understand (Marzano et al. 2001). This sample lesson model demonstrates two approaches to summarizing: paragraph shrinking and rule based. Developed by Fuchs et al. (2007), paragraph shrinking is primarily a technique for generating a main-idea statement, or summary, of an individual paragraph. In the rule-based strategy developed by Brown, Campione, and Day (1981), students follow a set of rules or steps that produce a summary. In this lesson model, sample text is used to represent a passage at students' independent reading level. The same model can be adapted and used to enhance summarization instruction for literary or informational text in any commercial reading or content-area program—as long as the text is at the appropriate level.

PARAGRAPH SHRINKING

Direct Explanation

Explain to students that to make a summary, readers first identify what is important and then synthesize and restate that information in their own words. Tell them that today they will learn to shrink the information in a paragraph into a main-idea statement. Then they will learn how to synthesize the individual main-idea statements into a summary. Display the Steps of Paragraph Shrinking, such as the example shown on the following page. Explain to students that paragraph shrinking has three steps and then read them aloud. Point out that paragraph shrinking will help them to figure out the most important ideas in what they are reading.

STEPS OF PARAGRAPH SHRINKING

1. Identify **who or what** (person, animal, place, or thing) a paragraph is mostly about.
2. Identify the **most important information** about the who or what.
3. **Shrink** all the information into one **main-idea statement** of 10 words or less.

Based on Fuchs et al. 2007.

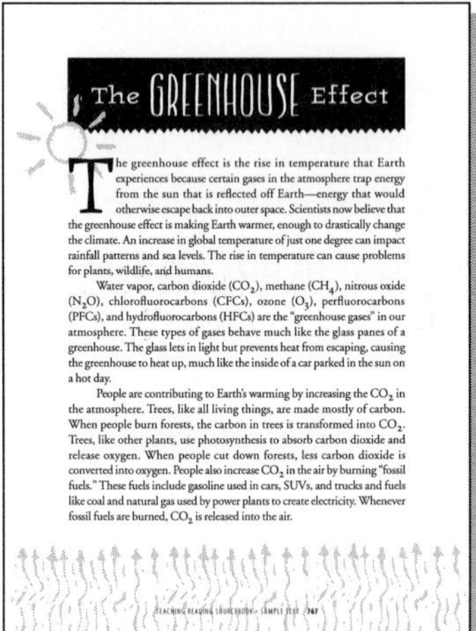

The GREENHOUSE Effect

The greenhouse effect is the rise in temperature that Earth experiences because certain gases in the atmosphere trap energy from the sun that is reflected off Earth—energy that would otherwise escape back into outer space. Scientists now believe that the greenhouse effect is making Earth warmer, enough to drastically change the climate. An increase in global temperature of just one degree can impact rainfall patterns and sea levels. The rise in temperature can cause problems for plants, wildlife, and humans.

Water vapor, carbon dioxide (CO_2), methane (CH_4), nitrous oxide (N_2O), chlorofluorocarbons (CFCs), ozone (O_3), perfluorocarbons (PFCs), and hydrofluorocarbons (HFCs) are the "greenhouse gases" in our atmosphere. These types of gases behave much like the glass panes of a greenhouse. The glass lets in light but prevents heat from escaping, causing the greenhouse to heat up, much like the inside of a car parked in the sun on a hot day.

People are contributing to Earth's warming by increasing the CO_2 in the atmosphere. Trees, like all living things, are made mostly of carbon. When people burn forests, the carbon in trees is transformed into CO_2. Trees, like other plants, use photosynthesis to absorb carbon dioxide and release oxygen. When people cut down forests, less carbon dioxide is converted into oxygen. People also increase CO_2 in the air by burning "fossil fuels." These fuels include gasoline used in cars, SUVs, and trucks and fuels like coal and natural gas used by power plants to create electricity. Whenever fossil fuels are burned, CO_2 is released into the air.

TEACHING READING SOURCEBOOK • SAMPLE TEXT 767

Teach/Model

Distribute copies of "The Greenhouse Effect." Then read the first paragraph aloud as students follow along. Referring to the chart, tell students that you are going to model how to use the steps of paragraph shrinking.

Paragraph 1

The greenhouse effect is the rise in temperature that Earth experiences because certain gases in the atmosphere trap energy from the sun that is reflected off Earth—energy that would otherwise escape back into outer space. Scientists now believe that the greenhouse effect is making Earth warmer, enough to drastically change the climate. An increase in global temperature of just one degree can impact rainfall patterns and sea levels. The rise in temperature can cause problems for plants, wildlife, and humans.

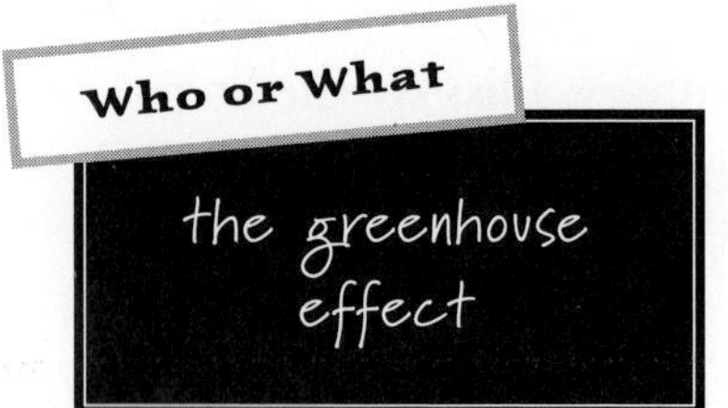

Say: *First I'll identify who or what the paragraph is mostly about. The main, or most important, who or what is always a person, animal, place, or thing. There can be more than one who and what in a paragraph, but only one is the most important. The main who or what in this paragraph is* the greenhouse effect—*a thing.* Print the who or what on the board.

Most Important Information

It is making Earth warmer and changing the climate, which could cause problems for living things.

Say: *Now that I've identified* the greenhouse effect *as the most important who or what, I need to identify the most important information about it. I think the most important information about the greenhouse effect is that it's making Earth warmer and changing the climate, which could cause problems for living things.* Print the most important information about the who or what on the board.

Shrink

The greenhouse effect is making Earth warmer and changing the climate, ~~which could cause problems for living things.~~

Ask: *What's the first step in paragraph shrinking?* (identifying who or what a paragraph is mostly about) Ask: *What's the second step in paragraph shrinking?* (identifying the most important information about the who or what) Say: *The next step is shrinking that information into a really good main-idea statement. When you make a main-idea statement, the fewer words, the better. Good main-idea statements have 10 words or less.*

Say: *Here is my main-idea statement for this paragraph: The greenhouse effect is making Earth warmer and changing the climate, which could cause problems for living things.* Print the main-idea statement on the board.

Main-Idea Statement

The greenhouse effect is making Earth warmer and changing the climate.

Say: *Now I'll count the words in my statement to see if I have less than 10. The main who or what counts as only 1 word. That leaves 9 words to say the most important thing about the who or what. In this case, the main who or what is* the greenhouse effect. Count the words. Say: *Oh, I have 16 words in my statement. That's too many. I have to shrink it. I'll try deleting the last part of the sentence.* On the board, cross out the last part of the sentence. Then count the words again. Say: *Now I have 9 words. The greenhouse effect is making Earth warmer and changing the climate.*

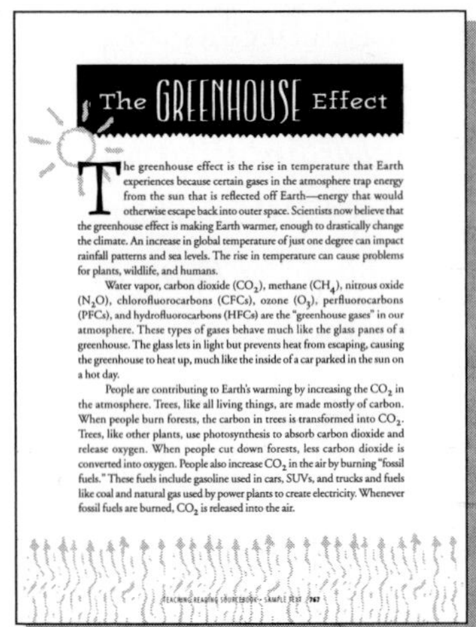

The GREENHOUSE Effect

The greenhouse effect is the rise in temperature that Earth experiences because certain gases in the atmosphere trap energy from the sun that is reflected off Earth—energy that would otherwise escape back into outer space. Scientists now believe that the greenhouse effect is making Earth warmer, enough to drastically change the climate. An increase in global temperature of just one degree can impact rainfall patterns and sea levels. The rise in temperature can cause problems for plants, wildlife, and humans.

Water vapor, carbon dioxide (CO_2), methane (CH_4), nitrous oxide (N_2O), chlorofluorocarbons (CFCs), ozone (O_3), perfluorocarbons (PFCs), and hydrofluorocarbons (HFCs) are the "greenhouse gases" in our atmosphere. These types of gases behave much like the glass panes of a greenhouse. The glass lets in light but prevents heat from escaping, causing the greenhouse to heat up, much like the inside of a car parked in the sun on a hot day.

People are contributing to Earth's warming by increasing the CO_2 in the atmosphere. Trees, like all living things, are made mostly of carbon. When people burn forests, the carbon in trees is transformed into CO_2. Trees, like other plants, use photosynthesis to absorb carbon dioxide and release oxygen. When people cut down forests, less carbon dioxide is converted into oxygen. People also increase CO_2 in the air by burning "fossil fuels." These fuels include gasoline used in cars, SUVs, and trucks and fuels like coal and natural gas used by power plants to create electricity. Whenever fossil fuels are burned, CO_2 is released into the air.

TEACHING READING SOURCEBOOK • SAMPLE TEXT 767

Follow the same procedure with the next two paragraphs, guiding students as they follow the steps of paragraph shrinking.

PARAGRAPH 2

- **Who or what:** greenhouse gases
- **Most important information about the who or what:** They behave like the glass panes in a greenhouse and prevent heat from escaping Earth's atmosphere.
- **Main-idea statement:** Greenhouse gases prevent heat from escaping Earth's atmosphere.

PARAGRAPH 3

- **Who or what:** people
- **Most important information about the who or what:** They are contributing to the greenhouse effect by increasing the carbon dioxide in the atmosphere by destroying forests and burning fossil fuels.
- **Main-idea statement:** People are contributing to the greenhouse effect.

For more practice in paragraph shrinking, see CSR (Collaborative Strategic Reading), p. 720.

Then say: *To summarize the whole passage, let's combine our three main-idea statements.* Print the final summary on the board and ask a volunteer to read it aloud.

The greenhouse effect is making Earth warmer and changing the climate. Greenhouse gases prevent heat from escaping Earth's atmosphere. People are contributing to the greenhouse effect.

RULE-BASED SUMMARY STRATEGY
• Substitute a more general term for a list of specific terms.
• Delete redundant information.
• Delete information that is not absolutely necessary, or central, to overall meaning.
• Select or create a topic sentence.

Based on Brown and Day 1983.

RULE-BASED SUMMARY STRATEGY

Direct Explanation

Explain to students that to summarize effectively, readers have to delete, substitute, or rephrase information. Tell students that you are going to show them how to use the rule-based strategy for summarizing, a set of rules they can follow to produce a summary. Display a Rule-Based Summary Strategy teaching chart, such as the example shown above. Then read aloud and explain each rule. Say: *The first rule is to substitute a more general term for a list of specific terms. A general term is a term whose meaning encompasses the meaning of other more specific terms; for example,* tree *for* pine, oak, *and* maple. *The second rule is to delete redundant information. A redundant phrase or word has the same meaning as a phrase or word used elsewhere in the passage. The third rule is to delete information that is not absolutely necessary, or central, to overall meaning of the passage. For example, in a passage about airplane travel today, information about how people used to travel could be interesting but not necessary to overall meaning. The last rule is to select or create a topic sentence. A topic sentence should contain the main idea. Sometimes the main idea is explicitly stated, and other times it is not.*

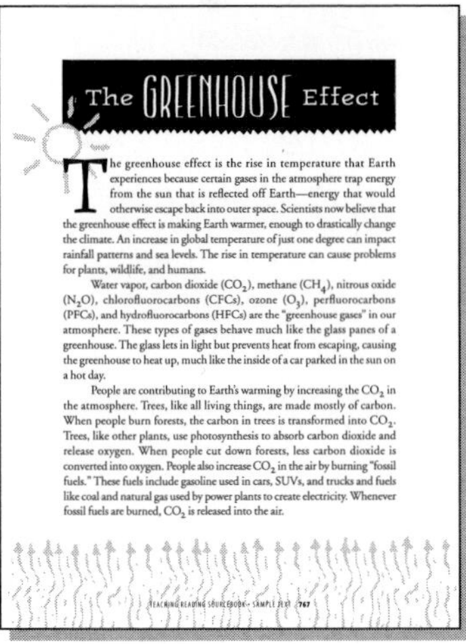

The GREENHOUSE Effect

The greenhouse effect is the rise in temperature that Earth experiences because certain gases in the atmosphere trap energy from the sun that is reflected off Earth—energy that would otherwise escape back into outer space. Scientists now believe that the greenhouse effect is making Earth warmer, enough to drastically change the climate. An increase in global temperature of just one degree can impact rainfall patterns and sea levels. The rise in temperature can cause problems for plants, wildlife, and humans.

Water vapor, carbon dioxide (CO_2), methane (CH_4), nitrous oxide (N_2O), chlorofluorocarbons (CFCs), ozone (O_3), perfluorocarbons (PFCs), and hydrofluorocarbons (HFCs) are the "greenhouse gases" in our atmosphere. These types of gases behave much like the glass panes of a greenhouse. The glass lets in light but prevents heat from escaping, causing the greenhouse to heat up, much like the inside of a car parked in the sun on a hot day.

People are contributing to Earth's warming by increasing the CO_2 in the atmosphere. Trees, like all living things, are made mostly of carbon. When people burn forests, the carbon in trees is transformed into CO_2. Trees, like other plants, use photosynthesis to absorb carbon dioxide and release oxygen. When people cut down forests, less carbon dioxide is converted into oxygen. People also increase CO_2 in the air by burning "fossil fuels." These fuels include gasoline used in cars, SUVs, and trucks and fuels like coal and natural gas used by power plants to create electricity. Whenever fossil fuels are burned, CO_2 is released into the air.

TEACHING READING SOURCEBOOK • SAMPLE TEXT 767

Teach/Model

Referring to the Rule-Based Summary Strategy chart, tell students that you are going to model how to apply the rules. Explain that you will first create a summary of each paragraph in the passage and then construct a summary of the whole passage by combining the individual summaries. Distribute copies of "The Greenhouse Effect." Read the first paragraph aloud as students follow along.

Paragraph 1

The greenhouse effect is the rise in temperature that Earth experiences because certain gases in the atmosphere trap energy from the sun that is reflected off Earth—energy that would otherwise escape back into outer space. Scientists now believe that the greenhouse effect is making Earth warmer, enough to drastically change the climate. An increase in global temperature of just one degree can impact rainfall patterns and sea levels. The rise in temperature can cause problems for plants, wildlife, and humans.

Paragraph 1 Summary

The greenhouse effect is the rise in temperature that Earth experiences because certain gases in the atmosphere trap energy from the sun that is reflected off Earth. Scientists believe the greenhouse effect is changing the climate, which can cause problems for all living things.

THINK ALOUD *First, I'll skim the paragraph for lists of specific terms. I see a list of terms in the last sentence:* plants, wildlife, and humans. *I think I can substitute a more general term for this list. How about the term* all living things? *Now I'll apply the second rule by looking for redundant, or repeated, information. I notice a few phrases that mean almost the same thing:* rise in temperature, making Earth warmer, increase in global temperature. *The phrases all describe the greenhouse effect, so I'll use that term. To apply the third rule, I'll look to see if I can delete any information not central to overall meaning. I think I can take out the second part of the first sentence:* energy that would otherwise escape back into outer space. *Also, although the third sentence provides some interesting specific details about the greenhouse effect's impact on the climate, the information is not absolutely necessary for overall meaning. I'll keep the word* climate *and combine it with the information in the last sentence. Now that I've applied the first three rules, I need to make sure there is a topic sentence that contains an explicitly stated main idea. Well, I think what is left of the first sentence makes a good topic sentence.*

Read the second paragraph aloud as students follow along.

Paragraph 2

Water vapor, carbon dioxide (CO_2), methane (CH_4), nitrous oxide (N_2O), chlorofluorocarbons (CFCs), ozone (O_3), perfluorocarbons (PFCs), and hydrofluorocarbons (HFCs) are the "greenhouse gases" in our atmosphere. These types of gases behave much like the glass panes of a greenhouse. The glass lets in light but prevents heat from escaping, causing the greenhouse to heat up, much like the inside of a car parked in the sun on a hot day.

Paragraph 2 Summary

Greenhouse gases prevent heat from escaping, like the glass panes in a greenhouse.

THINK ALOUD *First I'll skim the paragraph for lists of specific terms. Right away, I see a long list of the names of individual greenhouse gases. I'm going to substitute the general term* greenhouse gases *for the list. I see that* types of gases *and* greenhouse gases *mean the same thing. The information is redundant. I'm going to keep the term* greenhouse gases. *Now, the two analogies about the glass panes in a greenhouse and the parked car are helpful but not necessary to overall meaning. I need only know that greenhouse gases prevent heat from escaping. Now that I've applied the first three rules, I'll select a topic sentence containing the main idea. In the second sentence, if I replace* these types of gases *with* greenhouse gases, *it'll be a good topic sentence.*

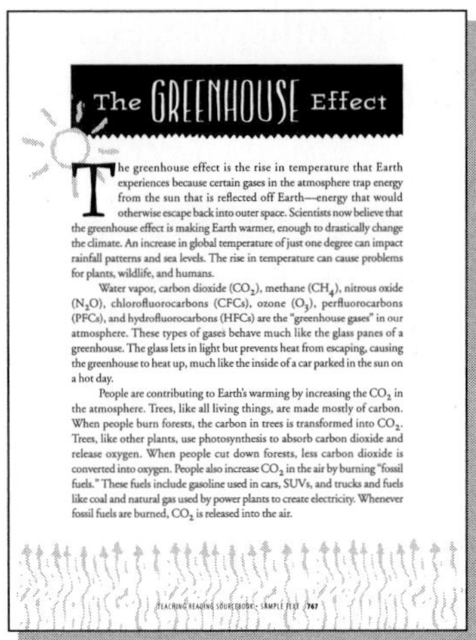
The GREENHOUSE Effect

The greenhouse effect is the rise in temperature that Earth experiences because certain gases in the atmosphere trap energy from the sun that is reflected off Earth—energy that would otherwise escape back into outer space. Scientists now believe that the greenhouse effect is making Earth warmer, enough to drastically change the climate. An increase in global temperature of just one degree can impact rainfall patterns and sea levels. The rise in temperature can cause problems for plants, wildlife, and humans.

Water vapor, carbon dioxide (CO_2), methane (CH_4), nitrous oxide (N_2O), chlorofluorocarbons (CFCs), ozone (O_3), perfluorocarbons (PFCs), and hydrofluorocarbons (HFCs) are the "greenhouse gases" in our atmosphere. These types of gases behave much like the glass panes of a greenhouse. The glass lets in light but prevents heat from escaping, causing the greenhouse to heat up, much like the inside of a car parked in the sun on a hot day.

People are contributing to Earth's warming by increasing the CO_2 in the atmosphere. Trees, like all living things, are made mostly of carbon. When people burn forests, the carbon in trees is transformed into CO_2. Trees, like other plants, use photosynthesis to absorb carbon dioxide and release oxygen. When people cut down forests, less carbon dioxide is converted into oxygen. People also increase CO_2 in the air by burning "fossil fuels." These fuels include gasoline used in cars, SUVs, and trucks and fuels like coal and natural gas used by power plants to create electricity. Whenever fossil fuels are burned, CO_2 is released into the air.

TEACHING READING SOURCEBOOK • SAMPLE TEXT 767

Guided Practice

Ask a volunteer to name the rules of summarizing. Then explain to students that they should keep the rules in mind as you guide them in summarizing the last paragraph. Then read the third paragraph aloud as students follow along.

Paragraph 3

People are contributing to Earth's warming by increasing the CO_2 in the atmosphere. Trees, like all living things, are made mostly of carbon. When people burn forests, the carbon in trees is transformed into CO_2. Trees, like other plants, use photosynthesis to absorb carbon dioxide and release oxygen. When people cut down forests, less carbon dioxide is converted into oxygen. People also increase CO_2 in the air by burning "fossil fuels." These fuels include gasoline used in cars, SUVs, and trucks and fuels like coal and natural gas used by power plants to create electricity. Whenever fossil fuels are burned, CO_2 is released into the air.

Paragraph 3 Summary

People are contributing to the greenhouse effect. They are increasing the CO_2 in the atmosphere by burning forests, cutting down trees, and burning fossil fuels.

Ask: *Is there a list of specific terms that we can replace with one more general term?* (yes, cars, SUVs, and trucks in the seventh sentence) Ask: *What general term can we replace it with?* (motor vehicles) Ask: *Is there any redundant, or repeated, information in the first sentence?* (The phrase *Earth's warming* means almost the same thing as *greenhouse effect.* We can use *greenhouse effect.*) Ask: *Any more repeated or redundant information?* (Possible responses: *The word* people *is repeated three more times.* Trees *and* all living things, trees *and* other plants, *and* forest *and* trees *mean almost the same thing.*) Ask: *From what remains, can we delete any information not necessary, or central, to overall meaning?* (Possible responses: *The second and fourth sentences give some interesting specific details about trees, but the details are not absolutely necessary for overall meaning. The same is true for the phrase* and therefore more stays in the air *in the fifth sentence and the phrase* used

by power plants to create electricity *in the seventh sentence.*) Say: *Now that we've applied the first three rules, let's select a topic sentence.* Ask: *What is the topic sentence?* (The first sentence is the topic sentence.)

Say: *Now let's put the summaries of paragraphs 1, 2, and 3 together. Let's combine the individual paragraph summaries to make a summary of the whole passage.* Ask: *Can we apply any of the rules to the passage summary?* (Possible response: *Delete the third sentence. In the first sentence, replace* certain *with* greenhouse.)

Passage Summary

The greenhouse effect is the rise in temperature that Earth experiences because ~~certain~~ greenhouse gases in the atmosphere trap the energy from the sun that is reflected off Earth. Scientists believe the greenhouse effect is changing the climate, which can cause problems for all living things. ~~Greenhouse gases prevent heat from escaping, like the glass panes in a greenhouse.~~ People are contributing to the greenhouse effect. They are increasing the CO_2 in the atmosphere by burning forests, cutting down trees, and burning fossil fuels.

LESSON MODEL FOR

Multiple-Strategy Instruction

Benchmark

- ability to coordinate a repertoire of strategies to guide comprehension

Strategy Grade Level

- Grade 3 and above

Prerequisites

- Introducing The Vocabulary Strategy, p. 555
- Practicing The Vocabulary Strategy, p. 562
- QAR, p. 702
- Strategies for Summarizing, p. 711

Grouping

- whole class
- small group or pairs

Sample Text (Resources)

- "Pioneers on the Oregon Trail" Complexity Level: Grades 4–5

Materials

- copies of "Pioneers on the Oregon Trail"

Source

- *Collaborative Strategic Reading: Strategies for Improving Comprehension* (2001) by Janette K. Klingner, Sharon Vaughn, Joseph Dimino, Jeanne S. Schumm, and Diane Bryant. Frederick, CO: Sopris West.

CSR (Collaborative Strategic Reading)

Collaborative Strategic Reading (CSR) combines two instructional approaches: comprehension strategies instruction and cooperative learning (Klingner and Vaughn 1999; Klingner et al. 2001). Originally developed for upper-elementary students, CSR is also effective for middle-school students (Brown 2002). In CSR, instruction is scaffolded. Initially, the teacher models each of the strategies for the whole class. Eventually, students collaboratively implement the strategies in heterogeneous groups in which each student performs a defined role.

This sample lesson model, based on CSR, focuses on introducing and practicing strategies. In this lesson model, sample text is used to represent a selection at students' independent reading level. The same model can be adapted and used to enhance comprehension instruction for informational text in any commercial reading or content-area program—as long as the text is at the appropriate level.

Direct Explanation

Display a copy of the CSR Strategies teaching chart, such as the example shown below. Tell students that you will be teaching them Collaborative Strategic Reading, or CSR. Explain the term by telling students that *collaborative* means "working together" and that *strategic reading* is a "plan or strategy for understanding and remembering what they read." Review the chart with students. Explain that CSR has four main strategies to help them understand what they read: Preview, Click and Clunk, Get the Gist, and Wrap Up. Point out that Preview is used before reading, Wrap Up is used after reading, and Click and Clunk and Get the Gist are used many times during reading.

CSR STRATEGIES

BEFORE READING: PREVIEW Scan • Brainstorm What You Know • Predict What You Will Learn
DURING READING: CLICK AND CLUNK • GET THE GIST
AFTER READING: WRAP UP Ask and Answer Questions • Review What You Learned

Based on Klingner et al. 2001.

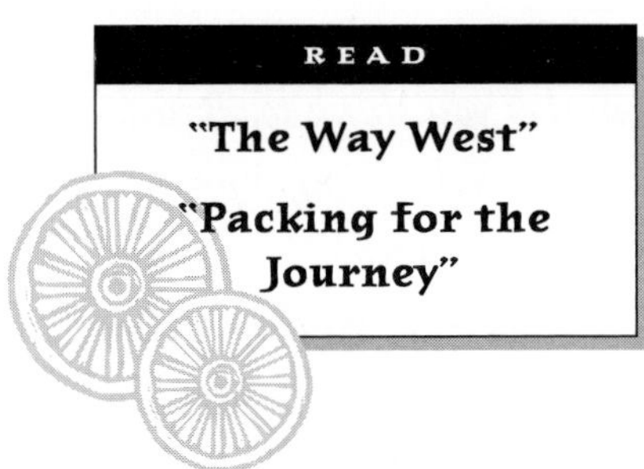

Teach/Model

Continue displaying the CSR Strategies teaching chart. Give students copies of "Pioneers on the Oregon Trail." Tell them that you will use the first two sections of the selection to model how to use CSR strategies.

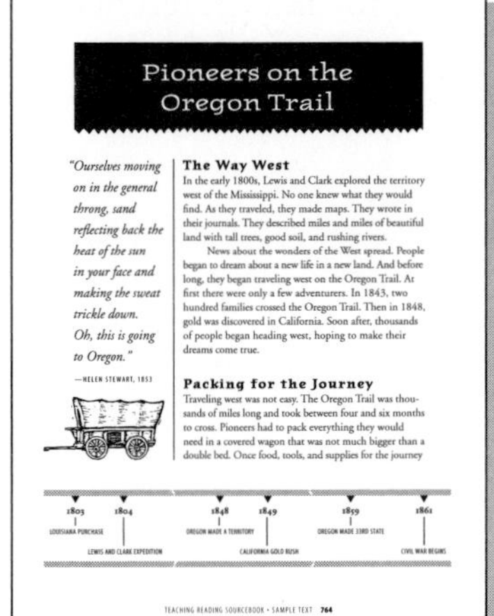

Pioneers on the Oregon Trail

"Ourselves moving on in the general throng, sand reflecting back the heat of the sun in your face and making the sweat trickle down. Oh, this is going to Oregon."

—HELEN STEWART, 1853

The Way West

In the early 1800s, Lewis and Clark explored the territory west of the Mississippi. No one knew what they would find. As they traveled, they made maps. They wrote in their journals. They described miles and miles of beautiful land with tall trees, good soil, and rushing rivers.

News about the wonders of the West spread. People began to dream about a new life in a new land. And before long, they began traveling west on the Oregon Trail. At first there were only a few adventurers. In 1843, two hundred families crossed the Oregon Trail. Then in 1848, gold was discovered in California. Soon after, thousands of people began heading west, hoping to make their dreams come true.

Packing for the Journey

Traveling west was not easy. The Oregon Trail was thousands of miles long and took between four and six months to cross. Pioneers had to pack everything they would need in a covered wagon that was not much bigger than a double bed. Once food, tools, and supplies for the journey

1803 LOUISIANA PURCHASE
1804 LEWIS AND CLARK EXPEDITION
1848 OREGON MADE A TERRITORY
1849 CALIFORNIA GOLD RUSH
1859 OREGON MADE 33RD STATE
1861 CIVIL WAR BEGINS

TEACHING READING SOURCEBOOK • SAMPLE TEXT 764

BEFORE READING: Preview

Pointing to this heading on the CSR Strategies teaching chart, explain to students that good readers preview a selection before reading it. Tell them that previewing has three steps: scanning the text, brainstorming what you already know about the topic, and predicting what you will learn.

SCAN Point to this heading on the teaching chart. Explain to students that "Pioneers on the Oregon Trail" is informational text and that informational texts often have graphic features such as titles, headings, maps, illustrations, captions, boldface text, italic text, and sidebars. Explain that to preview a selection, you first scan the text for these features. Say: *I'll begin my preview by scanning the first page. I see the title "Pioneers on the Oregon Trail" at the top of the page. This is the topic of the selection. Then I see two boldface headings, "The Way West" and "Packing for the Journey." I see a sidebar with italicized text in it. The text is a quote. Below the quote, I see a picture of a covered wagon. At the bottom of the page, I see a time line of historical events.*

Brainstorms
My Brainstorms—
• pioneers traveled in covered wagons
• pioneers traveled from east to west

BRAINSTORM WHAT YOU KNOW Pointing to this heading on the teaching chart, say: *Using what you saw during my scan of the text, you then brainstorm what you already know about the topic. From cowboy movies, I know that pioneers traveled in covered wagons. I also know that the pioneers traveled from east to west.* As you brainstorm, record your ideas on the board.

Predictions

My Predictions—
I Will Learn About
- the pioneers' journey
- what the journey was like
- how and what the pioneers packed

PREDICT WHAT YOU WILL LEARN Pointing to this heading on the teaching chart, say: *After you think about what you already know about the topic, you then predict what you will learn from what you are reading. Predictions are based on clues in the text and what you already know about the topic. When you make a prediction, you then tell what makes you think so. Based on the title, headings, and picture of the covered wagon, I predict I will learn about the pioneers' journey west to Oregon in covered wagons. Based on the quote, I predict I will learn what the journey was like for the pioneers. Based on the second heading, I predict that one of the things I will learn is how and what the pioneers packed for the journey.* As you generate the predictions, record them on the board. Keep them displayed for later reference in Wrap Up.

DURING READING: Click and Clunk • Get the Gist

The Vocabulary Strategy

1. **Look for Context Clues**
2. **Look for Word-Part Clues**
3. **Guess the Word's Meaning**
4. **Try Out Your Meaning in the Original Sentence**

SEE ALSO . . .

LESSON MODELS
Introducing The Vocabulary Strategy, p. 555
Practicing The Vocabulary Strategy, p. 562

CLICK AND CLUNK Remind students that when they are reading they should actively monitor their comprehension by noticing what they do understand, noticing what they do not understand, and then using appropriate fix-up strategies to resolve problems or confusion. Tell them that in CSR this process is called Click and Clunk. Pointing to the heading on the teaching chart, say: *Words or concepts whose meanings we understand "click," like a train rolling down the track. Words or concepts whose meanings we don't understand "clunk," like hitting an obstacle. When you hit a word-meaning clunk, you can use a fix-up strategy, such as The Vocabulary Strategy, to help you figure it out. Remember, The Vocabulary Strategy is a strategy for figuring out the meaning of an unfamiliar word by using context and word-part*

CLUNK

territory = big area of land

clues in combination. Explain to students that you are going to show them how to use the first four steps of The Vocabulary Strategy to figure out a word-meaning clunk.

Read aloud the first paragraph of "The Way West." Say: *I'm not sure what the word* territory *means; the word is unfamiliar to me. That's a clunk.* Print the word *territory* on the board. Say: *Step 1 of The Vocabulary Strategy says to look for context clues. I'm going to read the words, phrases, and sentences surrounding* territory *to see if I can find any context clues. In the fifth sentence, I think I may have found a synonym clue for* territory, *the phrase "miles and miles of beautiful land."* Territory *might have something to do with land. Step 2A says to try to break the word into parts. I don't see a meaningful prefix or suffix. So I'll skip to Step 3. Step 3 says to use the context clues I found in Step 1 to guess the meaning of the word. Because of the phrase "miles and miles," I think a territory might be a big area of land. Step 4 says to try out my meaning in the original sentence, to see whether or not it makes sense in context. I'm going to substitute* big area of land *for* territory. *"Lewis and Clark explored the big area of land west of the Mississippi." That makes sense.* Print the meaning on the board.

Paragraph Shrinking

1. **Identify who or what.**
2. **Identify the most important information about the who or what.**
3. **Shrink all the information into one main-idea statement of 10 words or less.**

Fuchs et al. 2007.

SEE ALSO . . .

LESSON MODEL: Strategies for Summarizing, p. 711

GET THE GIST Remind students that good readers can identify the most important ideas in what they are reading. They can shrink the information in a paragraph into a main-idea statement that tells the most important idea. Pointing to the heading on the teaching chart, say: *In CSR this paragraph-shrinking process is called Get the Gist.* Remind students that they have already learned about paragraph shrinking. Explain to them that you are going to use the Steps of Paragraph Shrinking to get the gist of the first paragraph.

Reread the first paragraph of "The Way West." Say: *First I'll identify who or what the paragraph is mostly about. The main who or what in this paragraph is* Lewis and Clark. *Now I'll identify the most important information about the who or what. I think the most important information about Lewis and Clark is that*

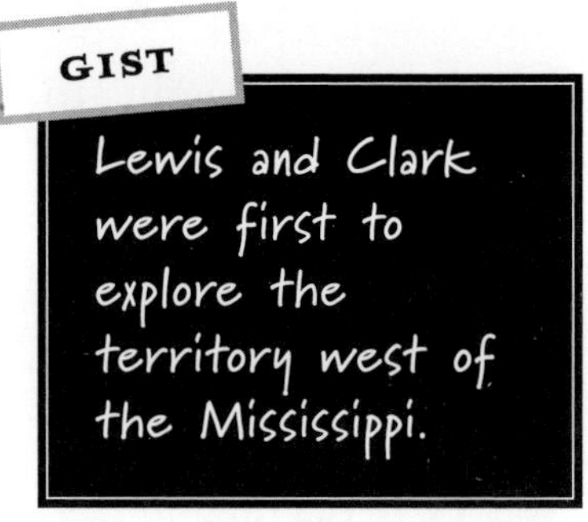

they explored the territory west of the Mississippi, describing it in maps and journals. Finally, I'll shrink the information into a really good main-idea statement of 10 words or less. Here is my main-idea statement, or gist: Lewis and Clark were first to explore the territory west of the Mississippi. Print the gist, or main-idea statement, on the board.

CLICK AND CLUNK Read aloud the second paragraph of "The Way West." Say: *In this paragraph everything is clicking for me. I don't have any clunks.*

GIST

People traveled west, hoping to make their dreams come true.

GET THE GIST Reread the second paragraph of "The Way West." Say: *Now I'm going to get the gist of this paragraph. The main who or what in this paragraph is* people. *I think the most important information about people is that they traveled west on the Oregon Trail, hoping to make their dreams come true. Here is my main-idea statement: People traveled west on the Oregon Trail, hoping to make their dreams come true. Oh, I have 14 words and I'm allowed to have only 10. I have to shrink it. People traveled west, hoping to make their dreams come true. That's 10.* Print the gist, or main-idea statement, on the board.

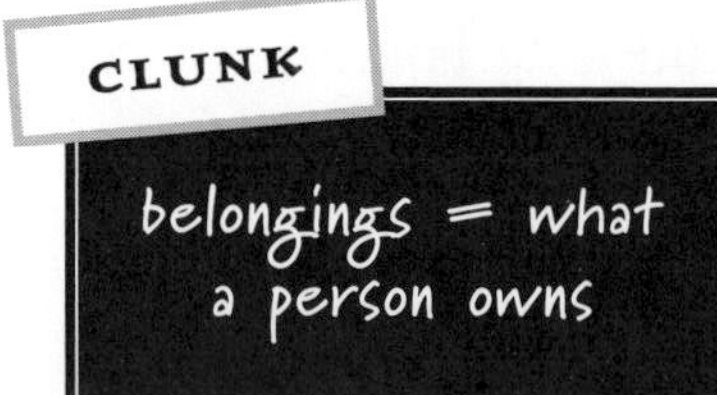

CLICK AND CLUNK Read aloud "Packing for the Journey." Say: *I have a clunk. I'm not sure what the word* belongings *means. Print the word* belongings *on the board.* Say: *Step 1 of The Vocabulary Strategy says to look for context clues. The word* personal *in the same sentence might be a context clue. In the sixth sentence,* special treasures *might be a context clue. Belongings could be special personal things. Step 2 says to look for word-part clues. I see two word parts: root word* belong *and suffix* –ings. *The root word of* belongings *is* belong. *If something belongs to you, you own it. Step 3 says to guess the meaning of the word. I think belongings might be what a person owns. Step 4 says to try out my meaning in the original sentence, to see whether or not it makes sense. I'm going to substitute* what each person owned *for* personal belongings. *"As a result, there was no room left for what each person owned." That makes sense.* Print the meaning on the board.

GIST

The pioneers could fit only necessary things in the covered wagons.

GET THE GIST Reread "Packing for the Journey." Say: *Now for the gist. The main who or what in this paragraph is* what the pioneers could take. *I think the most important information is they could take only food, tools, and supplies because the covered wagons were very small. Here is my main-idea statement: The pioneers could fit only necessary things in the covered wagons.* Print the gist, or main-idea statement, on the board.

AFTER READING: Wrap Up

Pointing to this heading on the CSR Strategies teaching chart, explain to students that after reading they will wrap up. Tell them that Wrap Up has two parts: asking and answering questions and reviewing what they have learned.

ASK AND ANSWER QUESTIONS Pointing to this heading on the teaching chart, say: *When you ask and answer questions, you think about the kinds of questions a teacher might ask on a test. I'm going to model by generating questions about what we just read. Focusing on the ideas in my main-idea statements, or gists, I'll begin each question with* who, what, when, where, why, *or* how. *I'll make sure that the answers to my questions reflect three different types of QAR: Right There, Think and Search, and Author and Me. Here are my questions.* Print the questions shown below on the board. Then read aloud each question and provide the answer. Ask students to identify the type of QAR.

Question	Answer	QAR
Who explored the territory west of the Mississippi in the early 1800s?	Lewis and Clark	Right There
What did the pioneers leave behind?	They left behind personal belongings, comforts of home, special treasures, and family and friends.	Think and Search
Why do you think people were willing to pack up and head west?	They thought they would get rich.	Author and Me

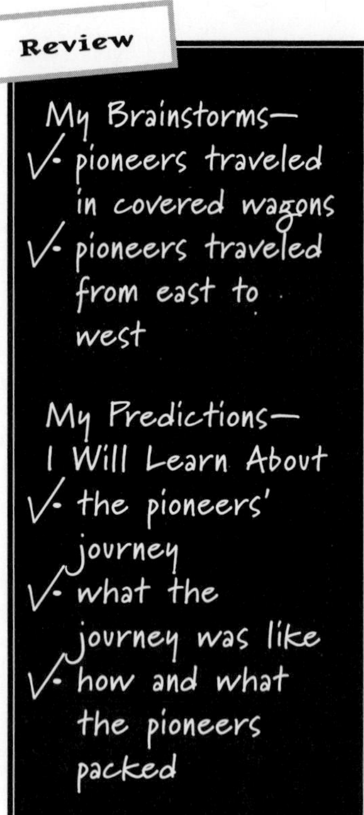

Review
My Brainstorms—
✓• pioneers traveled in covered wagons
✓• pioneers traveled from east to west
My Predictions—
I Will Learn About
✓• the pioneers' journey
✓• what the journey was like
✓• how and what the pioneers packed

REVIEW WHAT YOU LEARNED Pointing to this heading on the teaching chart, say: *In the second part of Wrap Up, you review by noting the important information that you learned. To review, it helps to first go back to the lists of brainstorms and predictions you made in Preview and confirm or revise them.* Pointing to these lists on the board, say: *Both of my brainstorms and both of my predictions were confirmed in the text. I predicted that I would learn what the journey was like for the pioneers, specifically about how and what they packed. From the text, I learned that it was a long journey and that the pioneers could pack only the essentials that would fit in the wagon.*

Say: *I also learned other information, so now I'm going to jot down my review. I learned that people knew about the West from Lewis and Clark. After gold was discovered in California in 1848, thousands of pioneers crossed the Oregon Trail in covered wagons in search of a new life. The Oregon Trail was thousands of miles long and took several months to cross. The pioneers could bring with them only what was necessary to survive.*

READ

"Wagons Ho!"

"Landmarks on the Oregon Trail"

Guided Practice

Continue displaying the CSR Strategies teaching chart. Tell students that you are going to guide them in applying CSR strategies as they read the next two sections of the selection.

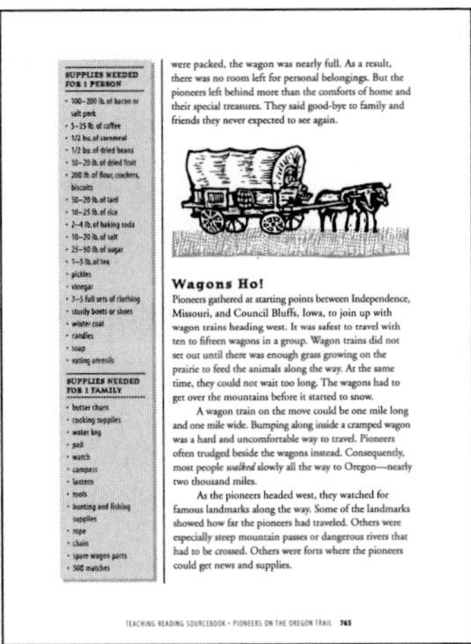

SUPPLIES NEEDED FOR 1 PERSON

- 100–200 lb. of bacon or salt pork
- 5–25 lb. of coffee
- 1/2 bu. of cornmeal
- 1/2 bu. of dried beans
- 10–20 lb. of dried fruit
- 200 lb. of flour, crackers, biscuits
- 10–20 lb. of lard
- 10–25 lb. of rice
- 2–4 lb. of baking soda
- 10–20 lb. of salt
- 25–50 lb. of sugar
- 1–5 lb. of tea
- pickles
- vinegar
- 3–5 full sets of clothing
- sturdy boots or shoes
- winter coat
- candles
- soap
- eating utensils

SUPPLIES NEEDED FOR 1 FAMILY

- butter churn
- cooking supplies
- water keg
- pail
- watch
- compass
- lantern
- tools
- hunting and fishing supplies
- rope
- chain
- spare wagon parts
- 500 matches

were packed, the wagon was nearly full. As a result, there was no room left for personal belongings. But the pioneers left behind more than the comforts of home and their special treasures. They said good-bye to family and friends they never expected to see again.

Wagons Ho!

Pioneers gathered at starting points between Independence, Missouri, and Council Bluffs, Iowa, to join up with wagon trains heading west. It was safest to travel with ten to fifteen wagons in a group. Wagon trains did not set out until there was enough grass growing on the prairie to feed the animals along the way. At the same time, they could not wait too long. The wagons had to get over the mountains before it started to snow.

A wagon train on the move could be one mile long and one mile wide. Bumping along inside a cramped wagon was a hard and uncomfortable way to travel. Pioneers often trudged beside the wagons instead. Consequently, most people *walked* slowly all the way to Oregon—nearly two thousand miles.

As the pioneers headed west, they watched for famous landmarks along the way. Some of the landmarks showed how far the pioneers had traveled. Others were especially steep mountain passes or dangerous rivers that had to be crossed. Others were forts where the pioneers could get news and supplies.

TEACHING READING SOURCEBOOK • PIONEERS ON THE OREGON TRAIL 765

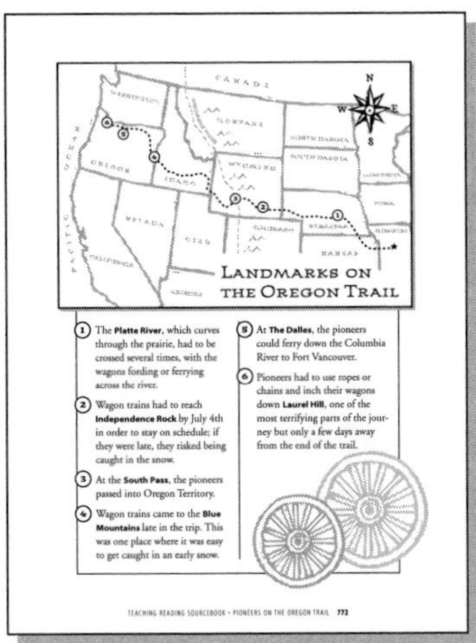

1. The **Platte River**, which curves through the prairie, had to be crossed several times, with the wagons fording or ferrying across the river.
2. Wagon trains had to reach **Independence Rock** by July 4th in order to stay on schedule; if they were late, they risked being caught in the snow.
3. At the **South Pass**, the pioneers passed into Oregon Territory.
4. Wagon trains came to the **Blue Mountains** late in the trip. This was one place where it was easy to get caught in an early snow.
5. At **The Dalles**, the pioneers could ferry down the Columbia River to Fort Vancouver.
6. Pioneers had to use ropes or chains and inch their wagons down **Laurel Hill**, one of the most terrifying parts of the journey but only a few days away from the end of the trail.

TEACHING READING SOURCEBOOK • PIONEERS ON THE OREGON TRAIL 772

BEFORE READING: Preview

Remind students that good readers preview a selection before reading it. Ask: *What are the parts of the Preview strategy?* (scanning the text, brainstorming what you already know about the topic, and predicting what you will learn)

SCAN Remind students that the topic of the selection is pioneers on the Oregon Trail. Then ask them to scan the next two sections of the selection. Ask: *What graphic features do you see on the next two pages?* (sidebar list of supplies, boldface subtitle "Wagons Ho!," a map showing the landmarks on the Oregon trail, numbered callouts explaining the landmarks on the map, pictures of a covered wagon pulled by oxen and wagon wheels)

BRAINSTORM WHAT YOU KNOW Ask: *What do you do during brainstorming?* (You think of what you already know about the topic.) Have students use what they saw while scanning the text to brainstorm what they already know about the topic; for example, they might be familiar with one of the landmarks on the Oregon Trail. Record their ideas on the board.

PREDICT WHAT YOU WILL LEARN Ask: *What is a prediction?* (It is an educated guess based on clues in the text and what you already know about the topic.) Have students use what they saw while scanning the text and what they already know about the topic to make a prediction about what they might learn by reading the section; for example, they might predict that they will learn all about wagon trains. Record their predictions on the board.

DURING READING: Click and Clunk • Get the Gist

Pointing to the CSR Strategies teaching chart, ask: *What CSR strategies do you use during reading?* (Click and Clunk and Get the Gist)

CLICK AND CLUNK Ask: *What does it mean when reading clicks?* (You understand everything.) Ask: *What does it mean when reading clunks?* (You do not understand the meaning of something.) Say: *I'm going to read aloud the first paragraph of "Wagons Ho!" Write down any clunks on a piece of paper, and we will talk about them after I finish reading.* Read the paragraph aloud. Then ask: *Are there any clunks about what I just read?* (no) *Is everything clicking?* (yes) Now read aloud the next two paragraphs. Then ask: *Do you have any clunks about what I just read?* (Possible responses: *I don't know the meaning of* cramped, uncomfortable, *and* trudged. *I'm not sure what a* landmark *is.*) Ask: *What can we do to figure out a clunk?* (Use a fix-up strategy, such as The Vocabulary Strategy.) Have students apply the steps of The Vocabulary Strategy.

GIST

Wagon trains left early to avoid snow in the mountains.

GET THE GIST Say: *In CSR, you get the gist after reading each paragraph or section of text.* Ask: *What do you do to get the gist?* (shrink a paragraph into a gist, or main-idea statement, of 10 words or less) Say: *Let's follow the steps of paragraph shrinking to get the gist of the first paragraph of "Wagons Ho!"* Ask: *Who or what is the paragraph mostly about?* (Possible response: *wagon trains*) *Print* wagon trains *on the board.* Ask: *What is the most important information about the wagon trains?* (Possible response: *They had to set out early enough so they could get over the mountains before it started to snow.*) Print the information on the board. Ask: *Who can shrink this information into a gist of 10 words or less?* (Possible response: *Wagon trains had to set out early enough so they could get over the mountains before it started to snow.*) Print the gist on the board. Ask: *How many words in this gist?* (19 words) Say: *That's too many words. Shrink it.* (Possible response: *Wagon trains left early to avoid snow in the mountains.*)

Follow the same procedure for the next two paragraphs. Possible gists, or main-idea statements, include the following:

"Wagons Ho!"

- Paragraph 1: Pioneers often walked the trail to avoid the uncomfortable ride.
- Paragraph 2: Famous landmarks on the trail helped the pioneers during their journey.

AFTER READING: Wrap Up

Remind students that after reading a whole selection or section of text, they will wrap up. Ask: *What are the two parts of the Wrap Up strategy?* (asking and answering questions, reviewing what you've learned)

ASK AND ANSWER QUESTIONS Remind students that the first thing they should do when they wrap up is to think of questions a teacher might ask on a test. Then have them develop questions about the section of text. To guide students, ask: *What words should your questions begin with?* (who, what, when, where, why, or how) *What types of QAR?* (Right There, Think and Search, and Author and Me) After each question is generated, print it on the board. Then call on a student to answer it, label the question type, and explain the reason for the label.

Possible Question	Answer	QAR
How big was a wagon train?	A wagon train could be one mile long and one mile wide.	Right There
What was important about the timing of the trip?	They couldn't leave until there was enough grass growing to feed the animals. They had to get there before it started to snow.	Think and Search
What do you think would be the most challenging landmark on the Trail? Why?	Laurel Hill, because their covered wagons could be destroyed and they were almost at the end.	Author and Me

REVIEW WHAT YOU LEARNED Remind students that when they review, they jot down the important information that they learned. Then lead students in writing a list of important information they learned by reading this section of text. (Possible responses: *For safety, wagons traveled in big groups, called trains. Timing of the trip was very important because the animals needed to graze. The trip was long and uncomfortable, and many people walked. Landmarks were important in guiding and supporting the journey.*)

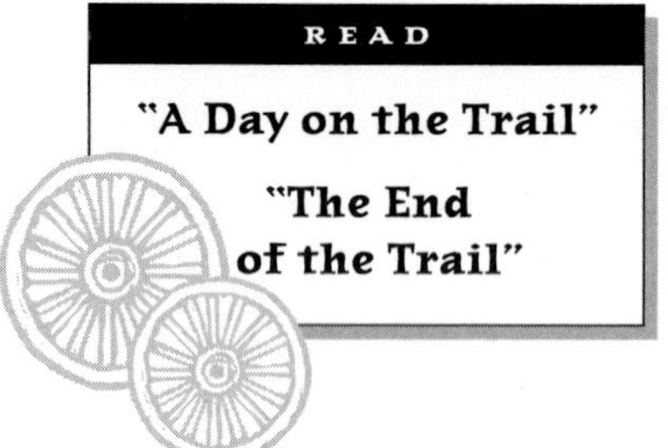

A Day on the Trail

If you were traveling in a wagon train on the Oregon Trail, you tried to travel at a steady pace. On a good day, you could go about fifteen miles. On a stormy day or over a bad part of the trail, you might go only one mile.

You would wake up at daybreak. Morning chores, including fixing breakfast, milking the cows, taking care of the animals, and packing up the wagon, would take a couple of hours. Then you would hitch up the mules or oxen and set out.

At noon you would find a place to stop and rest. Animals would graze and get water. You would eat a meal, rest, and make any repairs that were needed. Then you would set out again and keep going until four or five o'clock. You had to stop in time to get your chores done before nightfall.

Now the evening meal had to be cooked, which might mean gathering firewood, hunting or fishing, picking berries, and so on. Wagon repairs, cleaning and mending clothes, and other chores could be done. If you were lucky, you might find time to rest and relax. Musicians might pull out fiddles and harmonicas for singing and dancing by the campfire. Then it was time to go to bed, so that you could get up and do it again.

DID YOU KNOW?

Pioneers would milk their cows in the evening. Then in the morning, they would put the cream into the churn and set the churn inside the wagon. The constant rocking motion of the wagon would turn the cream to butter by the time they stopped for supper.

The End of the Trail

After four or five months of traveling, pioneers finally reached the Willamette Valley. Oregon City was the end of the Oregon Trail, where pioneers staked their claims to ranchland and farmland. Then the hard work really began.

The first winter in Oregon could be very hard. Supplies were low, and the weather turned rainy and cold. It was important to get busy and clear your land and build a cabin before the start of winter. But the end of the trail was where the dream of living in the West began. The pioneers who survived the trip had risked everything for a new life in the West.

TEACHING READING SOURCEBOOK • PIONEERS ON THE OREGON TRAIL 767

Partner Practice

BEFORE READING: Preview

Have pairs of students construct a preview of the last page of the selection, "A Day on the Trail" and "The End of the Trail." Remind them to first scan the text, then brainstorm and write down what they know about the topic, and finally write down their predictions about what they might learn. For example, after scanning the text, students might notice the headings, sidebar text, and the pictures of the cow and the tree. When brainstorming, students might connect to what they know about camping in the wilderness. Students might predict that they will learn about the daily routines of the pioneers and about what it was like for the pioneers once they reached the end of the trail. Circulate among students, providing assistance as needed.

DURING READING: Click and Clunk • Get the Gist

CLICK AND CLUNK Have pairs of students read the last page of the selection aloud, a paragraph at a time. After reading a paragraph, have them identify any clunks and then use fix-up strategies, such as The Vocabulary Strategy, to figure out what the clunks mean. Possible clunks include the words *pace* (the speed at which something moves or happens), *daybreak* (the time when light first appears in the sky at the beginning of the day, dawn), and *nightfall* (the time when it becomes dark and night begins, dusk), and the idiom *staked their claims* (to announce that something belongs to you, or literally to mark with posts a piece of land belonging to the government that you claim for yourself).

GET THE GIST After figuring out the clunks for a paragraph, have students follow the Paragraph Shrinking Steps to get the gist, or develop a main-idea statement, about the same paragraph. Possible gists, or main-idea statements, include the following:

"A Day on the Trail"
- Paragraph 1: A wagon train tried to travel at a steady pace.
- Paragraph 2: In the morning, pioneers got ready to set out.
- Paragraph 3: At noon, pioneers ate, rested, fed animals, and made repairs.
- Paragraph 4: In the evening, pioneers gathered food, did chores, and relaxed.

"The End of the Trail"
- Paragraph 1: Pioneers staked their claim at the end of the trail in Oregon City.
- Paragraph 2: Surviving the first winter in Oregon required hard work.

AFTER READING: Wrap Up

Have students work in pairs to wrap up the section. Give them some time to generate teacher-like questions. When they are finished, call on different students to ask their questions and call on other students to answer them. Student responses should include answering the question, labeling the question type, and explaining why the label is appropriate. Questions might include: What kinds of things did the pioneers do on a typical day on the trail? How many miles could the pioneers travel in a single day? Why was it important to get chores done before nightfall? How long did it take the pioneers to reach the end of the trail? Why did hard work begin at the end of the trail? To review, have pairs of students confirm or adapt their list of brainstorms and predictions and jot down the most important ideas they learned from reading. Call on students to share what they learned. Circulate among students, providing assistance as needed.

Cooperative Practice: Read a New Selection

Once students are proficient in using CSR with the support of the teacher, they implement the strategies while working in heterogeneous cooperative learning groups. In these groups, students assist one another in the comprehension of the text (Klinger et al. 2007). Different student roles include (Klingner et al. 2001):

Leader
Clunk Expert
Gist Expert
Announcer
Encourager

- Leader: Guides the group by saying what to read next and what strategy to apply next.
- Clunk Expert: Reminds the group of the steps to follow when trying to figure out a clunk.
- Gist Expert: Guides the group in developing a gist, or main-idea statement.
- Announcer: Asks different group members to read or share an idea. Makes sure that all members of the group participate.
- Encourager: Watches the group and gives positive feedback. Evaluates how well the group works together.

LESSON MODEL FOR

Directed Discussion

Benchmarks

- ability to focus on text content through teacher-directed discussions
- ability to engage in discussions to grapple with text meaning
- ability to recognize the intentions, biases, and fallibility of authors
- ability to recognize that poor comprehension may be due to poorly written text

Strategy Grade Level

- Grade 3 and above

Grouping

- whole class
- small group

Sample Text (Resources)

- "The Greenhouse Effect" Complexity Level: Grades 6–8

Materials

- copies of "The Greenhouse Effect"

Source

- *Improving Comprehension with Questioning the Author* (2006) by Isabel L. Beck and Margaret G. McKeown. New York: Scholastic.

QtA (Questioning the Author)

Developed by Isabel Beck and Margaret McKeown (Beck et al. 1997; Beck and McKeown 2006), QtA is a directed-discussion approach designed to build students' understanding of text ideas. Discussion is at the heart of QtA. In QtA, teacher-posed questions, or Queries, are the main instructional tool for discussion, supported by Discussion Moves that help orchestrate student participation and development of ideas.

This sample lesson model provides an overview of and sample script for the QtA approach. In this lesson model, sample text is used to represent a selection at students' independent reading level. The same model can be adapted and used to enhance comprehension instruction for literary or informational text in any commercial reading or content-area program—as long as the text is at the appropriate level.

Planning

QtA lesson planning has three goals: (1) to identify the major understandings and potential obstacles in the text, (2) to segment the text, or determine where to stop reading and initiate discussion, and (3) to develop Initiating Queries and potential Follow-Up Queries (Beck and McKeown 2006).

QtA Queries

QtA Queries are teacher questions designed to assist students in dealing with, and grasping, text ideas as students encounter them. They are intended to support students in building an understanding of major text ideas, and to help them discover the difference between knowing what an author says and inferring what an author means. There are two types of Queries: Initiating Queries and Follow-Up Queries. An Initiating Query is an open-ended question designed to start a discussion about a segment of text. A Follow-Up Query is a more detailed question developed during the lesson, in response to the discussion as it unfolds. Incorporating students' responses or specific terms from the text, Follow-Up Queries are designed to help focus the content and direction of a discussion. Such queries assist students in integrating and connecting ideas to build meaning.

QtA Queries

Type	Purposes	Examples
INITIATING QUERIES open a discussion or set it in motion.	• To make public the messages or ideas presented by an author • To draw attention to important text ideas • To remind students that important text ideas are written by an author	• What is the author trying to say here? • What do you think the author wants us to know? • What is the author talking about? • What is the important message in this section? • What big idea do you think the author is trying to tell us about? • With all that, what do you think the author wanted us to know? • What has the author just told us?
FOLLOW-UP QUERIES move a discussion along and guide students along productive lines of thought.	• To encourage students to consider the ideas behind an author's words	• So what does the author mean? • That's what the author said, but what does the author mean? • Does the author explain this clearly?
	• To guide students to relate information from different parts of a text • To connect to ideas that have been learned or read previously • To see that a connection or linking piece of information may be missing from the text	• Does that make sense with what the author told us before? • How does that fit with what the author told us before? • How does this connect to what the author told us here?
	• To help students figure out an author's possible reasons for including certain information	• Does the author tell us why? • Why do you think the author tells us that now?

Based on Beck and McKeown 2006.

QtA Discussion Moves

There are six basic types of QtA Discussion Moves, or tools a teacher can use to manage discussion. Marking, Turning-Back, and Revoicing are moves that productively use what students offer during a discussion. Recapping, Modeling, and Annotating are moves that involve the teacher stepping into the discussion in a more direct way (Beck et al. 1997).

QtA Discussion Moves

Move	Description	Example from Sample Script
MARKING	Drawing attention to an idea to emphasize its importance and to use it as a basis for further discussion	Oh, I think I get it now. Amira thinks the gases are thick, and Sophie says the gases trap the heat.
TURNING-BACK ...to Students	Turning responsibility back to students for thinking through and figuring out ideas	And what do the gases do? Can anyone say more about that?
...to Text	Turning students' attention back to the text as a source for clarifying thinking and keeping discussion on track	It seems that specific effects aren't the author's focus here. Let's read further to see what direction the author will take.
REVOICING	Interpreting what students are struggling to express so their ideas can become part of the discussion	So, Noah is suggesting that the author is trying to persuade people to stop destroying forests.
RECAPPING	Reviewing or highlighting major ideas and understandings developed so far	So destroying forests and burning fossil fuels are two ways people add to the amount of carbon dioxide in the atmosphere.
MODELING	"Making public" the processes in which readers engage in the course of reading	As a reader, I can visualize that—I'm picturing a big thick cloud of gases around Earth.
ANNOTATING	Providing information to fill in gaps or point out sources of confusion in a text	I know that fossil fuels are formed from the remains, or fossils, of plants and animals.

Based on Beck and McKeown 2006.

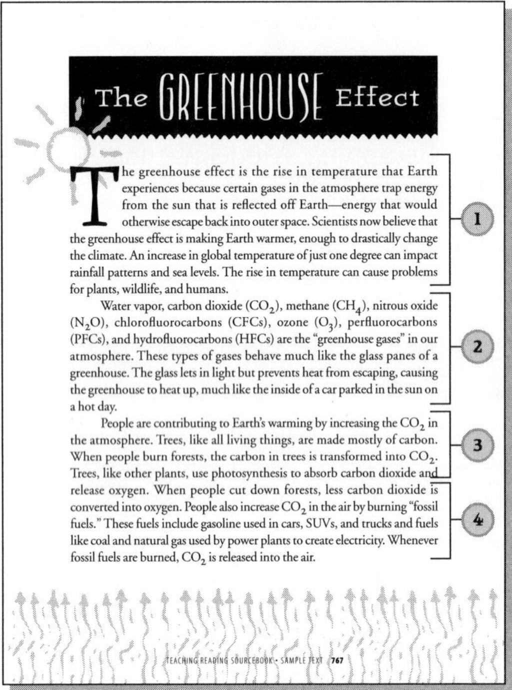

The GREENHOUSE Effect

The greenhouse effect is the rise in temperature that Earth experiences because certain gases in the atmosphere trap energy from the sun that is reflected off Earth—energy that would otherwise escape back into outer space. Scientists now believe that the greenhouse effect is making Earth warmer, enough to drastically change the climate. An increase in global temperature of just one degree can impact rainfall patterns and sea levels. The rise in temperature can cause problems for plants, wildlife, and humans. (1)

Water vapor, carbon dioxide (CO_2), methane (CH_4), nitrous oxide (N_2O), chlorofluorocarbons (CFCs), ozone (O_3), perfluorocarbons (PFCs), and hydrofluorocarbons (HFCs) are the "greenhouse gases" in our atmosphere. These types of gases behave much like the glass panes of a greenhouse. The glass lets in light but prevents heat from escaping, causing the greenhouse to heat up, much like the inside of a car parked in the sun on a hot day. (2)

People are contributing to Earth's warming by increasing the CO_2 in the atmosphere. Trees, like all living things, are made mostly of carbon. When people burn forests, the carbon in trees is transformed into CO_2. Trees, like other plants, use photosynthesis to absorb carbon dioxide and (3) release oxygen. When people cut down forests, less carbon dioxide is converted into oxygen. People also increase CO_2 in the air by burning "fossil fuels." These fuels include gasoline used in cars, SUVs, and trucks and fuels like coal and natural gas used by power plants to create electricity. Whenever fossil fuels are burned, CO_2 is released into the air. (4)

TEACHING READING SOURCEBOOK • SAMPLE TEXT 767

QtA in Action: A Sample Script

This sample script illustrates what a QtA lesson might actually look like in action. In the sample, the teacher reads aloud "The Greenhouse Effect" as students follow along on copies of the passage.

 *Teacher reads aloud the first segment of text.*

MRS. E.: What big idea do you think the author is trying to tell us about? (Initiating Query)

AARON: The greenhouse effect.

MRS. E.: So, this paragraph describes the greenhouse effect. (Marking) Does the author explain it clearly? (Follow-Up Query)

AMIRA: I had trouble understanding the first sentence.

MRS. E..: Yes, the author's first sentence is pretty long, which makes it confusing. (Annotating) It helped me to break the sentence into parts and look at each idea. (Modeling) Why don't we try that? What are all the ideas the author presents in this one sentence? (Turning-Back to Students)

SOPHIE: The greenhouse effect is the rise in temperature that Earth experiences.

MIA: The greenhouse effect happens because certain gases in the atmosphere trap energy from the sun.

MRS. E.: So, to make the connection that the trapped energy is creating the rise in temperature, I had to know that heat is a form of energy. (Annotating) What else is the author telling us in that sentence? (Follow-Up Query)

NOAH: The energy from the sun is reflected off Earth.

MRS. E.: And what does the author say about why the energy isn't escaping back to outer space? (Follow-Up Query)

AARON: Because it's being trapped.

MRS. E.: How? (Follow-Up Query)

MIA: By the gases.

MRS. E.: So the author tells us that the greenhouse effect is making Earth warmer. (Recapping) What does the author tell us about the impact of this? (Follow-Up Query)

AMIRA: It's changing the climate.

SOPHIE: It's bad for plants, wildlife, and humans.

MRS. E.: The author says, "The rise in temperature can cause problems for plants, wildlife, and humans," but what does the author mean? (Follow-Up Query)

NOAH: A warmer temperature could affect the health of living things.

MRS. E.: Does the author tell us how? (Turning-Back to Text)

NOAH: Not really. The author only says that it causes problems.

MRS. E.: So the author doesn't give us specific information about the problems. (Annotating) I can use what I know about how heat affects living things. I know that my plants wilt when it gets too hot. (Modeling)

AMIRA: I get really lazy when it's too hot.

MRS. E.: The text tells us that the greenhouse effect might cause problems for living things but doesn't go into specifics. It seems that specific effects aren't the author's focus here. Let's read further to see what direction the author will take. (Turning-Back to Text)

2 *Teacher reads aloud the next segment of text.*

MRS. E.: What has the author just told us? (Initiating Query)

MIA: What the greenhouse gases are.

SOPHIE: And what they do.

MRS. E.: And what do the gases do? Can anyone say more about that? (Turning-Back to Students)

AMIRA: They make the greenhouse effect.

MRS. E.: Does the author explain how the greenhouse effect got its name? (Follow-Up Query)

MIA: Because it works like a greenhouse.

MRS. E.: And what does the text say about how a greenhouse works? (Turning-Back to Text)

AARON: The glass traps the heat.

MRS. E.: So in a greenhouse, the glass traps the heat. (Marking) But I'm still confused about what that has to do with this list of gases. Sophie, what do you think? (Turning-Back to Students)

SOPHIE: The gases trap the heat.

MRS. E.: How do you think the gases do that? (Turning-Back to Students)

AMIRA: The gases must be thick, like a wall.

MRS. E.: Oh, I think I get it now. Amira thinks the gases are thick, and Sophie says the gases trap the heat. (Marking) As a reader, I can visualize that—I'm picturing a thick cloud of gases around Earth. (Modeling) The cloud of gases is so thick that it can trap heat, like when all the windows of a car are closed on a hot day. (Recapping)

AARON: Hey, we always put a sunshield over the windshield of our car to keep it cool inside. The shield reflects the heat from the sun. Why can't we put a sunshield around Earth to keep it from getting too hot?

NOAH: But how would you keep Earth from getting too cold?

MRS. E.: Aaron got us thinking of potential solutions for the greenhouse effect. I think there's a career in that somewhere, Aaron. (Revoicing) Maybe reading the rest of the passage will help us to brainstorm more ideas for reducing the greenhouse effect. (Turning-Back to Text)

3 *Teacher reads aloud the next segment of text.*

MRS. E.: With all that, what do you think the author wants us to know? (Initiating Query)

AMIRA: People are making the situation worse.

MRS. E.: Wow! So, before, Aaron had an idea about how people could reduce the greenhouse effect, and now Amira says the author is telling us what people are doing that could *increase* the greenhouse effect. (Revoicing, Recapping) What, specifically, does the author say people are doing? (Turning-Back to Text)

MIA: Cutting down forests.

SOPHIE: And burning them.

MRS. E.: What does the author say happens when people burn trees? (Follow-Up Query)

AARON: The carbon in the trees is turned into carbon dioxide.

MRS. E.: And then what happens to that carbon dioxide? (Follow-Up Query)

NOAH: It goes into the atmosphere.

MRS. E.: Okay, so I get that burning trees produces carbon dioxide, which goes into the atmosphere. But then in the next sentence, the author says that trees *absorb* carbon dioxide. Does the author explain this clearly? (Follow-Up Query) How can trees do both things—produce and absorb?

MIA: Well, the author says that during photosynthesis trees absorb carbon dioxide and release oxygen.

AMIRA: But burning trees produce carbon dioxide.

MRS. E.: So, what happens when trees are cut down for logs? (Follow-Up Query)

MIA: There's fewer of them to absorb carbon dioxide.

SOPHIE: So the carbon dioxide goes into the atmosphere.

MRS. E.: And then what? (Follow-Up Query)

Aaron: It adds to the amount of greenhouse gases.

Mrs. E.: So let's make sure we got this straight. The author is trying to say that if we cut trees down, they can't absorb carbon dioxide from the atmosphere. And when we burn trees, the fire creates even more carbon dioxide. (Recapping) Why do you think the author is telling us this? (Follow-Up Query)

Noah: So we will stop cutting and burning trees.

Mrs. E.: So, Noah is suggesting that the author is trying to persuade people to stop destroying forests. (Revoicing) Let's see what the author tells us in the rest of this paragraph. (Turning-Back to Text)

Teacher reads aloud the last segment of text.

Mrs. E.: What is the important message in this section? (Initiating Query)

Sophie: Don't drive cars.

Mrs. E.: So, Sophie thinks the author is trying to persuade people to reduce their driving. (Revoicing) Why would that be important, Mia? (Turning-Back to Students)

Mia: Because cars use gas.

Mrs. E.: What does the author tell us about gas and coal? (Follow-Up Query)

Aaron: They are fossil fuels.

Mrs. E.: Fossil fuels. I know that fossil fuels are formed from the remains, or fossils, of plants and animals. (Annotating) How does the author's information about fossil fuels connect to what we read about the trees? (Follow-Up Query)

Amira: When people burn fossil fuels, carbon dioxide is released, just like when they burn trees.

Mrs. E.: So destroying forests and burning fossil fuels are two ways people add to the amount of carbon dioxide in the atmosphere. (Recapping) And what does all of this have to do with the greenhouse effect, again? (Turning-Back to Text)

Sophie: Carbon dioxide is one of the greenhouse gases.

Aaron: That's what's causing global warming.

Mrs. E.: So, the author describes ways people are increasing the greenhouse effect, which Aaron points out is also referred to as global warming. (Marking) What do you think the author wants us to take away from all of this? (Follow-Up Query)

Noah: As I said before, stop cutting down trees.

Mrs. E.: So, Noah thinks one purpose might be to persuade or call people to action. (Marking) What do the rest of you think?

Amira: I think the author hints at that but doesn't give any real suggestions.

Mrs. E.: So, Amira suggests that persuasion might be the author's secondary purpose. What do you think the author's primary purpose is? Mia? (Turning-Back to Students)

Mia: Well, mostly, the author explains the greenhouse effect.

Mrs. E.: Right, the text's primary purpose is to inform us about the greenhouse effect. But the author also shows a bit of bias on the topic—there's some persuading going on here, too. (Recapping) I think the author would approve if we spent the last few minutes brainstorming more ideas for reducing the greenhouse effect, like Aaron's idea about the giant sunshield.

LESSON MODEL FOR

Integrated Content-Area Reading

Benchmarks

- ability to apply multiple comprehension strategies
- ability to gain conceptual understanding from content-area texts
- motivation to read independently and engagement with text

Strategy Grade Level

- Grade 3 and above

Grouping

- whole class
- small group or pairs
- individual

Materials

- none

Source

- http://www.corilearning.com

CORI (Concept-Oriented Reading Instruction)

Concept-Oriented Reading Instruction (CORI) is a program designed by John Guthrie and Allan Wigfield to incorporate reading strategy instruction with inquiry science—a theme-based integrated approach in which motivational practices provide the framework (Guthrie 2005–6). In CORI, science instruction is paired with the strategic reading of informational and literary texts, supported through student writing. The objectives of CORI are to increase students' reading comprehension, science knowledge, and motivation to read independently (McPeake and Guthrie 2007; Guthrie 2005–6).

This sample lesson model gives an overview of the CORI framework. The same approach can be adapted and used to enhance comprehension instruction tied to content-area reading, especially science. More detailed information is available on the CORI Web site.

Comprehension Strategy Instruction

In CORI, explicit comprehension strategy instruction is embedded in science content. CORI comprehension strategies include activating background knowledge, questioning, organizing graphically, structuring story, and summarizing. CORI also includes an inquiry strategy used for seeking and finding specific information in both print and electronic texts. Although they may be called by different names, CORI comprehension strategies (see the chart on the following page) are basically the same as the ones described earlier in this section of the Sourcebook.

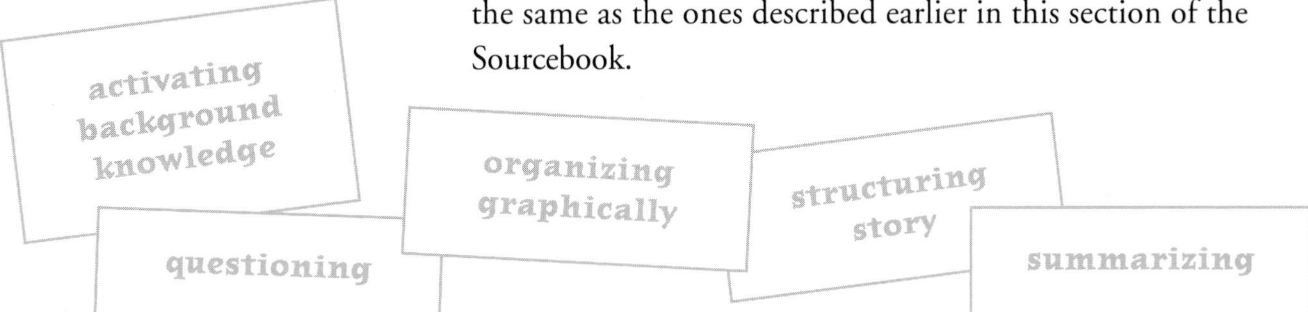

CORI: Comprehension Strategies	
CORI Strategy Name	**Sourcebook Cross-References**
Activating Background Knowledge	Connecting to World Knowledge, pp. 618, 689 Predicting, pp. 619, 689
Questioning	Asking Questions/Elaborative Interrogation, pp. 620, 690 Answering Questions/QAR, pp. 620, 691 Lesson Model: QAR (Question-Answer Relationships), p. 702
Organizing Graphically	Graphic Organizers, p. 684 Lesson Model: Semantic Map, p. 470 Lesson Model: Semantic Feature Analysis, p. 474 Lesson Model: Concept of Definition Map, p. 516
Structuring Story	Story Structure, p. 634 Recognizing Story Structure, p. 636 Lesson Model: Story Structure, p. 651
Summarizing	Summarizing, pp. 622, 693 Lesson Model: Strategies for Summarizing, p. 711

Science Learning Goals

In CORI, science learning is achieved through the integration of the reading and science curricula. The goals for science learning fall into two categories: process goals and content goals.

CORI: Science Goals		
Goal	**Purpose**	**Examples**
SCIENCE PROCESS	To develop skills needed to effectively observe scientific phenomena, ask relevant and informed questions, gather and compare appropriate information, and formulate an informed assessment of scientific concepts	Observe, analyze, synthesize, and compare and contrast scientific observations
SCIENCE CONTENT	To develop deep knowledge of science content	Survival of birds Hidden worlds of the woodland

Based on McPeake and Guthrie 2007.

Support for Motivation

A fundamental goal of CORI is to increase students' reading engagement and motivation to read. This is achieved through teaching practices that emphasize interest, ownership, social interaction, confidence, and content mastery. Motivational practices provide the framework for daily instruction.

CORI: Motivational Practices

Practice	Purpose	Examples
RELEVANCE Providing real-world purposes for reading by connecting to students' direct or recalled experience and background knowledge	To increase students' intrinsic motivation to read through interest-building activities	• Observational instruction • Hands-on instruction
CHOICE Providing an autonomy-supportive environment in which control of instruction and learning is shared between teacher and students	To afford students opportunities to take ownership over their reading and to pursue their own interests	• Students selecting high-interest texts • Students giving input on topics of study • Students selecting partners or groups • Students determining options for expressing or demonstrating learning
COLLABORATION Providing opportunities for social interaction during instruction	To generate enthusiasm for the text and its content	• Having students work in pairs or small groups • Encouraging students to exchange ideas with peers • Encouraging students to share what they are learning
SUCCESS Assuring proficient performance of instructional tasks	To build students' confidence in their capacity to comprehend content-area text	• Setting realistic instructional goals • Matching texts to students' independent reading level • Providing a wide variety of theme-based texts • Making students aware of their content knowledge expertise • Making students aware of their strategy use • Sharing students' successes and achievements • Providing positive feedback and encouragement
CONCEPTUAL THEME Providing integrated, theme-based instruction	To offer an instructional context in which students are reading for deep understanding of content	• Directly stating content theme • Relating concepts to each other • Connecting reading to concepts • Creating graphic organizers about concepts • Providing both literary and informational texts related to the theme

Based on McPeake and Guthrie 2007.

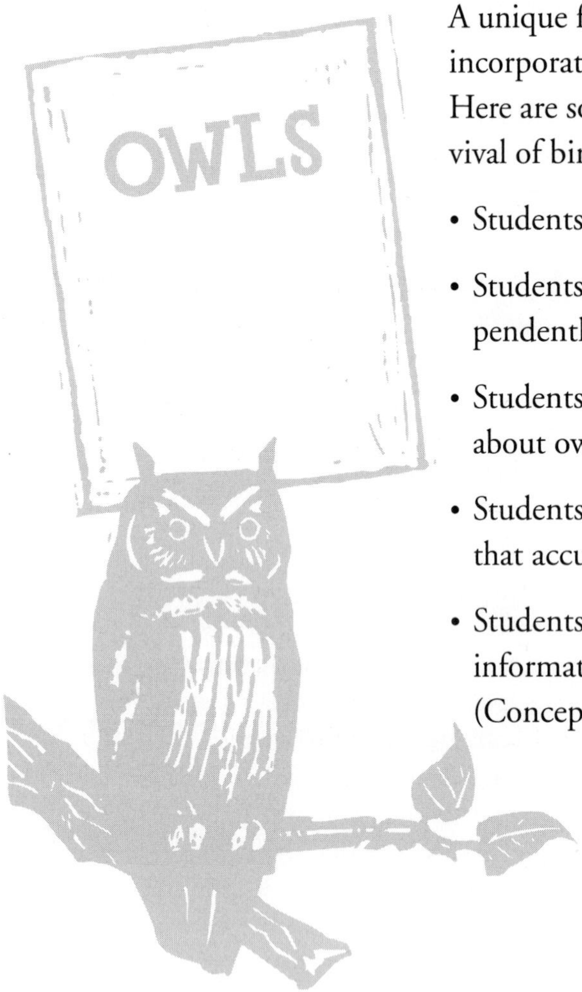

Motivational Practices in Action

A unique feature of CORI is that motivational practices are incorporated into and drive each phase of daily instruction. Here are some examples from a theme-based unit on the survival of birds (McPeake and Guthrie 2007).

- Students go on a habitat walk to observe birds. (Relevance)
- Students chose a theme-related narrative book to read independently, such as *White Bird* (Bulla 1990). (Choice)
- Students work in pairs to generate and answer questions about owls. (Collaboration)
- Students praise each other for successfully creating a poster that accurately shows how birds live. (Success)
- Students make a graphic organizer about owls, based on information they read in a chapter of a book about owls. (Conceptual Theme)

Comprehensive Reading Model

core reading program
strategic supplemental intervention
intensive intervention

Comprehensive Reading Model

SEE ALSO . . .

The Big Picture, p. 1

Implementing instructional practices based on the most current scientific reading research is key to ensuring achievement for all learners. A focal instructional goal in education is for every student to meet or exceed grade-level reading expectations. Therefore, when school districts have an organized, coherent, and comprehensive plan for effective reading program implementation across all schools, more students have a greater likelihood of reaching this goal. In order to meet the varied needs of learners in a school setting, many successful school districts use a three-tier model for reading instruction. In this model, each tier represents a specific type of instruction that increases in intensity based on student need. Tier I provides quality, research-based instruction for all students, and Tiers II and III deliver intensive intervention for students most at risk for reading difficulty. The coordination of a three-tier model with the response-to-intervention process (RtI) and a thorough plan for implementation supplies the architecture for a comprehensive reading model.

Levels of Learners

Benchmark (Tier I)

Strategic (Tier II)

Intensive (Tier III)

Three-Tier Model of Instruction

The three-tier model is a model of prevention, linking scientifically based reading research to practice, assessment, and professional development. Tier I includes implementing research-based core reading programs for most students, Tier II includes strategic interventions and support for students who could use a boost, and Tier III includes intensive and sustained interventions for students who are way behind their peers. Assessment data (e.g., screening, progress monitoring, and diagnostic) determine the instruction delivered in each tier. Data can also inform the

THREE-TIER MODEL

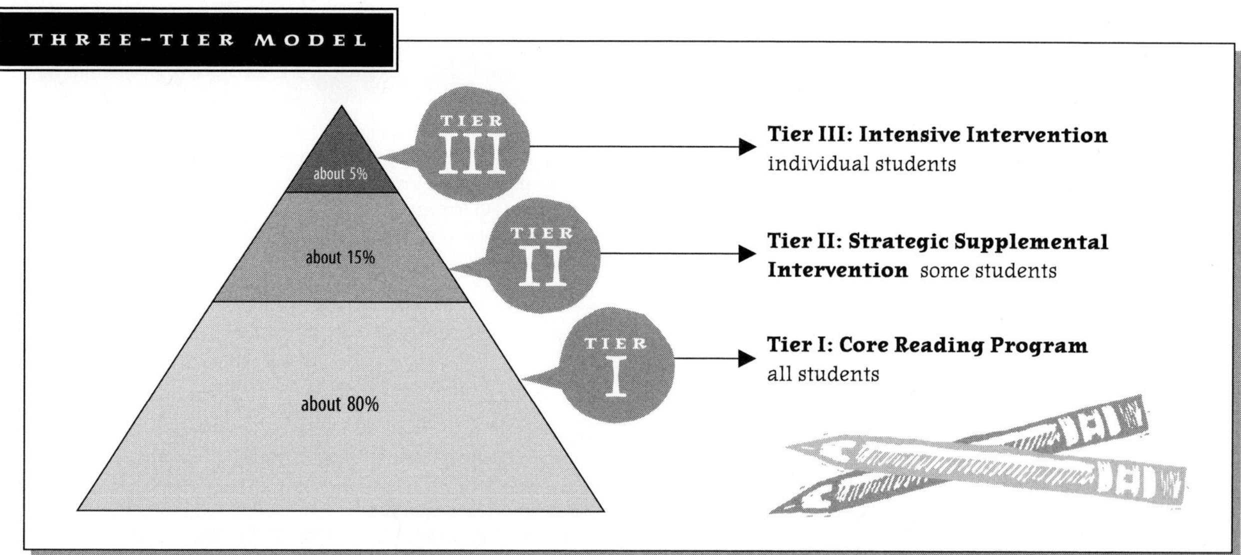

Based on National Association of State Directors of Special Education 2006.

> The three-tier model is more than a quick fix; it is a commitment to changing the process of providing quality reading instruction for all students.
>
> —VAUGHN GROSS CENTER FOR READING AND LANGUAGE ARTS, 2005

intensity, frequency, and duration of professional development support at the district, school, or classroom level. Ultimately, the three-tier model provides a system that is quick to respond to students' changing needs and is essential for preventing reading difficulties in most children. Each instructional tier is intended to support teachers in implementing research-based practices at levels of fidelity designed to improve student achievement (National Association of State Directors of Special Education 2006).

When a scientifically validated core reading program is solidly implemented in the general education classroom (Tier I), the majority of students should be able to meet proficiency within their grade level. Unfortunately, this is not the case for many schools, especially those who serve large numbers of students who are disadvantaged. In this case, the triangle may actually be inverted, with the majority of students needing intensive intervention. To meet grade-level expectations, students attending these schools will need specialized intervention instruction to accelerate their progress. A concentrated effort will have to be made to implement the three-tier model fully in order to increase student achievement. A failure to do so will impact students' quality of education and future success.

Three-Tier Model of Instruction

		Tier I Core Reading Program	Tier II Strategic Supplemental Intervention	Tier III Intensive Intervention
Focus	Elementary School	Quality, comprehensive reading instruction for all students	Strategic intervention programs, strategies, and procedures that support, enhance, and/or supplement Tier I core reading program instruction	Customized, stand-alone, intensive, and sustained interventions for students who still have acute reading difficulties, despite efforts in Tiers I and II
	Secondary School	Quality, comprehensive language arts instruction for all students		
Type of Learner	Elementary School	All students working at advanced, benchmark, strategic, or intensive levels	Students not making adequate progress in Tier I	Seriously at-risk students not making adequate progress in Tiers I and II
	Secondary School	Students working at or above grade level and students receiving added strategic supplemental intervention		
Type of Teacher	Elementary School	Classroom teacher	Classroom teacher and/or support staff, as determined by school site administration	Support staff, as determined by school site administration
	Secondary School	English/language arts teacher		
Program	Elementary School	Research-based reading program targeting the five essential components: phonemic awareness, phonics, reading fluency, vocabulary, and comprehension	Specialized, research-based supplemental reading program that targets specific student weaknesses	Sustained, research-based intensive stand-alone reading program that targets specific student weaknesses
	Secondary School	Research-based language arts program that focuses on vocabulary, comprehension, reading fluency writing, and advanced thinking and reasoning skills		
Instructional Support	Elementary and Secondary Schools	Explicit, systematic instruction with repeated opportunities for practice and review	Explicit, systematic supplemental instruction with repeated opportunities for practice and review; supports Tier I	Explicit, systematic instruction designed and customized to meet students' needs; includes an acceleration plan
Instructional Time	Elementary School	At least 90 minutes per day	At least 30 additional minutes per day	At least two additional 30-minute sessions per day or one 90-minute session
	Secondary School	One or two periods in middle school; one period in high school	One additional period	Two- or three-period block
Classroom Setting/Grouping	Elementary School	General education classroom with flexible groupings	Appropriate setting designated by school; homogeneous small-group instruction (e.g., about six students)	Appropriate setting designated by school; homogenous small-group instruction (e.g., about four students)
	Secondary School	Advanced placement, honors, or regular English	Additional reading support class and/or ELD class; homogeneous small-group instruction	Intensive intervention class; size of small group determined by program guidelines
Assessment Plan	Elementary School	Fall screening for all students, plus winter and spring progress monitoring; additional progress monitoring using program-specific assessments	Diagnostic assessment to determine specific needs for intervention, plus progress monitoring biweeky	Diagnostic assessment to determine specific needs for intervention, plus progress monitoring weekly or biweekly; additional progress monitoring using program-specific assessments
	Secondary School	Screening at least once a year for all students, plus progress monitoring using program-specific assessments		
Professional Development	Elementary and Secondary Schools	Ongoing training specific to core reading/language arts program and aligned to research	Ongoing training that is specific to core reading/language arts program and/or supplemental program; additional components to support struggling readers	Ongoing training that is specific to intensive intervention program; additional components to support struggling readers

Tier I: Core Reading Program

To reduce the number of students at risk for reading problems, in Tier I, high-quality, comprehensive reading/language arts instruction based on assessment data is provided for all students.

Instructional Goal

The goal of Tier I instruction is to ensure that the majority of students' needs can be met in the general education classroom through the implementation of research-based programs and practices that focus on the five essential reading components. This instruction is intended to reduce the number of students at risk for reading failure. Since instruction at this tier targets students who are above, at, or slightly below grade level, differentiated instruction is critical. The Tier I classroom can be organized homogeneously or heterogeneously, depending on the curriculum. In both organizational groupings, differentiated instruction based on individual needs should occur daily.

Assessment

In Tier I, assessment data are used collectively to determine students' instructional needs as well as to identify students who may be at risk for reading failure—students who may benefit from Tier II or Tier III support. Students who are identified as reading on grade level, or benchmark, will most likely benefit from Tier I instruction alone. Tier I assessment includes

- screening once a year, usually in fall;
- winter and spring progress monitoring using curriculum-based measurement (CBM) or independent screening/benchmark assessments;
- end-of-year outcome assessment (particularly for upper-grade students);
- specific core reading program assessments.

Professional Development

Tier I professional development must focus on how to teach the core reading curriculum and how it connects to the five essential reading components. At the school level, it is critical to have both initial and advanced professional development as well as follow-up training. This scaffolded professional development should address specific school and teacher needs and incorporate in-class coaching, lesson modeling, and side-by-side (Bessellieu 2006). At both the grade and school levels, adequate planning time should be allotted for teachers and support personnel to meet. Professional development also should include assessment administration and analysis of data so that teachers can differentiate effectively in Tier I and identify students who are in need of Tier II or Tier III intervention.

Three-Tier Model

Tier I: Core Reading Program

Tier II: Strategic Supplemental Intervention

Tier III: Intensive Intervention

Tier II: Strategic Supplemental Intervention

In Tier II, additional instructional support (i.e., programs, strategies, procedures) is provided to students who, according to assessment data, are not making adequate progress in Tier I. Tier II instruction also may supplement or enhance a weak curriculum component of the core reading program.

Instructional Goal

The goal of Tier II instruction is to provide sufficient additional assistance to enable students to improve their skills in order to be successful in Tier I instruction. This is often accomplished through specific preteaching, reteaching, and targeted review. In Tier II, instruction is more intensive, more explicit, and more focused than it is in Tier I. In addition, group size is smaller and instructional time is increased beyond the core reading block. At the middle- and high-school levels, Tier II instruction not only includes specific preteaching, reteaching, and targeted review using age-appropriate materials related to the core reading program, but also may include targeted intervention, as indicated by diagnostic assessment, in areas such as multisyllabic word reading and fluency. An additional reading support class may be necessary to implement this instruction in middle or high school.

Reading problems could be diminished if individual differences in skill development were addressed at the time they are first noticed, rather than waiting for these differences to become pronounced.

—O'CONNOR, FULMER, HARTY & BELL 2005

...across the grades, students identified as at-risk for reading difficulties need sustained support to improve reading outcomes over time.

—VAUGHN & CHARD, 2006

Three-Tier Model

Tier I: Core Reading Program

Tier II: Strategic Supplemental Intervention

Tier III: Intensive Intervention

Assessment

Students who are not making sufficient progress in Tier I and/or are identified as strategic on the screening assessment will most likely benefit from Tier II instruction. Progress monitoring for students in this tier should be conducted biweekly, targeting essential reading skills, oral reading fluency, and comprehension. Diagnostic assessment will accurately identify instructional strength and weakness in order to provide targeted support.

Professional Development

Tier II professional development is tied to the curriculum and students' specific needs. It focuses on assessment administration and analysis of data. Training should be provided for any supplemental programs. Support at the school level should include initial, advanced, and follow-up training. Part of that support should be setting aside additional time for classroom teachers and teachers who provide intervention to discuss student data and plan for instruction. Support at the classroom level should include in-class coaching.

Tier III: Intensive Intervention

In Tier III, intensive instructional support is provided for students who are significantly below grade level and who may have severe reading difficulties.

Instructional Goal

Tier III provides specifically designed and customized instruction for students who continue to have acute difficulties in reading, despite Tier I and Tier II efforts (Vaughn and Chard 2006). Ideally, if Tier I instruction is robust and if Tier II strategic support is sufficient, only a small percentage of students will require Tier III instruction. Instruction should accelerate learning, with the goal for students to catch up in one or two years. This tier of intervention may or may not include students in need of special education services (National Association of State

Directors of Special Education 2006). Instruction must be extremely focused, explicit, and intensive and targeted specifically to the skill needs of the students. Instructional grouping is usually smaller than Tier II, and instructional time is significantly increased. In some elementary schools, Tier III instruction replaces the core reading program with a specially engineered reading intervention program. At the middle- and high-school levels, Tier III instruction may be an intensive intervention class of two or more periods that replaces the regular English class.

Assessment

Students who are identified as intensive on the screening assessment and significantly below grade level will most likely benefit from Tier III instruction. Progress monitoring for students in this tier should be conducted weekly or biweekly to ensure adequate progress and learning. Diagnostic assessment should also be administered to accurately identify areas of strength and weakness in order to provide targeted instruction to meet specific student needs within Tier III.

Movement through Tier I, Tier II, and Tier III is a dynamic process, with students entering and exiting as needed.

—VAUGHN GROSS CENTER FOR READING AND LANGUAGE ARTS, 2005

Professional Development

Tier III professional development is tied to the curriculum and students' specific needs. It focuses on assessment administration and analysis of data, how to provide students with increased opportunities for practice and review with corrective feedback, and how to accelerate student progress. Support at the classroom level should focus on in-class coaching. School-level support should include setting aside additional time for classroom teachers and those teachers who provide intervention to discuss student data and plan for instruction.

Features of RtI

High-quality, research-based instruction in general education classroom

Universal screening assessment for all students

Frequent progress monitoring

Research-based Tier II and Tier III interventions

Measures of instructional fidelity

Problem-solving teams

Bradley, Danielson, and Doolittle 2005.

A key premise in RtI … is the need to ensure that the first tier of reading instruction is adequate, if not exemplary.

—JUSTICE, 2006

Response to Intervention (RtI)

RtI is part of the federal legislation for identifying students for special education placement, the Individuals with Disabilities Education Act (IDEA). Even though many schools still may use discrepancy between IQ and achievement to identify learning disabilities and student eligibility for special education, IDEA advocates the use of the RtI process as an alternative determination for such educational decisions. Providing services to students who struggle, the RtI process is applied within the three-tier model.

The foundational structure of RtI is built upon providing early intervention to all students, rather than waiting for students to fail. With RtI, all students—whether they are found to have a formal learning disability or not—receive targeted intervention instruction to meet their specific learning needs. Student progress at each tier is closely monitored and instructional decisions are based on student responsiveness to instruction (Fuchs et al. 2003; Tilly 2002; Vaughn 2003). Ultimately, the implementation of RtI within the three-tier model may reduce the number of students in special education because the program calls for providing effective instruction and intensified intervention to students in general education first, before making referrals to special education (Vaughn and Chard 2006). As these students receive increasingly intense interventions according to need, only those students who do not show sufficient progress are then formally evaluated for special education (Fletcher 2006; Klingner and Edwards 2006).

Problem-Solving Teams

Problem-solving teams are an integral part of the RtI process. Teams provide the structure for general, intervention, and special-education teachers to work closely together to identify problems, make instructional decisions, and evaluate the effectiveness of interventions (Denton 2006). Team members may include a school principal, counselor, special education teacher,

A problem-solving method provides educators with a consistent step-by-step process to identify problems and evaluate the effectiveness of interventions.

—NATIONAL ASSOCIATION OF STATE DIRECTORS OF SPECIAL EDUCATION, 2006

psychologist, Title I teacher, reading specialist, speech and language pathologist, grade-level general education teacher, and others. These teams meet regularly to analyze data and use the problem-solving method shown below to evaluate student progress and determine "next steps" in the intervention process.

Problem-Solving Method

A clear decision-making, or problem-solving, process should be in place at each tier of instruction. Four basic questions form the cyclical structure of problem solving:

1. What is the problem? Identify the problem a student is having.
2. Why is it happening? Analyze why the student is not meeting instructional goals.
3. What should be done? Make an instructional plan for the student, based on the analysis.
4. Did it work? Evaluate the student's assessment data to determine whether the instructional plan was effective or needs to be modified (Tilly 2002).

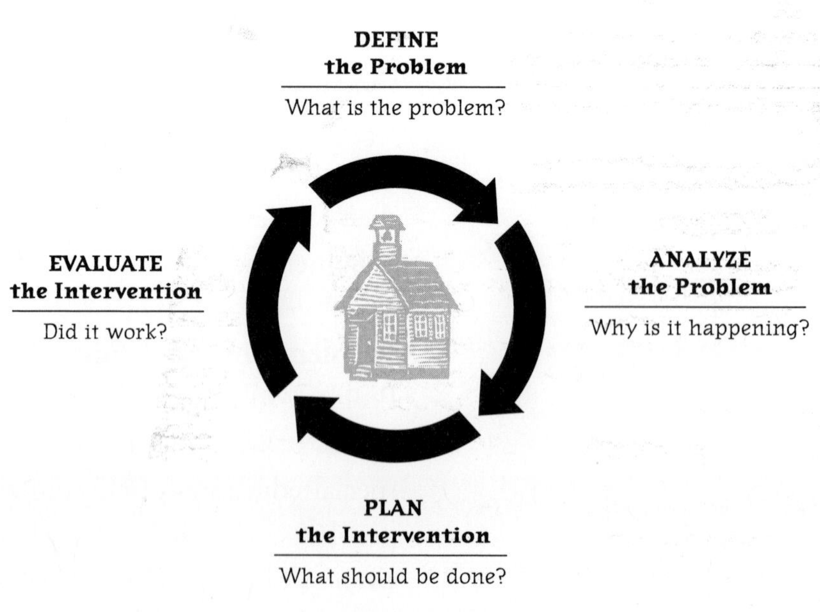

Based on National Association of State Directors of Special Education 2006.

Plan for Implementation

The comprehensive reading model provides an instructional framework to ensure that all students succeed. It requires well-designed and ongoing professional development to equip educators with the knowledge base they need for effective reading instruction and data analysis; it requires the selection and implementation of appropriate tools at each tier that are tightly linked to the research; and, finally, it requires committed and dedicated support systems to ensure smooth implementation and success for all students.

In order to fully implement a comprehensive reading model, districts or schools need to have in place an organized and thorough implementation plan. Following is a list of components that should be part of any plan. Because the components are interrelated, full implementation of each component is critical to ensuring success at the district, school, and classroom levels. Many of these same components have been implemented successfully in diverse schools—from schools managed by the Bureau of Indian Affairs to large urban districts in California and Georgia.

Choose a Reading Program and Prepare the Staff

- Select research-based instructional materials based on student data: core reading program (Tier I), strategic supplemental intervention (Tier II), and intensive intervention (Tier III).
- Fully implement the core reading program, including training of staff, and hiring and training of coaches and administrators.
- Create an instructional pacing plan and time line.
- Allocate instructional time for reading; build a schedule that incorporates intervention and protects reading time.

Designing, implementing, and sustaining effective reading programs is everybody's business.

—DIAMOND, 2006

Design a Comprehensive Assessment System

- Design a Tier II and Tier III assessment plan that incorporates screening, diagnostic, progress monitoring, and outcome assessments; design a process to evaluate student progress.
- Establish regular data study sessions at district, site, and grade or department levels to analyze the data and use it to plan instruction and interventions.

Create a Problem-Solving Model

- Select members of a problem-solving team; allocate time to meet on a consistent basis.
- Establish a system for problem solving and decision making.

Develop a Plan for Tiered Interventions

- In Tiers I and II, implement programs that provide extra support for students somewhat below grade-level expectations.
- In Tier III, implement a targeted, intensive intervention program for students performing significantly below grade-level expectations.

Provide Professional Development

- Provide ongoing, differentiated classroom-based support.
- Provide coach and administrator training informed by student performance data.

Develop a Procedure for Monitoring Program Implementation

- Develop a procedure for monitoring and sustaining program implementation.
- Recalibrate and adjust the procedure based on annual outcome data.

For printable PDFs of the Resources section, go to www.corelearn.com/SB2Resources.html

Resources

Alaska Adventure

Jake Mays and his dad spent two weeks visiting Alaska. They flew to Anchorage and then took a train south to a lodge in Seward, a small harbor town surrounded by the Kenai mountain range. From there they took day trips around the area to see and experience the sights. Jake found it all so enticing that he never wanted to leave.

Every day brought a new adventure. They traveled by ferry and sailboat on the marine highways through straits and inlets. They paddled sea kayaks up narrow fjords lined with ice cliffs. They saw whales, otters, puffins, sea lions, and eagles. They spent a day on a fishing schooner catching salmon for dinner. Jake snapped pictures of every new vista.

"Mom is not going to believe how awesome the scenery is!" he said. "Next time, we have to coordinate the schedule so that she can come with us."

On the flight home, they pored over the map, already planning the return trip. Jake thought it would be exciting to do some backpacking on Mount McKinley, the tallest peak in North America.

"Wouldn't it be fun to explore the state's interior? We could travel north from Anchorage to visit Denali National Park. I heard that the fishing is first class, and there is plenty of wildlife to see."

"That's true," said Dad. "Still, it is hard to resist the idea of retracing the route we just traveled. Now that we're expert kayakers, we should paddle around the capes and coves and lagoons of the Alaska Peninsula." Dad pointed at the chain of volcanic islands separating the Pacific Ocean from the Bering Sea. "The Aleutian archipelago stretches for more than a thousand miles. We could spend a lifetime on the water just exploring this part of the Ring of Fire."

"Well, that settles it," said Jake. "We just need to come back and stay longer."

"You've got that right," said Dad.

MAP

STATE OF ALASKA

Alaska Adventure

Jake Mays and his dad/spent two weeks visiting Alaska.//They flew to Anchorage/and then took a train south/to a lodge in Seward,/a small harbor town/surrounded by the Kenai mountain range.//From there/they took day trips around the area/to see and experience the sights.//Jake found it all so enticing/that he never wanted to leave.//

Every day brought a new adventure.//They traveled by ferry and sailboat/on the marine highways/through straits and inlets.//They paddled sea kayaks/up narrow fjords/lined with ice cliffs.//They saw whales,/otters, puffins,/sea lions,/and eagles.//They spent a day/on a fishing schooner catching salmon for dinner.//Jake snapped pictures/of every new vista.//

"Mom is not going to believe how awesome the scenery is!" he said.//"Next time,/we have to coordinate the schedule/so that she can come with us."//

On the flight home,/they pored over the map,/already planning the return trip.//Jake thought it would be exciting/to do some backpacking/on Mount McKinley,/the tallest peak/in North America.//

"Wouldn't it be fun/to explore the state's interior?//We could travel north/from Anchorage/to visit Denali National Park.//I heard/that the fishing is first class,/and there is plenty of wildlife to see."//

"That's true,"/said Dad.//"Still,/it is hard to resist/the idea of retracing/the route we just traveled.//Now that we're expert kayakers,/we should paddle/around the capes and coves and lagoons/of the Alaska Peninsula."//Dad pointed at the chain/of volcanic islands/separating the Pacific Ocean/from the Bering Sea.//"The Aleutian archipelago stretches/for more than a thousand miles.//We could spend a lifetime/on the water/just exploring this part of the Ring of Fire."//

"Well,/that settles it,"/said Jake.//"We just need/to come back/and stay longer."//

"You've got that right,"/said Dad.

Albert Einstein Asks a Question

BY JOHN ROSS

ALBERT EINSTEIN was born in Ulm, Germany, in 1879. When he was five, he was sick in bed for a time. His father gave him a compass. "But why does the needle always point north?" asked the boy. "I don't know why," his dad confessed. Later, the young Einstein studied the subject and found out the answer. And he never stopped asking questions after that. "The most important thing is to keep asking questions," Einstein would always tell young people who wanted to become scientists.

Einstein did not do well in school. His teachers said he was slow to learn. "Albert will never amount to very much," said the principal. But Einstein's mind wasn't slow. It was really working much faster than the school principal could ever have imagined. He wanted to know how everything worked. He thought a lot about space and time. He thought a lot about energy. He thought about atoms and how all the energy inside them could explode outward. He thought about how light travels in waves. He wondered what would happen to a person if he or she traveled at the speed of light, and he guessed that person would never grow old.

Einstein's scientific theories forever changed our understanding of the world. He called his ideas "theories" or "thought experiments." He tested his experiments by making pictures in his mind and using his imagination like a laboratory. These thought experiments were so hard to explain that sometimes only a few people in the whole world could understand what Einstein was thinking. Einstein's most famous theory is the theory of relativity. This is how he explained the theory of relativity: "If you sit with a pretty girl for an hour, it seems like only a minute. But if you sit on a hot stove for a minute, it seems like an hour. That's relativity."

In 1933, Albert Einstein fled Germany and went to the United States. From then until his death in 1955, he taught at Princeton University in New Jersey. There, he enjoyed sailing, playing the violin, putting together jigsaw puzzles, and building houses from playing cards. Einstein rode his bicycle everywhere; he thought driving was way too complicated.

When Einstein wanted to think, he often went for a walk. He usually wore a long overcoat and a black hat on top of his wild white hair (which was always uncombed). He would bring a notepad with him, to take notes on his "thought experiments." Sometimes he would get so lost in his own thoughts that he would get lost for real. Einstein would have to ask neighbors for directions home.

When this famous scientist died at the age of 76, he left his brain to science. Scientists wanted to see if it was different from the average human brain. Nothing unusual turned up—until quite recently. In June 1999, a research team from Canada announced that Einstein's brain is fifteen percent wider than normal in one particular area. This area seems to have something to do with mathematical thinking. Maybe having a wider area *caused* Einstein to be a math genius. Maybe having a wider area is the *result* of Einstein's being a math genius. Or maybe this larger area doesn't mean either of these things. Hmmm. Maybe it has to do with asking all those questions.

BMX Bikes

BMX bikes should have 20-inch wheels. The bolts should be tight. Take off any lights, and take off the kickstand.

Bike height is from 10 to 13 inches. A short bike can go fast, but your feet can hit the ground on turns. A tall bike has room for turns, but it jerks at top speed.

Choose the size of the wheelbase for the way you ride. Short is good for ramp riding and jumping. Long is good for going down hills.

Hot bikes are made for cool moves. To pop a wheelie, pump hard on the pedals. Shift your weight to the back of the seat. Pull up on the front wheel. It will lift the wheel off of the ground. You will be able to ride for a long way with your front wheel up high.

BMX Bikes

BMX bikes should have 20-inch wheels. The bolts 8
should be tight. Take off any lights, and take off the kickstand. 20

Bike height is from 10 to 13 inches. A short bike can go 33
fast, but your feet can hit the ground on turns. A tall bike has 47
room for turns, but it jerks at top speed. 56

Choose the size of the wheelbase for the way you ride. 67
Short is good for ramp riding and jumping. Long is good for 79
going down hills. 82

Hot bikes are made for cool moves. To pop a wheelie, 93
pump hard on the pedals. Shift your weight to the back of the 106
seat. Pull up on the front wheel. It will lift the wheel off of the 121
ground. You will be able to ride for a long way with your front 135
wheel up high. 138

The Case of the Blue Carbuncle

BASED ON A STORY BY SIR ARTHUR CONAN DOYLE

"What are you investigating today?" I asked my friend Sherlock Holmes as I walked into his apartment. He did not reply, so I moved in to see what he was holding under his magnifying glass.

"Why, Holmes!" I exclaimed. "It's just an old hat. What's so valuable about it?"

"Nothing whatsoever," he replied. "I'm only studying the hat to find the owner of the goose."

"The goose?!" I asked, perplexed.

"The facts are these, Watson," explained Holmes. "Police Commissioner Peterson was walking home last night. He saw a man ahead carrying a fat goose. At Goodge Street, a rough gang appeared and knocked off the man's hat. The man swung his walking stick to fight back, and Commissioner Peterson rushed to help. Startled, the man dropped the goose and ran. The gang scattered, too, leaving Peterson with the goose and the hat."

"Which, surely, he returned to their owner?" asked I.

"There's the problem. True, the owner's name—Henry Baker—is stitched inside the hat. But there are hundreds of Henry Bakers in London. It would be impossible to find the right one. So, Peterson brought the hat to me. He took the goose home to cook before it spoiled."

Just then, the door flew open. Peterson rushed in. "The goose, Mr. Holmes!" he gasped. "See what my wife found in its crop!" He held out a dazzling blue stone. It was no bigger than a bean, but it sparkled like a star.

Sherlock Holmes whistled. "Peterson! Do you know what you have there?"

"It's the Countess of Morcar's blue carbuncle!" I cut in.

"Precisely," replied Holmes. "I have the newspaper article right here:

'. . . Police arrested plumber John Horner. Hotel Cosmopolitan manager James Ryder reported to police that Horner fixed a pipe in the countess's room on the day of the robbery. Horner, who has a criminal record, claims he is innocent.'

"The question is: How did the stone get from jewelry box to bird?"

Holmes took a pencil and paper and wrote: "Found on Goodge Street: 1 goose, 1 black felt hat. Mr. Henry Baker can have same—221B Baker Street. 6:30 p.m. this evening."

"Peterson, put this ad in all the papers and bring me a new goose!"

At 6:30 sharp, Henry Baker knocked on Holmes's door. Holmes handed Baker his hat. Then he explained that he had eaten Baker's goose but was offering another one in its place. Baker thanked Holmes, unconcerned that it was a different goose.

"By the way," asked Holmes, "could you tell me where your goose came from? It was delicious."

"Oh, yes, from my favorite inn," replied Baker. "The Alpha."

"So now we know Baker isn't the thief," Holmes remarked after Henry Baker had left. "I say we eat dinner later. Let's follow this clue while it's still hot."

We arrived at the Alpha Inn and ordered tea. "This tea should be wonderful if it's as good as your geese," Holmes told the innkeeper.

"My geese?" asked the innkeeper hesitantly.

"Yes, I heard about them from Henry Baker."

"Aha! Them's not our geese," the innkeeper answered. "I got them from a man named Breckinridge in Covent Garden."

After tea, we headed for Covent Garden and found a stall with the name Breckinridge. Holmes approached and said, "I want a goose—same kind you sold to the Alpha Inn. Where'd you get them?"

Breckinridge fumed, "Why's everybody asking about those geese? 'Where did they come from? Where did they go?' I'm tired of it!"

"I bet you five pounds those were country geese," said Holmes.

"You lose," said Breckinridge. "They're town geese. Look here at my register."

Holmes read, "Mrs. Oakshott, 117 Brixton Road, number 249."

Holmes threw down his money with a huff. As we walked away, he laughed, "Anything for a bet! We'll visit Mrs. Oakshott tomorrow. Shall we have dinner, Watson? Chicken sounds good tonight."

We were interrupted by shouts. Mr. Breckinridge was yelling at a rat-faced little man, "Enough of you and your geese! Go away!"

"This might save us a trip to Brixton Road," whispered Holmes. "Let's see about this fellow." Holmes went up to the man and touched his shoulder. He jumped. "What do you want?" he cried.

"I heard you asking about geese," said Holmes. "I believe I can help you."

"Who are you? What could you know about it?" said the rat-faced man.

"My name is Sherlock Holmes. It is my business to know things. I know you are looking for a goose raised by Mrs. Oakshott. She sold it to Breckinridge. He sold it to the Alpha Inn. They sold it to Henry Baker."

"Oh, sir, you're just who I am looking for!" exclaimed the man.

"Before we talk, tell me your name."

The man looked sideways and answered, "John Robinson."

"No, your real name," said Holmes.

The man turned red, "Well, then. It's James Ryder."

"Ah, yes. Manager of the Hotel Cosmopolitan. Come to my place. I'll tell you everything."

Back at his apartment, Holmes began, "You want to know what became of that goose?"

"Oh, yes!"

"It came here. And a remarkable bird it was. No wonder you want to know about it. It laid an egg, after it was dead. The brightest little blue egg I ever saw. See?" Holmes held up the blue carbuncle. It gleamed in the firelight. Ryder stared, motionless.

"The game's over, Ryder," said Holmes. "You knew Horner had a criminal record, so the police would go after him. You gave Horner a job in the countess's room. When he finished, you took the gem. Then you called the police."

"Don't turn me in!" Ryder begged. "I swear I'll never do wrong again!"

"We'll talk about that," replied Holmes, "but first, tell me, how did the gem get into the goose and away from you? Tell the truth; it's your only hope."

Ryder confessed, "After Horner's arrest, I had to hide the stone. I went to my sister's on Brixton Road, where she and her husband, Oakshott, raise geese.

"In their yard, I got an idea. My sister had offered me a goose to take home. I grabbed one and put the stone down its throat. Suddenly, the goose jumped out of my arms back into the flock! To my relief, I recognized the bar on its tail and caught it again. When I got home and opened the goose, the stone was nowhere to be found! I ran back to my sister's, but she had just sold the whole flock to Breckinridge, including one of her two bar-taileds. The rest you know."

My friend Holmes got up and threw open the door. "Get out!" he yelled.

Ryder crashed down the stairs, slammed the door, and ran away.

Holmes said, "I look at it this way, Watson. Ryder is too afraid to become a criminal. Now, I think it's time we investigate another bird. Let's hope our dinner doesn't set off another wild goose chase."

Common Sense: An Anansi Tale

Anansi, the spider, was full of mischief. He loved to play jokes and pull pranks on people. One day, he decided to collect all the common sense in the world. Everyone uses these little bits of good judgment every day. "If," Anansi thought, "I alone had all of this sensible information, I could sell it back to people when they needed it." Anansi imagined people lining up to pay him for answers to the simplest questions: *Anansi, what should I wear when it's cold outside? What should I do when I am hungry?*

"This is a brilliant scheme," thought Anansi. "I will have all the common sense in the world, and all the money in the world, too!"

So Anansi got a sack and started collecting common sense. *Brush your teeth to prevent cavities! Put your socks on before your shoes!* Anansi put them all in his sack.

The sack was soon bursting at the seams. "I need to find a better place to keep the common sense," thought Anansi. Just then he spied a calabash growing on a vine. It looked like a giant pumpkin. Anansi hollowed out the calabash. Then he stuffed all of the common sense inside and kept collecting.

When Anansi had gathered up every bit of common sense, he thought, "Now I just have to find a good place to hide it."

Anansi set off through the jungle to find just the right hiding place. He dragged the calabash under ferns and over logs. He waded through streams. He trudged from shrub to bush to hedge. He hiked up muddy trails and slid down steep hillsides. Finally Anansi found the tallest tree in the jungle.

"This is the perfect hiding place," he said. "The calabash will be safe and sound. No one would ever guess that I have hidden such a valuable treasure in such an unusual place."

Using a thick rope, Anansi tied the heavy calabash around his neck so that it dangled in front of him like a locket on a necklace. He started up the tree trunk, but climbing was hard. The calabash flopped and swayed. It banged Anansi's belly. It bruised his knees and elbows. The rope burned the back of his neck. But even though Anansi was aching and battered, he did not stop. The thought of getting rich kept him going.

As Anansi was struggling upward, he heard someone giggling below him. He looked down and saw a small boy leaning against the tree trunk.

Anansi called down to the boy. "What is so funny?" he asked.

"*You* are," said the boy. "Anyone with a pinch of common sense knows that it is easier to carry things on your back—especially if you are climbing a tree. How foolish can you get?"

The boy's words made Anansi furious! Anansi thought he had collected all the common sense in the world. How could he have missed the one piece he needed most? The thought made Anansi madder and madder. Finally he lost his temper and swung the calabash with all his might against the tree trunk.

The calabash shattered into a million pieces. The common sense spilled out and pieces got caught in a breeze. The breeze blew little pieces of common sense all over the world. And that explains why today everyone has a little bit of common sense to use and a little bit of common sense to share. But, as you yourself know, nobody got all of it. It was Anansi who made it happen that way.

The GREENHOUSE Effect

The greenhouse effect is the rise in temperature that Earth experiences because certain gases in the atmosphere trap energy from the sun that is reflected off Earth—energy that would otherwise escape back into outer space. Scientists now believe that the greenhouse effect is making Earth warmer, enough to drastically change the climate. An increase in global temperature of just one degree can impact rainfall patterns and sea levels. The rise in temperature can cause problems for plants, wildlife, and humans.

Water vapor, carbon dioxide (CO_2), methane (CH_4), nitrous oxide (N_2O), chlorofluorocarbons (CFCs), ozone (O_3), perfluorocarbons (PFCs), and hydrofluorocarbons (HFCs) are the "greenhouse gases" in our atmosphere. These types of gases behave much like the glass panes of a greenhouse. The glass lets in light but prevents heat from escaping, causing the greenhouse to heat up, much like the inside of a car parked in the sun on a hot day.

People are contributing to Earth's warming by increasing the CO_2 in the atmosphere. Trees, like all living things, are made mostly of carbon. When people burn forests, the carbon in trees is transformed into CO_2. Trees, like other plants, use photosynthesis to absorb carbon dioxide and release oxygen. When people cut down forests, less carbon dioxide is converted into oxygen. People also increase CO_2 in the air by burning "fossil fuels." These fuels include gasoline used in cars, SUVs, and trucks and fuels like coal and natural gas used by power plants to create electricity. Whenever fossil fuels are burned, CO_2 is released into the air.

Marine Mammals

MAMMALS ARE WARM-BLOODED ANIMALS. Marine mammals, such as whales, live in the ocean. Unlike fish, marine mammals cannot breathe underwater. They can dive very deep to find food. They can stay under the water for a long time. However, it is impossible for them to stay below the surface for an indefinite amount of time. They regularly need to resurface to get air.

One marine mammal is the largest animal ever to be found on Earth. This huge creature, called a blue whale, can be 90 feet long. It can weigh more than 100 tons. The blue whale is also the loudest animal on earth. It makes a deep, resounding rumble that has no comparison on land or sea. Whenever the blue whale has the impulse to talk to other whales, it sends out a noise that travels uninterrupted through the ocean. Other whales react when they hear the call even if they are many miles away.

The blue whale requires an unusual amount of food each day. You might think that it hunts big game in the sea, but you would be incorrect. It lives on an infinite number of extremely tiny creatures. They are called krill. With its mouth gaping wide, the whale swims into a school, or group, of krill. The whale scoops up the krill, along with a big mouthful of seawater. In place of teeth, the whale has rows of fringe-like filters called baleen. Baleen is made of material that looks like stiff bristles or hairs. It acts like a strainer. It lets the seawater flow out of the whale's mouth but traps the krill.

Blue whales may be mighty giants, but they are endangered. Though once they were abundant, today very few blue whales remain on our planet. Overhunting caused an imbalance in their population. New laws help to protect them and increase their numbers. We should be grateful for the caring people who have united, with a goal of ensuring the survival of these wonderful creatures.

Percussion Instruments

From primitive cave dwellers to modern city dwellers, people have always played percussion instruments. A percussion instrument is any musical instrument that you play by striking or hitting using either sticks or your hands. There are many kinds of percussion instruments, including drums, cymbals, and xylophones.

Of all the percussion instruments, drums are the most prevalent. They are commonly found all over the world. Every culture has developed its own type of drum. The drums may differ from culture to culture, place to place, and group to group, but all of them possess the same basic elements. They usually have a hollow shell, or frame, and a round drumhead.

The shell can come in many shapes and sizes. Shells are usually made out of metal or wood. They can be shallow like a snare drum's or deep like a conga drum's. They can be shaped like a cereal bowl, an hourglass, or even a kettle. The shell acts like a speaker to amplify the sound, or make it louder. A small drum, like a bongo, will sound faint compared to the huge noise made by a big bass drum used in a marching band.

The drumhead is usually made from an animal hide. The animal hide, or skin, is stretched tight over the drum shell. When the drummer hits the drumhead, it vibrates, or moves very quickly back and forth. This vibration creates a resonant, or deep and rich, sound. A drum's pitch depends on the size and the tightness of the drumhead. A smaller, tighter drumhead makes a higher-pitched sound.

Drumbeats are like beating hearts. You can hear their rhythms through the ages.

Pioneers on the Oregon Trail

"Ourselves moving on in the general throng, sand reflecting back the heat of the sun in your face and making the sweat trickle down. Oh, this is going to Oregon."

—HELEN STEWART, 1853

The Way West

In the early 1800s, Lewis and Clark explored the territory west of the Mississippi. No one knew what they would find. As they traveled, they made maps. They wrote in their journals. They described miles and miles of beautiful land with tall trees, good soil, and rushing rivers.

News about the wonders of the West spread. People began to dream about a new life in a new land. And before long, they began traveling west on the Oregon Trail. At first there were only a few adventurers. In 1843, two hundred families crossed the Oregon Trail. Then in 1848, gold was discovered in California. Soon after, thousands of people began heading west, hoping to make their dreams come true.

Packing for the Journey

Traveling west was not easy. The Oregon Trail was thousands of miles long and took between four and six months to cross. Pioneers had to pack everything they would need in a covered wagon that was not much bigger than a double bed. Once food, tools, and supplies for the journey

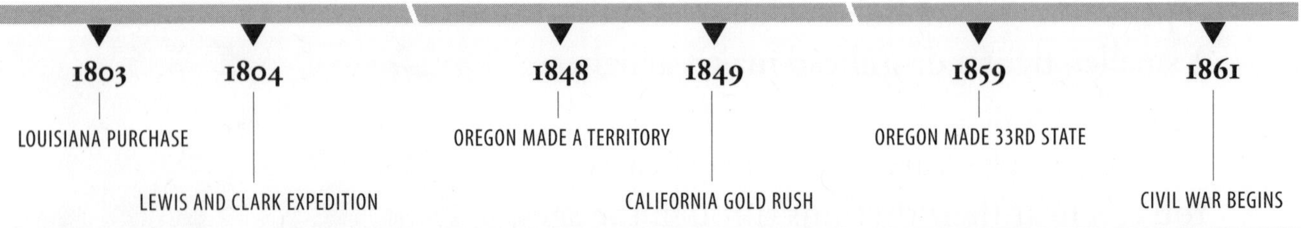

SUPPLIES NEEDED FOR 1 PERSON

- 100–200 lb. of bacon or salt pork
- 5–25 lb. of coffee
- 1/2 bu. of cornmeal
- 1/2 bu. of dried beans
- 10–20 lb. of dried fruit
- 200 lb. of flour, crackers, biscuits
- 10–20 lb. of lard
- 10–25 lb. of rice
- 2–4 lb. of baking soda
- 10–20 lb. of salt
- 25–50 lb. of sugar
- 1–3 lb. of tea
- pickles
- vinegar
- 3–5 full sets of clothing
- sturdy boots or shoes
- winter coat
- candles
- soap
- eating utensils

SUPPLIES NEEDED FOR 1 FAMILY

- butter churn
- cooking supplies
- water keg
- pail
- watch
- compass
- lantern
- tools
- hunting and fishing supplies
- rope
- chain
- spare wagon parts
- 500 matches

were packed, the wagon was nearly full. As a result, there was no room left for personal belongings. But the pioneers left behind more than the comforts of home and their special treasures. They said good-bye to family and friends they never expected to see again.

Wagons Ho!

Pioneers gathered at starting points between Independence, Missouri, and Council Bluffs, Iowa, to join up with wagon trains heading west. It was safest to travel with ten to fifteen wagons in a group. Wagon trains did not set out until there was enough grass growing on the prairie to feed the animals along the way. At the same time, they could not wait too long. The wagons had to get over the mountains before it started to snow.

A wagon train on the move could be one mile long and one mile wide. Bumping along inside a cramped wagon was a hard and uncomfortable way to travel. Pioneers often trudged beside the wagons instead. Consequently, most people *walked* slowly all the way to Oregon—nearly two thousand miles.

As the pioneers headed west, they watched for famous landmarks along the way. Some of the landmarks showed how far the pioneers had traveled. Others were especially steep mountain passes or dangerous rivers that had to be crossed. Others were forts where the pioneers could get news and supplies.

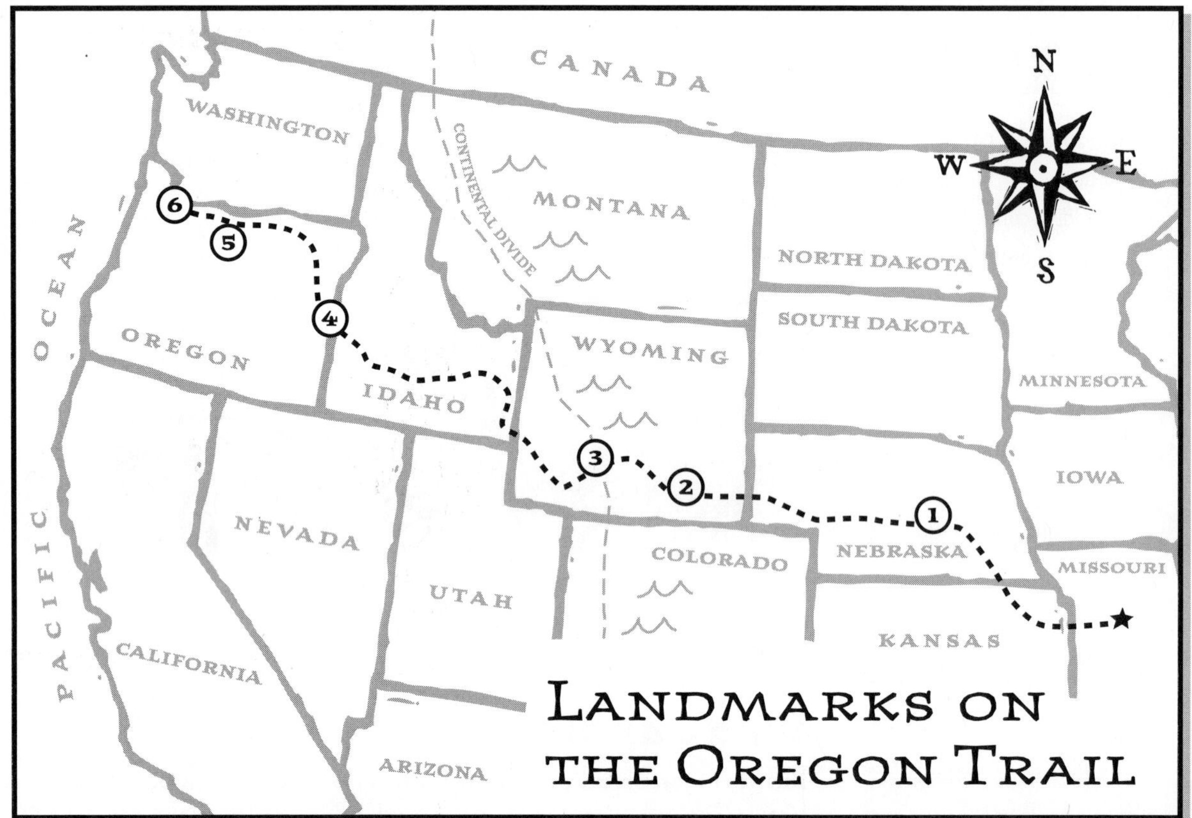

1. The **Platte River**, which curves through the prairie, had to be crossed several times, with the wagons fording or ferrying across the river.

2. Wagon trains had to reach **Independence Rock** by July 4th in order to stay on schedule; if they were late, they risked being caught in the snow.

3. At the **South Pass**, the pioneers passed into Oregon Territory.

4. Wagon trains came to the **Blue Mountains** late in the trip. This was one place where it was easy to get caught in an early snow.

5. At **The Dalles**, the pioneers could ferry down the Columbia River to Fort Vancouver.

6. Pioneers had to use ropes or chains and inch their wagons down **Laurel Hill**, one of the most terrifying parts of the journey but only a few days away from the end of the trail.

DID YOU KNOW?

Pioneers would milk their cows in the evening. Then in the morning, they would put the cream into the churn and set the churn inside the wagon. The constant rocking motion of the wagon would turn the cream to butter by the time they stopped for supper.

A Day on the Trail

If you were traveling in a wagon train on the Oregon Trail, you tried to travel at a steady pace. On a good day, you could go about fifteen miles. On a stormy day or over a bad part of the trail, you might go only one mile.

You would wake up at daybreak. Morning chores, including fixing breakfast, milking the cows, taking care of the animals, and packing up the wagon, would take a couple of hours. Then you would hitch up the mules or oxen and set out.

At noon you would find a place to stop and rest. Animals would graze and get water. You would eat a meal, rest, and make any repairs that were needed. Then you would set out again and keep going until four or five o'clock. You had to stop in time to get your chores done before nightfall.

Now the evening meal had to be cooked, which might mean gathering firewood, hunting or fishing, picking berries, and so on. Wagon repairs, cleaning and mending clothes, and other chores could be done. If you were lucky, you might find time to rest and relax. Musicians might pull out fiddles and harmonicas for singing and dancing by the campfire. Then it was time to go to bed, so that you could get up and do it again.

The End of the Trail

After four or five months of traveling, pioneers finally reached the Willamette Valley. Oregon City was the end of the Oregon Trail, where pioneers staked their claims to ranchland and farmland. Then the hard work really began.

The first winter in Oregon could be very hard. Supplies were low, and the weather turned rainy and cold. It was important to get busy and clear your land and build a cabin before the start of winter. But the end of the trail was where the dream of living in the West began. The pioneers who survived the trip had risked everything for a new life in the West.

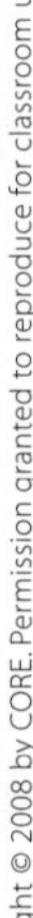

Studying the Sky

ASTRONOMY is the study of the planets, stars, and galaxies. People have been watching the movement of the sun, moon, planets, and stars since ancient times. So astronomy is a very, very old science.

From early times, people tried to make models of the universe. For many years, no one wanted to believe that the sun was the center of the solar system. It took a long time for people to accept this heliocentric model, with the earth orbiting around the sun with the other planets.

It is interesting to study the night sky like the astronomers from centuries ago. You can see even the most distant stars with your eyes alone. And you may be able to identify constellations, or groups of stars. Constellations make pictures in the sky, such as Canis Major (the Great Dog) or Ursa Minor (the Little Bear).

A telescope can be used to see faraway things more clearly. With a telescope, you can see details like the craters of the moon and other features of the lunar landscape, the moons of Jupiter, and the rings of Saturn.

Astronomy is like taking a trip back in time. This evening you can look at the same planets and stars that ancient astronomers observed so long ago.

TV Dinner

BY THE SAN FRANCISCO MIME TROUPE

Characters
Announcer: a TV announcer
Madam Video: Video Central's evil empress
Cosmo and Dodo: two raccoons
Pauline: a twelve-year-old TV fanatic
Henrietta: Pauline's pet guinea pig

ANNOUNCER: Pauline watches too much TV. She's behind on homework, forgets to wash the dishes, and has no time to play with Henrietta, her pet guinea pig. One night Henrietta is "pignapped" by two raccoon servants of Madam Video. Pauline sets out to find her.

ANNOUNCER: The setting is Madam Video's control room at Video Central. The walls are lined with TV monitors. Cosmo and Dodo are playing around. Henrietta is strapped to a special chair. Madam Video enters the room.

MADAM: *(speaking to audience)* Hi, kids. What a glorious night for my experiment—full moon, low-lying fog. If my Video Visor invention works—which lets you watch more TV in less time—I'll rule the mind of every kid within reach of this tower. *(to Cosmo)* Have you found me a subject?

COSMO: A perfect subject, primed and ready, your coldness.

MADAM: *(to Cosmo)* Excellent. Have some Bubbleicious Gum. If all goes well tonight, I'll show you something really special: six segments of "South Park"—uncut, prime stuff.

COSMO: Uncut, ooh, wow! Kyle and Stan and Cartman and Kenny. Awesome!

MADAM: Place the Video Visor on the subject. *(as Cosmo goes to do so, Madam sees the subject)* What is this?

HENRIETTA: I'm a guinea pig.

COSMO: It is a guinea pig, your monstrosity, just as you ordered.

MADAM: *(chasing raccoons)* You fools! You lazy bums! You, you—animals! I ask for a guinea pig to conduct my experiment and you bring me a . . . a . . .

COSMO: A guinea pig.

MADAM: I can't bear it. The experiment is ruined. It's worthless. You'll pay for this. I'm cutting you off. No TV.

COSMO: No TV? No, please, I can't stand it. *(falls on floor in a fit)*

DODO: Can we have just an hour's worth? Fifteen minutes?

MADAM: I'm pulling the plug.

DODO: No "Jeopardy"?

COSMO: How about Discovery Channel?

MADAM: Nothing. Not even bowling *(raccoons cry)* . . . until you bring me a real live child. *(an alarm sounds)* The video alarm! *(scans video screen)* A little girl is approaching. Perfect timing. Quick, lock that pig in the pantry. And get out of sight. *(raccoons obey, and Madam also hides)*

PAULINE: *(peeks in, stage right)* Henrietta? Henrietta? Where are you? *(walks around room)* Wow, look at all those TVs. This place is like a dream come true. *(turns on a TV)*

ANNOUNCER: Hello, America. Welcome to your favorite new show, "Reality Idiots". *(squabbling voices are heard)*

PAULINE: Oh, this is the show where people will do anything just to be on TV. *(turns off first TV and turns on another)*

ANNOUNCER: Got milk? It's fast food that's good for you.

PAULINE: *(to audience)* Milk? Yuk. *(turns off second TV)*

MADAM: *(entering)* Hello, dear.

PAULINE: Uh, are you real?

MADAM: As real as anything you'll ever see.

PAULINE: Hi, uh, my name is Pauline. I, uh, didn't mean to bust in, but . . . I'm looking for my pet. Two raccoons pignapped her and I gotta find her.

MADAM: Those naughty raccoons—they only wanted to play. But I scolded them, gave them all lettuce sandwiches, and then put them down for a nap. Why don't we let them sleep? *(taking Pauline to chair)* You and I can watch television.

PAULINE: Great—I didn't expect to end up in such a safe place. Can we watch "24"? My parents aren't into it.

MADAM: Anything you like, dear. Do you watch a great deal of television?

PAULINE: Not too much—only six hours a day. *(Madam puts Video Visor on her)* What's this?

MADAM: My new Video Visor. It lets you watch more TV in less time.

PAULINE: Wow. *(Madam turns on Visor)* What an awesome monitor! I could watch this forever.

MADAM: *(triumphantly)* You will, you will. *(calls)* Cosmo, Dodo! *(the raccoons enter)*

DODO: Yes, your repulsiveness.

COSMO: Coming, your grease. *(Pauline can tell that something's wrong and begins to struggle)*

MADAM: Program thirty minutes of commercials in ten seconds. *(raccoons bump into each other; Dodo programs the computer and Cosmo goes to read printout)*

COSMO: Maximum and rising.

MADAM: Brain activity?

DODO: Minimum and falling.

MADAM: *(removing Visor)* Little girl, can you hear me?

PAULINE: Yes.

MADAM: Try a Grease Burger . . .

PAULINE: . . . so tasty and good for you!

MADAM: Tired all day? Can't sleep at night? Ask your doctor about . . .

PAULINE: . . . Snooze Away. Side effects may include bad breath and pimples.

MADAM: What do you want for Christmas, little girl?

PAULINE: Webkins, an American Girl doll, and Baby Mastercharge. I answered all the questions, what's my prize?

MADAM: Stupid. *(to audience)* This is thrilling. *(back to Pauline)* What's your favorite food?

PAULINE: Baby Bottle Tops, Jolly Ranchers, Air Heads, Wing Pops . . . *(singing)* Wing Pops, Wing Pops, Wing Pops.

MADAM: It works! It works! My Video Visor works! First the raccoons, then the children. From this tower, I'll beam programs to make everyone in the entire world my obedient slaves.

COSMO AND DODO: *(dancing and singing)*

Madam Video will rule the world. Rule the world.
You will buy things you don't need. You don't need.
No one will remember how to read. How to read.
You may think her plan's insane,
But no one will dare complain.
You'll all be too busy watching your TVs.

Weekend Campout

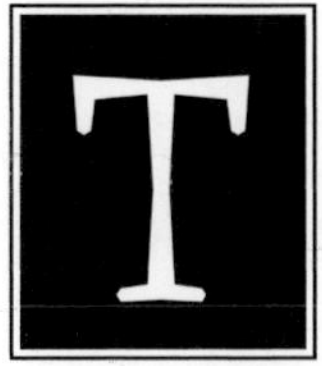HE FRANCO FAMILY loves to be outdoors. They spend almost every weekend camping. Fay Franco adores camping more than anything. She will even pitch her tent in the backyard just to sleep outside.

Fay has been to lots of campgrounds. Mar Vista Shores is her favorite. The campsites are in the tall trees. Each spot has a beach view.

At Mar Vista Shores, noisy birdcalls wake Fay early. She hears loud squawking and jumps up for breakfast. Then she packs a picnic. Fay and her dad drive to the trailhead. It is the place where the hiking trails start. They choose a path to take. Dad carries a daypack. It holds a first aid kit, sweatshirts, food, and water. The path leads sharply uphill to a waterfall. It is a steep climb! They hungrily devour their lunch by the riverbank. From the rocks, Fay can watch the water plummet over the cliff.

In the afternoon, Fay and her mom go to the seashore. Mom is a rock hound. She hunts for neat-looking stones. Fay makes sandcastles. Using wet sand, she builds high walls and towers. Sometimes she pokes around the tide pools. She looks for crabs and starfish in the rocks along the beach.

At dinnertime, the Franco family usually has a sunset cookout. They light a campfire. They roast hotdogs. The sky turns pink over the water. Nighttime falls. Fay gets into her sleeping bag. She looks up to see the stars twinkle overhead.

Fay thinks that weekend campouts are almost perfect. The only flaw comes when it is time to go home.

Weekend Campout

THE FRANCO FAMILY loves to be outdoors. They spend almost 10
every weekend camping. Fay Franco adores camping more 18
than anything. She will even pitch her tent in the backyard 29
just to sleep outside. 33

Fay has been to lots of campgrounds. Mar Vista Shores is her 45
favorite. The campsites are in the tall trees. Each spot has a beach view. 59

At Mar Vista Shores, noisy birdcalls wake Fay early. She hears 70
loud squawking and jumps up for breakfast. Then she packs a picnic. 82
Fay and her dad drive to the trailhead. It is the place where the hiking 97
trails start. They choose a path to take. Dad carries a daypack. It holds 111
a first aid kit, sweatshirts, food, and water. The path leads sharply 123
uphill to a waterfall. It is a steep climb! They hungrily devour their 136
lunch by the riverbank. From the rocks, Fay can watch the water 148
plummet over the cliff. 152

In the afternoon, Fay and her mom go to the seashore. Mom is a 166
rock hound. She hunts for neat-looking stones. Fay makes sandcastles. 177
Using wet sand, she builds high walls and towers. Sometimes she 188
pokes around the tide pools. She looks for crabs and starfish in the 201
rocks along the beach. 205

At dinnertime, the Franco family usually has a sunset cookout. 215
They light a campfire. They roast hotdogs. The sky 224
turns pink over the water. Nighttime falls. Fay 232
gets into her sleeping bag. She looks up to 241
see the stars twinkle overhead. 246

Fay thinks that weekend campouts 251
are almost perfect. The only flaw comes 258
when it is time to go home. 265

ACTIVITY MASTER

CONCEPT OF DEFINITION MAP

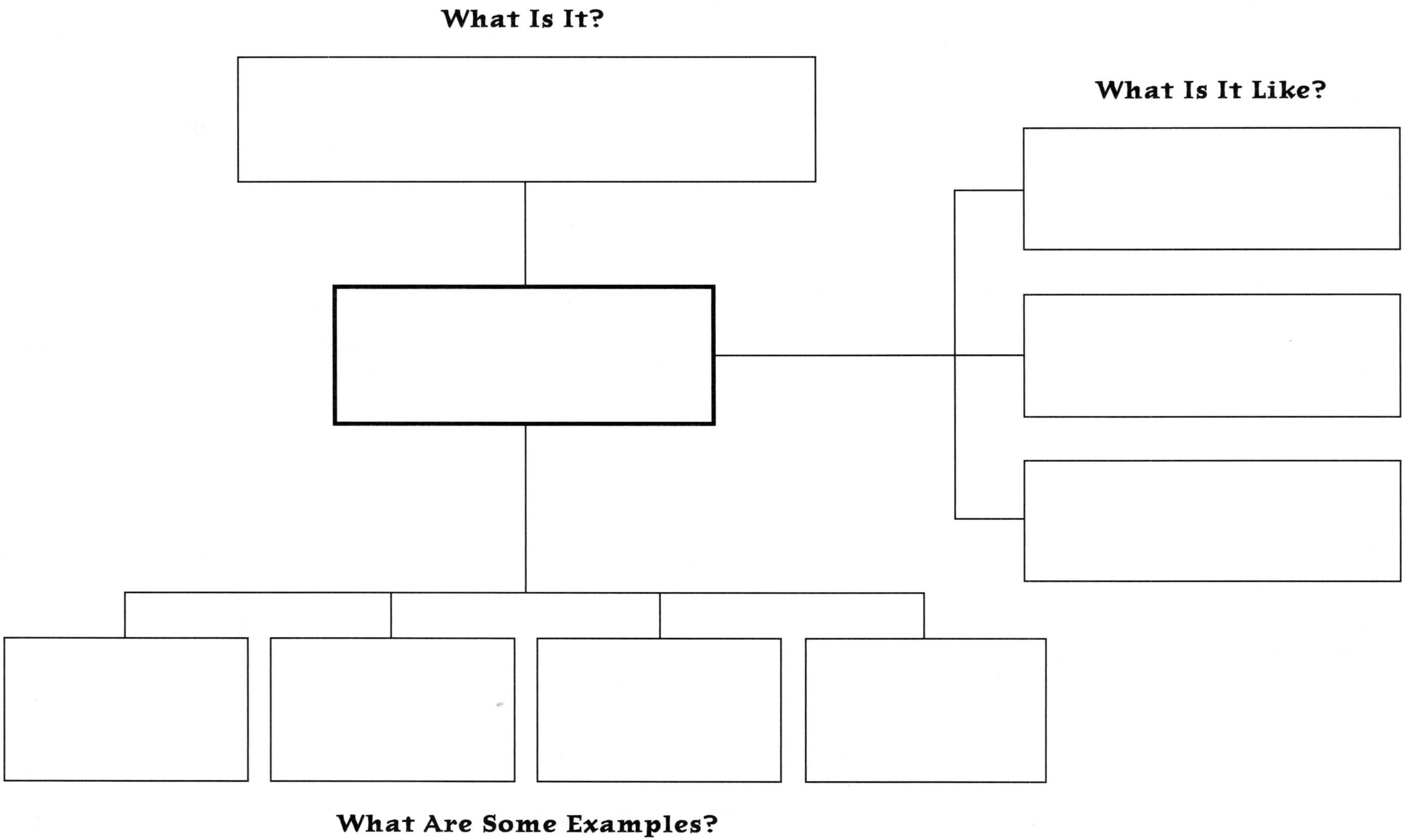

What Is It?

What Is It Like?

What Are Some Examples?

ACTIVITY MASTER

ELKONIN CARD

ACTIVITY MASTER

FIVE-SENSES SIMILE WEB

tastes like . . .

smells like . . .

feels like . . .

looks like . . .

sounds like . . .

ACTIVITY MASTER

LETTER PICTURE WORKSHEET

1

3

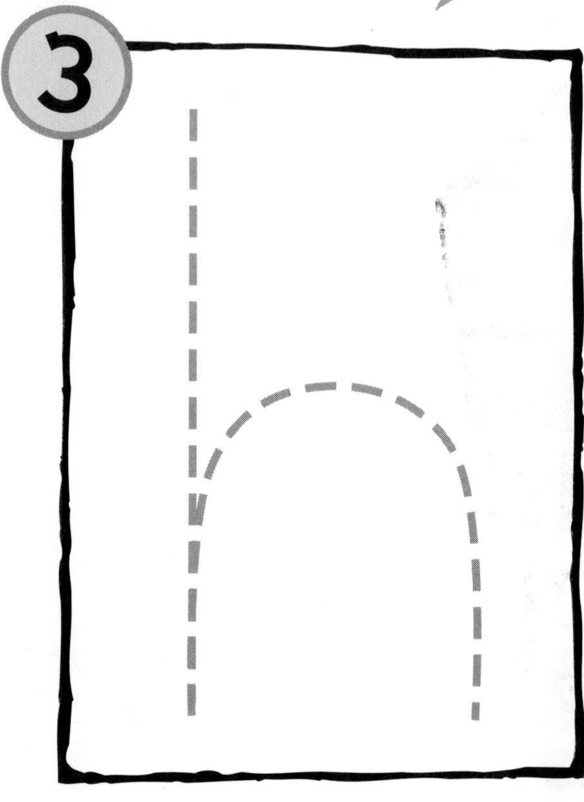

2

4

PAVE MAP

1 Context Sentence:

2 Target Word:

3 Predicted Meaning:

7 Word Image

4 Sentence Using Word's Predicted Meaning:

5 Word's Dictionary Definition:

6 Revised Sentence Using Verified Definition:

PREDICTIONS Worksheet

Title: ______________________________ Pages/Paragraphs: __________

Predict		Verify/Decide		
Prediction	What Makes Me Think So?	Keep Looking	Reject	Confirm

Prosody Assessment Summary Form

Student Name ______________________ Grade ____________

Teacher ______________________ Date ____________

Passage ______________________

Overall Score ______________________

Circle the score that best captures the characteristics of the student's reading.
A score of 1 or 2 indicates nonprosodic reading, or that the student has not yet achieved a minimum level of prosody for the grade- or difficulty-level of the passage. A score of 3 or 4 indicates prosodic reading.

Comments	Score	Prosody Assessment Rating
	1	• Equally stresses each word in a sentence • Reads primarily word by word • Often pauses after every word and within words • Chunks words with no attention to author's syntax or does not chunk them at all • Does not change pitch to reflect end marks • Reads in a monotone • Reads from one sentence to the next without pausing for punctuation
	2	• Equally stresses each word in a sentence or stresses the unimportant words in a sentence • Reads primarily in two-word phrases, but sometimes word by word • Often pauses within phrases • Chunks words with little attention to author's syntax • Occasionally changes pitch to reflect end marks • Occasionally uses voice to reflect character's emotions or actions • Pauses between sentences only when there is a period
	3	• Stresses the most important words in a sentence • Reads primarily in three- or four-word phrases • Often pauses between phrases, but occasionally pauses within them • Often chunks words appropriately, preserving author's syntax • Often changes pitch to reflect end marks • Usually uses voice to reflect character's emotions or actions • Usually pauses at commas and end marks
	4	• Stresses all appropriate words in a sentence • Reads primarily in larger, meaningful phrases • Consistently pauses at the end of clauses and sentences • Consistently chunks words appropriately, preserving author's syntax • Consistently changes pitch to reflect end marks • Consistently uses voice to reflect character's emotions or actions • Consistently pauses appropriately at all punctuation

QAR (Question-Answer Relationships) Worksheet

QAR

Title: ____________________ Pages/Paragraphs: __________

Question	Answer	QAR

SAY-IT-AND-MOVE-IT BOARD

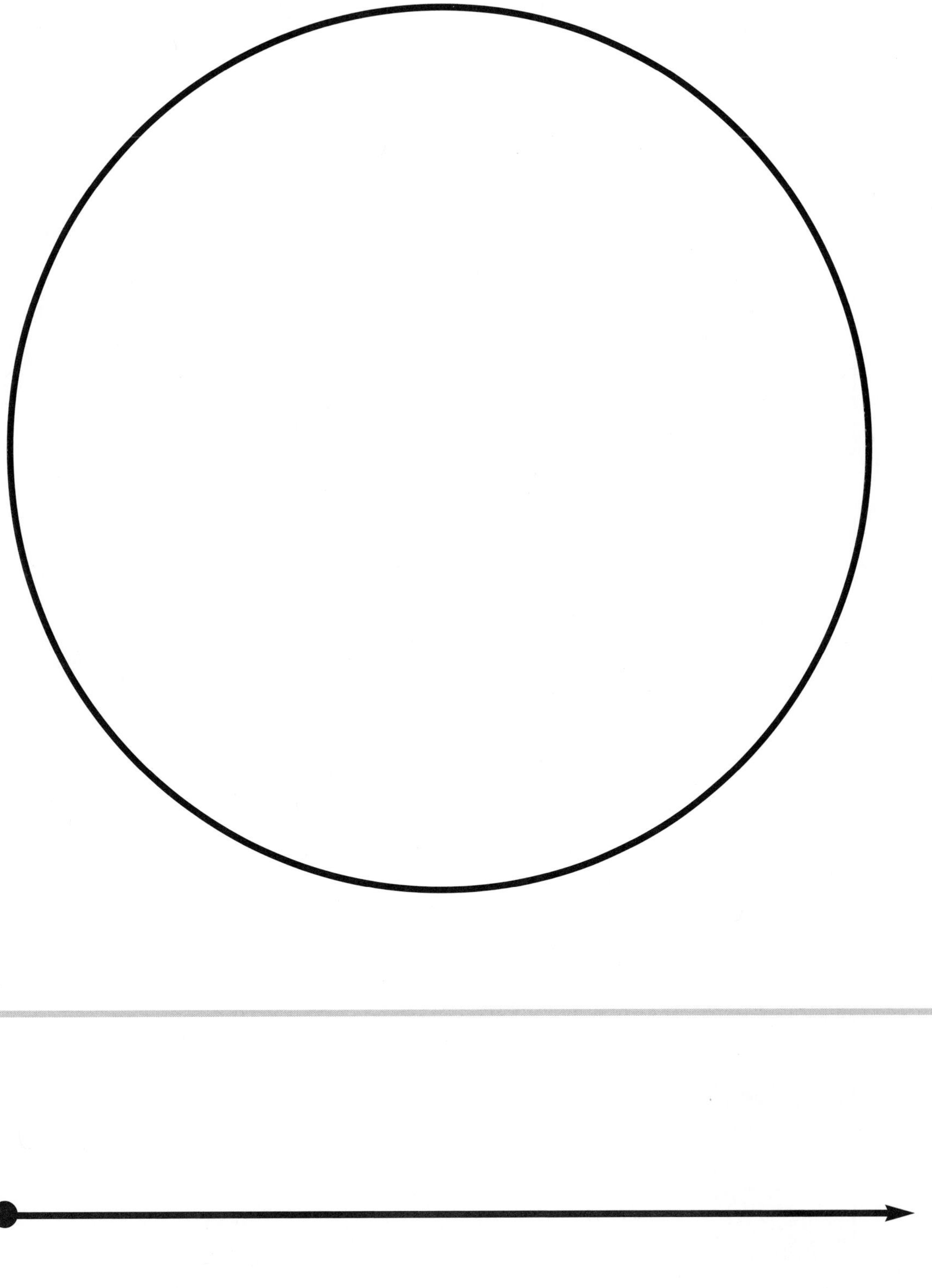

Story Map

TITLE:

Setting

Characters

PLOT

Problem

Sequence of Events

Outcome

Theme

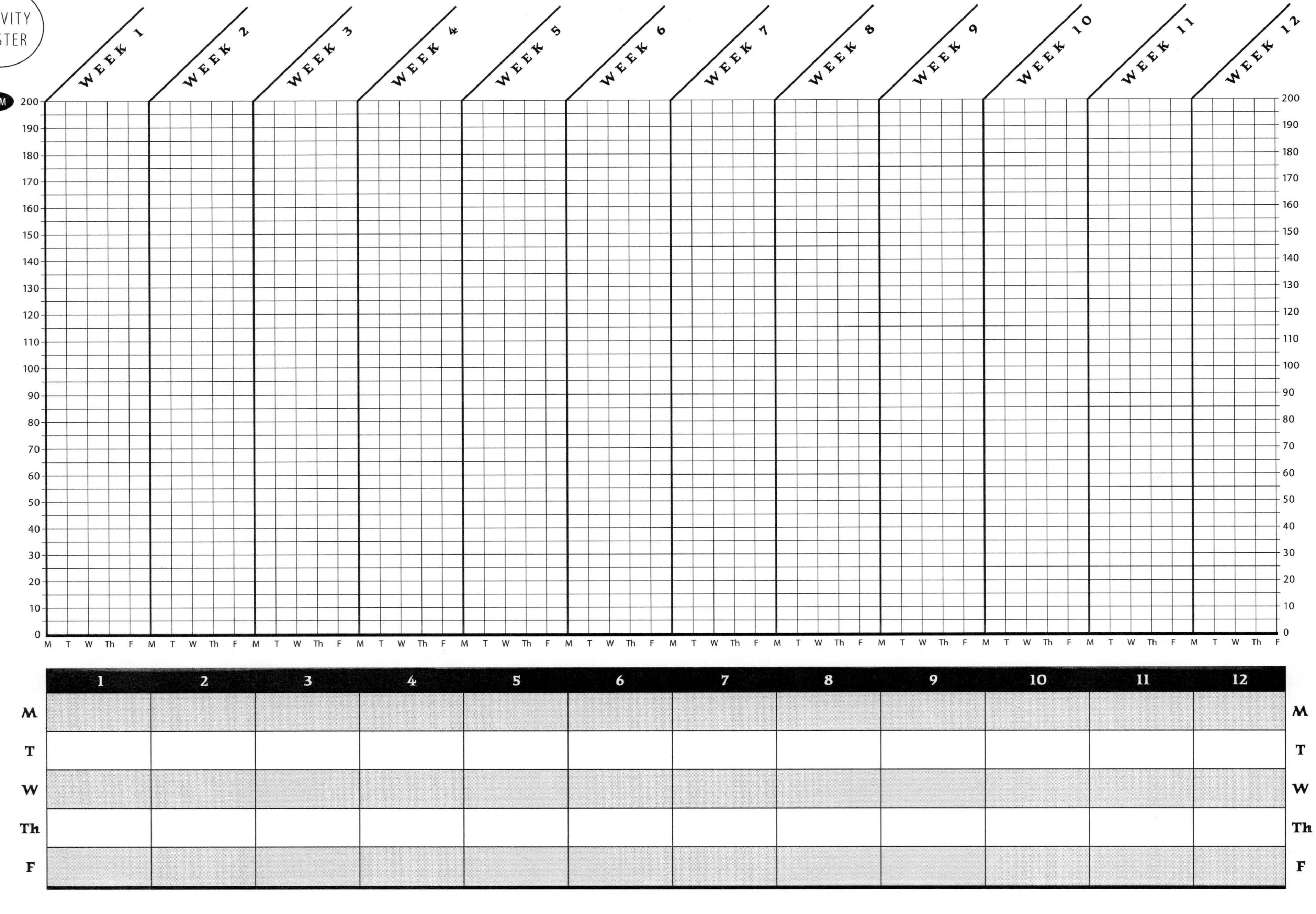

	1	2	3	4	5	6	7	8	9	10	11	12	
M													M
T													T
W													W
Th													Th
F													F

STUDENT PROGRESS GRAPH

Name ______________________ Grade ________

Final Goal & Date ______________________

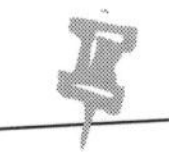

Name: ______________________ Date: ______________

Title: ______________________________________

PERSONAL Response

CREATIVE Response

CRITICAL Response

Vocabulary HOTSHOT Notebook

VOCABULARY WORD ______________________

Encounters	Word or Word in Family	Place and Source I Saw, Heard, or Used It classroom • school • home conversation • book • TV • other	How It Was Used (sentence or phrase)	It Means . . . (as used in this specific context)
First Time Date: ______				
Second Time Date: ______				
Third Time Date: ______				

Hotshot Points ______

Vocabulary HOTSHOT Notebook

VOCABULARY WORD ______________________

Encounters	Word or Word in Family	Place and Source I Saw, Heard, or Used It classroom • school • home conversation • book • TV • other	How It Was Used (sentence or phrase)	It Means . . . (as used in this specific context)
First Time Date: ______				
Second Time Date: ______				
Third Time Date: ______				

Hotshot Points ______

ACTIVITY MASTER

The Vocabulary Strategy Worksheet

Vocabulary Word

Context Sentence(s) ____________________

____

____

1 Look for Context Clues

Context Clues	Signal Words or Punctuation	Type of Context Clue

2 Look for Word-Part Clues

A. Can You Break the Word into Parts? Circle **yes** or **no**.
(If you can't, skip to Step 3.)

A. Word Broken into Parts

	Word Part	Meaning
B. What Is the Root Word?		
C. What Is the Prefix?		
D. What Is the Suffix?		
E. Put the Meanings of the Word Parts Together		

Prefix + Root Word • Root Word + Suffix • Prefix + Root Word + Suffix

3 I Guess the Word Means . . .

4 My Meaning Substituted in the Original Sentence

Does your meaning make sense in the sentence? Circle **yes** or **no**.

5 Dictionary Says . . .

Was your meaning close to the dictionary definition? Circle **yes** or **no**.

WORD MAP

SYNONYM

ANTONYM

EXAMPLE

NONEXAMPLE

ACTIVITY MASTER

WORD-PART WEB

TEACHING CHART

TYPES OF HELPFUL CONTEXT CLUES

Type	Description	Example Sentence
Definition	The author provides a direct definition of an unfamiliar word, right in the sentence. • SIGNAL WORDS: *is, are, means, refers to*	A conga *is* a barrel-shaped drum.
Appositive Definition	A type of definition clue. An appositive is a word or phrase that defines or explains an unfamiliar word that comes before it. • SIGNAL WORD: *or* • SIGNAL PUNCTUATION: set off by commas	At night you can see constellations, *or* groups of stars, in the sky.
Synonym	The author uses another word or phrase that is similar in meaning, or can be compared, to an unfamiliar word. • SIGNAL WORDS: *also, as, identical, like, likewise, resembling, same, similarly, too*	My dog Buck travels everywhere with me. My friend's canine buddy travels everywhere with him, *too*.
Antonym	The author uses another word or phrase that means about the opposite of, or is in contrast with, an unfamiliar word. • SIGNAL WORDS: *but, however, in contrast, instead of, on the other hand, though, unlike*	I thought the movie would be weird, *but* it turned out to be totally mundane.
Example	The author provides several words or ideas that are examples of an unfamiliar word. • SIGNAL WORDS: *for example, for instance, including, like, such as*	In science we are studying marine mammals *such as* whales, dolphins, and porpoises.
General	The author provides some nonspecific clues to the meaning of an unfamiliar word, often spread over several sentences.	Einstein rode his bike everywhere. He thought driving a car was way too complicated.

TEACHING CHART

THE VOCABULARY STRATEGY

To figure out the meaning of an unfamiliar word that you come across while reading:

1. **Look for Context Clues** in the Words, Phrases, and Sentences Surrounding the Unfamiliar Word
2. **Look for Word-Part Clues** Within the Unfamiliar Word
   A. Try to Break the Word into Parts. (If you can't, skip to Step 3.)
   B. Look at the Root Word. What does it mean?
   C. Look at the Prefix. What does it mean?
   D. Look at the Suffix. What does it mean?
   E. Put the Meanings of the Word Parts Together. What is the meaning of the whole word?
3. **Guess the Word's Meaning** (Use Steps 1 and 2.)
4. **Try Out Your Meaning in the Original Sentence** to Check Whether or Not It Makes Sense in Context
5. **Use the Dictionary**, if Necessary, to Confirm Your Meaning

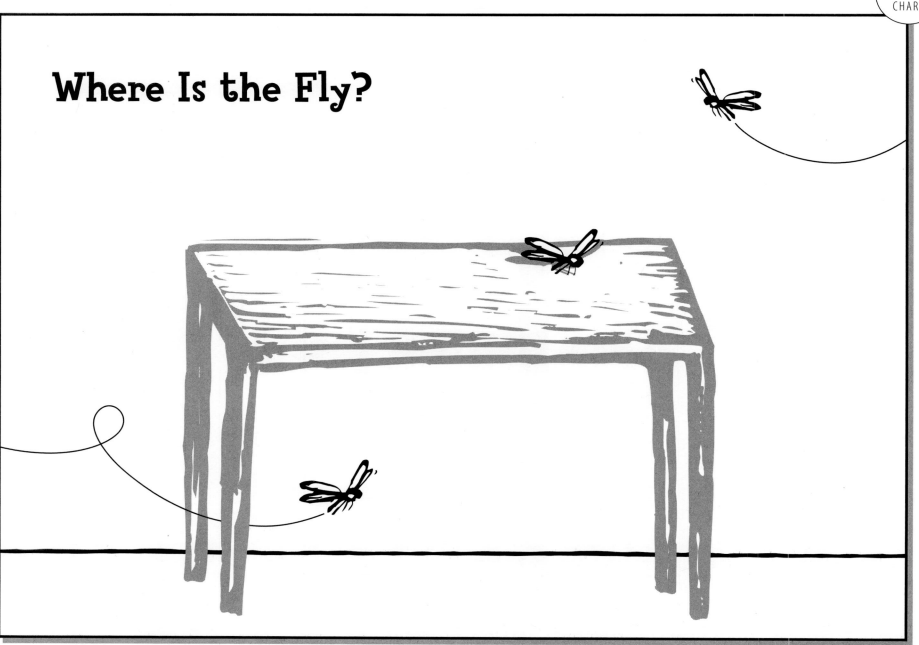

Where Is the Fly?

Connect to Theory Answer Key

SECTION II: EARLY LITERACY

PAGE 85

- English consonant letter names that begin with the sound that the letter frequently stands for: *b, d, j, k, p, t, v, z*
- English consonant letter names that end with the sound that the letter frequently stands for: *f, l, m, n, r, s, x*

PAGE 89

It may not be necessary to devote the same amount of instructional time for each letter-sound correspondence. More instructional time may need to be devoted to introducing the consonant letter sound for letters *c, g, y, h,* and *w,* and the short-vowel sound for the letters *a, e, i, o,* and *u.*

PAGE 117

Word	Phonemes/Number	Backward	New Word
ice	/ī/ /s/, (two)	/s/ /ī/	sigh
own	/ō/ /n/, (two)	/n/ /ō/	no
top	/t/ /o/ /p/, (three)	/p/ /o/ /t/	pot
let	/l/ /e/ /t/, (three)	/t/ /e/ /l/	tell
face	/f/ /ā/ /s/, (three)	/s/ /ā/ /f/	safe
easy	/ē/ /z/ /ē/, (three)	/ē/ /z/ /ē/	easy
meets	/m/ /ē/ /t/ /s/, (four)	/s/ /t/ /ē/ /m/	steam

SECTION III: DECODING AND WORD RECOGNITION

PAGE 173

1a. analytic phonics
1b. synthetic phonics

2a. synthetic phonics
2b. analogy phonics

3a. synthetic phonics
3b. embedded phonics

PAGE 182

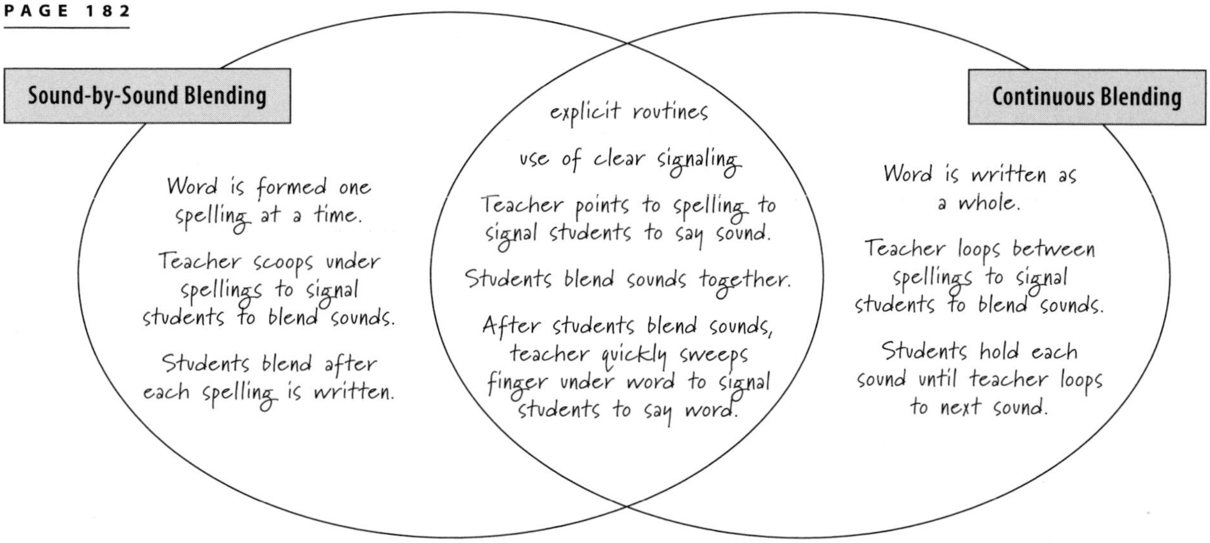

Sound-by-Sound Blending	Both	Continuous Blending
Word is formed one spelling at a time. Teacher scoops under spellings to signal students to blend sounds. Students blend after each spelling is written.	explicit routines use of clear signaling Teacher points to spelling to signal students to say sound. Students blend sounds together. After students blend sounds, teacher quickly sweeps finger under word to signal students to say word.	Word is written as a whole. Teacher loops between spellings to signal students to blend sounds. Students hold each sound until teacher loops to next sound.

PAGE 185

Decodable Text Analysis of *Bass Lake*

Word Types	Identified Words in Text	Percentage of Words in Text
Wholly Decodable Words	and, like, hike, Bass, Lake, for, week, fill, packs, will, need, hike, in, lake	14 words or 44%
Introduced Irregular Words	to, every, they, to, a, they, their, all, they, they, to, the	12 words or 37%
Nondecodable Words	Gail, Sue, year, go, with, then	6 words or 19%

Criteria for Nondecodable Words: The following sound/spellings have not been introduced: /ā/*ai;* /ōō/*ue;* /ē/*ea;* /ō/*o;* /th/*th;* and /TH/*th.*

PAGE 245

Permanently Irregular Words

Possible Answers (depending on a program's phonics scope & sequence): *the, of, to, was, you, are, they, from*

PAGE 263

Syllable Types

closed	**vowel combination**	**consonant-*le***
top with clip twist	heat snow toy noun	
open	**vowel-consonant *e***	***r*-controlled**
me go hi	side broke trade	park hurt verb thorn

PAGE 265

Syllable Divisions

VC/CV	V/CV	VC/V	VC/CCV	VCC/CV	Less Common
system distant center accept pictures observed	believe Minor features details people solar even Major craters	study planets Saturn models			ancient science

SECTION IV: READING FLUENCY

PAGE 332

- The first-grade student is below the normal, expected, and appropriate range.
- The second-grade student is within the normal, expected, and appropriate range.
- The fourth-grade student is below the normal, expected, and appropriate range.
- The sixth-grade student is within the normal, expected, and appropriate range.

PAGE 369

Melvin
- Passage One: instructional level
- Passage Two: independent level
- Passage Three: frustration level

Monica
- Passage One: frustration level, not appropriate for fluency instruction
- Passage Two: instructional level, most appropriate for teacher-assisted reading
- Passage Three: independent level, most appropriate for independent reading

SECTION V: VOCABULARY

PAGE 497

English/Spanish Cognates in "Marine Mammals":

animals/animals
marine/marino
ocean/océano
impossible/imposible
air/aire
creature/criatura
comparison/comparación
impulse/impulso
react/reaccionar
number/número
group/grupo
filters/filtros
material/material
giants/gigantes
abundant/abundante
planet/planeta
population/población
protect/proteger

False English/Spanish Cognate in "Marine Mammals":
miles/miles (In Spanish, *miles* means "thousands.")

PAGE 577

Layers of the English Language

- Anglo-Saxon: table, made, branch, book, airplane, after
- Latin: respectful, predict, pedestrian, instructor, export, audit, omit
- Greek: telephoto, phonogram, micrometer, geocentric, grapheme, astrology

SECTION VI: COMPREHENSION

PAGE 639

Possible Questions for Each Level of Bloom's Taxonomy: "The Case of the Blue Carbuncle"	
1. Knowledge	What was the blue carbuncle?
2. Comprehension	Can you explain how the goose was involved in the case?
3. Application	How could James Ryder have avoided mixing up the geese?
4. Analysis	How does this story compare or contrast with other mysteries you've read or seen on TV? Write a comparison describing the similarities and differences.
5. Synthesis	How could you adapt "The Case of the Blue Carbuncle" to fit modern times? Write your own updated version of the mystery.
6. Evaluation	How effective was the author in developing the mystery? (e.g., Were you intrigued and interested? Did the ending surprise you?) Support your answer.

PAGE 690

Elaborative Interrogation: Possible Why Questions and Answers

- Why do the names of the four lobes of the brain make sense? (Possible answer: *The frontal is in the front. I don't know enough about the other words yet, but as I learn more I can tell why their names make sense.*)
- Why does it make sense that the left side of the brain is associated with language and reading? (Possible answer: *I remember hearing that the left side of the brain controls the right side of the body. Most people write with their right hand. Writing is a form of language, so that makes sense to me. It may not be scientifically accurate, but it's helping me remember that the right side controls language. If I get new information, I can update my answer later.*)

PAGE 693

Constructing Mental Images: Possible Think Alouds

- *To remember how the neurotransmitter works, I'm picturing neon green goo drifting from one set of tentacles into another.*
- *Like a key in a lock. So the second neuron has this tailor-made receptor, not just the same kind of synapse. I'm picturing my green goo having a little more shape, like a cube of Jell-O. It's floating over to a perfectly matched empty cube on the next cell.*
- *Now I'm imagining that as soon as the chemical cube lands in the empty cube, poof, it turns back into a spark. Well, this may not be the most technically accurate description, but it's helping me get the basic idea of what's happening.*

References

Adams, G., and S. Brown. 2007. *The six-minute solution: A reading fluency program (intermediate level).* Longmont, CO: Sopris West.

Adams, M. J. 1990. *Beginning to read: Thinking and learning about print.* Cambridge, MA: MIT Press.

Adams, M. J. 2001. Alphabetic anxiety and explicit, systematic phonics instruction: A cognitive science perspective. In S. B. Neuman and D. K. Dickinson (eds.), *Handbook of early literacy research* (pp. 66–80). New York: Guilford.

Adams, M. J., S. A. Stahl, J. Osborn, and F. Lehr. 1990. *Beginning to read. Thinking and learning about print: A summary.* Champaign, IL: Center for the Study of Reading, Reading Research and Education Center, University of Illinois at Urbana-Champaign.

Afflerbach, P. 2002. Teaching reading self-assessment strategies. In C. C. Block and M. Pressley (eds.), *Comprehension instruction: Research-based best practices* (pp. 96–114). New York: Guilford.

Allen, K. A., G. F. Neuhaus, and M. C. Beckwith. 2005. Alphabet knowledge: Letter recognition, naming, and sequencing. In J. R. Birsh (ed.), *Multisensory teaching of basic language skills* (2nd ed.). Baltimore, MD: Paul H. Brookes.

Allington, R. L. 1983. Fluency: The neglected goal. *Reading Teacher* 36, pp. 556–561.

Allison, A. W., and R. B. Shrigley. 1986. Teaching children to ask operational questions in science. *Science Education* 70, pp.73–80.

Almasi, J. F. 2003. *Teaching strategic processes in reading.* New York: Guilford.

Alvermann, D. E. 2001. Reading adolescents' reading identities: Looking back to see ahead. *Journal of Adolescent and Adult Literacy* 44, pp. 676–690.

Alvermann, D. E., and A. J. Eakle. 2003. Comprehension instruction: Adolescents and their multiple literacies. In A. P. Sweet and C. E. Snow (eds.), *Rethinking reading comprehension* (pp. 30–140). New York: Guilford.

Anderson, E., and J. T. Guthrie. 1999. Motivating children to gain conceptual knowledge from text: The combination of science observation and interesting texts. Paper presented at the annual meeting of the American Educational Research Association, Montreal, April.

Anderson, R. C. 1996. Research foundations to support wide reading. In V. Greany (ed.), *Promoting reading in developing countries.* Newark, DE: International Reading Association.

Anderson, R. C., and P. Freebody. 1981. Vocabulary knowledge. In J. Guthrie (ed.), *Comprehension and teaching research review* (pp. 77–117). Newark, DE: International Reading Association.

Anderson, R. C., E. H. Hiebert, J. A. Scott, and I. A. G. Wilkinson. 1985. *Becoming a nation of readers: The report of the Commission on Reading.* Champaign, IL: Center for the Study of Reading and National Academy of Education.

Anderson, R. C., and W. E. Nagy. 1992. The vocabulary conundrum. *American Educator* 16, pp. 14–18, 44–47.

Anderson, R. C., and P. D. Pearson. 1984. A schema-theoretic view of basic processes in reading comprehension. In P. D. Pearson, R. Barr, M. L. Kamil, and P. Mosenthal (eds.), *Handbook of reading research,* Vol. 1 (pp. 255–291). New York: Longman.

Anderson, R. C., P. T. Wilson, and L. G. Fielding. 1988. Growth in reading and how children spend their time outside of school. *Reading Research Quarterly* 23(3), pp. 285–303.

Anderson, T. H. 1980. Study strategies and adjunct aids. In R. J. Spiro, B. C. Bruce, and W. F. Brewer (eds.), *Theoretical issues in reading comprehension.* Hillsdale, NJ: Erlbaum.

Anderson, V., and M. Roit. 1998. Reading as a gateway to language proficiency for language-minority students in elementary grades. In R. M. Gersten and R. T. Jimenez (eds.), *Promoting learning for culturally and linguistically diverse students.* Belmont, CA: Wadsworth.

Anglin, J. M. 1993. Vocabulary development: A morphological analysis. *Monographs of the Society for Research in Child Development* 58(10) (Serial No. 238).

Archer, A., M. Gleason, and V. Vachon. 2003. Decoding and fluency: Foundation skills for struggling older readers. *Learning Disability Quarterly* 26, pp. 89–101.

Archer, A., M. Gleason, and V. Vachon. 2006. *REWARDS: Reading excellence: Word attack and rate development strategies.* Longmont, CO: Sopris West.

Armbruster, B. 1996. Considerate texts in D. Lapp, J. Flood, and N. Farnan (eds.), *Content area reading and learning: Instructional strategies* (2nd ed.). Boston: Allyn & Bacon.

Armbruster, B., F. Lehr, and J. Osborn. 2001. *Put reading first: The research building blocks for teaching children to read.* Jessup, MD: National Institute for Literacy.

Armbruster, B., F. Lehr, and J. Osborn. 2002. *A child becomes a reader.* Jessup, MD: National Institute for Literacy.

August, D., M. Carlo, C. Dressler, and C. Snow. 2005. The critical role of vocabulary development for English language learners. *Learning Disabilities: Research & Practice* 20(1), pp. 50–57.

August, D., and T. Shanahan, eds. 2006. *Developing literacy in second-language learners: A report of the National Literacy Panel on language-minority children and youth.* Mahwah, NJ: Erlbaum. http://www.erlbaum.com/august.

Aylward, E. H., T. L. Richards, V. W. Berninger, W. E. Nagy, K. M. Field, A. C. Grimme, A. L. Richards, J. B. Thomson, and S. C. Cramer. 2003. Instructional treatment associated with changes in brain activation in children with dyslexia. *Neurology* 61, pp. 212–219.

Baker, L. 2002. Metacognition in comprehension instruction. In C. C. Block and M. Pressley (eds.), *Comprehension instruction: Research-based best practices* (pp. 77–95). New York: Guilford.

Baker, L., and A. L. Brown. 1984. Metacognitive skills and reading. In P. D. Pearson, R. Barr, M. L. Kamil, and P. Mosenthal (eds.), *Handbook of reading research,* Vol. 1 (pp. 353–394). White Plains, NY: Longman.

Ball, E. W., and B. A. Blachman. 1991. Does phoneme awareness training in kindergarten make a difference in early word recognition and developmental spelling? *Reading Research Quarterly* 26, pp. 49–66.

Bannon, E., P. J. Fisher, L. Pozzi, and D. Wessel. 1990. Effective definitions for word learning. *Journal of Reading* 34.

Baumann, J. F., E. C. Edwards, E. M. Boland, S. Olejnik, and E. J. Kame'enui. 2003. Vocabulary tricks: Effects of instruction in morphology and context on fifth-grade students' ability to derive and infer word meanings. *American Educational Research Journal* 40(2), pp. 447–494.

Baumann, J. F., E. C. Edwards, G. Font, C. A. Tereshinski, E. J. Kame'enui, and S. Olejnik. 2002. Teaching morphemic and contextual analysis to fifth-grade students. *Reading Research Quarterly* 37(2), pp. 150–176.

Baumann, J. F., G. Font, E. C. Edwards, and E. Boland. 2005. Strategies for teaching middle-grade students to use word-part and context clues. In E. H. Hiebert and M. L. Kamil (eds.), *Teaching and learning vocabulary: Bringing research to practice.* Mahwah, NJ: Erlbaum.

Baumann, J. F., N. Seifert-Kessel, and L. A. Jones. 1992. Effect of think-aloud instruction on elementary students' comprehension monitoring abilities. *Journal of Reading Behavior* 24, pp. 143–172.

Bear, D. R., M. Invernizzi, S. Templeton, and F. Johnston. 1996. *Words their way: Word study for phonics, vocabulary, and spelling instruction.* Upper Saddle River, NJ: Prentice-Hall.

Bear, D. R., M. Invernizzi, S. Templeton, and F. Johnston. 2000. *Words their way: Word study for phonics, vocabulary, and spelling instruction* (2nd ed.). Upper Saddle River, NJ: Prentice-Hall.

Beck, I. L. 1997. Response to "overselling phonics." *Reading Today* 17.

Beck, I. L. 2006. *Making sense of phonics: The hows and whys.* New York: Guilford.

Beck, I. L., and M. G. McKeown. 1985. Teaching vocabulary: Making the instruction fit the goal. *Educational Perspectives* 23(1), pp. 11–15.

Beck, I. L., and M. G. McKeown. 2001. Text talk: Capturing the benefits of read-aloud experiences for young children. *Reading Teacher* 55, pp. 10–20.

Beck, I. L., and M. G. McKeown. 2006. *Improving comprehension with questioning the author.* New York: Scholastic.

Beck, I. L., M. G. McKeown, R. L. Hamilton, and L. Kucan. 1997. *Questioning the author: An approach for enhancing student engagement with text.* Newark, DE: International Reading Association.

Beck, I. L., M. G. McKeown, and L. Kucan. 2002. *Bringing words to life: Robust vocabulary instruction.* New York: Guilford.

Beck, I. L., C. Perfetti, and M. G. McKeown. 1982. The effects of long-term vocabulary instruction on lexical access and reading comprehension. *Journal of Educational Psychology* 74.

Beck, I. L., S. F. Roth, and M. G. McKeown. 1985. *Syllasearch.* Allen, TX: Developmental Learning Materials.

Bell, R. Q. 1968. A reinterpretation of the direction of effects in studies of socialization. *Psychological Review* 75, pp. 81–95.

Bereiter, C., and M. Bird. 1985. Use of thinking aloud in identification and teaching of reading comprehension strategies. *Cognition and Instruction* 2, pp. 131–156.

Bergman, J. L. 1992. SAIL—A way to success and independence for low-achieving readers. *Reading Teacher* 45, pp. 598–602.

Berninger, V. W. 1999. The "write stuff" for preventing and treating writing disabilities. *Perspectives* 25(2), pp. 20–22.

Berninger, V. W., R. B. Abbott, K. Vermeulen, and C. M. Fulton. 2006. Paths to reading comprehension in at-risk second-grade readers. *Journal of Learning Disabilities* 39, pp. 334–351.

Berninger, V. W., K. Vermeulen, R. B. Abbott, D. McCutchen, S. Cotton, J. Cude, S. Dorn, and T. Sharon. 2003. Comparison of three approaches to supplementary reading instruction for low-achieving second-grade readers. *Language, Speech, & Hearing Services in Schools* 34, pp. 101–116.

Bessellieu, F. 2006. Learning centered coaching: Teacher support for instruction and achievement. Paper presented at the Reading First Leadership Meeting, Boise, ID.

Bhattacharya, A. 2006. Syllable representation in written spellings of sixth and eighth grade children. *Insights on Learning Disabilities* 3(1), pp. 43–61.

Bhattacharya, A., and L. Ehri. 2004. Graphosyllabic analysis helps adolescent struggling readers read and spell words. *Journal of Learning Disabilities* 37, pp. 331–348.

Biancarosa, G., and C. Snow. 2006. *Reading next: A vision for action and research in middle and high school literacy: A report to the Carnegie Corporation of New York* (2nd ed.). Washington, DC: Alliance for Excellent Education.

Biemiller, A. 2001. Teaching vocabulary: Early, direct, and sequential. *American Educator,* Spring.

Biemiller, A. 2003. Vocabulary: Needed if more children are to read well. *Reading Psychology* 24, pp. 323–335.

Biemiller, A. 2004. Teaching vocabulary in the primary grades. In J. F. Baumann and E. J. Kame'enui (eds.), *Vocabulary instruction: Research to practice.* New York: Guilford.

Biemiller, A. 2005a. Size and sequence in vocabulary development: Implications for choosing words for primary grade vocabulary instruction. In E. H. Hiebert and M. L. Kamil (eds.), *Teaching and learning vocabulary: Bringing research to practice.* Mahwah, NJ: Erlbaum.

Biemiller, A. 2005b. Vocabulary development and instruction: A prerequisite for school learning. In D. Dickinson and S. Neuman (eds.), *Handbook of early literacy research,* Vol. 2. New York: Guilford.

Biemiller, A. 2010. *Words worth teaching: Closing the vocabulary gap.* Columbus, OH: SRA/McGraw-Hill.

Biemiller, A., and C. Boote. 2006. An effective method for building meaning vocabulary in primary grades. *Journal of Educational Psychology* 98(1), pp. 44–62.

Biemiller, A., and M. Slonim. 2001. Estimating root word vocabulary growth in normative and advantaged populations: Evidence for a common sequence of vocabulary acquisition. *Journal of Educational Psychology* 93(3), pp. 438–520.

Bishop, A. G. 2003. Prediction of first-grade reading achievement: A comparison of fall and winter kindergarten screenings. *Learning Disability Quarterly* 26(3), pp. 189–200.

Bjorkland, D. F. 1989. *Children's thinking: Developmental function and individual differences.* Monterey, CA: Brooks/Cole.

Blachman, B. A. 1995. Identifying the core linguistic deficits and the critical conditions for early intervention with children with reading disabilities. Paper presented at the annual meeting of the Learning Disabilities Association of America, Orlando, FL, March.

Blachman, B. A. 2000. Phonological awareness. In M. L. Kamil, P. B. Rosenthal, P. D. Pearson, and R. Barr (eds.), *Handbook of reading research,* Vol. 3 (pp. 483–502). Mahwah, NJ: Erlbaum.

Blachman, B. A., E. W. Ball, R. Black, and D. M. Tangel. 2000. *Road to the code: A phonological awareness program for young children.* Baltimore, MD: Paul H. Brookes.

Blachowicz, C., and P. Fisher. 2002. *Teaching vocabulary in all classrooms* (2nd ed.). Upper Saddle River, NJ: Merrill/Prentice-Hall.

Blachowicz, C., and P. Fisher. 2004. Keep the "fun" in fundamental: Encouraging word awareness and incidental word learning in the classroom through word play. In J. F. Baumann and E. J. Kame'enui (eds.), *Vocabulary instruction: Research to practice.* New York: Guilford.

Blanton, W. E., K. D. Wood, and G. B. Moorman. 1990. The role of purpose in reading instruction. *Reading Teacher* 43(7), pp. 486–493.

Bleich, D. 1978. *Subjective criticism.* Baltimore, MD: Johns Hopkins University Press.

Blevins, W. 2001. *Teaching phonics & word study in the intermediate grades.* New York: Scholastic.

Blevins, W. 2006. *Phonics from A to Z: A practical guide* (2nd ed.). New York: Scholastic.

Block, C. C. 2004. *Teaching comprehension: The comprehension process approach.* Boston: Pearson Education.

Block, C. C., and M. Pressley. 2003. Best practices in comprehension instruction. In L. M. Morrow, L. B. Gambrell, and M. Pressley (eds.), *Best practices in literacy instruction.* New York: Guilford.

Bloom, B. S. 1956. Taxonomy of educational objectives. *Handbook I: Cognitive domain.* New York: McKay.

Bloome, D. 1988. Locating the learning of reading and writing in classrooms: Beyond deficit, difference, and effectiveness models. In. C. Emihovich (ed.), *Locating learning: Ethnographic perspectives on classroom research* (pp. 87–114). Norwood, NJ: Ablex.

Blum, I. H., and P. S. Koskinen. 1991. Repeated reading: A strategy for enhancing fluency and fostering expertise. *Theory into Practice* 30(3), pp. 195–200.

Boles, D. B., and J. E. Clifford. 1989. An upper- and lowercase alphabetic similarity matrix, with derived generation similarity values. *Behavior Research Methods, Instruments, & Computers* 21, pp. 579–586.

Boote, C. 2006. Vocabulary: Reasons to teach it. *New England Reading Association Journal* 42.

Bradley, R., L. Danielson, and J. Doolittle. 2005. Response to intervention. *Journal of Learning Disabilities* 38(6), pp. 485–486.

Bravo, M. A., E. H. Hiebert, and P. D. Pearson. 2005. *Tapping the linguistic resources of Spanish/English bilinguals: The role of cognates in science.* Berkeley: Lawrence Hall of Science, University of California.

Breznitz, Z. 2006. *Fluency in reading: Synchronization of processes.* Mahwah, NJ: Erlbaum.

Brown, A. L., J. C. Campione, and J. D. Day. 1981. Learning to learn: On training students to learn from texts. *Educational Researcher* 10, pp. 14–24.

Brown, A. L., and J. D. Day. 1983. Macro rules for summarizing texts: The development of expertise. *Journal of Verbal Learning and Verbal Behavior* 22, pp. 1–14.

Brown, H., and B. Cambourne. 1987. *Read and retell: A strategy for the whole-language/natural learning classroom.* Portsmouth, NH: Heinemann.

Brown, R. 2002. Straddling two worlds: Self-directed comprehension instruction for middle schoolers. In C. C. Block and M. Pressley (eds.), *Comprehension instruction: Research-based best practices* (pp. 337–350). New York: Guilford.

Brown, R., M. Pressley, P. Van Meter, and T. Schuder. 1996. A quasi-experimental validation of transactional strategies instruction with low-achieving second-grade readers. *Journal of Educational Psychology* 88, pp. 18–37.

Bruck, M., and R. Treiman. 1990. Phonological awareness and spelling in normal children and dyslexics: The case of initial consonant clusters. *Journal of Experimental Child Psychology* 50.

Bryant, P. 1990. Phonological development and reading. In P. D. Pumfrey and C. D. Elliot (eds.), *Children's difficulties in reading, spelling, and writing: Challenges and responses.* London: Falmer Press.

Buckingham, B. R., and E. W. Dolch. 1936. *A combined word list.* Boston: Ginn.

Bulla, C. R. 1990. *White bird.* New York: Random House.

Burns, M. S., P. Griffin, and C. E. Snow (eds.). 1999. *Starting out right: A guide to promoting children's reading success.* Washington, DC: National Academies Press.

Bus, A. G., and M. H. van IJzendoorn. 1988. Mother-child interactions, attachment, and emergent literacy: A cross-sectional study. *Child Development* 59(5), pp. 1262–1272.

Bus, A. G., and M. H. van IJzendoorn. 1999. Phonological awareness and early reading: A meta-analysis of experimental training studies. *Journal of Educational Psychology* 91, pp. 403–414.

Calderón, M., D. August, R. Slavin, D. Duran, N. Madden, and A. Cheung. 2005. Bring words to life in classrooms with English-language learners. In E. H. Hiebert and M. L. Kamil (eds.), *Teaching and learning vocabulary: Bringing research to practice.* Mahwah, NJ: Erlbaum.

Canney, G., and R. Schreiner. 1977. A study of the effectiveness of selected syllabication rules and phonogram patterns for word attack. *Reading Research Quarterly* 12, pp. 102–124.

Carbo, M. 1981. Making books talk to children. *Reading Teacher* 35, pp.186–189.

Carlisle, J. F., and C. A. Stone. 2005. Exploring the role of morphemes in word reading. *Reading Research Quarterly* 40(4), pp. 428–449.

Carlo, M., D. August, B. McLaughlin, C. Snow, C. Dressler, D. Lipman, T. Lively, and C. White. 2004. Closing the gap: Addressing the vocabulary needs of English language learners in bilingual and mainstream classrooms. *Reading Research Quarterly* 40.

Carnine, D. W., and D. Kinder. 1985. Teaching low performing students to apply generative and schema strategies to narrative and expository materials. *Remedial and Special Education* 6(1), pp. 20–30.

Carnine, D. W., J. Silbert, E. J. Kame'enui, S. G. Tarver, and K. Jungjohann. 2006. *Teaching struggling and at-risk readers.* Upper Saddle River, NJ: Pearson.

Carr, E., and D. Ogle. 1987. K-W-L Plus: A strategy for comprehension and summarization. *Journal of Reading* 30(7), pp. 626–631.

Carreker, S. 2005. Teaching reading: Accurate decoding and fluency. In J. R. Birsh (ed.), *Multisensory teaching of basic language skills* (2nd ed.). Baltimore, MD: Paul H. Brookes.

Carrick, L. U. 2000. The effects of Readers Theatre on fluency and comprehension in fifth grade students in regular classrooms. Unpublished doctoral dissertation, Lehigh University, Bethlehem, PA.

Carrillo, M. 1994. Development of phonological awareness and reading acquisition: A study in Spanish. *Reading and Writing: An Interdisciplinary Journal* 6, pp. 279–298.

Carroll, J. B., P. Davies, and B. Richman. 1971. *The American Heritage word frequency book.* Boston: Houghton Mifflin.

Carver, R. P. 2003. The highly lawful relationships among pseudoword decoding, word identification, spelling, listening, and reading. *Scientific Studies of Reading* 7, pp. 127–154.

Chall, J. S. 1983. *Stages of reading development.* New York: McGraw-Hill.

Chall, J. S. 1996. *Learning to read: The great debate* (3rd ed.). New York: McGraw-Hill.

Chall, J. S., and E. Dale. 1995. *Readability revisited: The new Dale-Chall readability formula.* Brookline, MA: Brookline Books.

Chall, J. S., and V. A. Jacobs. 2003. Poor children's fourth-grade slump. *American Educator* 27(1), pp. 14–15. http://www.aft.org/pubs-reports/american_educator/spring2003/chall.html.

Chall, J. S., and H. M. Popp. 1996. *Teaching and assessing phonics: A guide for teachers.* Cambridge, MA: Educator's Publishing Service.

Chan, L. K., P. G. Cole, and J. N. Morris. 1990. Effects of instruction in the use of a visual-imagery strategy on the reading-comprehension competence of disabled and average readers. *Learning Disability Quarterly* 13, pp. 2–11.

Chard, D. J., S. Vaughn, and B. Tyler. 2002. A synthesis of research on effective interventions for building fluency with elementary students with learning disabilities. *Journal of Learning Disabilities* 35, pp. 386–406.

Chiappe, P., L. S. Siegel, and A. Gottardo. 2002. Reading-related skills of kindergartners from diverse linguistic backgrounds. *Applied Psycholinguistics* 23, pp. 95–116.

Chomsky, C. 1970. Reading, writing, and phonology. *Harvard Educational Review* 40, pp. 287–309.

Ciardiello, A. V. 1998. Did you ask a good question today? Alternative cognitive and metacognitive strategies. *Journal of Adolescent & Adult Literacy* 42(3).

Clay, M. 1993. *An observational survey of early literacy achievement.* Portsmouth, NH: Heinemann.

Clay, M. 2000. *Concepts about print.* Portsmouth, NH: Heinemann.

Coalition for Evidence-Based Policy. 2003. *Identifying and implementing educational practices supported by rigorous evidence: A user friendly guide.* Washington, DC: U.S. Department of Education.

Colman, D., and S. Pimentel. 2012. Revised publishers' criteria for the common core state standards in English language arts and literacy. Modified 04/12/12. www.corestandards.org/assets/Publishers_Criteria_for_3-12.pdf.

Common Core State Standards Initiative. Frequently asked questions. http://www.corestandards.org/frequently-asked-questions.

Corcoran, C. A., and A. D. Davis. 2005. A study of the effects of Readers Theater on second and third grade special education students' fluency growth. *Reading Improvement* 42(2), p. 105.

Coyne, M. D., D. J. Chard, R. P. Zipoli, Jr., and M. F. Ruby. 2007. Effective strategies for teaching reading comprehension. In M. D. Coyne, E. J. Kame'enui, and D. W. Carnine (eds.), *Effective teaching strategies that accommodate diverse learners* (3rd ed.). Upper Saddle River, NJ: Pearson Education.

Coyne, M. D., D. Simmons, and E. J. Kame'enui. 2004. Vocabulary instruction for young children at risk of experiencing reading difficulties: Teaching word meanings during shared story reading. In J. F. Baumann and E. J. Kame'enui (eds.), *Vocabulary instruction: Research to practice*. New York: Guilford.

Cunningham, A. E. 1990. Explicit versus implicit instruction in phonemic awareness. *Journal of Experimental Child Psychology* 50, pp. 429–444.

Cunningham, A. E. 2005. Vocabulary growth through independent reading and reading aloud to children. In E. H. Hiebert and M. L. Kamil (eds.), *Teaching and learning vocabulary: Bringing research to practice.* Mahwah, NJ: Erlbaum.

Cunningham, A. E., and K. E. Stanovich. 1997. Early reading acquisition and its relation to reading experience and ability 10 years later. *Developmental Psychology* 33(6), pp. 934–945.

Cunningham, P. M. 1998. The multisyllabic word dilemma: Helping students build meaning, spell, and read "big" words. *Reading and Writing Quarterly* 14(2), pp. 189–218.

Curtis, M. E., and R. Glaser. 1983. Reading theory and the assessment of reading achievement. *Journal of Educational Measurement* 20, pp. 133–147.

Curtis, M. E., and A. M. Longo. 1999. *When adolescents can't read: Methods and materials that work.* Cambridge, MA: Brookline Books.

Daane, M. C., J. R. Campbell, W. S. Grigg, M. J. Goodman, and A. Oranje. 2005. *Fourth-grade students reading aloud: NAEP 2002 special study of oral reading* (NCES 2006–469). Washington, DC: U.S. Department of Education, Institute of Education Sciences, National Center for Education Statistics.

Dale, E. 1965. Vocabulary measurement: Techniques and major findings. *Elementary English* 42, pp. 82–88.

Dale, E., and J. O'Rourke. 1981. *Living word vocabulary.* Chicago: World Book/Childcraft International.

Deno, S. L., and D. Marston. 2006. Curriculum-based measurement of oral reading: An indicator of growth in fluency. In S. J. Samuels and A. E. Farstrup (eds.), *What Research Has to Say About Fluency Instruction.* Newark, DE: International Reading Association.

Deno, S. L., D. Marston, and P. Mirkin. 1982. Valid measurement procedures for continuous evaluation of written expression. *Exceptional Children* 48, pp. 368–371.

Deno, S. L., D. Marston, M. R. Shinn, and G. Tindal. 1983. Oral reading fluency: A simple datum for scaling reading disability. *Topics in Learning and Learning Disabilities* 2(4), pp. 53–59.

Denton, C. 2006. Responsiveness to intervention as an indication of learning disability. *Perspectives* 32(1), pp. 2–7.

Diamond, L. 2005. Assessment-driven instruction: A systems approach. *Perspectives,* Fall, 33–37.

Diamond, L. 2006. Triage for struggling adolescent readers. *School Administrator,* April.

Dickinson, D. K., and S. B. Neuman. 2006. Introduction. In D. K. Dickinson and S. B. Neuman (eds.), *Handbook of early literacy research,* Vol. 2. New York: Guilford.

Dickson, S. V., D. C. Simmons, and E. J. Kame'enui. 1998. Text organization: Research bases. In D. C. Simmons and E. J. Kame'enui (eds.), *What reading research tells us about children with diverse learning needs: Bases and basics.* Mahwah, NJ: Erlbaum.

Dodge, B. 1997. *Some thoughts about WebQuests.* Retrieved September 19, 2006, from http://webquest.sdsu.edu/about_webquests.html.

Dole, J., S. Valencia, E. Greer, and J. Wardrop. 1991. The effects of prereading instruction on the comprehension of narrative and expository text. *Reading Research Quarterly* 26, pp. 142–159.

Dowhower, S. L. 1991. Speaking of prosody: Fluency's unattended bedfellow. *Theory in Practice* 30(3), pp. 158–164.

Doyle, B. G., and W. Bramwell. 2006. Promoting emergent literacy and social-emotional learning through dialogic reading. *Reading Teacher* 59(6), pp. 554–564.

Dreher, M. J. 2002. Children searching and using information text: A critical part of comprehension. In C. C. Block and M. Pressley (eds.), *Comprehension instruction: Research-based best practices* (pp. 289–304). New York: Guilford.

Dreher, M. J., and A. Dromsky. 2000. Increasing the diversity of young children's independent reading. Paper presented at the National Reading Conference, Scottsdale, Arizona, December.

Dressler, C. 2000. The word-inferencing strategies of bilingual and monolingual fifth graders: A case study approach. Unpublished qualifying paper, Harvard Graduate School of Education, Cambridge, MA.

Duke, N. K. 2000a. Print environments and experiences offered to first-grade students in very low—and high—SES school districts. *Reading Research Quarterly* 35(4), pp. 456–457.

Duke, N. K. 2000b. 3.6 minutes per day: The scarcity of informational texts in first grade. *Reading Research Quarterly* 35(2).

Duke, N. K. 2004. The case for informational text. *Educational Leadership* 61(6), pp. 40–44.

Duke, N. K. 2006. Building and assessing informational literacy in the primary grades. Paper presented at the Colorado Council of the International Reading Association, Denver, CO, February.

Duke, N. K., and P. D. Pearson. 2002. Effective practices for developing reading comprehension. In A. E. Farstrup and S. J. Samuels (eds.), *What research has to say about reading instruction* (3rd ed., pp. 205–242). Newark, DE: International Reading Association.

Durgunoglu, A. Y., W. E. Nagy, and B. J. Hancin-Bhatt. 1993. Cross-language transfer of phonological awareness. *Journal of Educational Psychology* 85(3).

Durkin, D. 1993. *Teaching them to read* (6th ed.). Boston: Allyn & Bacon.

Durrell, D. 1963. *Phonograms in primary grade words.* Boston: Boston University Press.

Dutro, S., and C. Moran. 2003. Rethinking English language instruction: An architectural approach. In G. G. García (ed.), *English learners: Reaching the highest level of English literacy* (pp. 227–258). Newark, DE: International Reading Association.

Eagleton, M., and Dobler, E. 2007. *Reading the Web: Strategies for Internet inquiry.* New York: Guilford.

Eccles, J., A. Wigfield, R. D. Harold, and F. Blumenfeld. 1993. Age and gender differences in children's self- and task perceptions during elementary school. *Child Development* 64, pp. 830–847.

Edwards, E. C., G. Font, J. F. Baumann, and E. Boland. 2004. Unlocking word meanings: Strategies and guidelines for teaching morphemic and contextual analysis. In J. F. Baumann and E. J. Kame'enui (eds.), *Vocabulary instruction: Research to practice.* New York: Guilford.

Ehri, L. C. 1995. Phases of development in learning to read words by sight. *Journal of Research in Reading* 18, pp. 116–125.

Ehri, L. C. 2002. Phases of acquisition in learning to read words and implications for teaching. In R. Stainthorp and P. Tomlinson (eds.), *Learning and teaching reading* (pp. 7–28). London: British Journal of Educational Psychology Monograph Series II.

Ehri, L. C. 2004. Teaching phonemic awareness and phonics: An explanation of the National Reading Panel meta-analysis. In P. McCardle and V. Chhabra (eds.), *The voice of evidence in reading research* (pp. 153–186). Baltimore, MD: Paul H. Brookes.

Ehri, L. C. 2006. More about phonics: Findings and reflections. In K. A. Dougherty Stahl and M. C. McKenna (eds.), *Reading research at work: Foundations of effective practice.* New York: Guilford.

Ehri, L. C., N. D. Deffner, and L. S. Wilce. 1984. Pictorial mnemonics for phonics. *Journal of Educational Psychology* 76(5), pp. 880–893.

Ehri, L. C., and S. McCormick. 1998. Phases of word learning: Implications for instruction with delayed and disabled readers. *Reading and Writing Quarterly* 14, pp. 135–163.

Ehri, L. C., S. R. Nunes, D. M. Willows, B. V. Schuster, Z. Yaghoub-Zadeh, and T. Shanahan. 2001. Phonemic awareness instruction helps children learn to read: Evidence from the National Reading Panel's meta-analysis. *Reading Research Quarterly* 36(3), pp. 250–287.

Ehri, L. C., and T. Roberts. 2006. The roots of learning to read and write: Acquisition of letters and phonemic awareness. In D. K. Dickinson and S. B. Neuman (eds.), *Handbook of early literacy research*, Vol. 2 (pp. 113–131). New York: Guilford.

Ehri, L., and M. Snowling. 2004. Developmental variation in word recognition. In C. A. Stone, E. Silliman, B. Ehren, and K. Apel (eds.), *Handbook of language and literacy development and disorders* (pp. 433–461). New York: Guilford.

El-Dinary, P. B. 1993. Teachers learning, adapting and implementing strategies-based instruction in reading (doctoral dissertation, University of Maryland, 1993). *Dissertation Abstracts International* 54, 5410A (University Microfilms No. 9407625).

Eldredge, J. L. 1990. Increasing the performance of poor readers in the third grade with a group-assisted strategy. *Journal of Educational Research* 84, pp. 69–77.

Elkonin, D. B. 1963. The psychology of mastering the elements of reading. In B. Simon and J. Simon (eds.), *Educational psychology in the USSR.* London: Routledge and Kegan Paul.

Englemann, S., L. Meyer, L. Carnine, W. Becker, J. Eisele, and G. Johnson. 1999. *Corrective reading: Decoding strategies.* Columbus, OH: SRA/McGraw-Hill.

Espin, C. A., and A. Foegen. 1996. Validity of general outcome measures for predicting secondary students' performance on content-area tasks. *Exceptional Children* 62, pp. 497–514.

Ezell, H. K., and L. M. Justice. 2000. Increasing the print focus of adult-child shared book reading through observational learning. *American Journal of Speech-Language Pathology* 9, pp. 36–47.

Fisher, D., and N. Frey. 2004. *Improving adolescent literacy: Strategies at work.* Columbus, OH: Pearson Prentice-Hall.

Fitzgerald, J., and A. B. Teasley. 1986. Effects of instruction in narrative structure on children's writing. *Journal of Educational Psychology* 78(6).

Fletcher, J. 2006. The need for Response to Intervention models of learning disabilities. *Perspectives* 32(1), pp. 12–15.

Flynn, R. M. 2004. Curriculum-based Readers Theatre: Setting the stage for reading and retention. *Reading Teacher* 58(4), pp. 360–365.

Foorman, B. R., D. Chen, C. Carlson, L. Moats, D. J. Francis, and J. M. Fletcher. 2003. The necessity of the alphabetic principle to phonemic awareness instruction. *Reading and Writing* 16, pp. 289–324.

Foorman, B. R., D. J. Francis, T. Beeler, D. Winikates, and J. M. Fletcher. 1997a. Early interventions for children with reading problems: Study designs and preliminary findings. *Learning Disabilities: A Multidisciplinary Journal* 8, pp. 63–72.

Foorman, B. R., D. J. Francis, K. C. Davidson, M. W. Harm, and J. Griffin. 2004. Variability in text features in six grade 1 basal reading programs. *Scientific Studies of Reading* 8(2), pp. 167–197.

Foorman, B. R., D. J. Francis, S. E. Shaywitz, B. A. Shaywitz, and J. M. Fletcher. 1997b. The case for early reading intervention. In B. A. Blachman (ed.), *Foundations of reading acquisition and dyslexia: Implications for early intervention* (pp. 243–264). Mahwah, NJ: Erlbaum.

Foorman, B. R., and J. K. Torgesen. 2001. Critical elements of classroom and small-group instruction promote reading success in all children. *Learning Disabilities Research & Practice* 16, pp. 203–212.

Fordham, N. 2006. Crafting questions that address comprehension strategies in content reading. *Journal of Adolescent & Adult Literacy* 49(5), pp. 390–396.

Fountas, I. C., and G. S. Pinnell. 1996. *Guided reading: Good first teaching for all children.* Portsmouth, NH: Heinemann.

Francis, D. J., M. Kieffer, N. Lesaux, H. Rivera, and M. Rivera. 2006. *Practical guidelines for the education of English language learners: Research-based recommendations for instruction and academic interventions.* Portsmouth, NH: RMC Research Corporation, Center on Instruction.

Francis, D. J., S. E. Shaywitz, K. K. Stuebing, B. A. Shaywitz, and J. M. Fletcher. 1996. Developmental lag versus deficit models of reading disability: A longitudinal, individual growth curves analysis. *Journal of Educational Psychology* 88(1), pp. 3–17.

Freedman, S. W., and R. C. Calfee. 1984. Understanding and comprehending. *Written Communication* 1.

Fry, E. 1998. The most common phonograms. *Reading Teacher* 51, pp. 534–547.

Fry, E. 2004. *1000 instant words.* Westminster, CA: Teacher Created Resources.

Fuchs, D., L. S. Fuchs, P. G. Mathes, and D. C. Simmons. 2007. Peer-assisted learning strategies: Reading methods for grades 2–6. Unpublished teacher manual available from Douglas Fuchs, Department of Special Education, Vanderbilt University, 0228 GPC, 230 Appleton Place, Nashville, TN 37203-5721.

Fuchs, D., D. Mock, P. L. Morgan, and D. L. Young. 2003. Responsiveness-to-intervention: Definitions, evidence, and implications for the learning disabilities construct. *Learning Disabilities Research and Practice* (18)3, pp. 157–171.

Fuchs, L. S., and D. Fuchs. 1992. Identifying a measure for monitoring student reading progress. *School Psychology Review* 21(1), pp. 45–58.

Fuchs, L. S., and D. Fuchs. 1999. Monitoring student progress toward the development of reading competence: A review of three forms of classroom-based assessment. *School Psychology Review* 28, pp. 659–671.

Fuchs, L. S., D. Fuchs, C. L. Hamlett, L. Walz, and G. Germann. 1993. Formative evaluation of academic progress: How much growth can we expect? *School Psychology Review* 22, pp. 27–48.

Fuchs, L. S., D. Fuchs, M. K. Hosp, and J. Jenkins. 2001. Oral reading fluency as an indicator of reading competence: A theoretical, empirical, and historical analysis. *Scientific Studies of Reading* 5, pp. 239–256.

Fuchs, L. S., D. Fuchs, and L. Maxwell. 1988. The validity of informal reading comprehension measures. *Remedial and Special Education* 9(2), pp. 20–28.

Fukkink, R. G., and K. de Glopper. 1998. Effects of instruction in deriving word meaning from context: A meta-analysis. *Review of Educational Research* 68, pp. 450–469.

Gambrell, L. B., and R. J. Bales. 1986. Mental imagery and the comprehension-monitoring performance of fourth- and fifth-grade poor readers. *Reading Research Quarterly* 21, pp. 454–464.

Gambrell, L. B., and P. Koskinen. 2002. Imagery: A strategy for enhancing comprehension. In C. C. Block and M. Pressley (eds.), *Comprehension instruction: Research-based best practices* (pp. 305–318). New York: Guilford.

Garcia, G. E. 2003. The reading comprehension development and instruction of English-language learners. In A. P. Sweet and C. E. Snow (eds.), *Rethinking reading comprehension* (pp. 30–140). New York: Guilford.

Garner, R. 1987. *Metacognition and reading comprehension*. Norwood, NJ: Ablex.

Gaskins, I. W., and T. T. Elliot. 1991. *Implementing cognitive strategy instruction across the school: The Benchmark manual for teachers.* Cambridge, MA: Brookline Books.

Gersten, R., and S. Baker. 2001. *Topical summary: Practices for English-language learners.* Eugene, OR: National Institute for Urban School Improvement.

Gersten, R., L. S. Fuchs, J. P. Williams, and S. Baker. 2001. Teaching reading comprehension strategies to students with learning disabilities. *Review of Educational Research* 71, pp. 279–320.

Gill, D., and M. Kozloff. 2004. *Introduction to Reading First.* Wilmington: University of North Carolina, Wilmington. http://people.uncw.edu/kozloffm/Introduction_to_Reading_First.htm.

Graesser, A. C., J. M. Golding, and D. L. Long. 1991. Narrative representation and comprehension. In R. Barr, M. L. Kamil, P. Mosenthal, and P. D. Pearson (eds.), *Handbook of reading research*, Vol. 2 (pp. 171–204). White Plains, NY: Longman.

Graesser, A. C., and N. K. Person. 1994. Question asking during tutoring. *American Educational Research Journal* 31, pp. 104–137.

Graham, S., and K. Harris. 2005. *Writing better: Effective strategies for teaching students with learning difficulties.* Baltimore, MD: Paul H. Brookes.

Graves, M. F. 2000. A vocabulary program to complement and bolster a middle-grade comprehension program. In B. M. Taylor, M. F. Graves, and P. Van Den Broek (eds.), *Reading for meaning: Fostering comprehension in the middle grades.* New York: Teachers College Press.

Graves, M. F., C. Juel, and B. B. Graves. 2004. *Teaching reading in the twenty-first century* (3rd ed.). Boston: Allyn & Bacon.

Graves, M. F., and S. M. Watts-Taffe. 2002. The place of word consciousness in a research-based vocabulary program. In A. E. Farstrup and S. J. Samuels (eds.), *What research has to say about reading instruction.* Newark, DE: International Reading Association.

Graves, M. F., S. M. Watts, and B. B. Graves. 1994. *Essentials of classroom teaching: Elementary reading.* Boston: Allyn & Bacon.

Griffin, C. C., L. D. Malone, and E. J. Kame'enui. 1995. Effects of graphic organizer instruction on fifth-grade students. *Journal of Educational Research* 89(2), pp. 98–107.

Guirao, M., and A. M. B. Manrique. 1972. Fonemas, sílabas y palabras del español de Buenos Aires. *Filología* 16, pp. 135–165.

Gunn, B. K., D. C. Simmons, and E. J. Kame'enui. 1998. Emergent literacy: Research bases. In D. C. Simmons and E. J. Kame'enui (eds.), *What reading research tells us about children with diverse learning needs: Bases and basics.* Mahwah, NJ: Erlbaum.

Guthrie, J. T. 2005–2006. Concept-oriented reading instruction. College Park: Department of Human Development, University of Maryland. http://www.cori.umd.edu.

Guthrie, J. T., and P. Mosenthal. 1987. Literacy as multidimensional: Locating information and reading comprehension. *Educational Psychologist* 22, pp. 279–297.

Guthrie, J. T., and S. Ozgungor. 2002. Instructional contexts for reading engagement. In C. C. Block and M. Pressley (eds.), *Comprehension instruction: Research-based best practices* (pp. 275–288). New York: Guilford.

Guthrie, J. T., P. Van Meter, G. R. Hancock, A. McCann, E. Anderson, and S. Alao. 1998. Does Concept-Oriented Reading Instruction increase strategy-use and conceptual learning from text? *Journal of Educational Psychology* 90(2), pp. 261–278. http://www.cori.umd.edu/research/publications/1998-guthrie-vanmeter-etal.pdf.

Guthrie, J. T., and A. Wigfield. 2000. Engagement and motivation in reading. In M. L. Kamil, P. B. Mosenthal, P. D. Pearson, and R. Barr (eds.), *Handbook of reading research*, Vol. 3 (pp. 403–422). New York: Erlbaum.

Guthrie, J. T., A. Wigfield, P. Barbosa, K. C. Perencevich, A. Taboada, M. H. Davis, N. T. Scafiddi, and S. Tonks. 2004. Increasing reading comprehension and engagement through Concept-Oriented Reading Instruction. *Journal of Educational Psychology* 96, pp. 403–423.

Hall, S. L., and L. C. Moats. 1999. *Straight talk about reading: How parents can make a difference during the early years.* Lincolnwood, IL: NTC/Contemporary Publishing Group.

Hanna, P. R., J. S. Hanna, R. E. Hodges, and E. H. Rudorf, Jr. 1966. *Phoneme-grapheme correspondences as cues to spelling improvement.* Washington, DC: U.S. Office of Education.

Hansen, J. 2004. *"Tell me a story": Developmentally appropriate retelling strategies.* Newark, DE: International Reading Association.

Harris, A. J., and M. D. Jacobson. 1972. *Basic elementary reading vocabularies.* New York: Macmillan.

Harris, B., and G. Von Harrison. 1988. Teaching a core vocabulary of high-frequency irregular words to beginning readers. Paper presented at the Annual Meeting of the California Educational Research Association, San Diego, November 12–13.

Harris, T. L., and R. E. Hodges. 1995. *The literacy dictionary.* Newark, DE: International Reading Association.

Hart, B., and T. R. Risley. 1995. *Meaningful differences in the everyday experience of young American children.* Baltimore, MD: Paul H. Brookes.

Hasbrouck, J. E. 2006. Drop everything and read—but how? *American Educator*, Summer.

Hasbrouck, J. E., and G. A. Tindal. 2006. Oral reading fluency norms: A valuable assessment tool for reading teachers. *Reading Teacher* 59(7), pp. 636–644.

Hayes, D. P., and M. Ahrens. 1988. Vocabulary simplification for children: A special case of "motherese"? *Journal of Child Language* 15, pp. 395–410.

Hayes, D. P., L. T. Wolfer, and M. F. Wolfe. 1996. Schoolbook simplification and its relation to the decline in SAT-verbal scores. *American Educational Research Journal* 33, pp. 489–508.

Heilman, K. M., K. Voeller, and A. W. Alexander. 1996. Developmental dyslexia: A motor-articulatory feedback hypothesis. *Annals of Neurology* 39, pp. 407–412.

Henry, M. K. 1997. The decoding/spelling continuum: Integrated decoding and spelling instruction from pre-school to early secondary school. *Dyslexia* 3.

Henry, M. K. 2003. *Unlocking literacy: Effective decoding & spelling instruction.* Baltimore, MD: Paul H. Brookes.

Hintze, J. M., and T. J. Christ. 2004. An examination of variability as a function of passage variance in CBM progress monitoring. *School Psychology Review* 33, pp. 204–217.

Hirsch, E. D., Jr. 1987. *Cultural literacy: What every American needs to know.* Boston: Houghton Mifflin.

Hirsch, E. D., Jr. 2006. *Building knowledge: The case for bringing content into the language arts block and for a knowledge-rich curriculum core for all children.* Washington, DC: American Federation of Teachers. http://www.aft.org/pubs-reports/american_educator/issues/spring06/hirsch.htm.

Hofmeister, A. M. 1992. *Handwriting resource book.* http://www.usu.edu/teachall/text/langart/programs/writing.htm.

Hosp, M.K., J.L. Hosp, and K.W. Howell. 2007. *The ABCs of CBM: A practical guide to curriculum-based measurement.* New York: Guilford.

Hudson, R. F., L. High, and S. A. Otaiba. 2007. Dyslexia and the brain: What does current research tell us? *Reading Teacher,* 60(6), pp. 506–515.

Hudson, R. F., H. B. Lane, and P. C. Pullen. 2005. Reading fluency assessment and instruction: What, why, and how. *Reading Teacher* 58(8), pp. 702–714.

Hudson, R. F., J. K. Torgesen, H. B. Lane, and S. J. Turner. 2006. Predictors of decoding fluency: Explaining individual differences in children. Unpublished manuscript.

Hutchins, E. 1991. The social organization of distributed cognition. In L. Resnick, J.M. Levine, and S. D. Teasley (eds.), *Perspectives on socially shared cognition* (pp. 283–307). Washington, DC: American Psychological Association.

Idol, L. 1987. Group story mapping: A comprehension strategy for both skilled and unskilled readers. *Journal of Learning Disabilities* (20)4, pp. 196–205.

Jenkins, J. R., and R. Dixon. 1983. Vocabulary learning. *Contemporary Educational Psychology* 8, pp. 237–280.

Jenkins, J. R., L. S. Fuchs, P. van den Broek, C. Espin, and S. L. Deno. 2003. Sources of individual differences in reading comprehension and reading fluency. *Journal of Educational Psychology* 95, pp. 719–729.

Johns, J. L. 1993. *Informal reading inventories.* DeKalb, IL: Communitech.

Johnson, D. D. 2001. *Vocabulary in the elementary and middle school.* Boston: Allyn & Bacon.

Johnson, D. D., B. H. Johnson, and K. Schlichtling. 2004. Logology: Word and language play. In J. F. Baumann and E. J. Kame'enui (eds.), *Vocabulary instruction: Research to practice.* New York: Guilford.

Joseph, J., K. Nobel, and G. Eden. 2001. The neurobiological basis of reading. *Journal of Learning Disabilities* 34, pp. 566–579.

Just, M. A., and P. A. Carpenter. 1987. *The psychology of reading and language comprehension.* Needham Heights, MA: Allyn & Bacon.

Justice, L. M. 2006. Evidence-based practice, response to intervention, and the prevention of reading difficulties. *Language, Speech, and Hearing Services in Schools* 37, pp. 284–297.

Justice, L. M., and H. K. Ezell. 2000. Enhancing children's print and word awareness through home-based parent intervention. *American Journal of Speech-Language Pathology* 9, pp. 257–269.

Justice, L. M., and H. K. Ezell. 2002. Use of storybook reading to increase print awareness in at-risk children. *American Journal of Speech-Language Pathology* 11, pp. 17–29.

Justice, L. M., and H. K. Ezell. 2004. Print referencing: An emergent literacy enhancement strategy and its clinical applications. *Language, Speech, and Hearing Services in Schools* 35, pp. 185–193.

Justice, L. M., and J. Kaderavek. 2002. Using shared storybook reading to promote emergent literacy. *Teaching Exceptional Children* 34, pp. 8–13.

Justice, L. M., and C. Lankford. 2002. Preschool children's visual attention to print during storybook reading. Manuscript in review.

Justice, L. M., and P. C. Pullen. 2003. Promising interventions for promoting emergent literacy skills: Three evidence-based approaches. *Topics in Early Childhood Special Education* 23(3), pp. 99–113.

Kamil, M. L. 2004. Vocabulary and comprehension instruction: Summary and implications of the National Reading Panel finding. In P. McCardle and V. Chhabra (eds.), *The voice of evidence in reading research.* Baltimore, MD: Paul H. Brookes.

Kamil, M. L., and E. H. Hiebert. 2005. Teaching and learning vocabulary: Perspectives and persistent issues. In E. H. Hiebert and M. L. Kamil (eds.), *Teaching and learning vocabulary: Bringing research to practice.* Mahwah, NJ: Erlbaum.

Keehn, S. 2003. The effect of instruction and practice through Readers Theater on young readers' oral reading fluency. *Reading Research and Instruction* 42(4), pp. 40–62.

Kim, H. S., and M. L. Kamil. 2003. Electronic and multimedia documents. In A. P. Sweet and C. E. Snow (eds.), *Rethinking reading comprehension* (pp. 166–175). New York: Guilford.

Kindler, A. 2002. *Survey of the states' limited English proficient students and available educational programs and services, 2000–2001 summary report.* Washington, DC: National Clearinghouse for English Language Acquisition and Language Instruction Educational Program. http://www.ncela.gwu.edu/policy/states/reports/seareports/0001/sea0001.pdf.

Kintsch W., and J. M. Keenan. 1973. Reading rate as a function of the number of prepositions in the base structure of sentences. *Cognitive Psychology* 5, pp. 257–274.

Klingner, J. K., and P. Edwards. 2006. Cultural considerations with Response to Intervention models. *Reading Research Quarterly* 41(1), pp. 108–117.

Klingner, J. K., and S. Vaughn. 1999. Promoting reading comprehension, content learning, and English acquisition through Collaborative Strategic Reading (CSR). *The Reading Teacher* 52, pp. 738–747.

Klingner, J. K., S. Vaughn, and A. Boardman. 2007. *Teaching reading comprehension to students with learning disabilities.* New York: Guilford.

Klingner, J. K., S. Vaughn, J. Dimino, J. S. Schumm, and D. Bryant. 2001. *Collaborative strategic reading: Strategies for improving comprehension.* Longmont, CO: Sopris West.

Koskinen, P. S., and I. H. Blum. 1986. Paired repeated reading: A classroom strategy for developing fluent reading. *Reading Teacher* 40, pp. 70–75.

Kucan, L., and I. L. Beck. 1997. Thinking aloud and reading comprehension research: Inquiry, instruction and social interaction. *Review of Educational Research* 67, pp. 271–299.

Kuhn, M. R., and P. J. Schwanenflugel. 2006. Fluency-oriented reading instruction: A merging of theory and practice. In K. A. Dougherty Stahl and Michael C. McKenna (eds.), *Reading research at work: Foundations of effective practice.* New York: Guilford.

Kuhn, M. R., and S. A. Stahl. 1998. Teaching children to learn word meanings from context: A synthesis and some questions. *Journal of Literacy Research* 30, pp. 119–138.

Kuhn, M. R., and S. A. Stahl. 2003. Fluency: A review of developmental and remedial practices. *Journal of Educational Psychology* 95(1), pp. 3–21.

LaBerge, D., and S. J. Samuels. 1974. Toward a theory of automatic information processing in reading. *Cognitive Psychology* 6, pp. 292–323.

Lane, H. B. 2006. Conceptualizing reading: What have we learned from scientifically based reading research? Invited presentation at the New York State Reading First Conference, Brooklyn, August.

Lane, H. B., and S. A. Allen. 2010. The vocabulary-rich classroom: Modeling sophisticated word use to promote word consciousness and vocabulary growth. Reading Teacher 63(5), pp. 362–370.

Lane, H. B., and P. C. Pullen. 2004. *A sound beginning: Phonological awareness assessment and instruction.* Boston: Allyn & Bacon.

Lane, H. B., P. C. Pullen, M. R. Eisele, and L. Jordan. 2002. Developing phonological awareness: An essential goal of early reading instruction. *Preventing School Failure* 46, pp. 101–110.

Lane, H. B., P. C. Pullen, and R. F. Hudson. 2006. Identifying essential instructional components of literacy tutoring for struggling beginning readers. Paper submitted for publication.

Lane, H. B., and T. L. Wright 2007. Maximizing the effectiveness of reading aloud. *Reading Teacher* 60(7).

Lapp, D., N. Frey, and D. Fisher. 2012. *Text complexity: Raising rigor in reading.* Wilmington, DE: International Reading Association.

Lehr, F., and J. Osborn. 2005. *A focus on comprehension.* Honolulu: Pacific Resources for Education and Learning (PREL). http://www.prel.org/programs/rel/rel.asp.

Liang, L. A., and J. Dole. 2006. Help with teaching reading comprehension: Comprehension instructional frameworks. *Reading Teacher* 59(8), pp. 742–753.

Liberman, I. Y., D. Shankweiler, and A. M. Liberman. 1989. The alphabetic principle and learning to read. In D. Shankweiler and I. Y. Liberman (eds.), *Phonology and reading disability: Solving the reading puzzle* (IARLD Research Monograph Series). Ann Arbor: University of Michigan Press.

Lyon, G. R. 2002. Reading development, reading difficulties, and reading instruction: Educational and public health issues. *Journal of School Psychology* 40, pp. 3–6.

Mandler, J. M. 1987. On the psychological reality of story structure. *Discourse Processes* 10, pp. 1–29.

Mandler, J. M., and N. S. Johnson, 1977. Remembrance of things parsed: Story structure and recall. *Cognitive Psychology* 9, pp. 111–151.

Marzano, R. J., D. J. Pickering, and J. E. Pollock. 2001. *Classroom instruction that works: Research-based strategies for increasing student achievement.* Alexandria, VA: Association for Supervision and Curriculum Development (ASCD).

Mason, J. M. 1980. When do children begin to read: An exploration of four-year-old children's letter and word reading competencies. *Reading Research Quarterly* 15, pp. 203–227.

Mastropieri, M. A., and T. E. Scruggs. 1998. Enhancing school success with mnemonic strategies. *Intervention in School and Clinic*, March.

Mayer, R. E. 1997. Multimedia learning: Are we asking the right questions? *Educational Psychologist* 32(1), pp. 1–19.

McFeely, D. C. 1974. Syllabication usefulness in a basal and social studies vocabulary. *Reading Teacher* 27, pp. 809–814.

McKenna, M. C., D. J. Kear, and R. A. Ellsworth. 1995. Children's attitudes toward reading: A national survey. *Reading Research Quarterly* 30(4), pp. 934–956.

McKeown, M. G., and I. L. Beck. 2004. Direct and rich vocabulary instruction. In J. F. Baumann and E. J. Kame'enui (eds.), *Vocabulary instruction: Research to practice.* New York: Guilford.

McKeown, M. G., I. L. Beck, R. C. Omanson, and M. T. Pople. 1985. Some effects of the nature and frequency of vocabulary instruction on the knowledge and use of words. *Reading Research Quarterly* 20, pp. 522–535.

McPeake, J. A., and J. T. Guthrie. 2007. *Concept Oriented Reading Instruction (CORI) Teacher Training Module, Grades 35.* Available from John T. Guthrie, University of Maryland, Department of Human Development, 3304 Benjamin Building, College Park, MD 20742.

McTighe, J., and E. T. Lyman, Jr. 1988. Cueing thinking in the classroom: The promise of theory-based tools. *Educational Leadership* 45, pp. 18–24.

Mercer, C. D., and A. R. Mercer. 2004. *Teaching students with learning problems* (7th ed.). Upper Saddle River, NJ: Merrill/Prentice-Hall.

Mewhort, D. J. K., and A. L. Beal. 1977. Mechanisms of word identification. *Journal of Experimental Psychology: Human Perception and Performance* 3, pp. 629–640.

Mewhort, D. J. K., and A. J. Campbell. 1981. Toward a model of skilled reading: An analysis of performance in tachistoscoptic tasks. In G. E. Mackinnon and T. G. Walker (eds.), *Reading research: Advances in theory and practice* 3 (pp. 39–118). New York: Academic Press.

Meyer, M. S., and R. H. Felton. 1999. Repeated reading to enhance fluency: Old approaches and new directions. *Annals of Dyslexia* 49, pp. 283–306.

Miller, G., and P. Gildea. 1987. How children learn words. *Scientific American* 27, pp. 94–99.

Millin, S. K., and S. D. Rinehart. 1999. Some of the benefits of Readers Theater participation for second-grade Title I students. *Reading Research and Instruction* 39(1), pp. 71–88.

Moats, L. C. 2000. *Speech to print: Language essentials for teachers.* Baltimore, MD: Paul H. Brookes.

Moats, L. C. 2005. *Language essentials for teachers of reading and spelling (LETRS). Module 10, reading big words: Syllabication and advanced decoding.* Longmont, CO: Sopris West.

Moats, L. C. 2007. Whole-language high jinks: How to tell when "scientifically-based reading instruction" isn't. Washington, DC: Thomas B. Fordham Institute. http://edexcellence.net/foundation/publication/publication.cfm?id=367.

Moats, L. C., and B. Rosow. 2003. *Spellography: A Student Road Map to Better Spelling.* Longmont, CO: Sopris West.

Moffett, J., and B. J. Wagner. 1992. *Student-centered language arts: K–12* (4th ed.). Portsmouth, NH: Heinemann.

Moran, C., and R. Calfee. 1993. Comprehending orthography: Social construction of letter-sound systems in monolingual and bilingual programs. *Reading and Writing: An Interdisciplinary Journal* 5, pp. 205–225.

Morrow, L. M. 1990. Assessing children's understanding of story through their construction and reconstruction of narrative. In L. M. Morrow and J. K. Smith (eds.), *Assessment for instruction in early literacy* (pp. 110–134). Englewood Cliffs, NJ: Prentice-Hall.

Morrow, L. M., M. Kuhn, and P. J. Schwanenflugel. 2006. The family fluency program. *Reading Teacher* 60(4), pp. 322–333.

Morrow, L. M., and J. K. Smith. 1990. The effects of group size on interactive storybook reading. *Reading Research Quarterly* 25, pp. 213–231.

Nagy, W. E. 1988. *Teaching vocabulary to improve reading comprehension.* Newark, DE: International Reading Association.

Nagy, W. E. 2005. Why vocabulary instruction needs to be long-term and comprehensive. In E. H. Hiebert and M. L. Kamil (eds.), *Teaching and learning vocabulary: Bringing research to practice.* Mahwah, NJ: Erlbaum.

Nagy, W. E., and R. C. Anderson. 1984. How many words are there in printed school English? *Reading Research Quarterly* 19, pp. 304–330.

Nagy, W. E., R. C. Anderson, and P. A. Herman. 1987. Learning word meanings from context during normal reading. *American Educational Research Journal* 24, pp. 237–270.

Nagy, W. E., R. C. Anderson, M. Schommer, J. A. Scott, and A. Stallman. 1989. Morphological families in the internal lexicon. *Reading Research Quarterly* 24, pp. 262–282.

Nagy, W. E., I. N. Diakidoy, and R. C. Anderson. 1993. The acquisition of morphology: Learning the contribution of suffixes to the meanings of derivatives. *Journal of Reading Behavior* 25, pp. 155–170.

Nagy, W. E., G. E. Garcia, A. Y. Durgunoglu, and B. Hancin-Bhatt. 1993. Spanish-English bilingual students' use of cognates in English reading. *Journal of Reading Behavior* 25, pp. 241–259.

Nagy, W. E., P. A. Herman, and R. C. Anderson. 1985. Learning words from context. *Reading Research Quarterly* 20, pp. 233–253.

Nagy, W. E., and J. A. Scott. 2000. Vocabulary processes. In M. L. Kamil, P. Mosenthal, P. D. Pearson, and R. Barr (eds.), *Handbook of reading research*, Vol. 3 (pp. 269–284). Mahwah, NJ: Erlbaum.

Nation, K., and M. J. Snowling. 1998. Semantic processing and the development of word-recognition skills: Evidence from children with reading comprehension difficulties. *Journal of Memory & Language* 39, pp. 85–110.

National Association for the Education of Young Children. 1998. Learning to read and write: Developmentally appropriate practices for young children. *Young Children* 53(4), pp. 30–46.

National Association of State Directors of Special Education. 2006. *Response to intervention: Policy considerations and implementation.* Alexandria, VA: National Association of State Directors of Special Education.

National Center for Education Statistics. 2005. *The condition of education.* Washington, DC: U.S. Department of Education.

National Center for Education Statistics. 2011. *The nation's report card: Reading 2011* (NCES 2012–457). National Center for Education Statistics, Institute of Education Sciences, U.S. Department of Education, Washington, D.C.

National Governors Association Center for Best Practices, Council of Chief State School Officers. 2010. *Common core state standards for English language arts.* Washington DC: National Governors Association Center for Best Practices, Council of Chief State School Officers.

National Reading Panel. 2000. *Teaching children to read: An evidence-based assessment of the scientific research literature on reading and its implications for reading instruction.* Washington, DC: National Institute of Child Health and Human Development.

Neufeld, P. 2005. Comprehension instruction in content area classes. *Reading Teacher* 59(4), pp. 302–312.

Neuhaus Education Center. 2002. *Reading readiness.* Bellaire, TX: Neuhaus Education Center.

Neuhaus, G. 2003. What does it take to read a letter? *Perspectives on Dyslexia*, pp. 27–31. Winter.

Neuman, S. 1988. Enhancing children's comprehension through previewing. In J. Readence and R. S. Baldwin (eds.), *Dialogues in literacy research*, (Thirty-Seventh Yearbook of the National Reading Conference, pp. 219–224). Chicago, IL: National Reading Conference.

New Standards Primary Literacy Committee. 1999. *Reading & writing grade by grade: Primary literacy standards for kindergarten through third grade.* Washington, DC: National Center on Education and the Economy.

O'Brien, D. G. 1998. Multiple literacies in a high-school program for "at-risk" adolescents. In D. E. Alvermann, K. A. Hinchman, D. W. Moore, S. F. Phelps, and D. R. Waff (eds.), *Reconceptualizing the literacies in adolescents' lives* (pp. 27–49). Mahwah, NJ: Erlbaum.

O'Brien, D. G. 2001. "At-risk" adolescents: Redefining competence through the multiliteracies of intermediality, visual arts, and representation. *Reading Online* 4(11). http://www.readingonline.org/newliteracies/lit_index.asp?

O'Connor, R. E. 2007. *Teaching word recognition: Effective strategies for students with learning difficulties.* New York: Guilford.

O'Connor, R. E., D. Fulmer, K. Harty, and K. Bell. 2005. Layers of reading intervention in kindergarten through third grade: Changes in teaching and student outcomes. *Journal of Learning Disabilities* 38(5), pp. 440–455.

O'Connor, R. E., and J. R. Jenkins. 1999. Prediction of reading disabilities in kindergarten and first grade. *Scientific Studies of Reading* 3, pp. 159–197.

Ogle, D. M. 1986. K-W-L: A teaching model that develops active reading of expository text. *Reading Teacher* 39(6), pp. 564–570.

Olsen. J. Z. 2003. *Handwriting without tears®.* Cabin John, MD: Jan Z. Olsen.

Osborn, J., and F. Lehr. 2003. *A Focus on Fluency.* Honolulu: Pacific Resources for Education and Learning.

O'Shea, L. J., and P. T. Sindelar. 1983. The effects of segmenting written discourse on the reading comprehension of low- and high-performance readers. *Reading Research Quarterly* 18, pp. 458–465.

Otero, J., J. A. Leon, and A. C. Graesser (eds.). 2002. *The psychology of science text comprehension.* Mahwah, NJ: Erlbaum.

Palincsar, A. S., and A. Brown. 1984. Reciprocal teaching of comprehension-fostering and comprehension-monitoring activities. *Cognition and Instruction* 1, pp. 117–175.

Pardo, L. S. 2004. What every teacher needs to know about comprehension. *Reading Teacher* 58(3), pp. 272–280.

Pearson, P. D., and L. Fielding. 1991. Comprehension instruction. In R. Barr, M. L. Kamil, P. Mosenthal, and P. D. Pearson (eds.), *Handbook of reading research*, Vol. 2. White Plains, NY: Longman.

Pearson, P. D., and M. C. Gallagher. 1983. The instruction of reading comprehension. *Contemporary Educational Psychology* 8, pp. 317–344.

Pearson, P. D., and D. N. Hamm. 2005. The assessment of reading comprehension: A review of practices—past, present, and future. In S. G. Paris and S. A. Stahl (eds.), *Children's reading comprehension and assessment.* Mahwah, NJ: Erlbaum.

Pearson, P. D., and D. Johnson. 1978. *Teaching reading comprehension.* New York: Holt, Rinehart & Winston.

Perfetti, C. A. 1985. *Reading ability.* New York: Oxford Press.

Perfetti, C. A. 1986. Continuities in reading acquisition, reading skill, and reading disability. *Remedial and Special Education (RASE)* 7, pp. 11–21.

Pikulski, J. J. 2006. Fluency: A developmental and language perspective. In S. J. Samuels and A. E. Farstrup (eds.), *What research has to say about fluency instruction.* Newark, DE: International Reading Association.

Pikulski, J. J., and D. J. Chard. 2005. Fluency: Bridge between decoding and reading comprehension. *Reading Teacher* 58(6).

Pinnell, G. S., J. J. Pikulski, K. K. Wixson, J. R. Campbell, P. B. Gough, and A. S. Beatty. 1995. *Listening to children read aloud.* Washington, DC: U.S. Department of Education, National Center for Educational Statistics.

Pressley, M. 2000a. *Comprehension instruction: What works.* Reading Rockets. http://www.readingrockets.org/articles/68.

Pressley, M. 2000b. What should comprehension instruction be the instruction of? In M. Kamil, P. Mosenthal, P. D. Pearson, and R. Barr (eds.), *Handbook of reading research*, Vol. 3 (pp. 545–561). Mahwah, NJ: Erlbaum.

Pressley, M. 2002a. Comprehension strategies instruction: A turn-of-the-century status report. In C. C. Block and M. Pressley (eds.), *Comprehension instruction: Research-based best practices* (pp. 11–27). New York: Guilford.

Pressley, M. 2002b. *Reading instruction that works: The case for balanced teaching* (2nd ed.). New York: Guilford.

Pressley, M., and P. Afflerbach. 1995. *Verbal protocols of reading: The nature of constructively responsive reading.* Hillsdale, NJ: Erlbaum.

Pressley, M., and C. C. Block. 2002. Summing up: What comprehension instruction could be. In C. C. Block and M. Pressley (eds.), *Comprehension instruction: Research-based best practices* (pp. 383–392). New York: Guilford.

Pressley, M., P. B. El-Dinary, I. Gaskins, T. Schuder, J. L. Bergman, J. Almasi, and R. Brown. 1992. Beyond direct explanation: Transactional instruction of reading comprehension strategies. *Elementary School Journal* 92(5), pp. 513–555.

Pressley, M., and K. R. Hilden. 2005. Commentary on three important directions in comprehension assessment research. In S. G. Paris and S. A. Stahl (eds.). *Children's reading comprehension and assessment.* Mahwah, NJ: Erlbaum.

Pressley, M., C. J. Johnson, S. Symons, J. S. McGoldrick, and J. A. Kurita. 1989. Strategies that improve children's memory and comprehension of text. *Elementary School Journal* 90(1), pp. 3–32.

Pressley, M., and R. Wharton-McDonald. 1998. The development of literacy, part 4: The need for increased comprehension in upper-elementary grades. In M. Pressley (ed.), *Reading instruction that works: The case for balanced teaching* (pp. 192–227). New York: Guilford.

Pressley, M., R. Wharton-McDonald, J. M. Hampson, and M. Echevarria. 1998. The nature of literacy instruction in ten grade-4/5 classrooms in upstate New York. *Scientific Studies of Reading* 2, pp. 59–191.

Pressley, M., E. Wood, V. E. Woloshyn, V. Martin, A. King, and D. Menke. 1992. Encouraging mindful use of prior knowledge: Attempting to construct explanatory answers facilitates learning. *Educational Psychologist* 27(1), pp. 91–109.

Pring, L., and M. Snowling. 1986. Developmental changes in word recognition: An information-processing account. *Quarterly Journal of Experimental Psychology: Human Experimental Psychology* 38, pp. 395–418.

Pullen, P. C. 2000. The effects of alphabetic word work with manipulative letters on the reading acquisition of struggling first-grade students (doctoral dissertation, University of Florida). *Dissertation Abstracts International* 61(8), 3108A.

Pullen, P. C. 2005. Effective practices for phonological awareness. TeachingLD.org *Online Journal.* Division of Learning Disabilities of the Council for Exceptional Children.

Pullen, P. C., and L. M. Justice. 2003. Enhancing phonological awareness, print awareness, and oral language skills in preschool children. *Intervention in School and Clinic* 39(2), pp. 87–98.

Pullen, P. C., H. B. Lane, J. W. Lloyd, R. Nowak, and J. Ryals. 2005. Effects of explicit instruction on decoding of struggling first grade students: A data-based case study. *Education and Treatment of Children* 28, pp. 63–76.

RAND Reading Study Group. 2002. *Reading for understanding: Towards an R & D program in reading comprehension.* Santa Monica, CA: RAND Corporation.

Raphael, T. E. 1982. Question-answering strategies for children. *Reading Teacher* 36, pp. 186–190.

Raphael, T. E. 1986. Teaching question/answer relationships, revisited. *Reading Teacher* 39, pp. 516–522.

Raphael, T. E., and K. H. Au. 2005. QAR: Enhancing comprehension and test taking across grades and content areas. *Reading Teacher* 59(3), pp. 206–221.

Raphael, T. E., S. Florio-Ruane, M. George, N. L. Hasty, and K. Highfield. 2004. *Book club plus! A literacy framework for the primary grades.* Lawrence, MA: Small Planet Communications.

Raphael, T. E., M. Kehus, and K. Damphousse. 2001. *Book club for middle school.* Lawrence, MA: Small Planet Communications.

Raphael, T. E., L. S. Pardo, and K. Highfield. 2002. *Book club: A literature-based curriculum* (2nd ed.). Lawrence, MA: Small Planet Communications.

Raphael, T. E., and P. D. Pearson. 1985. Increasing students' awareness of sources of information for answering questions. *American Educational Research Journal* 22, pp. 217–236.

Rashotte, C. A., and J. K. Torgesen. 1985. Repeated reading and reading fluency in learning-disabled children. *Reading Research Quarterly* 20, pp. 180–188.

Rasinski, T. V. 1990. Investigating measures of reading fluency. *Educational Research Quarterly* 14(3), pp. 37–44.

Rasinski, T. V. 1994. Developing syntactic sensitivity in reading through phrase-cued texts. *Intervention in School and Clinic* 29(3).

Rasinski, T. V. 2000. Speed does matter in reading. *Reading Teacher* 54, pp. 146–150.

Rasinski, T. V. 2003. *The fluent reader: Oral reading strategies for building word recognition, fluency, and comprehension.* New York: Scholastic.

Rasinski, T. V. 2004. *Assessing reading fluency.* Honolulu: Pacific Resources for Education and Learning.

Rasinski, T. V., and J. Hoffman. 2006. Seeking understanding about reading fluency: The contributions of Steven A. Stahl. In K. A. Dougherty Stahl and M. C. McKenna (eds.), *Reading Research at Work: Foundations of effective practice.* New York: Guilford.

Readence, J. 2004. Semantic feature analysis. *Nevada Reading First Newsletter* 1(4).

Reitsma, P. 1983. Printed word learning in beginning readers. *Journal of Experimental Child Psychology* 36(3), pp. 321–339.

Reyna, V. F. 2004. Why scientific research? The importance of evidence in changing educational practice. In P. McCardle and V. Chhabra (eds.), *The voice of evidence in reading research* (pp. 47–58). Baltimore, MD: Paul H. Brookes.

Rodriguez, T. A. 2001. From the known to the unknown: Using cognates to teach English and Spanish-speaking literates. *Reading Teacher* 54(8), pp. 744–746.

Rosenblatt, L. M. 1978. *The reader, the text, the poem: The transactional theory of the literary work.* Carbondale, IL: Southern Illinois University Press.

Rosenblatt, L. M. 1995. *Literature as exploration* (5th ed.). New York: Modern Language Association.

Rosenshine, B. 2012. Principles of instruction: Research based strategies that all teachers should know. *American Educator,* Spring 2012.

Sadler, C. R. 2001. *Comprehension strategies for middle grade learners*. Newark, DE: International Reading Association.

Sadoski, M., and A. Paivio. 1994. A dual coding view of imagery and verbal processes in reading comprehension. In R. B. Ruddell, M. R. Ruddell, and H. Singer (eds.), *Theoretical models and processes of reading* (4th ed.), pp. 582–601). Newark, DE: International Reading Association.

Sakiey, E., E. Fry, A. Goss, and B. Loigman. 1980. A syllable frequency count. *Visible Language* 14(2), pp. 137–150.

Sameroff, A. J. 1975. Early influences on development. Fact or fancy? *Merrill-Palmer Quarterly* 1, pp. 267–294.

Samuels, S. J. 1988. Decoding and automaticity: Helping poor readers become automatic at word recognition. *Reading Teacher* 41, pp. 756–760.

Samuels, S. J. 1997. The method of repeated readings. *Reading Teacher* 32, pp. 403–408.

Samuels, S. J. 2006. Toward a model of reading fluency. In S. J. Samuels and A. E. Farstrup (eds.), *What research has to say about fluency instruction*. Newark, DE: International Reading Association.

Sandora, C., I. Beck, and M. McKeown. 1999. A comparison of two discussion strategies on students' comprehension and interpretation of complex literature. *Journal of Reading Psychology* 20, pp. 177–212.

Schatschneider, C., J. Buck, J. K. Torgesen, R. K. Wagner, L. Hassler, S. Hecht, and K. Powell-Smith. 2004. *A multivariate study of factors that contribute to individual differences in performance on the Florida Comprehensive Reading Assessment Test* (Technical Report No. 5). Tallahassee: Florida Center for Reading Research.

Scheerer-Neumann, G. 1981. The utilization of intraword structure in poor readers: Experimental evidence and training program. *Psychological Research* 43, pp. 155–178.

Schneider, W. 2003. *Automaticity in complex cognition*. Pittsburgh: Center for Cognitive Brain Imaging at Carnegie Mellon University. http://coglab.psy.cmu.edu/index_main.html.

Schreiber, P. A. 1980. On the acquisition of reading fluency. *Journal of Reading Behavior* 7, pp. 177–186.

Schreiber, P. A. 1991. Understanding prosody's role in reading acquisition. *Theory into Practice* 30, pp. 158–164.

Schuder, T. 1993. The genesis of transactional strategies instruction in a reading program for at-risk students. *Elementary School Journal* 94, pp. 183–200.

Schwanenflugel, P. J., A. M. Hamilton, M. R. Kuhn, J. M. Wisenbaker, and S. A. Stahl. 2004. Becoming a fluent reader: Reading skill and prosodic features in the oral reading of young readers. *Journal of Educational Psychology* 96 (1), pp. 119–129.

Schwartz, R. M., and T. E. Raphael. 1985. Concept of definition: A key to improving students' vocabulary. *Reading Teacher* 39, pp. 198–203.

Scott, J. A., and W. E. Nagy. 1997. Understanding the definitions of unfamiliar verbs. *Reading Research Quarterly* 32, pp. 184–200.

Scott, J. A., and W. E. Nagy. 2004. Developing word consciousness. In J. F. Baumann and E. J. Kame'enui (eds.), *Vocabulary instruction: Research to practice*. New York: Guilford.

Shany, M. T., and A. Biemiller. 1995. Assisted reading practice: Effects on performance for poor readers in Grades 3 and 4. *Reading Research Quarterly* 50(3), pp. 382–395.

Share, D. L. 2004. Knowing letter names and learning letter sounds: A causal connection. *Journal of Experimental Child Psychology* 88, pp. 213–233.

Share, D. L., and K. E. Stanovich. 1995. Cognitive processes in early reading development: Accommodating individual differences into a mode of acquisition. *Issues in Education: Contributions for Educational Psychology* 1, pp. 1–57.

Shaywitz, B. A., S. E. Shaywitz, B. A. Blackman, K. R. Pugh, R. K. Fulbright, P. Skudlarski, W. E. Mencl, R. T. Constable, J. M. Holahan, K. E. Marchione, J. M. Fletcher, G. R. Lyon, and J. C. Gore. 2004. Development of left occipitotemporal systems for skilled reading in children after a phonologically-based intervention. *Biological Psychiatry* 55(9), pp. 926–933.

Shaywitz, S. E. 2003. *Overcoming dyslexia: A new and complete science-based program for reading problems at any level*. New York: Vintage Books.

Shaywitz, S. E., M. D. Escobar, B. A. Shaywitz, J. M. Fletcher, and R. Makuch. 1992. Distribution and temporal stability of dyslexia in an epidemiological sample of 414 children followed longitudinally. *New England Journal of Medicine* 326, pp. 145–150.

Shaywitz, S. E., J. M. Fletcher, J. M. Holahan, A. E. Shneider, K. E. Marchione, K. K. Stuebing, D. J. Francis, K. R. Pugh, and B. A. Shaywitz. 1999. Persistence of dyslexia: The Connecticut longitudinal study at adolescence. *Pediatrics* 104, pp. 1351–1359.

Shefelbine, J. 1990. A syllable-unit approach to teaching decoding of polysyllabic words to fourth- and sixth-grade disabled readers. In J. Zutell and S. McCormick (eds.), *Literacy theory and research: Analysis from multiple paradigms* (pp. 223–230). Chicago: National Reading Conference.

Shefelbine, J., and J. Calhoun. 1991. Variability in approaches to identifying polysyllabic words: A descriptive study of sixth graders with highly, moderately, and poorly developed syllabication strategies. In J. Zutell and S. McCormick (eds.), *Learner factors/teacher factors: Issues in literacy research and instruction* (pp. 169–177). Chicago: National Reading Conference.

Shefelbine, J., L. Lipscomb, and A. Hern. 1989. Variables associated with second, fourth, and sixth grade students' ability to identify polysyllabic words. In S. McCormick and J. Zutell (eds.), *Cognitive and social perspectives for literacy research and instruction* (pp. 145–149). Chicago: National Reading Conference.

Shefelbine, J., and K. Newman. 2004. *SIPPS: Systematic instruction in phoneme awareness, phonics, and sight words. Challenge level, polysyllabic decoding* (2nd ed.). Oakland, CA: Developmental Studies Center.

Shin, E. C., D. L. Schallert, and W. C. Savenye. 1994. Effects of learner control, advisement, and prior knowledge on young students' learning in a hypertext environment. *Educational Technology Research & Development* 42(1), pp. 33–46.

Shinn, M. 1998. *Advanced applications of curriculum-based measurement*. New York: Guilford.

Silven, M., and M. Vauras. 1992. Improving reading through thinking aloud. *Learning and Instruction* 2, pp. 69–88.

Simmons, D. C., and E. J. Kame'enui. 2000. *Overview of big ideas in beginning reading*. Institute for the Development of Educational Achievement, College of Education, University of Oregon. PowerPoint presentation.

Slingerland, B. H. 1971. *A multisensory approach to language arts: Book I*. Cambridge, MA: Educators Publishing Service.

Snow, C. E. 2003. Assessment of reading comprehension: Researchers and practitioners helping themselves and each other. In A. P. Sweet and C. E. Snow (eds.), *Rethinking reading comprehension*. New York: Guilford.

Snow, C. E., S. M. Burns, and P. Griffin. 1998. *Preventing reading difficulties in young children*. Washington, DC: National Academies Press.

Snow, C. E., and A. P. Sweet. 2003. Reading for comprehension. In A. P. Sweet and C. E. Snow (eds.), *Rethinking reading comprehension*. New York: Guilford.

Spear-Swerling, L. 2006. The importance of teaching handwriting. LD Online. http:/ldonline.org/spearswerling/10521.

Spear-Swerling, L., and R. J. Sternberg. 2001. What science offers teachers of reading. *Learning Disabilities Research & Practice* 16(1), pp. 51–57.

Speece, D. L., and K. D. Ritchey. 2005. A longitudinal study of the development of oral reading fluency in young children at risk for reading failure. *Journal of Learning Disabilities* 38, pp. 387–399.

Spires, H. A., and T. H. Estes. 2002. Reading in Web-based learning environments. In C. C. Block and M. Pressley (eds.), *Comprehension instruction: Research-based best practices* (pp. 115–125). New York: Guilford.

Stahl, S. A. 1992. Saying the "p" word: Nine guidelines for exemplary phonics instruction. *Reading Teacher* 45, pp. 618–625.

Stahl, S. A. 1999. *Vocabulary development.* Cambridge, MA: Brookline Books.

Stahl, S. A. 2005. Four problems with teaching word meanings (and what to do to make vocabulary an integral part of instruction). In E. H. Hiebert and M. L. Kamil (eds.), *Teaching and learning vocabulary: Bringing research to practice.* Mahwah, NJ: Erlbaum.

Stahl, S. A., and C. H. Clark. 1987. The effects of participatory expectations in classroom discussion on learning of science vocabulary. *American Educational Research Journal* 24, pp. 541–556.

Stahl, S. A., and K. A. Dougherty Stahl. 2004. Word wizards all! Teaching word meanings in preschool and primary education. In J. F. Baumann and E. J. Kame'enui (eds.), *Vocabulary instruction: Research to practice.* New York: Guilford.

Stahl, S. A., A. M. Duffy-Hester, and K. A. Dougherty Stahl. 1998. Everything you wanted to know about phonics (but were afraid to ask). *Reading Research Quarterly* 33(3).

Stahl, S. A., and M. M. Fairbanks. 1986. The effects of vocabulary instruction: A model-based meta-analysis. *Review of Educational Research* 56(1), pp. 72–110.

Stahl, S. A., and K. Heubach. 2006. Fluency-oriented reading instruction. In K. A. Dougherty Stahl and Michael C. McKenna (eds.), *Reading Research at Work: Foundations of effective practice.* New York: Guilford.

Stahl, S. A., K. Heubach, and B. Cramond. 1997. *Fluency-oriented reading instruction* (Reading Research Report No. 79). Athens, GA: National Reading Research Center.

Stahl, S. A., and B. A. Kapinus. 1991. Possible sentences: Predicting word meanings to teach content area vocabulary. *Reading Teacher* 45, pp. 36–38.

Stahl, S. A., and M. R. Kuhn 2002. Making it sound like language: Developing fluency. *Reading Teacher* 55(6).

Stahl, S. A., and W. E. Nagy. 2000. *Promoting vocabulary development.* Austin: Texas Education Agency.

Stanback, M. L. 1992. Syllable and rime patterns for teaching reading: Analysis of a frequency-based vocabulary of 17,602 words. *Annals of Dyslexia* 42, pp. 196–221.

Stanovich, K. E. 1986. Matthew effects in reading: Some consequences of individual differences in the acquisition of literacy. *Reading Research Quarterly* 21(4), pp. 360–406.

Stanovich, K. E. 1991. Word recognition: Changing perspectives. In R. Barr, M. L. Kamil, P. Mosenthal, and P. D. Pearson (eds.), *Handbook of reading research*, Vol. 2 (pp. 418–452). New York: Longman.

Stanovich, K. E. 1993. Romance and reality. *Reading Teacher* 47(4), pp. 280–291.

Stanovich, K. E. 1994. Does dyslexia exist? *Journal of Child Psychology and Psychiatry* 35, pp. 579– 595.

Stanovich, K. E., and P. Stanovich. 1995. How research might inform the debate about early reading acquisition. *Journal of Research in Reading* 18(2), pp. 87–105.

Stanovich, P. J., and K. E. Stanovich. 2003. *Using research and reason in education: How teachers can use scientifically based research to make curricular and instructional decisions.* Washington, DC: National Institute for Literacy, Partnership for Reading. http://www.nifl.gov/partnershipforreading/publications/pdf/Stanovich_Color.pdf.

Stayter, F. Z., and R. Allington. 1991. Fluency and the understanding of texts. *Theory into Practice* 30, pp. 143–148.

Stecker, S. K., N. L. Roser, and M. G. Martinez. 1998. Understanding oral reading fluency. In T. Shanahan and F. V. Rodriguez-Brown (eds.), *47th yearbook of the National Reading Conference* (pp. 295–310). Chicago: National Reading Conference.

Sternberg, R. J. 1987. Most vocabulary is learned from context. In M. G. McKeown and M. E. Curtis (eds.), *The nature of vocabulary acquisition.* Mahwah, NJ: Erlbaum.

Stoller, F., and W. Grabe. 1995. Implications for L2 vocabulary acquisition and instruction for L1 vocabulary research. In T. Huckin, M. Haynes, and J. Coady (eds.), *Second language reading and vocabulary learning.* Norwood, NJ: Ablex.

Swanborn, M. S., and K. de Glopper. 1999. Incidental word learning while reading: A meta-analysis. *Review of Educational Research* 69, pp. 261–285.

Sweet, R. W., Jr. 2004. The big picture: Where we are nationally on the reading front and how we got here. In P. McCardle and V. Chhabra (eds.), *The voice of evidence in reading research* (pp. 13–44). Baltimore, MD: Paul H. Brookes.

Sweller, J. J. 1994. Cognitive Load Theory, learning difficulty, and instructional design. *Learning and Instruction* 4, pp. 95–312.

Sweller, J., J. Van Merrienboer, and F. Paas. 1998. Cognitive architecture and instructional design. *Educational Psychology Review* 10, pp. 251–296.

Taylor, B. M., and R. W. Beach. 1984. The effects of text structure instruction on middle-grade students' comprehension and production of expository text. *Reading Research Quarterly* 19, pp. 134–146.

Taylor, B. M., and B. J. Frye. 1992. Comprehension strategy instruction in the intermediate grades. *Reading Research and Instruction* 32(1), pp. 39–48.

Taylor, G., P. Pearson, D. Peterson, and M. Rodriguez. 2003. Reading growth in high-poverty classrooms: The influence of teacher practices that encourage cognitive engagement in literacy learning. *Elementary School Journal* 104, pp. 3–28.

Teale, W. H., and E. Sulzby. 1996. Emergent literacy: New perspectives. In R. Robinson, M. McKenna, and J. Wedman (eds.), *Issues and trends in literacy instruction* (pp. 139–143). Boston: Allyn & Bacon.

Templeton, S. 1997. *Teaching the integrated language arts.* Boston: Houghton Mifflin.

Therrien, W. J. 2004. Fluency and comprehension gains as a result of repeated reading: A meta-analysis. *Remedial and Special Education* 25(4), pp. 252–261.

Tilly III, W. D. 2002. School psychology as a problem solving enterprise. In A. Thomas and J. Grimes (eds.), *Best Practices in School Psychology* IV, pp. 25–36. Bethesda, MD: National Association of School Psychologists.

Topping, K. 1987. Paired reading: A powerful technique for parent use. *Reading Teacher* 40, pp. 608–614.

Torgesen, J. K. 1998. Catch them before they fall: Identification and assessment to prevent reading failure in young children. *American Educator* 2(1–2), pp. 32–39.

Torgesen, J. K. 2002. The prevention of reading difficulties. *Journal of School Psychology* 40, p. 6.

Torgesen, J. K. 2004. Preventing early reading failure. *American Educator*, Fall.

Torgesen, J. K. 2006. *A comprehensive K-3 reading assessment plan: Guidance for school leaders.* Portsmouth, NH: RMC Research Corporation, Center on Instruction.

Torgesen, J. K. 2007. Research related to strengthening instruction in reading comprehension: Part 2. Paper presented at Reading First Comprehension Conference, Atlanta, January.

Torgesen, J. K., and S. R. Burgess. 1998. Consistency of reading related phonological processes throughout early childhood: Evidence from longitudinal, correlational, and instructional studies. In J. Metsala and L. Ehri (eds.), *Word recognition in beginning reading* (pp. 161–188). Hillsdale, NJ: Erlbaum.

Torgesen, J. K., D. D. Houston, L. M. Rissman, S. M. Decker, G. Roberts, S. Vaughn, J. Wexler, D. J. Francis, M. O. Rivera, and N. Lesaux. 2007. *Academic literacy instruction for adolescents: A guidance document from the Center on Instruction.* Portsmouth, NH: RMC Research Corporation, Center on Instruction.

Torgesen, J. K., and R. F. Hudson. 2006. Reading fluency: Critical issues for struggling readers. In S. J. Samuels and A. E. Farstrup (eds.), *What research has to say about fluency instruction.* Newark, DE: International Reading Association.

Torgesen, J. K., C. A. Rashotte, and A. Alexander. 2001. Principles of fluency instruction in reading: Relationships with established empirical outcomes. In M. Wolf (ed.), *Dyslexia, fluency, and the brain* (pp. 333–355). Parkton, MD: York Press.

Trabasso, T., and E. Bouchard. 2002. Teaching readers how to comprehend text strategically. In C. C. Block and M. Pressley (eds.), *Comprehension instruction: Research-based best practices* (pp. 176–200). New York: Guilford.

Treiman, R. 1992. The role of intrasyllabic units in learning to read and spell. In P. B. Gough, L. C. Ehri, and R. Treiman (eds.), *Reading acquisition* (pp. 65–106). Hillsdale, NJ: Erlbaum.

Treiman, R. 2005. Knowledge about letters as a foundation for reading and spelling. In R. Malatesha, R. M. Joshi, and P. G. Aaron (eds.), *Handbook of orthography and literacy.* Mahwah, NJ: Erlbaum.

Treiman, R., and B. Kessler. 2003. The role of letter names in the acquisition of literacy. In R. Kail (ed.), *Advances in child development and behavior* 31, pp. 105–135.

Treiman, R., B. Kessler, and T. C. Pollo. 2006. Learning about the letter name subset of the vocabulary: Evidence from US and Brazilian preschoolers. *Applied Psycholinguistics* 27, pp. 211–227.

Treiman, R., R. Tincoff, K. Rodriguez, A. Mouzaki, and D. J. Francis. 1998. The foundations of literacy: Learning the sounds of letters. *Child Development* 69, pp. 1524–1540.

Treiman, R., S. Weatherston, and D. Berch. 1994. The role of letter names in children's learning of phoneme-grapheme relations. *Applied Psycholinguistics* 15, pp. 97–122.

Tunmer, W. E., M. L. Herriman, and A. R. Nesdale. 1988. Metalinguistic abilities and beginning reading. *Reading Research Quarterly* 23, pp. 134–158.

Vaughn Gross Center for Reading and Language Arts. 2005. *Introduction to the 3-tier reading model* (4th ed.). Austin: The University of Texas System/Texas Education Agency.

Vaughn, S. 2003. How many tiers are needed for response to intervention to achieve acceptable prevention outcomes? Paper presented at the National Research Center on Learning Disabilities Responsiveness-to-Intervention Symposium, Kansas City, MO.

Vaughn, S., and D. Chard. 2006. Three-tier intervention research studies: Descriptions of two related projects. *Perspectives* 32(1), pp. 29–34.

Vaughn, S., and S. Linan-Thompson. 2004. *Research-based methods of reading instruction: Grades K-3.* Alexandria, VA: Association for Supervision and Curriculum Development (ASCD).

Vellutino, F. R. 2003. Individual differences as sources of variability in reading comprehension in elementary school children. In A. Polselli Sweet and C. E. Snow (eds.), *Rethinking reading comprehension.* New York: Guilford.

Vellutino, F. R., and D. M. Scanlon. 2002. The interactive strategies approach to reading intervention. *Contemporary Educational Psychology* 27, pp. 573–635.

Venezky, R. L. 1970. *The structure of English orthography.* The Hague: Mouton.

Vygotsky, L. S. 1978. *Mind in society: The development of higher psychological processes.* Cambridge, MA: Harvard University Press.

White, T. G., J. Sowell, and A. Yanagihara. 1989. Teaching elementary students to use word-part clues. *Reading Teacher* 42, pp. 302–308.

White, T. J., M. A. Power, and S. White. 1989. Morphological analysis: Implications for teaching and understanding vocabulary growth. *Reading Research Quarterly* 24, pp. 283–304.

Whitehurst, G. J. 1992. Dialogic reading: An effective way to read to preschoolers. http://www.readingrockets.org/.

Whitehurst, G. J., F. L. Falco, C. J. Lonigan, J. E. Fischel, B. D. DeBaryshe, M. C. Valdez-Menchaca, and M. Caulfield. 1988. Accelerating language development through picture-book reading. *Developmental Psychology* 24, pp. 552–558.

Williams, J. P. 1993. Comprehension of students with and without learning disabilities: Identification of narrative themes and idiosyncratic text representations. *Journal of Educational Psychology* 85, pp. 631–641.

Williams, J. P. 2002. Using the theme scheme to improve story comprehension. In C. C. Block and M. Pressley (eds.), *Comprehension instruction: Research-based best practices* (pp. 126–139). New York: Guilford.

Williams, J. P. 2005. Instruction in reading comprehension for primary-grade students: A focus on text structure. *Journal of Special Education* 39(1), pp. 6–18.

Williams, J. P., and K. B. Stafford. 2005. Addressing the challenges of expository text comprehension: Text structure instruction for children in the primary grades. *CASL News* 10, Winter.

Wolf, B. J. 2005. Teaching handwriting. In J. R. Birsh. (ed.), *Multisensory teaching of basic language skills* (2nd ed.). Baltimore, MD: Paul H. Brookes.

Wolf, M., and P. G. Bowers. 1999. The double-deficit hypothesis for the developmental dyslexias. *Journal of Educational Psychology* 91, pp. 415–438.

Wood, E., M. Pressley, and P. H. Winne. 1990. Elaborative interrogation effects on children's learning of factual content. *Journal of Educational Psychology* 82, pp. 741–748.

Wood, P., J. Bruner, and G. Ross. 1976. The role of tutoring in problem solving. *Journal of Child Psychology and Psychiatry* 17, pp. 89–100.

Worden, P. E., and W. Boettcher. 1990. Young children's acquisition of alphabet knowledge. *Journal of Reading Behavior* 22, pp. 277–295.

Worthy, J., and K. Prater. 2002. "I thought about it all night": Readers Theatre for reading fluency and motivation. *Reading Teacher* 56.

Wylie, R., and D. Durrell. 1970. Teaching vowels through phonograms. *Elementary English* 47.

Young, A., and P. G. Bowers. 1995. Individual difference and text difficulty determinants of reading fluency and expressiveness. *Journal of Experimental Child Psychology* 60, pp. 428–454.

Zeno, S. M., S. H. Ivens, R. T. Millard, and R. Duvvuri. 1995. *The educator's word frequency guide.* Brewster, NY: TASA.

Zevenbergen, A. A., and G. J. Whitehurst. 2003. Dialogic reading: A shared picture book reading intervention for preschoolers. In A. van Kleeck, S. A. Stahl, and E. B. Bauer (eds.), *On reading books to children: Parents and teachers* (pp. 177–200). Mahwah, NJ: Erlbaum.

Zhurova, L. Y. 1963. The development of analysis of words into their sounds by preschool children. *Soviet Psychology and Psychiatry* 2, pp. 17–27.

Index

A

B

C

D

T

U

V

CHARTS AND TABLES

SAMPLE LESSON MODELS